ABOUT THE EDITORS

Mary Lawlor is a Lecturer in Marketing at the Dublin Institute of Technology, Mountjoy Square. She is a marketing graduate of DIT and a postgraduate of Trinity College. Prior to taking up her position in DIT, she worked with Allergan Pharmaceuticals as Sales Manager and subsequently as a lecturer in Marketing at Carlow Institute of Technology. She has several years' experience as a marketing consultant. Her research interests are in services marketing, service quality and direct marketing. She is a course tutor for the Diploma in Direct Marketing at the DIT; she teaches on the postgraduate diploma course in Database Marketing and as a guest lecturer for the Institute of Advertising Practitioners in Ireland. She has presented papers on healthcare marketing at several conferences. She is a member of the IDMA and serves on the education committee. She is also a member of the Institute of Direct Marketing in the UK. She is on the editorial board of the *Journal of Database Marketing*.

John Keane is the chief executive and joint owner of the Response Group of companies. He was founding Chairman of the IDMA in 1988 and remained on the IDMA board until 1997. He has represented Irish Direct Marketing on the Board of FEDMA and was involved in the preparation of arguments to the European Commission on behalf of the industry. He remains an active member of the IDMA and the Marketing Institute of Ireland. He is a commerce graduate of UCD and a member of the editorial board of the *Journal of Database Marketing*. He has presented papers and chaired several conferences both in Ireland and abroad. He was part of the adjudication panel for the Best of Europe Campaigns and the Irish awards. He is a pioneer of direct marketing in Ireland, with 25 years' experience in marketing at national and international level.

DIRECT MARKETING IN IRELAND

Theory and Practice

Edited by
Mary Lawlor
John Keane

Oak Tree Press
Dublin

Oak Tree Press
Merrion Building
Lower Merrion Street
Dublin 2, Ireland
http://www.oaktreepress.com

A catalogue record of this book is
available from the British Library.

ISBN 1-86076-092-9

Printed in Ireland by Colour Books Ltd.

CONTENTS

PART FOUR: EMERGING TECHNOLOGIES

PART FIVE: IMPLEMENTATION OF THE
DIRECT MARKETING STRATEGY

LIST OF CONTRIBUTORS

Mairead Brady is a research fellow at the Dublin Institute of Technology, Mountjoy Square. Previously she worked in direct marketing as new product co-ordinator for Golden Pages Ltd.

Áine Cassidy is Customer Development and Marketing Manager at Ark Life Assurance Co. Ltd. She is on the board of the Irish Direct Marketing Association.

Pat Cody is joint Managing Director of Kompass Ireland Ltd. since its establishment in 1985. He is a founding member and chairman of the IDMA and a member of the Marketing Institute of Ireland.

Joseph Coughlan is a Lecturer in Finance and Information Management at the Dublin Institute of Technology, Mountjoy Square. He is national secretary of the Management Science Society of Ireland.

Peter Crotty is General Manager and Client Services Director with Dialogue Direct Marketing. He is a member of the education committee of the IDMA.

Laura Cuddihy is a Lecturer in Marketing and Sales Management at the Dublin Institute of Technology, Mountjoy Square. Her teaching and research interests are in selling, sales management and sales promotion.

Kieran Devenish BCL, ACII, has worked in the insurance industry for over 25 years. Formerly Chairman of the Irish Direct Marketing Association (IDMA), he currently represents the Association on the Board of the Federation of European Direct Marketing in Brussels.

Geraldine Doherty is Creative Director with Target Marketing Ltd. She is a graduate of the College of Art and Design. She has received numerous gold awards at the IDMA, FEDMA and the IDMN.

David Fitzgerald is the New Business Development Director of Response Tech. Ltd., a member of the Response Group.

Edel Foley is a Lecturer in Direct Marketing at the DIT Mountjoy Square. An author of several best-selling books and articles in marketing and management, she is also an examiner with the Marketing Institute of Ireland and a member of the IDMA, the IDM and the Strategic Planning Society.

Valerie Gannon is a Lecturer in Communications at the Dublin Institute of Technology, Mountjoy Square. She previously spent eight years in industry.

J. Cyril Gavaghan is a Lecturer in Direct Marketing and Marketing Communications at Tralee Institute of Technology. He is a member of the Marketing Institute.

Robert Hayes McCoy is Managing Director of Robert Hayes McCoy and Associates. He has received numerous awards for excellence from the IDMA, Best of Europe and FEDMA. He is a founding member and former board member of the IDMA.

John Jameson is a lecturer in Marketing Research, Marketing and Business Planning at DIT Mountjoy Square. He has extensive experience as a consultant in the SME and multinational sectors in Ireland and abroad.

Ben Kealy is Marketing Manager with EBS Building Society, which he joined in 1984. He worked in the brand network before moving to marketing at EBS in 1990.

Marie Keane is a Lecturer in Marketing at the Dublin Institute of Technology, Mountjoy Square. She has ten years experience in marketing and customer service with AIB Bank PLC.

Aileen Kennedy is a Lecturer in Services Marketing at the Dublin Institute of Technology, Mountjoy Square.

Michael Killeen is a Director of Dialogue Direct Marketing. He teaches on the Diploma in Direct Marketing at DIT and is vice chairman of the IDMA. He is currently Chairman of the International John Caples Awards programme for Ireland.

Frank Lalor is Managing Director of Lalor International Holdings. He was one of the founder members of the Irish Direct Marketing Association. He was the first Irish person to receive the "Best of

Europe" Gold Award, and has received major Direct Marketing Awards in the US and Ireland.

Margaret-Anne Lawlor is a lecturer in Marketing Communications in DIT, Mountjoy Square and is also a visiting Lecturer in Marketing at Trinity College.

Alan Leibert is Managing Director of Virtual Precincts Ltd, a SmartZone electronic shopping mall. He is also a consultant in the computer and emerging and technology industries.

Darren McGee is Business Development Manager with Delta Systems Ltd. He previously worked in database roles with Kompass Ireland and Canon Ireland. He is a founding member of the Young Direct Marketing Association.

Cathy McGennis is Data Analysis Manager at PMI Ltd. Prior to this, she set up the SPSS office in Ireland.

Matt Moran is Business Development Manager with An Post, based in Cork. He served as Regional Chairman of the Marketing Institute in the southern region in 1994/95.

Michelle Morris is Client Service Director with OgilvyOne Worldwide.

Gerry Mortimer is a Lecturer in Marketing Management at DIT Mountjoy Square. He has considerable experience as a consultant to Irish industry and to Irish and international development agencies.

Bill Moss is Joint Managing Director of Bill Moss and Associates. He is a founding member of The Irish Direct Marketing Association and served as its chairman for 1998.

Bernice O'Connor is a Marketing Officer in sales and marketing for television and radio with RTE. She is a member of the Marketing Institute of Ireland.

Michael O'Donovan is Assistant Commissioner in the office of the Data Protection Commissioner.

Aidan O'Driscoll is a Lecturer in Marketing and Strategic Management at the DIT Mountjoy Square. He is founder and editor of *Irish Marketing Review*. He is a Fellow of the Marketing Institute of Ireland

and was a visiting professor at the University of Ulster for the 1997/98 academic year.

Gerard O'Neill is Managing Director of Amárach Consulting. He has authored numerous reports including the IDMA *Focus on the Future* report.

Joanne Reader is New Market Development Manager at Barclays Merchant Services in the UK. She has been involved in the development and implementation of the Visa Cash electronic purse in Leeds.

Joy Redmond is a Strategic Research and Development student at the DIT, Mountjoy Square. She is also an honours marketing graduate of DIT.

Eddie Rohan is a Lecturer in Marketing Research. For many years he has been involved in taught postgraduate courses at the DIT.

Donncha Ryan is a Lecturer in Operations Research at the DIT, Mountjoy Square. He teaches on the Diploma in Direct Marketing.

Helen Seymour is an Associate Director with Dimension Ltd. She is chairperson of the Irish Institute of Sales Promotion Consultants.

Tom Trainor is Sales Director, Corporate Business in Telecom Éireann. He is an active member the Sales Institute of Ireland and of the Editorial Review Board of the *International Journal of Selling and Key Account Management*.

Marian Wallace is Account Director in the direct marketing division of Creative Solutions. She has seven years' experience in direct marketing in both Ireland and the UK.

Susan Wheeler is founder and Managing Director of TMS (Ireland) Ltd., the largest telemarketing agency in Ireland, and has carried out campaigns for companies such as Microsoft, AIB and HMV Ticketline. She is a Director of the Irish Direct Marketing Association.

Rosita Wolfe is a market analyst with Telecom Ireland International. She holds a first class honours marketing degree from DIT and was An Bord Trachtala marketing graduate of the year in 1995.

This book is dedicated to the memory of John Tierney, who died tragically in 1997. John, who was at a very early stage of his career, will be forever remembered with great fondness

ACKNOWLEDGEMENTS

Through the process of bringing this book to its final stages, many valuable relationships have been developed between education and practice. We are indebted to numerous people who have contributed to this textbook, knowingly and unknowingly. It is a collaboration of effort between academics and practitioners in marketing and information technology, a close alignment of scholarly thinking and practice and a signal that the academy and the marketplace are in synchronisation.

Contributors from the Dublin Institute of Technology and the IDMA deserve our sincere thanks; Paul O'Sullivan, DIT, for his continued motivation, genuine interest and sound advice for the project; the academics who have given generously of their time and written enthusiastically about Irish direct marketing, drawing from their research, knowledge and experience. Thanks also to J. Cyril Gavaghan from the Institute of Technology, Tralee. We are indebted to all the direct marketing practitioners who have contributed chapters, case material and illustrations from many of the award-winning Irish campaigns with which they have been involved.

We thank the Irish Direct Marketing Association which has supported this project from its inception. A sincere word of gratitude to Aine Cassidy for her ongoing support and encouragement and her facilitation of the links between the DIT and the IDMA. Special thanks also to the Board of the IDMA, the Education committee and the Publicity committee.

In addition, the co-operation and interest of the following companies, with whom the contributors worked closely for this project, have been much appreciated: Ark Life; Bloomfield-Tesco; Baileys; Cockburn Port; Eircell; EBS Building Society; Lever Bros.; Matchmaker; Max Florists; Mitsubishi; and Open University.

Thanks to the library staff at DIT whose assistance to many of the contributors was greatly appreciated. Our special thanks to Ciaran Collins from Astra Pharmaceuticals for his patience in reading drafts and editing copy. The team at Oak Tree Press have inspired confidence throughout this project. We greatly acknowledge the professionalism of David, Brian, Jenna and Janet.

Lastly, we would like to thank each of our partners, Mary Keane and Edmund Butler for their ongoing support and encouragement over the last year.

We hope that this text will provide insights into Irish direct marketing for students and practitioners at a strategic and operational level and that the text stimulates discussion and debate on current issues, directions for future research and case study development.

Mary Lawlor
John Keane
May 1998

FOREWORD

In 1989, when I addressed the Irish Direct Marketing Association's first annual conference, I congratulated the founders on their foresight in developing an association with objectives to grow, develop and watch over the future of this marketing tool.

I doubt that even the founders could have envisaged the rapid advancement we have seen in service support technologies since then. The development of these technologies has catapulted the growth of database and loyalty marketing, and not least the huge advances being made in the area of telemarketing.

Direct marketing has been singled out by governments as a major employment growth area and, almost every month, the IDA seem to be announcing new projects and new jobs in telemarketing-related businesses. Just as this growth is set to continue internationally, so also has there been enormous growth in the indigenous Irish market. In such a short period, the use of direct marketing as a key element in the overall marketing strategies pursued by most Irish companies has been staggering. But its use will not be confined to commercial companies. I expect that political parties, voluntary groups and not-for-profit organisations will also be using the direct marketing approach with increasing frequency in the future.

Technology has influenced and will continue to influence the way we live, how we communicate, how we buy and sell. Direct marketing will, I believe, play a vital role in fulfilling consumer needs.

The writing of *Direct Marketing in Ireland* is timely, given that the industry is about to face the challenges of the new millennium. The next chapter of Irish direct marketing can be firmly set on the foundation of the past ten years. This book, written by academics and practitioners working in tandem, is a celebration of a new professional industry; it is an enduring record which will act as a source of valuable information for both students and practitioners.

Ruairi Quinn, TD
Leader of The Labour Party

INTRODUCTION

Mary Lawlor *and* John Keane

Marketing communications and the wider industry which supports it has witnessed a world-wide technological revolution over the past 20 years. Not since the industrial revolution of the nineteenth century have there been such rapid advances in technology.

The key difference in the twentieth-century revolution has been in the accelerated degree of innovation brought about following the initial inventions; in the main, this is evident in the computer systems which now drive almost all production and service industries.

Technology has dramatically changed the world we live in and continues to change it (at times it seems almost daily); it affects how we study, work, play. Just consider the growth in mobile phone usage in Ireland: in the two years to 1998, ownership grew by almost 300 per cent to 500,000 units. These figures simply illustrate a marketing landscape in perpetual change, moving from the concept of mass marketing in the 1970s to today's almost "one-to-one" scenarios. Other examples range from designer clothing to small-run, highly targeted desk-top published magazines, none of which would have been an economical prospect 15 years ago.

Over the past five years in Ireland, we have witnessed exponential growth in all the general areas of direct marketing. Now, and in the near future, this growth is concentrated in the areas of database and relational marketing. A whole new sub-set of marketing has emerged within the Irish market. Indeed, the very technology that has driven this growth has also fuelled consumer demands in ways not witnessed before.

As manufacturers and service suppliers seek to grasp the changing environment, more and more will rely on the potential of direct marketing to relate to customers; to supply goods and services; and to process orders from customers.

A revolution driven by technology has now begun to permeate the Irish social structure; the processes and approaches necessary to meet this change has caused a paradigm shift in marketing theory.

More and more academic writers and marketing practitioners are finding it impossible to work within the traditional definitions of marketing and even of direct marketing. Other than the acceptance of the general principle that marketing is firstly a philosophy — that is, a way of doing things which starts with an understanding of a customer's needs — very little of the definitions we have grown up with will remain valid as we seek to comprehend the beginnings of a revolutionary shift in consumer needs for delivery and communication channels.

New thinking and new approaches are required. The concept of integrated marketing will mean a much closer linkage between all of the communication tools. The challenge now presented by Irish consumers will undoubtedly bring to the fore an entrepreneurially driven and imaginative marketing community.

As more opportunities to enter the Irish, European and world markets grow, so also will the industry's responsibilities in managing its technologies, to use properly its new-found customer data/ information tools. As Europe moves inextricably towards a truly single market bereft of national and institutional barriers to new entrants, there are increasing demands for industries to put strong regulation firmly in place at national level. Whether this regulation will remain "self-regulatory" or "governmental" will depend on those in the industry and how they use their new-found data.

The challenge to practitioners and educators is to address the changing marketing paradigm in the development and delivery of educational programmes. Knowledge management is a critical success factor for companies whose employees engage in lifelong learning to ensure that their skills remain relevant and valued. This book attempts to provide a text and a source of reference for students at all stages of learning; full-time, part-time, distance or in-company learning. The previously unpublished cases in the book will hopefully facilitate discussion and analysis.

The cases illustrate how these companies are operating outside the traditional defining boundaries of distribution and communication and how competition in their industries has shifted from product and quality to process management, response handling and fulfilment.

This book is divided into five parts. Part One covers direct marketing strategy; Part Two deals with database strategy; Part Three examines issues of communications strategy; Part Four considers the emerging technologies; while Part Five relates to strategy implementation.

Direct Marketing Strategy

The first part deals with direct marketing in an overall marketing strategy context. It introduces direct marketing, and deals with key decisions involved in branding, pricing and in the allocation of the marketing budget across customer acquisition and retention activity.

In **Chapter 1**, Aidan O'Driscoll defines direct marketing and examines the reasons for its growth in Ireland over the last decade. He positions direct marketing within a wider relationship marketing context. In **Chapter 2**, Frank Lalor traces the development of direct marketing in Ireland from the 1970s, and discusses the challenges currently facing the direct marketing industry. Mary Lawlor and Michael Killeen define branding and examine the main challenges facing brand owners in **Chapter 3**. They present ways to build brands using more interactive marketing approaches in conjunction with advertising. A case history of Mitsubishi illustrates some of the issues raised in the chapter.

Cyril Gavaghan defines and emphasises the need for customer acquisition in **Chapter 4**. He considers the process involved in developing an acquisition programme and concludes with an acquisition case history of Max Florists. Aileen Kennedy and Margaret-Anne Lawlor (**Chapter 5**) focus on the economics, benefits and philosophy underpinning retention programmes, while Marian Wallace's case study demonstrates how Lever Bros. have used information to target promotions and communications to their valued customers.

In **Chapter 6**, John Jameson examines the pricing options and the factors to consider in developing a pricing strategy. These issues are then raised by Gerry Mortimer in a case history of Eircell in the mobile phone market.

Database Strategy

The second part of the book deals with database strategy. It considers the main issues involved in managing a database: how to use, extract and analyse the data for the purpose of segmentation, targeting and tracking. Privacy issues in data collection and storage are also examined.

Darren McGee (**Chapter 7**) discusses the mechanics of the database management process and provides a framework for choosing and implementing a marketing database solution.

Donncha Ryan and Cathy McGennis, in **Chapter 8**, argue that data correctly applied can lead to profitable and sustainable levels of performance through research, accurate testing and response analysis. They demonstrate key data applications with a case history of Bloomfields-Tesco.

In **Chapter 9**, Eddie Rohan and Dave Fitzgerald examine different approaches to segmentation and the various systems and software available to the direct marketer. The authors describe in detail how Matchmaker can be used in geodemographic profiling.

Mailing lists, data protection and other privacy issues are dealt with by Kieran Devenish in **Chapter 10** and by Michael O'Donovan, Bill Moss and Pat Cody in **Chapter 11**.

Communications Strategy: Offers, Media and Creativity

The third part demonstrates how sales promotion integrates with direct marketing to make appropriate offers to the target market. The personal and non-personal media of direct marketing are detailed, as are the creative approach to copywriting and visuals for direct marketing communications.

In **Chapter 12**, Laura Cuddihy and Helen Seymour examine the historical development of sales promotion, the sales promotion tools that are available and how sales promotion can be integrated with direct marketing to achieve a targeted and measurable communications programme.

Mary Lawlor, Tom Trainor and Susan Wheeler examine the reasons for the growth of telemarketing in Ireland and internationally in **Chapter 13**. They overview the typical applications of telemarketing and conclude with the strategic considerations involved in the introduction of inbound and outbound telemarketing. A case history of telemarketing in Baileys illustrates the key issues involved.

Edel Foley and Matt Moran (**Chapter 14**) trace the development of direct mail and the key strategic considerations in strategy development and the authors use the case of Cockburns Port to illustrate how direct mail was employed by the company in their creative strategy.

Mairead Brady and Rosita Wolfe make a case for print media. **Chapter 15** tracks the changes that are taking place and profile the structure of the media in Ireland. The chapter also presents the case for the role of inserts in direct marketing. Michelle Morris uses the Open University to illustrate the effective use of print media and inserts in a direct marketing campaign. Robert Hayes McCoy and Ger Doherty explain how copy and design work together in **Chapter 16**.

Emerging Technologies

The fourth part of the book deals with emerging technologies, including the Internet, digital and interactive television, smart cards, virtual shopping technologies and the implications of these technologies for direct marketing in an Irish context.

Bernice O'Connor looks at television as an evolving medium in **Chapter 17**, tracking the changes that are taking place in terrestrial television and considers the development of digital and interactive television. In **Chapter 18**, Ben Kealy and Peter Crotty consider direct response advertising on television and how direct response buying differs from buying conventional advertising. The factors involved in using the medium effectively are highlighted, as are the key measures of effectiveness. The chapter concludes with a case history of the EBS Building Society.

Joseph Coughlan and Joy Redmond trace the development of the Internet in **Chapter 19**, and suggest the various ways that companies can use the Internet to communicate with their target market. Alan Leibert (**Chapter 20**) explores the possibilities of virtual shopping while Joanne Reader (**Chapter 21**) outlines the growth in the use of smart cards. She raises the issues that their success has created, together with details of the background to smart cards and the associated benefits for marketers and consumers, finishing with a case study of one application of the smart card, the electronic purse. In

Chapter 22, Áine Cassidy details how sales and marketing technologies can be integrated and gives a case history of Ark Life Ltd.

Implementation of Direct Marketing Strategy

The fifth part deals with the implementation of direct marketing strategy. Valerie Gannon, in **Chapter 23**, takes the reader through the main stages of the campaign management process, including budgeting, and draws on some useful and practical tools from the sphere of project management. In **Chapter 24**, Marie Keane and John Keane explore the issues involved in planning and managing fulfilment and customer care and complaint management, while Martin Biddle gives guidelines on the preparation of a mailing for the lettershop. Finally, in **Chapter 25**, Gerard O'Neill forecasts the future potential growth of direct marketing.

PART ONE

Direct Marketing Strategy

Chapter 1

THE ART AND SCIENCE OF DIRECT MARKETING

Aidan O'Driscoll

Overview

There is an ongoing debate about whether marketing is a science or an art. This debate situates marketing somewhere along a continuum, with science at one end and art at the other. At its simplest, the "science" view considers marketing as properly constituting a set of robust general principles, amenable to accurate measurement and likely to have predictable performance outcomes. The "art" focused, humanistic view, on the other hand, sees marketing as a less precise discipline, with few universal imperatives, where the experience, intuition and expertise of its practitioners are crucial. Where one lands along this continuum depends in no small part on how one defines marketing (Brown, 1996).

Much the same observation can be made about direct marketing, arguably the most exciting domain of marketing today. From one perspective, direct marketing is a quantitative activity, amenable to scientific methods where, for instance, the cost-benefit of a campaign direct from a supplier to a targeted group of buyers can be assessed accurately. Another perspective, cognisant of the rapidly changing technological and societal environment in which direct marketing operates, sees it as a veritable Pandora's Box of opportunity where managing profitable exchange along a direct channel between supplier and buyer is highly dependent on managerial intuition and judgement. Again, which perspective one endorses depends to a large extent on one's view of what exactly constitutes direct marketing.

The purpose of this chapter is to explain what direct marketing actually does constitute. It seeks to define, however tentatively, this important subfield of marketing and to set down some broad boundary parameters. The reader of this book is soon introduced to what may initially seem a bewil-

dering array of concepts and techniques: direct mail, telemarketing, geo-demographics, database management, direct response marketing, loyalty schemes, to name just a few. Hopefully, this chapter provides an integrating framework, a set of reference points, so that the student and interested practitioner can piece together the challenging puzzle that is successful direct marketing.

The chapter falls into four sections. The first explores some definitions of direct marketing. The aim is not to offer one definitive version, but rather to introduce the reader to the range of concepts and concerns that underpin these definitions. The hope is to convey a "feel" for what direct marketing is about, not some easily remembered definition. The second section examines the reasons behind the phenomenal growth in direct marketing over the last decade or two: the changing nature of the consumer, fractionalism of communication media, reconfigured channels of distribution, and new forces and methods for compiling highly individualised customer information.

The third section argues that, in order to comprehend this growth fully, it is necessary to examine wider changes that have been taking place in the marketing landscape — how markets, consumer behaviour, technology and the nature of organisations have undergone significant transition. It postulates that a significant evolution — a paradigm shift — has been occurring in marketing thinking and practice. The fourth section positions direct marketing within this wider, shifting marketing landscape. In sum, the contention is that direct marketing is conceived most usefully within a broadened understanding of marketing that focuses on the individual relationship — what is referred to as relational and relationship marketing.

TOWARDS A DEFINITION OF DIRECT MARKETING

Direct marketing claims a long heritage. The names *Reader's Digest* and *Family Album* have been around for half a century; the first markets magazines and books, the second clothing and household goods. These firms avoid any intermediaries, dealing directly with their customers, use mail service to communicate and distribute, make extensive use of catalogues and assiduously develop subscriber lists. In the US in the nineteenth century, mail order firms such as Sears were primary vehicles for the supply of goods to the pioneering West because of its underdeveloped wholesale and retail channels. William Lucas published a gardening catalogue in England in 1667. In Venice in 1498, a book catalogue was published by one Aldus Manutius. In 1086, William the Conqueror created the Domesday Book as a record of what each of his subjects owned, arguably the first substantive consumer database (Evans, 1994).

But the study of such historical provenance is of limited use. Today's direct marketing industry is fundamentally different from yesteryear's direct mail endeavour. During the last twenty years, direct marketing has become enveloped in technology. Information, computing and communications technologies have brought — even jerked — direct marketing into a new era. The pace of change has been dramatic. So it is not surprising that the perceptions and definitions of direct marketing continue to evolve.

FIGURE 1.1: SELECTED DEFINITIONS OF DIRECT MARKETING

Direct marketing is getting your ad message direct to the customer or prospect to produce some type of immediate action (Kobs, 1979).

Direct marketing is an interactive system of marketing that uses one or more advertising media to effect a measurable response and/or transaction at any location (DMA, 1981).

Direct marketing is an all-encompassing catch-all that covers direct mail, telephone marketing and mail order (Gosden, 1985).

Direct marketing is a relational marketing process of prospecting, conversion, and maintenance that involves information feedback and control at the individual level by using direct response advertising with tracking codes (Bauer and Miglautsch, 1992).

Direct marketing is a form of marketing in which push-only promotional efforts are supported by an evolving database that will ultimately include demographic and longitudinal response (i.e. query and/or sales) data for targeted entities (Murrow and Hyman, 1994).

Direct marketing is broadly defined, in media terms, as any direct communication to a consumer or business recipient that is designed to generate a response in the form of an order (direct order), a request for further information (lead generation), and/or a visit to a store or other place of business for purchase of a special product(s) or service(s) (traffic generation) (DMA, 1995).

Figure 1.1 offers six arbitrarily selected definitions of direct marketing laid out in chronological order. Reading through them, it is clear that a number of key ideas and themes run through most: direct, highly focused communication, direct response, interaction, feedback and measurement, information and data management. It is also apparent that with the advent of the 1990s, definitions of direct marketing become more widely embracing and comprehensive. The Direct Marketing Association (DMA), the professional representative body of the industry in the US, first promulgated its (still) official definition in 1981. By 1995, its thinking, as evidenced by a specially commissioned report, becomes more encompassing and specific.

It is worthwhile to look more closely and "break down" one definition. Let us choose that of Bauer and Miglautsch (1992). Their definition consists of four properties, moving from general to specific characteristics: (i) relational marketing; (ii) the process of prospecting, conversion, and maintenance; (iii) information feedback and control at the individual level; and (iv) direct response advertising with tracking codes. Let us consider each property, but in reverse order.

Advertising that encourages and enables a direct response is a distinguishing characteristic of direct marketing. Linking such advertisements to tracking codes enables responses to be tracked, measured and analysed (e.g. a magazine ad will have a tracking code in an alpha and/or numeric code printed on the mail-back coupon that identifies the specific ad in the magazine to which a consumer might respond). It also facilitates the development of a customer file of transactions for future marketing decisions.

Information feedback and control at the individual consumer or organisation level is a second necessary characteristic of direct marketing. It is essentially facilitated by the tracking codes. Customer and transaction data provide a key information base to market further. For example, a direct marketer might develop customer segmentation models for selecting particular customers for various types of special mailings or contacts (e.g. frequent mailings to highly valued customers or reactivation mailings to dormant customers).

Prospecting or name acquisition is the ongoing activity of finding new customers for building customer data files. Conversion involves seeking to change the status of a respondent to a customer (i.e. a purchaser of a minimum order size). Maintenance involves ensuring ongoing/repeat-buying behaviour on the part of the customer. It can include regular contact with customers, new product selection and testing by customers, profitability analysis (e.g. lifetime value analysis of customer) and other marketing and market research activities that help retain the customer's interest and increase the profitability of the customer file.

The ongoing marketing process of prospecting, conversion, and maintenance lead to the "relational marketing" property of direct marketing, according to Bauer and Miglautsch. Focusing on developing and maintaining a continuing relationship between marketer and customers means, in practice, some minimum of regular repeat contact by direct response advertising mailings (or telephone calls) to customers *and* repeat orders from customers.

This explanation of direct marketing is not offered as definitive. Rather it attempts to set out broad parameters of direct marketing activity, so that the student may deepen their knowledge as they read through the book. Direct marketing is not only growing at a dramatic rate; it is an activity with many component parts and an increasing number of constituent players. Figure 1.2 illustrates the direct marketing process in action.

FIGURE 1.2: DIRECT MARKETING PROCESS IN ACTION

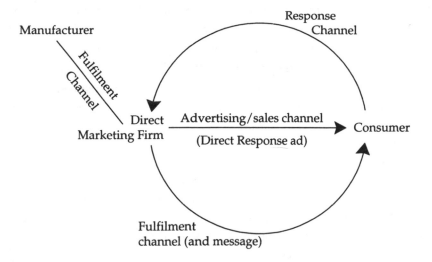

The direct marketing (DM) firm and the manufacturer may be one and the same, in which case the fulfilment channel between the manufacturer and the DM firm in the diagram is redundant. (Fulfilment refers to fulfilling an order for a product/service once it has been requested by a customer.) However, many direct marketing firms do not manufacture the product/service they market, e.g. Family Album or QVC, the TV shopping organisation.

The direct marketing firm in Figure 1.2 transmits an advertising/ sales message (direct response ad) to the consumer (prospects or customers). The advertising message can be transmitted via a variety of media: magazines, newspapers, TV, radio, mail service, the Internet, even over the telephone. The consumer responds by mail or phone (response channel). The firm then sends the merchandise directly to the consumer via mail or courier service (fulfilment channel). In addition to the merchandise, the fulfilment channel can use the opportunity to carry another direct response advertisement. Again, this presents a simplified version of the direct marketing process. Figure 1.2 must be refined further if it is to accommodate growing forms of direct marketing activity; for example, large manufacturers and retailers like Nestlé and Tesco writing directly to customers to encourage them to remain brand loyal and to buy their goods when shopping.

Some firms using direct marketing execute the whole process themselves — carry it out in-house. However, direct marketing is becoming increasingly complex and logistically sophisticated. Thus, many firms outsource or contract out many parts of the process. In turn, many specialist firms are growing to provide dedicated services in this domain: fully integrated direct mail houses; coupon handling specialists (17 million money-off coupons were redeemed in Irish supermarkets in 1996!); response fulfilment experts (generally 80 per cent of responses arrive within two weeks of the final mailing date, a sizeable potential "bottleneck"); specialists in database management, in address validation, in static profiling and in lifestyle analysis. Add to these direct marketing consultancies, sales promotion specialists, specialist publishing houses and the services of advertising agencies and integrated marketing communication agencies, and we see a very sizeable portfolio of players in the direct marketing industry.

THE GROWTH OF DIRECT MARKETING

The reasons for the growth in direct marketing over the last two decades are many and interrelated. They include changes in the nature of the consumer, fractionalisation of communication media, reconfigured channels of distribution, and new forces and methods for compiling highly individualised customer information.

Customers

The era of the trusting, easily defined, homogeneous consumer has faded. The customer to whom the marketer is now appealing has become increasingly knowledgeable, sceptical and demanding — basically, harder to persuade. Their ongoing loyalty and interest in repurchasing cannot be taken for granted. Younger consumers, for whom consumption is often an act of self-expression and empowerment, present a particular challenge. There has been a shift away from the "nuclear" towards the "cellular" family, with households working less *en famille* as each member behaves more individualistically. The ability of the direct marketer to segment into smaller "micro" categories, to personalise product offerings, and to develop databases has become crucial.

Communications Media

This increasing heterogeneity and segmentation in customer profiles, allied to the increasing array of communication modes, have produced audience fragmentation and decreased effectiveness in traditional mass marketing appeals. The result is shrinking audiences for individual media and escalating media costs, as well as media proliferation and "clutter" (Meenaghan, 1995). Technology, greater leisure time availability and changing socio-economic and demographic factors have resulted in a fractionalisation of advertising media, particularly TV and print. New magazines and newspaper titles, extra national, regional and even global television channels, the development of the World Wide Web, the Internet and multi-media instruments have all conspired to make the marketer's job of communicating with the target audience more difficult. Furthermore, consumers are not helping the advertiser by video-recording TV programmes and "zapping the commercials" (Kitchen, 1986). Direct marketing has the possibility to circumvent this clutter as the message can be tailored and communicated in customised fashion — in a mailshot, for example.

Initiatives pioneered by An Post and Telecom Éireann during the 1980s were an important catalyst in the development of direct marketing in Ireland. Established by legislation as commercially focused semi-state companies in the early part of the decade, such postal and telecommunications work was formerly the responsibility of the Department of Posts and Telegraphs. An Post set up PostAim, a service which enabled companies to target mail at different postal districts at reduced cost. Telecom Éireann upgraded what was a fairly antiquated telecommunications infrastructure into a state-of-the-art one. This put Ireland to the fore in telematics and facilitated the development of the "call centre" and telemarketing industries.

Channels of Distribution

An important feature of the past decade has been the increasing sophistication, abetted by new technology, in channels of product and service distribution. Just-in-time delivery modes, automated teller machines (ATMs) and electronic point-of-sale (EPOS) systems are all in widespread use. Powerful new players have arisen along the distribution chain. In the food and clothing industries, for example, retailing structures have become very concentrated with a smaller number of retailers controlling a greater share of the market than was previously the case. One result of this has been the rise of so-called "distributor own brands" (DOBs) and a challenge to the preeminence of manufacturers' brands. Another is the impressive ability of retailers to build databases on their customers. These structural changes have significant implications for marketing strategy, marketing communications policy and decisions on the extent to which conventional mass marketing appeals (e.g. a TV ad) are supported by directly targeted communication (e.g. a personalised letter).

Individualised Customer Information

The extent to which the marketer can now assemble information and data about individual customers is, in many regards, awesome. Indeed, it is understandable that such activity leads to concern about rights of privacy, and that it is increasingly subject to legislation (O'Malley et al., 1997). Demographic data segments customers according to age, gender and social grade. Psychographic data provides information on their lifestyle, attitudes and beliefs. The commercial availability, since the early 1980s, of national census data was an important fillip to the direct marketing industry and aided the development of geodemographics. Whereas demographic profiles are often based on sample surveys of 1,000, a census counts the whole population. Names and addresses cannot be revealed from the census, but aggregated statistics for each district can. In the UK, each of these districts amounts to a grouping of around 170 households. When such data are linked with a postcode (one postcode for 15 households approximately) and with the electoral register, it is virtually possible to identify households and their characteristics. MOSAIC and OMNIDATA are examples of European information systems which provide such data commercially to clients.

In the Irish market, Matchmaker provides a similar service for geodemographic profiling. The census divides the Republic of Ireland into some 3,500 unique district electoral divisions (DEDs). Information on every household is aggregated and available at DED level on characteristics such as age and sex, family composition, occupation and employment status, cars per household, education levels and so on. Each DED or neighbourhood tends to be relatively homogeneous. Thus, a financial services company selling educational savings plans could target DEDs where the number of children under the age of 15 is high and unemployment levels are low. In many countries, such profiling can also draw on financial data in the form of customers' credit status — indeed, an important origin of direct marketing lies in credit referencing information (Evans, 1998).

Electronic point-of-sale (EPOS) systems provide retailers with information on customers' actual purchasing behaviour; this history of sales transactions confirms the recency, frequency and monetary value (RFM) of purchases. Link this transactional data to the personal information which larger retailers get from encouraging customers to join loyalty and affiliation schemes and from customers' responses to various media offers (e.g. coupon redemption), and one appreciates the potential direct marketing abilities of such companies.

To reiterate: detailed, accurate, individualised information about customers is now available to the direct marketer. They can use this customised data, in Bauer and Miglautsch's terminology, to prospect, convert and maintain such individuals. Data fusion (Evans, 1998) of geodemographic, psychographic/lifestyle, credit status, transactional and media response information creates a powerful database. Such creation is facilitated by the growth in computing and neural-network software technology. This fusion of static profile and transaction-related data brings us into an era of "biographics" (Muranyi, 1997) where the direct marketer can literally write the biography of their customer. Perhaps George Orwell's Big Brother has arrived. But one thing is certain. Nash's (1984) conception of direct marketing as being essentially "about the mailing list" seems redolent of the steam engine in comparison with the jet-like sophistication of the database instrument a decade or so later.

A CHANGING MARKETING LANDSCAPE

Marketing's heyday was the 1960s. The marketing concept held full sway and marketing commanded a pre-eminent status and authority in the firm. Conventional marketing wisdom was exemplified by multinational firms, often manufacturers of fast-moving consumer goods, which made successful mass marketing appeals to consumers of largely predictable purchasing habit. It was an era of strong and consistent economic growth, well-established modes of manufacturing and delivery, and traditional hierarchical organisation in the firm. The intervening decades have seen the commercial environment change substantially. Markets, consumer behaviour, technology and the nature of organisations have undergone significant transition.

Markets and Consumer Behaviour

Slowed by the oil crises of the 1970s, Western markets now show more modest levels of growth. However, the services sector has grown consistently and much more substantially than the manufacturing sector, whose growth had been central to the development of the large industrial enterprise and the multinational firm. Governments have adopted more market-based, *laissez-faire* economic polices, which have involved considerable deregulation. While increasing fragmentation is observable in many markets as the popularity of vertical integration recedes, this appears to be accompanied by more complex networks and interdependencies in the resulting market structures. Novel channels of distribution and concentration of firms along parts of the value chain have changed the rules of the game in many respects. Furthermore, globalisation of competition has become an underlying feature of markets.

Not surprisingly, consumers have also changed. They have become more sophisticated, sceptical and literate; they are not only more difficult to persuade but also to retain. The issue of customer retention has profoundly influenced marketing thinking and practice. A number of influential US studies focused on the economics of holding on to, and doing more business with, a firm's existing client base, compared to the costs and benefits of getting new customers. It was found that in mature markets it costs five times as much to attract a new customer as to maintain the goodwill of an existing customer (Peters, 1987). The longer a customer stays with a business, the greater their contribution to profitability; this arises from both cost savings and additional revenues (Reichheld, 1993). One study showed, using a range of examples, how a five per cent decrease in defections can contribute from 12 to 85 per cent more profits (Reichheld and Sasser, 1990). Establishing a personal relationship or bond with a customer helps such retention.

Technology

The revolutionary role of information and communications technology (ICT) on media, distribution channels and customer data collection was addressed earlier. The last two decades have also seen important new modes of manufacturing and service technology firmly take root in organisations. The provenance of total quality management (TQM), world class manufacturing (WCM), just-in-time workflows and supply chain management lies in Japanese methods of production. These approaches stress multidisciplinary integration, parallel as well as sequential tasking, speed to market, high product quality and dedicated customer service. They highlight the failure of conventional Western "chimney-stack" management, with its functional "bunkers" — including marketing — embodying an abstract notion of "marketing orientation" with regard to corporate commitment to customers and markets, combined with a practical unwillingness to get out in the field and "deliver" on customer service and satisfaction. In this regard, the production and operations departments of firms that have implemented manufacturing and service methods such as TQM and WCM, with their driven customer focus, have stolen a march on (if not the clothes of!) marketing.

Organisation Design

Not surprisingly, organisations are changing profoundly in their structure. The possibilities and demands of new technology, real-time communication, innovative products and services and intensifying global competition have necessitated flatter structures and consequentially greater empowerment at lower levels of the organisation (Boehm and Phipps, 1996). Hierarchy has been overlaid with heterarchy, and a growing emphasis on *process* complements concern with function. The functional departmental hegemony, implicit in the organisational models of the post-war years, has been reduced in favour of approaches involving cross-functional teams, stressing customer-focused tasks and shared learning. High levels of vertical and horizontal integration have been replaced by modalities such as out-sourcing, partnering, strategic alliances and networks.

In the early 1990s, Procter and Gamble, the original "inventor" of the brand management system in the US of the 1930s, switched from brand to category management — i.e. all shampoos or diapers managed as a unit — and evolved multidisciplinary customer business development teams with managers from production and sales as well as marketing (George et al., 1994). The brand management model had worked spectacularly well during the era of high consumer trust, effective mass advertising, growing prosperity, homogeneous demand, poorly developed distribution channels and, above all, manufacturer power. A different marketing landscape has led to a reappraisal of existing modes of organising for brand/ product management and for the "effective delivery" of marketing company-wide. A renewed emphasis on trade marketing has developed; manufacturers and retailers are working more closely together and using techniques such as efficient consumer response (ECR). New organisational forms are evolving in the competitive struggle for survival and growth.

Paradigm Shift in Marketing

What is noteworthy about this evolving marketing environment is the scale and unrelenting pace of the change. The life cycles of many products and services are becoming shorter than the time it takes for the firm to nurture the necessary competencies and expertise to develop and market such products. Thus, it is not surprising that many have spoken with unease about the future of marketing, e.g. "marketing's mid-life crisis", "a function without a cause" (Brady and Davis, 1993). The widely quoted *Marketing at the Crossroads* study observed much introspection and found many marketing departments trying to find a new role and relevance within the organisation (Coopers and Lybrand, 1993).

Yet marketing's ills do not appear terminal. There is much evidence of regeneration, fresh thinking and reinvented approaches. Leading international companies like Procter and Gamble, Lever Bros., Kelloggs, Kraft Foods Inc. and Irish-based firms like Superquinn, Dunnes Stores and Tesco have developed large databases about their customers and now complement their traditional advertising with highly targeted one-to-one communication. Such direct marketing approaches are redefining the notion of market segmentation.

Such innovative practice characterises a general shift in marketing thinking which has been taking place since the late 1980s. Marketing theory and teaching had been very much rooted in managing the 4Ps of the marketing mix and in addressing the high-street consumer, with an emphasis on fast-moving consumer goods (FMCGs), competitive modes of behaviour and a short-term, transactional focus (often referred to as a classic Kotlerian approach, after the influence of Philip Kotler's books). This view of marketing was challenged by many who argued that it represented a very limited, and largely American, comprehension of marketing activity. The Nordic school of marketing (Håkansson, 1982; Gummesson, 1987; Gronroos, 1994) made the case that consumer goods marketing was only the tip of the value-creating "iceberg" and that in business-to-business marketing, long-term relations, stable networks, partnerships and co-operative modes of behaviour were to be observed.

Furthermore, understanding services marketing, the fastest growing sector in most developed economies, required a broadened if not altered perspective. Marketing practice in many successful companies evolved towards viewing the customer, not merely as someone to whom something is sold at a profit, but as a possible longer-term partner in mutual business development. The importance of relationships between buyer and seller, between client and firm, took hold. Kotler himself suggested (1991) that marketing is now characterised by "a movement away from a focus on exchange

— in the narrow sense of transaction — and towards a focus on building value-laden relationships and marketing networks". This new thinking about marketing, a so-called paradigm shift, argues that conventional marketing must embrace a wider network approach with an emphasis on interaction, relational marketing, and order fulfilment and service expertise (Murray and O'Driscoll, 1996).

What Exactly Do We Mean by Relationship Marketing?

Relationship marketing can mean different things to different managers. Some direct marketing personnel involved in building databases and mailshooting prospective buyers present their work as relationship marketing. Such communication may have the potential to build a meaningful relationship, but it represents a weak conception of relationship. On a deeper level, some argue that loyalty and affiliation programmes, often referred to as loyalty marketing, which involve regular communication with and perhaps some gift or benefit giving to a customer, amount to relationship marketing. Whether or not the customer feels they also have a relationship with the firm is a moot point. Managers who truly embrace relationship marketing go further and argue that both parties — firm and customer — must feel clearly that they benefit in a positive way from the exchange.

The leading academic proponents of relationship marketing would concur with this latter view and make the case that relationship marketing is a new way of doing marketing — a reinvention of the marketing concept. Gronroos encapsulates this perspective in his 1995 relationship-focused definition of marketing:

> The purpose of marketing is to establish, maintain, enhance and, where necessary, terminate relationships with customers and other partners, at a profit, so that the objectives of the partners involved are met. This is achieved by a mutual exchange and fulfilment of promises.

This is the perspective taken in this chapter. Given the widespread (mis)use of the terms relationship and relationship marketing, there is a real danger that, like Gresham's Law, according to which bad money drove out good money in the seventeenth century, these terms may become debased and undervalued — a little like the use of the term excellence today. However, the underlying concepts and thinking are robust and relevant.

Relationship marketing aims to close the loop between getting and keeping customers. To develop this notion, we can take the long-established concept of the "ladder of loyalty" and add a few rungs to create the "relationship ladder" (see Figure 1.3). The idea here is that there are a number of identifiable stages in the development of a long-term customer relationship. At the foot of the ladder is the prospect or the target market. Classical marketing has tended to focus on the means by which this individual or organisation might be converted into a customer. However, in the relationship marketing model, a "customer" is someone who has done business with the firm once or occasionally. The step beyond this is the client. A client is someone who will do business with the organisation on a repeat basis, but may be neutral or even negative about the company. For example, some of a bank's clients might have less than positive views about the institution, but stay with it out of inertia rather than loyalty.

It is only when a client is converted into a supporter that the strength of the relationship becomes apparent. These people like being associated with the organisation and they may even be persuaded to become advocates — to actively recommend the firm to others. Such bank supporters may boast to others about the benefits of "my bank". The final step on the ladder is where the customer is now a partner; both parties strive together to identify ways in which mutual advantage can be gained from the relationship. In this approach, the emphasis in relationship marketing is upon finding appropriate means to move customers up the ladder and keep them there. Conventional marketing, on the other hand, has tended to focus on the winning of customers and building share of market without any significant attempt to develop strategies for customer retention and for "share of customer" (Peppers and Rogers, 1995).

FIGURE 1.3: THE RELATIONSHIP LADDER OF CUSTOMER LOYALTY

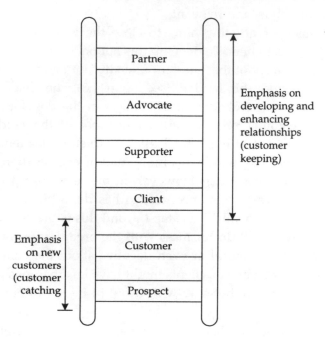

Source: Payne et al. (1995), p. viii.

There are clear benefits to a firm from a relational approach. But a relationship is by definition a two-sided affair with mutual advantage to both parties. What are the benefits to the customer? Ideally, they gain from the firm having a deeper and ongoing understanding of their wants and needs, which allows it to offer a value-for-money bundle of benefits over time such that the customer remains happy to bestow loyalty to the firm. An example might be a financial institution which courts a customer over their adult lifetime by providing a tailored range of services and products to meet their changing needs. However, customers do not always perceive such mutuality of benefit, nor indeed do they always want to enter into a "relationship".

Some kinds of transactions make the initiation of a relationship problematic. For example, a good purchased on impulse, on a once-off decision, or the case of low-involvement products. Indeed, relational marketing is most likely to be successful where both firm and customer perceive the purchasing stakes to be rising — where purchase decisions require more buyer involvement, and order generation, fulfilment and service support require greater investment on the part of the firm. Many firms attempt to lock-in customers in a variety of ways — for example, through the creation of switching costs, exit barriers, training schemes, even affiliation clubs. While such approaches do indeed achieve repeat purchase, yield profit to the firms, at least in the short to medium term, and represent a type of structural bonding, they cannot be categorised truly as exercises in relationship marketing. Genuine relationships require trust and commitment from both parties. They also require a respect for privacy.

Building a Relationship

Buyer loyalty and repurchase must be won on a voluntary, non-coercive basis in true relational exchange. Furthermore, some customers simply do not want a relationship with a company, for various reasons. In the case of financial services, some clients prefer to deal with a bank at arm's length and purchase services from a number of institutions. Other customers may be well disposed to the idea of a relationship with a firm. But the firm fails to deliver from its side, and the customer defects to a competitor. Such an occurrence is often indicative of a firm's inability to listen to its customers' grievances and its failure to understand the nature of consumer complaint behaviour.

Firm-buyer relationships are by nature complex, varying considerably in their viability, intensity and length. The firm considering a more relational approach with its customers must assess at least three important factors:

1. *The nature of the exchange*: is the transaction one where a mutually satisfying relationship can indeed be nurtured, or one where it will always remain difficult to establish? A personal service like a retail bank has many possibilities to foster a relational approach. A seller of holiday souvenirs to tourists has few.

2. *Building blocks of the relationship*: if a relationship looks feasible, how is it best pursued? What actions will enhance it, given the particular array of product, market and competitive behaviour? A car dealer, for example, may place a customer who has purchased a particular model, and who has indicated certain lifestyle interests, on a mailing list for regular information updates about new model innovations in order to create enthusiasm about a

possible new purchase. A specialist component manufacturer may work very closely with a number of client companies, providing first-rate service back-up, liaising on R&D and offering the clients new and better solutions in their operations. A local grocer may use friendliness, personal service, delivery and credit availability as the basis of relationship building with customers in winning their loyalty away from competing supermarket chains. In fact, many smaller local firms seem intuitively better at relationship management than bigger companies. The large firm can usefully imitate aspects of small firm practice in relationship marketing.

3. *Researching customer needs*: a thorough and unrelenting ambition on the part of the firm to understand the precise, and changing, needs and expectations of its customers characterises successful relationship marketing. Firms display great innovation in pursuing this, from running focus groups, commissioning lifestyle research, using point-of-sale terminals and telemarketing, to simply listening to and observing buyers and consumers in the marketplace. As we have seen, current research methods and computing technology facilitate an increasing ability to segment markets and customers on a variety of bases.

Many companies are now complementing their traditional mass advertising appeals with highly targeted one-to-one communication with customers, which offers the possibility of dialogue and relationship development. General Motors joined with Mastercard to offer the GM Card, and by the mid-1990s had a database of over 12 million GM cardholders; it surveys them to learn what they are driving, when they next plan to buy a car, and what kind of vehicle they would like. If a cardholder expresses an interest in, say, sport-utility vehicles, the card unit mails out information on its jeep line and passes the cardholder's name to the appropriate division (*Business Week*, 1994). Such targeted offerings garner a considerably higher response rate than the typical two to three per cent for the unsolicited mail referred to by some as junk mail, and may be seen as a way of nurturing closer firm-customer relations. However, not all such database marketing should be equated with relationship building. Much of it involves undifferentiated direct mail techniques and telemarketing, where the notion of a mutually satisfactory relationship remains very tenuous.

SETTING DIRECT MARKETING IN
A RELATIONSHIP MARKETING CONTEXT

This chapter proposes that direct marketing is best considered in the wider context of relationship marketing. Relationship marketing focuses on the creation and maintenance of satisfying, mutually profitable relationships. So ultimately does direct marketing, although, as discussed later, some direct marketing activity may antagonise customers and stifle relations. Nonetheless, the concepts and constructs of relationship marketing help explain to the direct marketer what they are, or should be, about. A direct marketer happy with Bauer and Miglautsch's (1992) definition of direct marketing should be content "to buy into" Gronroos' (1994) definition of relationship marketing. It leads, at least, to a more customer-centred rather than media-focused conception of direct marketing (McGowan, 1995). It is worthwhile to consider further three dimensions of this interconnection: the relative role and costs of mass marketing and high definition marketing communication; whether direct marketing is tactical or strategic; and the danger of database marketing intrusion into customers' privacy.

Mass Marketing and High Definition Marketing Communication

When marketers seek to inform and persuade their customers, they have many communications media available. These can be classified in a graduated way from mass media towards highly targeted media. With traditional mass media such as TV, radio, print press and posters, the communication message or appeal is broadcast to a large audience. While many potential buyers are in the audience, there are likely many others for whom the message is of little or no interest. The approach is analogous to firing a shotgun. High definition marketing communication media, on the other hand, use a much more targeted, one-to-one approach, similar to a rifle. The appeal is individualised. Personalised letters in direct marketing activity are an example.

Consider a manufacturer of garden tools. They may try to develop brand awareness for their products by advertising them on prime-time TV. They will certainly "hit" many gardeners. They may advertise them on a specialist gardeners' programme on radio. Again, they will appeal to many gardeners, though not necessarily more than with their first stratagem. But they are targeting more precisely. They may attempt to achieve public relations coverage in gardening magazines. They may use sales promotion techniques in key garden centres and DIY outlets. Again, the message is being channelled in a focused way. The manufacturer may also develop a database of dedicated gardeners and seek to establish their brand franchise by individualised, highly defined communication.

No one stratagem is intrinsically more or less effective. Which approach, or mix of approaches, is adopted depends on the feasibility and costs of each route *relative* to their effectiveness and benefit. Where the marketer chooses along the mass marketing to high definition marketing continuum depends on a number of factors. Each factor must be considered carefully to assess the relative cost-effectiveness of different approaches. Figure 1.4 suggests that these factors can be grouped under four headings: consumer tastes; information and communications technology (ICT) effectiveness; market dynamics; and the nature of the product or service.

Consumer Tastes

If consumer tastes and values are fairly homogeneous, mass media tend to be cost-effective. It has been argued that the increasingly heterogeneous nature of today's consumer means more individualised attention will likely be successful. But how much more successful? And at what cost? Some direct marketing pundits maintain that mass marketing is dead. The evidence is far from clear. Fanning (1997) points out that an effective loyalty marketing programme for a major brand in the Republic of Ireland could cost up to £1 million and adds:

> it is always worth remembering why advertising became the force it is today — because of its ability to deliver large audiences at very low prices. An advertisement on the national television network (RTE) can still deliver a thousand house-

wives for about £8. To reach a thousand housewives through relationship marketing would cost significantly more.

FIGURE 1.4: KEY DIMENSIONS OF MASS MARKETING AND HIGH DEFINITION MARKETING COMMUNICATION

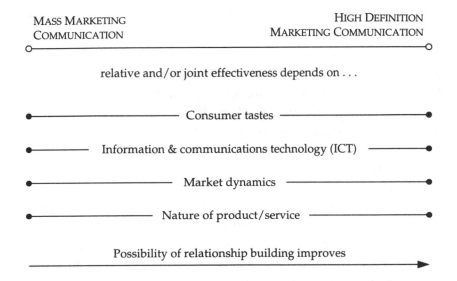

Furthermore, in many nascent developing countries (e.g. South America and China), the consumer remains homogeneous and brand awareness, to pull the consumer up the loyalty ladder, is best achieved by mass advertising. Thus the marketer evaluates the cost-benefits of different communication approaches in the light of evolving consumer attitudes and values.

Information and Communications Technology (ICT)

Such evaluation must also take place in regard to the current status of ICT. The veritable explosion of ICT over the past two decades has provided many more media and made high definition marketing communications more feasible, accurate and cheaper. I have already highlighted the way in which Postaim and the development of a first-rate telephone network contributed to the growth of direct marketing in Ireland. The development of a satellite TV "gardeners' world" channel might enable our hypothetical garden tool company to employ targeted direct response TV advertising. As technology continues to expand, more products and markets will become amenable to highly selective and one-to-one marketing. But the issue of the (relative) costs and effectiveness of such media must be borne in mind.

Market Dynamics

The structure of and competitive behaviour in the marketplace also have a bearing on the choice of communication media. In a market with strong "gatekeepers" or in a mature market with oligopolistic tendencies, where key players traditionally use mass media, high definition marketing communication presents an opportunity for winning competitive advantage. Part of the reason large food manufacturers are initiating one-to-one dialogue with consumers is to circumvent the power of large retailers. Drink manufacturers, acknowledging powerful distributor and trade networks, are using highly targeted, imaginative sales promotion and direct marketing practices aimed at these intermediaries in order to win their brand loyalty and to encourage them to push manufacturers' products to the final consumer. Other manufacturers eschew distributors and retailers altogether and supply directly to the final user in a traditional direct marketing approach; in so doing they may use a combination of mass marketing and highly defined marketing communication methods. Dell Computers sells and supplies directly to its customers and uses a mixture of broadly and highly defined marketing communication.

Nature of Product/Service

The characteristics of the product or service obviously have an important role in choosing a mode of communication. Business-to-business and industrial products with a high level of customisation in design are likely to employ highly defined channels. A manufacturer of specialist industrial refrigeration equipment will have a very focused approach to their target market. Unilever, on the other hand, uses mass advertising in promoting its ice cream to the gigantic Chinese market. When a service is small and localised, its communications activity will be limited and well defined, perhaps only amounting to promoting word-of-mouth endorsement. As a service goes national and international, standardises its operations and possibly licenses them under a business format franchise (e.g. McDonald's), its marketing communications adopt more mass appeal. Yet many such services are increasingly complementing this broad communication with individualised approaches (e.g. financial and insurance services).

Thus the marketer, in making decisions about marketing communication, must carefully consider these four dimensions. The outcome of such consideration may be broadly dispersed or highly defined communication. Or it may be an optimal combination of both, depending on issues of cost-effectiveness. Equally, the direct marketer must fully understand the issues at play here. It is only then that the range, possibilities and likely effectiveness of different direct marketing activity can be assessed. An affiliation programme incorporating telemarketing, at the expense of existing TV advertising, may become a realistic, and winning, option.

Further, it is only then that the direct marketer can speculate on the level of response and longer-term loyalty they might win from customers. As Figure 1.4 suggests, as one moves across the continuum towards high definition marketing communication, the possibility of relationship building improves. Interaction and personalised exchange become a reality, and the largely passive dimension of the customer in mass communication recedes. While there are many difficulties and pitfalls involved in establishing relationships and partnerships with customers, the process only becomes feasible when individualised one-to-one dialogue — whether by mail, phone, "virtual" contact, other electronic circuitry, and/or face to face — becomes possible.

Direct Marketing: Tactical or Strategic?

Is direct marketing tactical or strategic? The contention in the preceding section — that the use of direct marketing is predicated on decisions about relevant marketing communication — makes this question redundant. Indeed, the notion of strategic direct marketing is unhelpful. It is redolent of the sophistic thinking of many managers and educators who seek to legitimise their particular domain or sub-field of marketing by rushing to label it as strategic. It is symptomatic of an ever-hopeful "me too, me too" syndrome. Furthermore, attempts by some writers (Cook, 1994) to suggest tactical versus strategic uses for direct marketing come across as confusing.

The job of the marketing manager, along with other senior managers in the firm, is to develop a marketing strategy. The marketing strategy determines the choice of market in which the firm intends to compete. It involves scrutiny of customer need, understanding the firm's competencies in the light of market need, assessment of marketing assets and liabilities, and the development of marketing objectives and a broad strategy to serve the chosen market, all within the wider context of the firm's strategic management. Operationalising, managing and implementing this strategy involves a set of crucial decisions about product positioning, the choice and characteristics of the product/service, its price, distribution, selling and communication. In this context, direct marketing activity may (or may not) have a relevant and powerful role to play. This is the only sense in which direct marketing is strategic.

In the context of the overall marketing strategy, direct marketing should have a balanced and integrative part to play in winning and keeping satisfied and loyal customers. In this line of thinking, traditional categories such as above-the-line (e.g. mass media such as TV and press), below-the-line (e.g. sales promotion and merchandising), and even beyond-the-line (e.g. sponsorship and telesales) promotion/communication seem dated and unhelpful to the marketer. A mindset which considers a portfolio of opportunities, where complementarity rather than exclusivity becomes a guiding principle, is required. Getting that balance and level of integration right requires considerable competence on the part of the firm's marketing management and its advisers — the better the balance, the greater the synergistic (2 + 2 = 5) effect. Figure 1.5 describes how Tesco is now complementing its traditional mass advertising appeals with highly targeted one-to-one communication with customers.

The concept of integrated marketing communications (IMC) refers to getting this equilibrium right in marketing communications — for instance, getting the right mix of mass and highly defined communication presented in Figure 1.4. But getting it right is difficult, and firms, their marketing personnel and their outside providers and consultants are very much still in a learning mode. Much can go wrong. Organisational behaviour and structures may mean that direct marketing remains a separate function from sales, PR, and so on, and each tries to maintain its own integrity by keeping vital information, even customer lists, to itself. As Goften (1996) points out:

> there's nothing more sad than the spectacle of an ad agency deploying one concept and a PR agency pursuing another. It's not only a crime against the economic use of resources but no service at all to either client or consumer.

FIGURE 1.5: TESCO MARKETS TO THE NEXT GENERATION

Tesco operates a chain of 600 supermarkets throughout the UK and Ireland. It has grown dramatically over the last decade to outperform and out-position its rivals, with a sharply focused value-for-money philosophy for its customers. "Tesco's mission is to create value for the customer", says Tim Mason, its marketing director. "No decision, however big or small, is taken in the company unless the answer to the question 'does it add value for the customer?' is positive." This concern for the customer permeates the organisation, from the consultative staff forums among its 150,000 employees, its innovative product policy (it is into financial services and is the largest retailer of petrol in the UK) to its marketing communication.

Tesco features on any national list of big advertising spenders. But it is increasingly complementing such mass advertising expenditure with more individualised marketing communication. The conduit for doing this is its affiliation club. Shoppers who sign up receive a Tesco clubcard. Depending on the amount they purchase, they are entitled to bonus points, discounts and special offers. As part of this loyalty scheme, Tesco communicates regularly with members — who amounted to 11 million by the end of 1997.

It does so mainly through its highly targeted clubcard magazines. These are lifestyle and feature magazines which carry relevant product information in appealing settings. Based on the personal information supplied by customers on joining, and linked to other information sources such as replies to coupons and special offers, the firm can segment its market into a range of groupings based on life-stage, interests in holidays, food and home shopping. Life-stage, in turn, segments into seven categories: students, young mothers, young adults, families with small children, families with older children, older adults, and over-60s. Tesco believes the magazines enable dialogue with its customers and encourages a long-term relationship with the store and its products. "It helps build up emotional loyalty . . . and loyalty is emotional", says William Sieghart, who heads the specialist publishing agency which produces the magazines on behalf of Tesco.

Tesco had over 5,000 different customised magazines by the end of 1997. Company surveys indicate that 60 per cent of recipients read them cover to cover and 77 per cent take them up and read them in parts. The cost? Not as high as you might at first think. For a cost to Tesco of £1 per year per customer mailed, four magazines can be posted incorporating information on some 200 products! As such costs reduce and the feasibility of segmenting further increases — through various forms of data "fusion" of personal, geodemographic and transactional/EPOS information — the possibility of one-to-one communication with the customer becomes a reality.

Tesco has particular ambitions for its baby club magazine. Mothers-to-be are encouraged to register with the firm, and are sent six different magazines in the subsequent 18 months: during the first three months of pregnancy; during months three to six of pregnancy; during the three months after birth; during months three-to-six and six-to-twelve; and finally on the baby's first birthday — and the baby receives a present as well! For many mothers, such communication leads to a significant bonding to Tesco and its products. In 1996, 300,000 out of the 750,000 babies born in the UK were enlisted in Tesco's baby club!

Source: Mason (1997) and Sieghart (1997).

Direct Marketing: Intimacy or Intrusion?

Direct marketers know they have the chance to build a strong rapport and mutually satisfying relationship with their customers. The database represents a powerful technology for achieving this. But it can be a double-edged weapon, sometimes acting to stifle relations. Many consumers feel vulnerable and lacking control, knowing that so much information about them is available to firms, and possibly shared between firms. They feel their privacy being threatened more than they perceive a firm's wish to relate to them on a personal level. In effect, such consumers see as intrusion what direct marketers view as promoting intimacy. "The volume of direct marketing communications and marketers' acquisition, manipulation, and sale of information are exacerbating consumer 'privacy' concerns" (O'Malley et al., 1997). (See also Chapter 10 in this volume.)

To minimise these dangers, there is a need for greater transparency in intentions and actions, and for more attention to database accuracy and integrity. Firms should make clear to consumers what they are about and stress the potential mutual benefits of a relational approach. Information about consumers must be accurate and up-to-date and not sold or shared, unless by unambiguous consent on the part of the consumer; there is a need for customer-friendly databases, as distinct from user-friendly ones. Relationship building involves behaviour and an etiquette that transcends mere legalistic interpretation. Issues of trust, commitment, respect, mutuality of interest, adaptation and sensitivity to privacy and to private "space" all underpin it.

O'Malley et al. (1997) conclude that direct marketers:

> . . . can show their commitment to the relationship by maintaining accuracy, engaging in dialogue, and respecting individual privacy. Consumers must also show commitment if the relationship is to be successful, and the willing provision of accurate information for relationship building is one aspect of this. Finally, companies must ensure that their behaviour will continue to instil consumer trust. Without these elements, exploitation and manipulation exist, not a meaningful relationship.

CONCLUSIONS

Direct marketing is one of the fastest growing and most challenging domains of marketing today. While direct marketing activity is becoming more varied and sophisticated, all such activity shares certain characteristics: targeted communication intended to encourage quick, measurable, direct response; database development; and the use of one-to-one dialogue to encourage relationship building. Arguably, any more precise definition of direct marketing will prove self-limiting, considering the discipline's rapidly evolving nature.

It is contended that direct marketing is best comprehended in the context of relationship marketing. Direct marketers need to embrace the full extent of the paradigm shift implicit in relationship marketing and understand the concepts and constructs of a relational approach. The aim of best direct marketing practice is the creation and maintenance of mutually satisfying, profitable partnerships with customers. In a concrete sense, direct marketers appreciate the marketing communication options facing their firms along the continuum from mass marketing to highly defined marketing communication; these options involve consideration of four key dimensions: consumer tastes; information and communications technology (ICT) effectiveness; market dynamics; and the nature of the product or service. Such assessment and decision-making is, of course, done in the light of the firm's overall marketing strategy. It is only then that direct marketing becomes an integrated and synergistic activity in the marketing and corporate ambitions of the firm.

There are difficulties ahead. The extent to which it is possible to build relationships with consumers is as yet unknown (Barnes, 1995). The dynamics and protocol of nurturing relationships need further study. There is the danger of consumers reacting to what they consider to be an invasion of privacy. Little is known of consumers' behavioural and psychological response to direct marketing appeals (Evans et al., 1997); we know whether they respond or not, but we do not know *why*. So conclusions about the long-term cost-effectiveness of, say, loyalty programmes remain tenuous, and many manufacturers and retailers are coy about their ultimate "profitability".

Yet much first-rate direct marketing practice continues to emerge. The successful firm today is essentially a learning organisation; and knowledge about direct marketing is still at an early stage of development (DeTienne and Thompson, 1996). At times, direct marketing seems to be riding a rollercoaster of technology. But the technology must be the servant of a set of beliefs and assumptions which govern the success of direct marketing activity. At the heart of these beliefs and assumptions lies the notion of relationships and relationship building — and not just neural networks and database building.

REFERENCES TO CHAPTER 1

Barnes, J.G. (1995), "Establishing Relationships — Getting Closer to the Customer may be More Difficult than you Think", *Irish Marketing Review*, Vol. 8, pp. 107–116.

Bauer, C.L. and J. Miglautsch (1992), "A Conceptual Definition of Direct Marketing", *Journal of Direct Marketing*, Vol. 6, No. 2, p. 10.

Boehm, R. and C. Phipps (1996), "Flatness Forays", *The McKinsey Quarterly*, No. 3, pp. 32–48.

Brady, J. and I. Davis (1993), "Marketing's Mid-life Crisis", *The McKinsey Quarterly*, No. 2, pp. 17–28.

Brown, S. (1996), "Art or Science? Fifty Years of Marketing Debate", *Journal of Marketing Management*, Vol. 12, No. 4, pp. 3–12.

Business Week (1994), "Database Marketing: a Potent New Tool for Selling", 5 September.

Cook, S. (1994), "Database Marketing: Strategy or Tactical Tool?", *Marketing Intelligence and Planning*, Vol. 12, No. 6, pp. 4–7.

Coopers and Lybrand (1993), *Marketing at the Crossroads*, London: Coopers and Lybrand.

DeTienne, K. and J. Thompson (1996), "Database Marketing and Organisational Learning Theory: Toward a Research Agenda", *Journal of Consumer Marketing*, Vol. 13, No. 5, pp. 12–34.

Direct Marketing Association (1981), "Defining Direct Marketing", *Newsletter*.

Direct Marketing Association (1995), *Economic Impact: US Direct Marketing Today*, special study conducted by The WEFA Group for the DMA, New York.

Evans, M., M. Patterson, L. O'Malley and S. Mitchell (1997), "Consumer Reactions to Database-based Supermarket Loyalty Schemes", *The Journal of Database Marketing*, Vol. 4, No. 4, pp. 307–320.

Evans, M (1998), "From 1086 and 1984: Direct Marketing into the Millennium", *Marketing Intelligence and Planning*, Vol. 16, No. 1, pp. 56–67.

Evans, M. (1994), "Domesday Marketing?", *Journal of Marketing Management*, Vol. 10, No. 5, pp. 409–31.

Fanning, J. (1997), "Is the End of Advertising Really all that Nigh?", *Irish Marketing Review*, Vol. 9, No. 1, pp. 15–25.

George, M., A. Freeling and D. Court (1994), "Reinventing the Marketing Organisation", *The McKinsey Quarterly*, No. 4, pp. 43–62.

Goften, K. (1996), "Integrating the Delivery", *Marketing*, 31 October, pp. viii–ix.

Gosden, F.F. (1985), *Direct Marketing Success*, New York: Wiley, p. 7.

Gronroos, C. (1994), "Quo Vadis Marketing? Towards a Relationship Marketing Paradigm", *Journal of Marketing Management*, Vol. 10, pp. 347–60.

Gummesson, E. (1987), "The New Marketing — Developing Long-term Interactive Relationships", *Long Range Planning*, Vol. 20, No. 4, pp. 10–20.

Håkansson, H. (ed.) (1982), *International Marketing and Purchasing of Industrial Goods: an Interaction Approach*, Chicester: John Wiley & Sons.

Kitchen, P. (1986), "Zipping, Zapping and Nipping", *International Journal of Advertising*, Vol. 5, pp. 343–52.

Kobs, J. (1979), *Profitable Direct Marketing*, Chicago: Crain Books, p. 2.

Kotler, P. (1991), "From Transactions to Relationships to Networks", Paper presented to the Trustees of the Marketing Science Institute, Boston, November.

McGowan, M. (1995), "Direct Marketing — Irish Perspectives", in T. Meenaghan and P. O'Sullivan (eds.), *Marketing Communications in Ireland*, Dublin: Oak Tree Press.

Mason, Tim (1997), "Marketing Planning at Tesco", address to the Strategic Planning Society — Irish Region, Dublin, 9 October.

Meenaghan, T. (1995), "Marketing Communications in transition", in T. Meenaghan and P. O'Sullivan (eds.), *Marketing Communications in Ireland*, Dublin: Oak Tree Press.

Muranyi, N.R. (1997), "Database Marketing in FMCGs: What is the State of the Art?", *The Journal of Database Marketing*, Vol. 4, No. 1.

Murray, J.A. and A. O'Driscoll (1996), "Reconsidering the Management of Marketing", *Irish Marketing Review*, Vol. 9.

Murrow, J.L. and M.R. Hyman (1994), "Direct Marketing: Passages, Definitions, and Déjà Vu", *Journal of Direct Marketing*, Vol. 8, No. 3, p. 51.

Nash, E.L. (ed.) (1984), *The Direct Marketing Handbook*, New York: McGraw-Hill.

O'Malley, L., M. Patterson and M. Evans (1997), "Intimacy or Intrusion? The Privacy Dilemma for Relationship Marketing in Consumer Markets", *Journal of Marketing Management*, Vol. 13, No. 6, pp. 541–59.

Payne, A., M. Christopher, M. Clark and H. Peck (1995), *Relationship Marketing for Competitive Advantage: Winning and Keeping Customers*, Oxford: Butterworth-Heinemann.

Peppers, D. and M. Rogers (1995), "A New Marketing Paradigm: Share of Customer, Not Market Share", *Managing Service Quality*, Vol. 5, No. 3, pp. 48–51.

Peters, T. (1987), *Thriving on Chaos*, Basingstoke: Macmillan, p. 91.

Reichheld, F.F. (1993), "Loyalty-based Management", *Harvard Business Review*, March–April, pp. 64–73.

Reichheld, F.F. and W.E Sasser (1990), "Zero Defections: Quality Comes to Services", *Harvard Business Review*, September–October, pp. 105–11.

Sieghart, William (1997), "Loyalty Marketing — The Tesco Story", address to The Marketing Institute's National Marketing Conference, Dublin, 16 October.

Chapter 2

REFLECTIONS ON DIRECT MARKETING IN IRELAND

Francis G. Lalor

Overview

My early exposure to direct marketing came from overseas companies and international experiences. These translated into Irish activity with organisations like Time, Reader's Digest, *and* Encyclopaedia Britannica. *Then to involvement with Bank of Ireland, An Post, Irish Life, Newsweek International and other organisations who pioneered the use of this "new" marketing discipline in Ireland and abroad.*

Attendance at international direct marketing seminars and symposia in Europe and the United States from the early and mid-1980s — and the establishment of relationships with industry people who are "gurus" in their own right — has given me an opportunity to view Irish direct marketing development from a different perspective.

This chapter is a personal perspective on the growth of direct marketing in Ireland. You will perhaps be surprised that a chapter in a book called Direct Marketing in Ireland *lacks emphasis on* Irish *specifics. That's for one simple reason. The techniques that we apply in Ireland are universal — not unique to Ireland. All we do in direct marketing is tailor successful formulae and practices to Irish market size, profile, circumstances and needs — because direct marketing is about satisfying those needs first, and continuing a relationship that is profitable and right for both parties.*

This chapter is designed to be an easy read, with one overriding objective — to fascinate you about direct marketing in the same way as it has fascinated me for over 30 years. But also, to make you realise that you're studying direct marketing at a time when it has come of age in Ireland and has an uncharted but highly exciting and profitable future.

THE COMMERCIAL BEGINNINGS OF
DIRECT MARKETING IN IRELAND

Direct marketing was alive and well in Ireland since before the 1950s. The Book Clubs that were tamed for censored Ireland. The clothing catalogues that promised you ten whole months to pay. The Shannon Mail Order Catalogue for US customers. Cash's Mail Order Catalogue that made use of the names and addresses of tourists to Irish stores who wanted postal delivery of Irish purchases to their overseas homes. The Bullworker Press advertisements that promised you a tremendous physique — or your money back. The host of develop and print "off-the-page" photographic operators who competed for your holiday or Christmas film, and competed savagely on price.

The hardy ones remain to this day.

Some "mail order" experiences that I had in the teens and twenties of my life illustrate two things: a surprisingly lively range of activity in the leisure, learning and literary sectors and a complete lack of Irish identification with these commercial ventures:

- The Reader's Digest Sweepstakes offers in the early 1960s that *convinced* me I had been selected as a winner of a fabulous Silver Shadow Rolls Royce. I eagerly waited for the morning post as a teenager to get that confirmation that never came.

- The advertising course by the School of Careers in London that I responded to through an advertisement in a magazine — a course that was an excellent example of a mid-1960s version of what we now call Distance Learning.

- The *National Geographic* that's been mailed to me without interruption — month after month — since I got my first subscription as a gift in 1959. That's almost 40 years of lifetime value from that first commitment!

This is not about nostalgia. It's about the realisation that direct marketing is not new to Ireland. But nobody called it direct marketing then!

In the early 1980s, I carried out informal research into what percentage of newspaper and magazine advertisements carried a coupon or other response device. Seventeen per cent of all advertisements had a reply device of some sort. (That compares to around 50 per cent today.)

Direct response was alive!

In the 1970s, every one of the 12,000 members of the Heron Book Club series in Ireland was held on card index and members' names and addresses were screened onto address labels for sequential monthly despatch of the next book in the monthly cycle.

Mail order was alive and well, too.

There were no data protection laws then, and no computer records. That came later. The advertisements and mailing pieces were brash and ugly. Looked down on by the advertising agency profession, they were designed for one purpose only — to maximise on qualified response and minimise on cost per enquiry and conversion to order. And they worked.

In those heady days of direct response, the low acquisition cost achieved by Irish activity when compared to UK experience made the Mail Order parent companies very envious indeed. Take a bow Family Album, Oxendales Catalogues and Reader's Digest!

Then the insurance and financial services revolution began to happen in earnest.

A visit from two senior executives from the west of Ireland in May 1987 introduced me to the vision of the first direct motor insurance marketing initiative. I became part of a marketing and operational team with the responsibility to develop and control the direct marketing package from a zero base. The company was Celtic International; the direct initiative Celtic Autoline.

Direct marketing computer-driven database communication by phone and mail was alive!

Bank of Ireland asked us to carry out the first major direct marketing audit of any financial institution in the same year. The race was on.

Or, more directly, the *realisation* that direct marketing was worthy of a serious part of their marketing activity was on — the realisation that their customer database was more than a computerised record of financial transactions.

THE MYSTIQUE OF DIRECT MARKETING

There's been a mystique surrounding direct marketing that's been difficult to displace. In parallel with this mystique has been a confusion in the minds of senior business people that direct marketing is "direct mail" or "mail order".

Add to that the historical indifference, fear of the unknown and lack of profit potential that advertising agencies have seen in direct marketing — and the misguided economics of new customer acquisition to the detriment of existing customer profitability — and you had a business cocktail destined for possible disaster rather than dynamic growth.

This has been the history of direct marketing world-wide. This has been the history of direct marketing in Ireland.

Over the years, we traded successfully by knowing our customers on a one-to-one basis: knowing their likes and dislikes; understanding how we could marry the benefits of our offerings to the real and perceived needs that they believed they wanted to fulfil; using that on-going relationship to more fully understand the process, the ease of repeat sale rather than the difficult acquisition of the first customer.

That is what direct marketing is about today. And that is what Irish business and commerce has begun to understand in the short history of direct marketing in Ireland.

AN UNDERSTANDING OF THE DIRECT MARKETING PROCESS

A basic understanding of the direct marketing process is an essential prelude to an understanding of the Irish experience.

Direct marketing is an aspect of total marketing. The most concise definition is that in Pete Hoke's *US Direct Marketing* magazine:

> Direct marketing is an interactive system of marketing that uses one or more advertising media to effect a measurable response and/or transaction at any location, with this activity stored on database. (March 1998)

But this definition does not do full justice to the process and the *outcome* of that information being held on database. Because the catchment of name, address and other enhanced information is the potent nucleus of a marketing tool that has a power and potential in excess of any other marketing method available.

Direct marketing practice confirms in measurable terms what is a fact in general marketing and communication: it costs money to buy the first customer — to make the first sale. You make money on repeat business with that customer.

This equation is not generally possible to measure in mainstream, branded, FMCG, consumer product or service marketing, particularly where there is a single or multi-tiered distribution chain. At best, marketers can attempt to measure cost per order from in-company financial monitoring, analysis and market information, and from industry monitoring services.

But that measurement and research cannot provide the most essential consequence of all — an ability to know each customer on a one-to-one basis and to relate to each customer in a manner which directly addresses their status, wants and desires.

Two service industry examples will illustrate this ability to use direct marketing as a powerful one-to-one relationship marketing tool: insurance and publishing.

Insurance

Motor insurance is one case in point. Through use of proven press, radio, TV and direct distribution media, direct response driven material invites a prospect to phone or write for a motor insurance quote.

From this mass of enquiries three things emerge:

1. A database of warm prospects who have willingly provided relevant information on age, sex, car type, driving record, other drivers, name, address, telephone number, etc.

2. An established cost per enquiry for each medium used

3. A data protection construction that allows for further contact on this and other product categories.

The second stage then follows:

1. A completed proposal is sent to all who have qualified for a quote

2. A certain percentage respond and convert to policyholders

3. An established cost per order for each medium used emerges.

The third stage is where the database comes into its own:

1. Three weeks before renewal, a re-activation procedure commences

2. A letter and renewal proposal form is mailed to the known policyholder with a renewal offer that relates directly to that customer. Telephone follow-up is made as a matter of course to slow responders

3. At a small percentage of the original cost of *enquiry* (not cost per order) in excess of 85 per cent will purchase again — if the offer is right!

But the use of the database doesn't stop with this renewal cycle. It is used to:

1. Cross-sell and up-sell add-ons and other insurance products

2. Encourage the introduction of friends and colleagues to the service

3. Sell related financial services products like motor and home loans

4. Comprehensively analyse the marketing cost of access and retention

5. Analyse the composition of customers, level of uptake by type of product and offer, profit thresholds by business sector and type, geographic and sociographic performance by area, measure the gains and losses against specific competition, etc.

The combination of the percentage enquiry level achieved and the optimum percentage conversion rate to order has a dramatic effect on the business achieved, the average cost per order (CPO) and the resultant economics of the lifetime value of customer. Fulfilment and customer servicing play an equally important role.

Publishing

The example given above was two-stage. In the case of a magazine subscription offer, the process is single stage. An invitation to subscribe is made through print or broadcast media, with the recipient being invited to commit to a subscription purchase at that stage.

Response percentages for (say) promotional inserts in credit card statements would typically attract what would appear to be a very small percentage response, a mere 0.30 per cent. The cost of that first sale could well be in excess of the gross subscription revenue. But the value is in the repeat opportunities. As early as 18 weeks before the first subscription is due to terminate, the first in a series of up to eight letters with a personalised order form is mailed. This series continues, for up to four weeks after the expiry date, to those who have not yet renewed.

An industry average for first time renewal is around 50 per cent of original subscribers. But subsequent renewal mailings to that existing base generate around 80 to 85 per cent renewal/retention. The methodology of acquiring first-time subscriptions at an apparent loss is now more than justified by the very low repeat cost of sale, the very high retention level and the real lifetime value of the subscriber.

Other profitable exercises for subscription magazines include:

- Re-activation programmes, where lapsed subscribers are encouraged to renew. This achieves very high and cost-effective results.

- Donor/donee programmes, where the subscriber is encouraged to give gifts of the publication to friends and associates.

- Donor renewal programmes, where the donor is encouraged to renew the gift subscriptions and consider additional gift subscriptions also.

- Donee programmes, where the receiver of the gift subscription is invited to subscribe in the event of the gift not being repeated by the donor.

All of these programmes are only possible because of the existence of the subscriber database and its regular use at a very low cost of access.

Tracking, Fulfilment and Customer Servicing

There is an unwritten rule among direct marketers that every cost of access must be monitored and analysed. While the three initial costs to monitor are cost per thousand access (CPT), cost per enquiry (CPE) and cost per order (CPO), the average order value (AOV) and lifetime value (LTV) are highly relevant to the direct marketing equation. No medium should be contemplated without first considering the consequences for these values.

Fulfilment may appear to be a mundane aspect of marketing. But it is by far the most important aspect in the new and developing relationship between prospect and customer. It is the completion of the loop, the bringing home of the customer. If left to disparate forces to complete, it is likely to fall apart and invalidate other aspects of the marketing effort. This cannot be over-emphasised.

Customer servicing fits in this same category. The "personality" of the customer servicing facility must be a mirror image of earlier direct communication and must be committed to fulfilling the promise made in the print or broadcast offer.

Too often, other values take over which are alien to the personality, intent and promise made in the first instance. But that's a separate subject, beyond the scope of an overview such as this.

THE POPULARISATION OF DIRECT MARKETING IN IRELAND

I invited a number of direct marketing industry peers to give me their thoughts on what they considered to be the dominant threshold that each could associate with the growth of direct marketing in Ireland.

The formation of the Irish Direct Marketing Association, the launch of Postaim and the highly attended and acclaimed Murray Raphel Seminars were the recurring reasons given. But I see these as astute reactionary forms to the emergence of what has become a relentless new force in marketing.

Others astutely identified a combination of factors that included the recession in the early 1990s (focusing the marketing mind on accountability and profitable sales); the revolution of information technology that has provided us with tools at a sophistication and price unheard of a few short years ago; and the belated realisation that "the customer is king" — a realisation that has brought "relationship marketing" to the forefront of marketing philosophy.

"Relationship *selling*" is what successful direct marketing is all about. But "selling" has become an obsolete word in sophisticated marketing and academic circles. It should be brought back in direct marketing vocabulary.

We get carried away by marketing jargon and creative strategies where cleverness of presentation and unity of image supersede the most basic considerations that drive traders to success or failure.

Those traders have to ask themselves:

- Are they making their proposition in the right place, to the right person, at the right time and in the easiest and most convenient way?

- Are they exposing a product or service (an offer or proposition) which has an immediate appeal and encouragement to act now — at a price that is attractive to their customer and that allows for a profit margin?

- Are they answering vital questions which the buyer has in mind before purchasing?

- Do they know this new customer well enough to ensure that they makes repeat sales as a consequence of this first sale?

The realisation that modern technology could turn the equivalent of the street trader's sensible goals into a mass marketing discipline for business was — to my mind — the turning point in direct marketing growth in Ireland.

External and internal changes and influences propel this attitude of mind, priority of direction and growth. A few pivotal influences can be identified:

- The huge growth in home phones (allied to the increasing pressures on time that modern life dictates);

- The breakdown of EU trading barriers (the fear of competitive attack and the need to protect home market share);

- The financial services revolution (car insurance, personal loans, mortgages and banking on demand by phone);

- The emergence of technology-driven call centres (encouraged by global centralisation of international customer services, lowering of telephone tariffs, sophisticated communications and computer technology, and the IDA's opportunistic grant-aided approach to this modern phenomena);

- The advance of the Internet (psychologically and electronically creating a world-wide direct marketing village within reach of all). I call the Internet "the next generation of direct marketing". It has all the tools that a direct marketer has yearned for, but never had until now. It has an immediacy and regression analysis edge that will influence how we do business for good. And it has particular significance for an island like Ireland that is technologically advanced and internationally oriented.

The Internet is a new marketing "media" for local opportunity. But think of it globally and it transcends this to reach new dimensions and horizons.

WHAT ARE THE MAJOR OBSTACLES TO FUTURE GROWTH?

Another question raised by me with my mentors — what are the major obstacles to the future growth of direct marketing in Ireland? The responses to this question were diverse and thought provoking. They should be taken as a challenge to those at the early stages of a direct marketing career. They are definitely being seriously addressed by the direct marketing industry at present:

> "Intrusive DM messages — in particular, cold calls to home addresses (invasion of privacy). In relation to mail, poor targeting (irrelevance) coupled with high mail volumes (seen as wasteful and irritating). If we alienate the consumer, our growth will be retarded." — *Kieran Devenish, Group Planning and Marketing, Eureko Ireland Holdings and IDMA Chairperson 1996–97.*

> "EU laws and the lack of access to good quality consumer databases with targeting capabilities." — *Pat Cody, Managing Director, Kompass Ireland and former IDMA Chairperson.*

"The biggest single factor is the lack of willingness of consumers to accept this way of doing business. I do not believe sufficient time and effort is taken to explain the benefits of dealing direct — scary application forms, complicated phone numbers and postage regulations (although currently improved) are just some of the consumer objections to parting with cash." — *Damian Ryan, Managing Director, RyanHo Publishing and Board Member, IDMA.*

"Its future is still being inhibited by many factors. Lack of appreciation of direct marketing as a marketing tool by businesses; inadequate education; confusion between below-the-line, sales promotion and direct marketing; hesitancy of mainstream advertising agencies to get involved, due partly to it not being seen as a lucrative area for them and fear of the unknown." — *Kathleen Treanor, Prime Programme Manager, International Post Corporation, Brussels and former IDMA Chairperson.*

"A surprising fear of public reaction due to poor understanding of basic principles." — *Adrian Taheny, Group Development Manager, FBD Insurance and former IDMA Chairperson.*

"The future growth of direct marketing in Ireland will be hampered by size of market, as the economies of scale are only reached once large volumes are mailed/contacted. I feel with a small market this is not always possible. Due to this cost consideration Irish companies do not regularly carry out tests and thus we roll out full mailings/direct marketing programmes which may not be profitable and are subsequently abandoned. This is in direct contrast with companies in the UK and the US, who would test market a small portion of the population and then, based on results, continue to increase their use of direct marketing in its most profitable form." — *Ewan Byrne, Managing Director, Family Album and former IDMA Chairperson.*

THE EXPERIENCE GAP AND COMPETITIVE PITCHING

Lack of direct marketing experience by Irish marketers and practitioners is an obstacle to growth. Go back to my memories of what influenced me in the 1960s. These were mainly UK and US organisations who were tapping the Irish market by direct response advertising and by direct mail. They had the benefit of hindsight — or elaborate testing and roll-out in other markets that allowed them to operate in Ireland without too much fear of getting it wrong.

It's refreshing now to see Irish organisations like Celtic Hampers and Telephone Marketing Services (TMS) being bought over by a UK catalogue company (GUS) and a US telemarketing organisation (Sitel) respectively. A tribute to both Irish companies and their appeal to international giants.

Reflecting on successful direct marketing organisations in Ireland, the situation is mainly in the reverse, with some obvious exceptions, like the Response Group who have bought into *overseas* specialist companies. I am of the opinion that the UK, US and international direct marketing businesses still represent the majority of direct marketing turnover in Ireland — and the centre of knowledge in this marketing discipline.

Apart from direct marketing's use by financial services and a nucleus of dedicated Irish FMCG organisations, our Irish-sourced volume is low.

It is also not as focused or targeted as I would like direct marketing to be.

In relation to education, the more sophisticated we become in selection and targeting, the more difficult it is to get credible matching and sufficient roll-out potential. This has led to us becoming "instant experts", where we tend to make decisions based on limited knowledge and little or no valid testing. A formula must be found to change this dangerous equation.

We have an increasing level of overseas experience: Irish practitioners returning from the UK or the US to take up careers in financial services or in the new breed of direct response agencies; or a number of international advertising agencies who've bought in to Irish-owned ad agencies and decided to form dedicated direct marketing/direct response agency subsidiaries.

This in turn has brought a dangerous culture that is more akin to mainstream agency operation: the free agency presentation or pitch for business. However wrong this is for mainstream agencies, it is very wrong for both client and DM agency in Ireland.

Direct marketing solutions do not come from a quick and clever creative pitch — they come from an in-depth relationship with clients, a deep understanding of client philosophy, strategy and vision, a knowledge of customer composition and segmentation, and a relationship that transcends second-guessing and third-degree treatment.

In direct marketing, the relationship must be long-term and intimate. Otherwise, it will not develop in a deliberate way and will result in the too-often-heard protestation: "I tried direct mail [sic] once, and it didn't work"!

There is also evidence of confrontation between mainstream advertising agencies, below-the-line promotions companies and direct marketing consultants/direct response agencies. Business is being sought where lines of professional demarcation are blurred.

This has been perpetrated to some degree by large financial institutions, where direct marketing has often been used as another method of access to gain market share at any cost. The soul of direct marketing solicitation is in its accountability, selectivity and future database worth, not as an indiscriminate buyer of business.

Too much lip service has been paid to regression analysis and data interrogation. It is only by knowing your customer intimately that real bottom-line opportunity can be realised.

TOMORROW'S MARKET IS TODAY'S CUSTOMER

Readily available research tells us that customers who have only bought one product (say motor insurance) lack loyalty and are as likely to move as they are to stay. They become more persistent as more products are purchased. A customer with three or more products (say home insurance, life cover and a savings plan from the same company) is likely to remain a customer for their lifetime.

But to be effective and improve profits, this must operate in an environment where the cost of re-selling is low.

Intelligent use of customer information can deliver on this requirement. Enhancing and maintaining that information in an up-to-date form naturally becomes an essential part of that equation.

The gathering of information must be transparent for its use to be effective. But when a two-way dialogue has been established and customer relationship marketing is implemented throughout the distribution system, there will be a dramatic rise in service satisfaction, response, order value, lifetime profitability and loyalty.

By following database-driven, customer-guided marketing principles throughout the organisation's activities, the customer will be involved as an equal partner in the marketing and service functions.

Acquiring and using greater quantities of customer information and encouraging partnership with customers will change the typical marketing campaigns of the past to personal dialogues with each individual customer. Such an approach will create long-term customer relationships based on trust and satisfaction between buyer and seller.

Involving each customer in a meaningful one-to-one relationship throughout the spectrum of activities — in a such a way that the customer's privacy is protected completely and that information is given freely and obtained transparently — will create a powerful asset and information base for creative marketing action.

This greatly enhanced customer database will begin to identify accurately who should be offered specific products and at what critical time. Cross-selling opportunities will become clear and targeted. Customer life cycles will be extended. Wasted and intrusive communications will be minimised, and in time eliminated. Informed and willing customer feedback will identify new market opportunities and new products, and provide invaluable information for accurate product pricing and superior service.

We operate in a small market with an adult consumer universe of around 2.5 million people and a core business universe of around 80,000 companies. This makes it all the more imperative for us to relate in the most sophisticated way to each customer. Acquiring a new customer is an expensive business; knowing that customer and directly servicing their individual needs is the profitable outcome.

A VALUABLE SOURCE OF PRACTICAL KNOWLEDGE AND IRISH EXPERIENCE

This book provides a unique insight into the practice and theory of direct marketing from an Irish perspective. I believe that you will be fascinated by how it relates to different marketing disciplines, media and attitudes to customer relationships.

If you are already in marketing, it will fundamentally influence how you view communications. If you are a new student to marketing, it will provide you with a cost-effective and focused approach to marketing that I would have loved to have had on my bookshelf when I began my own career in marketing.

You will be challenged by direct marketing in a more intense way than any other marketing discipline, for one simple reason — it's so measurable. But that challenge is its appeal. Accept the challenge and read on!

POST SCRIPT

The value of a PS in a letter is one of the first things you'll learn about in direct marketing communication. But there are lots of other practices and principles that relentlessly work, and continue to work.

On reviewing my friend Jerry Reitman's book, *Beyond 2000: The Future of Direct Marketing*, where he invited 28 of the world's leading experts to predict changes and challenges, I was impressed by the unshakeable realism of Bob Stone's "30 Timeless Direct Marketing Principles". Over his career in direct marketing, Bob Stone[1] identified 30 principles that proved true more than 90 per cent of the time. With small variations, these principles are universal and as applicable to Ireland as elsewhere in the world.

Study these as my added value to this chapter. Because they'll save you a lot of mistakes I made before I discovered the infallibility of these principles through hard and costly experience.

1.   All customers are not created equal. Give or take a few percentage points, 80 per cent of repeat business for goods and services will come from 20 per cent of your customer base.

2.   The most important order you ever get from a customer is the second order. Why? Because a two-time buyer is at least twice as likely to buy again as a one-time buyer.

3.   Maximising direct mail success depends first on the lists you use, second on the offers you make, and third on the copy and graphics you create.

---

[1] Bob Stone, Chairman Emeritus of Stone and Adler, Inc., has contributed greatly to the direct marketing community through his writing and teaching. His book, *Successful Direct Marketing Methods*, has become an essential handbook for Direct Marketing students — and practitioners — around the world. He is the recipient of numerous awards and is a member of the US Direct Marketing Hall of Fame.

4. If, on a given list, "hotline" names don't work, the other list cate-
    gories offer little opportunity of success.

5. Merge/purge names — those that appear on one or more lists —
    will outpull any single list from which these names have been
    extracted.

6. Direct response lists will almost always outpull compiled lists.

7. Overlays (enhancements) on lists, such as lifestyle characteristics,
    income, education, age, marital status, and propensity to respond
    by mail or by phone will always improve response.

8. A follow-up to the same list within 30 days will pull 40–50 per
    cent of the first mailing.

9. "Yes/No" offers consistently produce more orders than offers
    that don't request "no" responses.

10. The "take rate" for negative-option offers will always outpull
    positive-option offers by at least two-to-one.

11. Credit card privileges will outperform cash with order by at least
    two-to-one.

12. Credit card privileges will increase the size of the average cata-
    logue order by 20 per cent or more.

13. Time limit offers, particularly those that give a specific date, out-
    pull offers with no time limit practically every time.

14. Free gift offers, particularly where the gift appeals to self-interest,
    outpull discount offers consistently.

15. Sweepstakes, particularly in conjunction with impulse purchases,
    will increase order volume by 35 per cent or more.

16. You will collect far more money in a fund-raising effort if you
    ask for a specific amount from the purchaser. Likewise, you will
    collect more money if the appeal is tied to the specific project.

17. People buy benefits, not features.

18. The longer you can keep someone reading your copy, the better
    your chances of success.

19. The timing and frequency of renewal letters is vital. But I can report nothing but failure over a period of 40 years in attempts to hype renewals with "improved copy". I've concluded that the "product" — the magazine, for example — is *the factor* in making a renewal decision.

20. Self-mailers are cheaper to produce, but they practically never outpull envelope-enclosed letter mailings.

21. A pre-print of a forthcoming ad, accompanied by a letter and a response form, will outpull a post-print mailing package by 50 per cent or more.

22. It is easier to increase the average dollar amount of an order than it is to increase percentage of response.

23. You will get far more new catalogue customers if you put your proven winners in the front pages of your catalogue.

24. Assuming items of a similar appeal, you will always get a higher response rate from a 32-page catalogue than from a 24-page catalogue.

25. A new catalogue to a customer base will outpull cold lists by 400–800 per cent.

26. A print ad with a bind-in card will outpull the same ad without a bind-in up to 600 per cent.

27. A direct response, direct sale TV commercial of 120 seconds will outpull a 60-second direct response commercial better than two-to-one.

28. A TV support commercial will increase response from a newspaper insert by up to 50 per cent.

29. The closure rate from qualified leads can be from two to four times as effective as cold calls.

30. Telephone-generated leads are likely to close four to six times greater than mail-generated leads.

REFERENCES TO CHAPTER 2

Stone, Bob (1994), *Successful Direct Marketing Methods*, 5th edition, Chicago, IL: NTC Business Books.

Reitman, Jerry (1994), *Beyond 2000: The Future of Direct Marketing*, Chicago, IL: NTC Business Books.

Chapter 3

BUILDING BRANDS THROUGH DIRECT MARKETING

Mary Lawlor *and* Michael Killeen

Overview

Brand strategy is often viewed as a distinct task from direct marketing. However, a direct marketing approach that uses customer information contributes to developing awareness and brand loyalty for companies today.

Much of the recent branding literature refers to the early 1990s as an era of turbulence for the marketing world (Brown, 1996; Muranyi, 1995; King, 1991). On 2 April 1993, now referred to as "Marlboro Friday", Philip Morris announced that they were cutting the price of Marlboro cigarettes, one of the world's strongest brands. This was followed by shock headlines in the popular press and panic in corporate boardrooms. Now companies like Coke, Microsoft and Disney are proving that having a strong name may be the ultimate competitive weapon (Light, 1997).

How the stock markets react to what a firm does with a brand can indicate how investors view these strategies. Research findings by Aaker and Jacobson (1994) clearly indicate that firms who invested in their brands and who focused on long-term goals for brands experienced the largest gains in brand equity and stock return. Branding creates value for consumers, the firm and its stockholders. In a dynamic marketing environment, today's brand owners are leveraging the power of the direct interface with the customer and rethinking their approach to building brands.

This chapter defines branding and examines the main challenges to brands, including a discussion on the increased power of intermediaries, new approaches to distribution and communication among competitors, and more demanding consumers. The factors considered important in building brands are then outlined. We discuss how to build brands using more interactive direct marketing approaches in conjunction with advertising.

DEFINITION OF A BRAND

While a product has been defined as "anything that meets the needs of customers", brands exist to identify and distinguish a firm's particular offering. Doyle (1990) suggests that brand awareness alone is not the hallmark of a successful brand. He defined a successful brand as:

> A name, symbol, design, or some combination, which identifies the "product" of a particular organisation as having a sustainable differential advantage.

A brand identifies the source of a promise and is considered a shortcut in communication: the values offered by brands are often communicated through simple advertising themes. Customers should have a reason to prefer a firm's brand to those of its competitors and the brand should not be easily imitated by competitors. If brands can maintain a sustainable differential advantage, they can be treated as an asset for the company. Bird (1996) points out that

> The brand and its image results from what you are and what you do, the way you deal with your customers, the products you have sold, the value you have offered. These activities will do more for your brand and its image than anything else.

An example of this is American Express, whose card members expect recognition and service superior to that offered to the average credit card holder. Recognition is at the heart of the long-running slogan, "Membership has its Benefits". This reflects how American Express has maintained its differentiation by increasing the range of services and privileges available to card members.

Ballygowan is one of the great success stories of Irish branding. The company has positioned the brand in the mind of consumers around the image of purity using the core proposition "No Other Water" and has achieved a dominant share of the market, both in Ireland and the UK.

Guinness is recognised as a company that is committed to brand building. The company spent IR£15 million in 1996/97 on the Guinness "Big Pint" campaign to give the brand a more accessible image among the younger generation. Research had shown that the Guinness brand needed to be imbued with more impact and aggression and to be lowered from a pedestal upon which many drinkers placed it. It was seen to be "out of step" with the mores of the "just-do-it" generation raised on aggressive brands like Nike, Marlboro, Levi's and Virgin.

THE BRAND CHALLENGE

Established and new brands compete in a rapidly changing marketing environment with increased power residing with intermediaries. Competitors are employing radically different approaches to marketing, using new channels of communication and distribution to reach consumers who are more sophisticated and demanding. The following section describes the marketing environment in which brands compete.

Changing Role of Retailers

In consumer markets, the strongest new competition comes from retailer private label products, which are taking a growing share in many categories. The trend is most visible for grocery and DIY goods, but private label is also emerging in more expensive, high technology product categories such as consumer electronics, photography and computers.

In the UK grocery market, private label share exceeds 30 per cent in most supermarkets. In excess of 50 per cent of the products sold in Sainsbury's are the retailer's own label while Marks & Spencer sell their own label exclusively. According to Lambkin (1996), the penetration of own label in Ireland is four per cent — the lowest in Europe. A report in *Checkout Ireland* (1996) suggests that the arrival of the British multiples in Ireland will have a major effect on premium own brand labels. It is suggested that UK multiples will gain share by the promotion of loyalty schemes and rewarding high-spending customers. Retail brands provide higher margins for retailers who determine the shelf space and position given to their own and manufacturer brands. They reproduce the features and benefits of manufacturer brands, and add the values associated with their own retailer brand. Retailers need invest little in research, do not need to market each product separately, have guaranteed distribution, and can compete at lower prices. Increased consumer promotions demanded by both retailer and customer has resulted in greater brand promiscuity and brand switching among consumers.

In many retail sectors, specialist retailers offer wide selections of goods at low prices. They spend little on their sites or their merchandising and compete at prices even lower than the multiples.

Retailers have become very sophisticated marketers, building powerful databases that enable them to have a greater understanding of their customers' needs and behaviour. In essence, they have established a closer relationship with customers than manufacturers have. Retailers control the interface with their customers and have exploited the many opportunities to build closer relationships with customers, appearing almost as "virtual manufacturers".

Brand managers are required to develop a greater understanding of the consumers who purchase their brands. The emphasis must shift to identifying the customers who account for most of the brand's sales. Manufacturers must continuously explore new ways to communicate and establish a dialogue with the consumer.

Changing Role of Marketing

Recent marketing literature has been critical of the traditional marketing function (Brady et al., 1993) and has suggested that marketing is "not picking up the signals and is facing a mid-life crisis". Pearson (1996) highlighted that marketing has experienced marginalisation, with little evidence of marketers becoming business managers. He suggests that marketing is lacking in credibility because it is rarely accountable. Further criticisms have pointed to marketing as being a "big spending" function lacking innovation and relying more on low risk brand and line extensions. Much of the contribution to company growth has derived from other functions employing total quality management, benchmarking, just-in-time, logistics and database techniques. More recently, however, firms in many sectors have re-engineered their approach to marketing and customers.

Firms in numerous industries have chosen to communicate and sell direct to the consumer, exemplified by Dell Computers and Direct Line Insurance in the UK. Dell sees itself as a "manu-tailer". Information and flexible manufacturing technologies enable economies of large-scale production, resulting in a high degree of product customisation to the individual level. It manufactures all its PCs to individual customer orders. Dell's growth is founded on a standard of customer service that established manufacturers could not match through their dealer networks and sales forces.

The common advantage enjoyed by the new competition is ownership of the customer interface. Companies are building their own brands by developing direct links to their customers. According to Shocker et al. (1994):

> . . . new competitors are leveraging their established relationships with customers to penetrate markets rapidly. In every market, power resides with whomever is in direct contact with the customer. A new form of branding is evolving: "relationship branding". You brand and promote not only the product but the relationship as well. How well the company interacts with the customer to create added value.

In an over-branded world, the biggest challenge today does not lie in more brands, or further brand extensions. Firms are focusing their attention on fewer, bigger and stronger brands. Procter & Gamble has devised "Wash and Go" as a one-formulation product suitable for all hair types, while its competitors continue to extend their brands. Research findings indicated that consumers required more simplified product sets. Firms are revisiting the marketing rules derived from the classic brands and returning to basics in their approach to building brands.

Brand managers in companies such as Lever Bros., Heinz and Masterfoods are beginning to capture more data about individual customers. This information, stored on a database, can be used to target segments and generate more powerful and personal communications to their customers (Linton, 1995).

Masterfoods' Whiskas cat food campaign in Ireland identified and targeted "cat lovers" from information collected from "take-ones" in the aisles of supermarkets. They captured information about the names of the owners, their cats and the brands they consume and followed up with a personalised letter to the cat owner offering free samples and a gift for their cats. More efficient use can be derived from marketing budgets when key customers can be identified as individuals and targeted with relevant messages motivating the customer to buy the company's brand.

The challenge to brand managers is how to adapt proactively to harsh new market realities in increasingly open markets. The companies that control the interface with customers have the opportunities to build relationships, targeting customers who they know are likely to buy more or are willing to pay more. These strong relationships make it less attractive for customers to migrate to competitors.

The Changing Consumer

Increased competition and changing demographics have altered the customer decision-making process in general, and brand choice in particular. Increased competition exposes customers to new information and product/service alternatives that have potential to influence their tastes and preferences (Shocker et al., 1994). As a result, customers are more questioning and less trusting. They want more choice and better information about the products that they consume. There is a great sense of immediacy among today's consumers who seek immediate information and benefits from the brands that they purchase. They are more demanding and seek products and services that are designed to meet their needs as individuals (Pearson, 1996). Aware of the increased choices on offer, they expect to be rewarded for their custom. Constrained by a reduction in disposable income, they seek better value for their money. Consumers expect high quality brands and personal added values, variants, style and fashion changes. They are less tolerant of brands that do not contribute to their own values (Susman, 1996).

Brand managers must recognise that customer satisfaction and "relationships" with a brand provide the best protection from competition. Satisfied customers, who can interact with the brand, buy more, are willing to pay more, incur lower sales and service costs, and provide referrals (Jones et al., 1995). Brand managers are increasingly charged to develop and communicate a strong and consistent brand image through a variety of traditional and direct media. The optimum media mix to communicate with customers is increasingly being decided by information, collected at household (micro) and store (macro) levels, on consumers' brand preferences, socioeconomic characteristics and sensitivity to sales promotions.

This section of the chapter has considered some of the issues facing brand builders. Firms competing in markets characterised by an increase in the power of distributors, demanding and volatile customers, and competitors with re-engineered communication and distribution strategies, are faced with the challenge of building their customer base and their margins. The consensus among marketing academics and practitioners is that success will depend on a firm's brand building skills. King (1991) suggests that a firm should establish a competitive advantage in an area of marketing and employ all its assets to develop and maintain brands that certain consumers really want. The following section discusses the key factors in building a successful brand and the direct methods employed to communicate the brand to the target market.

KEY FACTORS IN BUILDING BRANDS

Like any company asset, a brand will depreciate without further support and investment in its quality, service levels and the brand image and associations.

Successful brands are treated as assets and brand equity is the term that is used to describe the value of a brand name. Aaker (1991) defines brand equity as:

> A set of brand assets and liabilities linked to a brand, its name and symbol, that add to or subtract from the value provided by a product or service to a firm and/or to that firm's customers.

He groups the assets underlying brand equity into five categories:

1. *Brand Loyalty*: Customers who are loyal to a brand will purchase more and speak favorably about the brand;

2. *Name Awareness*: Successful brands strive to achieve high levels of awareness;

3. *Perceived Quality*: The consumers' perception of brand quality influences their purchasing behaviour;

4. *Brand Associations*: Customers may favourably (or unfavourably) associate the brand with some positive (or negative) aspect;

5. *Other Assets*: Relationships with intermediaries, patents and trademarks contribute to the equity of the brand.

Advertising, both image and direct response, sales promotion, electronic media, the relationships between the company's staff and their customers all contribute to developing brand awareness, creating brand loyalty, building associations, and influencing consumers' perceptions of brand quality. Table 3.1 summarises how direct marketing can influence the consumer's decision-making process before and after purchasing the brand on a one-to-one level. It also highlights the brand building activities required to strengthen the customer's relationship with the brand, from awareness to loyalty and ultimately to association with other brands within a brand family.

TABLE 3.1: BRAND BUILDING THROUGHOUT THE BUYING PROCESS USING DIRECT MARKETING

Consumer decision-making process before purchase	Customer acquisition	Interactive communications before purchase	Brand building before purchase
1. Problem Recognition	Suspect	Image and Direct Response Advertising,	Brand Awareness
2. Information Search	Prospect	Interactive Response Media, On-demand information, Internet, Electronic Media, Video, CD	Brand Knowledge
3. Evaluation of Alternatives	Prospect	Interactive Response Media, On-demand information, Electronic Media, Video, CD, Catalogues	Brand Preference
4. Purchase	Customer	Direct Mail, Telemarketing	Brand Choice

Consumer decision-making process after purchase	Customer retention	Interactive communications after purchase	Brand building after purchase
5. Post purchase evaluation	Customer	Telemarketing	Brand Reinforcement
6. Repeat Purchase	Loyal Customer	Customer publications, Events, Remote and personal sales contact	Brand Loyalty
7. Purchase from Brand Family	Loyal Customer	Database telemarketing Cross-selling	Brand Associations

BUILDING BRANDS THROUGH IMAGE ADVERTISING

Today's famous brands were created by mass marketing and built by television advertising. Marketers have traditionally built brands by reaching a mass television audience at low costs. Television image advertising is powerful and involving, perceived by many as engaging, entertaining and compelling. It can communicate the features, benefits and values of the brand to motivate customer choice in a very powerful way. Image advertising can contribute to brand building by increasing awareness of the brand in the consumer's mind through repetition of the brand name and the image associated with it. Image advertising can also influence a consumer's preference for a brand. However, it is not considered the communication of choice for conveying product knowledge or building relationships with the consumer after a purchase has been made.

Today's brand marketers are faced with an increase in the number of channels. This has resulted in more fragmented audiences, lower entry costs, more advertisers, higher media costs and lower production values. According to Mediaworks, the real cost of advertising on RTE television increased by nine per cent in 1996 as more advertisers chased fewer viewers. The cost per thousand (CPT) for adult RTE viewers in 1996 was £4.43 compared to £4.08 in 1995.

An increase in the level of advertising has resulted in advertising clutter, making each message harder to communicate, and less likely to be received. Advertising is increasingly required to engage the consumer more closely, allowing them to make a direct response to the advertiser. Future advertising will be targeted to individual households. The database developed from customer contact will be used to match future messages to customer interests (Susman, 1996).

Growth in Direct Response Advertising

Increasingly, advertisers invite customers to respond to press and television advertising. Direct response advertising motivates customers to take direct action towards an experience of, and relationship with a brand. According to British Telecom and Channel 4, direct response telephone numbers are included in one in four television advertisements in the UK, double the figure for 1993 (*Go Direct*, 1997).

Direct contact with customers creates impact and is engineered for two-way communication. It enables and urges the consumer to talk back to the brand. It enables the medium to record the reactions of the consumer and to fine-tune the advertiser's next message, customising the benefits to individual customers. Direct response enables marketers to understand what individual customers have and want in their own lives. This approach to virtual branding will be different to different people. It can assist the marketer in moving the consumer through the decision-making process from problem recognition to purchase and repeat purchase.

Image or Direct Response Advertising?

The philosophies and methods of brand image advertising and direct response advertising are different. Pearson (1996) outlines the key differences between image and direct response advertising:

- Brand image advertising is emotive, direct response is rational

- Brand image advertising works by changing beliefs, direct response advertising work by changing behaviour

- Brand image advertising is imaginative, direct response advertising is factual

- Brand image advertising appeals to the emotions and senses, direct response advertising appeals to needs and desires — even to greed and ambition.

In addition, McCorkell (1997) highlights further differences between the two types of approach:

- Brand image advertising sets out to *inform* and make the customer *feel*, which is a positioning exercise. Direct response advertising seeks to *inform*, wants people to *feel*, but also to *take action*.

The fundamental difference is that brand image advertising communicates ideas, whereas direct response traditionally communicates offers. The awareness set up by conventional advertising and the action demanded by direct marketers is crucial.

Direct response advertising is designed to build the brand and to achieve immediate results. Image advertising builds the brand and market share over time. In contrast, a direct response campaign with the same creative execution almost always suffers falling response over time; the first advertisements attract the best prospects and the later advertisements pull fewer, lower value respondents.

Image advertising is evaluated on recall and brand awareness, image and preferences. The advertising is reinforcing, building over time. Consistent creative advertising usually runs for an extended period of time, often for years (Light, 1997).

The brand manager can employ image and response advertising to create a synergy between enhancing brand awareness and the call to action.

Double Duty Advertising

Rapp and Collins (1995) refer to "double duty" advertising that combines image and response advertising in a single execution. Double duty advertising balances image building and response generation. This mix offers new and exciting benefits to both consumers and marketers. Dell Computers, one of the fastest growing businesses in the world over the last decade, built its brand and market share using double duty advertising. For Dell's UK launch, the challenge was twofold: to build the brand and to generate immediate sales directly from advertising. In the early days, virtually all sales could be linked to advertising: today, the brand is so well established that a steady flow of leads is received irrespective of advertising. But initially, the advertising budget for each month was determined by the sales generated from advertising in the past month. This illustrates how marketing can fund its own investment.

Federal Express, one of the world's largest courier companies, sought to increase brand awareness among international express shippers in Ireland. The company used radio, business press and posters, in conjunction with a "teaser" direct mail campaign. A series of teaser postcards was mailed to 5,000 existing customers and potential customers prior to the opening of its new sorting facility in Dublin; a second direct mail campaign followed the opening. The company has switched resources from TV advertising to a "double duty" campaign, which they have found to be more cost-effective in targeting international express shippers.

Interactive communications with the customer can be controlled, tested and measured, resulting in greater accountability. Investment can be planned against increased sales and against the long-term value of the customer relationships created. A company can generate more sales and profits by redirecting its marketing spend towards targeted media. Redirecting spend towards existing customers, away from prospects, can result in a more effective use of marketing funds.

Brand marketers must determine the objectives for the brand and to create a synergy between image and response advertising. This is not as simple as adding coupons and telephone numbers to image advertising. The integration of advertising and direct response is interactive advertising. This combination results in a more salient, involving and effective communication.

Image and direct response advertising can be complementary. Image advertising creates awareness and draws attention to the rational appeal and call to action of direct response advertising.

Image advertising also communicates the brand's positioning, which is crucial in markets with intense competition. Response executions reinforce and complement the image advertising, picking up on the interest created and moving the prospects toward an inquiry or sale. The two forms of advertising should be co-ordinated, sharing personality, tone of voice and company-brand values.

BUILDING BRANDS THROUGH SALES PROMOTION

The brand manager can use sales promotion in direct marketing to create and maintain name awareness, influence consumers' perceptions of the brand, build loyalty and associate the brand with some positive aspect.

Sales promotion has taken an increasing share of the marketing budget, at the expense of advertising, because it can achieve a measurable increase in short-term sales. As with advertising, the long-term effects of sales promotion are poorly measured. Research by the LMC Group in the US shows that consumer sales promotion was ranked by 79 per cent of marketers surveyed as a very important marketing activity for brand building (Brown, 1996).

Sales promotions can be strategically employed as part of an overall brand strategy to build brands in conjunction with advertising and direct marketing. They can be tactically used to generate and increase sales during specific periods in a sales cycle.

Aer Lingus has been successful in challenging the price discounting strategy led by Ryanair. Their strategy involves the targeting of relevant added value promotions to their key customers. The company has established a joint promotion campaign with the Custom Shirt Group and Blarney Woollen Mills. Participating customers can avail of special discounts through their membership of the Aer Lingus frequent flyer programme. This can influence consumers' perceptions of the Aer Lingus brand by its association with a high quality sales promotion, while also rewarding loyal customers.

Sales promotions can leverage the brand, in terms of image, awareness and sales, in a way that advertising rarely does. Other studies have shown that when advertising is combined with sales promotions, sales increase anywhere from 25 to 250 per cent. When sales promotions are accurately targeted, based on consumers' purchasing habits, they can achieve a greater response and are more cost-effective than mass promotions.

American Express extracts information from its database to target consumer promotions based on how and where its cardholders spend their money, rather than where they live. They can work out the offers that best suit the buying habits of each customer. Customised promotional offers increase the response and reduce the costs of such offers. One wine merchant that used this system showed the cost/response of this new selling channel amounted to 28p per response, as opposed to as much as £42.16 using traditional "junk" mail (Lloyd, 1996).

The brand manager must identify the strategic and tactical role of sales promotions in building brands and to develop sales promotions that are targeted to specific customer segments.

Consumers are educated to expect a deal and to buy when the product is on offer. Only sales from certain promotions result in incremental revenue or attract new users to the brand. The brand manager must use promotions to target new customers to try the brand and ultimately to persuade them to remain loyal to it.

Carefully planned sales promotions can contribute to building brands in a cost-effective way, adding value to the brand through a continuing relationship, motivating existing customers to increase the share of the brand in their purchasing repertoire. Information on customers' responsiveness to different promotions can be tracked using database technology, leading to more tailor-made campaigns.

BUILDING THE BRAND THROUGH INTERACTIVE MEDIA

Brands are being communicated through existing and new interactive media to reach clearly defined audiences. The telephone, fax and direct mail are well-established methods of encouraging interaction between the company and its customers. Emerging interactive media include the Internet, e-mail, interactive television and kiosks. These interactive media can build brands in the same way as traditional media can, but, in addition, the nature of interactive media imply brand values of accessibility, responsiveness and convenience.

- *Telephone*: Companies that include Freephone numbers in their advertising and on their packaging make their brand more accessible to prospective and established customers. Accessible companies can provide immediate technical support and listen to customer complaints. It is well established from research (Jones, 1995) that fast resolution of customers' complaints leads to increased levels of customer satisfaction. Carelines on product packaging and marketing literature add brand value by demonstrating access and responsiveness. A free helpline or information service adds value by demonstrating the company's commitment to its customers.

  Companies can also remind customers by mail or phone when a service is due for the products purchased, to ensure that the brand delivers optimum performance. This communicates quality values to the customer.

- *Internet*: Companies are using the Internet to maintain an ongoing dialogue with customers and in many cases customers are encouraged to transact business on-line. International Data Corporation predicts that there will be £750 million in on-line transactions in 1997 — only one per cent of the on-line audience say they go on-line specifically to shop. A report published by 3Com Ireland predicts that electronic transactions between consumers and businesses are forecast to reach IR£4.3 billion by the year 2001; business-to-business transactions are expected to reach IR£40 billion within the same time-scale (*Sunday Business Post*, 1997).

  Several Irish financial services companies, mortgage brokers and financial advisers have designed sites to provide on-line services and to offer product and lending information. AIB Bank and Bank of Ireland have created Internet banking sites that enable customers to view and manage their accounts and to pay bills to nominated utilities and credit card companies, and AIB intends to offer customers the facility to buy and sell shares.

A recent survey conducted by Cap Gemini (Ireland) revealed that retailers expect 13 per cent of their sales to be via home shopping by 1999, rising to 26 per cent by 2007. Electronic channels and high street outlets can co-exist for the retailer. It is forecast that international competition in electronic commerce will be intense (*Go Direct*, 1997).

A significant obstacle to electronic commerce is the lack of security in sending credit card details over the Internet. The development of Secure Electronic Transmission (SET) will enable the Internet to develop as the next new marketplace.

- *E-mail*: Using E-mail to respond to customer inquiries associates the brand with accessibility, responsiveness and convenience. Moneycorp, an Irish mortgage broker, offers a quotation service to prospective house buyers. The website provides an "easy-to-navigate" design, enabling prospective customers to request basic information and a response is e-mailed within 24 hours, promising further contact. This is also a means of providing faster, more efficient feedback from customers than from traditional surveys of buyer attitudes and intentions.

- *Interactive Home Shopping*: This emerging technology enables the customer to access a company through a home PC and is a natural development of ordering products over the telephone. Developments in this area will enable customers to have live contact with the company's staff and view products in a "virtual" showroom.

- *CD-ROM*: The National Gallery has launched a CD-ROM which brings the viewer on a virtual tour of the gallery. It enables the customer to view 100 works of art. Users can access information on each artist, find out the history of the paintings, and even zoom in on certain parts of the work of art.

- *Kiosks*: Electronic shopping kiosks in shopping centres and retail outlets are providing the customer with greater access to a company's products and services.

- *Smart Cards*: Emerging smart card technologies are providing very flexible and secure methods of ordering and paying for products over the Internet, through kiosks and for home shopping. In addition, smart cards will enable the customer to download and upload cash and data from a company.

The direct marketing applications of these media are dealt with in later chapters. Table 3.2 summarises the customer services that are pivotal to building brands and how interactive media are increasingly being employed to deliver services.

TABLE 3.2: INTERACTIVE MEDIA TO DELIVER CUSTOMER SERVICE

Customer Services	Interactive Media
Customer queries	Telemarketing, e-mail
Customer help-line	Telemarketing
Complaint handling	Telemarketing/Internet/e-mail
Technical support	Telemarketing/Internet/CD-ROM
Service guarantees	Direct mail
Service reminders	Telemarketing, direct mail, Internet/e-mail
Customer satisfaction surveys	Telemarketing, Internet, direct mail
Home shopping	Home shopping networks/Interactive TV
On-line shopping	Internet
	Kiosks
Flexible ordering and payment	Internet
	Smart card
	Electronic purse, credit and debit cards

Companies can provide product information, deal with complaints, and give technical support to customers as they move through the buying process from initial contact to purchase and after sales. Companies can further build brands after the sale through providing customer service carelines, reminding customers to service the product and carry out customer satisfaction research. The provision of home shopping and on-line shopping to customers adds value to the brand by providing increased convenience and greater accessibility to the brand for the customer.

BUILDING THE BRAND THROUGH STAFF

A company, whether it is offering a pure service to the market place or a physical product with a service element, can build its brands through the staff it employs.

The quality and personality of a company and the people behind a product or brand matter to the customer. To build and sustain their brands, companies need to inject the commitment and personality of their people into their brand values.

Pearson (1996) emphasises that

> Differentiation through people is stronger than any media advertising, explaining why fast-growing companies like Virgin or The Body Shop rarely advertise, yet have two of the most distinct brands in the international marketplace. Yet most companies invest in media advertising without backing up their promise with investment in the customer interface. The result is dissatisfaction and loss of sales.

When customers respond, the company must match the promise made in advertising; otherwise money spent on advertising is wasted. Each staff member shares responsibility for the customer, beginning with those who interact directly with customers. Brand marketers must clarify the customer contact strategy and ensure that this is understood not only by customer-contact staff, but also by staff across the entire company (Vavra, 1992). Relationship marketing builds brands by building relationships and trust between customers and company. It is the staff in the company that deliver the promise to customers; they are part of the brand, which is ultimately the summation of all customer experiences with the brand.

BUILDING BRANDS THROUGH CUSTOMER RELATIONSHIPS

There is consensus among academics and practitioners that building relationships is important in today's marketplace. Many companies have shifted their emphasis from a transactional to a relational approach with their customers. They have redesigned their business processes around customer segments using multidisciplinary teams to manage important relationships. However, companies need to recognise that not all of their customers want to have a relationship with their brand, nor indeed is it profitable for a company to want a relationship with all of its customers.

Pearson (1996) suggests that a company may have a passive relationship with its prospects and some of its frequent customers. He maintains that a customer's interest in a relationship with the company depends on the importance of a product category and the strength of the customer's association with brands in that category. He sees the challenge for brand managers to activate relationships with those customers who have a high lifetime value. If a company analyses its customer database, it is probably true to say that the "Pareto" principle exists. This suggests that 80 per cent of its business comes from 20 per cent of its customers. A company needs to identify this small group of customers to communicate and reward them appropriately. Companies can concentrate their efforts on building relationships with this vital group of customers.

O'Neill (1996) points out that, in Ireland, companies will only want to have a relationship with their most profitable customers, segmenting their market by profit and lifetime values. Nearly half of all Irish consumers — and four out of ten UK consumers "would be more likely to buy from a company that keeps in touch".

Direct marketing is an efficient and effective system of communication, bringing the company closer to its customers. According to Pearson (1996):

> Power in business resides with the owner of the customer interface, yet most companies have no experience of controlling or managing the customer interface. The potential of direct relationships with individual customers, and the process required to manage these relationships are key challenges for brand owners.

Relationships with customers enhance marketing effectiveness. The customer is more receptive to an offer from a recognised brand or company. If the company or brand name is known, sales increase by a factor of three. When the customer has an active relationship with the company or brand, sales increase by a factor of six.

Selling more brands to the same customer, rather than to different customers, contributes to the competitive value of the company brand. This is becoming the norm in many of today's companies. Brand managers are required to target a more selective customer base, selling new versions of the product or a range of brands within a family to these customers. Rapp and Collins (1995) point out the numerous opportunities for building database-driven relationships with existing customers to maximise sales and profits. A customer relationship is both a private advertising medium and an individual distribution channel. As the relationship with the customer evolves, the following strategies can be considered:

Re-sell

This strategy aims to maximise repeat sales. With this strategy, the company motivates more purchases of the brand. In addition to re-minder advertising on television, direct marketers can capture names and addresses of customers to facilitate interaction with the customer and increase brand loyalty. The company can establish a reward pro-gramme, recognising their best customers.

Customised promotional offers can be targeted at specific seg-ments. Debenhams in Dublin have built a database from applications for store cards and have launched frequent-shopper programmes, in which customer spend accrues for rewards and special benefits. A series of personalised letters is mailed to its customer base to make special offers and to invite customers to special shopping events. This increases store traffic and adds value to the customer relationship outside the store.

Telecom Éireann stimulate international call traffic to customers who are known to have family living abroad. They use their database to identify those customers who call regularly to the USA and pres-ent special offers to these customers prior to national events in America such as Thanksgiving and Independence Day.

Up-sell

This strategy involves maximising the revenue per sale per customer and encourages customers to purchase improved versions of the company's products.

With a sophisticated database, the company can target certain customers to upgrade to deluxe models of the more profitable products. When BMW introduced its new 7 Series, the company offered test-drives to a highly targeted group of company owners and managing directors. The offer included a "test-drive" weekend for two at the Sheen Falls Hotel in Kenmare, with a new BMW. The campaign achieved its objective of encouraging test drives and selling the BMW 7 Series car.

Keep-sell

The company aims to maximise customer loyalty by retaining long-term customers. Establishing a strong relationship with them is considered to be a way of avoiding the need for discounting. Effort is also focused on upgrading customers who buy the brand infrequently to become more profitable loyal customers. Loyalty cannot be bought from a customer — it must be earned. Aer Lingus have tapped into this philosophy in a highly creative way. When a customer arrives at the ticket desk, the check-in staff have the option to upgrade that particular passenger, based on known data and value of the customer.

Cross-sell

Multi-product/service companies can use the database to extract recency, frequency and customer value information to introduce customers to other products in the company's portfolio. Ulster Bank, for example, recently successfully launched their new 24-hour telephone banking service to targeted customers through a highly sophisticated segmentation strategy. The service, called "Anytime", allows customers to schedule bill payments, receive a list of recent transactions and receive account balance details. Customers also have access to an interactive voice response (IVR) facility and a team of advisers is available from 8 a.m. to 10 p.m.

The Irish Permanent Bank targeted its existing deposit account and mortgage customers in a switching campaign to encourage customers to switch their current account from other banks. It offered five different current accounts, depending on the level of service required. The bank waived the £30 management charge for new customers for the first year and reimbursed customers who incurred a fee from their former bank for canceling a direct debit.

In the direct motor insurance market, Premier, which is owned by Bank of Ireland, cross-sells motor insurance to Bank of Ireland's one-million strong customer base. Similarly, the ICS Building Society targeted 7,500 customers on its database with a pilot offer of a pre-approved car loan up to £10,000. These customers have equity in their homes and a good credit rating. The offer encouraged customers to take advantage of the government "scrappage" scheme and included one year's free membership of a motor-assisted service worth £65 to the customer.

Add-sell

This strategy aims to maximise line extension. When a company extends a brand beyond its original category, it can use information from the database to introduce the brand extension to its customers who have already bought from that company. This strategy reduces the cost and risk of launching the brand extension through traditional methods.

In October 1997, Eircell introduced the Eircell Visa Card to its existing customers. When a customer uses the credit card, they are rewarded with "talking points", giving them a reduction on their Eircell telephone bill.

New-sell

This strategy aims to maximise new-venture success. Companies can use customer information from their databases to enter new, unrelated markets.

In 1997, Tesco (UK) launched a baby mail order catalogue targeted at mothers and mothers-to-be, based on information it holds on its 9.5-million Clubcard holders throughout its 568 stores in Britain. Cardholders receive extra points when they purchase prams and baby clothes from the catalogue. This proactive strategy is designed to attract customers from Mothercare (see also Aidan O'Driscoll's chapter).

Friend-sell

This strategy strives to maximise advocacy and referrals. Companies can use the power of positive word-of-mouth by formally setting up a system to manage advocacy and referral by its best customers. MCI, a long-distance telecommunications carrier in the US, has a "Friends and Family" loyalty programme, which is recognised as one of the most sophisticated "friend-get-friend" programmes world-wide. MCI customers call within a designated circle of callers and are offered discounts of up to 20 per cent on all calls. What makes this different to other telecommunications programmes is how MCI per-suades its customers to collaborate in recruiting new customers. Each member gets a programme guide and calling-circle status report, listing current members as well as nominees who have chosen not to participate. This report is used to encourage members to recruit new customers into their circles and increase the discount value that they receive.

Brand managers can create more opportunities for contact with the customer and strengthen the relationship with those customers who have a high lifetime value. Brands can be managed to compete through the relationships they build with their customers, as well as through product features, benefits and values. The emphasis shifts to the quality of service, which becomes an important element in differentiating the brand. By moving service providers closer to customers, the company can add value to the brand and generate increased revenues and profits.

SUMMARY

A company must continuously invest in its brands to create value for the firm, its customers and shareholders. A strong brand creates a competitive advantage for a company and differentiates the company's brand from the competition. Brands today must compete in a very competitive environment where retailers have increased power over manufacturers and closer relationships with their customers. The role of marketing is undergoing radical change and greater accountability is required from the spend on marketing. Customers are also demanding more value at lower prices; in addition, they expect convenience, fast response times from staff and back-up and support for the products they buy long after purchase. They expect to be informed of better offers that a company may have and often may prefer to take the initiative themselves to contact the company. Customers today will only develop relationships with brands that they know and have grown to trust and respect. Brand managers can use the interactive media of direct marketing to enable one-to-one communication with their valued customers while simultaneously building their brands.

CASE HISTORY: MITSUBISHI APRICOT

Mitsubishi have been very successful worldwide in building their brands. Worldwide sales of all Mitsubishi companies are now well in excess of US$200 billion, or five times the GNP of Ireland. Since the launch of the Apricot PC in Ireland in 1995, they have succeeded in becoming the number one home PC brand. The company entered the home PC market in Ireland with a brand name that was unknown, in a market saturated by other brands. They selected the very best dealers that shared their belief in providing a professional and expert approach. These selected dealers became part of a network of relationships that transcended normal business relationships and played a crucial role in building the brand.

The Mitsubishi brand is a symbol of the perceptions the customers have of the company. The company believed that the most effective way of enhancing the total product concept was through branding. It sought to build into the brand a consumer perception of quality and desirability. The company believes that branding has to be a long-term commitment. They built two fundamental principles into their brand: the selective dealer network and the consumer perceptions of quality and desirability. The brand has to communicate value to the customers, not just price. It has to deliver quality and not just quantity; the brand also promises reliability, service and customer backup. The brand, in essence, has to communicate and practice an ethical system in the marketplace. This philosophy results in the company achieving market leadership in most of the product markets in which it operates.

Based on their experience as market leaders in the consumer electronics market over the last 16 years, the company set out to develop the Apricot computer campaign. Research showed much confusion and a lack of knowledge among consumers in the home PC market. The advertising and marketing campaigns of existing PC manufacturers were targeted at IT managers who had a knowledge of PCs. Findings also revealed that most PC advertisements were too technical and not relevant to the consumer's lifestyle. The key aim of the home consumer is to purchase the right computer for their children, with good value and appropriate software.

Positioning

The company designed imaginative visuals aimed at a consumer life-style, positioning the product around an educational theme that had relevance for parents. The positioning emphasised that both children and parents could become educated and entertained in multimedia technology with Apricot and the software offer. The key message was "Mitsubishi is a brand you can trust, which stands for quality, technology and innovation — and it makes PCs".

The visuals were imaginative, full of impact and consumer life-style driven. The visuals in the direct mail letter illustrated the Apricot being used in a family setting, which clearly positioned the product as a user-friendly computer for all the family. The company used the following strapline in their first advertisement for the Apricot:

At last, a computer worthy of the name Mitsubishi

followed by another advertisement challenging the consumer to:

Make Apricot a part of your children's future

A subsequent advertisement included the strapline:

B.A. — Bachelor of Apricot

The final Christmas commercial demonstrated an Apricot PC wrapped up with all the other Christmas gifts under the tree.

The Campaign

The direct mail campaign (see letter in Figure 3.1) was based on re-search that sought to profile the home PC buyer. Findings pointed to a lack of knowledge among consumers and a desire for value from a brand that they could trust. Hewlett Packard and AST were not rec-ognisable brand names in the consumer's brand repertoire. However, Mitsubishi is a consumer brand that consumers already had in their homes.

FIGURE 3.1: MITSUBISHI CAMPAIGN LETTER

October 1996

Mr A.B. Sample
Any Street
Any Town
Any County

TOMORROW'S WORLD OF EDUCATION & ENTERTAINMENT

Dear Mr Sample,

Imagine a world where you travel around the globe at the touch of a button . . . where your children your children learn about history, space travel and exotic creatures through words, pictures and sound . . . where you run for your life and save the universe from an alien invasion!

Welcome to the world of multimedia from Mitsubishi Computers.

With multimedia the world of education and entertainment is brought to life — through words, pictures, animation and brilliant stereo sound.

You can bring this wonderful world of learning to life with a Mitsubishi home computer.

Learn more . . . get more done . . . have more fun

A Mitsubishi home computer will help your children to get ahead in education. Easy to use, yet highly advanced, it's also the ideal way to introduce them to the kind of technology they'll be using when they grow up.

For you, it's a convenient way to manage your finances, a personal organiser and a business tool. Everyone can have fun with it too! And with the Internet on everyone's lips, our systems also give you access to this vast storehouse of practical and educational information.

£500 worth of exclusive offers!

*Because we want to bring the world of multimedia to life in your home, we've put together **an exclusive package of offers worth up to £500 when you buy a Mitsubishi home computer!***

If you have children at school or college or if you are a teacher, you will be entitled to claim a copy of Microsoft Office® Professional '95 — the world's most popular suite of office software — worth £400 — at no extra cost!

Plus free access to the Internet for 3 months and a free copy of one of Microsoft's leading educational multimedia software packages — worth nearly £100!

We've also put together an exclusive finance offer to help you spread the payments on your home computer.

Simply call 1850 33 55 88 NOW!

All you have to do is call this number for your nearest participating Mitsubishi dealer. Then, go for a free in-store demonstration of a Mitsubishi home computer.

Win a family holiday to Eurodisney, Paris!!

When you've had your demonstration you'll receive a free Mitsubishi designer T-shirt and automatic entry into our free draw to win a fantastic family holiday in Eurodisney, Paris!

So look inside — there's never been a better time to introduce your family to the exciting and educational benefits of multimedia!

Yours sincerely,

Des Hughes
Marketing Manager
Mitsubishi Computers

P.S. Hurry! These exclusive offers from Mitsubishi Computers are subject to availability and must end 31st January 1997.
P.P.S. You could also win a fantastic Mitsubishi colour TV! Just complete & return the short questionnaire opposite to enter this free draw.

The Offer

The Apricot was targeted at certain family income levels and potential buyers were given a finance option. In addition, the offer included software to the value of £400 at no additional cost and three months' free access to Internet software from Ireland On-line, which was valued at £100. To overcome the fear factor among parents and to prompt prospects to trial, the company invited potential customers to a free demonstration with their dealers. Respondents to this offer were included in a free draw for a holiday to EuroDisney, Paris.

Prospects had four months in which to take up the offer. This was considered a reasonable time for interested parties to respond and take up the offer of an in-store demonstration. A low-call phone number was included in the letter to provide inquirers with the names of Mitsubishi dealers. A questionnaire was included with the direct mail letter, which captured demographic data and information on the ownership of other electronic products and cars. This enabled the company to build a database to facilitate future cross-selling and up-selling marketing activity from the range of Mitsubishi brands.

Results

From 1996–97, the Apricot achieved a four per cent market share, which was directly linked with the direct market campaign.

Source: Adapted from a paper "A is for Apricot" presented by Fergus Madigan to the Marketing Institute, January 1997.

REFERENCES TO CHAPTER 3

Aaker, D.A. (1991), *Managing Brand Equity: Capitalising on the Value of a Brand Name*, New York: The Free Press.

Aaker, D.A. and Jacobson, R. (1994), "Brand Building Pays off for Stockholders", *Advertising*, 18 July, p. 13.

Bird, D. (1996), *Commonsense Direct Marketing*, Third Edition, London: Kogan Page.

Brady, John and Ian Davis (1993), "Marketing's Mid-life Crisis", *The McKinsey Quarterly*, No. 2, pp. 17–28.

Brown, J. (1996), "Retailers, Partners in Brand Building", *Advertising Age*, 14 August.

Checkout Ireland (1996), "Grocery Fact File" in *Checkout Yearbook and Buyer's Guide*, Dublin, pp. 3–34.

Doyle, P. (1990), "Building Successful Brands: The Strategic Options", *The Journal of Consumer Marketing*, Vol. 7, No. 2, Spring, pp. 5–19.

Go Direct (1997), "Direct Response Telephone Numbers", No. 20, September, p. 9.

Jones, Thomas O. and Sasser, W.E., Jr. (1995), "Why Satisfied Customers Defect", *Harvard Business Review*, November/December, pp. 88–99.

King, S. (1991), "Brand Building in the 1990s", *The Journal of Consumer Marketing*, Vol. 8, No. 4, pp. 43–51.

Lambkin, M. (1996), *The Irish Consumer Market*, Dublin: The Marketing Society, pp. 72–77.

Light, Larry (1997), "Brand Loyalty Management", *The Prentice Hall Marketing Year Book*, Englewood Cliffs, NJ: Prentice Hall.

Linton, I. (1995), *Database Marketing: Know What Your Customers Want*, London: Pitman Publishing.

Lloyd, C. (1996), "Junk Mail will do Nicely", *The Sunday Times*, 14 April.

Madigan, Fergus (1997), "A is for Apricot", Paper presented to the Marketing Institute, January.

McCorkell, G. (1997), *Direct and Database Marketing*, London: Kogan Page.

Muranyi, N.R. (1995), "Database Marketing in FMCGs: What is the State of the Art?", *The Journal of Database Marketing*, Vol. 4, No. 1, pp. 13–20.

O'Neill, G. (1996), *Focus on the Future: The Coming Boom in Direct Marketing*, Dublin: Henley Centre.

Pearson, S. (1996), *Building Brands Directly*, New York: New York University Press.

Rapp, S. and T.L. Collins (1995), *The New Maximarketing*, New York: McGraw-Hill.

Shocker, A.D., R.K. Srivastava and R.W. Ruekert (1994), "Introduction — Challenges and Opportunities Facing Brand Management, *Journal of Marketing Research*, Vol. XXXI, Special Issue, pp. 149–158.

Sunday Business Post (1997), "Online Banking Fast Becoming a Reality", 23 November, p. 35.

Susman, A. (1996), "New Media and Brand Reformation", *Advertising Age*, August, p. 18.

Vavra, T.G. (1992), *After-Marketing: How to Keep Customers for Life Through Relationship Marketing*, Homewood, IL: Irwin.

Chapter 4

CUSTOMER ACQUISITION

J. Cyril Gavaghan

Overview

It is a truism of business that nothing happens until a sale is made. It is only then that the purchasing department has a reason to purchase, the production department a reason to produce, the accounts department has something to account for and so on. But a sale cannot be made until a customer is acquired and hence the importance of studying customer acquisition, whether in the context of direct marketing or of general marketing.

This chapter defines and emphasises the need for customer acquisition. It considers the process involved in developing an acquisition programme and concludes with an acquisition case history of Max Florists.

DEFINITION

Customer acquisition may be defined as:

> The identification and recruitment of new customers (Holder, 1992).

Despite its brevity, this definition succinctly explains the function of customer acquisition. In addition, however, it is useful to note that the act of identifying potential customers is alternatively referred to as prospecting and the potential customer is alternatively referred to as a prospect. A prospect may be defined as a person who can benefit from and can afford the product that the company is selling. Awareness of this definition gives guidance to the direct marketer in directing relevant market offerings and messages at relevant target markets and allows the direct marketing student to distinguish between direct mail and junk mail, and between telemarketing and nuisance telesales calls.

THE ONGOING NEED FOR CUSTOMER ACQUISITION

Every company, irrespective of its industry or market, has an ongoing need for the acquisition of new customers. There are three major reasons for this acquisition requirement: to replenish the loss due to natural customer attrition, to replace customers lost to competitors, and to fuel new growth.

Replenishing Losses Due to Natural Customer Attrition

Natural customer attrition is the result of the market offering of the company being no longer suited to the needs of some members of the existing customer list. Customer attrition occurs through no particular fault of the company itself but is occasioned by one of six reasons:

- *Customers Grow Out of a Market*: Many current members of the teenage market will not be in it next year — they have progressed through the family life cycle

- *Altered Economic Situation*: Students graduate, join the professional sector and can afford more expensive products

- *Changed Tastes*: People's tastes and therefore their product requirements change

- *Reduced Loyalty*: Improved education standards and wider experiences have increased personal sophistication and confidence and engendered a desire to try new things.

- *Migration*: People migrate for work purposes and therefore are no longer in the market area.

- *People Die*.

Replacing Customers Lost to Competitors

Customers buy from competitors for the sake of change, for the improved offering of that competitor, as a result of perceived inadequacies of service, product quality or price on the part of the existing supplier, or for a plethora of other reasons. These reasons are often highly personal, sometimes irrational, but always important to the individual customer or ex-customer. Failure to provide adequate customer service is often cited as the main reason why customers are lost.

It should be noted that between attrition and competition, experience would indicate that a company may lose up to one in five customers every year. This emphasises the need for effective customer retention plans. There is no point in going to the expense of acquiring new customers only to lose them again.

Fuelling New Growth

Even if a company were to replace all customers lost through attrition and competition, it would still be performing at a level no higher than it performed at in the previous trading periods. It would be doing no more than running on the spot; in not being proactive, in not constantly innovating and improving, it would almost certainly be overtaken by competitors. Additional customers are needed to fuel new growth, to improve on the company's position in previous trading periods. More customers bring higher turnover, greater profit and more market share.

Additionally, the constant acquisition of new customers recognises that the most profitable period in a customer relationship is usually shortly after that customer's recruitment. The first time a company deals with a customer will often be unprofitable or at least of greatly reduced profitability. It is feasible for a company to operate on this basis, to treat the first sale as a "loss leader", knowing that sales to the customer in the immediate future will be the most profitable of the company-customer relationship. After this period, however, the level of profitability reduces until the customer is lost through attrition or competition. These sequential periods of low, fast-growing, mature and then declining profitability may be referred to as the natural customer life cycle. It behoves the direct marketer to be cognisant of this life cycle in planning campaigns. New customers are constantly required to replace those of reducing profitability.

THE CUSTOMER ACQUISITION PROCESS

A well-planned customer acquisition programme may be regarded as a seven-stage process, as depicted in Figure 4.1.

The customer acquisition programme should not be regarded as an independent programme or as an end in itself, but as a forerunner to a customer retention programme. There is no point in acquiring customers unless they are retained.

FIGURE 4.1: THE CUSTOMER ACQUISITION PLAN

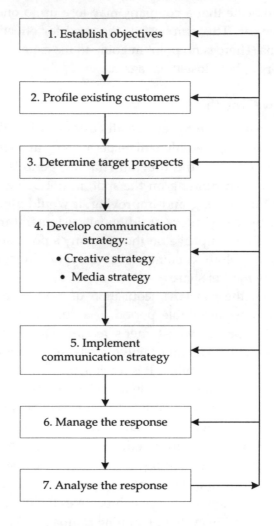

ESTABLISHING OBJECTIVES

As with all aspects of business planning, it is essential that objectives are set for a customer acquisition programme. The setting of objectives imposes a desirable discipline on programme managers and ensures that the value of proposed campaigns, and all elements of those campaigns, are evaluated in advance of their implementation.

Direct marketing campaigns are distinguishable from other promotional campaigns on the basis of their differentiating characteristics — controllability, measurability, and accountability. These characteristics mean that the objectives to be established for a direct marketing customer acquisition programme are likely to be more tangible and quantifiable than the objectives typically associated with a general advertising campaign such as awareness, recall, share of mind and so on.

The desired percentage response rate to the campaign is an objective often associated with direct marketing campaigns. It is a tribute to the discipline that its measurability allows for the response rate to be quantified. However, it is an objective that is not associated with campaigns of any other element of the promotions mix. Response rate does not allow for comparison of the relative effectiveness of those mix elements — it gives no indication of the type of response, it gives no concession to the more relevant measures of marketing success such as sales, number of new customers, or average order value, and it makes no contribution to budget allocation decisions. As McCorkell (1994) suggests:

> The first step towards straight thinking is to rid your mind of response rates as a valid measure. Cost-per-response may be a valid measure. Cost-per-order is often a valid measure. Cost-per-sale is certainly a valid measure.
>
> If you think in terms of these unit costs, you are now able to make inter-media comparisons, comparing direct mail with inserts, door drops, space advertisements or broadcast media advertising. This is a prerequisite for the sensible allocation of a direct response budget.

With response rates eliminated from consideration, the typical objectives of a customer acquisition programme might be specific, quantifiable measures of:

- The allowable cost-per-order
- The number of new customers
- The average order value
- The sales value
- The sales volume.

All of these objectives are closely interrelated: the desired number of new customers is based on sales value and average order value, while average order value is obviously based on sales value and number of new customers, and so on. More importantly, from a direct marketing perspective, all other objectives may be premised on the allowable cost-per-order concept, which is explained in the next section.

The statement of campaign objectives should also specify the type of respondent that is sought. Four types of respondent are possible:

- *Purchasers* buy directly off-the-page or television, usually by means of a credit card. This is the respondent sought by advertisers on TV shopping channels.

- *Trialists* wish to try a sample of the product before committing themselves to purchase. The Book Club of Ireland, for example, facilitates this response by offering a 14-day trial period before committing oneself to membership of the club. The lethargy of human nature dictates that once one has accepted the product on trial it is easier to accept the offer rather than reject it and have the trouble of returning it.

- *Evaluators* are at a point in the adoption process where they are attempting to make an objective evaluation of the product in question relative to alternative means of satisfying the need. Insurance companies such as Guardian Direct seek this type of respondent in their direct response advertisements by inviting them to ring their low-cost telephone number — 1850 28 28 20 — for a quotation.

- *Information seekers* have an interest in the product or product type and therefore require further information to satisfy this interest. They are not yet in a position to evaluate the offer. A direct response press advertisement with a response device that allows the respondent to add their name and address to the sentence "Please send me further information on . . .". In completing the coupon, respondents are notifying the marketer of their interest.

Allowable Cost-Per-Order

The allowable cost-per-order (or allowable cost-per-new-customer) is a standard measure for controlling direct marketing activities. In addition to being an objective in its own right, it is, probably more importantly, a calculation that guides the framing of all other campaign objectives. Identifying the allowable cost-per-order is more than just establishing a budget and a desirable number of new customers and dividing one by the other to establish how much the direct marketer can afford to spend on each new customer. That involves no more than spending money simply because it is available to spend and is a profligate approach to budgeting. The allowable cost-per-order takes a more disciplined approach to setting the target by focusing on the profitability per customer.

Essentially, this approach involves the preparation of a pro-forma profit-and-loss account of the likely average order or average customer. The profit-and-loss account only takes account of expected direct costs, the estimated required contribution to fixed costs and the company's "desired" profit. It excludes promotion costs on the basis that the purpose of preparing the account is to establish how much the company can afford to allocate to this expense.

Table 4.1 below presents a worked example of the allowable cost-per-order approach.

TABLE 4.1: ALLOWABLE COST-PER-ORDER — A WORKED EXAMPLE

Selling price per unit		£60.00
Less Expected returns (5%)		−£3.00
Net sales value per unit		£57.00
Direct costs:		
Cost of goods	£18.00	
Cost of order fulfilment	£5.00	
Expected bad debts (5%)	£3.00	−£26.00
Contribution to break-even		£31.00
Estimated required contribution to fixed costs	£10.00	
Desired profit per unit	£6.00	−£16.00
Allowable promotional cost per order		**£15.00**

When applied in a direct marketing context, its most common application, allowable cost-per-order takes a short-term view in only accounting for the first transaction in the company-customer relationship. As identified previously, it is an accepted marketing maxim that the first customer transaction is likely to be unprofitable, or of reduced profitability, and that true profitability only occurs from transactions from retained customers. In assuming a short-term view, the allowable cost-per-order approach only takes account of the immediate value of the customer and ignores the future lifetime value (LTV) of that customer. Of course, the approach may be adapted to take account of LTV and in so doing will usually permit the investment of a higher cost-per-order.

Additionally, the allowable cost-per-order may also be criticised on the basis that:

- It treats promotion budgets as a function of sales rather than vice versa. It implies that the more a company sells the more it should, or can afford to, spend on promotions, rather than maximising its profits. This is tantamount to the "affordable method" of setting the promotions budget (Kotler, 1994).

- It requires an accurate prediction of sales volume in order to pre-determine direct unit costs.

PROFILING EXISTING CUSTOMERS

Profiling is the analysis of existing customers for the purpose of identifying their common characteristics of consumer decision-making importance. In identifying the characteristics of existing customers, and the methods originally used to acquire them, the profiling process recommends the methods and media that might be employed to acquire new customers.

Profiling emphasises the importance of systematically collecting and maintaining relevant information on all established customers in a well-managed database. This information may then be used to maximise the value of the customer relationship over its life and be used as the basis of initiating new relationships.

The process of profiling should categorise customers on the basis of their value to the company. Applying the Pareto principle — or the 80/20 rule as it is more commonly known — a company is likely to find that 20 per cent of its customers account for 80 per cent of its sales and vice versa. It will find that some customers are more valuable than others. That top 20 per cent should be analysed and described and then customer acquisition programmes designed to find more prospects just like those better customers. The economic logic of this approach ensures that time and money are allocated in proportion to the sales or profit potential of prospective new accounts.

Four classes of information should be maintained on customers in the consumer market, as listed below:

- *Personal*: Sociographic, geographic, lifestyle

- *Behavioural*: Average order value, recency, frequency

- *Promotional*: Method of acquisition, responsiveness to promotion types, incentives and media

- *Product*: Product-type preferences, model, price range.

In the business-to-business market, customers may be profiled on the basis of type of business, size of business, geographic location, transaction data, and so on.

A particularly important extension of profiling concerns the use of existing customer referrals as an acquisition source. A profile analysis of the referee usually also reveals much about the referral, on the basis that "birds of a feather flock together".

DETERMINE TARGET PROSPECTS

Determining target prospects, the succeeding step to the profiling activity, involves deciding which specific prospects or prospect types should be the target of the company's customer acquisition efforts. Typically, the target to use will be prospects with characteristics (profiles) most like those of the company's best existing customers. In the event of this segment having already been saturated, the direct marketer will be obliged to cast the net further. The decision on which targets to use will be based on the potential of each prospect-type source and on the associated costs of acquiring each type. Figure 4.2 below, explained in the succeeding sections, provides guidance for the decision-maker in these respects.

FIGURE 4.2: SOURCES AND RELATIVE COSTS OF NEW CUSTOMERS

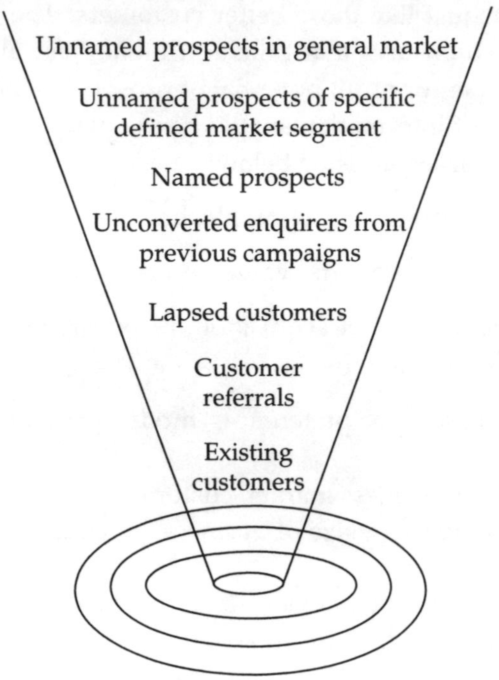

Unnamed prospects in general market

Unnamed prospects of specific
defined market segment

Named prospects

Unconverted enquirers from
previous campaigns

Lapsed customers

Customer
referrals

Existing
customers

Sources of Prospective Customers

Seven sources of prospects for customer acquisition programmes
may be identified. These sources are listed on the target board presented in Figure 4.2 and are explained below.

The economic value of each source varies. This variation in value
is also demonstrated in Figure 4.2. In examining the figure, the
reader should be aware that as one moves in towards the central circle, the identified prospect sources offer:

• Less cost per sale

• Greater cost-per-contact or cost-per-thousand (CPT) contacts

• Greater knowledge of each prospect

• More specific targetability

• Greater potential value per prospect

• Lower volume of prospects.

Each of these criteria is of particular importance in planning a customer acquisition programme.

Existing Customers

The obvious and best source of prospects for a company introducing a new product. They know the company, its products, its service, its quality, and so on, and are obviously satisfied with it. Microsoft, for example, introduces its new software products by post, initially to customers of its other products, the mailing list being derived from the completed registration cards from those previous purchases.

Customer Referrals

Customers who are satisfied with a company's product, price, service, quality and so on are usually agreeable to referring that company to their friends or referring their friends to the company. An incentive is sometimes offered by the marketer to encourage such referrals. This approach to customer acquisition is usually called a "friend-get-a-friend" or "member-get-a-member" scheme. Celtic Insurance, for example, in campaigning to increase their customer numbers, invite existing policy holders to refer other suitable motorists to the company — the incentive offered for making the referral being a £20 discount off the customer's own next policy renewal premium.

Lapsed Customers

They preferred the company's marketing mix once. As customers they were satisfied with the company as a supplier at one time. The problem tends to be that most companies do not know why those customers lapsed, because they never asked them. It may have been something very trivial that has already been forgotten, or that they just fancied a change, or that they temporarily grew out of the market, or a plethora of other reasons. The great advantage is that the company does not have to introduce itself to lapsed customers.

Unconverted Enquirers from Previous Campaigns

These are people who made enquiries of the company in response to previous campaigns but who were not converted into customers at the time. In making the enquiry, they were expressing an interest in the product, the company, and the offer. The reason for the failure to convert might be something as simple as the time being inappropriate, and maybe it is appropriate now. Insurance companies, for example, who generate responses to their broadcast advertisements through 1800 or 1850 telephone numbers will continue to target those respondents with a renewed offer on an annual basis, once they have established the policy renewal date. The potential problem associated with this source of customer is, from a measurability and accountability perspective, which campaign should be attributed with the ultimate success?

Named Prospects

The company may contact prospects by direct mail or by telephone having acquired a list of names, addresses and phone numbers of people who match a particular desirable profile. When the company is using a list of names of people who are neither customers, lapsed customers or enquirers, the contact will be referred to as a cold-mailing or cold-phoning. Cold-mailings/phonings fulfil the same functions as direct response advertising, magazine inserts, and so on, their particular advantage being that, depending on the quality and precision of the list, they are more specifically targeted. MBNA International Bank, for example, introduced their Visa card option by direct mail to a targeted list of suitable named prospects.

Unnamed Prospects of Specific Defined Segments

In the absence of a list, but where the desirable prospect type is known, this segment may be accessed by means of such media as advertising or inserts in specialist publications, trade shows, or door drops. For example, Precision Marketing Information (PMI) use this customer source when they advertise their customer information analysis service in *Deadline*, the magazine of the Irish Direct Marketing Association, which is aimed specifically at those in the direct marketing industry. PMI use the following appeal: "Nobody knows your customers better than you. But nobody knows how to find others like them better than PMI — Ireland's customer information specialist."

Unnamed Prospects in General Market

The company aims at the general market through the broadcast media such as TV, national/local radio, and the national/local press. The purpose is typically to generate a direct response from prospects so that the company is better positioned to attempt converting them into customers. In many instances, however, the purpose may be a direct off-the-page or off-the-screen sale or product-trial request. The latter is typically the objective in the case of an advertisement or an insert from an organisation such as the Book Club of Ireland.

Lists generated from enquiries to campaigns aimed at the latter three groups outlined above automatically move those enquirers up to at least the status of "unconverted enquirers" for future campaigns, thereby improving the targetability of the prospect and reducing the cost per contact. In other words, it moves the prospect nearer to the central circle in Figure 4.2, with all the attendant advantages of such movement for the direct marketer.

Cost of Customer Acquisition

The cost of acquiring a new customer depends on:

1. The media and methods used to target prospects, and

2. The status of the company's relationship with the target prospects.

The costs associated with recruiting customers increase on a per-customer basis as one moves through the alternative customer sources in the order they are listed in Figure 4.2. This also indicates that the cost of recruiting customers rises with the volume of customers sought. The recruitment cost of a few well-targeted prospects, such as those recommended by existing customers, will usually be substantially less than that associated with recruiting among a large number of loosely targeted or untargeted prospects.

DEVELOP COMMUNICATION STRATEGY

The development of a direct marketing communication strategy involves making decisions regarding both the creative strategy and the media strategy.

The Creative Strategy

The creative strategy is the message, or series of messages, to be aimed at the target market for the purpose of eliciting the desired response to achieve the campaign objectives. Developing this strategy will involve making decisions on the offer, the appeal, the incentive, the style and the tone of the communication.

In designing a creative strategy, the target audience at whom the communication will be aimed is of paramount importance. Even if the direct marketer uses a poorly formulated message but aims it at the right target market, the campaign may nonetheless be somewhat successful. It does not matter, however, how creative the message is if it is aimed at the wrong target market — such a campaign cannot possibly succeed.

In addition to the needs, wants and characteristics of the target audience, the direct marketer must also be cognisant of the following factors in formulating the message:

- The product position or personality

- The objectives of the campaign

- The desired response type

- The chosen medium (there is an interdependent relationship between the chosen medium and the creative strategy — each influences the decision in relation to the other).

The creative content in a direct marketing communication should be evaluated on its commercial applicability rather than its artistic merit. Its job is to pull response, to sell. Therefore, while creativity should not be factored out of the creative process, nor indeed be formulised, it is nonetheless appropriate that the message designer might consider a series of predetermined steps in designing the message. This adherence to a system imposes a pragmatic discipline on the designer that ensures the development of a message specifically formulated to achieve the campaign objectives. The AIDA (attention, interest, desire, action) model is one basic, though very useful, model on which to base the creative design process (Strong, 1925).

The AIDA model suggests that a communication should be designed to guide the prospective customer through four distinct and successive stages leading to a positive response. Lawlor (1995: 34) described the principle of AIDA on the basis that a marketing communication founded on it:

> should be a substitute for a sales presentation, by creating awareness of a product, leading to generation of interest, and desire for the product, which then, it is hoped, will lead to purchase. On first sight, there would appear to be four separate objectives and distinct intentions. However, they do, in fact, constitute a continuum focused on achieving sales.

Some marketing communication theorists (Colley, 1962) have incorrectly described AIDA as a communication-school model which dictates that campaign objectives be generation of awareness, or interest or desire or action. The reality however is, as Lawlor (1995: 35) contends, that "AIDA sees action/sale as the intended outcome of all campaigns".

Writing over 70 years after its development, Bird (1993) is still in absolute agreement with the AIDA principle. He censures British marketers in saying:

> A 1980 survey of senior British marketing people revealed that 80 per cent thought advertising had some primary purpose *other* than selling. Many see this as a comfortable state of affairs. If nobody knows what advertising should do, how can the content (or results) be evaluated?

When the communication is in a direct marketing context, whether as a single communication or a planned series of communications, and the objective is not a sale, then it defeats the intrinsic purposes of the discipline — measurability, accountability and control.

Follow-up strategies should be designed as an innate element of the overall campaign, not as an afterthought to it. Follow-up is of particular importance in customer acquisition campaigns. The initial contact will often not sell, but by introducing the company and the offer it will pave the way for subsequent contacts. This point is emphasised in the Max Florists case study at the end of this chapter.

Media Strategy

The dividing line between direct marketing media and general marketing media is becoming increasingly vague as the promotions mix becomes more and more integrated. It is no longer possible to describe a medium as strictly a general marketing medium, and few can be described as strictly a direct marketing medium. As McGowan (1995) says:

> It is now possible to argue that that all media can be classified as direct marketing media, including even the mass-marketing mainstay of broadcast television. In determining the likely number of direct media, it is not so much a question of whether a medium is first and foremost a direct marketing medium, but the extent to which it accommodates the techniques of direct marketing communications.

TABLE 4.2: THE MEDIA OF DIRECT MARKETING

Print Media	Electronic Media	Distribution Media*
• Direct mail: addressed and unaddressed	• Telephone (and associated technologies)	• Lists
• Press: local/national (direct response advertising)	• Facsimile	• Door-to-door
• Press supplements	• Television	• Referral systems
• Freesheets	• Radio: local/national	• Electronic networks
• Leaflets/inserts/ flyers/bangtails	• Electronic catalogues	• On-pack or via physical products
• Magazines: general consumer, professional and industrial	• Computer diskettes/ CD-ROM	
• Posters	• Computer on-line marketplaces	
• Catalogues	• Electronic kiosks	
• On-pack		

* The traditional dichotomy of print and electronic leads to the exclusion of other "media" which may essentially be described as "distribution" media.

Source: Adapted from McGowan (1995), p. 536.

Table 4.2 lists 22 alternative media which may be used effectively in a direct marketing customer acquisition programme. This is not intended to be an exhaustive list but merely an indication of the main media available. The committed direct marketer will use each of these, and many more in addition.

In choosing the medium to use for a particular customer acquisition programme, the direct marketer should consider the following factors:

- Media habits of target audience

- Responsiveness of audience to promotion types (established from profiling)

- Characteristics of product and each medium's ability to portray it to full effect

- Suitability of medium for creative strategy

- Absolute cost of medium

- Specific medium's cost-per-thousand

- Ability of medium to complement or project the desired product position

- Level of credibility of medium

- Medium's coverage (geographic, demographic, sociographic)

- Medium's audience/readership/listenership size

- Level of audience specialisation

- Level of customisation

- Possibility of feedback

- Ability to evaluate campaign's effectiveness

- Level of flexibility

- Speed of message delivery.

Having made the medium selection decision, the usage of the medium will then need consideration. Specifically, the marketer must consider:

- Size/length of message

- Allocation of budget across selected media

- Timing of various campaign stages

- Frequency of message placement

- Timescales: creative, production and printing lead times, for example.

A more detailed treatment of this topic and of the virtues and relative merits of the various media options that are available is presented elsewhere in this volume.

Direct Marketing and the Law of Diminishing Returns

The law of diminishing returns is of particular importance to the direct marketer. This law suggests that:

> Incremental units of a given factor of production, other factors being held constant, will yield increasing returns up to a certain point, beyond which diminishing returns will set in. This point is not fixed and will vary with changes in technology and the other inputs. However, at any given point in time, it is theoretically possible to determine the optimum allocation of inputs which will maximise total output (Baker, 1991).

The law of diminishing returns implies that increasing the size of the advertisement, the size of the campaign budget, the weight of the mailing pack, the number of times the advertisement is placed, and so on, beyond a particular optimum point will not increase the response on a proportional basis. As Goodwin (1992) states, "larger spaces normally result in more responses (although *not* in proportion to increased costs)".

In direct marketing, this optimum point may be established through testing proposed campaigns in advance of their implementation and through analysis of historical information from previous campaigns or similar campaigns in the market segment. Testing differs from research in that it involves the implementation of the proposed campaign in a test-marketing situation, such that the market's reaction may be measured and the likely performance and profitability of the campaign evaluated. Testing ensures that only efficient and effective campaigns are implemented.

Testing the efficacy of a proposed campaign, whether through cognisance of the law of diminishing returns or otherwise, benefits the direct marketer by:

- Minimising financial risk

- Protecting the company's image through saving prospects in general from poorly constructed direct marketing campaigns

- Maximising possible response

- Reducing costs

- Predicting the future, thus being better positioned to justify the proposed campaign

- Stimulating creativity by establishing a benchmark that must be exceeded in future improved versions of the campaign.

The effects of the law of diminishing returns are clearly illustrated in Table 4.3. ·

TABLE 4.3: TYPICAL RESPONSE PATTERN FOR SUNDAY SUPPLEMENT ADVERTISEMENT

Week(s)	Proportion of Total
1	69%
2	16%
3	4%
4	3%
5	2%
6	1%
7–15	5%
Total	100%

Source: Goodwin (1992), p. 7.1–10.

MANAGE THE RESPONSE

Response management — or fulfilment as it is referred to in direct marketing — is the task of fulfilling the demands of customers and potential future customers. The required approach to managing response will vary in accordance with the specific type of response received. While it must be acknowledged that no two responses will be exactly alike, they can nonetheless be divided into three general categories:

- Off-the-page/screen purchases

- Product trial requests

- Information requests (for the purpose of satisfying interest in the product or of evaluating it).

These three response types are directly in line with the respondent types identified earlier. Potential subsequent customer contacts in the form of product returns and customer complaints must also be taken into account in the planning process.

Customer, or enquirer, satisfaction is the objective of response management. Satisfaction occurs when a customer's experience of dealing with a company matches their prior expectations. These expectations are formed from previous experiences, word-of-mouth and promises made by the marketer. It therefore behoves the marketer to take account of the exigencies of response management in developing the communication strategy.

ANALYSE THE RESPONSE

Analysis of the campaign response fulfils the dual function of being a management control device for monitoring the successful implementation of the current campaign and the informational premise of future campaigns. The latter function is of particular importance in direct marketing. Access to relevant information on the outcome of previous campaigns allows for continuous improvement in future campaigns. Analysing the response tells the direct marketer:

- The efficiency and effectiveness of the campaign

- The appropriateness of the established objectives

- The type of response

- The type and profile of respondents

- The accuracy of the target market

- The effectiveness of the media strategy

- The relevance of the offer

- The attractiveness of the incentive, and

- The additional research and testing needed with regard to the clarity and format of the communication.

As a result of its overall contribution, analysis of response may be regarded as not only the final stage of one campaign, but the initial stages of future campaigns in the direct marketer's ongoing acquisition of customers.

CASE HISTORY — MAX FLORISTS

Max Florists was established in the 1950s at Bachelors Walk in Dublin's city centre. Thirty years later it had developed into one of the city's premier florists, employing seven people. However, by the late 1980s, the business was no longer experiencing growth, so management initiated the preparation of a customer acquisition plan.

At the outset, the options of relocation or a multi-site strategy were considered. These options would facilitate the company approaching an entirely new, though relatively unknown, market segment. Consideration of these options was also necessitated due to the fact that at this time retailing in Ireland was undergoing a major transition. Retailers were moving from the high street to the out-of-town shopping centre (Parker, 1990; Parker, 1991). These out-of-town shopping centres all tended to have a florist shop and/or a flower stall. Customers increasingly shopped in these centres to avoid the congestion of town and city centre. In shopping there, they also fulfilled their requirements for flowers. This move out of town by the market also reduced the passing traffic in the city centre, thus reducing the city centre florist's potential for impulse purchases. Other city centre florists had already taken the out-of-town option by this time and were now successfully operating a multi-site strategy.

After due consideration, it was established that through lack of both fixed and working capital, Max Florists was unable to go with the out-of-town trend and therefore was obliged to expand the business internally from its existing single-site location.

Developing the Campaign

A profile of the shop's existing customers identified four main business sectors:

- Loyal customers who call to shop
- Passing trade
- Credit card orders by phone
- Corporate accounts.

Given the single-site constraint, it was decided that, of these four customer types, the corporate sector offered the greatest opportunity for development. As this sector purchased flowers by credit card, or on credit, and required delivery, it was therefore indifferent to its florist's location; consequently, Max's single-site location would not be an impediment. The company considered a number of media for acquiring new customers from this sector, including radio and press advertising, trade magazine and Golden Pages advertising, and direct mail.

It was decided that direct mail would be the most efficient and effective means of delivering a business-to-business message that emphasised the value of flowers as a corporate medium. As this was the company's first ever use of the technique, the direct marketing agency PHS (Ireland) was appointed to develop and manage the direct mail campaign.

Initial research by PHS confirmed that location was not a primary consideration for a business requiring flowers. More importantly, it also identified that the main evaluative criteria of potential corporate customers would be quality of flowers and customer service, reliability and value. The research also established the type of businesses that were buying flowers. The findings of this research became the premise on which a detailed creative brief was developed and was used to guide the design of all elements of the campaign. The brief, developed mutually by the client and the agent, was in three sections — the campaign objectives, the creative content, and the mailing list (Exhibit 4.1).

The importance of the mailing list was repeatedly emphasised throughout the campaign development process, as it was recognised that it did not matter how creative the message was — if it was aimed at the wrong target market, it would still fail.

To fulfil the requirements of the brief, a specially selected team comprising company and agency staff was brought together. This team consisted of:

- An expert in the product — flowers
- An expert in database management and control
- An expert in the area of direct mail.

EXHIBIT 4.1: THE MAX FLORISTS DIRECT MAIL CAMPAIGN BRIEF

The Campaign Objective

The objective for the first year of this direct mail campaign is to open 400 new corporate accounts that will remain active in future years. This objective is to be achieved within a total budget of £2,500 and within the constraints of the company's existing facilities and staff.

The Creative Content

There are four main issues to be addressed in developing the creative content of the campaign, as follows:

1. The need to deliver a message that reflects the quality of the product that is being sold.

2. The need to deliver the message in such a way as to gain attention — for example, personalised invitation, laser printed letter and envelope.

3. The need to present the message in such a way that will incentivise the recipient to react.

4. The need to present the offer in such a way that will simplify the recipient's ability to react — for example Freepost and/or Freephone.

The Mailing List

The mailing list should:

1. Be personalised to the decision-maker or those in a capacity to influence the decision process — for example, the marketing manager, the PR manager, the financial manager or the chief executive.

2. Be concentrated on the greater Dublin area.

3. Be concentrated initially on the service business sector, as marketing research and analysis of existing accounts indicates the greater potential of this area.

The Mail Shot

An initial and follow-up mailing were designed simultaneously. The design of each was based on simplicity and functionality. The initial mailing consisted of a personalised envelope, a brief personalised letter which introduced the offer and incentive and a detailed invitation card which reinforced that offer and invitation. All three items were connected by a shared headline *"There are many beautiful things, but the silent beauty of a flower surpasses them all"*.

The mailing invited the recipient to register as a corporate account holder with Max Florists in order to avail of "the highest standard of service, in the shortest possible time with a guarantee of quality". It then listed the various elements of the service that Max Florists could offer its corporate clients.

To encourage response, recipients were offered the incentive of placing their first order to the value of £25 free of charge. In addition to encouraging a positive response, this incentive was designed to indicate Max Florists' confidence in their own service. Additionally, to make response as easy as possible, respondents were offered a Freepost facility.

The follow-up letter, posted ten days later, was designed to remind recipients of the offer and included the same invitation card. To achieve an immediate connection with the original letter the follow-up mailing was also presented under the headline *"There are many beautiful things, but the silent beauty of a flower surpasses them all"*. The invitation card is reproduced in Exhibit 4.2.

Having placed their order for £25 worth of free flowers, respondents received the flowers within 24 hours, together with an invoice for the £25. The invoice was accompanied by a credit note for the same amount. The existence of an invoice and credit note ensured that an account in the name of Max Florists was opened in the company's books and an account in the company's name was established in Max Florists' books. Now, if the company needed flowers in the future, it would naturally contact the supplier with whom it had the account.

Some time later, the account holder was issued with a statement showing a zero balance. This statement was issued with a gift of a desktop calendar which maintained the name of Max Florists' and its phone number prominently in the mind of the new account holder.

EXHIBIT 4.2: TEXT FROM MAX FLORISTS' INVITATION CARD

There are many beautiful things,
but the silent beauty of a flower surpasses them all

Max Florists is one of Dublin's longest established florists, situated at the centre of Dublin for over 25 years. Our floristry skills and techniques are expert and we work with the widest possible selection of top quality produce only.

One thing we have come to realise is that today's client requires the highest standard of service, in the shortest possible time with the guarantee of quality. We provide that service.

As part of the service we offer:
 Guaranteed same-day delivery of Dublin orders placed before 5 p.m.
 Same-day delivery of orders for the rest of Ireland and the UK if placed
  before noon.
 Flowers delivered world-wide with Interflora.
 Weekly flower arrangements for reception or board rooms.
 Promotional flowers — add that extra touch to your next sales promotion.
 Champagne, wine or chocolates delivered with flowers.
 Major functions, banquets, AGMs or sales conference displays.
 Company crest or logo in floral display.
 Prompt quotation service.
 Funeral or memorial service flowers.

And your Invitation . . .

We know our service is best — so confident are we that we are certain once you have sampled our service, you will be more than happy to place your company's account with us. This is why we are inviting you to send your first order to the value of £25 **free of charge****. Simply complete the card below and return it to us FREEPOST, or phone us today at 731222.*

P.S. All major Credit Cards accepted by telephone.

*Limited to flower value of £25.00 in Dublin area only.

✂--

Company Account Registration
Name: _____   Persons authorised to place
Address: _____   telephone orders: _____
_____   _____
              _____

Telephone: _____

Free of charge order:
Recipient: _____   Message on card: _____
Address: _____   _____
_____   _____
              _____

Date of Delivery:_____   _____

Testing the Mail Shot

The mail shot was tested prior to implementation to establish if modifications were necessary to any part and to:

1. Determine how acceptable the offer was and

2. Predict a likely response rate so that the resources required for efficient fulfilment could be determined in advance of implementation.

A total of 150 units were mailed as the test sample. The mailings were made over a three-week period in batches of 25, 50 and 75 in each of the three weeks, respectively. These volumes were used to establish the volume of response that the company could most efficiently fulfil. All mail recipients who had not responded were sent the follow-up mailing ten working days later.

The positive response from the test was 58 (39 per cent), and of those 58 respondents, 43.29 per cent of the total number of mail recipients converted to active accounts. That is, 74 per cent of those who responded positively to the offer became active accounts.

A number of significant findings emerged from the test:

1. The spend per new account was substantially higher on average than initially assumed.

2. On the basis of the test results, an annual mailing of 1,400 would be sufficient for the initial objective to be achieved.

3. The follow-up letter, through its reminder effect, outpulled the initial mailing by a ratio of 2:1.

4. Fifty units was the most suitable weekly mailing volume to allow efficient fulfilment within the existing company resources.

Campaign Results

Consequent to the positive test results, the campaign was launched on 1 March. The mail shot was posted in weekly volumes of 50, as this was the volume indicated most appropriate by the test findings. No mailings were made in weeks which included occasions traditionally associated with flower-giving such as Valentine's Day, Mother's Day and Christmas, as the demand generated by these occasions already stretched existing resources sufficiently.

At the end of the first year of using the mail shot, the target of 400 new, active accounts was exceeded by 25 per cent, with a higher than anticipated average order value per account. The response rate achieved over the year was 37 per cent, only two percentage points down on the 3-week test results. Additionally, these figures were achieved without having to inject management or capital resources beyond those initially budgeted for. The company was now acquiring sufficient numbers of new customers and had returned to its desirable growth position without following the multi-site strategy.

As a bonus, the campaign won first prize in the 1988 An Post/*Business and Finance* Direct Marketing Awards, which generated much positive publicity for the company.

REFERENCES TO CHAPTER 4

Baker, M.J. (1991), *Marketing: An Introductory Text*, Fifth edition, London: Macmillan, p. 102.

Bird, D. (1993), *Commonsense Direct Marketing*, Third Edition, London: Kogan Page, p. 13.

Colley, G. (1962), *Defining Advertising Goals for Measuring Advertising Results*, New York: Association of National Advertisers.

Goodwin, J. (1992), "Media Planning and the Role of Press Advertising" in *The Practitioner's Guide to Direct Marketing*, London: The Direct Marketing Centre, pp. 7.1–23.

Holder, D. (1992), "Finders Keepers — The Basics of Customer Acquisition and Customer Retention" in *The Practitioner's Guide to Direct Marketing*, London: The Direct Marketing Centre, p. 2.2.

Kotler, P. (1994), *Marketing Management: Analysis, Planning, Implementation and Control*, Eighth edition, Englewood Cliffs, NJ: Prentice Hall, p. 611.

Lawlor, K. (1995), "Advertising as Communication" in T. Meenaghan and P. O'Sullivan (eds.), *Marketing Communications in Ireland*, Dublin: Oak Tree Press.

McCorkell, G. (1994), "What Happened to the Good Old Days" in *The Best of Graeme McCorkell*, London: Institute of Direct Marketing, p. 33.

McGowan, M. (1995), "Direct Marketing — Irish Perspectives" in T. Meenaghan and P. O'Sullivan (eds.), *Marketing Communications in Ireland*, Dublin: Oak Tree Press, p. 536.

Parker, A.J. (1991), "Retail Environments: Into the 1990s", *Irish Marketing Review*, Vol. 5, No. 2, pp. 61–72.

Parker, T. (1990) "The Changing Nature of Irish Retailing" in R.W.G. Parker and A.J. Parker (eds.), *Ireland: A Geographic Perspective*, London: Routledge, pp. 237–270.

Schiffman, L.G. and L.L. Kanuk (1994), *Consumer Behavior*, Fifth edition, New York: Prentice Hall International, pp. 81–84.

Smith, P.R. (1993), *Marketing Communications: An Integrated Approach*, London: Kogan Page, pp. 50–54.

Strong, E.C. (1925), *The Psychology of Selling*, New York: McGraw Hill, p. 9.

Chapter 5

CUSTOMER RETENTION

Aileen Kennedy *and* Margaret-Anne Lawlor

Overview

This chapter looks at the economics, benefits and philosophy behind reten-
tion programmes. Key literature on retention in general is reviewed. The
focus then moves to the challenges specifically facing companies dealing
with consumer markets. Though relationship marketing is acknowledged as
a facilitator of retention, this chapter intentionally avoids a discussion of
relationship-building strategies, while acknowledging retention as one com-
ponent of such a strategy.

THE IMPORTANCE OF CUSTOMER RETENTION

The growth in importance of retention marketing, described by
Barnes (1994) as one of the 3Rs of the new marketing paradigm (relationships, retention and recovery), is driven by numerous factors.
Increased competition means that firms find it difficult to differentiate their market offering and constantly seek some type of sustainable competitive advantage. Costs of marketing are simultaneously
rising, as is the number of companies vying for the individual
consumer's/customer's attention.

It has also been generally accepted that acquiring new customers
is much more expensive than retaining existing customers (Reichheld
and Sasser, 1990). This is most obvious in the area of direct marketing, where the costs of acquiring and keeping customers can be accurately quantified (Stone et al., 1996). However, consumers are
becoming more sophisticated and discerning, increasing the challenge for companies trying to retain an existing customer base.
Within services literature, there is acknowledgement of the need to
decrease the "churn factor" — customers lost to the organisation —

or as Reichheld and Sasser (1990) describe them, the "scrap heap" — customers who will not come back.

THE ECONOMICS AND BENEFITS OF RETENTION

Customers who stay longer with a company have an increased customer lifetime value (Stone et al., 1996). With each additional year of a relationship, customers become less costly to serve. Over time, the loyalty life cycle plays out, loyal customers even become business builders, buying more, paying premium prices and bringing in new customers through referrals (O'Brien and Jones, 1995).

Reichheld and Sasser (1990) suggest that as a customer's relationship with the company lengthens, profits rise — the suggestion being that companies can boost profit by almost 100 per cent by retaining just five per cent more of their customers, and as such, companies should strive for "zero defections".

Free advertising or positive word-of-mouth generated by satisfied customers and the spillover effect on referrals is also an anticipated benefit of successful customer retention. Higher customer profitability also occurs, as the costs of recruiting customers is lower. The cost of sales is reduced, as existing customers are usually more responsive and operating costs decline, with lower maintenance costs for existing customers. Finally, as the company gains experience with its customers, it can serve them more efficiently. All of these factors will combine to produce a steadily increasing stream of profits over the course of the customer's relationship with the company (Reichheld and Sasser, 1990).

Retaining customers makes it difficult for competitors to enter a market or increase their market share (Buchanan and Gillies, 1990). Even in low growth businesses, there is generally a regular churn of customers; 20 per cent of customers may defect each year to the competition. In this case, the most powerful way to grow is to increase retention (Rosenberg and Czepiel, 1984).

LIFETIME VALUE OF THE CUSTOMER

Retention marketing is adopted to create profit. Small once-off transactions by customers do not fulfil this objective. Continuous purchases over a lengthy period of time increase revenue at a reduced cost; hence the focus on the "stream of earnings" which every customer has the potential to generate, if you can coax them to stay! For example, British Airways has calculated that a frequent business flyer is worth in excess of £10,000 over their lifetime. Dominos Pizza, a US fast-food chain, has calculated that a single customer purchasing regularly over a ten-year period is worth $5,000 to the firm (Buchanan and Gilles, 1990).

WHICH CUSTOMERS TO RETAIN?

For most companies, a blind attempt to retain all customers may be counter-productive. The key to increasing profitability and competitive strength may be to get rid of customers who will never be profitable and focus on recruiting and retaining high lifetime value customers (Stone at al., 1996) or the "right customers". These are not necessarily the easiest to attract or the most profitable in the short term, but those who are likely to do business with the company over time (Reichheld, 1993). Stone et al. (1996) discuss the case of commercial banking, where in some cases banks have found that 10 per cent of their customers are responsible for 100 per cent of the profit, the remainder being loss-making. Some of these unprofitable customers will eventually become profitable, such as students, who will in time generate a lifetime value as mentioned previously. In such cases, the suggestion is that companies should look to customer management systems to identify which customers to acquire and retain and which to discourage.

To make such decisions, management needs access to information that will allow for discriminating among customers, or quality segmentation. Rather than following market share, companies should be committed to developing "quality share", achieving their largest share among customers who will provide the greatest profits (Barnes, 1994). In companies such as financial services and the business-to-business sector, customer information is readily available. For example, credit card companies often offer lower interest rates to customers with better credit profiles and superior payment histories (O'Brien and Jones, 1995). Other companies serving "anonymous" customers are at a disadvantage in terms of retention strategies (Barnes, 1994). Retailers have aggressively addressed this issue through the introduction of loyalty cards, generating customer information which may in turn facilitate a retention programme.

BASIC COMPONENTS OF A RETENTION STRATEGY

This section draws on Hamilton and Howcraft (1995) and outlines the main components that constitute the basis of a retention strategy.

Management Commitment

Improving customer retention may involve investments of both capital and time on the part of any organisation. Management commitment is also necessary to establish a corporate culture conducive to maximising customer retention (Hamilton and Howcraft, 1995). Within services and industrial markets, emphasis must also be put on establishing and maintaining a customer-focused culture where the value of customer retention, based on enhancing relationships with customers, is valued.

Retention Information Systems

At the core of a retention strategy is the ability to identify and track customers, and as such, organisations must have access to or develop new methods of tracking and analysing causes of customer defection, using this information to strengthen customer relationships and maximise customer retention.

Employees

In high contact situations, employees/front-line staff must have the power to deal with customer problems immediately to lead to customer satisfaction and so retention. This presupposes their access to appropriate customer information simultaneously. A further discussion of this point is beyond the scope of this chapter, but has been well developed within services literature.

ALTERNATIVE CUSTOMER RETENTION STRATEGIES

Various suggestions have been put forward in the literature as to how to retain customers. Differences emerge depending on whether the service, industrial or consumer market is under consideration.

Defections Management

In the case of service industries, Reichheld and Sasser (1990) discuss the need for an organisation to adopt a "zero defections" culture to reduce customer churn. They define defection management as a "systematic process which attempts to retain customers before they defect" and is facilitated by tracking reasons why customers leave, using this information to reduce further defections. They suggest that, for the credit insurance sector, by reducing the defection rate by five per cent, a company could boost profits by 25 per cent plus. The positive effect on profit of defections management is consistent across industries as diverse as software (reducing defections by five per cent can boost profits by 35 per cent), industrial distribution (45 per cent), and car services (81 per cent). It has also been shown that closing the "retention gap" in banking has a direct effect on profit. For every one per cent improvement a bank makes and sustains in its customer retention rate, operating earnings will improve by 20 per cent (Gilliam, 1994). Similar defection programmes are discussed in various contexts such as logistics (Copacino, 1997) and banking (Gilliam, 1994). Geller (1997) outlines 15 basic steps to follow for a direct marketing retention programme (Table 5.1).

TABLE 5.1: GUIDELINES FOR A DIRECT MARKETING CUSTOMER RETENTION PROGRAMME

1.	Deliver a high quality/high value product
2.	Make every single contact count
3.	Know your customers
4.	Know when your customers defect
5.	Keep your company at the top of your customer's mind
6.	Modify your product/service mix
7.	Always close the loop in your marketing programme
8.	Deliver excellent customer service
9.	Keep your customer retention programmes human
10.	Use partnerships to build customer retention
11.	Do the unexpected
12.	Use your database to maximise the personalisation of offers
13.	Identify the timing and frequency of promotions
14.	Utilise retail and catalogue synergy
15.	Another customer retention strategy is online marketing.

Source: Geller (1997), p. 58–62.

DeSouza (1992) outlines the key steps to be taken by a company designing a successful customer retention plan: measure customer retention (assuming this is feasible); interview former customers (are they defecting due to price, product, service factors or due to technological, organisational or market factors); analyse complaint and service data; and finally identify switching barriers. Waterhouse and Morgan (1994) discuss the application of defection management within Lloyds Bank and how this financial institution tackled the issue of increasing customer retention rates through research on defections and satisfaction.

Marketing Approaches for Customer Retention

Rosenberg and Czeipel (1984) discuss the concept of a "customer retaining mix", as opposed to the traditional mix aimed specifically at acquiring customers. The elements of this marketing mix for customer retention are product extras, reinforcing promotions, sales force connections, specialised distribution and post purchase communication. They reinforce the idea of not targeting all customers equally, and altering the company's approach to existing customers with the objective of increasing retention rates.

"Locking in" Customers

It may be inherently easier within business-to-business markets to manage customer retention. Jackson (1985) suggests that long-term relationships between individual buyers and sellers can be established and specifically designed to increase the switching costs that customers will face. Within the highly competitive arena of retail banking, one means of increasing retention has been to increase customer-switching costs. Effectively, the customer becomes "locked in" by such tools as long-term mortgages, with penalties for switching. The same idea relates to airline frequent flyer programmes, as collectors feel they cannot switch (Barnes, 1994; McKenzie, 1995). Given the competitive environment, such retention strategies are unlikely to prevail, and evidence suggests that retail banks are now focusing on more proactive approaches to retention via customer care programmes, quality customer service and building relationships with customers (Ennew and Binks, 1996).

Rewarding Customers

Many companies have adopted the approach of rewarding customers with tangible and often financial incentives for continued custom, largely through the adoption of loyalty programmes. Such programmes seek to reward customers for their patronage and to stimulate return shopping trips. Loyalty schemes also offer a valuable opportunity to collect data about customers in terms of the frequency and value of their custom, brand preferences, individual responses to coupons, competitions and other sales promotions, as well as valuable demographic information about their households. The use of such schemes is examined in detail later in this chapter.

STAGES IN RETENTION STRATEGY

As mentioned above, retention strategies tend to differ amongst consumer, industrial and service sectors. The remainder of this chapter will focus on the concept of retention practices/programmes in the consumer market.

Stone et al. (1996) offer the view that the existence of binary relationships, whereby customers exhibit 100 per cent loyalty to one organisation, is quite rare. Given the plethora of "me-too" choices in many consumer markets, marketers have been somewhat misguided in believing that they could "ensnare customers in lifetime monogamous relationships" (Mitchell, 1996). Most relationships between company and customer may develop in stages, whereby newly acquired, current and lapsed customers exhibit different buying patterns at each stage. In order to isolate different segments, the crucial factor is the ability to collect, analyse and track customer information (Stone and Woodcock, 1995). Most companies maintain a database of sorts either in terms of the maintenance of basic accounting records and sales data or under the guise of the formalised marketing information system (MIS). The gathering and management of customer information allows the company to isolate different types of customer according to their status as newly acquired, current or lapsed.

Stone et al. (1995) suggest that there are five stages in a retention strategy: welcome, up-selling, cross-selling, renewal and reactivation. The different stages serve to prescribe various courses of action available to a retention marketer when addressing new, current and lapsed customers.

Welcome

The welcome stage offers an opportunity to welcome and reassure new customers, as well as collecting additional customer information. The objective is to reduce dissonance or lingering doubts in the customer's mind and also to generate positive attitudes — "I *have* made the right decision in choosing to deal with Company X". Instead of using this as a selling opportunity, the emphasis is on educating customers, explaining company procedures and, most importantly, thanking buyers for their custom. For example, the car manufacturer, Mitsubishi, offers a welcome pack to new buyers, comprising an audio tape and car manual. The audio tape congratulates the "proud owner" and also gives details regarding servicing procedures, warranties, etc.

New members of the Statoil Premium Club reward scheme receive a personalised letter of welcome offering 100 Welcome Points as well as explaining how one's points can be used to make donations to charity, to enjoy cash-back prizes or else to choose gifts from the Premium Club's catalogue. The appropriateness of a welcome strategy will depend on the anticipated lifetime value of the customer. For example, many airlines and car manufacturers aspire to retain customers for the duration of their lifetime.

Up-selling

Apart from stimulating repeat business, the company should encourage the customer to purchase a more valuable version of the product or service than is currently being consumed. The up-selling technique seeks to generate "trading up". The objective is to increase the profitability generated by existing customers. Car dealers are arguably past masters of this technique. A potential car buyer with a certain price in mind might be encouraged by a persuasive salesperson to purchase additional "extras" such as power steering or a sunroof.

Continuing with the auto theme, up-selling is frequently used by car manufacturers who seek to encourage current customers to trade up to a larger and more expensive model.

There are many techniques which can be used to up-sell, including discounts, incentives and customer clubs. In 1991, British Airways awarded platinum cards to 1,200 of their most influential flyers with the aim of offering exclusive benefits to this customer segment.

Another mode of up-selling would be an explanatory newsletter or catalogue detailing the company's range of goods. Kilroy's Superstores, located in the Irish midlands, sell a wide range of household goods and have used newsletters, targeted at loyal customers, with a view to announcing pending special offers and sales. One past innovation involved sending customers a sachet of coffee designed to offer a pleasing start to the day of the sale.

The timing for employing up-selling techniques depends on the expected replacement period for the product. The replacement cycle for, say, a car would be estimated by analysing customers' buying patterns. If a database indicates that customers tend to change their cars every three years, then the time to draw a customer's attention to new and more expensive models might be six months before the probable purchase date.

Cross-selling

The cross-selling stage seeks to change customer behaviour by introducing buyers to new product and service categories of which they might previously have been unaware. Techniques used to inform customers about such offerings include catalogues and newsletters.

Cross-selling may be crucial to the long-term survival of a company. If it is perceived that an organisation offers a narrow range of goods, the buyer may be pushed in the direction of the competitor who is seen to offer a wide range of continuously improving goods.

Examples of cross-selling would include *The Sunday Times* newspaper's promotion of its Wine Club to readers. The National Geographic Society introduces its subscribers to a wide range of travel-based offerings such as maps, videos and travel magazines. Clarks International, the shoe manufacturer, dispatched mailings to its regular customers with a view to encouraging mothers to purchase shoes for their children at Clarks outlets. Methods of cross-selling across households, for example to husbands, were also examined.

When considering the use of this technique, it is crucial that particular care is taken if the objective is to remove unwanted inventory or old lines of stock by selling it to the buyer. A customer who is encouraged to purchase useless or obsolete stock will probably be lost to the company in the long term.

Renewal

Many products and services require annual or regular renewal, such as car insurance, healthcare subscriptions and membership of clubs and societies. The renewal technique involves the careful timing of appropriate and personalised communications prior to the renewal date, with a view to reinforcing repeat purchase. Such communications generally take the form of a personalised letter to the customer. It is imperative that such communication occurs *before* the renewal date, *on* the renewal date and *after* the renewal date so as to maximise the number of reminders to the customer.

A certain period of time must be allowed after the final renewal date to allow for unexpected events which may have prevented customers from receiving the communications, e.g. postal strikes, absence due to holidays, etc. After this period of time, the customer is considered to have become lapsed.

Reactivation

The reactivation stage aims to attract lapsed or inactive customers who have not responded to communications. Customers may be *temporarily dormant* if they have merely forgotten to renew their relationship with the company and have every intention of doing so in the future. Alternatively, customers may be *permanently lost* if, for example, they have moved out of the target market. This might apply to a teenager who subscribes to a particular teen magazine for a certain number of years. However, as such people grow older, they inevitably move out of the target readership.

A customer might also be permanently lapsed if there is a perceived problem in the delivery of the product or service. Dissatisfaction with product quality or pricing might result in a customer terminating the relationship with the seller. Reichheld (1993) emphasises the need for organisations to ascertain the deep-rooted causes of customer defection. It is vital that the reasons for lapsed customers are thoroughly investigated by the company; a dissatisfied customer has the power of word-of-mouth to laud or deride a company.

RETENTION TECHNIQUES

In each of the five stages of a retention strategy, the organisation has a wide range of mechanisms or techniques at its disposal with which it can seek to retain customers (Table 5.2). Such options allow the company to advise customers about new product or service offerings. Alternatively, customers may be rewarded for their patronage by virtue of special offers such as bonus points, premiums, cash-back vouchers, etc. It must be emphasised that a fundamental *raison d'être* for such schemes is the customer information which is duly generated (Hartley, 1997). Customers can only be retained in the long term if the company continually innovates with a view to improving its selling proposition. In essence, such innovation is dependent on ongoing transactional data which can be used to construct a meaningful picture of a customer complete with changing requirements and preferences over a long period of time.

TABLE 5.2: RETENTION TECHNIQUES

- Members' magazines
- Reward/loyalty schemes
- Delayed payment schemes
- Catalogues
- Events/invitations
- Store cards and credit accounts
- Advance sale previews

This chapter will focus specifically on loyalty schemes as a means of customer retention. The loyalty/reward technique seeks to develop a symbiotic relationship between customer and company whereby the customer is offered monetary or non-monetary incentives as a reward for patronage. The company benefits by gaining advantage through enhanced knowledge of customers.

The grocery retail sector exemplifies this concept with participating companies including Tesco, Safeways and Marks and Spencer in the UK (Palmer and Beggs, 1997). Irish retailers have followed suit, using customer databases to build relationships with customers by offering discounts and products in proportion to the amounts spent in store, as in the case of Dunnes Stores, Superquinn and the new entrant Tesco. Petrol stations have been another area where loyalty schemes have been enthusiastically adopted, as in the cases of Texaco, Shell, Statoil, etc. Airline frequent flyer programmes (FFPs), originating with American Airlines in 1981, have also swept through that particular sector. Fashion and furniture retailers are now adopting this concept also; for example, the Burton Group, Austin Reed, Harvey Nichols, and department store account cards.

Despite such a high level of activity, doubt has been expressed as to the ability of such schemes to enhance the firm's long-term competitive advantage. The first firm to innovate in the market will reap a competitive advantage, but this will soon be copied — as was the case of Superquinn in the Irish marketplace. With airlines, FFPs have become the norm for the customer and part of their expectation rather than the exception.

The majority of schemes offer rewards either directly related to the product or combined with third-party benefits, with airlines offering car rental facilities to enhance the service proposition. The vast majority of these schemes are driven by database marketing. The recent launch of the Tesco Clubcard reflects the increasing focus on customer retention and lifetime value. In the UK, an estimated 25 million consumers participate in loyalty programmes.

The question is, do such schemes promote lasting customer loyalty? According to the British Consumer Association's *Which?* magazine, loyalty cards do not appear to buy loyalty, with just three per cent of people saying they now shop exclusively in one supermarket chain because of the schemes. Also, customer loyalty schemes do not compensate for marketing weakness, as a good product with a strong brand image will generally promote greater loyalty than schemes (McKenzie, 1995). Also, loyalty schemes may not be suited to the product as high average transaction value, high lifetime value and frequent purchase patterns provide a basic "must" for most loyalty schemes (Hawkes, 1996).

Loyalty programmes may appear attractive as a low-cost method of gathering information and improving customer retention rates. However, while customer retention has been shown to be more profitable than continual customer replacement, it remains unclear whether such programmes are effective compared with more expensive but possibly more rewarding activities such as developing customer care programmes, which add to the customer's perceived value (Palmer and Beggs, 1997). Loyalty schemes therefore emerge as one possible retention tactic within consumer markets, the success of which is largely determined by the company's industry and strategic position (McKenzie, 1995). An interesting discussion of these points can be found in Palmer and Beggs (1997).

REVIEWING THE MULTIMEDIA COMMUNICATION CHANNELS

A company which is innovating and improving its selling proposition must communicate this information to the customer body. Enhanced product offerings, improved customer service facilities and attractive promotional offers are among the many messages that a customer-friendly organisation may choose to bring to the attention of a target audience. McCorkell (1997) numbers catalogues, mailings, newspapers and telemarketing among the retention media that can be used to communicate such information to current customers (Table 5.3).

TABLE 5.3: RETENTION MEDIA

- Telemarketing
- Mailings
- Catalogues
- Inserts/enclosures
- Newspapers/bulletins
- Miscellaneous (birthday cards, thank you notes)

Source: McCorkell (1997), p. 197.

The authors would suggest that other media options such as *direct response broadcast advertising*, *Internet* and *electronic kiosks* can be added to this list, as they too afford an opportunity to the customer for interaction and dialogue with the company.

As always, the final media vehicle choice is governed by factors such as its ability to reach a target audience, technical properties and the atmosphere or image lent to the creative message.

Telephony/Telemarketing

The growth of telemarketing is due to its twin benefits of speed and convenience, as well as the facility for out-bound and in-bound lead generation. Telemarketing is ideal for the "welcome" stage of the retention strategy, whereby customers can be contacted with a view to simply thanking them for their custom. It can also be used for up-selling and cross-selling stages.

The use of telemarketing in the Irish motor insurance industry was pioneered by Celtic Autoquote in 1988. They sought to target existing and new customers by virtue of the perception that tele-insurance offers both convenience and value for money to the subscriber.

For a fuller discussion of telemarketing, see Chapter 13.

Direct Mail

O'Rourke (1997) suggests that the following facilities may be offered by direct mail as part of a retention programme:

- Maintaining the loyalty of existing customers
- Upgrading the value of existing customer
- Launching new products
- Cross-selling and reactivating
- Building traffic to retail outlets.

Direct mail is particularly popular with financial institutions and charities in Ireland. In 1996, Trocaire and An Post embarked on a mailing campaign targeting 5,000 Trocaire donors and 7,000 An Post customers. The reasoning behind the campaign was to promote the TAP (Trocaire/An Post) swipe card in order to facilitate the payment of donations to Trocaire through the Post Office. The card could be presented at any Post Office, a donation made and a receipt given to the cardholder.

The objectives were to inform individuals of Trocaire's activities and to emphasise the need for continuing support. The campaign also aimed to encourage the application for and regular use of a TAP card. The desired response rate for the campaign was 7 per cent. A mailshot was dispatched to the 12,000 customers, enclosing a letter of introduction, a brochure and a reply coupon. The outcome of the campaign was a resounding success, with an actual response rate of 15 per cent. Direct mail is further discussed in Chapter 14.

Catalogues

The immediate benefit of using a catalogue to communicate with existing customers is that it facilitates armchair shopping — the customer can order an item from the comfort of home. For years, catalogues were utilised by the traditional mail order suppliers — fashion houses, book clubs, etc. Stone et al. (1995) have likened this medium to "the perpetual mailshot" or "the ever-attendant sales person".

Catalogues particularly lend themselves to a retention programme because they can be used to build databases of customer buying patterns and thence a "scoring system" can be developed to distinguish between frequent customers, infrequent customers, etc. Catalogues can also be used to test new products and services amongst existing customers in advance of a roll-out introduction.

Inserts/Enclosures

Inserts are cards or leaflets which may be enclosed (loosely or bound) in a newspaper or magazine. Their popularity derives from cost-effectiveness (greater responsiveness generated than space advertising) and their eye-catching nature.

Coupon books and product samples are frequently distributed to customers using this method. For example, many women's magazines include samples of cosmetic products or may offer a cash-back voucher to the reader.

Newspapers/Direct Response Press Advertising

This option is particularly useful if the objective is to generate volume enquiries and to construct/enhance a customer database. It has been suggested that 85 per cent of all large press advertisements offer a coupon or telephone number with a view to eliciting an immediate response, while many companies also extend an invitation to the reader to visit their website.

In autumn of 1997, Tesco ran a series of press advertisements with a view to receiving customer feedback on the retailing experience provided by Tesco/Quinnsworth. Readers were invited to submit their ideas and suggestions to the company with the objective of revealing customers' shopping priorities. Cody (1996) alludes to the importance of customer feedback and suggests that the act of prioritising the exploration of customers' needs will result in further sales and customer-driven innovations.

Inserts and direct response press advertising are dealt with in detail in Chapter 15.

Miscellaneous

Simple gestures like birthday cards and thank you notes may be used as a gesture of goodwill towards the customer. Quinn (1990) describes how customers who celebrate their birthday on the day they visit a Superquinn store may be presented with a birthday cake as they depart from the outlet.

In December 1997, the same retail outlet dispatched a mailshot to its Superclub members, thanking them for their custom and offering them a number of bonus points if a certain volume of shopping was completed within a specified time period.

In the Christmas period of 1997, Tesco mailed a large number of its Clubcard members with a £3 voucher as a way of thanking its higher spending customers for their patronage.

Direct Response Television

Nash (1995) suggests that direct response advertising is designed to produce an immediate inquiry, order or donation, by virtue of offering a contact address and/or telephone number.

The objective in DRTV is to deliver a brand or corporate message by suggesting that "this company is responsive, approachable and open for business" (Smyth, 1997).

DRTV is particularly popular in the Irish financial services industry, whereby the use of a Freefone 1800 or CallSave 1850 telephone number encourages current and prospective customers to contact the particular institution at a zero/reduced cost. Chapter 18 looks at DRTV in more detail.

Direct Response Radio

Because listening to the radio is essentially a secondary activity, advertising has to work even harder than on television to catch the audience's attention. Guardian Direct, one of the largest spenders on radio advertising in Ireland, has successfully used this direct response medium because the telephone number (1850 28 28 20) combined with a catchy musical jingle makes the call to action quite memorable. Again, direct response radio advertising lends itself to lead generation as well as inbound and outbound communication with existing customers.

Internet

Although it has been in existence for over 30 years, it is only in the last five or so years that the Internet has made its presence felt amongst direct marketers. This medium can be likened to a computerised Golden Pages directory, offering the properties of movement, music and colour. Unlike television and radio advertising, an Internet site involves the user actively — the latter chooses to "click on" to a home page. Thus the user is controlling the information which is consumed. Irish companies such as Gaeltarra, Kenny's Bookshop, the House of Ireland and Texaco have designed successful websites which have been used to inform customers about new product offerings as well as allowing individuals to order goods from the privacy and comfort of their home.

The Internet is discussed further in Chapter 19.

Electronic Kiosks

McGowan (1995) suggests that the use of computer kiosks placed at customer-contact locations facilitates the collection of potential/ current customer data as well as allowing the end-user to control the information being provided. Electronic kiosks are often used by financial institutions, whereby touch-screen computers seek to reduce the necessity for a customer to queue in line, waiting to catch the attention of a busy employee.

It should be noted that many shoppers exhibit signs of discomfort towards computer technology and may be reluctant to use an unfamiliar medium. In addition, kiosks, and indeed other forms of electronic shopping preclude the individual from physically handling the product, trying it on if necessary, etc.

DETERMINING THE CREATIVE MESSAGE

Having chosen the communication channel(s) that will be used to target certain customers, the next task is to assemble the creative message. A message can consist of three basic building blocks — text, sound and visuals. Stone et al. (1995: 214) contend that:

> Creativity is above all about ideas that work. Direct marketing is essentially about making a sale. Combining the two . . . leads to creative ideas that work to make a sale (or generate a lead that will produce a sale). Whether your objectives are visual, original, clever or aesthetically pleasing, they must achieve your objective.

It has been suggested that any attempt to examine the creativity in a promotional campaign can be likened to an attempt to explain a joke. The humour and appeal is lost in the process of explanation. Nevertheless, Belch and Belch (1995) contend that creativity is "the ability to generate fresh, unique and appropriate ideas that can be used as solutions to communication problems". From an advertising perspective, Schultz and Tannenbaum (1988) suggest that "creative advertising understands that people do not buy products — they buy product benefits". Charles Revson echoed this sentiment with his oft-quoted statement: "in the factory, we make cosmetics, in the store, we sell hope".

Thus, it follows that the development of a creative message must derive from an understanding of customers' information needs — what benefits are being sought and what do customers need to know and remember about our product or service offering?

Prior to the launch of the Ford Ka in December 1996, Ford decided to use a mailing campaign to generate awareness of and interest in the new car marque. The first mailshot was dispatched to prospects in November 1996. The creative execution consisted of a letter accompanied by an intriguing teaser brochure. The outer envelope outlined the key proposition — *Style is Nothing Without Substance*. A second mailing in December comprised a personalised letter and a Ka brochure, giving details of Ford dealerships, prices and other data.

The creative message should endeavour to guide the receiver through a series of steps or a "hierarchy of effects" — awareness, interest, desire, action. The consumer of the message must be informed about the existence of a certain product or service offering. Interest may be aroused by drawing attention to the features and benefits of the offering and by demonstrating the relevance and/or aspirational nature of the offering. In order to generate desire, the receiver must be presented with a credible unique selling proposition (USP) or a compelling reason why one needs to purchase the product (action stage) and why it is better than its competitors.

The following are suggested guidelines for evaluating the creative message:

- What are your first impressions of the message?

- Is it saying something new/interesting?

- Does it contain a unique selling proposition?

- Will your audience relate to the language and style of the message?

- Is there a clear offer? Can the following question be easily answered by the customer — "What's in it for me?"

- Is the offer credible or is it too good to be true?

- Have you used clichés, jargon or unintelligible words?

- What is the visual appeal of the message? For example, this question can apply to:

  - a direct mailing (colour and size of stationery and typeface)

  - a direct response television advertisement (number of times the brand/company name and contact telephone number are flashed on the screen, the appeal of company spokesperson appearing in the advertisement)

  - an Internet website (colours, graphics and symbols used)

- Is there an immediate call to action? e.g. "Telephone lines open until midnight tonight!".

THE IMPORTANCE OF CONTINUAL TESTING

Very few promotional campaigns offer an ironclad guarantee of success. There is a risk that a target audience might not receive the message, may misunderstand it or may be sceptical or unwilling to respond. Other potentially damaging factors would include the employment of an unsuitable medium, badly executed creative offer or poor timing.

With a view to maximising the effectiveness of a campaign, it is essential that continuous testing of the various elements which comprise a retention programme be employed. Testing has been defined as:

> The planned and scientific inclusion and measurement of alternative marketing elements or combinations in a campaign in order to improve systematically future campaign performance and profitability (IDM, 1995).

Another factor driving the need for continuous testing is the prudent aspect of minimising, where possible, the costs of making mistakes (McCorkell, 1997).

The objective is to test two or more alternatives amongst a small sample of current or potential customers to determine the optimum option. For example, two versions of a mailshot, using different typefaces, might be dispatched to a small number of customers with a view to ascertaining which version generates the greater response.

GATHERING CUSTOMER DATA

A detailed knowledge of customers' needs and past purchasing habits helps a firm in building long-term customer relationships, ensuring customer loyalty and increasing the possibility of cross-selling (Fletcher et al., 1990).

One of the key objectives governing the use of retention programmes is database construction and management. Information can be difficult and expensive to gather, store, manage and manipulate. Therefore, it is vital from the outset that the marketer has a clear and concise understanding of the information that will prove relevant to the organisation's operations. Information can be gathered from many sources:

1. *Sales Records*: May generate the following information — name and address of customer, frequency of custom, method of payment, value of custom.

2. *List Brokers*: These are intermediaries who sell or rent lists of contacts. In Ireland, Kompass is probably the best-known industrial list supplier, offering information on companies in over 90 industry sectors and 20,000 industry subsectors. In the consumer

marketing arena, Precision Marketing Information Ltd. (PMI) has developed the Irish Consumer Marketing Database (ICMD), which provides demographic and lifestyle data.

3. *Public Sources*: Such sources generate contact names and addresses, e.g. Electoral Register, Golden Pages, telephone directories.

4. *Promotional Sources*: Competitions, money-off coupons, customer satisfaction surveys, in-store credit cards and loyalty schemes are among the many options which can be employed with a view to amassing customer data.

Categories of Data to Capture

Information which is captured via the retention techniques outlined above (loyalty schemes, store card applications, coupons, etc.) may be organised under the following headings:

1. *Customer Demographics*: Name, addresses and age of the individual, family details (number of children and ages), occupation details

2. *Value of Custom*: value of the individual's shopping trip; lifetime value of customer

3. *Frequency of Custom*: How often does the customer do business with the organisation? What time of the day/week is most popular? Does frequency vary according to special offers, e.g. the use of bonus points on slack days?

4. *Products Purchased*: Does the customer exhibit an allegiance to own brands or to manufacturer brands? Is the individual a heavy or light user of certain products? Are there product categories that generate high levels of brand loyalty? How responsive is this person to newly introduced products?

5. *Price*: How price sensitive is the customer? How responsive is the customer to special offers such as discounts and added-value incentives?

GAINING VALUE FROM INFORMATION

One should consider the relative usefulness of data in terms of its ability to facilitate the identification of marketing opportunities and/or the resolution of marketing problems. Information is undoubtedly a crucial corporate asset and credence must be given to the logical argument that better-informed decisions lead to improved product/service offerings, which in turn will lead to increased profitability.

For instance, the database may yield 500 shoppers who regularly purchase a certain brand of shampoo. The retailer might use this information to make promotional offers targeted at these users, such as a personalised money-off coupon to be used against certain accompanying products, e.g. conditioners and bath gel. In this manner, the retailer introduces the customer to new products and may also give that individual an incentive to increase the usage rate of the product.

BUILDING A RETENTION BUDGET

The objective of a retention programme is to maximise sales and profit amongst existing customers. The *raison d'être* for most companies is not only profit maximisation, but also survival in the marketplace. Economic theory suggests that the marketer will continue to add promotional effort as long as the profit contribution from the additional sales is greater than the cost of the promotional effort. However, a difficulty arises in terms of allocating an optimum financial budget to the promotional campaign (McCorkell, 1997).

Traditionally, many companies have used an arguably haphazard method of budget allocation, whereby an amount was set for the campaign and then the monies were sub-divided between different tasks, e.g. producing, printing and dispatching catalogues, etc.

There are many budget-setting techniques available to a marketer (percentage of sales, same as last time, competitive parity, affordable method) but the preferred (while not always the most popular) is the objective and task method.

This technique requires the manager to specify clear objectives for the retention programme (e.g. maintain loyalty of current customers, up-sell more valuable products/services, increase the value of existing customers). The tasks to be undertaken in order to meet these objectives are then planned and costed.

Consider the example of a loyalty programme operating on the basis of a customer completing an application form and presenting a "swipe card" to the checkout operator. Points are duly awarded to the customer and, ultimately, they may select various gifts from a catalogue. Assuming that the objectives are to reward customers and to increase their purchasing propensity, the costs involved might be as follows:

- *Agency costs*: design, copy and artwork consultancy

- *Printing costs*: application forms, swipe cards and catalogues

- *Mailing costs*: customer communications, statement of points awarded, envelopes handling and dispatch, postage, customer service correspondence

- *Fulfilment costs*: opening and sorting of customer correspondence, data capture, selection, packing and dispatch of selected gifts, return postage

- *Staff communication*: training costs

- *Overheads*: staff, facilities.

From a marketing communications perspective, the budget may frequently come under threat when profit margins are in doubt or in the event of an economic downturn. It is important to realise that the financial allocation to any promotional programme should be regarded in the same light as, say, an investment in manpower or machinery. The budget for a retention programme must be viewed as an investment in the long-term welfare of the company and indeed the company's brand(s).

SUMMARY

The importance of customer retention cannot be underestimated in today's competitive marketplace. As increasing competition militates against sustainable competitive advantage, the cost of marketing communications is also experiencing an upward movement. It is now widely acknowledged that customer retention incurs lower costs than does customer acquisition and a further development of this argument suggests that a proportion of existing customers will be more attractive to the company in the long term.

Various strategies may be employed with a view to retaining customers, including defections management and the development of a customer retention mix. Recognising that customers may be categorised as newly acquired, current or lapsed, retention strategy literature suggests five separate course of action which may be targeted at such a divergent customer body — namely welcoming, up-selling, cross-selling, renewal and reactivation. There are a variety of retention techniques at the disposal of the direct marketer; this chapter has focused on the loyalty scheme.

A review of the communication channels offers numerous options that lend themselves to the retention objectives of informing and rewarding existing customers, while guidelines are suggested for evaluating the creative message. The importance of continual testing and budgeting is examined with a view to maximising the effectiveness of a retention campaign, while minimising an ever-present risk of failure. A key argument in this chapter is the premise that the enhancement of customer relationships is dependent on the collection and management of pertinent customer data.

CASE HISTORY: LEVER '90S LIVING — THE USE OF DATABASE MARKETING FOR CUSTOMER RETENTION

Marian Wallace

Industry Background

Market Size

The Irish household cleaning market is worth approximately £85 million. The sector is broken down into a number of subsectors, the largest of which is the detergent segment, which accounts for over half the total value of the market. The rest of the market is divided into various types of cleaners, e.g. washing up liquid, toilet cleaner, bleach and multi-purpose cleaner (Table 5.4).

TABLE 5.4: IRISH HOUSEHOLD CLEANING MARKET BREAKDOWN

Product	Value
Detergent	£45m
Toilet Cleaner	£7m
Washing up Liquid	£6m
Air Freshener	£5.2m
Rubber Gloves	£5m
Multi-purpose cleaner	£4.2m
Bleach	£3.5m
Ancillary products (cloths, scouring pads etc.)	£3.5m
Furniture Polish	£2.5m
Window cleaner	£2.5m

The overall market continues to grow annually and there is a high level of product development in all sectors.

Market Trends

The detergent sector has moved from a position of having a large number of lines and varieties per brand — e.g. standard powder, concentrates, liquids — to a position where most brands have begun to streamline the number of variants under one brand name. Whilst there is a professed brand loyalty among consumers to a certain extent, special promotions and offers continue to be the deciding factor in most detergent purchases.

Market Growth

Lever's detergent brand Persil and Procter & Gamble's (P&G) Ariel are virtually neck-and-neck in terms of market share, with less than 0.5 per cent dividing their share of the market. P&G dominate the overall market with their portfolio of detergent brands — Ariel, Daz, Bold and Fairy — holding a 55 per cent share of the market. Lever produce almost all of the other popular brands, i.e. Persil, Surf and Radion.

Lever brand Jif leads the hard surface cleaners sector and now has a range of products including separate bathroom and kitchen cleaners. This sector is growing at a rate of 28 per cent per annum. Lever brand, Domestos, has a 60 per cent share of the bleach market.

Market Outlook

What is already a fragmented market continues to further divide as a number of task-specific products and the variety of formulas continue to grow. Surface cleaners such as powders or creams are now broken down further into products for the bathroom and kitchen and the range of formulas has grown to include gels, mousse, and micro liquids. Detergents, on the other hand, which have had a range of liquids and concentrated powders, are now rationalising in response to consumer confusion over the array of products on offer.

Soap Powders

The £45 million detergent market is controlled by two multinationals, Lever Brothers and Procter & Gamble, with their two main brands Persil and Ariel. Ariel has a sales figure based on value sales at RSP of £10 million, Persil has a sales value of £9 million, Bold £7 million plus, Daz £6 million, Surf £3 million and Radion £3 million. Comfort fabric conditioner from Lever Brothers has a sales value of £4 million.

Within the premium sector, Persil dominates the market. Persil regained this lead after losing sales with the controversy over the launch of Persil Power in 1996. Early in 1998, the entire Persil range was relaunched in the UK and Ireland at a cost of millions. The range now contains a new "Stain Release System". Radion and Surf, the two other Lever detergent brands, received heavy advertising support in the last year, and both are performing well in the market.

Detergents are an extremely fragmented market. Certain major companies will market what is essentially the same product under a number of different brand names. This tactic ensures that the company's products are spread across a lot of shelf space in the retail trade. In Ireland, the washing detergent and household cleaner industry has reached maturity, with stable brand shares and a limited potential for market growth. There is little difference between products in terms of performance. Differentiation between brands is mainly in the product claims made, their marketing strategies and in packaging. Because of the limited growth potential in the market, brands have had to focus their brand marketing strategies on achieving an increased share of consumers' overall spend in individual product categories.

"Own label" products have yet to make an impact in the detergent market, accounting for less than five per cent of total sales. Advertising has positioned the major brand names firmly in customers' minds.

However, Lever's 1996 Laundry Detergents Report predicts that the pendulum will swing back to simplicity and that the market will reduce to a single powder and a single liquid format. The report also states that concentrated powders will disappear as consumers drift back to the traditional box powders, believing them to be better value for money.

In the UK, sales of big box powders have increased by 30 per cent over the past three years, while concentrated powders have fallen by 18 per cent. However, detergents are one sector where loyalty to well-known brands is strong.

How Lever Brothers Markets its Brands

Lever Brothers is one of the leading manufacturers of washing detergents and household cleaning products. Lever Brothers markets its household brands internationally. In Ireland, it supplies detergent brands, Persil and Surf, fabric conditioner Comfort and leading household products Jif and Domestos. In the dishwasher detergent market, their main brand is Sun.

Distribution

In the fast-moving consumer goods sector (FMCG), distribution is a key factor in the success of a brand. All major Lever brands achieve full distribution in the retail grocery trade.

Retail Display and Promotional Strengths

Another key factor in the success of a brand is its display and positioning in grocery stores. Persil, Domestos and Jif achieve prominent positioning in grocery multiples at regular periods throughout the year when the brand is on promotion. To illustrate how Lever Brothers markets its brands, this case history focuses on Persil, Lever's leading washing detergent brand.

The Marketing Mix

Brands such as Persil use a mix of marketing media to increase sales volume and support awareness of the brand.

Sales Promotions

Achieving distribution and product display in the retail environment is vitally important in attracting consumers to the brand at the point of sale. To achieve sales volume, a series of brand promotions in stores are planned throughout the year. These promotions involve "special packs" — one free product from the Lever portfolio, e.g. Jif Cream, Dove Cream Bar — banded on to the standard box of Persil powder.

Additional sales building activity in stores throughout the year includes on-pack promotions and competitions. These are designed to build repeat purchase among consumers. A very successful on-pack promotion was developed for Persil in 1996. This offered customers the opportunity to collect *"Mr Men"* books. Consumers collected tokens from packs purchased and redeemed them for *Mr Men* books. The promotion was designed to appeal to families with children, who are considered to be heavy users of detergent.

Advertising

Brand awareness and image are maintained through television, radio and press advertising. Product differentiation is difficult to sustain, so brand relaunches such as new formulations or new packaging create brand promotion opportunities. Product "events" create opportunities for large-scale advertising, such as the recent Persil advertising campaign which focused on the "Stain Release System", Persil's latest formulation. This also created the opportunity to re-name the Persil variants and create new core propositions as follows:

- *Biological variant*: Re-named *Persil Performance Biological* with the proposition "Unbeatable Cleaning Across the Wash"

- *Non-Biological variant*: Re-named *Persil, The Original Non-Biological* with the proposition "Unbeatable Non-Bio cleaning — suits even a baby's skin"

- *Persil Colour variant*: Renamed *Persil Colour Care Biological* with the proposition "Brilliant cleaning — helps keep colours vibrant".

The Persil brand has created a premium image which is supported by mass market advertising.

Direct Marketing

Customer loyalty to the brand is supported by direct marketing. The customer database has been developed by gathering names of consumers that have responded to brand promotions since 1995.

Customer Loyalty Programme

In a mature market, there is little difference between brands in terms of performance. Differentiation between brands is mainly in the product claims made, their marketing strategies and in packaging. Because there is very limited growth potential in the market, brands are dependent on increasing their market share for growth. They must now focus on building their share of the market by achieving an increased share of a consumer's overall spend on detergents.

Mass advertising has traditionally been the method for building brand share. This continues to be the main focus of marketing spend. It is acknowledged that the level of advertising spend by major brands in this sector has successfully fended off the threat of own label brands.

However, increasing media fragmentation means that mass advertising audiences are diminishing. Coupled with the almost universal acceptance by advertisers that direct marketing can generate business growth, giving them a competitive edge, investment in direct marketing continues to rise.

Database Building

In the FMCG sector, a number of devices can be used to collect name and address information for database applications. Sales promotion techniques such as coupon door drops (where the redeemer's name and address is requested as a condition of redemption) and on-pack promotions are used for data collection. Other devices such as member-get-member are also used once a direct mail programme commences.

The Lever Programme

The programme was developed in 1995 and is targeted at Lever consumers in the Republic of Ireland and Northern Ireland.

Objectives of Campaign

1. Identify and target high value consumers

2. Develop a one-to-one dialogue with the target consumers, i.e. households with children

3. Develop loyalty to key Lever brands

4. Drive incremental profit.

To date, five campaigns have been developed from Lever's consumer database. The programme consists of regular direct mail campaigns to Lever customers providing information and offers on lead brands Persil, Comfort, Jif and Domestos. (Dishwasher detergent brand, Sun, has its own direct marketing programme targeted specifically at dishwasher owners.)

The format used to promote the above brands is a consumer lifestyle magazine called *Lever '90s Living*. This "magalogue" contains lifestyle features such as fashion, interior design and gardening and includes advertorial and usage information on each brand. The design of the magazine is based on a typical women's magazine such as *Woman's Way*.

Features include:

- *The Outdoor Room*: Summer edition feature on garden furniture, including Jif cleaning advice.

- *Washful Thinking*: Washing tips from consumers and a competition to win a washing machine.

- *Brighter Bathrooms & Kitchens*: Advice on brightening up bathrooms and kitchens with accessories and colour, which included Domestos cleaning tips.

Also included in each edition are personalised money-off coupons on primary and secondary brands, competitions, a Prize Bond collection scheme and special offers, e.g. free mail-in for a Persil CD-ROM.

The Prize Bond collection scheme is an ongoing promotion designed to encourage consumers to continue to purchase Lever brands. Consumers have the opportunity to save bar codes from Lever product packs and exchange them for a £5 Prize Bond for one year. Each consumer that applies is assigned a Prize Bond number for one year, which goes into the weekly Prize Bond draw. Prize Bond winners are published in each edition of the magazine.

Each campaign includes a response device, such as coupons and questionnaires, incorporating a unique identity number for each consumer. By capturing the response information, the database is updated with purchase behaviour and questionnaire information on customer lifestyle, family size and brand purchasing behaviour. In addition, customers are also encouraged to participate in the campaign and are invited to write in with comments and any washing/cleaning hints they would like to share with other readers.

Success of the Programme to Date

The programme achieves success in a number of key areas:

- The personalised nature of each communication has contributed significantly to higher coupon redemption (i.e. product purchase) than other coupon distribution techniques such as non-personalised door drops

- Qualitative customer research and customer feedback confirms that consumers think very favourably of the programmes, and enjoy reading the magazine and participating in the competitions and promotions within the programme

- The programme generates trial and cross-selling by promoting new variants and product lines with personalised coupons.

REFERENCES TO CHAPTER 5

Barnes, J. (1994), "Relationship Marketing: A Useful Concept for all Firms?", Working Paper No. 94-2, Centre for Quality and Services Management, Dublin: University College Dublin.

Belch, G. and M. Belch (1995), *Introduction to Advertising and Promotion: An Integrated Marketing Communications Perspective*, Homewood, IL: Irwin.

Buchanan, R.W.T. and S. Gillies (1990), "Value Managed Relationships: The Key to Customer Retention and Profitability", *European Management Journal*, Vol. 8, No. 4, December, pp. 523–526.

Cody, P., (1996), "Information for Better Marketing", *Sunday Business Post*, 25 February.

Copacino, W. (1997), "The Value of Customer Retention", *Logistics Management*, Vol. 36, May, p. 37.

DeSouza, G. (1992), "Designing a Customer Retention Plan", *Journal of Business Strategy*, Vol. 13, No. 2, March/April, pp. 24–28.

Ennew, C.T. and M.R. Binks (1996), "The Impact of Service Quality and Service Characteristics on Customer Retention: Small Businesses and Their Banks in the UK", *British Journal of Management*, Vol. 7, No. 3, September, pp. 219–230.

Fletcher, K., C. Wheeler and J. Wright (1990), "The Role and Status of UK Database Marketing", *The Quarterly Review of Marketing*, Autumn, pp. 7–14.

Geller, L. (1997), "Customer Retention Begins with the Basics", *Direct Marketing*, Vol. 60, No. 5, September, pp. 58–62.

Gilliam, T.K. (1994), "Closing the Customer Retention Gap", *Bank Marketing*, Vol. 26, No. 12, December, pp. 51–54.

Hamilton, R. and J.B. Howcraft (1995), "A Practical Approach to Maximising Customer Retention in the Credit Card Industry", *Journal of Marketing Management*, Vol. 11, pp. 151–163.

Hartley, M. (1997), "It Wouldn't Stop Me Going Somewhere Else: Supermarket Customers and Their Loyalty Cards", *Proceedings of the 31st Academy of Marketing Annual Conference*, Manchester, 8–10 July.

Hawkes, P. (1996), "The Customer Loyalty Challenge", *Admap*, January, pp. 47–48.

IDM (1995), *The Practitioner's Guide to Direct Marketing*, London: Institute of Direct Marketing.

Jackson, B.B. (1985) "Build Customer Relationships that Last", *Harvard Business Review*, November/December, pp. 120–128.

McCorkell, G. (1997), *Direct and Database Marketing*, London: Kogan Page.

McGowan, M. (1995), "Direct Marketing — Irish Perspectives" in Meenaghan, T. and O'Sullivan, P. (eds.), *Marketing Communications in Ireland*, Dublin: Oak Tree Press.

McKenzie, S. (1995), "Customer Loyalty: Finders Keepers", *Marketing Week*, 30 June, pp. 41-42.

Mitchell, A. (1996), "No Rewards for Buying Loyalty Ruse", *Marketing Week*, 7 June, pp. 24–25.

Nash, M. (1995), *Direct Marketing: Strategy, Planning and Execution*, Third Edition, New York: McGraw Hill.

O'Brien, L. and C. Jones (1995), "Do Rewards Really Create Loyalty?", *Harvard Business Review*, May–June, pp. 75–82.

O'Rourke, J. (1997), *The Power of Post*, An Post Brochure, September/October, Dublin: An Post.

Palmer, A. and R. Beggs (1997), "Loyalty Schemes: Congruence of Market Structure and Success" in *Proceedings of the 31st Academy of Marketing Annual Conference*, Manchester, 8–10 July.

Quinn, F. (1990), *Crowning the Customer*, Dublin: O'Brien Press.

Reichheld, F. (1993), "Loyalty Based Management", *Harvard Business Review*, Vol. 71, No. 2, pp. 64–73.

Reichheld, F. and W. Sasser (1990), "Zero Defections: Quality Comes to Service", *Harvard Business Review*, September/October, pp. 105–111.

Rosenberg, L.J. and J.A. Czepiel (1984), "A Marketing Approach for Customer Retention", *Journal of Consumer Marketing*, Vol. 1, pp. 45–51.

Schultz, D. and S. Tannenbaum (1988), *Essentials of Advertising Strategy*, Lincolnwood, IL: NTC Business Books.

Smyth, A. (1997), "Direct Response Television", Brochure presented at Special Session of Academy of Marketing and the American Marketing Association Conference, Manchester, 7–10 July.

Stone M., N. Woodcock and M. Wilson (1996), "Managing the Change from Marketing Planning to Customer Relationship Management", *Long Range Planning*, Vol. 29, No. 5, pp. 675–683.

Stone, M. and N. Woodcock (1995), *Relationship Marketing*, London: Kogan Page.

Stone, M., D. Davies and A. Bond (1995), *Direct Hit: Direct Marketing with a Winning Edge*, London: Pitman Publishing.

Waterhouse, K. and A. Morgan (1994), "Using Research to Help Keep Good Customers", *Marketing and Research Today*, August, pp. 181–194.

REFERENCES TO CASE STUDY

Direct Marketing Information Service (UK) (1997), "Sector Intelligence Report on Household Goods and Toiletries".

Muranyi, N.R. (1995), "Database Marketing in FMCGs: What is the State of the Art?", *The Journal of Database Marketing*, Vol. 4, No. 1, pp. 13–20.

Chapter 6

PRICING AND THE DIRECT MARKETING OFFER

John Jameson

"There are two fools in every market. One charges too little; the other charges too much."

— *Russian proverb (Jober, 1995)*

Overview

Pricing is one of the most important considerations a manager faces in constructing a marketing offer. Price too high and the offer will not be taken up; price too low and the company forgoes profitability. Establishing the right price level can be difficult, and is perhaps as much an art as a science.

The growth of direct marketing has reinforced the importance of price within the offer. Direct marketing allows a greater scope for creativity in pricing strategy than that commonly available in the more traditional channels, where a national price may be the custom. Direct marketing allows for greater scope to adjust price up or down, even within the same campaign, in line with company objectives and customer requirements.

For many companies, however, pricing is often the last element considered in a campaign, seen more as a technical problem to be solved rather than a marketing element that can dictate the success or failure of the offer.

In some market situations, such as insurance or professional services, pricing may not even be part of the initial offer. The price may be calculated only in response to a specific detailed enquiry initiated by the potential customer as a result of the direct marketing appeal.

Settling on the right price is critical to the success of the firm, but it can be a difficult process. Market demand, customer reaction, price elasticity, competitive reaction, and costs all need to be evaluated. Despite the difficulty, however, formal consideration of the many pricing influences can help the manager to make more effective decisions.

In general, the aim of the pricing strategy is very straightforward: to price the offer to maximise company objectives. It is often suggested, however, that pricing requires work and that effective pricing requires a lot of work — researching the market, evaluating competition and assessing costs. The central requirement of good pricing is always to budget properly and test price (Jones, 1992). This will ensure that the profit objectives of the campaign can be met.

DEFINING PRICE

In broad terms, price may be viewed as any resource that the customer exchanges in return for the benefits obtained from the offer. It is defined simply by Hutchings as "the value placed on that which is exchanged" (Hutchings, 1995). It can range from the customer's attention and time through to money exchanged in return for a product or service, and can be called many names, including a licence, a fare, a premium, a toll, a fee, a deposit, a fine, a rent, a commission.

Whatever it is called, price can be viewed as having at least two distinct elements:

- A basic price or value — what customers pay for the core offering

- Premium price or value differential — what consumers will pay for the extended or "augmented product" (Mudie, 1997).

Dibb et al. (1997) suggest that while price may be expressed in a variety of ways, it is important to remember that the purpose of the concept is to quantify and express the value of the items in a market exchange.

In a broader sense, price includes the activities used by the company to highlight the value of the offer, including credit propositions (Bacon, 1994).

THE ROLE OF PRICE

The role of price within any marketing programme is of critical importance to the success of the campaign and the satisfaction of the customer. It fulfils many roles, some symbolic, some economic, and all are important.

The Symbolic Meaning of Price

Price can have a symbolic dimension, which organisations use to convey meaning to customers about their offerings. This is particularly so in consumer markets where price can be used to confirm or reinforce a customer perception of a product. A high price can emphasise the quality of a product and an improved status associated with its ownership, while a low price can emphasise a bargain and attract customers. In both cases, price is part of the offer which the customer buys, and from which they derive an element of satisfaction. In a direct marketing context, price is useful in facilitating the determination of value in the absence of a product or service.

Consumer decision-making is typically portrayed as a non-rational process in which customers have difficulty in weighing up the various features and attributes of competing products or services. In such situations, price becomes a simple objective criterion against which decisions can be made with less effort.

Price–Quality Relationship

The price–quality relationship is an important concept within marketing strategy, and is held to exist mainly based on experience rather than research findings. Most of the research on the topic has been exploratory; however, there does seem to be evidence of a general relationship, with a large body of experience and anecdotal evidence to support it. It particularly applies to products whose quality is difficult to judge and whose brands are believed to vary widely in quality — in short, the perception that "you get what you pay for".

The relationship can be viewed from two perspectives:

- Firstly, evidence suggests that customers are likely to choose the offering that they perceive as having the highest quality among a set of offerings with similar prices.

- Secondly, in the absence of objective criteria on which to judge competing offers, customers tend to use price as the main criterion for choosing the best value. Where customers are unable to judge offers due to lack of knowledge, lack of understanding, too little or too much information, price may to used to simplify the decision. Even in business-to-business markets, price is often used as an indicator of value and an important decision variable.

The price–quality relationship has important implications for the direct marketer, including:

- The use of price to infer quality about products or services prior to purchase or inspection

- The use of price to differentiate the offer from competition in the mind of the customer.

Direct marketing, with its greater need to communicate value and comparability among offers, needs to use price as a communication mechanism, underpinning all other elements of the marketing mix.

The Economic Role of Price

Fundamentally, pricing the direct marketing offer is an economic consideration. From an economic perspective, pricing decisions are critical in establishing the economic viability and profitability of a campaign. It is the sole revenue-generating mechanism open to marketers. In the short term, the price set must enable the marketer to cover costs, while in the long term it will dictate the overall profitability of the campaign.

The following equation illustrates the interrelated role of price in overall success:

Profits = Total Revenue – Total Costs

Profits = (Price × Volume) – Total Costs

Profits = (Price × Volume) – ([Variable Costs × Volume] +
        Fixed Costs)

Price affects the organisation's profit equation in several ways.

It directly influences the revenue generated through its impact on the quantities sold, while at the same time it has an indirect impact, as it is a major determinant of total costs through its impact on quantities sold. This price–volume relationship is at the heart of pricing as an important marketing activity.

The concept of *"break-even"* analysis is often used by marketers to establish the base level at which an offer covers its variable costs and above which it starts to contribute to profitability. At the break-even point, profit is zero. It is the point at which the contribution earned is equal to the fixed costs incurred. Above the break-even point, the contribution is applied to the profits; below the break-even point, each unit left unsold deepens the loss.

Price is a critical element in determining the volume sold and in turn the variable costs incurred. Consider the following example.

> *A producer of craft pottery has the following data:*
>
> Price of the unit: £100
>
> Variable Cost of the unit: £60
>
> Fixed Costs of the plant: £120,000
>
> Contribution to Fixed Costs and Profits = Price − Variable Cost (£100 − £60 = £40)
>
> Break-even Point = Fixed Costs/Unit Contribution to Fixed Costs and Profits (£120,000/£40 = 3,000 units)

FIGURE 6.1

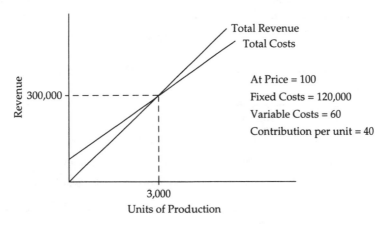

To break even at a price of £100, the producer will have to sell 3,000 units; if however the price can be increased to £120, then the break-even point comes down to 2,000 units.

> Price of the unit: £120
>
> Variable Cost: £60
>
> Fixed Cost: £120,000
>
> Contribution to Fixed Costs and Profit = Price − Variable Cost (£120 − £60 = £60)
>
> Break-even Point = Fixed Costs/Unit Contribution to Fixed Costs and Profits (£120,000/60 = 2,000 units)

FIGURE 6.2

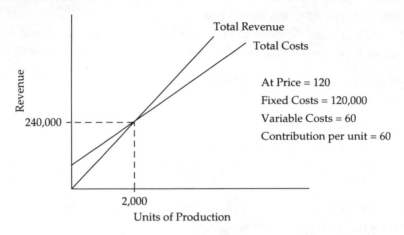

An important consideration, however, is the relationship between the price and the demand at that price. It may well be that at the higher price of £120 the company will sell only 1,500 units, reducing the contribution to fixed costs and profits by £30,000 (see Table 6.1).

TABLE 6.1: BREAK-EVEN ANALYSIS AT VARYING PRICES AND VOLUMES

Price	Volume	Contribution	Fixed Costs	Result
£100	3,000	£40	£120,000	Break-even
£120	2,000	£60	£120,000	Break-even
£120	1,500	£60	£120,000	£90,000 (£30,000 short of break-even)

Pricing decisions can be made using the break-even approach in either arithmetical or graphic form. The break-even chart is a graphic representation of the relationship between costs, volume and price. By plotting the volume and associated costs, management can readily observe how profitable each level of output is, given a price per unit.

As well as enabling management to balance costs and volume, price is the most common method used by customers to *evaluate an offering*. Consumers rarely act with total rationality and cannot always judge quality from product attributes (Hutchings, 1995), especially in areas in which their purchasing experience is low. Price is often the criterion against which an offer can be judged to be accept-able or not.

Price tends to be an objective concept, easy to identify, determine and compare. Concepts like value, on the other hand, tend to be somewhat more subjective. An offering's value is often in the mind of the beholder, and can give rise to opportunities to vary pricing, or price discrimination.

Price, perhaps more than any other aspect of the marketing mix, establishes whether or not a market exists for the offering. *Demand only exists at a price*, so pricing decisions are critical if an offer is to succeed.

Price itself is a powerful mechanism in *regulating demand*. When setting prices, marketers often use sensitivity analysis to establish effective price points at which varying degrees of demand exist. The concept of *elasticity of demand* is helpful in understanding the reaction of demand to different price points.

Price elasticity of demand (E) is defined as:

$$E = \frac{\% \text{ Change in the quantity demanded}}{\% \text{ Change in price}}$$

- Demand is "inelastic" where $E < 1$: changes in price cause a smaller change in demand (see Figure 6.3a)

- Demand is "elastic" where $E > 1$: changes in price cause a greater change in demand (see Figure 6.3b).

FIGURE 6.3: ELASTIC AND INELASTIC DEMAND

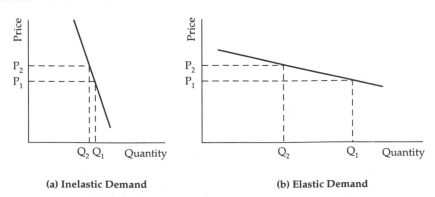

(a) Inelastic Demand   (b) Elastic Demand

Source: Dibb et al. (1997), p. 588.

Elasticity is generally negative for normal goods, where a price increase can be expected to result in a volume decrease. The extent of this volume decrease is a function of the degree of elasticity, with elastic demand resulting in a greater decrease in demand.

To complicate matters further, it is evident that an offer's degree of price elasticity is not the same at all levels. The degree of price elasticity often depends on the direction and size of the price change. Demand may be inelastic for small changes in price, but elastic for more dramatic changes (Mudie, 1997).

A further demand consideration relevant to pricing an offer involves prestige pricing. Prestige pricing occurs whenever buyers' desire for the offer increases with price. Their sensitivity to the product or its performance increases more than their sensitivity to price. As a result, the demand curve for a prestige good slopes upwards, indicating the price range within which a price increase will result in an increase in demand.

FIGURE 6.4: DEMAND CURVE FOR PRESTIGE PRODUCTS

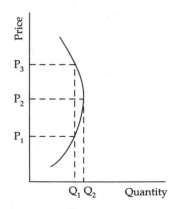

Source: Dibb et al. (1997), p. 587.

DETERMINANTS OF PRICE

In common with traditional marketing, direct marketers need to consider and understand the many variables that will influence the pricing decision. There are many interrelated variables which a firm should take into account when making pricing decisions, any one or combination of which could be crucial in the development of an appropriate price.

The Customer

Customer knowledge is a crucial element in the design of an effective pricing strategy. Without a thorough knowledge of the customer's level of interest in the offer, their ability and willingness to buy and their experience as purchasers, pricing becomes a guess rather than a considered decision. Good pricing begins with thorough research of the customer. Other considerations include:

- Customer demand, and the ability of the customer to pay
- Perceived value of the product by the customer
- Elasticity of demand or the willingness of the customer to buy
- Seasonal spending patterns
- Susceptibility of the customer to psychological factors.

The Competition

Competition defines and regulates the boundaries within which effective pricing occurs. Knowledge of competitors, their objectives, policies and tactics are useful in allowing the company to set and adjust prices as market conditions change. Some competitive considerations include:

- The price of similar offers from competitive suppliers
- The market segment in which the offer is placed
- Competitive reaction to changes in price
- Price flexibility in the market
- Market share enjoyed by the competition.

The Environment

The business environment imposes a set of conditions or context in which pricing decisions are made. Generally, they are the same for all competitors; however, careful monitoring of the changing business environment can highlight emerging opportunities early. Some of the environmental considerations include:

- Local, national and international policies

- The country's general economic situation

- Societal factors

- Political decisions

- Legal limitations imposed

- Geographical characteristics

The Company

Perhaps the greatest impact on pricing strategy stems from the company itself. Its profit and market objectives, cost structure, and competitive intention to a large extent dictate price strategy. Some of the company considerations include:

- Costs

- Long- and short-term profit objectives

- Organisational and marketing objectives

- Volume sales required

- Production costs involved

- Type and cost of promotional material

- Brand image and quality of the offer and company

- Ability of the company to produce and supply

- Strategies adopted, e.g. market share and profit level

- Policy on discounts and allowances

- Life cycle stage of the offer.

THE EFFECTS OF PRICE ON COSTS AND PROFIT

Analysing the effect of price on costs and profits requires a consideration of the cost structure of the organisation and of demand within the market. While demand can be viewed as varying from elastic to inelastic, depending on the offer's desirability, costs can generally be viewed as either fixed or variable. The various elements are summarised in Table 6.2.

TABLE 6.2: COST, VOLUME, PRICE RELATIONSHIPS

	Element	Formula	Example
A	Price	A	£100
B	Volume	B	3,000 units
C	Revenue	A × B	£100 × 3,000 units =£300,000
D	Variable Costs (per unit)	D	£60 × 3,000 units = £180,000
E	Contribution	C – D	£300,000 – £180,000 = £120,000
F	Less Fixed Costs	E – F	£120,000 – £120,000 = £0

Costs can generally be divided between fixed and variable, with variable costs changing in response to volume sales. Each unit sold will contribute towards the overall profitability of the offer, allowing the marketer to judge the effect of different combinations of price and cost. Sensitivity analysis is often used to establish the optimum price at which an offer is made available to the market.

While costs alone should never determine price, they do have an important influence on the price-setting process.

As outlined in an earlier section, price has a direct effect on organisation revenue and profits. Perhaps more than any other marketing component, it relates directly to the generation of total revenue and total costs through the volumes sold.

Price affects the profit equation in several ways. It directly affects the equation, as it is a major component of total revenue. It also has an indirect impact, as it can be a major determinant of the volume sold. In addition, price influences total costs through its impact on volumes sold.

The costs and profits associated with a direct marketing programme — communication costs, offer costs, administration, packaging costs, and profit — all have to be paid for through the establishment of an offer price which will be judged acceptable to a significant number of customers. Knowledge of customer demand, the competition, the market environment and company costs are the building blocks for the construction of an effective pricing strategy.

LIFETIME VALUE OF A CUSTOMER

A concept becoming increasingly important in marketing, and particularly so in direct marketing, is that of the "lifetime value" of a customer. It is important to consider each potential customer not as a once-off sale but rather as a long-term asset, capable of delivering to the company a stream of income into the future. Lifetime value analysis is a technique used to establish the potential value of a customer at different retention rates and over different periods of time. Pricing an offer with reference to the lifetime value is useful, but needs to be done carefully to avoid expensive mistakes.

Customer lifetime value is the net present value (NPV) of the profit that a company stands to make on the average new customer during a given number of years (Hughes, 1994). An example will serve to illustrate.

TABLE 6.3: LIFETIME VALUE OF A CUSTOMER

		Year 1	Year 2	Year 3	Year 4	Year 5
Revenue						
A	Customers	1,000	400	180	90	50
B	Retention rate	40%	45%	50%	55%	60%
C	Average yearly sales/customer	£150	£150	£150	£150	£150
D	Total revenue	£150,000	£60,000	£27,000	£13,500	£7,500
Costs						
E	Cost	50%	50%	50%	50%	50%
F	Total costs	£75,000	£30,000	£13,500	£6,750	£3,750
Profits						
G	Gross profit	£75,000	£30,000	£13,500	£6,750	£3,750
H	Discount rate	1%	1.2%	1.44%	1.73%	2.07%
I	NPV profit	£75,000	£25,000	£9,375	£3,902	£1,812
J	Cumulative NPV profit	£75,000	£100,000	£109,375	£113,277	£115,089
K	Lifetime value/ customer	£75	£100	£109.375	£113.277	£115.089

Source: Adapted from Shimp (1997).

Assume a retailer has a database of 1,000 customers (**A**). The analysis examines the net present value of each customer over a five-year period.

- **B** describes the retention rate — indicates the likelihood of customers remaining customers over the five-year period

- **C** identifies the average yearly sales to each customer

- **D** identifies the total revenue (**A** × **C**)

- **E** identifies the cost, as a percentage of revenue, of selling the offer to the customers

- **F** identifies total costs (**E** × **D**)

- **G** computes the gross profit

- **H**, the discount rate, is a critical component of NPV and indicates the changing value of money due to the passing of time. For convenience, the discount rate is taken as the prevailing bank interest rate. Money received in the different time periods needs to be adjusted to present values using an adjustment formula:

$$D_R = (1+i)^n$$

where D_R equals the discount rate; i equals the interest rate; and n equals the number of years before the money will be received.

As an example, the discount rate in year 3 is 1.44, because the company will have to wait two years to receive the profit that will be earned in year 3,

$$(1 + 0.2)^2 = 1.44$$

- **I** identifies the Net Present Value profit and is determined by taking the reciprocal of the discount rate $(1/D_R)$ (e.g. $1/1.44 = 0.69$), and multiplying by the gross profit, **G**.

- **J** identifies the cumulative NPV profit over the years

- **K** identifies the lifetime value per customer, which shows the average value of each of the customers over the life of the offer.

Lifetime value analysis is an important tool in setting up, managing and evaluating the direct marketing programme. The LVA identifies a number of strategic issues which should concern the marketer: It forces the marketer to consider measures to improve the campaign by focusing on three key requirements:

- *The Retention Rate*, the larger the number of retained customers and the longer the retention duration, the more valuable the customer will be.

- *The Sales Volume* will be a function of the offer's purchase and consumption rate, frequency and quantity.

- *Direct Costs* are those costs directly attributable to the establishment and implementation of the direct marketing channel.

Lifetime value analysis can be used to undertake sensitivity analysis on a campaign before implementation. As a result the marketer can identify how best to focus the effort to maximise overall profitability.

PRICING OBJECTIVE

In constructing the pricing elements of the offer consideration of the pricing objectives, pricing strategies will help to identify the appropriate pricing methods available to the company. Pricing objectives are overall goals that describe what the firm wants to achieve through its pricing efforts (Dibb et al., 1997). An organisation must be clear on what it is trying to achieve by way of its overall business and marketing objectives before it can set the price on its offering. Each price may have different implications for the organisation's profit, sales revenue and market share. Companies usually set pricing objectives according to different categories, as in Table 6.4 (Hutchings, 1995).

Seven common pricing objectives can be identified (Dibb et al., 1997):

1. *Survival*: The first and foremost business objective. Organisations may sometimes use the flexibility of price to increase sales, incurring short-term losses in the process, to ensure survival. Price is the most immediate marketing component available to the organisation to influence demand.

2. *Maximum Current Profit*: Although profit maximisation is a much-stated objective, it is rarely achievable due to the difficulty in

measuring its attainment. As a result of this difficulty, profit objectives tend to be set at levels acceptable to the owners and management and expressed as absolute monetary amounts or return on investment or profit growth relative to a previous year.

TABLE 6.4: PRICING OBJECTIVES

1.	**Image**	*Setting a fair price*
	Emphasising product quality	
	Concentration on market retention	
	Prestige objectives	
2.	**Economic**	*Cash flow*
	Corporate survival	
	Return on Investment	
	Break-even analysis	
3.	**Sales**	*Unit growth*
	Geographical areas	
	Market share growth	
	Sales maximisation	
4.	**Profit**	*Target returns*
	Profit maximisation	
	Geographical areas	
5.	**Stability**	*Retention of status quo*
	Meeting the competition	
	Using non-price competition	

Source: Adapted from Hutchings (1995), p. 256.

3. *Return on Investment (ROI)*: Return on investment is a profit-related pricing objective, which although often explicitly stated by management, is difficult to achieve as relevant cost and revenue data are generally not available at the time of setting prices.

4. *Maximum Current Revenue (Cash Flow)*: Pricing to maximise current revenue involves the setting of prices to recover cash as fast as possible, which may be justified in some situations such as a short life-cycle market. This pricing objective usually involves the use of high prices, which may retard the development of the market and/or attract competitors. The strategy tends to over-simplify the value of price in contributing to profits.

5. *Market Share*: Many firms establish pricing objectives to maintain or increase their market share in the belief that market share leads to profits. Care must be exercised, however, in the pricing methods used to obtain market share. Profitable market share should be the objective, rather than market share *per se*. It is often suggested that market share is vanity, while profit is sanity.

6. *Product Quality Leadership (Premium Pricing)*: A company may set for itself a non-economic objective such as quality leadership, which in turn may have an impact on the price required to sustain and reinforce the objective.

7. *Status Quo*: A status quo objective generally involves an organisation endeavouring to maintain the current situation within the market, and involve it minimising price as a competitive tool. Status quo pricing can reduce a firm's risks by helping to stabilise demand for its products.

PRICING STRATEGIES AND METHODS

Whatever the objectives chosen, companies implement their decisions through a series of pricing strategies and pricing methods. Some typical approaches to pricing involve:

Cost-Based Pricing

A pricing method where an amount or percentage is added to the cost of the product. Although denounced by marketers and economists, cost-based pricing is a common pricing method used by many firms. Its ease of calculation and implementation makes it a popular method. Cost-based methods are generally favoured whenever there is a difficulty in establishing demand forecasts, or where a company has a large number of products for which developing demand forecasts may be impractical. Two cost-based methods are most popular:

1. *Cost Plus*: A method in which a specified amount or percentage is added to the seller's cost after that cost is determined.

2. *Target Profit Pricing*: A method in which the company sets a price to achieve a specified target return.

Value-Based Pricing

Perceived Value = Perceived Worth − Perceived Price

Perceived value is a calculation which customers make implicitly; it is a function of what they receive by way of benefits for what they pay by means of money, resources time or attention. Wherever the perceived price is lower than the perceived worth, customers will judge the offer as good value, and wherever the customer perceives the perceived price to exceed the perceived worth, the offer will be judged as poor value for money.

Competition-Based Pricing

A pricing method whereby a company considers costs and revenue to be secondary to competitors' prices. Prices are set by reference to competitor prices rather than costs or market demand.

Many companies have no clear pricing policy, with final prices often market-inspired (Hutchings, 1995), i.e. set at the market level already established by competitors, which management know from experience will be accepted by consumers. A typical competition-based pricing method would be *going rate pricing*, where the company bases its price largely on competitors' prices with little attention paid to its own costs or to demand. When demand elasticity is difficult to measure, the going rate price tends to be used to reflect the collective wisdom of the industry concerning the price that will yield a fair return.

There are a number of tactical pricing methods used within competition-based pricing to establish the offer price; the main methods include (Hutchings, 1995):

1. *Customary Pricing*: Fixing an offer's price within a band or range to which the customer has become accustomed

2. *Differential Pricing*: Charging different prices for essentially the same offer according to location or type of customer, and value or size of the order

3. *Diversionary Pricing*: Concealing the real price while incorporating additional charges for necessary extra services

4. *Dumping*: Products offered in bulk at prices below cost

5. *Experience Curve Pricing*: The setting of prices at low levels in anticipation of cost reductions through volume and production economies of scale

6. *Loss Leader Pricing*: Pricing below cost to attract customers in the hope that they will buy additional normally priced profitable items

7. *Market Pricing*: Pricing dictated by fluctuating supply and demand conditions, especially in commodity markets

8. *Predatory Pricing*: Pricing designed to accept short-term losses in exchange for long-term gains, as an attempt to exclude competitive offers

9. *Prestige Pricing*: Pricing used to convey high quality, status or image due to high price level

10. *Price Discrimination*: Pricing policy in which different prices are charged to different buyers for minimal differential offerings

11. *Professional Pricing*: Pricing in situations where an objective value of the service offered is difficult

12. *Promotional Pricing*: Prices set below normal level to reflect special promotions

13. *Psychological Pricing*: Pricing based on emotional responses, such as £9.99 instead of £10.00

14. *Single Price Strategy*: A policy in which a single price is charged to all buyers

15. *Special Event Pricing*: Prices raised or lowered to attract customers or regulate demand for once-off occasions

16. *Variable Pricing:* Pricing adjustments used to regulate demand on a daily, weekly or seasonal basis.

PRICING THE DIRECT MARKETING OFFER

In setting prices for the direct marketing offer, it is important for the marketer to collect as much relevant information regarding their customer, their costs, their market and their competition. An understanding of the customer's evaluation of price and perceived value for money, as well as an understanding of market trends and competitors' pricing methods. In addition, effective pricing cannot be achieved without knowledge of demand, price elasticity and the relationship between demand, costs and profit. Ultimately, the marketer must choose pricing policies and methods in line with company objectives. The following stages of decision-making are useful in establishing pricing policy:

Develop Pricing Objectives

Pricing objectives provide the foundation for decisions about the later stages of the pricing plan. Objectives must be stated explicitly; they should be quantified and time-based. They should also be consistent with the organisation's overall business and marketing objectives. Organisations normally have multiple pricing objectives, some short-term and others long-term.

Research the Target Market's Evaluation of Price and Its Ability to Buy

Price depends on a number of considerations, such as the type of product, the type of target market and the purchase situation. By assessing the target market's evaluation of price, a company is in a better position to know how much emphasis to place on price. Understanding the customer's buying power, buying habits and buying intentions can help the company correctly assess the market's evaluation of price.

Determine Demand

For most normal products, the quantity demanded increases as price decreases. There is an inverse relationship between price and the quantity demanded. As long as the marketing environment and the buyers' need, ability, willingness, and authority to buy remain stable, this fundamental relationship will continue. The classic demand curve identifies the quantities that are expected to be sold at different price levels.

There are, however, types of demand that do not conform to the classic demand curve. Prestige products, for example, sell better at higher prices than at lower prices.

Demand elasticity is a measure of the sensitivity of demand to changes in price. It is defined as the percentage change in demand relative to a given percentage change in price. Knowledge of an offer's elasticity is useful in guiding management towards effective price points, as well as providing insight into price adjustments over the life of the offer.

If the company can determine the price elasticity of demand for its products, it is much easier to set price. Inelastic demand results in a change in the same direction in total revenue. With elastic demand, a change in price will cause an opposite change in revenue.

An evaluation of the offer to determine its demand function and elasticity is critical to the development of an effective price.

Analysis of Demand, Cost and Profit Relationships

There are two useful approaches to understanding demand: marginal analysis and break-even analysis. Marginal analysis is used to identify the optimum price volume position at which the sale of additional units reduces the overall revenue of the firm.

Evaluation of Competitors' Prices

Knowledge of competitive pricing objectives, strategies and tactics can be useful in devising the company's own pricing strategy and tactics. In addition, such knowledge often highlights gaps or opportunities. For many companies, the pricing task is reduced to an evaluation and matching of competitors' prices. The task is thus simplified, but in the process a company may lose the opportunity to earn higher profitability, especially if they have a superior offer. Competition-based pricing depends almost totally on competitors as a reference point.

Selecting a Pricing Policy

Pricing policies help companies solve the practical problems of establishing prices. Common pricing policies include:

- *Price Skimming*: Pricing policies in which a company charges the highest possible price to the most price-insensitive buyers.

- *Penetration Pricing*: A policy in which prices are set below the prices of competing offers in a price-sensitive market in order to penetrate the market and produce a larger unit sales volume

- *Psychological Pricing*: Pricing methods designed to encourage purchases that are based on emotional rather rational responses

- *Promotional Pricing*: Pricing related to the short-term promotion of a particular offer.

Development of a Pricing Method

Three main methods are commonly used in pricing:

- *Cost-Oriented Pricing*, a method whereby a monetary amount or percentage is added to the cost of the product. Cost-based methods are simple and easy to implement; however, they fail to take into consideration the economic aspects of supply and demand. The most widely used cost based methods are Cost Plus Pricing and Mark-up Pricing.

- *Demand-Oriented Pricing*, a method based on the level of market demand for the product, resulting in a high price when demand is strong and a low price when demand is weak. Price differentiation is a common method of pricing based on demand in different segments.

- *Competition-Oriented Pricing*, a method in which costs and profits are considered secondary to competitors' prices.

Determine the Specific Offer Price

The final price, together with its tactical plan for adjustment, is developed out of the detailed analysis of the target customer, demand, price elasticity, costs and competitive factors. In addition, the company's objectives and their intended use of price will have a role to play. Price is a complex mechanism with economic, competitive and psychological roles to play. In the end, however, the price decided upon must help to attract customers in sufficient numbers and at a sufficient level of demand to justify the company's efforts and ensure adequate profitability for future survival.

CASE HISTORY: REVIEWING THE PRICE AT EIRCELL

Gerry Mortimer

The Review

In mid-1996, Eircell management reviewed the company's pricing policy for its mobile phone networks. Several factors prompted this review. The review was made under time pressure, given the imminent arrival of competition and the perceived need to make any price changes and communicate them to customers prior to the launch of the competitive product.

The Background

In April 1996, Eircell had been established as a separate subsidiary of Telecom Eireann, operating the only two mobile phone networks in Ireland. The networks were TACS (analogue), established in 1985 and GSM (digital) launched in 1993. Telecom Eireann itself had experienced recent change with a minority share being sold to Swedish and Dutch telecom interests.

The key factor in the need to re-examine the pricing structure lay in the imminent arrival of competition in the form of Esat Digifone. Esat had been awarded the second GSM licence in October 1995 and was expected to enter the market in time for Christmas 1996.

There were also other factors in the area of pricing that needed to be addressed. There was a realisation that pricing needed to be simplified. Pricing methods had become unnecessarily complex. Pricing was based on a monthly rental and on charges for calls made. Both were different for TACS and GSM users. In general, tariffs were higher for GSM users, as it was seen as a more modern network that would eventually replace TACS. GSM was more secure, was supposed to offer clearer service, could be used in conjunction with other equipment such as laptop computers and could be used internationally. However, it was in GSM that Eircell would face competition. It was also likely that the new competition would target heavy users who were not receiving any special rates from Eircell. There was therefore a perceived need to reward high users through a sliding scale of tariffs. Perhaps, above all, there was a view that an "easy to buy/easy to sell" philosophy was needed to ensure that both customers and sales agents clearly understood prices and that agents could effectively communicate the nature of the pricing arrangements to customers.

The Mobile Phone Market

The mobile phone market was growing rapidly. However, by 1996, market penetration in Ireland, at six per cent of the adult population, was still lower than the UK at ten per cent, the US at 15 per cent and Scandinavia (where there were particular features) at 30 per cent. All of these markets were continuing to grow. Market penetration in Ireland was expected to reach 20 per cent by the year 2000. In addition to the existing customers, there were a further 450,000 customers to be fought for, if these projections were accurate.

Eircell did not sell mobile phones. These were normally sold through independent retail outlets, though Telecom Eireann, Eircell's parent, also had a retail operation. Eircell licensed retailers or agents and enabled customers to connect to their network. Where there was strong competition, operators such as Eircell frequently subsidised the retailer or agent in an effort to encourage the agent to persuade a new customer to connect to that network. The agent or retailer might pass some or all of that subsidy to the potential customer in a reduced price for the phone. Eircell had developed a number of such incentives as competition loomed. Eircell was, however, constrained in its actions. Because of its dominant position, it was subject to strict scrutiny by the telecom regulator. Thus, for example, if a customer switched from Eircell to Esat, Eircell would be required to inform a caller to the customer of the switch for a period of 3 months. The new Esat service would operate using an 086 prefix and could give a customer the same number as they previously had with the TACS prefix (088) or the Eircell GSM prefix (087). Eircell recognised that Esat would win customers in a growing market and that customers might also switch to Esat from Eircell. The company was keen to minimise that switching. It recognised the value of its existing customer base, who could be considered to be the innovators and early adopters in the mobile phone market.

Existing Pricing Policy

At the time of the price review, three options existed for customers. These were as follows:

1.	**GSM (087):**	Rental £20.00 per month
	Less special discount for limited coverage	(£5.00) per month
	Calls peak 8 a.m. – 8 p.m., Mon–Fri	25p per minute
	Off-peak calls	17p per minute
2.	**Analogue Business (088)**	Rental £20.00 per month
	Special discount	nil
	Calls peak 8 a.m. – 8 p.m., Mon–Fri	22.33p per minute
	Off-peak calls	15p per minute
3.	**Eircell Personal**	Rental £20.66 per month
	Included calls to value	£11.00
	Additional calls peak	43.98p per minute
	Additional calls off-peak	14.64p per minute
	Additional calls weekend	10.98p per minute

All rates were subject to VAT at 21 per cent. All national calls had a minimum 30 seconds charge and were billed at 10-second intervals. Separate pricing arrangements applied to international calls. Unlike the land-based system, all mobile calls within Ireland (excluding Northern Ireland) were charged at the same rate. There was therefore no distinction between local and long-distance calls.

The Proposed Pricing Solution

The new pricing review was to be branded Eirtime. Five separate tariffs were proposed, which would apply to both analogue and GSM networks. The different tariffs would be inclusive of varying levels of calls and would be as follows:

Option	Charge Monthly	Inclusive Minutes	National Call Per Minute Rates	
			Peak	*Off-peak*
Eirtime	£10	0	45.0p	22.5p
Eirtime 30	£20	30	30.0p	15.0p
Eirtime 60	£30	60	25.0p	12.5p
Eirtime 180	£60	180	20.0p	10.0p
Eirtime 480	£120	480	18.0p	9.0 p

All prices quoted exclude VAT. The number of inclusive minutes represented the number of minutes that were included with the rental charge before any charges were made. No distinction was to be made between peak and off-peak inclusive minutes. Once a subscriber used up their inclusive minutes, the national call rates applicable to that option came into operation. Unused inclusive minutes could not be retained and lapsed at the end of the billing period (one month) if not used. Customers using the existing tariffs were not obliged to switch to Eirtime tariffs. However, Eircell estimated that 95 per cent of existing subscribers would benefit from the change. Once customers changed they could not change back, though they could switch between the different Eirtime options at the end of each billing period. New customers would only be able to choose from the five Eirtime options.

Communicating the New Price Structure

The price changes required communication with three separate groups:

- Existing customers
- Potential customers
- Agents.

The launch incorporated the following timetable and events:

Date	Activity
Sunday 22 September	Press announcement
Friday 27 September	Existing customer mailshot
Monday 30 September	Options team/help desk opens
Week of 14 October	Agent training
Monday 21 October	Full launch
	Ad campaign

The mailshot to existing customers incorporated a recommendation as to which was the most suitable option, based on an analysis of each customer's previous six-months usage.

A high level of secrecy surrounded the price changes until the press announcement on 22 September. The Esat launch was imminent and Eircell was keen that Esat would not have any advance notice of its tariff changes. Per second exact billing was also introduced at the same time.

REFERENCES TO CHAPTER 6

Bacon, M.S. (1994), *Do-It-Yourself Direct Marketing: Secrets for Small Business*, New York: John Wiley & Sons, pp. 154–158.

Dibb, S., L. Simkin, W.M. Pride and O.C. Ferrell (1997), *Marketing Concepts and Strategy*, Third European Edition, New York: Houghton Mifflin, pp. 557–580.

Hughes, A.M. (1994), *Strategic Database Marketing*, Chicago: Probus, p. 17.

Hutchings, A. (1995), *Marketing: A Resource Book*, London: Pitman Publishing.

Jobber, D. (1995), *The Principles and Practice of Marketing*, New York: McGraw-Hill, p. 326.

Jones, S.K. (1992), *Creative Strategy in Direct Marketing*, London: NTC Business Books, p. 149.

Mudie, P. (1997), *Marketing: An Analytical Perspective*, London: Prentice Hall, p. 156.

Shimp, T.A. (1997), Advertising, Promotion and Supplemental Aspects of Integrated Marketing Communications, Fourth Edition, New York: The Dryden Press.

PART TWO

Database Strategy

Chapter 7

DATABASE STRATEGY IN AN IRISH CONTEXT

Darren McGee

Overview

Managers, realising the benefits of retention and information-based strategies, have recently turned to marketing databases (MDBs) and database marketing (DBM) to enhance their marketing activities. The MDB is now seen by Irish managers as the ideal tool to help them keep customers, cross-sell products to these customers and recruit new customers with a similar profile to that of their existing base.

This chapter deals with the area of database marketing management and strategy in an Irish context. In the first section, the author presents the results of an innovative piece of research into the marketing database management practices of Irish firms, focusing on the business-to-business sector. The following sections then present a practical discussion of the mechanics of the DBM process and a common-sense framework for choosing and implementing an MDB solution.

MARKETING DATABASE MANAGEMENT PRACTICES IN IRELAND — THE STUDY

Introduction

Koschnick defines marketing as the "total system of interacting business activities designed to plan, price, promote and distribute want-satisfying products and services to present and potential customers" (quoted in Baker, 1984: 119). This definition echoes other varying assertions that marketing is about satisfying customer wants or needs at a profit (Kotler, 1991; Dibb et al., 1991). In recent years, due mainly to soaring mass media costs, there has been a strong focus on developing relationships with a firm's existing customers. Other costs in the background of this focus are the higher costs of identifying and converting new customers. This has led to the advent of relationship marketing. The theoretical focus of relationship marketing is on getting 100 per cent loyalty or advocacy of the company's products by all customers, through dyadic interaction.

In essence, the trend in relationship marketing has been towards individualised, retention or one-to-one marketing, and the growth of DBM is rooted in the philosophy of small businesses, the concept of getting and staying closer to the customer (Shaw and Stone, 1988: 7).

Cross and Smith (1995: 28) highlight their variation of relationship marketing, called "customer bonding", where the strategies pursued recognise that each marketing element plays a role in forming one or more type of customer bond. The types of customer bond highlighted by Cross and Smith are highlighted in Table 7.1. It is interesting to note the similarity between these "bond types" and the "loyalty ladder" as developed by Murray Raphel in recent years.

TABLE 7.1: TYPES OF CUSTOMER BOND

Type of Bond	Purpose
Awareness	Captures share of mind
Identity	Bond based on emotions/shared values
Relationship	Bond based on dialogue
Community	Sharing in your customer's lifestyle
Advocacy	When customers become champions

Source: Cross and Smith, 1995: 28

Jackson (1985) pondered the viability of getting close to a customer in a sustainable fashion. She identified a spectrum upon which the relationship exists, from a mere transaction to a fully-fledged dyadic partnering. Jackson hypothesised that the customer's main aim was to maximise the value from any transaction with the company, while the company was the party with the most vested interest in developing a long-term relationship, with a view to maximising the lifetime value (LTV) of that particular customer.

DBM aims to create "barriers to exit", for the customer, hence creating a structural bond. This in turn makes it less attractive for the customer to change to another supplier company. This method of "locking-in" a customer is an information-based strategy, as identified by Webster (1995: 11), where products or processes are evolved to build value for customers (Mitchell, 1995: 6). DBM plays a central role in Webster's new marketing concept, where marketing's primary role is to provide information to decision-makers within the company. Webster sees the truly market-driven company as one where all decisions are based on customer information. This echoes Peters and Waterman's ideas of closeness to the customer (Peters and Waterman, 1988). DBM aims to fulfil the relationship marketing goals of increased market share, sales productivity and the development of a large core group of loyal customers.

Research Methodology

Over the past few years, faced with increased competition, brand proliferation and consumer demands, marketers have begun to realise the benefits of reaching consumers on a more individual basis (McCutcheon and Wang, 1995: 69).

Technological developments have assisted in this change to an individualised focus by making it more cost-effective to reach narrowly targeted micro-segments of the population. Traditional mass marketers are now disaggregating their vast amounts of marketing information to deliver highly tailored messages to narrowly targeted segments, to elicit certain behaviour. However, in many cases, due to lack of proper use and management of information and insufficient planning, what often results is the creation of one-time buyers, not loyal repeat customers. Gregory estimates that 80 per cent of data collected by organisations is never turned into useful information.

The research objective was to examine effective database management in Ireland. Throughout the secondary research, several core areas of database management emerged. These highlight the information needed to build an effective database. Each one of these variables when adequately examined provides a piece of the final picture of database management practices in Ireland.

System Description

System description refers to the actual location of the database in the organisation. For an MDB to be fully effective, it should be networked throughout as large a number of departments and staff as possible. If a database is on a standalone machine in the marketing department, then the staff at the contact points with customers will not have access to those customers' past purchase/preference/credit histories. This is ineffective management and use of an MDB. Another important aspect to the system description is the level of integration between a company's databases. In an ideal world, a telemarketing executive dealing with a client should be able to access a customer's file and look at all their details, including past purchases and credit history. The advantages of such a scenario are obvious. In reality, however, the marketing and accounts databases are often discrete entities operated by remote departments in an organisation. In this instance, the company is not fully utilising the information it already has on each customer, nor is it providing customer contact staff with a full on-line picture of any individual customer's dealings with that company. Without organisation-wide integration, the database lacks effectiveness as a marketing tool.

Content

The content of the database is the level of information that the database actually stores on each customer or account. This covers the actual quality of the data being "trapped" about customers and prospects. In order to be fully effective, the database should allow the users of the system to input a wide variety of data about customers. Courtheoux (1984) identified the fields that are essential for both industrial and consumer MDBs. These generally include demographic information, purchase history and some type of future purchase predictive score. Courtheoux's recommendations were used in the section of the questionnaire dealing with content of the database.

Applications

The profitable use of the database should be the main reason for its development. It is one thing to have a powerful database with lots of information; unless it provides some tangible benefit to the company, it will erode resources. Through the secondary research, there are implications that many of the companies who use an MDB only use it as a computerised mailing list. In other words, the information on the database is only used in sending direct mail pieces. The functions of an MDB are much more diverse than simple mailing list generation and management. Some of the other uses for a database include management of prospects/contacts, telemarketing, profiling, loyalty programmes, customising product offerings and cross-selling. This list is by no means exhaustive, but by examining it one can see the bigger picture of the functions of an MDB.

Measurement/Analysis of the Database

One of the distinguishing features of database marketing, and indeed the direct marketing activity that databases facilitate, is the accountability of database marketing versus traditional mass marketing. Mailshots can be tracked using a database to test the level of sales by geographic region. Indeed, the customers/prospects who were converted as a result of a particular ad can be tracked over their time with the company to provide a cost-benefit analysis on advertising spend involved. Companies can also segment their customer databases to identify their more profitable customers to target with certain promotions, remembering that database marketing is built on the Pareto Principle — that all customers are not the same and should not be treated equally. Thus, measurability and accountability are two key features of database marketing. By using a database, a company can analyse its customer base to determine characteristics of its best/biggest customers, and then target prospects with a similar profile. Through data mining and profiling, the company can benefit multi-fold from its database activity.

Data Management

This basically refers to the way in which new data are sourced for introduction into the organisation's database, and the way in which existing information is cleaned, i.e. updated or de-duplicated. This is an essential element of any database research, since the data itself is the lifeblood of the MDB. If this data is out of date or inaccurate, the effectiveness of the database is compromised. It is useful to remember here that it is the data that allows marketing communications and promotions to be targeted, while the database software only allows one to manipulate that data. There are two main sources of new data — external and internal. External data may be purchased from a large information-based company such as Kompass or Dun and

Bradstreet. The external data may be used to add records to a database or alternatively to enhance records already on the database. Internal data are data that are captured each time the customer/prospect has a contact with the company.

Defining the Population

For the purposes of this survey, the population under consideration was all companies in the Republic of Ireland currently using an MDB. The sampling units were the companies in question, and the sampling element was the marketing manager in these organisations. The marketing manager was chosen as a result of the interviews at the exploratory phase of the research. From these interviews, it emerged that the marketing manager was the person charged with the maintenance of the customer/prospect database. It should be noted that in companies where the title Marketing Manager did not exist, the default contact was Sales Manager and then Managing Director, as the latter contacts would carry the role and duties in such firms. The sample size was 370. It was judgementally selected, based on consultation with industry experts who had knowledge of companies using MDBs.

Mail Interview

The mail interview was the chosen method of contact for this piece of research. A number of measures were introduced to combat low response rates. Firstly, only companies who used a database were targeted. This meant that the communication was relevant to them. Secondly, the cover letter was designed in accordance with direct mail copy-writing guidelines to encourage a higher response rate. The letters and labels were all personalised through mail-merging the sample list.

In all, there were 94 questionnaires returned by the cut-off date of 27 July 1996. Of these, nine were unusable due to the spurious data provided. The following results are based on the 85 usable returns, which represents a 23 per cent response rate to the mail questionnaire.

Statement and Interpretation of Findings

System Description

If the database is stand-alone or only networked within one department, it limits viewing access to those in close geographic proximity. In such cases, there is the risk that the MDB will become static, since the information about customers on the database is not a complete picture. Thirty-seven per cent of companies in this study are located on stand-alone machines and 48 per cent are networked in one or two departments.

This conflicts with best MDB practice, which suggests that the extent of the network closely correlates with the effectiveness of the database. If the MDB is networked throughout the organisation, then every department dealing with a client will add to the record on that customer. This means that past purchases, credit history, product preferences, promotional responses and recent complaints can all be recorded in one central place.

Findings from this study also show that the vast majority (68 per cent) of companies have more than one MDB. Some companies used a separate MDB for separate business units, some separated by function, i.e. customer service database, warranty administration database and direct mail database. This leads to duplication of effort, since the individual databases have to be maintained and managed. It also means that some information on the same customer is being stored in two isolated databases, which means that the front line customer contact staff do not have full information on a given account in a single database.

Seventy-four per cent of the companies have separate marketing and accounts databases. These companies will forego the benefits of having an integrated system, while also incurring the cost of running two separate databases. This is a strategic issue in the increasing tendency towards global competition in the Irish marketplace.

The level of write access, which is concerned with the accessibility of the database within the organisation, proved disappointing. Each individual who has customer contact should have access to log each customer contact to the respective records on the database. Only 47 per cent of the companies report that all of their staff have access to amend records on the database, while 52 per cent of companies stated that write-access to the database is restricted to certain staff.

Content

The level of data on the database defines the scope of any marketing activity that the MDB supports. It is essential to have fields that include demographic information, purchase history and some type of future predictive score. In both industrial and consumer MDBs, there was a distinctly poor level of data. In both instances, there were very high incidences of companies with no "predictive score" field. This, it could be assumed, is a symptom of weak statistical analysis of the MDB, which means ineffectual use and hence management of the MDB. Other key indicator fields missing in a large number of both industrial and consumer MDBs were the "offer exposure" and "offer response" fields. This also reflects a lack of commitment to analysis of the MDB. In addition, there was a noticeable lack of consistency in demographic information gathered. Some consumer marketers actually had an MDB without a field for age (23 companies), sex (20 companies) or title of the customer/prospect (5 companies). Lifestyle information was also lacking in a large number of consumer MDBs. This presents a very poor view of the data element of consumer MDBs.

Industrial marketers also highlighted a poor level of basic classification data, in addition to large numbers of databases that lack a customer history facility or offer exposure and response fields. This would seem to indicate that the MDB is limited at both the strategic and tactical levels, since mailshots won't reach the target population, while segmental analysis is impossible if no record is kept of the customers who actually buy the company's products. It is apparent from the survey that the level of data on MDBs is poor. However, some companies forwarded lists of extra fields that their MDBs contain, in addition to up-to-date basic information. The inclusion of fields, such as whether the customer is a golfer, illustrate the creative thinking behind successful DBM methods, and highlight the flexible nature of DBM.

It is interesting to note, in an atmosphere of changing communication channels, that 52 companies did not include a field for the e-mail address of the customer company, while 66 companies did not facilitate the recording of the Internet address of the customer.

Applications

The application or use of the MDB indicates the level of strategic thinking that lies behind the use of the MDB. Interestingly enough, 77 per cent of the companies stated that they used the MDB for both strategic and tactical purposes.

FIGURE 7.1: USES OF THE MARKETING DATABASE (NUMBER OF COMPANIES

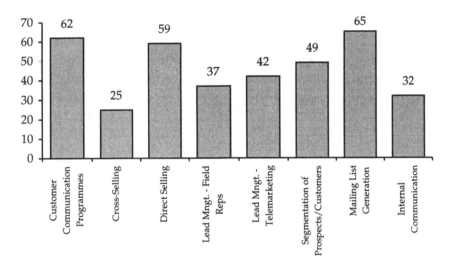

However, of the companies who managed the MDB on a mixed tactical/strategic basis, only 29 per cent used the MDB for cross-selling — possibly one of the most strategic uses of MDB. Mailing list generation was used by 77 per cent of companies. There are indications that the MDBs are being used for strategic purposes, such as the high number of companies using their MDB for customer communication programmes and segmentation.

However, companies who stated that they use the MDB for both strategic and tactical purposes are not making use of the full spectrum of applications available to them. Although mailing list generation was highlighted as the main use for the MDB, there was an awareness of alternative uses. These included customer communication programmes (73 per cent) and segmentation of customer/ prospect base (58 per cent). In addition, 50 per cent of companies used the MDB for lead management in a telemarketing context, while

43 per cent used it for lead management for field representatives. A surprisingly low number of companies used the MDB for co-ordinating internal communication about customers (37 per cent).

Measurement/Analysis of the Database

The accountability of DBM activity has already been identified as a distinguishing feature. Data mining and profiling allows the company to identify prospects with similar characteristics to their most profitable customers.

FIGURE 7.2: FACTORS IN EVALUATING THE DBM ACTIVITIES (NUMBER OF COMPANIES)

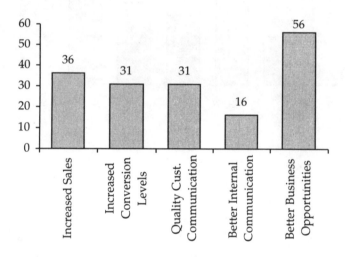

The frequency of evaluation of the MDB activities is a key indicator of the effectiveness of MDB management. Over half of the respondents evaluated the performance of MDB at least once a month. However, there were 25 companies who evaluated the MDB activities either once a year or never. Evaluation of the MDB is ineffective if carried out at such distant intervals. Any effective MDB management programme should include a function to evaluate the activities on a regular basis. In this instance, the majority of companies seem to have an effective evaluation function, with 60 companies evaluating the DMB activities at least every quarter.

The evaluation parameters offer valuable clues as to the strategic intent of the companies using MDBs. The identification of better business opportunities was the most common variable used, yet there was also a strong focus on sales and increased conversion rates. This would seem to indicate a mixed tactical/strategic evaluation procedure. Although industry wisdom recommends that the MDB be evaluated on a long-term basis, it is reasonable to evaluate the MDB in terms of some immediate benefit to the company. In this respect, the evaluation parameters used by companies seem to indicate a healthy evaluation environment for MDBs.

The effectiveness of MDB management is boosted by indications that the most common evaluator of the MDB is either the marketing manager or marketing executive. The marketing manager is charged with evaluation of the MDB in the majority of companies across the spectrum, from companies who use the MDB for mailing lists to companies who use it for customer communication. In addition, the managing director evaluates the MDB in 19 per cent of cases.

FIGURE 7.3: ROLE OF PERSONNEL IN EVALUATING THE MARKETING DATABASE (PERCENTAGE OF CASES)

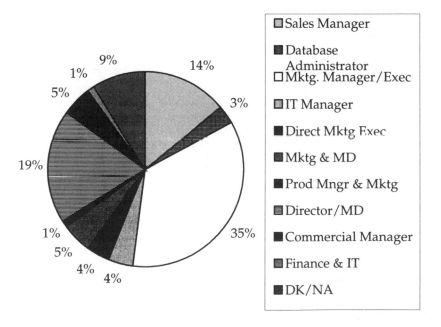

Database Management

One core area of data management is data cleaning, which "is concerned with the correction of errors and discrepancies in the data that

has been collected, and the elimination of undesirable record dupli-
cations" (Gorski and Ingram, 1994: 61). Data cleaning includes for-
matting the data, validation, enhancement and de-duplication of
data. In the vast majority of cases, the companies conducted some
level of data cleaning. Only nine companies admitted that no data
cleaning was conducted on their MDB. At the other end of the scale,
29 companies clean their data either monthly or weekly. The 29 companies who clean the MDB quarterly or 6-monthly would seem to
represent a healthy data cleaning practice, while companies who
conduct data cleaning on an annual basis face a mammoth chore and
longer periods with inaccurate data on the MDB. The low number of
companies using external agencies for cleaning prevented the comparison of internal and external cleaning with respect to age of the
data. Given the complex nature of data cleaning, it is surprising that
only five per cent of companies use the expertise of an external
agency to fulfil their data-cleaning needs.

The age of data on the MDBs of respondent companies offers a
further insight into the health of data on existing MDBs. The responses from this question would seem to contradict the claims of
regular cleaning. Only 21 per cent of companies stated that all data
on the MDB was less than six months old, yet 68 per cent of companies claim they clean the MDB at least once every six months. This
incongruity seems to point to some confusion among respondents
about the relationship between data cleaning and accuracy of data.

A common internal source of data for the MDB is customer data
that already exists on the accounts system of the company. However,
in the study only half of the respondents use the accounts data as a
source for the MDB. This suggests that companies are ignoring vast
amounts of existing data in their search for knowledge about their
customers. Forty per cent of companies stated that the biggest problem with management of the MDB is getting the accounts data into a
useful form for marketing. Without accounts data, the company has
an incomplete picture of the customer. Companies that do use accounts data as a source for the MDB report a number of difficulties in
"getting the accounts data into a useful form for marketing purposes". These include lack of resources, transfer of paper records,
differing levels of accuracy, relevancy, recency, and irregular formats
of the data.

In this instance, it may prove difficult or impractical to use ac-counts data in the MDB. To facilitate ease of transfer, data entry to both databases should be in accordance with a standard inputting procedure with supervision. This ensures that all relevant data is captured on initial contact with the customer/prospect, alleviating the problem of incomplete demographic data highlighted earlier.

Relationship of the MDB to Other Marketing Activities

The impact of the MDB on Irish business practice is reflected in Fig-ure 7.4. One can readily note that the vast majority of companies now regard the MDB as an essential tool in their marketing activities. In addition, the majority (75 per cent) of companies agreed that the im-plementation of an MDB has improved their business. This statement is reinforced by the benefits that the companies derive from Database Marketing (DBM) activity. These include top-line benefits such as sales increases, as well as more qualitative benefits such as better customer communication and lead qualification. One interesting area of benefit is in sales force management. The MDB makes it possible to supervise sales force activity and performance, and in addition, some companies have reduced the size of the field sales force, since the MDB can be used to substantially qualify leads and maximise face-to-face selling time.

FIGURE 7.4: "MARKETING DATABASE IS NOW AN ESSENTIAL TOOL TO MY MARKETING ACTIVITIES"

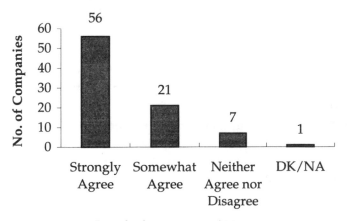

Level of Agreement/Disagreement

The MDB plays an increasingly important role in a large number of Irish companies. However, DBM is still in its infancy in Ireland, highlighted by the fact that 70 per cent of the MDBs in this research were under three years old, with 34 per cent of these less than one year old.

Conclusions

System

From the research conducted, it has been established that most companies who operate an MDB do so on a network, while nearly half the respondents stated that they allow all staff the access to modify records on the database. This is the optimal scenario and is an encouraging sign for the DBM industry in Ireland. However, there are still a number of concern areas that warrant mention at this stage:

- Over one third of companies run the MDB from a standalone machine

- Almost half of the companies with a networked MDB restrict the network to one or a few departments.

- Less than half the companies stated that they allowed all company staff access to modify records on the MDB

- Less than one-third of the companies have a single, integrated MDB, while other companies have multiple MDBs — up to ten individual MDBs in some cases

- There is scarce representation of multi-departmental representation in the development and implementation of the MDB.

These areas present stumbling blocks to the effective management of MDBs in Ireland. All of the above are symptomatic of companies who are not aware of the benefits of operating a single integrated MDB, which continually updates customer records with every contact. The lack of involvement by other departments in the development and implementation of the MDB would seem to indicate a narrow marketing/sales focus, instead of an enterprise-wide vision of the capabilities of a fully integrated MDB.

Level of Data Stored on the MDB

The level of data currently stored on the majority of Irish MDBs is a cause for concern. The most basic demographic and psychographic data were missing. In addition, predictive data and response data were missing. Almost half the companies reported that the data on the database was not updated at every customer contact. The conclusion from this finding is that the data on most Irish databases is gathered on a reactive basis, or as a by-product of some other process, as opposed to being a process in itself (data gathering). Irish companies need to develop a more proactive approach to data capture, to ensure that at least all basic demographic, psychographic and contact data are obtained. Companies should provide training to customer contact staff in order to educate them as to the data requirements of the company and the need to capture all details upon initial contact with the customer/prospect. Most companies stated that there is standard inputting procedures and supervision of inputting within their organisation. It would appear that these procedures are ineffectual, given the fields contained on the majority of databases. It is recommended that the companies review data entry procedures and supervision in the light of these findings. The actual data content on the MDBs represents an obstacle to effective MDB management. It can be concluded that the management of data collection for the database has been ineffective in most companies to this point.

Application/Use of the MDB

There was a distinct lack of utilisation of the full range of MDB applications. This is especially true of issues such as cross-selling that are at the heart of DBM. It is suggested that the low number of companies using the MDB for cross-selling may be due to a lack of knowledge about the full range of MDB applications. The large number of companies who use the MDB solely as a mailing list generator echoes this fact.

Evaluation

There was a healthy evaluation cycle in most companies, combined with sensible evaluation parameters. Most companies evaluated the MDB in a hybrid manner of top line sales increases, in line with better business opportunities and customer communications. As with any business initiative, evaluation is paramount in order to achieve objectives and there is an effective level of MDB evaluation in Irish companies.

Data Management

Irish MDB managers, for the most part, conduct data cleaning internally, while only a minority of companies use external agencies to clean the data on their MDB. The fact that external agencies are not used to any great proportion is highlighted by the knowledge that the majority of data on existing MDBs is more than six months old. Companies would benefit from specialist knowledge from an external agency in the context of MDB cleaning, since the task is a complex one. Although companies may think that they are cleaning the data on the MDB, the age of the data on existing MDBs proves otherwise.

There is also evidence that companies are using a mix of internal transactional data and externally sourced lists. The conclusion is that the perceived high quality and accuracy of externally sourced lists provides a stimulant for the growth of DBM in Ireland. Fifty per cent of companies do not use data from the accounts database as a source of data for the MDB. This may be due in part to the difficulties encountered in merging the two databases. In order to increase the viability of using accounts data as a source of data for the MDB, the author recommends that data collection procedures be standardised across departments, to ensure compatibility of data fields and formats.

General Marketing Database Management Issues

The MDB is generally accepted as a valuable tool for marketers, but this research has highlighted that the MDB is now an essential marketing tool for most companies. In addition, most companies are prepared to state that their business has improved as a result of the implementation of an MDB, in terms of increased inquiries, sales and customer communications, among others.

Overall, this study has shown that the management of MDBs in Ireland to date has been ineffective. There seems to be a basic level of understanding of some DBM concepts, and ignorance or misunderstanding of others. One major area of concern for DBM practitioners should be the actual data on the MDB, and currently the state of this data is far from ideal. There is also an evident lack of analytical thinking behind the use of DBM, which leads to the suspicion that many companies still consider the MDB to be a mailing list generator. However, DBM is in its early days in this country, and as such it is too early to judge conclusively. The major positive outcome of this research was the overall awareness by managers of shortcomings in existing practices and a willingness to improve. This would suggest future improvements in the effectiveness of all areas of DBM management.

Finally, it is suggested that DBM management is still a vastly unexplored field. This study used non-probability sampling and as such, no statistical certainty can be attached to any of the findings. However, this study has highlighted many areas for further research, including the threats that DBM presents to traditional sales force management and issues relating to data-entry supervision.

DATABASE MARKETING — THE WAY IT WORKS

Figure 7.5 illustrates the Database Marketing (DBM) framework. This framework highlights the main flow of information around the MDB and marketing activity, while also emphasising the aims of DBM — to increase profits by maximising customer loyalty.

Essentially, all databases begin with a "data" element. This data comes from a variety of sources, including field sales staff, customer service records, internal accounts systems, telesales staff and externally available lists. This data, used in conjunction with database software, enables the company to add value to, and derive tangible benefit from, lists of names and addresses. The use of reporting functions on the MDB or indeed external report-writing software allows the company to profile, score and segment its existing customer base. This will present the company with a picture or "profile" of its best customers, most profitable customers, worst paying customers, etc. Once this profiling exercise is complete, the company is in a position to target the selected new prospect groups with communications designed to appeal to that particular type of prospect based on the company's experience with similarly profiled existing customers. Profiling also helps the company to avoid unprofitable company types, or to reduce its bad debt exposure.

FIGURE 7.5: DATABASE MARKETING — A FRAMEWORK

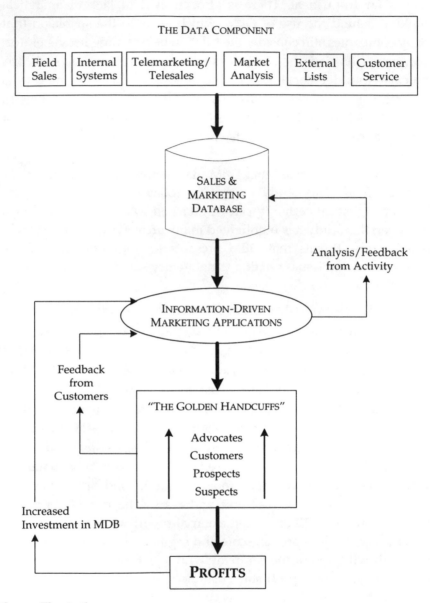

Source: The Author

The objective of profiling and scoring is to convert suspects to customers and maximising customer loyalty/repeat purchases by delivering relevance — hence avoiding a lot of wastage typically associated with mass marketing techniques. In essence, the database is used to lock the customer in, by applying the "golden handcuffs", or Jackson's (1985) structural bond as discussed earlier. Above all, the main objective of DBM is to increase profits and decrease the cost of sales.

One of the most important elements of the Database Marketing process is feedback, which occurs at multiple levels:

1. Once the company has conducted any information-driven application, the results are fed back to the database to monitor what works well for the company, and what doesn't work at all. In this way, the MDB becomes a knowledge centre, the central brain of the company — keeping a history of all activity with each individual client over time (Information feedback: company side).

2. On a daily basis, a company will receive feedback from its customers. By using the MDB to log this feedback against individual client records, the company can build a picture of those clients' preferences and dislikes (Information feedback: customer side).

3. With an overall objective of increasing profitability, it is essential that as returns from the MDB investment increase, the company ploughs back some of this profit into the development of the MDB, ensuring that it is continually updated to keep in line with changes in the market and technology.

IMPLEMENTING A MARKETING DATABASE SOLUTION

Once a company decides to harness MDB technology to improve its business, it has a number of choices. Firstly, it can use an external database bureau to house its database and conduct all of the maintenance and cleaning exercise, export data for promotional activities and conduct all analyses on its behalf. This is an excellent solution for large companies with a large resource pool — although it could be argued that this takes some control out of the hands of the company itself.

Alternatively, the company can decide to house its MDB internally. In this situation, there is a choice to build a custom database from scratch on a package like Microsoft Access or to implement a contact management package and customise it to the particular requirements of the company. Developing a system from scratch will obviously be more expensive than implementing software that already exists. The main advantage of writing a package from scratch is that the entire package is developed from the ground up for that company. Unfortunately, like any customised product, this can mean that modifications are expensive, since changes to such a customised system would have to be made by programmers.

In addition, developing a system from the ground up could also mean that valuable resources are being expended "re-inventing the wheel" — in that there are a lot of alternative solutions which offer high degrees of in-built functionality. These alternative solutions come in the shape of contact management packages, the most common being GoldMine, Tracker and ACT! These alternatives can be altered slightly to provide a tight fit with the requirements of even the most diverse companies. Contact management packages also offer a high degree of user comfort — allowing the entire database to be configured by a staff member, reducing dependence on expensive programmers.

The choice of internal versus external database management would justify several chapters of discussion, and as such I have chosen to focus on internal implementation — since this is the MDB reality for most small and medium-sized Irish companies.

When designing an MDB system, there are a number of key areas that require consideration. These areas are represented in Figure 7.6.

Internal Considerations

Before any comparison of solutions is possible, the company must first carry out an introspective exercise. The MDB is not a solution to an organisation's ills, and as such the company may need to change its focus or method of business, to provide an environment where the MDB can flourish, providing all the aforementioned benefits.

In companies where there is a poorly defined or ineffective marketing function, the MDB is doomed to failure. The fact that the marketing perspective is not optimal would suggest that the mindset for evaluation and development of the MDB is also absent. Similarly, where top management is reluctant to believe in the benefits of implementing an integrated MDB, the effectiveness of the initiative is

FIGURE 7.6: IMPLEMENTING A MARKETING DATABASE SYSTEM — AS EASY AS IT LOOKS?

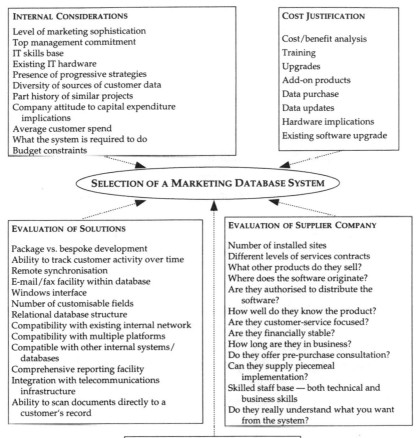

INTERNAL CONSIDERATIONS

Level of marketing sophistication
Top management commitment
IT skills base
Existing IT hardware
Presence of progressive strategies
Diversity of sources of customer data
Part history of similar projects
Company attitude to capital expenditure
 implications
Average customer spend
What the system is required to do
Budget constraints

COST JUSTIFICATION

Cost/benefit analysis
Training
Upgrades
Add-on products
Data purchase
Data updates
Hardware implications
Existing software upgrade

SELECTION OF A MARKETING DATABASE SYSTEM

EVALUATION OF SOLUTIONS

Package vs. bespoke development
Ability to track customer activity over time
Remote synchronisation
E-mail/fax facility within database
Windows interface
Number of customisable fields
Relational database structure
Compatibility with existing internal network
Compatibility with multiple platforms
Compatible with other internal systems/
 databases
Comprehensive reporting facility
Integration with telecommunications
 infrastructure
Ability to scan documents directly to a
 customer's record

EVALUATION OF SUPPLIER COMPANY

Number of installed sites
Different levels of services contracts
What other products do they sell?
Where does the software originate?
Are they authorised to distribute the
 software?
How well do they know the product?
Are they customer-service focused?
Are they financially stable?
How long are they in business?
Do they offer pre-purchase consultation?
Can they supply piecemeal
 implementation?
Skilled staff base — both technical and
 business skills
Do they really understand what you want
 from the system?

DATA CONSIDERATIONS

Type of data
Amount of data
People, address, accounts, activity data
Consumer vs. business records

Source: The Author

jeopardised. Top management support is essential for an MDB, since such support will enable the project team to overcome internal barriers to successful implementation. It is also worth mentioning at this stage that the support should be from all functions of an organisation, not just from sales and marketing. This is essential, since the MDB is in most cases a product of the information gathered in all functions of the company, and improving the quality of information gathering in all functions of the company can only improve the quality of the MDB.

The presence of progressive strategies would imply a healthier environment for implementing an MDB since such a management team should be able to see past the immediate evaluation parameters, and view the MDB as an investment with return, focused on the long-term for the company. This ability to focus on the MDB as a long-term investment will also manifest itself in the attitude of management towards the expenditure on the MDB. If the management attitude is that the MDB is an operating expense similar to commission cheques, then the MDB will be required to show a return in the very short term. Alternatively, if the company views the expenditure as an investment, there will be an appreciation of the long-term benefits of the MDB. One suggestion by industry experts to help the shift in focus to the long term has been to put the MDB on the company balance sheet — where it is viewed as an asset of the company. The actual size of the budget allocation for the MDB is paramount, since this budget, coupled with timing considerations, will dictate whether the company can build a database from scratch or whether they implement a package solution to their MDB needs. Cost justification will be discussed separately.

An internal IT audit will provide management with a picture of the state of IT development within the company. This audit should include existing hardware, software and skills levels of existing staff. This is an important consideration, since the MDB will depend heavily on these factors. Any shortcoming in these areas could present a stumbling block to the successful implementation of the MDB, and significant cost considerations in updating the IT infrastructure within the company. A marketing database is a piece of software, and as such the success of the MDB will be a function of the level of IT sophistication resident in the company.

When conducting the internal audit, the company should consider the extent to which turf or ownership issues will help or hinder the successful implementation of the MDB. Such issues should be identified and addressed during the implementation process, typically with a high level of training and education about the new system. The internal audit should conclude with a statement of what is required of the MDB. This statement/document can then be used to evaluate the progress of the MDB project — without an objective for the MDB, it will be difficult for the company to gauge the effectiveness of the MDB project.

Cost Justification

One of the biggest success killers of successful MDB implementation is the cost dynamic. This is especially true in Irish companies, where there is an apparent reluctance to pay for intangibles such as software, consultancy and training. The main shortfall here is that companies are prepared to pay a fixed price for installation of a system, but fall down when it comes to training staff to operate the system and to keep the information/system updated.

When costing the MDB project, companies should include consultancy fees — usually 60 per cent of MDB projects — the cost of data updates, and an allowance for future upgrades of software (e.g. upgrading from Windows 3.1 to Windows 95 to Windows NT4). The MDB should continue to evolve to keep pace with changes in the market and as such there should be an annual budget for the upkeep of the MDB.

If the MDB is intended for use by a field sales force, there are cost implications in providing these staff with laptops to access the information on the database. In addition, there is the cost of upgrading the hardware and telecommunications to allow reps to synchronise remotely with the main database in the company's premises.

Evaluation of Solutions

> The benefits of running an integrated [marketing] system are straightforward: keeping all customer details in one central area means that the most up-to-date information can be used by all the teams in an organisation. It is easier for new members of the salesforce to take over new territories, and reshuffles of staff are easier to carry out . . . direct marketing can take existing customer preferences into account (Dudman, 1995: 17).

In business, contacts are among the company's most valuable assets (Reichard and Yakal, 1995: 243). In recent times, the emphasis has switched from market management to customer management — that is, not how much market share a company can obtain but what share of each individual customer's spend it can get. A renewed emphasis on productivity of company staff and customer management, as well as a new focus on issues such as the Internet, mobile workforces, teleworking and converting customer information into tangible business benefit has driven the quest for integrated MDB software.

MDB packages today must share contact data and history throughout the organisation. In this regard, the MDB or contact manager provides the company with a "memory" of each individual customer. This is increasingly important since marketing practice in itself is undergoing a transformation, from the mass marketing period where customers were distant entities and companies had limited knowledge of them, to an individualised, one-to-one customer focus.

The term "database marketing" implies a high technology content, but the goal of database marketing practice is a traditional one: that of the focus on and complete knowledge of each individual customer by everyone in the organisation. Indeed, the networking capability is a prerequisite in the contact management software arena, and any contact manager worthy of the name is a workgroup tool, sharing the wealth of accumulated contact information across the organisation.

In reality, the term "marketing database" equates to "contact management software", since contact managers have developed to become more than information managers. These developments include links to fax-shot software, e-mail, Internet compatibility, word processing, call scheduling and the inclusion of customer history tracking fields. In addition, the cost of developing bespoke MDB software has proven prohibitive for most Irish companies. With the average package solution priced at around £350 per user, it is more attractive to procure such packages than embark on a slow development cycle. In addition to shorter implementation cycles, external packages have the advantage of an experience curve modified over time, being constantly improved — evolving from a crude MS-DOS version to slicker Windows "point and click" versions. Contact management packages have the advantage of low cost and networkability. In addition, software program modules can be written to transfer data from internal systems such as invoicing, service and inventory directly into each record on the MDB. In the Irish reality, once a company decides that it wants its own MDB, the choice of an MDB system is a choice of which package to implement.

To be an effective contact management package, the software must initially be a strong contact database. This ability is measured in a number of ways: the ability to import data from a variety of sources into both new and existing databases; and the ability to export. Also considered important are the ability to store different types of data and the level of flexibility to customise the interface of the contact manager to suit different applications. The capability to add, search, delete records, and the program's logging and reporting capabilities are also used in the selection of a contact manager (Reichard and Ya-kal, 1995: 244).

To be an effective workgroup contact manager, the package must first meet the requirements of the workgroup members, while permitting information to be shared on the network. It must have a solid foundation and the record formats must contain enough standard and customisable fields to satisfy users with the most demanding needs for detail (Reichard and Yakal, 1995: 243). Security is also an issue: where access to some data is restricted to certain personnel, the database should allow security to be assigned at different levels.

However, good contact management packages do much more than manage contacts. Possibly the most useful day-to-day uses of the contact management packages are personal scheduling and correspondence. Personal scheduling features include the arranging and tracking of meetings, tasks and phone calls. Scripting of telephone conversations and automating sequences of events also come under this heading, and are very important for companies involved in telemarketing (Reichard and Yakal, 1995: 244). Correspondence functionality includes the ability to send and track letters, faxes, e-mails and mass mailings using built-in functions or by transferring data into an external application such as MS Word, Exchange or fax broadcast software. The main advantage of contact managers is the ability to integrate all of the above features: there should be no need to switch from a contact screen to a calendar to schedule a meeting. Indeed, some advanced contact managers provide additional modules to allow users to scan correspondence from customers directly into the actual record on the MDB.

Effective contact management means capturing large amounts of detail. The more carefully the activities with the contact are documented, the more complete and useful the contact histories will be (Reichard and Yakal, 1995: 245). An effective contact management package should allow the user to pull up a contact record and, with a few mouse clicks, determine whether to call, write, e-mail, or schedule a future meeting with that particular contact, with full knowledge of the contact-company history. This ability to view a company's contacts history enables the user to prepare for conversation with the contacts, and tailor sales pitches or discounted deals to the preferences of the contact.

"The shared database is both the most basic and the most powerful feature of a group contact manager" (Reichard and Yakal, 1995: 248). At a most basic level, the shared database enables all users throughout the company to view static information, such as contact phone number, fax number and address, without duplication of effort. In this way, the shared database serves as a shared address file on every desktop in the organisation. On a more advanced level, the shared database allows group access to the dynamic information about a contact — the history of all interactions between the company and the contact in question.

An increasing number of companies are using software packages as opposed to bespoke software to fulfil their MDB needs, and as such managers are becoming involved in the process of package selection. Many managers, however, have little experience in the selection of such packages, and from bad previous experience are suspicious of help given by IT departments. This gulf between IT and marketing staff is, however, changing, while the diversity and rapidly changing nature of marketing users' requirements remains a challenge for IT (Gorski and Ingram, 1994: 1.29).

With over 200 software packages available world-wide, the selection of one package can be a daunting one for managers. However, a few players dominate the Irish MDB package market in Ireland, and this obviously simplifies the selection process.

The concentration of this market in Ireland is probably due to the limited sales potential on our island. However, an increasing number of suppliers are serving the Irish market from bases in England and Northern Ireland. This provides the Irish manager with a wider choice of packages, but also restricts the level of pre-sales consultation, interface customisation and after-sales service options available. In this respect, a domestic supplier, with a comprehensive training and after-sales programme in conjunction with a good core MDB package, would be a better option for an Irish company.

The choice of MDB package is specific to each individual company. In selection and implementation of such a package, however, the manager should bear in mind that the investment in MDB software is a long-term one, and as such any evaluation of the software should match this long-term perspective. To enhance the quality of the selection process, the manager should start with business objectives and examine what they expect the software to do, rather than look to the software as a "quick-fix" solution to business problems.

Data Considerations

While the selection of software solution to the MDB is important, the company must also focus its attention on the actual data requirements for their specific situation. The data for the MDB will often exist on paper records within the organisation, unless it is a start-up scenario. This can often present problems for the company if the data are from several internal sources that store the data in different formats and/or different media. This conversion is often the first step to be considered before indiscriminately "dumping" data into the MDB.

The next step for the company is to state what levels of data are to be stored about each record on the database. The type and level of information to be retained on the MDB will largely be a function of the type of business the company is in. Obviously, the data on a consumer marketer's database will differ greatly from that on a business-to-business database. In addition, companies in the same industry will often desire to have different fields of data on their respective databases. Logan (1995) identifies the main types of people, address, accounts and activity data that should be included in all good MDBs.

It is also imperative that the organisation establishes a data policy at the outset. This policy should govern the management and capture of data in all functions of the organisation, to ensure that the quality of the data on the database is maintained at a consistently high level. Typically, this data policy should include a Data Entry Protocol to govern the format of data to be entered into fields on the database, and a framework for performing periodical database maintenance, to include merging duplicate records and deleting (or purging) obsolete records from the MDB.

It is important that the data policy be cross-functional, because data on internal order processing systems often ends up in the MDB, causing problems with inconsistency of data formats and unnecessary duplicate accounts being created. Having all of the data in one format will significantly reduce the need to de-duplicate the MDB, and will enhance the quality and reliability of data transfers from other internal systems.

Supplier Company Considerations

When implementing a package solution to the MDB, as with any software purchase, there are a number of key considerations. The company needs to assure itself that the supplier has the resources to provide quality back-up on the MDB software, while also having a successful track record of MDB software implementation. The main areas of consideration when evaluating alternative supplier companies are as follows:

- *Customers*: How many installed sites are the suppliers involved with? What kind of companies — across industries, blue-chip organisations and different application environments?

- *Credibility*: Is the supplier authorised to distribute the software in Ireland? Where does the software originate? How close are the supplier's ties to the software originator?

- *Continuity*: Will the supplier be around in the foreseeable future to service the MDB software? Will updates be available from them?

- *Consultation*: Does the supplier offer pre-sales consultation focused on the client's specific business needs? If so, do they supply a needs document connecting business requirements to software solutions? Is the supplier company customer-focused or sales-oriented? Have they a mix of both technical and business skills?

- *Customisation*: What level of skills does the supplier possess to customise the packaged solution to clients' specific needs? What lead times are involved?

Once the decision has been made to progress with a particular supplier, it is paramount that the company obtains their advice on system design, data management, data suppliers and general DBM issues. The MDB supplier is an invaluable source of relevant, current information about changes in the market and impending developments in the MDB software arena.

REFERENCES TO CHAPTER 7

Baker, M. (1984), *Macmillan Dictionary of Marketing and Advertising*, London: Macmillan Reference Books.

Courtheoux, R. (1984), "Database Techniques: How to Tap a Key Company Resource", *Direct Marketing*, August, pp. 68–84.

Cross, R. and J. Smith (1995) "Customer Bonding and the Information Core", *Direct Marketing*, February, pp. 28–37.

Dibb, S., L. Simkin, W. Pride and O. Ferrell (1991), *Marketing Concepts and Strategies*, European Edition, Boston, MA: Houghton Mifflin.

Dudman, J. (1995) "Integrated Circuits", *Marketing Week*, 15 April.

Gorski, D. and J. Ingram (1994), *"The Price Waterhouse Sales and Marketing Software Handbook"*, Pitman, London.

Jackson, B.B. (1985), "Build Customer Relationships That Last", *Harvard Business Review*, November/December, pp. 102–118.

Kotler, P. (1991), *Marketing Management — Analysis, Planning, Implementation and Control*, Seventh Edition, Englewood Cliffs, NJ: Prentice Hall.

Logan, Russell (1995), "Getting to Know Your Database", in B. Halsey (ed.), *The Practitioner's Guide to Direct Marketing Part 1*, Middlesex: The Institute of Direct Marketing.

McCutcheon, S. and P. Wang (1995), "Leveraging Database Marketing to Create a More Customer Focused Organisation", *Journal of Database Marketing*, Vol. 3, No. 1, pp. 65–84.

Mitchell, A. (1995), "The Royal Ascent of the Shopper", *Marketing Week*, 21 July, pp. 6–7.

Peters, T. and B. Waterman (1988), *In Search of Excellence*, New York: Harper and Row.

Raphel, M. (1995), *Up the Loyalty Ladder — How to Make Your Customer Your Best Promoter*, Dublin: O'Brien Press.

Reichard, K. and K. Yakal, (1995) "Share the Wealth", *PC Magazine*, August, pp. 243–244.

Shaw, R. and M. Stone (1988), *Database Marketing*, Hants, UK: Gower Publications.

Webster, F. (1995), "Executing the New Marketing Concept", *Marketing Management*, Vol. 3, No. 1, pp. 10–14.

Chapter 8

MARKETING RESEARCH, TESTING AND ANALYSIS

Donncha Ryan *and* Cathy McGennis

Overview

Few areas in marketing have lent themselves so readily, and stand to benefit so much from the application of quantitative and statistical techniques as does direct marketing. The advancement of direct marketing, and database marketing in particular, owes much to the exponential explosion of data sources, the development of new marketing research systems and technologies (Blattberg et al., 1994), and the growing availability of advanced analytical and statistical techniques. Last but not least there is an increasing recognition of its important and potentially pivotal role, and the determination to utilise it to best effect towards the marketing goals being pursued.

Marketing decisions cannot be predicated on judgmental and experiential frameworks only. Effective and optimal decision-making makes references to all available and appropriate inputs. Evolving and emerging techniques and methodologies should be viewed as supplementing rather than supplanting standard decision frameworks. Recognition of the role of analytical marketing approaches has happily been greatly enhanced in recent years, with many advocates and proponents demonstrating the imperative and subsequent benefits of a scientific approach to marketing analysis.

Data are the lifeblood of any decision system, particularly in the case of direct marketing. The acquisition, analysis and actionable usage of data and information are the key to a successful and profitable market strategy and implementation. A commitment to putting in place the requisite systems and structures such as the IT and database function, the ongoing data issues, etc., are well recognised. In direct marketing, there is the added dimension of sustaining and improving response performance — which can only be properly addressed and investigated by a commitment to ongoing marketing research and testing.

This chapter seeks to address some of the issues pertaining to the direct marketer's love affair with data, together with its many forms and uses, which if correctly engaged can lead to profitable and sustainable levels of performance. The data trail leads one from the initial assessment of needs to the acquisition of the data, through to the analysis stage and finally to the data-driven actions. Data may be acquired through market research, for instance, accessed through a database tool, analysed via a statistical technique and acted upon to deliver a tenable and justifiable solution. The core issues in this chapter will revolve around:

- *Marketing research*

- *Testing*

- *Targeting and response analysis,*

and their place in the direct marketer's toolkit of approaches.

MARKET RESEARCH IN DIRECT MARKETING

Introduction

Direct marketing is a marketing approach in which a company markets its products or services directly to the end user. Knowing your market can be just as important as penetrating that market. No matter how good you think your product is, it is virtually impossible to sell a product that people do not want.

Traditionally, direct marketing has not utilised market research techniques to the same extent as other methods of marketing. However, the role of market research in direct marketing has recently increased in importance. One of the main reasons for this is the vast improvement and increased accessibility of customer databases. In addition, the direct marketing industry has moved out of the realm of the small to medium-sized professional into large international firms who respect the value of long-term planning and are not just happy to know that a product is sold, but need to know why.

Market research can be used in direct marketing in the following areas:

- Identifying target prospects

- Classifying different types of customer

- Developing creative media

- Assessing customer requirements

- Identifying important product features

- Understanding the marketplace

- Post-campaign analysis.

Types of Market Research

The American Marketing Association defines market research as:

> The systematic gathering, recording and analysis of data about problems relating to the marketing of goods and services. (Quoted in University of Strathclyde, Dept. of Information Science home page, www.dis.strath.ac.uk)

Generally there are two main types of market research:

- Qualitative research

- Quantitative research.

Qualitative Research

Qualitative research is mainly used prior to a quantitative study to assess consumers' attitudes and behaviours. The main techniques used to gather data for qualitative research are:

- *Group discussions*: A group of people invited to a venue, with an informal atmosphere created and discussion on the topic

- *In-depth interviews* One-on-one interviews where the individual in asked in detail about their views on particular topics.

Market research techniques can be used to ascertain what motivates people to respond to campaigns.

Useful qualitative information which could be collected to differentiate your customers include (Magson and McLelland, 1997):

- *Attitudes to price*: Price elasticity, price competitiveness, price vs. quality, payment method and ease

- *Attitudes to brand*: Brand values, level of brand attachment, brand importance

- *Service and satisfaction*: Do service levels match, exceed or fall short of expectation for the product or service?

- *Consumers' view of your competitors*: Their preferences and how they differentiate in your market

- *Product*: Availability and location, differentiation, fashion or trend, necessity vs. luxury or appropriateness to lifestyle.

Case 8.1 shows an example of a qualitative research project:

CASE 8.1: AN POST NATIONAL MAILING

An Post conduct a national mailing each year containing product information from the different sections of the organisation and third parties, and a lifestyle questionnaire. Fitzpatrick Marketing Research was employed to conduct a qualitative study into the consumer's perception of this pack and direct mail in general. A total of six discussion groups from Dublin, Cork and Galway were organised. Each group had a different profile, e.g. female, C2D, living in Dublin northside. The groups represented a cross-section of the target market, i.e. participants from the previous survey, non-participants and potential participants.

   Group discussions involved in-depth discussions with a small homogenous group of people, typically seven or eight, in convivial surroundings, during which the moderator steers the flow of conversation through an agreed list of topics. These topics included views on the An Post mailing and other direct mail campaigns. During these discussions respondents are invited to give their opinions in a free-flowing manner, thus allowing underlying attitudes and opinions to be thoroughly probed.

Quantitative Research

Quantitative research is concerned with the "how many" questions. The main techniques used to collect data for quantitative research are:

- Field interviews

- Mail questionnaires

- Telephone questionnaires.

Some examples of quantitative research projects follow:

CASE 8.2: EMPLOYEE RELATIONS SURVEY

Insight Statistical Consultancy conducted an employee relations survey in a manufacturing company. A sample of 250 employees was asked to complete a questionnaire. There were 98 questions that made a statement and asked for a rating on a Likert five-point scale (an attitude measurement scale). The results were analysed using a variety of techniques, including factor analysis. The factors found explained up to 85 per cent of the variance and ranged from "Mistrust and Insecurity" to "Rewarded and Motivated".

CASE 8.3: KNORR FOODS LOYALTY MAILING

Knorr Foods implements a quarterly postal mailing of 18,000 of its customers. Included in the mailing is product information, recipes, new product development and a customer satisfaction survey. Lifestyle and attitudinal information is also collected. This can show the change in consumers' eating habits, e.g. after the beef scare, the changeover to other meat products and the increase in the use of pasta and noodles. This information can be used by new product development to create products to suit changing customer habits and build on the relationship that Knorr has with its customers.

CASE 8.4: ESB SATISFACTION SURVEY

ESB mailed Gold Shield Home Owners with a customer satisfaction survey. This mailing also identified any particular problems which customers incurred; these were then followed up and addressed.

CASE 8.5: AC NIELSEN ESTABLISHMENT SURVEY

AC Nielsen carries out an annual survey using a random sample of 2,500 people from the population. The aim of this survey is to define the characteristics of the TV viewing population. Field interviews are used to collect the information for this survey, where the interviewers call to homes of the selected individuals.

Research Data

The perfect situation for describing customers is to have information on every individual in the country. However, this is a difficult goal and hence inferences have to be made about consumers. A company will hold a certain amount of data on its customers, but often this information does not go beyond basic transactional data such as the balance of their account. These internal data can be fused with third-party data to assist in describing your customers better and finding more of them. Some third-party data sets that can be used are as follows:

- Electoral register

- Census data

- Lifestyle databases

- Classification systems

- Geographic information.

Electoral Register

The electoral register is collected every year and contains names and addresses of all individuals eligible to vote in the country. The electoral register file does not contain personal information about individuals, only their names, addresses and various geographic and constituency classifications. Information can be inferred from the register by comparing the file from one year to another; for example, movers and attainers can be identified. Movers are individuals who have registered at an address for the first time and attainers are eighteen-year-olds who have registered at an existing household.

Census Data

The census is carried out in Ireland every five years; the last was carried out in 1996. Census data can be purchased from the Central Statistics Office. It is important to note that personal information is not available from the CSO. Strictest confidentiality on an individual basis is maintained. The CSO provide data on an aggregated basis, the smallest of which is the District Electoral Division (DED). There are approximately 3,440 DEDs within the country and there are over 1,700 variables of information available for these areas. This information ranges from age and gender to means of travel.

These data can be used to draw inferences about the population in certain areas. Customer data can also be analysed by assigning DED codes to customer records and analysing what areas your customers live in (for example, urban/rural, social class etc.).

The Central Statistics Office also has other data sets available which are useful for research, including the following:

- Household Budget Survey

- Agricultural Statistics

- Labour Force Survey

- Vital Statistics Report — summaries of births, deaths and marriages.

Lifestyle Databases

Lifestyle databases are commercially available, containing information on consumers collected by different methods from individuals. The principal method of collecting this information is mail questionnaires such as the PMI Ltd. lifestyle questionnaire. These are questionnaires with incentives, containing demographic and lifestyle questions. These lifestyle questions can be sponsored by different companies to collect specific information.

Profiling Data

Profiling systems attempt to classify individuals by the demographics of the area in which they live (e.g. "Money and Brains", "Young Suburbans"). A combination of census data, lifestyle data and statistical methods such as factor and cluster analysis are used to create these classifications. These data can be used in a variety of different ways — appended onto an existing customer database, for instance, or used independently for planning mailshots. Systems currently available in Ireland include:

- Neighbours (PMI Ltd.)

- MOSAIC (Experian).

Among the systems available in the UK are:

- MicroVision (Equifax Europe Ltd.)

- ACORN (CACI)

- PRIZM (Claritas Group).

Geographic Information

Geographic information systems (GIS) are playing an increasingly important role in the direct marketing industry. To capitalise on the power of GIS, geographic co-ordinates need to be assigned to data sets. Data from the Ordnance Survey is available on many different levels, from county to household level. An Post and the Ordnance Survey will launch a National Geocoded Address Directory, which details individual addresses and their geographic co-ordinates. Systems available in Ireland include:

- PrecisionMap (PMI Ltd.)

- Daonra (Gamma)

- Prospex (Beacon & Dodsworth).

Other Research Data

Other research data sets which are used for analysis are:

- *Target Group Index (TGI)*: These data are extracted from a questionnaire answered by a representative sample of the population, who supply information on their use of hundreds of products and services, and approximately 400 brands. Their consumption of print and broadcast media is also captured. Additionally, their attitudes are measured by responses to over 200 discriminatory statements. Irish Marketing Surveys produce these data.

- *AC Nielsen Trade Directory*: AC Nielsen conducted a census of the retail trade in Ireland. Each retail outlet in the 195 towns and cities in Ireland with a population in excess of 1,000 was visited. The exact business activity and address of the business were established. This data set consists of 38,000 prime retail outlets, broken down into 50 distinct retail trade categories.

- *Joint National Listenership Research (JNLR) and Joint National Readership Research (JNRR)*: The JNLR shows average weekday listenership patterns during a 12-month period. The JNRR provides data on readership and cinema attendance during a 12-month period. Both surveys are from a sample of approximately 5,000 adults aged 15+ in Ireland. The findings are based on personal interviews, conducted in-home, by Lansdowne Market Research.

Summary and Comment

Summary

Market research and database analysis have an ever-increasing role to play in the direct marketing process. Methods can be applied at the beginning of a campaign to ascertain the target audience. Research techniques can be used at various stages throughout the direct marketing cycle. If you have a current customer database, then database analysis techniques such as CHAID and data mining can be used to segment your data (see the next section on testing). If no customer data are available, external information (census data, research studies, etc.) can be used in the prospecting process.

Direct mail is one of the main methods of direct marketing. One of the main advantages of this method is that there is great opportunity to measure the success of a campaign. Figure 8.1 summarises the direct marketing cycle, with reference to a direct mail campaign.

FIGURE 8.1: THE USE OF MARKET RESEARCH IN THE DIRECT MARKETING CAMPAIGN CYCLE

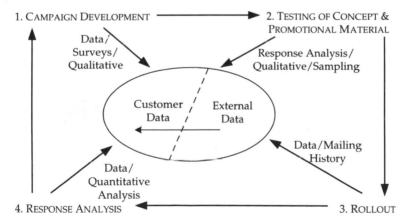

1. *Campaign Development*: The concept for the direct marketing campaign is developed using previous market research and customer data, e.g. the identification of high-responding segments.

2. *Testing of the Concept and Promotional Material*: Sample records are taken from the database to test different mailing designs and the content of the pack. The different concepts can then be assessed by analysing the responses of the sample and also by using qualitative methods.

3. *Rollout*: When the final campaign has been decided, the list can be generated from the customer database and/or an external list. Customers selected should be flagged for future analysis.

4. *Response Analysis*: The responders to the campaign are captured and entered into the database. These responders can then be analysed further to identify the high-responding consumers. The results of the response analysis can then be used for further concept development projects.

Comment

One of the main aims of using market research in the direct marketing area is to describe your customers better, identify your "best" customers and try to find more of them.

For example, our segment in Figure 8.2 depicts a segmented database. The segment A1 describes our "best" customers, such as customers whose orders have highest value. These customers can be described by using a combination of internal and external data and analytical techniques (e.g. married, with children, have a credit card). Now, campaigns can be designed to sell more products to this segment and to source prospects with similar characteristics.

FIGURE 8.2: SEGMENTED DATABASE

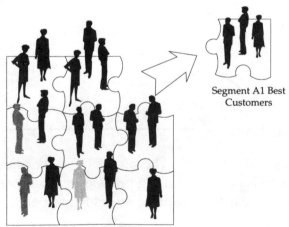

Segment A1 Best
Customers

The use of these geodemographic profiling techniques in Ireland has been somewhat inhibited by the lack of standard addresses and postcodes. The rate of development has not been as rapid as in other countries such as the United Kingdom, where postcodes are standard and there is a rich source of data available at this level. In the UK, profiling techniques have been used for nearly two decades and are now quite mature and varied. The feeling there now is that the ultimate target of one-to-one marketing may not be far away, and the current profiling techniques will help achieve that goal. The entrance into the Irish market of some of the UK's main players, Equifax and Experian, should increase awareness of the power of profiling and research tools in the direct marketing process.

Business information is tipped for huge growth in the next ten years as the use of technology and data-gathering increases; so too is the need to transform these data into information. The techniques and systems described in this chapter can aid this transformation.

TESTING IN DIRECT MARKETING

Introduction

At the heart of testing is the simple notion of discovering what marketing action or factors under our control work best in terms of evoking customer response and subsequent sustained involvement with a product or service.

Discovering what works, and repeating or improving it over time is undoubtedly an important element in contributing to the success of a company. Testing can take the form of a tentative first step in the case of a new product or service, or be a revisit and fine-tuning of a current product offering, ensuring its optimal viability, attraction and performance over its life cycle. It is a process of enquiry, but in its proper form is founded on sound statistical principles and practice. At a very basic level, testing can involve trying to establish which one of a number of mailing lists brings the best response or which media vehicle works best. A more complex situation might involve reference to statistical experimental design in identifying the optimal mix of components in a direct marketing campaign, where several factors at a time, rather than a single factor, are investigated.

Testing Benefits

Whatever the level of sophistication or complexity involved, certain benefits accrue from testing. Among the most obvious benefits are:

Risk Aversion

Testing is a recognition of, and response to, the inherent uncertainty involved in any marketing action and budget allocation. Normal risk aversion and caution suggests a measured, considered approach to any marketing decision. Testing appropriate samples in terms of size and representativeness goes a long way towards furnishing a reasonable prediction of likely customer response, thus facilitating a more productive and informed rollout.

The Factors

Testing allows you to build up a picture of the various factors which affect response to direct mailing programmes, and allows for measurement of their impact; which can be quantified through engaging modelling techniques for response analysis and prediction. This can in turn point out combinations and offers previously untried as being viable and worth adopting, or indeed identifying redundant or unprofitable offerings.

Information

Testing informs and thus allows for more certainty in marketing decisions, which in turn feed into other functional areas such as budget allocations, competitor and market share analysis, together with the attendant strategic implications.

Theory and Action

Testing is a natural offspring of market research, and can be viewed as a fundamental enquiry into consumers' perceptions, preferences and conceptualisations. Testing can contribute to theory building, theory validation or indeed to new avenues and directions for research. It is actionable in terms of its assessment of actual individual response to the stimuli presented via a real-life marketing setting.

Macro and Micro View

Testing by addressing immediate decision areas of a marketing programme promotes careful consideration of all aspects of the product and indeed the relationship with the consumer. This brings to the forefront of decision-making the macro and micro issues affecting response, and promotes an environment of constant enquiry across the entire marketing mix in the pursuit of ever-better performance.

Targeting

Testing explicitly recognises the value of both knowing and respecting your customer or prospect, by recognising the need for offering the optimal product bundle of attributes in the most efficient way. This is advanced by careful targeting or contacting of interested customers without using the blunt instruments of mass marketing, with its potential waste of valuable resources, not to mention the goodwill of poorly targeted prospects.

Change

Testing recognises and is an acknowledgement of the dynamic nature of marketing with its ever-shifting horizons of consumer tastes, demands and expectations, as well as the inevitable competitor activity. Testing is perhaps comparable to the surfer catching the waves (of opportunity) but constantly seeking the elusive better wave that is undoubtedly out there!

Testing Candidates

As in any activity, care needs to be taken when approaching or setting the levels of factors that have a considerable influence on the outcome. If experience or judgement suggest some factors as being dominant, then these may well be the obvious candidates for testing. If no prospective factors stand out, then one may well be faced with testing a variety of offers with a view to finding a promising combination. Although no hard and fast rules apply across all situations and contexts, it is generally accepted that the aspects to test include:

1. *Product*: The right product or service must be identified

2. *Offer*: The offer must match the segment requirements and be capable of evoking response. Issues involved might include incentives, payment terms, discounts, etc.

3. *Target Market*: Who is being targeted, what segments are being used and how have they been identified? What lists, internal or external, are being used?

4. *Price*: Obviously an extremely important component with direct implications for revenue and profitability. The price should be viable in terms of the product and the target market.

5. *Format/creative*: Establishing if the creative and format issues such as copy, colour of paper, envelope type, general layout, etc., can be tested.

6. *Contact strategy/timing/frequency*: Are the appropriate contact strategy and the right timing being employed? Some products/ services are time-sensitive in terms of demand, as determined by life cycles, seasonality, etc. Does mail plus telemarketing work as a better contact strategy than simply telemarketing? Finding the best contact frequency and building a relationship as opposed to incurring annoyance factors and wasted resources demands attention.

Figure 8.3 is an attempt to capture the various stages and milestones involved in going down the testing route, while Table 8.1 expands on the issues flagged in Figure 8.3.

FIGURE 8.3: THE "TESTING TRAIL"

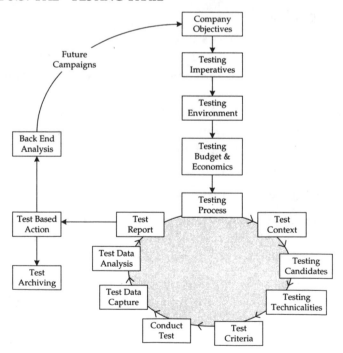

TABLE 8.1: THE TESTING TRAIL MILESTONES

Testing Imperatives	Testing Environment
• Recognising the needs/benefits of testing • A proactive approach • A scientific and rigorous approach	• Personnel and procedures in place • Tracking a dynamic market • A research/results focus
Testing Economics	**Test Context**
• The test budget • Large/small scale testing • Front end analyses • Break-even rates, lifetime values	• Reasons for the test • Importance of the test • Strategic/competitor issues • Comparative or predictive testing • Environment issues
Testing Candidates	**Testing Technicalities**
• Product/service • Offer • Price • Format/creative • Contact/timing • Any high impact factor	• Type of sampling technique • The type of experimental design used • Setting the sample size • Margins of error and significance levels • Test objectives/hypotheses addressed
Test Criteria	**Conduct Test**
• Response rates • Average order values • Conversion rates • Profit per unit mailed • Retention rates • Lifetime valuations • Return on investment • Cost per sale etc.	• Test must reflect full campaign • Monitor early results • Review and control of test
	Test Data Analysis
	• In-house or external agency • Basic/descriptive statistics • Advanced statistical/response analysis • Scenario analysis
Test Data Capture	**Test Based Action**
• Capture/coding/care	• Are the results decisive? • Partial or full rollout?
Test Report	• Further tests, reverse tests, retests?
• Conclusions/recommendations • Actionable summary • A decision support tool	• A new control? • Role of experience and judgement • External factors (competitor, deadlines etc.)
Test Archive	• Implementing and monitoring decisions
• Procedures and personnel assigned • Test objectives/rationale detailed • Test outcomes/reports detailed • Test actions and economics detailed • Test packs and samples available • A repository of recorded experience	**Back End Analysis** • Performance measurement • Profitability and budgeting • Tracking and lifetime valuations • Test/company objectives being realised?

Statistical Backdrop

In attempting to ascertain which factors and what levels of the factors work best, one must realise that testing involves elucidation and inference from part of the population under current conditions, to the whole population, hopefully under similar conditions. Thus no certainty can be conferred on any of the results deduced. Much has been written on the issue of statistical inference and hypothesis testing. In the case of direct marketing, given that there is an abundance of factors that could conceivably be tested, it is always worthwhile narrowing down the candidates to the main areas. In particular, factors likely to impact heavily on profitability and other performance measures constitute more compelling candidates for testing. Any testing involves outlay, and considerable cost may be associated with some tests. Consequently, it is important that the testing is justifiable in terms of a cost/benefit analysis. This requires quantifiability of all aspects, ranging from the measures to be tested to the likely monetary impact. A good testing programme and approach is hallmarked by a coherent set of measurable objectives that link to the wider marketing objectives pertaining to the targeted segments. This notion leads naturally to the concept of hypothesis testing, and the accompanying notions of confidence levels and levels of significance.

The Basics

The classic prescription in direct marketing in terms of testing involves testing one factor at a time whilst keeping other factors fixed. This isolation and study of a single factor allows assessment of its impact on performance, thus allowing decisions to be made regarding the optimal level of that factor. This approach suffers from an obvious over-simplification, in that it does not allow for an efficient study of interacting elements. Central to the process is the notion of a viable sample that is sufficiently large and representative of the target population, so that reliable estimates and reasonable inferences can be made from the results. The classic scenario involves probability samples from the population using one of a variety of sampling techniques. (The interested reader will find ample discussion of the various methods in any market research text.) The quantity of interest is measured using the sample data and inferences made. Typically either a point estimate or an interval estimate is computed or a hypothesis is tested, and on the basis of the sample data either validated, invalidated, or there exists insufficient information to come to a conclusion.

The Sample

Your sample constitutes your attempt to capture the essence of your target population, in structure and hopefully in behaviour. Given that you are likely to base future actions upon test results, you must have grounds for believing that your sample is a fair and representative snapshot of the population from which it was drawn. Ensuring this is the concern of sampling and survey methodologies (Scheaffer et al., 1990). Sampling can broadly be divided into two types, and further subdivided into their variants. These are the techniques of probability and non-probability sampling. Some examples of each type are as follows (Malhotra, 1993):

TABLE 8.2: SAMPLING APPROACHES

Some Probability sampling techniques	Non-probability sampling approaches
Simple random sampling	Quota sampling
Stratified sampling	Convenience sampling
Systematic sampling	Judgmental sampling
Cluster sampling	

Non-probability Sampling

One major consequence of the type of sampling conducted is the types of inferences and statistical estimation one can attempt. Non-probability samples do not generally allow for a proper assessment of sampling errors and easy sample size determination. Setting sample sizes in cases of non-probability sampling is not as well defined as in probability sampling. In many cases, non-probability sampling is employed in exploratory research, where preliminary results might be sought rather than conclusive research. Usage of non-probability sampling might be as a result of convenience, lower cost, the exploratory nature of the research, or where inferences to the population are not actively being sought. An application of non-probability sampling might be in concept or package tests, for instance. In setting sample size in cases of non-probability sampling, one is guided by allowable cost, past similar research projects, or even reference to an equivalent probability sampling approach. Whilst acknowledging the appropriateness and desirability of non-probability sampling, our main concern rests with probability sampling and its role in direct marketing.

Probability Sampling

Inclusion in a sample or test is dictated by probability and chance rather than simply by judgement. Each unit or individual has a particular probability of being selected. The simplest case is that of simple random sampling (SRS), where each individual has the same chance of being selected. The effect of this is that statistical inferences can be drawn. In particular, estimates of precision and sampling error are possible and confidence intervals can be generated.

Sample Size

Yes, size does indeed matter in testing programmes! A sample needs to be sufficiently large to ensure that reliable estimates can be obtained. The trade-off is typically between cost and accuracy. Obviously, cost increases with sample size, as does the precision of results. However, accuracy does not improve linearly with size; rather, diminishing returns to scale set in.

In general, many issues, both quantitative and qualitative, may well impact on the final sample size determination. These might range from list availability, resource constraints, the type of test design and analysis intended, importance of the test, population structure and so on.

The issue of sample size is generally addressed in the context of probability sampling (e.g. every N^{th} name on a list), with response rates, order values or profitability being the focus of attention. Thus in the case of a single sample/test one might be concerned with developing an estimate of the rollout response rate or likely profitability of the full campaign. The test gives an indication of likely response rates and whether break-even will be achieved.

Test Design

Testing is, as mentioned, fundamentally a process of enquiry. Limited resources are applied with a view to determining, for instance, the best combinations of factors for evoking response. It therefore makes compelling sense that tests be designed in the most efficient way possible. If the goal is to extract as much information as possible in the most cost-efficient way, and to develop statistically sound judgements, one must consider statistical experimental designs. The methodology of experimental design was developed in large part for the assessment and design of agricultural experiments, whereby yields due to different treatment combinations were under study. In the case of direct marketing, the yield may well be the response or conversion rate or lifetime valuations, and the treatments are the various offers, creatives, prices, etc.

Experimental design is a scientific approach to testing several factors at a time. The various components of a direct marketing programme such as price, list, copy, etc. are termed the *factors*, which in turn may be set at various *levels*. A *treatment* is a particular combination of factors and their levels. These treatments are then assigned to random segments of the population or house file. Assigning these treatments to the experimental units (e.g. individuals from a mailing list) is the concern of experimental design. The guiding principles of *replication, randomisation* and *blocking* are crucial for proper testing (Montgomery, 1991).

Replication or repetition of the treatment allows for the estimation of experimental error, and in cases where an average is being used in estimating the effect of a factor (e.g. average order value and the effect of method of payment), then replication allows for a better estimate of the effect. Randomisation involves ensuring that no systematic errors occur in results, by randomly allocating the experimental treatments. In cases where testing is carried out sequentially in time, the order of the tests should be randomised. Thus, randomisation helps reduce systematic bias. Blocking is used to increase the precision of a test. If a test is divided into groups which are relatively homogeneous — for example, different segments of a mailing list — these are viewed as blocks (Deere, 1996). If the same number of measurements are made on each treatment in each block and if the order in which the tests are carried out within a block is randomised, then we have what is termed a randomised block design.

Other types include so-called central composite designs (Hansotia, 1992), nested and hierarchical designs, split-plot designs and so forth. The reader who wishes to pursue a more detailed and comprehensive treatment of what is an area requiring some statistical knowledge and proficiency, is advised to consult texts on experimental design.

Advanced Analyses

There is a wealth of statistical techniques available that can be brought to bear in the context of data analysis for the direct marketer. Statistical and database software packages abound, and many analyses are but a few keystrokes away. It is worth reminding ourselves that with vastly increased computational power comes responsibility and justified caution. Appropriate application of advanced techniques requires care at several stages, and one must ensure that any underlying assumptions are adequately satisfied and data integrity ensured. Proper investigation and interpretation may in some cases require the attention of professional data analysts. Potentially far-reaching and costly decisions should not be founded on spurious or questionable data analysis, nor data integrity compromised by poor data capture, coding or care. Simple test designs may well result in simple analyses, whilst more complex statistical experimental designs generally merit more advanced analyses and help in the exploration of underlying relationships between variables.

Some of the techniques that might be employed are classical multivariate methods, whilst others are more recently developed approaches. The latter might include techniques such as neural networks and genetic algorithms, which tend to be computationally intensive, and data-driven algorithms. At the heart of the application of all these techniques, however, are the standard direct marketing concerns such as:

- Profiling high value customers and sourcing more
- Identifying likely respondents to direct marketing programmes
- Developing efficient acquisition and retention programmes
- Lifetime value enhancement
- Identifying cross-selling opportunities
- Developing efficient promotion and communication strategies and so forth.

Data sources, ranging from geodemographic and lifestyle data to electronic point-of-sale transactional data, have resulted in a potentially vast and rich vein of data for the analyst to scrutinise and utilise. Terminology such as data warehousing and data mining are suggestive of the modern problem/opportunity of a wealth of data held on databases awaiting analysis and action. Such analyses might result in the uncovering of unknown, complex or suspected relationships between variables of interest to the direct marketer. For example, a company with a complete transactional history of its customers, together with demographic and contact history, might use a neural network tool to predict future respondents to a particular promotion being planned, thus saving unnecessary contact and expense in the case of probable non-responders. Amex has been recorded as using neural network tools to scrutinise the hundreds of millions of entries on their databases to determine where and how the cardholders spend their money. This was with a view to customising their bills so that promotional offers would match the cardholders' purchase habits. Also, a response history over time can be generated so that, with market modelling, future likely response rates can be predicted (Lloyd, 1996). The list of possible beneficial uses is limited only by the technology and the imagination of the decision-makers.

The list of techniques in Table 8.3 makes reference to some of the methodologies and tools that can be brought to bear by the direct marketer, and some of the actionable outcomes resulting from their proper application. The list is by no means exhaustive and should only serve as a useful reference, linking techniques with quantitative issues that might be of concern to the direct marketer. A brief description follows for some of the main data analysis tools, and some simple examples prompt their potential application.

TABLE 8.3: A QUANTITATIVE TOOLKIT FOR DIRECT MARKETERS

Technique/tool	Typical application	Direct marketing uses
Analysis of Variance (ANOVA) Analysis of Covariance (ANCOVA)	Testing for treatment effects and interactions modelling	• Analysing results of test designs and finding best combinations of factors
Multiple Regression and its variants	Forecasting/ prediction Time series analysis	• Scoring and prediction • Contrasting and comparisons e.g. average order values of two lists
Logistic Regression	Prediction of whether an event occurs or not	• Scoring/ranking files developing a gains chart • Prediction of response
Multinomial Logit	Choice modelling in marketing research	• New product/concept evaluations
Discriminant Analysis	Classifying into groups profiling group members	• Profiling responders/ brand loyal consumers
Conjoint Analysis	Determining the relative importance of product attributes for new products or services development	• Segmenting and positioning • Market share estimation • Profitability analysis • Strategic advertising
Factor Analysis	Data reduction to facilitate insight or the application of other statistical analyses	• Reducing large numbers of variables to a smaller set of factors which can: • aid segmentation • point to optimal offerings
Multidimensional Scaling	Brand Mapping Perceptual Mapping Identifying the dimensions that describe consumer perceptions	• Developing positioning strategies • Segmentation analysis • Identifying "holes" in a market
Cluster Analysis	Generating clusters or classifications whereby units within clusters are "similar" and different from those in other clusters	• Segmentation of a database • Exploration of customer types for classification and profiling systems

TABLE 8.3 CONTINUED

Technique/tool	Typical application	Direct marketing uses
CHAID/CART	Interaction detection and breakdown Analysis of survey data and exploratory data analysis	• Segmenting a database using a designated criterion e.g. high or low aftersale level of support required in direct sales personal computers • ranking/gains charts • aids scoring model building
Loglinear Models	Categorical data analysis and multi-way contingency table analysis	• Testing for associations in multi-way tables • Predicting cell frequencies
RFM Analysis	Segmenting transactional databases across measures of activity and value	• Segmenting a database based on behaviour • Relationship marketing • Targeting and lifetime values
Neural Networks	Analysis of complex data structures, pattern recognition and forecasting	• Response analysis/ prediction • Segmentation • Use in conjunction with other tools in modelling
Automated Modelling	Model development and data mining	• Investigating data-driven solutions in modelling and data warehousing

Others might include: Correspondence Analysis (Sleight and Leventhal, 1992); Data Fusion approaches (Baker et al., 1989); Genetic Algorithms (Hurley et al., 1995); Expert Systems, Fuzzy Logic and Artificial Intelligence systems (Moutinho et al., 1994); Interactive Graphics; and so forth.

The following descriptions are of necessity brief and should primarily serve to highlight their potential uses within the direct marketing context. The reader who requires more detailed descriptions of the techniques and their features should refer to some of the suggested reading at the end of the chapter.

Conjoint Analysis

A firm developing a new product, concept or service may wish to determine which of a number of possible attributes or features of the product are the most important to the prospective buyer. Thus, a company might firstly identify the key attributes through previous research such as focus groups. Realistic and viable levels of these can then be tested, whereby various combinations of product attributes are presented in the form of a full concept, and preference scores or rankings can be assigned to each full concept by the candidates. A conjoint model can then be computed which allows both individual and group preferences to be computed and inferred. In this way, the most important attributes and the optimal levels to set them at can be identified as those giving the highest utility.

At a basic level, the model assumes that the total utility of a product is the sum of the individual part worths (utility scores) of the various attributes and their levels. Conjoint analysis can thus be employed as a segmentation device (Green and Krieger, 1991), whereby people who view certain attributes as being most important are grouped together. For example, a price-sensitive segment or a segment for which brand is an important consideration might be identified (Kucher and Hilleke, 1993). This might in turn feed into strategic advertising decisions, where emphasis is placed on attributes appealing to potentially promising segments. Geodemographic and lifestyle data, etc. might further allow the development of profiles and the targeting of similar customers. Conjoint analysis can also be used in conjunction with cost and market share estimates to help in modelling likely profitability of product offerings and help identify niche products.

CHAID (Chi-square Automatic Interaction Detector)

Consider a direct marketing concern such as a company mailing a catalogue to its customers and prospects. Targeting promising prospects represents a better return on investment. Consequently an outcome such as response/non-response or high/low order value might well be the initial focus of attention.

In the case of a categorical outcome variable such as response/ non-response, it would be of considerable interest and potential benefit to know which variables are most strongly associated with the desired outcome, and indeed what combinations offer the best chances of evoking a positive response from the rollout.

CHAID segments the population into segments defined by appropriate combinations and levels of the predictor variables through a process of splitting and merging (Magidson, 1993). The final results yield a number of segments that are mutually exclusive and cover all the tested units. Each segment is statistically different from all other segments in terms of the decision criterion (for example, response rate), and each segment is homogeneous with regard to the criterion, in that there is no appreciable difference between individuals within the particular segment in terms of response rate. The results are generally presented in either a tree diagram, which displays the various segments and describes them, or in the form of a gains chart. The latter facilitates the identification of the most responsive segments and only profitable segments need be targeted (Magidson, 1994).

This targeting naturally allows better allocation of resources and of course helps avoid unnecessary communication, cost and effort being expended. The catalogue mailer in a test mailing analysis might, for example, have found that the most responsive names were households with dual incomes, past purchase activity through direct mail, aged over 35 and urban. These might then be targeted in the rollout as the most promising segment, followed by other segments which are predicted to exceed break-even levels of response, or indeed sourced lists having individuals with the desired profile.

The CHAID analysis can be an end in itself as far as the analysis goes, or serve as a precursor to another technique. This might be the case in a follow-on logistic regression analysis, whereby likely interactions to include might be prompted by the initial CHAID analysis (Shepard, 1993). The CHAID might be used as a benchmark analysis and other tools or techniques compared to it in terms of their contribution to increased lifts in response rates and so forth.

The tree diagram in Figure 8.4 represents a CHAID analysis of a hypothetical file used by a company, say a bank, which is soliciting responses to a mailshot concerning a financial product. The issue of response to the mailshot is being studied, and various factors such as age, geocode, etc., of the prospects need to be investigated as segmenting variables, to aid in future targeting. The diagram shows that home-ownership was the most important factor, followed by age, and lastly the geocode area of residence. Other variables present were not found to be significant in the segmentation. The overall response rate was 1.32 per cent, but if home-owners are targeted, a response rate of 1.93 per cent could be expected. The nodes detail the numbers in each category and the corresponding response rate. For example, those in age category 6 and non-home-owners had the poorest response rates at only 0.81 per cent — obviously a segment to avoid contacting. Age categories 1–5 were merged, as were people in geocode 1 and 2 in the case of non-home-owners, as these were not found to be significantly different in response (Box 2).

FIGURE 8.4: A CHAID TREE DIAGRAM

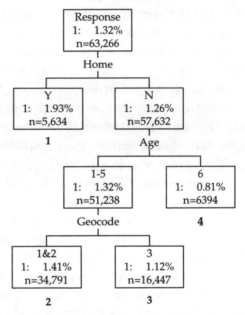

In all, the CHAID analysis identified four distinct segments (the four boxed nodes), each differing in response rates and profile.

These indicate the important interactions that might be investigated in a scoring model approach. Various tree sizes could be investigated, as could user-defined splits of the explanatory variables.

TABLE 8.4: A GAINS CHART

Tile	Size	Score	Index
20	12,653	1.64	124
40	25,306	1.52	115
60	37,960	1.48	112
80	50,613	1.41	107
100	63,266	1.32	100

Various gains tables can be generated which allow for better mailing decisions. For example, if various portions of the file are examined, one can judge expected performance. Going down the ranked file in steps of 20 per cent, one can see from Table 8.4 how the response rates (score) vary from 1.64 per cent for the top 20 per cent, which is 24 per cent above average (index = 124), down to the whole file, with a score of 1.32 per cent, which is given the index of 100.

CART (Classification and Regression Trees)

Another tree-based algorithm suitable for classification purposes is that of CART. In common with discriminant analysis, logistic regression, and CHAID, the technique allows for classifying prospects or respondents in a direct marketing programme. Unlike CHAID, the CART algorithm can handle both continuous and categorical explanatory variables. The CART approach typically involves using a portion of the data for constructing the tree (the learning data set) and the remaining data (holdout or validation data) can be used to compare various trees and subsequently choose an optimal tree (Haughton and Oulabi, 1993). This allows for the efficacy of the technique to be assessed and indeed performance compared to other benchmarks, or tools such as CHAID.

The CART approach consists of developing a series of binary splits, by selecting the best split on the best variable (Thrasher, 1991). Here, "best" means separating responders from non-responders, for instance. There are a usually a number of splitting criteria which can be applied, which address the issue of minimising the sample variance of the response variable. CART allows for user-specified priors and misclassification costs. For example, if the relative proportion of the two groups (respond:don't respond) was 3:97 — i.e. a response rate of three per cent — one can specify priors to reflect this. Misclassification costs allow one to include the issue of misclassifying. For instance, it is usually more expensive to misclassify a responder than to misclassify a non-responder. The technique builds and prunes trees until an optimal tree is arrived at, in terms of the level of accuracy it has in predicting response on the validation file or by cross-validation. CART also allows for detecting interactions and can thus feed into the development of predictive scoring models such as a logistic regression model.

CART is currently available as a standalone technique or as a companion technique to programmes such as CHAID, whereby the perceived weaknesses of one are counterbalanced by the differing strengths of the other (for example, the AnswerTree™ product by SPSS).

Discriminant Analysis

The issue of profiling and classification is one often encountered and mentioned in direct marketing. The ability to classify a person as being likely to be brand loyal or a heavy user as compared to not being, and generating a profile of what constitutes such a person, can prove useful so that similar persons can be identified and targeted from the house file or a rented list. The dependent variable of concern is thus typically categorical in nature — for example, classifying individuals as belonging to one of several possible groupings. A bank might classify a prospective applicant as potentially a good credit risk or not, or a company as likely to succeed or fail given its profile across a number of factors. In the case of a bank seeking cross-selling opportunities for one of its products, the factors to be used might include age, current account holders, number of years with the bank, home-owner, past query record, etc.

A discriminant analysis develops a scoring model that allows scores to be computed; the impact of each variable on the classification can thus be assessed. Discriminatory analysis can be exploratory or confirmatory and can be applied in the case of two or more a priori defined groups. As with most techniques, some assumptions are required for the proper use of the technique and violation of some or all of the assumptions can of course lead to misleading results (Hair et al., 1992). However, in any event, if one wishes to:

- Classify individuals into categories on the basis of their score across a number of explanatory variables

- Decide which of the variables are most important in terms of classifying power,

then two-group or multiple-group discriminatory analysis offers a potential solution. As an example, consider a direct marketing company using lists to cold-call prospects. In an effort to target the more receptive prospects, a test is carried out and data gathered across a range of variables. For instance, say the two categories are positive and negative reception to cold calling, whilst the other available information are age (X_1), income (X_2), number of dependants (X_3) and time at present address (X_4). A discriminant analysis might result in a so-called Z score being developed, whereby a discriminant function is computed where the coefficients allow a broad estimation of the impact of each factor in determining the classification of a given case. For example, if:

$$Z = .217X_1 + .201X_2 - .176X_3 - .103X_4 \qquad \text{(Equation 8.1)}$$

We would judge that age and income were the most useful variables for discriminating, with both having a positive impact. The other variables were less useful. Thus higher scores tended to place individuals in one category, and lower scores (e.g. high values for X_3 and X_4) tend to classify as belonging to the other group. Of course, there are the usual caveats as regards interpreting the output and the correct application of the technique. In the above example, the list could be scored using the Z function, ranked, and prospects identified accordingly. Misclassification results would generally be monitored to see if the model should be adjusted or if other variables are relevant.

Factor Analysis

Factor analysis is a set of statistical techniques that is often employed when a large number of variables need to be condensed down to a more workable or useful set of variables. Data reduction is the outcome of a factor analysis, whereby the original data is reduced to a smaller set of factors or dimensions with as little loss of information as possible (Morrison, 1990). Thus, an original data file consisting of, say, 60 variables per case, might following a factor analysis, be reduced to seven underlying dimensions which can be used in further analysis or as a basis for segmentation. Further analysis might take the form of regression or discriminant analysis. For example, a direct marketer might have attitudinal, lifestyle and demographic data and, following a factor analysis, might identify dimensions ranging from "conservative old-world values", to "progressive technos", and customise the offer or contact strategy accordingly. The dimensions or factors are identified, named and interpreted by the data analyst; of course, care in the use of the technique is required if used as a basis for subsequent action.

Multidimensional Scaling

Consider a company developing alternative positioning platforms in terms of its product or service. The company might highlight features such as benefits obtainable in a benefit positioning pitch, together with a price-positioning tactic. It is crucial to understand and evaluate your potential and current customers' perceptions, and the pivotal dimensions used by them in evaluating your product. Multidimensional scaling or perceptual mapping allows the analyst to compare objects, be they products, services, companies, etc., in terms of the respondents' perceptions regarding similarity or preferences among the objects (Green, Carmone and Smith, 1989). An object can be regarded as having both objective and perceived dimensions (for example, a particular model of personal computer having a particular price and memory specification, the brand name being a perceived dimension, whilst price and memory are objective). Insight can be generated about products or competitors. The analysis can help point to holes in the market or help in brand or company positioning strategies by identifying key dimensions used by customers.

Cluster Analysis

The direct marketer will often wish to group people together so that within each group a certain similarity prevails, whilst being different in some sense to people of different groups or clusters.

Cluster analysis provides a means of doing this segmentation task, whereby the technique reduces what may typically be a large data set into a small number of manageable clusters or groups. These groups can then be scrutinised and profiled using other techniques, and, from a marketing concern, different offers, communication strategies and so forth can be developed and better returns on marketing spend recovered. The technique of cluster analysis has been applied particularly to geodemographic data. The well-known UK neighbourhood classification systems were a result of the application of clustering techniques (Ozimek, 1993). The ACORN (A Classification Of Residential Neighbourhoods) system uses census data and clustering techniques to develop the various groupings, whilst PIN (Pinpoint Identified Neighbourhoods) uses a combination of principal component analysis and cluster analysis to produce the various groupings. MOSAIC similarly is a cluster solution in which census and non-census data are subjected to clustering algorithms.

Cluster analysis is a non-statistical technique and different issues may and often do impact heavily on the outcome. The number of clusters to form, the technique used (hierarchical or non-hierarchical), profiling, interpreting and validating are all issues that need careful consideration (Hair et al., 1992). As an example, consider a large shopping centre analysing its proposed catchment area in terms of the customer/prospect types present. Census data, household budget survey data together with GIS (geographic information systems) tools could be used, and cluster analysis, together with customer-type mapping, performed and profiles developed, thus identifying appropriate mixes of outlets to develop, etc. Another example might be a health and fitness centre catering for a certain profile of user, such as a cluster labelled "mudips" (mature urban dual income professionals). The centre can visually identify, in map format, the heavy concentrations of this customer type and make better-informed decisions.

Logistic Regression

In marketing, one is often concerned with the occurrence or non-occurrence of an event. The event in question might be purchase/non-purchase of a product, the response/non-response outcome of a direct mailshot, the success or failure of a new product, and so on. In cases such as these, where the outcome variable is binary, the standard regression approaches are not appropriate. Logistic regression is a technique tailored and developed to address situations where the dependent/outcome variable is dichotomous and one is concerned with estimating the probability that the event occurs or not. Estimating the likelihood, and finding the most important predictors and a functional form for their relationship with the binary outcome variable, can provide valuable information to the direct or database marketer. The approach involves modelling the natural logarithm of the odds as being a function of the explanatory variables, where the odds are simply the probability of occurrence, p, divided by the probability of non-occurrence, 1–p.

Logistic analysis possesses many of the strengths of standard regression in that it builds upon well-developed and understood theory (Hosmer and Lemeshow, 1989). It allows for statistical testing, confidence intervals and prediction, accommodates interactions and non-linear effects, diagnostic and residual analysis, customised and automated model building, etc.

Logistic regression models can be developed and compared in terms of efficiency with other techniques such as neural networks or CHAID (Furness, 1992). For instance, in a response analysis of test data the outcome variable might be response (coded 1 for response and 0 for non-response) to a test mailing by a charity soliciting contributions from its donor database for a humanitarian project. A logistic regression model might be estimated and result in an equation such as:

Logit = $\log_e$ (odds)

$$= A_0 + A_1X_1 + A_2X_2 + A_3X_3 + B_1D_1 + B_2D_2 + B_3D_1D_2 + B_4D_4 \quad \text{(Equation 8.2)}$$

where X_1 = number of years on patron database

X_2 = number of previous responses to previous special project solicitations

X_3 = average yearly donation

D_1 = 1 if standing order relationship in place, 0 otherwise

D_2 = 1 if male, 0 if female

D_3 = 1 if regular newsletter being received, 0 otherwise.

A_0, A_1, . . . B_4 are the model parameters, to be estimated from the data

The logistic regression model allows for:

- Scoring each individual on the database and developing a ranking procedure or gains chart to facilitate targeting of likely responders and classification by response

- Predicting response rates for individuals and developing a profile of typical responders so that prospects with a similar profile can be targeted

- Identifying and gauging the relative importance of the different explanatory variables in terms of their impact on the odds of responding

- Testing of various hypotheses of interest, such as whether using regular newsletters as a vehicle for relationship building and lifting response rates has a high impact.

RFM Analysis

RFM (recency, frequency, monetary value) analysis is an intuitively simple yet potentially powerful approach to segmenting your customer database and providing a basis for marketing action such as promotional mailing and relationship marketing. A customer database with fields detailing aspects of transactional history is a prerequisite. In particular, coding for recency of purchase (often coded 1 to 5, with 5 being assigned to the most recent quintile), frequency and monetary value and possibly product category, is applied and added to the database. Thus each customer has three codings added to their record (Hughes, 1994). If quintiles are used, the top 20 per cent are coded 5 down to a coding of 1 for the last 20 per cent. Hence, across the three measures, there are 125 possible RFM cells ranging from (555) down to (111). These are automatically updated with each transaction and consequently a profile by transactional behaviour is developed so that at a glance one can judge the value of a customer across these measures. Some database packages include RFM-type analysis as a standard feature, allowing prospect selection on bases such as pulling out customers with order values above some threshold, together with a recency requirement (for example the *Faststats* database package, from Appropriate Ltd.).

Test mailings can help identify profitable contact RFM cells so that rollout is directed only towards RFM cells exceeding break-even response rates. Typically an Nth sample (for example, every 40th name) is drawn from the full file and mailed. The response rate is then recorded for each RFM cell and compared to break-even response. Thus, winning cells (i.e. those exceeding breakeven) are chosen for rollout. This can easily be handled in an automated way by a spreadsheet, as can the issue of tracking RFM cells in terms of lifetime values, whereby longer-term concerns can be assessed, and relationship marketing programmes developed. If other overlay data, such as demographics, business-type codings, etc., are available, then an added return on the database investment is possible, if profile analysis is conducted on the best customer groupings and consequently like prospects can be targeted.

Multiple Regression

The statistical technique of regression is probably the best-known and most widely used of modelling approaches. In many ways it has been the workhorse of modelling, and over time a considerable bank of knowledge and experience has been built up in the marketing industry regarding its use and indeed misuse. In common with any proper application of a technique, one should be informed about its proper use and any assumptions underpinning its validity as a predictive or descriptive tool (Kleinbaum et al., 1988). Multiple regression in its simplest form involves relating a metric dependent variable to a set of explanatory or independent variables. A particular relationship may be posited and subsequently tested, or a range of possible models investigated to see which provides the best fit to the data. The generation of a predictive model is usually the goal of a regression analysis. From the data and model description of the relationship between the dependent and independent variables, one can then attempt to forecast the values for the dependent variable for given levels of independent variables. Hence, inferences for the population are possible and predictions or forecasts can be generated together with the testing of hypotheses. Rather than develop a discussion around the technicalities, a simple example is presented, illustrating a possible use and benefit of the technique.

Consider a large supermarket chain operating a loyalty card scheme in which promotions are tailored to the spending patterns of the customers. Bar-coded coupons are sent out and their redemption monitored for the test mailing group and the basket spend recorded.

The store might wish to model average basket spend with coupon use compared to non-coupon occasions. A linear regression model might result in the following:

$$Y = A_0 + A_1D_1 + A_2D_2 + A_3D_3 + A_4D_4 + A_5D_5 + A_6D_2D_3 + B_1X_1 + B_2X_2 \quad \text{(Eqn. 8.3)}$$

where Y = basket spend on coupon occasion

D_1 = 1 if previously redeemed coupons, 0 otherwise

D_2 = 1 if household size >4, 0 otherwise

D_3 = 1 if redeemer female, 0 if male

D_4 = 1 if resident in geocode 1, 0 otherwise

D_5 = 1 if resident in geocode 2, 0 otherwise

X_1 = length of time in months on loyalty card

X_2 = store index relating to frequency of visits, total spend and loyalty card points built up in the past six months

$A_0, \ldots, B_2$ are the model parameters estimated using the test data.

The model thus provides a description of the impact of the relevant variables on the variable under study, in this case basket spend. It has to be realised that omitting important variables, insufficient data, improper model specification or technique application, can all lead to a poor model and basis for marketing action. Notwithstanding these caveats, the model above lends potentially valuable insight into, and understanding of, the various interactions of marketing mix elements and customer profiles. For example, from the model the store might realise that targeting certain households according to their size and geographical location is more profitable, especially if promotions are directed and relevant to female shoppers. The impact of the loyalty card might be captured by variables like X_1 and X_2 and inferences drawn. The list of questions that might be addressed in the above context is indeed extensive and should serve to demonstrate the value of the technique and that of modelling in general.

Neural Networks

Developing a relationship between a set of input and output variables can be tackled quite successfully using regression-based approaches, if the relationship is of a relatively simple form. In cases of complex or highly non-linear relationships, a non-parametric algorithm may be the only approach. Thus, if the more traditional data analysis techniques are not useful or appropriate, and one seeks to investigate complex patterns and unearth trends in data, then neural network tools offer a way forward (McFarland, 1995).

Traditional statistical techniques often hinge on certain assumptions about the data and likely functional forms for the relationships between response and predictor variables. Neural computing generally requires no assumptions about the data and can be applied to a set of training data. This so-called learning approach can be supervised or unsupervised. In the supervised mode, the neural network trains on past data, where both the inputs (e.g. demographic and transactional data) and outputs such as response data are available. The neural network analyses the data and develops a set of predictions which are compared with the actual outputs, and continues to adjust the model until predicted outputs are as close a match as possible to the observed outputs (Shepard, 1993). This form of learning can be applied to the tasks of classification and prediction as might be required in time series forecasting.

The less widely used (from a marketing standpoint) unsupervised learning approach is often used to group and cluster data. In the unsupervised mode, the network could, for example, be used by a company with a strong brand. If large-scale advertising in various publications is seen as crucial, then commissioning research on the readership of these publications, obtaining a range of demographic, lifestyle and attitude data and analysing the data to group the audience into clusters would facilitate a more effective communication strategy, matching corporate objectives and image to the audience via the message and vehicle. This issue of applying neural networks to the task of market segmentation is one that has received considerable attention (Severwright, 1996).

Automated Modelling Tools

These refer to systems that allow for the investigation of a large range of modelling approaches to the data in an effort to determine which model works best. Thus, such a system might allow for predictive modelling and profiling to be conducted, and instead of manually trying to determine which of a multiplicity of potential modelling approaches works best for the data, a number of different models are fitted and the best chosen. Such modelling capabilities could be integrated with geodemographic and mapping products and segmentation tools to provide an integrated approach to developing solutions rather than first-stage type analysis.

Thus, as regards generating a "best" model, one needs to evaluate and compare competing models, which becomes an iterative process as models are developed, improved and compared with others. Intelligent search techniques are employed to identify the best model, and these can range from genetic algorithm search to the application of CHAID. An automated modelling tool might include the use of linear regression, logistic regression, RFM, CHAID, genetic algorithms and neural networks (for example, the *Model 1* software product by Group 1 Software Company). Consequently, literally hundreds of models can be generated, tested and compared using all the techniques, and a "best" model developed. The automated nature of the analysis allows for maximising the chances of finding a good model in what otherwise might be a nightmarish task of investigating a plethora of possible model types with a manual approach, and the possible attendant bias of the modeller.

Summary of Testing and Analyses

Testing involves commitment in terms of time, thought and resources. It needs to be approached in a structured and methodical way if the benefits are to be properly realised. Testing, if properly conducted, yields information and insight, at a price. Consequently, one should:

- Decide on what is to be tested and why. Experience and judgement may well play a major role at this stage.

- Detail the objectives, cost/benefits and quantify where possible.

- Decide on the budget to be allocated to testing; again a rationale as to its level is appropriate.

- Determine the structure of the testing — whether it is a simple or sophisticated testing process. Construct the test design, choose the sampling method and determine sample sizes having regard to practicality and statistical validity.

- Put in place a system or structure to advance the enquiry process that is testing, thus facilitating the actionable potential of test data. This will require commitment to, among other things: staff training; data capture, coding, care, archiving; analysis and implementation; and continual review and control.

- Decide on the range of analyses that are appropriate or available, recognising their inherent value or potential weakness as part of the decision support system. Analyses may range from basic summary statistics such as counts, frequencies and cross-tabulations, to the application of predictive models for use in targeting and segmentation or profiling.

- Retain a commitment to ongoing testing which may involve improving current controls, retesting or reverse testing, etc.

- Recognise the value of test information and the testing history of your company. Past test programmes give insight and potentially valuable information. A test campaign archive detailing past testing programmes and all relevant data and outcomes (information on what was tested and why, test descriptions, results summary, action taken, test packs, dates, source codes key and form numbering, etc.) can constitute a further return on investment and feed into current decision processes such as test budgets. In short: learn from *recorded* experience.

- Maintain a clear focus on the economics of your direct marketing test campaigns. Both front-end and back-end performances need to be measured and monitored. This involves a commitment to data. In the case of back-end performance, tracking each individual in terms of purchase history, source of origin, type of offers responded to, cross-selling, etc., can aid future marketing decisions and evaluation of current marketing efforts.

As regards the issue of data — given that data are generated by testing, analysed and acted upon — it is patently necessary to employ statistical and database tools, in order to produce sound and reasonable decisions. Utilising appropriate tools and techniques will go a long way towards getting the data to tell its story, which after all is the story of your customer, product, and environment. This is one particular story for which the ending is partially under our control, particularly if a commitment to marketing research, testing and analysis exists, and resources in terms of people, processes and technology are in place.

TABLE 8.5: SUMMARY OF SOME ISSUES MATCHED WITH POSSIBLE TECHNIQUES

Issues	Techniques
Profiling/Classifying	Discriminant Analysis Logistic regression
Segmentation	Cluster Analysis CHAID/CART Conjoint Analysis
Response Analysis Modelling	Multiple Regression Logistic Regression Neural Networks
Prediction/Planning/ Ranking/Targeting	Multiple/Logistic Regression Neural Networks/Genetic Algorithms
Data Reduction	Factor Analysis
Association	CHAID or Loglinear Analysis
Sampling issues	Marketing Research Sampling Theory
Profitability	Financial Modelling
Mapping	Correspondence Analysis Multidimensional Scaling
Tracking/Lifetimes	Spreadsheets/Database Analysis

MARKET RESEARCH CASE STUDY: BLOOMFIELDS

General Introduction

Cawley Nea Ltd., an Irish advertising and marketing agency, conducted a launch of a new high-quality supermarket campaign on behalf of its client Bloomfields. PMI Ltd. carried out research and analysis techniques for Bloomfields' direct mail campaign.

Background Information on Bloomfields

The client, Bloomfields, decided to use direct mail as a vehicle for promoting the opening of their first store in Dun Laoghaire. The store is a premium food hall with emphasis on quality, choice and customer service. Most previous direct marketing campaigns for retail outlets in the country to date have been cheap "special offer" unaddressed door-drops. This method works well for the general outlet. However, Bloomfields needed to look at a more upmarket and targeted series of mailing campaigns to position itself as the premium food hall.

It was decided that the mailing would contain an invitation letter to visit the store, a glossy brochure and redeemable coupons. A questionnaire was also placed on the reverse of the letter.

Identification of Prospects

As Bloomfields was a new store, this campaign was started without customers; hence the first stage was to identify prospects for the mailing. This was approached using a combination of lifestyle information held on PMI's Irish Consumer Marketing Database (ICMD) and the 1991 Census data. The analysis tools used were *PrecisionMap* Geographical Information System (GIS), *Neighbours* from PMI's suite of analysis tools, and the *SPSS* Statistical Software package.

Identification of District Electoral Divisions (DEDs)

Census information was used to identify suitable DEDs in Dun Laoghaire and its surrounding areas from which appropriate individuals would be selected for the mailing. The DEDs in the area were categorised according to the penetration of social classes A and B who reside in the division. This was calculated from 1991 Census data. This information was then displayed on a map in PrecisionMap (see Appendix A).

The map displayed the penetration of the A's and B's by shading the higher penetration. From this map, a number of target DEDs were selected based on their penetration of social class AB. These target DEDs were used as a basis to select suitable mailing prospects.

There can be several hundred households in a DED; as a result the data held at DED level is not as accurate as pure lifestyle information, which is at individual level. However, there was insufficient pure lifestyle information available for the scale of this mailing. Hence, a geographic level between individual and DED level had to be used to combine the volume of the census data with the accuracy of the household data (see Figure 8.5).

FIGURE 8.5: NUMBER OF PROSPECTS VS. ACCURACY OF DATA

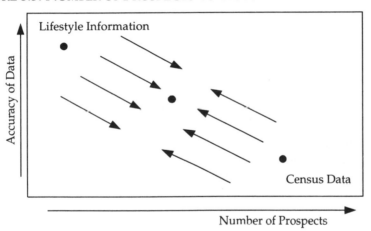

Identification of Thoroughfares

The lifestyle information held on the ICMD at an individual level was used to drill down into the data selected at DED level to define a smaller profile unit.

Consumers who had expressed an interest in food and wine in the target DEDs were selected off the ICMD. These prospects were then passed through PMI's *Neighbours* profile system. This profile system identifies the thoroughfares on which these customers live. Other consumers who live on these thoroughfares are then detected. Thoroughfares were classified by the penetration of food and wine enthusiasts who live on them and prospects were selected by this criteria.

For example, Dalkey Upper was selected as a target DED. Angle-sea Park is located in this DED; there are four (fictional) people inter-ested in food and wine living on that road, according to lifestyle information.

FIGURE 8.6: SAMPLE DED

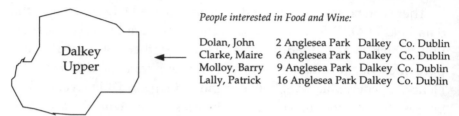

People interested in Food and Wine:

Dolan, John	2 Anglesea Park	Dalkey	Co. Dublin
Clarke, Maire	6 Anglesea Park	Dalkey	Co. Dublin
Molloy, Barry	9 Anglesea Park	Dalkey	Co. Dublin
Lally, Patrick	16 Anglesea Park	Dalkey	Co. Dublin

There are a total of 20 households on this thoroughfare, and four ex-pressed an interest in food and wine. Hence the penetration of peo-ple interested in food and wine is 20 per cent. The remaining 16 householders were identified as prospects.

Selection of Prospects

The combination of Census data at DED level and lifestyle informa-tion at household level allows us to profile a greater number of peo-ple with greater accuracy. The names and addresses of 50,000 targeted prospects were selected from the Irish Consumer Marketing Database (ICMD) based on the thoroughfare on which they live.

Mailing

The main objective of the mailing pack was to get people to actually visit the store. The pack was a high-quality one containing a letter, glossy brochure and coupons. The letter (see Appendix B) introduced the general manager and the main attractions of the store. The reader was invited to visit and share the new *shopping experience*. A total of eight coupons were included, which were redeemable in the store and were valid for approximately one month.

A questionnaire was positioned on the reverse of the letter, the objective of which was to find out about customer requirements and profiles. The questionnaire consisted of demographic, lifestyle and preference questions. One of the main aims of the mailing was to en-courage people to visit the store. Hence the reader was asked to return the completed questionnaire to the information desk in the store. The data collected from this questionnaire (Appendix C) could then become the basis of a customer database, as the responder would actually have shopped in the store.

A glossy colour brochure was included which introduced the store, the key personnel and "the many flavours of the food hall". A map of the store location was also included.

Questionnaire Analysis

These responders to the mailing are of a high quality, as they are not just passive responders, because they actually visited the store to return the questionnaire. Hence these responders can be classified as customers and can become the base of a customer database. The questions asked were therefore geared towards profiling the customers and being able to segment them for future campaigns.

Several types of questions were asked on the questionnaire. The first three questions were concerned with demographic information (age of respondent, composition of the household and ages of the children). All of this information helps build up a picture of the customer. For example. families with children under the age of five will have different needs to a more mature family with adult children.

The lifestyle section included questions on types of hobbies and interests that the customer has; this is useful information for creating a profile of the customer. This specific information can also be used for future in-store promotions — for example, inviting all customers interested in wine to a launch of a new range of wines.

As Bloomfields is a new store, it is of interest to see what store the customers usually visit for their weekly shopping. This information can also help in describing the customers — a typical Superquinn customer will differ from a typical Dunnes Stores customer.

The preference question related to the factors that influenced where they shopped. Responders were asked to rank these in order of importance. This information can lead to the store placing more emphasis on factors deemed more important to their customers.

The customer was given the opportunity to select which type of information they would like to receive from Bloomfields. This ensures that they receive information that is of interest to them.

Conclusions and Recommendations

This initial campaign was very successful in launching the Bloomfields store. It created awareness of the Bloomfields Food Hall with its individual and high calibre mailing. There was a good response to the questionnaire, as the respondents were of a high quality, having actually visited the store to return the questionnaire. Figure 8.7 shows a summary of the campaign process.

FIGURE 8.7: SUMMARY OF BLOOMFIELDS CAMPAIGN

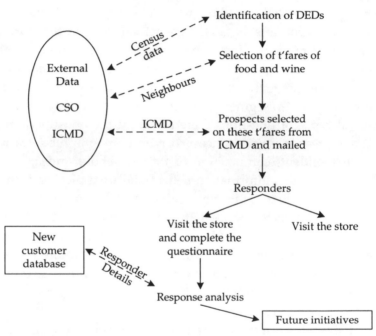

This exercise was also successful in collecting customer data as the initial phase in a database marketing programme. There are now many opportunities to work on in the future. Some suggestions for future project direction and development are outlined below.

Challenges of the Project

Many profiling and segmentation systems available in the world today are based on the postcode. The lack of postcodes in Ireland make the profiling of geodemographic data in this country a different science. The techniques used to profile the prospect base for the Bloomfields campaign circumvented this problem and allowed the available information to be used sensibly. The census data alone could have been used, but the addition of the pure lifestyle information refined the selection and led to more precise prospect targeting.

The aim of most organisations using direct mail today, and particularly that of Bloomfields with its high-calibre product, is to make sure that only interested parties receive their mailing and to avoid the "junk mail" label. The profiling methods used in this campaign provided a vehicle to achieve this goal.

Database Marketing

As previously mentioned, the data from this campaign has been collected taking into consideration the setting-up of a customer database. All other data collected on customers or prospects should be added to this database. Data on non-responders would also be useful to keep, whether it is to exclude from subsequent mailings or to profile against the responders. Particular to this mailing are the *invisible* responders, those who did respond to the mailing by visiting the supermarket but did not complete a questionnaire. Their response was not measured. One way of measuring these responders would be to personalise the coupons included in the mailing and hence track the coupon redemption back to a specific mailing.

As more data is collected on customers and the database grows, there will be more substance to segment the database. This means classifying your customers into similar groups (e.g. empty nesters, double income no kids, etc.). These groups can then be specifically targeted, based on the assessment of their needs.

There are a range of statistical techniques which can be used for this process, as described earlier (for example, factor and cluster analysis and CHAID analysis). The collection of data should always be consistent to facilitate the use of these models.

Further Analysis

During the post-campaign analysis, we looked only at the responders. However, as mentioned already, it is also useful to look at the non-responders to a campaign. At this stage in the project, we have little information on non-responders, outside of the DED and thoroughfare information, which was known for all 50,000 prospects. If the database itself is remailed, the responders and non-responders can be analysed based on the fields of information stored.

The data from the question referring to the factors which influence where you shop could also be investigated more. A multivariate technique such as multiple scaling could be used to analyse the relationships between each of the factors of influence. A perceptual map is a clear way to present the findings of this type of analysis.

Future Campaigns

Future campaigns can be based upon the results of this project, from mailing the specific interested individuals to profiling the responders and sourcing prospects with a similar profile. Bloomfields may, for example, decide to launch a new range of cooking sauces and mail invitations to those individuals who expressed an interest in cooking and new products.

A mailing history of persons mailed for campaigns and responses should be kept on the database, and after time a picture of the "best" mail-responsive customers can be drawn. Bloomfields can then tap into external databases such as the PMI's ICMD and select new prospects with a similar profile to their top customers.

APPENDIX A: PENETRATION OF ABS IN DUN LAOGHAIRE BY DED

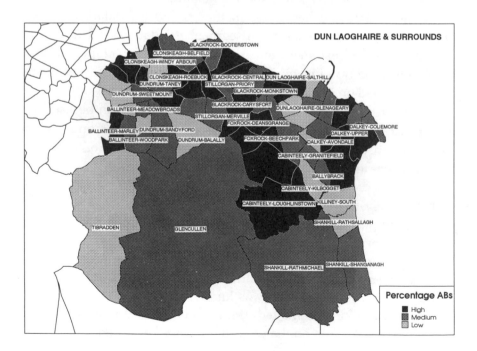

APPENDIX B: BLOOMFIELDS LETTER

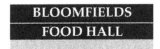

A. Name
Address
Address

May 1997

Dear Ms Name,

Something very exciting is happening in Dun Laoghaire — grocery shopping will never be the same again. I'm Tony Curran, General Manager of the new Bloomfields Food Hall and I'm delighted to tell you we're open from May 28th, here in the Bloomfields Centre right in the heart of Dun Laoghaire.

We have combined a stunning selection of the best, most tempting and delicious fresh foods with the widest range of branded grocery items, including many speciality items you won't find elsewhere. Added to this is our truly spectacular Off-Licence. "The Vine" at Bloomfields will be a wine lover's paradise.

All of this in a spectacularly spacious store with great wide aisles which allow you to browse at ease, and most importantly allows you to do all your grocery shopping under one roof.

You'll be welcomed and well looked after by our team, all of whom are highly trained and actively want to make sure that you enjoy every minute you spend with us.

Convenience is a big factor at Bloomfields. A very accessible large car park, and all the services you might need including free home delivery, to make your visit to Bloomfields hassle-free.

To make sure we are doing everything we possibly can for you, I would be very grateful if you would complete the enclosed questionnaire. You'll find the details if you just turn this page over.

I'm personally inviting you to come and visit us at your earliest opportunity — because I, with the rest of my staff, believe that we have created a shopping experience which I know you will enjoy. To add to your enjoyment I have enclosed a selection of tempting offers for you to try.

Yours sincerely,

Tony Curran
General Manager

BLOOMFIELDS FOOD HALL, BLOOMFIELDS CENTRE, GEORGE'S STREET LOWER, DUN LAOGHAIRE
TELEPHONE (01)230 1863. FAX (01)230 1879

APPENDIX C: BLOOMFIELDS QUESTIONNAIRE

QUESTIONNAIRE

1. Please indicate with an "X" your age group

    18–24 ☐   25–34 ☐   45–54 ☐   55–64 ☐   65+ ☐

2. How many people live in your home?

    Adults _____   Children under 18 _____

3. Number of children in each group

    Under 1 year _____   1–4 _____   5–9 _____   10–14 _____   15–17 _____

4. Interests and hobbies

    Gardening   ☐   Cooking ☐   Wine   ☐
    Theatre Arts   ☐   Food   ☐   Music   ☐

5. Which of these foodstores do you use for your weekly shopping?

    Superquinn ☐   Super Valu   ☐   Crazy Prices ☐   Dunnes   ☐
    Londis   ☐   Quinnsworth ☐   Centra   ☐   Other   ☐

6. Please rank in order of importance the following factors that may influence
    where you shop (where 8 is most important and 1 is least important)

    Special Promotions   _____
    Parking Facilities   _____
    Opening Times   _____
    Price   _____
    Quality of Products   _____
    Variety of Products   _____
    Loyalty Card   _____
    Convenience   _____

7. Please tick what information you would like to receive from Bloomfields in the future.

    Special Promotions   ☐   New Products   ☐   Product Advice   ☐

    Complete and return this questionnaire to our courtesy desk at Bloomfields
    before July 13th and you will be automatically entered into a draw for five
    luxurious Bloomfields Hampers

REFERENCES TO CHAPTER 8

Baker, K., P. Harris and J. O'Brien (1989), "Data Fusion: An Appraisal and Experimental Evaluation," *Journal of the Market Research Society*, Vol. 31, No. 2, pp. 153–212.

Barth, P.S. (1995), "Mining for Profits in the Data Warehouse," *Journal of Database Marketing*, Vol. 3, No. 1, pp. 285–296.

Blattberg, R., R. Glazer, W. Haas and J. Little (1994), *The Marketing Information Revolution*, Boston: Harvard Business School Press.

Bretton-Clark, *Conjoint Designer*, Version 3, (Software) User Manual, Morristown, NJ: Bretton-Clark.

Bretton-Clark, *Conjoint Segmenter*, (Software) User Manual, Morristown, NJ: Bretton-Clark.

Chatfield, C. (1983), *Statistics for Technology*, Third edition, Bristol and New York: Chapman and Hall.

Curry, D. (1992), *The New Marketing Research Systems*, New York: John Wiley.

Deere, R. (1996), "Modern Methods of Testing in Direct Marketing", *Journal Of Database Marketing*, Vol. 4, No. 1, pp. 51–64.

Dreze, X. and F. Zufryden (1997), "Testing Web Site Design and Promotional Content", *Journal of Advertising Research*, Vol. 37, No. 2, March/April, pp. 77–91.

Freund, J.E. (1992), *Mathematical Statistics*, Fifth edition, Englewood Cliffs, NJ: Prentice-Hall.

Furness, P. (1992), "Applying Neural Networks in Database Marketing: An Overview", *Journal of Targeting, Measurement & Analysis for Marketing*, Vol. 1, No. 2, pp. 152–169.

Gorski, D. and I. Ingram (1994), *The Price-Waterhouse Sales and Marketing Software Handbook*, London: Pitman.

Green, P., F. Carmone and S. Smith (1989), *Multidimensional Scaling: Concepts and Applications*, Boston, MA: Allyn and Bacon.

Green, P. and V. Srinivasan (1990), "Conjoint Analysis in Marketing: New Developments with Implications for Research and Practice", *Journal of Marketing*, Vol. 54, No. 4, October, pp. 3–19.

Green, P. and A.M. Krieger (1991), "Segmenting Markets with Conjoint Analysis", *Journal of Marketing*, Vol. 55, October, pp. 20–23.

Group 1 Software, *Model 1*, http://www.g1.com/model1/response.htm.

Hair, J.F., R.E. Anderson, R.L. Tatham and W. Black (1992), *Multivariate Data Analysis with Readings*, Third edition, London: Maxwell Macmillan.

Hansotia, B.J. (1992), *The Direct Marketing Handbook*, Second edition, Chapter 38, New York: McGraw-Hill.

Hansotia, B.J. (1992), "Determination of Panel Sizes in Designed Experiments", *Journal Of Direct Marketing*, Vol. 6, No. 4, pp. 17–27.

Haughton, D. and S. Oulabi (1993), "Direct Market Modelling with CART and CHAID", *Journal of Direct Marketing*, Vol. 7, No. 3, pp. 16–26.

Hosmer, D.W. and S. Lemeshow (1989), *Applied Logistic Regression*, New York: John Wiley and Sons.

Hughes, A.M. (1994), *Strategic Database Marketing*, Chicago, IL: Probus Publications.

Hurley, S., L. Moutinho and N.M. Stephens (1995), "Solving Marketing Optimization Problems using Genetic Algorithms", *European Journal of Marketing*, Vol. 29, No. 4, pp. 39–54.

Kleinbaum, D., L. Kupper and K. Muller (1988), *Applied Regression Analysis and Other Multivariable Methods*, Second edition, Boston, MA: PWS-Kent.

Kucher, E. and K. Hilleke (1993), "Value Pricing through Conjoint Measurement: A Practical Approach", *European Management Journal*, Vol. 11, No. 3, September, pp. 283–289.

Lloyd, C. (1996), "Junk Mail Will Do Nicely", *The Sunday Times*, 14 April.

Magidson, J. (1989), "CHAID, Logit, and Loglinear Modelling", *Marketing Research Systems*, Vol. 11, No. 130, pp. 101–114.

Magidson, J. (1993), *SPSS for Windows: CHAID*, Release 6.0.

Magidson, J. (1994), "The CHAID Approach to Segmentation Modelling", in R. Bagozzi (ed.), *Advanced Methods of Marketing Research*, Cambridge, MA: Oxford-Blackwell, pp. 118–159.

Magson, N. and J. McLelland (1997), "Choose your Friends", *New Perspectives*, No. 9, October, pp. 20–23.

Malhotra, N.K. (1993), *Marketing Research: An Applied Orientation*, Second edition, Englewood Cliffs, NJ: Prentice Hall.

McFarland, P. (1995), "Evaluating the Performance of Neural Networks for Rank Ordering Prospects", *The Journal of Database Marketing*, Vol. 3, No. 3, pp. 271–279.

Montgomery, D.C. (1991), *Design and Analysis Of Experiments*, Third edition, New York: Wiley.

Moore, W.L. and E.A. Pessemier (1993), *Product Planning and Management*, New York: McGraw-Hill.

Morrison, D.F. (1990), *Multivariate Statistical Methods*, Third edition, McGraw-Hill.

Moutinho, L., B. Curry, F. Davies and P. Rita (1994), *Computer Modelling and Expert Systems in Marketing*, New York: Routledge.

Norusis, M.J. (1993), *SPSS for Windows: Advanced Statistics*, Release 6.0.

Ozimek, J. (1993), *Targeting for Success: A Guide to New Techniques for Measurement and Analysis in Database and Direct Response Marketing*, New York: McGraw-Hill.

Picconi, M., A. Romano and C.E. Olson (1993), *Business Statistics: Elements and Applications*, New York: HarperCollins.

Roberts, M.L. and P.D. Berger (1989), *Direct Marketing Management*, Englewood Cliffs, NJ: Prentice Hall.

Sawtooth Software, *Adaptive Conjoint Analysis*, http://www.sawtoothsoftware.com/

Scheaffer, R.L., W. Mendenhall and L. Ott (1990), *Elementary Survey Sampling*, Fourth edition, London: PWS-KENT.

Severwright, J. (1996), "Market Segmentation Using Neural Networks", *Journal of Targeting, Measurement and Analysis for Marketing*, Vol. 5, No. 1, pp. 20–28.

Shepard, D. et al. (1993), *The New Direct Marketing*, London: Business One Irwin.

Sleight, P. and B. Leventhal (1992), "An Introduction to Multivariate Analysis Techniques and their Application in Direct Marketing for Locating Patterns within Data", *Journal of Database Marketing*, Vol. 3, No. 5, pp. 37–53.

SPSS, http://www.spss.com.

Thrasher, R. (1991), "CART: A Recent Advance in Tree Structured List Segmentation Methodology", *Journal of Direct Marketing*, Vol. 5, No. 1, pp. 35–47.

Zahavi, J. and N. Levin (1997), "Applying Neural Computing to Target Marketing", *Journal of Database Marketing*, Vol. 2, No. 1, pp. 5–22.

Chapter 9

SEGMENTATION IN DIRECT MARKETING

Eddie Rohan *and* David Fitzgerald

Overview

This chapter deals with methods of selecting one's customers — a topic which is obviously one of the most critical issues facing any marketing manager. As is apparent from other chapters, segmentation of customers is particularly critical in direct marketing where the customers to receive communications must be selected on an individual basis.

Even within the listings of contacts or existing customers that have been assembled by firms, many disparate groups exist — not all of whom merit further contact. Hence a variety of selection techniques exist to sort the profitable from the non-profitable. Segmentation of existing contacts is therefore the first and most relevant approach to be taken.

The second task addressed by the segmentation literature is how to identify the most rewarding customers from the vast number of potential prospects "out there". However, finding the proverbial "needle in the haystack" can prove elusive. In this section, attention is paid to the idea of geodemographic analysis, which has reached a high level of sophistication in the UK. The necessary conditions for their operation are described and the basic principles underlying such systems are examined.

A direct transfer of these systems to Ireland is inappropriate due to the absence of a detailed postcode system. However, such schemes have been adapted to Irish conditions and comparable services are now available on a commercial basis. One such application is described in detail in the case study.

Finally, some comments are made regarding future approaches to segmentation.

REVIEWING THE BASIC CONCEPT OF SEGMENTATION

Two simple ideas underlie the concept of segmentation as it is practised in marketing. Firstly, it is *not possible* for a firm to lavish attention equally on all its customers. Secondly, it is *not desirable* to do so. Not only may a substantial number of client accounts be dormant at any point in time, but an even larger number are of sufficiently low value that contacting them is a waste of resources. Clearly such realities demand that any organisation must focus on:

- How future approaches might be made only to the more valuable of one's existing customers and

- How new customers can be identified and accessed from the wider population.

Increasing Importance in the 1990s

The increasing emphasis on segmentation in order to target more effectively and to maximise profitability is the result of a number of causes:

- Increasing fragmentation of the market in terms of consumers, media and distribution channels has led to the movement from mass marketing towards one-to-one marketing

- Arising from this market fragmentation, there is a decreasing return on investment from the traditional methods of doing business — e.g. cost per thousand for TV advertising has increased but the reach in many cases has fallen because of the proliferation of TV channels

- The volume of available data on an individual is increasing substantially — it has been estimated that the amount of information stored on databases globally is doubling every ten months

- Available technology to store and manipulate data has become much more accessible as the price of personal computers has fallen as market penetration has increased

- Improved data analysis tools are much more accessible and easy to use for marketers (e.g. SPSS). Traditionally, the use of techniques such as Cluster Analysis or CHAID required a statistician and a large computer

- The costs of new customer acquisition have increased.

The Essence of Segmentation

The existence of many diverse groups within the wider population underlines the necessity of segmentation. While a market may be defined as "an aggregate of people who as individuals or as organisations have a need for certain products and have the ability, willingness and authority to purchase such products" (Dibb et al., 1997: 200), it cannot be presumed that they have uniform needs. Standard products are unlikely to satisfy them and they are likely to be differentiated in terms of spending levels, methods of communication and channels of distribution. The division of the total market into segments — i.e. homogenous subgroups that share similar characteristics — therefore appears to be the optimal solution. Not only can the diversity of customer needs be satisfied by concentrating resources on particular segments, but such an approach also permits a firm to operate with greater efficiency and improved margins.

Even within a firm's existing customer base, it has long been recognised that the Pareto Principle or the 80/20 rule should guide a firm's operations. Basically this relates to the observation that approximately 80 per cent of the revenue or profit of an organisation comes from just 20 per cent of its customer base. A firm will therefore ignore or neglect such customers at its peril.

Originally the imbalance between individual customers was first recognised in the business-to-business sector, where it is particularly pronounced, but it is also true that significant disparity has been found even in consumer markets. Put in a nutshell, the universal reality is that "all consumers are not created equal" (to quote the title of a book by Hallberg, 1995).

Such dissimilarity between customers is a core principle that underpins all marketing theory and drives all marketing practice. Essentially, a triad of concepts encompasses the view that marketing is concerned with the *selection* of particular customers, *targeting* products and services specially to their needs and judiciously *positioning* these offerings within the total available. Differentiation of one's total product on the basis of the special circumstances of a chosen segment is a fundamental principle in this regard.

SEGMENTATION AND DIRECT MARKETING

The necessity for segmentation is even more critical when one turns to direct marketing. This is due to the fact that the means of communication are now individualised. Irrespective of the chosen vehicle for making an offer (e.g. direct mail or telemarketing), judicious selection is critical to the success of the operation. Whether a prospect is identified individually or as a member of a group, the key issue is to sift them on the basis of market potential. The goal is to use customer analysis to restrict contact to those targets who offer the most potential and to ignore all those where at best responses will be negligible. As illustrated through the analogy of aiming a rifle with telescopic sights for targeting, rather than pointing a shotgun in the general direction of one's target, very refined selection procedures are used. Only those who meet fairly strict criteria should be approached in the first instance.

Sheer economics underpins such thinking, as the costs of incorrect choices are so apparent. Decisions taken by direct marketers come into sharp focus because the costs of communicating with each potential customer must be individually paid — even if Postaim or other methods of cost reduction are used. Hence the achieved "hit rates" for different subgroups can be clearly seen.

Furthermore, a return on investment can be quantified for each prospect or group of prospects. By examining the outcome of each communication and subtracting the costs of initiating the contact, the success or failure in choosing each particular target becomes quite apparent. Such transparency concerning the results of a campaign puts the spotlight clearly on the success or failure of the selection criteria that were employed in the first place.

This in turn leads to the quest for more discriminating tools which will produce higher response rates and so improve the cost-effectiveness of a campaign. Again, it is obvious that a comparison of different segmentation variables should be included in the testing procedures for any major direct marketing programme (see the chapter on testing in this volume).

Overall Approaches to Segmentation

In looking at how a firm may seek to segment markets, two overall approaches have proved necessary. One set of techniques is available for existing customers. Here the new business is sought through marketing additional products or services to such customers. The second approach is used where one is seeking out new customers from the overall population. In this case, an existing customer profile is used as an essential guide and the task centres on finding "look-alike" or "identikit" customers.

METHODS OF SELECTION FROM EXISTING CUSTOMERS

A customer database is usually the repository of a variety of information, only some of which may be of value. On the one hand, it may prove to be an invaluable resource as it provides data about actual purchasing behaviour on a longitudinal basis, as well as basic customer details. On the other hand, it may contain large numbers of out-of-date or redundant files which may have arisen from a variety of sources — old enquiries, complaints or responses to promotions, etc. In addition, many records may refer to transactions that occurred in the distant past. The likelihood is that any data that had been entered into the firm's computer system now exists in an undifferentiated manner. Enquirers, complainers, minor purchasers in the past and loyal customers are all likely to be lumped together. The result is that lists which can be produced either alphabetically or by date of first entry are unlikely to be immediately usable.

The first task is to identify the most valuable customers, i.e. those who have reached the most significant points on the "loyalty ladder". Business success hinges on these 25 per cent or so. Only when the database marketer has established procedures for their identification and isolation can the contact procedures move to other categories that, although of lesser importance, are still critical.

These customers may purchase in lower volume or to lesser value than the "core loyalists" but are still of major importance. They may provide little repeat business although their purchases have shown the firm's products to be part of their repertoire. The marketing task here is to seek to motivate these customers to the highest stage of loyalty, even to the extent of becoming "advocates" (Raphel and Raphel, 1995).

Even those who have made a single purchase may be considered to provide marketing opportunities. Not only have this group shown themselves to be aware of the company's products, but through their initial purchase they have indicated that a particular offering was superior to those of competitors. They have moved from being mere enquirers and might rightly be classified as customers in a real sense.

The task for marketers is to build on this relationship, however tenuous it may be. Perhaps they can be cultivated and moved from "one-time customers" to "regulars" on the loyalty ladder.

Other records on the customer database may have become redundant due to fact that contact with the firm was either peripheral or is now outdated. For this reason, flagging these accounts as dormant is essential. Alternatively, a decision may be taken to cull them entirely from the existing files as they have outlived their usefulness.

Customer Analysis in Business-to-Business Markets

The process of customer analysis can best be illustrated in business-to-business markets. These are defined as those where one's customers are other organisations who purchase a specific kind of product to re-sell, use directly in producing other products or use in general daily operations (Dibb et al., 1997: 200).

Documentary evidence of all customer transactions is retained on a database as a matter of course in these markets due to the fact that business is usually conducted by invoice. At a bare minimum, each invoice contains the identity of the purchaser, product details and cost information relating to each transaction. Such a paper trail then provides an ideal opportunity for deciding whether or not to re-contact any particular customer.

Because of these practices, the database in such markets is particularly easy to maintain. Analysis of invoices can identify the range of products purchased by each customer, size of order, frequency of order, the manner of payment and the length of credit taken. Through the use of running totals, the total amount purchased by a particular customer either historically or on an annual basis can be assessed and thus the value of each particular customer can be established. Ranking of customers by value is then a simple matter.

Once these rankings have been established, listings can be produced of those customers who meet any given criteria. There is, for example, no difficulty in extracting a list of the top 15 or 30 per cent of customers by value. In addition, by means of simple calculation or through a Lorenz curve, the proportion of turnover they account for can be both ascertained and demonstrated.

Furthermore, a detailed profile can be provided concerning the make-up of such a group as relevant details about the customer will be contained in their records or at least can be overlaid onto it. Typically, information such as geographical location, type of industry, SIC code, level of technology and size of company would be included in the basic record of each customer.

Standard Industrial Classification (SIC)

The SIC code (Standard Industrial Classification) is a key variable as it provides a system whereby the nature of a customer's business can be classified. The first two digits of a four-digit code indicate a major classification of industry, of which there are ten; for example:

01–09	Agriculture, Forestry, Fisheries
10–14	Mining
15–19	Construction
20–39	Manufacturing.

The final two digits of the four-digit SIC code classify individual organisations by sub-group and further details within the industry. For example, SIC code #2300 denotes manufacturers of clothing as detailed below:

SIC Number			Description
2300			Clothing and Footwear
	2310		Men's clothing
		2311	Suits and coats
		2312	Shirts
	2330		Women's clothing
		2331	Blouses and shirts
		2335	Dresses

The availability of listings of all the firms having the same SIC code is therefore a useful tool in seeking additional new business, particularly in unfamiliar markets.

Additional information regarding a firm's credit rating and its status as manufacturer, distributor, wholesaler or exporter as well as the names of key executives can also be acquired from business information providers such as Kompass or Dun and Bradstreet. The fact that such agencies operate on a world-wide basis means that international as well as national lists can be easily accessed. The specialist nature of these operations and the resources they put into building up the most complete directories possible ensures that available lists of potential customers are likely to be well focused.

In short, "profiling", or the creation of an accurate description of existing industrial customers, provides a platform whereby similar enterprises can be identified. This proves to be the most effective way to expand one's customer base successfully.

Customer Analysis in Consumer Markets

Similar strategies for the analysis of existing customers are possible in many consumer markets where the manner of doing business facilitates the keeping of records. For example, travel companies, car dealers, estate agents, banks, building societies, and insurance companies all regularly contact their customers at their home addresses and so are in a position to undertake pre-selection before contact. In this way, the strategy for segmenting markets according to customer characteristics is no different than in the case of industrial markets. Geographic, demographic, lifestyle and behavioural variables, as listed in Table 9.1, form the main categories used for this purpose.

Customers of direct marketing can be divided on the basis of their residence — region of the country, county, rural versus urban, density of population and the size of town or city. These variables may be important in that alternative channels of distribution may be either strong or weak in a particular region.

The behaviour of customers is also very likely to be dependent on their demographic characteristics, such as age, sex, number in the household or stage in the family life cycle. Product needs inevitably change with age, are different for men and women, and tend to reflect family commitments. The examination of existing customer records may show the impact of such variables and enable a detailed customer profile to be assembled.

TABLE 9.1: CONSUMER CATEGORIES

Geographic	Psychographic	Demographic	Behavioural
Region	Lifestyle	Sex	Usage rate
County	Personality type	Age	Frequency of purchase
Rural/Urban		Household size	Purchase occasion
Size of town/city		Family lifecycle stage	Benefits sought
Density of population		Income	Loyalty status
		Occupation	
		Social class	
		Education	
		Single/dual earner couple	

Obviously the impact of income on product choice is paramount, although actual income data may be absent in customer files due to the difficulty in gaining access to such confidential information. It will, however, be available as a matter of course where application is being made for various financial products such as banking services, mortgages and insurance services. Education, occupation and social class (as denoted by category of occupation) also indicate an individual's social status and have the advantage of being easier to record. For example, the classification section of most commercial market research questionnaires routinely includes these latter items, while the income question is conspicuous by its absence. Finally, when one is looking at customers on an international canvas, issues such as nationality, religion and race may be necessary to describe the type of customer that one is attracting.

The experience of market analysts, however, is that demographics are insufficient to distinguish between customers. While they may be identical in terms of demographics, their purchasing behaviour may show dramatic differences. Indeed, this rings true to our daily experience, as we all know 35-year-old married males with similar jobs who could not be more different in purchasing terms. So for many years now, profiling in terms of personality or psychographics has been used to capture such differences. Typically, this is attempted through the use of lifestyle questionnaires. These are usually composed of a large battery of items dealing with one's Activities, Interests and Opinions (AIO). Through cluster analysis grouping of likeminded consumers, particular patterns of purchasing behaviour may be found. The purchase of holidays or travel by different customer types might illustrate the potential of such lifestyle profiling.

The final category of segmentation variables relate to purchasing behaviour on the part of consumers. Typically, size of purchase, frequency of purchase and occasion of the purchase are examined. Customers are also distinguished on the basis of the benefits sought. For example, a database of car purchasers may be segmented on the basis of the use to which the vehicle is being put — high mileage travel by sales representatives, family transport vehicle or thirty-something status symbol.

While many of the variables mentioned in the above section apply to direct marketing databases, just as they apply to marketing in general, it must be realised that detailed customer analysis and selection is not always mandatory before using a particular database.

Highly Selective Consumer Lists

The listings that many of these companies possess may already be highly exclusive and require little by way of editing. This would arise where the entire database is sufficiently focused to afford significant business opportunities, while yet being sufficiently small that mailing costs are not prohibitive.

By way of example, a single transaction may attract a relatively well-off segment of the population and thereby give rise to a listing of such households. The entire membership of such a list might prove equally effective in generating business for allied products or services.

This might be illustrated by the targeting of teachers, nurses and gardaí by various financial institutions. By first negotiating with trade unions and staff associations to promote attractive group rates jointly for car insurance, these institutions gained access to large numbers of potential clients. All were relatively well-off families with the added advantage that they were in secure permanent employment. In time, the new databases afforded them opportunities to cross-sell a whole range of products — home insurance, income continuance plans, tax-based savings schemes and the long-term provision of educational funding for children. Undoubtedly, the considerable success of these institutions can be attributed to the value of the databases and the efficiency with which they were used.

Problems of Cash-based Consumer Markets

However, significant difficulties arise in other important consumer markets such as food, groceries and almost all areas of the leisure industry. Direct contact with customers has been traditionally hindered by the fact that cash transactions have been the norm, thus making customer names irrelevant. Because it is unnecessary to raise invoices to receive payment, it proves very difficult to know the identity of one's customers. While they might be described in general terms through formal and informal market research, the absence of names and addresses has made it impossible to conduct business with them directly.

EPOS Technology and Consumer Behaviour

In recent years electronic point of sale technology (EPOS) has provided a means through which this problem might be addressed, particularly in the case of food and grocery purchases. The capture of full details on each transaction at the point of sale has facilitated the introduction of sophisticated inventory systems. In addition, it has enabled the dynamics of customer purchasing to be efficiently tracked. For example, the impact of promotions or price reductions on brand loyalty can be monitored and evaluated.

The advent of the loyalty card in recent years marks a radical change in all of these operations. By means of such cards, transaction details can be automatically associated with specific customers. Nowadays many supermarkets and petrol stations have succeeded in persuading customers to use a personal card on each shopping occasion. Clocking up electronic points has proven attractive to consumers who feel that it provides real benefits in a way that is more efficient, less time-consuming and requires less effort than the collection of stamps, tokens or coupons. It is the registration details for such cards that enable the product choices to be linked to specific customers.

In this way the IT capability is no longer constrained and its true potential is becoming apparent. Without a single question being asked by a market researcher, patterns of purchases can be attributed to particular consumers and longitudinal patterns for each individual can be established. In this way, a valid association of brand preferences with demographics and other variables can be accurately established. More importantly, the inclusion of the name and address of the card holder facilitates communication between the retailer and its customers on an individual basis.

For example, prior to the introduction of the loyalty card, it must have been a source of frustration to retailers to be aware of the existence of a group of customers who spend, say, £500 per annum (about £10 a week) on wine at their local supermarket and yet not be able to communicate with them directly. Nowadays such a group can be identified and personally informed about a forthcoming wine sale.

Such relationship marketing is likely to be beneficial in the short term as well as contributing to building loyalty and consolidation of the long-term relationship between consumer and retailer.

Choices in Segment Selection

This example can also be used to illustrate the various options available to the database owner. On the one hand, the retailer may choose to contact *all* listed consumers irrespective of their wine-buying behaviour; *any* consumer who has made a wine purchase within a specified time period; or on the other hand, it may be confined to a small group whose purchases exceeded a specified minimum volume. The offer may even be localised to designated regions where competition is particularly keen. These choices depend on the circumstances and ultimately on the judgement of the marketer.

The above example shows that various selection criteria may be applied to the customer base. Generally, it is unusual for a database to be used in its entirety and selection is made of the most likely prospects on the basis of their purchasing history.

Recency, Frequency and Monetary Value (RFM)

Monitoring of consumption patterns over time constitutes the most basic form of segmentation. Typically, customers are organised in terms of criteria such as recency, frequency or monetary value (or

RFM as it is known in the literature). Although such principles are basically simple, they can be enhanced and made more complex and therefore become more practical and realistic. Such criteria are not necessarily implemented as single index segmentation systems but can be used in combination.

In examining the previous purchasing behaviour of consumers, it quickly becomes apparent that not all customers are of equal value. Names on a database may denote enquirers, ex-users, first-time users, and ongoing users, whether intermittent or regular. They may be light, medium or heavy in their usage rate, and in terms of loyalty may range from being very loyal to being switchers.

The manner in which such principles of segmentation are applied generally will be outlined with respect to the recency criterion.

Recency

Obviously, a customer who purchased the use of a hotel room only once, and that in late 1993, is less significant and merits less attention than a regular customer whose last visit was in the previous week or month. So if one focuses merely on the recency issue, it is clear that the record of a purchase from a new car dealer in 1990 is less pertinent that someone who purchased in 1996 or 1997. The benefit of recency as a segmentation variable is illustrated in Table 9.2 below, where responses or purchase rates are found to be higher for the more recent customers.

TABLE 9.2: TYPICAL RESPONSES BY RECENCY OF PURCHASE

Recency Quintile	Time	Mailed	Responses	Response Percentage	Index
5	<1 month	10,000	510	5.1%	213
4	1–<3 months	10,000	340	3.4%	142
3	3–<6 months	10,000	203	2.03%	85
2	6 mths – <1 year	10,000	99	0.99%	41
1	1 year and over	10,000	48	0.48%	20
Total		50,000	1,200	2.4%	100

As can be seen from this hypothetical example, quintile 5 (the 20 per cent who purchased most recently) have a response rate which is 2.13 times above the average for all customers. Contacting quintile 1 (those who have not purchased within the past year) is likely to prove worst of all and tends to result in an overall loss.

The benefits of segmentation on the recency criterion are therefore twofold. In the event of very limited resources, quintile 5 (the top 20 per cent) should be the first group to be contacted, followed by quintile 4 (the next best 20 per cent). The bottom 20 per cent could clearly be excluded because of their lack of response over time.

Frequency

Using a similar table to convert the results to percentages, the focus can be put on consumers who buy most frequently. The top 20 per cent in frequency terms can be identified and their purchasing behaviour monitored. Typically, the rate at which they respond to new offerings is found to be vastly superior to that of the average consumer.

Monetary Value

This is one of the most powerful discriminators with regard to future purchases. Therefore, it makes economic sense to identify those accounts that are highest in terms of monetary value and to target additional offerings to them. No particular method of assessing monetary value appears to be universally practised and it is calculated in a number of different ways. For example, use has been made of total value of purchases to date, cumulative annual purchases and average spend per transaction.

Use of Scoring Systems

These three concepts (RFM) can be combined so that each customer is given a composite score on recency, frequency and monetary value. Such a system can be illustrated in the following way.

The most valuable customers are those in the top 20 per cent on each criterion and score 555, while those who are least valuable score 111. These extremes could easily be translated into a simple composite score ranging from 15 (5+5+5) to 3 (1+1+1). Alternatively, a weighting scheme (which perhaps gives more weight to the monetary value criterion) could be devised. This might be found to give rise to a more acceptable composite score.

Lifetime Value

One limitation of the RFM criterion is that it is centred on behaviour from the past, whether immediate or quite distant, and fails to take anticipated future purchases into account. This difficulty can be overcome through the use of yet another measure — the LTV or Lifetime value of a customer. This criterion takes the life cycle of the relationship into account so that customers who may not be particularly valuable now may get a high rating if it is anticipated that at some point in the future their status will change. The importance of this criterion is exemplified by the high ratings given to third-level students by the financial institutions that assiduously target them — not because of their past or present behaviour, but because of their anticipated lifetime earnings.

Irrespective of whether RFM or LTV criteria are used, it is apparent that such criteria exemplify simple ways of identifying one's valued customers. Relationship building with these groups is obviously most beneficial and represents an optimisation of the limited resources that any firm possesses for such tasks.

On the other hand, the identification of the worst prospects and their separation from those to be actively pursued is a sensible strategy. By diverting resources away from appealing to these "lost causes", unnecessary expenditure is avoided. Segmentation works therefore in a twofold way: targeting the communication only at those from whom a high return is anticipated; while at the same time, reducing waste by not contacting those from whom a response is unlikely.

In all of the above discussion, it must be realised that a previous contact history is a prerequisite. These techniques are inapplicable when one is faced with a large population with whom one has never had any contact.

METHODS USED IN IDENTIFYING NEW CUSTOMERS

The second approach to segmentation is also very important, as it concerns the vast number of non-customers who might be approached by a business. Here the basic principle is to build on a profile of one's existing customers and then to "go out and get more like them". Phrases such as finding "lookalikes" through the use of an "identikit" are commonly used to describe this process.

"How can I get more of the same?" is the basic philosophy underlying such an approach. Obviously, such a strategy is not without its dangers and may produce a very myopic view of one's target market. It could lead to the acquisition of new customers who are mere "clones" of the existing customer profile and so narrow the customer profile too much. While one must be conscious of this danger, it certainly makes sense to use such knowledge in the first instance.

The Purchase of Highly Selective Lists

Given that direct contact with new customers will be made by post, the basic requirement is for well-targeted listings of new names and addresses. Such lists tend to be acquired from specialist firms who have accumulated large numbers of databases over time. In Ireland, An Post has published the "list of lists" which illustrates the variety of titles that can be accessed through list brokers.

A brief perusal of this publication shows that many of these lists are already segmented. For example, the available company lists are pre-selected by turnover, number of employees, type of business and whether or not they export. Alternatively, while a large list such as 80,000 Irish farmers can be made available, the list brokers can also deliver such a list in segmented form, so that communications can be targeted at those who specialise in sectors such as beef, cereals, milk, pigs or sugarbeet. The value of such lists for identifying new customers is obviously a matter for careful consideration, as they may duplicate existing customers and contain little that is of value.

On the consumer side, lists of households can be identified which fit very specific descriptions. For example lists of household containing children under one-year-old, or 10- to 14-year-olds are readily available. Indeed, house-owners can be divided depending on whether their home is detached, semi-detached or terraced. These specialist lists have been gleaned from many sources, but depend mainly on the gathering of information through enquiries, promotions, competitions and general lifestyle surveys.

The Electoral Register and DEDs

Another approach to generating leads is to access the entire Electoral Register. This represents the fullest and most up-to-date listing of the total adult population and can be used to identify groups of names and addresses which are likely to prove responsive to particular offerings. Typically, these lists are not purchased from the local authorities by the ordinary user but are accessed through specialist agencies who have expertise in their management. In the UK, these agencies work on microdata from the Office of National Statistics and have access to the total list of registered addresses through the Royal Mail's Postal Address File (PAF). In Ireland, the position is basically similar, with firms such as PMI (Precision Marketing Information) and Response Tech. Ltd. obtaining such data from the CSO. This is then used in their work on behalf of clients.

The Electoral Register in the Republic of Ireland is assembled by each local authority on an annual basis. While a draft register is published for viewing in January each year, the definitive register is published in April. Because of mobility and the personal preference of each individual, the register is an imperfect listing in the case of individuals. Names of former residents (including those who have died) take time to be removed from the register, while new residents frequently are not registered. This is particular relevant for young adults who are highly mobile and frequently may live at home and at different addresses throughout any one year.

While the identity of any particular resident is likely to be problematic, particularly for younger age groups, the register has more accuracy when addresses are considered. Omissions on any given street are more easily identified where house numbers are listed in sequential order. So the omission of 17 St Christopher's Road (between number 16 and number 18) is more likely to be noticed than "Dalriada", St Christopher's Road.

By monitoring the register over time, companies can find the length in residence of any particular household within the area, in addition to identifying mobile individuals within the population. It also provides household size in terms of adult voters.

Using Demographic Data from the Census

Demographics (or descriptions of the population in terms of age, gender, marital status and so on) have relevance in virtually all spheres of marketing, as can be illustrated in the following examples. Typically, a vast range of products relate to each stage in the family life-cycle. Examples such as baby food, clothes, bikes, college education, mortgages, housing, and pensions are clearly age-related. It makes sense therefore to seek out customers where higher than average concentrations of the requisite age-groups might to be found. But how can this be ascertained if these individuals are not customers and one is unable to enquire into the age status of one's customers? The answer is that such information is available from the Census. This source must be accurately described, as the level of information available is frequently misunderstood.

District Electoral Divisions

The Census of Population in the Republic is undertaken every five years; the last Census was in 1996. The manner in which this is organised is that the Republic is divided into some 3,440 separate geographical areas called District Electoral Divisions (DEDs). Each county in the Republic of Ireland has varying numbers of DEDs depending on its size and population density, but it is important to note that DEDs do not cross county boundaries. DED information is collected on a particular night (Sunday, 28 April 1996) and returns made for the 1.1 million plus households in the country. The information collected is aggregated together at DED level which forms the basic reporting unit for CSO data.

While it is essential to realise that data at individual household level is not and never will be provided by the Central Statistics Office due to the confidentially of the Census form, a large amount of data is available at a local or DED level. Each DED contains on average about 300 households, although the actual number varies according to the location of the DED and the corresponding population density. Within the 3,400 DEDs it is therefore possible to identify those localities where either the largest number or the greatest concentration of over 65-year-olds can be found. Alternatively, localities containing the highest number of young people can similarly be listed. In all cases, however, the DED is the unit of analysis, whether DEDs are taken individually, in groups, or even at county level.

All the statistical information contained in the many volumes of Census '96 can be purchased from the CSO at Urban District, Rural District, Town and DED levels. These Small Area Population Statistics (SAPS) are available on diskette and hence are useful for further processing by marketing analysts.

Although the level of disaggregation in Dublin City and County is slightly different to the national pattern, this also permits statistics relating to very narrow geographical areas to be used. About one million inhabitants live in approximately 340,000 households and in such an urban area the density of households per DED is higher than the national average. Census data referring to this population is disaggregated to 332 distinct DEDs, each containing an average of about 1,000 households. The narrow confines of these DEDs can be appreciated if one studies DED or ward maps of Dublin, which are available for purchase from the Ordnance Survey Offices. The fact that one can visit a large number of DEDs (five by the direct route or nine without a great deal of diversion) in a ten-minute walk from O'Connell Street to Croke Park in Dublin city verifies this point.

DEDs therefore hold the key to market segmentation at consumer level. Firstly, their inhabitants are described in detail within the Census micro reports. Secondly, their boundaries are mapped by the Ordnance Survey. Thirdly, and most importantly for direct marketing, the Register of Electors contains the name and address of each registered voter within DED boundaries.

The inter-relationships can be portrayed as in Figure 9.1.

FIGURE 9.1: LEVEL OF DETAIL AVAILABLE

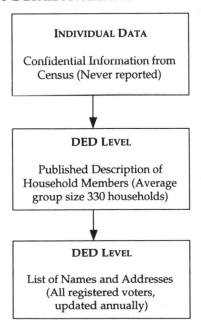

Benefits of Using DED Profiles

By way of illustration: a marketer who wished to target relatively wealthy individuals within the Fingal region of Dublin can use the SAPS data to obtain listings of those DEDs where at least 70 per cent of all households are headed by a chief income earner having an ABC1 occupation.

TABLE 9.3: DEDs WITHIN FINGAL ORDERED BY PERCENTAGE ABC1 SOCIAL CLASS

District Electoral Division (DED)	Percentage ABC1 Social Class*
Castleknock — Park	88%
Castleknock — Knockmaroon	82%
Castleknock North	81%
Malahide East	79%
Howth	77%
Malahide West	73%
Sutton	72%
Blanchardstown — Delwood	71%

As can be seen, a knowledge of the DED profiles enables the marketer to be quite selective.

Cost Projections at DED Level

A key benefit of using DEDs is that the number of households in each DED is known and the marketer can calculate costs depending on the number of DEDs selected. While they contain some 330 households on average nationally, some contain about 1,000.

Age Profiles at DED Level

Simple demographics such as age can be useful for market segmentation. For example, if one wishes to communicate with elderly consumers, then the ranking of DEDs in terms of the relative proportion of inhabitants over 65 years of age is likely to improve the targeting in addition to removing new suburban estates, where the proportion of such consumers is minimal. While no information is available on individual households, one is three times as likely to get successful responses from localities in which 30 per cent of the population is over 65 years old than in localities where only 10 per cent of the population is at that age. The odds of success are thereby improved by judicious selection.

At the other end of the age scale, it is perfectly understandable that age might be of critical importance to a supermarket chain in making a decision about the location of a new store. Management may decide on the new suburban localities containing high proportions of youngsters under five years of age. Not only are such suburbs unlikely to be serviced to any great extent by existing grocers but, as they are populated by families at the early stages of the life-cycle, they are also likely to consist of customers with the highest lifetime value.

Other Analyses at DED Level

Other data of relevance to marketers include gender and marital status, family composition and household size, occupation and social class grouping, employment status, number of cars, and level of education. While single factor demographics have the virtue of simplicity, the possibility of using multiple indices makes the targeting even more powerful.

For example, it is possible to identify groupings of DEDs which have high numbers of two-car households, many apartments, high levels of single people and low unemployment levels. Alternatively, areas showing a high density of ABC1 occupations and married couples with children under 15 may be of particular interest to financial services companies selling educational savings plans.

Typically, these different household types tend to dominate different DEDs within the many cities and towns throughout the country. It not surprising, therefore, that attempts have been made to classify DEDs in terms of a global labelling system. The following section sets out how this is done.

Classification of DEDs

A system of classification is implemented by undertaking a cluster analysis of the large number of DED descriptors to arrive at a small number of well-defined neighbourhood types. In this way, one can characterise particular locations by means of labels such as "Flats and Mortgages, Singles and Young Working Couples" or "Wealthy Suburbs, Large Detached Houses".

GEODEMOGRAPHICS

Geodemographics is based on geographical location and is now well advanced within the UK, where it was first applied to marketing at the Market Research Society conference in 1979 (see Baker et al., 1979). Originally developed by Richard Webber at the Centre for Environmental Studies, it had been used previously to identify areas of high deprivation in Liverpool. It was, however, shown to be equally effective in showing high levels of discrimination in spending behaviour and product usage. The essence of the system is to carry out analysis of the demographics of people where they live. Sleight (1997) refers to geodemographics as "locality marketing" or the mere combination of demographics and geography; he believes that it is demystified by realising that it is based on the truism that "birds of a feather flock together". Consumers are more likely to be similar to those who live in their immediate vicinity than to other randomly chosen individuals.

A number of well-known systems of describing neighbourhood types have been developed in the UK; these form the basis of the systems undergoing development in the Irish context. In the following discussion, it is valuable to reflect on the British experience, as a number of specialist companies work in this area. Their experience over many years means that their systems have become quite sophisticated.

SPECIALIST GEODEMOGRAPHIC AGENCIES IN THE UK

ACORN

The first and most influential system is ACORN (which is an acronym for A Classification of Residential Neighbourhoods). This service is offered by CACI — an international consultancy founded in the USA in 1962. This service might rightly claim to be the first organisation to offer such a service within the UK. While other systems now exist, each has taken the basic ACORN system and developed it in unique ways.

TABLE 9.4: MAIN ACORN TYPES

Category A	ACORN Groups	ACORN Types	% of Population
	1. Wealthy Achievers, Suburban area		
		1.1: Wealthy Suburbs, Large Detached Houses	2.6%
		1.2: Villages with Wealthy Commuters	3.2%
		1.3: Mature Affluent Home Owning Areas	2.7%
		1.4: Affluent Suburbs, Older Families	3.7%
		1.5: Mature, Well-Off Suburbs	3.0%
Thriving	2. Affluent Greys, Rural Communities		
		2.6: Agricultural Villages, Home Based Workers	1.6%
		2.7: Holiday Retreats, Older People, Home Based Workers	0.7%
	3. Prosperous Pensioners, Retirement Areas		
		3.8: Home Owning Areas, Well-Off Older Residents	1.4%
		3.9: Private Flats, Elderly People	0.9%

Source: CACI

As can be seen in Table 9.4, the ACORN system classifies areas at three distinct levels. Based on the 1991 Census, 79 different data items are screened from the thousands of items produced by the Census authorities for each of the 150,000 small enumeration districts (EDs) which cover Britain. These EDs are then clustered into types of areas with similar characteristics based on criteria such as age, sex, marital status, ethnic group, home ownership, car ownership, education, and occupational category. Each ED, which are relatively small areas comprising only 150 households on average, can then be described according to a basic ACORN Type.

The 54 neighbourhood types that have been identified can be further amalgamated into 17 groups that coalesce into six major ACORN Categories. The latter range from Category A who are the most established and affluent people, labelled "Thriving" to those people who endure the greatest hardship — Category F, labelled "Striving".

TABLE 9.5: THE DISTRIBUTION OF ACORN CATEGORIES IN THE UK

Category	Label	Percentage of the UK population
A	Thriving	19.7%
B	Expanding	11.6%
C	Rising	7.8%
D	Settling	24.0%
E	Aspiring	13.7%
F	Striving	22.7%

Source: CACI

Category A can be subdivided into three major groups which in turn represent further subdivisions. The full distribution of ACORN Types, Groups and Categories within the population of Britain is demonstrated in Table 9.6 on the following pages.

The entire system is quite effective, in that the 130,000 distinctive EDs can be classified into a relatively small number of descriptors. A marketing manager who knows which ACORN type or types are the most valuable users of their services is therefore able to gain listings of the many EDs through the country which share the same ACORN label. The inhabitants of all these localities therefore become targets, due to the fact that they share the same basic description as existing valued customers.

TABLE 9.6: THE ACORN SYSTEM IN THE UK

ACORN Groups	ACORN Types	'000s	%
1. Wealthy achievers, suburban areas	Wealthy suburbs, large detached houses	1,467	2.6
	Villages with wealthy commuters	1,824	3.2
	Mature affluent home-owning areas	1,548	2.7
	Affluent suburbs, older families	2,123	3.7
	Mature, well-off suburbs	1,718	3.0
2. Affluent greys, rural communities	Agricultural villages, home-based workers	924	1.6
	Holiday retreats, older people, home-based workers	399	0.7
3. Prosperous pensioners, retirement areas	Home-owning areas, well-off older residents	807	1.4
	Private flats, elderly people	542	0.9
4. Affluent executives, family areas	Affluent working families with mortgages	1,224	2.1
	Affluent working couples with mortgages, new homes	728	1.3
	Transient workforces, living at their place of work	201	0.3
5. Well-off workers, family areas	Home-owning family areas	1,486	2.6
	Home-owning family areas, older children	1,721	3.0
	Families with mortgages, younger children	1,276	2.2
6. Affluent urbanites, town & city areas	Well-off town and city areas	631	1.1
	Flats and mortgages, singles and young working couples	425	0.7
	Furnished flats and bedsits, younger single people	253	0.4
7. Prosperous professionals, metropolitan areas	Apartments, young professional singles and couples	653	1.1
	Gentrified multi-ethnic areas	557	1.0
8. Better-off executives, inner city areas	Prosperous enclaves, highly qualified executives	428	0.7
	Academic centres, students and young professionals	371	0.6
	Affluent city centre areas, tenements and flats	254	0.4
	Partially gentrified multi-ethnic areas	407	0.7
	Converted flats and bedsits, single people	497	0.9
9. Comfortable middle agers, mature home-owning areas	Mature established home-owning areas	1,890	3.3
	Rural areas, mixed occupations	1,985	3.5
	Established home-owning areas	2,299	4.0
	Home-owning areas, council tenants, retired people	1,520	2.7

TABLE 9.6 CONTINUED

ACORN Groups	ACORN Types	'000s	%
10. Skilled workers, home-owning areas	Established home-owning areas, skilled workers	2,580	4.5
	Home-owners in older properties, younger workers	1,743	3.0
	Home-owning areas with skilled workers	1,765	3.1
11. New home owners, mature communities	Council areas, some new home-owners	2,176	3.8
	Mature home-owning areas, skilled workers	1,762	3.1
	Low-rise estates, older workers, new home-owners	1,608	2.8
12. White collar workers, better-off multi-ethnic areas	Home-owning multi-ethnic areas, young families	642	1.1
	Multi-occupied town centres, mixed occupations	1,038	1.8
	Multi-ethnic areas, white-collar workers	614	1.1
13. Older people, less prosperous areas	Home-owners, small council flats, single pensioners	1,088	1.9
	Council areas, older people, health problems	971	1.7
14. Council estate residents, better-off homes	Better-off council areas, new home owners	1,375	2.4
	Council areas, young families, some new home-owners	1,711	3.0
	Council areas, young families, many lone parents	898	1.6
	Multi-occupied terraces, multi-ethnic areas	487	0.8
	Low-rise council housing, less well-off families	1,015	1.8
	Council areas, residents with health problems	1,099	1.9
15. Council estate residents, high unemployment	Estates with high unemployment	645	1.1
	Council flats, elderly people, health problems	383	0.7
	Council flats, very high unemployment, singles	495	0.9
16. Council estate residents, greatest hardship	Council areas, high unemployment, lone parents	1,056	1.8
	Council flats, greatest hardship, many lone parents	518	0.9
17. People in multi-ethnic, low-income areas	Multi-ethnic, large families, overcrowding	366	0.6
	Multi-ethnic, severe unemployment, lone parents	570	1.0
	Multi-ethnic, high unemployment, overcrowding	301	0.5
Unclassified		291	0.5
Total		**57,353**	**99.8**

Source: CACI

Making Contact by Means of ACORN Classification

The task of contacting these potential customers is facilitated by the fact that all households in the UK have a postcode. The postcode system is very narrowly defined, to the extent that the 25 million households between them are identified by about 1.6 million postcodes — each containing about 15 addresses. This means that each ED contains an average of about 10 postcodes. The matching of these postcodes with the relevant ED provides the mechanism through which all the households in the various EDs that share a common ACORN description in Britain can be contacted by post.

While this is all very well in theory, the matter of matching postcodes, through which customers may be contacted, to EDs, wherein their demographic profile is known, has proved to be more difficult than anticipated. Digitised mapping of individual addresses and digitised mapping of the centroids (weighted centre) of the EDs has proven to be the most successful system. The result of this system is that listings of individual addresses can be used to contact the members of any group of EDs which share the same ACORN type label. Thus listings of all addresses with an ACORN label "Affluent working couples with mortgages, new homes" can be accessed. As this type contains over two per cent of the population, this list will contain over a half a million households which broadly fit this description.

Geodemographics and Survey Data

ACORN relies solely on UK Census data in allocating EDs to cluster types. However, when survey data relating to national purchasing behaviour (the Target Group Index or TGI, which is based on a sample of 25,000 respondents) was analysed using ACORN classifications, it was found to discriminate very well between consumers. This led to its use in conjunction with other survey data such as the National Readership Survey (NRS) and other data such as the AGB panel data. Over time, a number of specific applications were developed which enabled expenditure zones, drive-times and catchment areas to be examined in quite close detail. Another product which is now under CACI management is Financial ACORN. This product was originally developed by Pinpoint under the label FiNPiN and resulted from analysing the Financial Research Survey data by ED.

At present, separate ACORN analysis can also be organised for London, Scotland, Northern Ireland, and the Rest of the UK.

The success of the ACORN system led to a number of competitors, each of which has introduced some new feature into the way their particular geodemographic system is designed or implemented. At present (1998), CACI faces five main competing systems in the UK.

MOSAIC

This system, which was developed by CCN (now Experian), uses Census data to define its cluster types but, in addition, information from other sources is utilised. The main sources of such information are county court judgements, electoral register data, credit data and information from the Postal Address File. Details of county court judgements can be obtained at postcode level from the Lord Chancellor's Office in the UK. Close analysis of the electoral registers is particularly useful, as it can show the number of adults in a household. In addition, "stable residents" who are at the same address for years can be distinguished from those who are "movers". The credit data examines the frequency and types of credit references that are carried out for individuals wishing to get a credit or charge card, get a store charge card or apply for a loan from a finance house. These results are not available at an individual level but are aggregated at the level of postcode and can be expressed in terms of their existence within the community. The clustering occurs at two levels with 11 and 52 cluster types being used to describe EDs throughout Britain. As might be noted, the final output is not dramatically different from that contained in the ACORN system. The name MOSAIC is particularly apt when colour-coded output is shown on an area map.

An advantage of the MOSAIC system is that, while other geodemographic products operate at ED level (where all postcodes within an ED share the same classification), it distinguishes at postcode level. Thus, neighbouring postcodes, even within the same ED, can be allocated into different MOSAIC clusters.

SUPERPROFILES

This system belongs to Credit and Marketing Services Ltd. (CDMS), a subsidiary of Littlewoods. This grouping system is the most detailed and potentially precise, using as many as 150 clusters. Ten "lifestyles" and 40 "target markets" are also identified, with the latter ranked each year on the basis of the annual TGI data from 1 to 40 in terms of affluence. So while the basic Census data may not have changed from one decade until the next census data is available, the market-based data is updated annually. In this way, the problem of ageing Census data is limited to some extent.

DEFINE

This relatively new system, developed by Equifax, is like MOSAIC in that it uses credit reference data to supplement that available from the Census. However, its clustering procedure is undertaken through the use of Census data only, with credit risk and financial activity data used to divide its 56 clusters into ten credit-related groups.

NEIGHBOURS and PROSPECTS

This system, supplied by EuroDirect, is based exclusively on census data and develops 41 neighbourhood types that are aggregated into 11 groups.

PRIZM

PRIZM was launched by Claritas UK in 1996. This classification system, which has its roots in the American system of the same name, is unique in that it contains no census data but relies on demographic information contained within the lifestyle questionnaires to which it has access. These questionnaires were originally designed and implemented by CMT (Computerised Marketing Technologies) and NDL (National Demographics and Lifestyles) and have been completed by as many as 17 million separate households, or 75 per cent of the UK total. These large-scale questionnaires are made possible through a mixture of sponsorship and list rental. Sponsors will pay for the exclusive results of questions relating to the use of their products, while other information relating to general lifestyle behaviour and overall attitudes is available for rental or sale.

Many of these questionnaires are distributed through the print media. Information is generally gleaned from warranty cards and media-distributed questionnaires. In the latter case, customers who complete questionnaires are granted money-off vouchers for products marketed by the sponsoring organisations. The output of such questionnaires is cluster-analysed and then related to postcodes so that targeting is possible. The resultant system is organised at three levels: four life-stage groups, 19 life-stage/income groups and 72 types, which can be used as appropriate.

Comparison of the Various Systems

Detailed analysis of the systems listed above undertaken by Sleight (1997) and Ozimek (1993) shows that each of the available systems has particular advantages and none is particularly superior. This view is echoed by Leventhal (1995), who states that each system has its adherents who have found that it has worked very well in their own circumstances.

GEODEMOGRAPHICS: AN IRISH PERSPECTIVE

This section examines segmentation in direct marketing from the Irish perspective, with particular emphasis on geodemographic profiling. Some examples are used to illustrate its practical application. All of the data analysis techniques detailed earlier are equally applicable in the Irish context, as anywhere else, subject to sufficient information being available to apply them nationally. Given that these techniques have already been explained in some detail, it is not proposed to revisit them again.

Census Information

The key advantages in using the Census as the base for geodemographic profiling are that it is conducted nationally, it is mandatory (i.e. it must be completed by all the population) and it is quantifiable. Therefore it provides a true measurement of the demographics of the population. The Census collects approximately 1,700 individual pieces of information on such data as:

- Age
- Household composition
- Stage in the family life cycle
- Occupation
- Social class and socio-economic status

- Gender

- Car ownership

- Housing (i.e. mortgage paid or outstanding, rented accommodation analysis)

- Education standards

- Travel to work.

Given that the Census is collected every five years, it can immediately highlight trends in population movement, changes in age profiles, etc. By mapping these trends across each different release of the Census it becomes easy to identify the changes which are taking place within the structure and nature of the population as a whole and their consequent effects on the surrounding infrastructure. This information is vital to marketers because they must be aware of any emerging demographic trends which can adversely effect how and where they do business and their potential impact on profitability.

DEDs and Consumer Behaviour

These trends can be analysed by individual DED and the information can then be aggregated together into groups of DEDs, thus creating a sales territory or a catchment area which can be analysed in terms of business potential and profitability. So, for example, a bank may analyse its customer base in terms of the level of penetration it has within its catchment area for car loans versus the total number of cars for that DED or catchment area.

The year 1996 marked the introduction of the Irish Consumer Marketing Database (ICMD) which has expanded our knowledge of consumer behaviour at DED level. Set up by Precision Marketing Information Ltd. (PMI), a joint venture between An Post and Equifax Inc., the world's largest provider of consumer information data, this database aims to provide information on the 2.6 million adults within the Republic. Addresses of the 1.1 million households have been gathered from the Electoral Registers of 1995, 1996 and 1997. In addition, product usage and lifestyle data are included, which have been assembled from various national surveys conducted in recent years. Other lifestyle information can be used where clients have conducted their own surveys. At present the demographic section of

the database contains about 150,000 records and includes information on age, residency, family size, household composition, financial
requirements, newspaper choice, hobbies and interests. This represents about one household in every eight (13 per cent).

By analysing the available lifestyle data at DED level, it is possible
to target likely users of a company's products in a more precise manner. A comparison can also be made of the profile of a firm's existing
customer base relative to the ICMD. In this way, one may acquire
additional prospects from the national database.

Finally, PMI has subdivided the 3,400 DEDs to arrive at 85,000
thoroughfares (streets/roads/townlands), each of which has been
assigned its own classification code. Although such a Neighbours
system offers more refined targeting than DEDs (which are approximately 25 times larger), its success depends on the build-up of accurate non-census data.

Geographical Information Systems

The use of this information can be further enhanced through dis-
playing the information on maps via a Geographical Information
System (GIS). Not only does this reflect the importance that geography has for most businesses, it also provides clear visual output from
the system. Information presented in a spreadsheet or tabular format
can be difficult to understand but information colour-coded or
shaded and displayed on a map is easily understandable (see Figure
9.2).

On-screen maps showing the distribution of supermarket customers in various residential areas offer a powerful illustration of the
impact of such presentations. Overlaying charts which show the
number of existing customers, non-customers, over 65-year-olds,
two-car households, or low proportions of unemployed people onto
product-related data can produce colour-coded maps which show
performance and potential in a very striking and simple manner.

FIGURE 9.2: COUNTY KERRY — % POPULATION CHANGE 1991–96

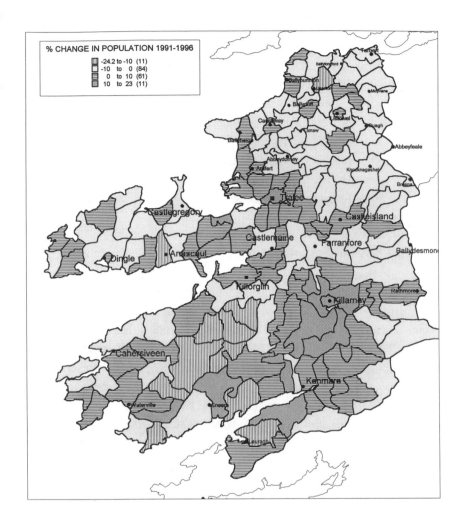

The base maps for the Republic of Ireland can be purchased from the Ordnance Survey Office and are available at county, town, and DED level. Additional layers such as the national road network, rivers and canal network or rail track location can also be provided.

Some would say that the gap between each Census collection is problematic in that new developments constructed in the intervening period cannot be included until the next release becomes available. Certainly this has been a problem in the UK, where the Census is collected every ten years. Allied to the fact that the level of information collected is not as detailed as in Ireland, this has facilitated the growth in lifestyle companies like NDL to service the UK market. In the Irish context, this is certainly less of a problem due to the five-year survey period.

DEDs and Market Segmentation

So how can this bank of demographic information be applied to assist in more effective segmentation? The starting point is to analyse the existing customer database in terms of the customer type, products purchased, frequency and value of purchases, lifestyle information, etc. This will highlight information on product groupings by distinct customer types, cross-sell opportunities, etc. Once this has been completed, the customer database should then be compared against the DED to analyse performance by DED or catchment area and to identify additional information that could be incorporated into the segmentation model — for example, drive-time analysis calculations from a number of different locations to a specific branch or store. This will not only reveal information about the various different customer profiles, DED or catchment area penetration levels, but it may also highlight information about how you do business.

DEDs are the key to understanding markets, as illustrated in Figure 9.3.

FIGURE 9.3: THE CENTRALITY OF DEDS

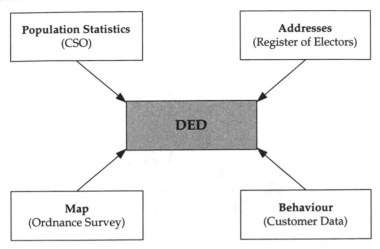

Until recently, the principal difficulty in the utilisation of the available Census information in conjunction with a customer database was in the allocation of the customer database records to the correct DED. As can be seen in Figure 9.4, a street or townland can be divided across a number of DEDs. The implications of allocating customer records to an incorrect DED can have serious implications in that it skews the profile of your existing customer base and any subsequent calculations of business potential and profitability will be incorrect.

Individual Addresses in an Irish Context

How therefore does one allocate customer database records to the correct DED? In essence, this involves matching at individual address level to ensure that the correct DED code is being appended.

However, this matching presents a problem due to the lack of standardisation of Irish addresses and the consequent inconsistencies in structure and content. This has in fact proved to be a significant problem in the management of customer data and customer databases. The uniqueness of the Irish market is that nearly all addressed mail gets delivered as a result of local knowledge. Minor address variations may not affect delivery but they can cause problems when trying to de-duplicate to identify how many actual customers there are as opposed to the number of accounts and, more

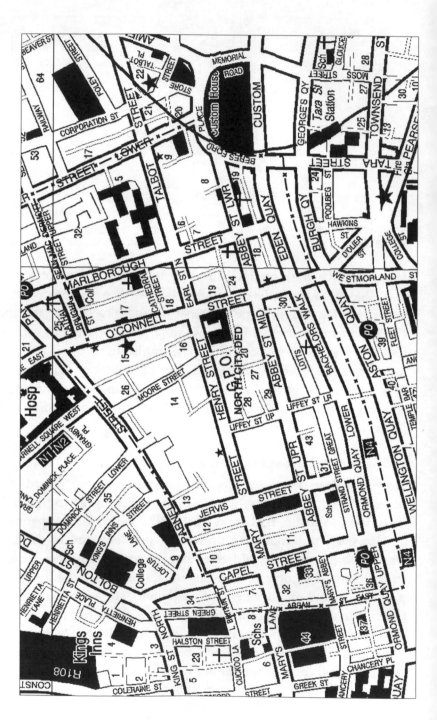

FIGURE 9.4: DUBLIN NORTH CITY DED

importantly, which accounts are attributable to which customer. This problem is increased considerably when there are numerous different sources of input to the database, thus making detailed database analysis difficult to achieve. For example, if an insurance company allows its brokers to register new policies online to the main database, it is probable that different brokers will use different address variations and abbreviations in entering the policy information.

The UK, through the provision of Royal Mail's PAF, has been able to overcome these difficulties. The Royal Mail provides quarterly updates to PAF incorporating all new addresses that have been created. At present such a service is not available in Ireland and there are no immediate plans for a similar service to be implemented.

To that extent it has been left to the private sector to overcome these difficulties (see list of specialist firms in the Appendix). Response Tech. Ltd. has developed a product called Matchmaker — an address validation, geodemographic profiling and mapping product specifically for the Irish market. Matchmaker facilitates better planning and targeting:

- Through comprehensive standardisation, verification and correction of all household addresses

- By appending the correct DED codes to the validated addresses

- Through its GIS module, an ability to analyse market profile and penetration and present this information on a map.

This means that the kind of geodemographic systems available in Britain since the early 1980s can be replicated here, although at a slightly larger geographical level.

THE FUTURE

The rapid growth in data analysis and customer segmentation will continue in Ireland as more and more businesses become aware of the power that customer databases can provide. This will be based on the use of geodemographics and lifestyle in the consumer market allied to the information retained on the customer database. This will facilitate the development of one-to-one marketing along similar lines to that evidenced in the UK and US.

There will be considerable development in the whole area of customer modelling and behavioural prediction using the latest methods like data mining, neural networks, etc., as the amount of available information increases in Ireland. This will be particularly true for the large financial institutions and supermarkets, who are pursuing this at the moment. For example, loyalty cards are not just about rewarding the customer and incentivising them with relevant offers; they also allow marketers to identify purchase patterns, products and values and these can then be used to predict customer behaviour.

It is likely that "data fusion", or the merging of market research data with database information, will also increase in the future. This is a system whereby the results of market research in which information is given anonymously will be married into large-scale databases such as the electoral register. The essential difference between data fusion and geodemographics is that, while the latter works at group level (i.e. Electoral District level), the former tries to match survey responses with customers who are identical on a number of key variables. Although the technique was first described in the late 1980s (see Baker et al., 1989), little has been published in the meantime. However, recent work by Leventhal (1997) on the FRS (Financial Research Survey, sample 60,000) has shown that the technique could provide excellent new information.

CASE STUDY: USING MATCHMAKER

An international FMCG company used Matchmaker to assist in identifying supermarket catchment areas within a sales territory where sales were steadily declining against the "supermarket own brand" label. This decline amounted to 2.5 per cent nationally over a two-year period and could be attributed to an improvement in the quality of the own label product allied to a cheaper price point. Nationally, each percentage point decline represented a multi-million pound decrease in sales.

Through Matchmaker, two locations of similar size and with similar demographic profiles were identified and selected for analysis. The starting point was to create a database of known existing users of the branded product. The details of all respondents to sales promotion activity for the previous three years across the entire country were identified and extracted for address validation and de-duplication. This amounted to just over one million sales promotion applications.

Analysis of Sales Promotion Data

These sales promotion applications were address validated, which resulted in some 75 per cent of the address data on file being updated or enhanced and two per cent of the file being rejected from the process due to insufficient address information. The address validated data was then de-duplicated at family level to identify the number of promotions responded to by each individual family, as in some cases an individual may have applied more than once to a specific promotional offer. Alternatively, different individuals within the same family may have responded to the same sales promotion and will thus have to be identified as being two applications from the same family. As a result of the address standardisation and enhancement achieved through Matchmaker, the de-duplication process was far easier to implement and netted down to 270,000 family records (averaging 3.7 applications per family) containing some 375,000 individual family members. Obviously, the number of sales promotion applications received varied across families, with some having been more responsive than others.

Each household was analysed in terms of the number and type of promotions responded to. Each promotion required a number of tokens to be collected and submitted to verify the promotion application. Using this information, allied to the number of cases sold on which the promotion was available, it was possible to allocate a consumption weighting to each sales promotion offer in terms of the volume of product which had to be consumed to attain the required number of tokens to enter the promotion. This allow for the allocation of consumption classifications to the different households based on the promotions responded to.

Profiling Existing Customers

In addition, market research information generated through consumer panels and other independent market research findings were also analysed for modelling purposes. These findings indicated that the key factors influencing consumption were:

- Family size

- Number and ages of children

- Age of the mother

- Social class.

Combining this information with sales information by sales territory, it was possible to draw some conclusions about the profile of existing consumers. Each of the key factors influencing consumption were incorporated into a scoring model based on the weightings they attained through the independent research activity. The maximum score achievable was 100. This information was then mapped using the GIS module in Matchmaker, actual sales information was compared against predicted sales information, and the variations analysed.

Mailing Strategy

Of the 270,000 households on the database a selection of the heaviest households (in terms of consumption) nationally were selected for mailing. The mail pack included a questionnaire designed to gather information on the key consumption criteria identified in the market research activity, the supermarket where the main shopping was done, as well as the actual consumption of the branded product per month. Money-off coupons for the branded product were included and these coupons had a personalised barcode printed on them enabling the users of the coupons to be tracked. All recipients were also informed that all completed responses would be entered into a prize draw. The overall response rate to the mailing was 55 per cent and over 85 per cent of the respondents completed the questionnaire in full. The consumption information received from the respondents led to many families having their consumption category being reclassified.

Using this consumption information and the data collected on the key consumption factors in the questionnaire, the weightings attached to the key consumption criteria could be revalidated using factor and discriminant analysis. This resulted in some modification to the scores allocated to each of the individual criteria and the scoring model was subsequently revised to take account of this. New maps reflecting potential sales were then designed incorporating the revised scoring routine (see Figure 9.5).

Test Design

On the basis of the information received from the questionnaire, two areas of similar profile were selected for testing. Each of these areas had shown a decline in market share almost in line with the overall national average. The objective was to see if the decline in market share could be arrested or even reversed, by targeting the catchment areas where there were significant numbers matching the demographic profile of existing heavy, medium and potential future heavy users. A secondary objective was to recruit heavy, potential heavy and medium users of the branded product who were not currently on the database. The trial was scheduled to last for a 12-month period.

All DEDs in both catchment areas were then profiled using the scoring routine devised. Given that the maximum score attainable was 100, any DED attaining a score of less than 30 was excluded on the basis that the potential returns were unlikely to be high enough to justify the investment involved. Once this DED analysis was completed, the selected catchment areas were finalised and ready for testing.

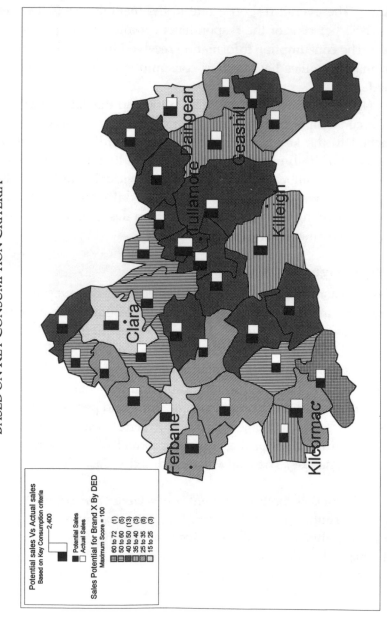

FIGURE 9.5: POTENTIAL SALES ANALYSIS BY DED FOR BRAND X — USING A SCORING MODEL BASED ON KEY CONSUMPTION CRITERIA

All families on the database within one of the selected catchment areas were then de-duplicated against all families on the Electoral Roll (ER) in that catchment area. This necessitated address validation of the ER data in order to facilitate accurate de-duplication. All records on the ER which did not match any record on the promotions database were then mailed with a mail pack containing personalised money-off coupons and a questionnaire similar to that sent to all sales promotion respondents. Total quantity mailed was approximately 6,500 households. The response rate to this mailing was 38 per cent, but the actual number meeting the target demographic profile for heavy responders and medium users in terms of age profile, household composition, etc. that responded was just under 78 per cent — a ratio of 4:1.

An ongoing contact strategy was then developed for heavy, potential future heavy and medium users of the branded product who had responded to the mailings. They received a total of six mailings over the 12-month period, which, although product-related, were designed to be generally informative and appeal to various members of the family. Some of the mailings contained money-off coupons for the branded product or other products within the FMCG company's product range. Non-respondents to previous mailings were offered two additional opportunities to enter the scheme during this 12-month period.

Light user families were not included in the programme as, based on the calculations, it was believed that it was not cost-effective to include them. This was because market research had indicated that although they might constitute 43 per cent of all the households who purchase the branded product, they account for less than ten per cent of the overall volume sold.

All new responses to sales promotion offers within this specific catchment area were also incorporated onto the database as part of the regular programme, subject to their meeting the consumption classification criteria.

The other selected catchment area — i.e. the control group catchment area — received no direct mail contact from the database and continued to do business in the same way as it had prior to the establishment of the database.

The pricing policies, distribution, advertising and promotional support remained at the same level as it had prior to establishment of the trial. No discrimination in terms of additional support was given to either area during the duration of the trial.

Case Study Findings

Following the 12-month evaluation period, the results were analysed across the selected catchment areas. The control group catchment area, which had had been allowed to continue doing business in an unchanged fashion, had continued to decline and had suffered an additional one per cent drop in market share.

On the other hand, the test area, even allowing for the direct mail couponing activity on the branded product, had shown an increase of six per cent in market share. Post-test research indicated that this could be attributed to the careful targeting and messages delivered by the contact programme which had engendered new loyal users to the branded product, as well as re-introducing lapsed purchasers to the product.

The success of the test was such that this campaign is being introduced nationally by the FMCG company in question.

APPENDIX: GEODEMOGRAPHIC PROFILING COMPANIES IN THE REPUBLIC OF IRELAND

Gamma
14 Clanwilliam Square
Dublin 2
Tel: 01 662 0476
Contact: Fergal O Neill

PMI Limited
Alexandra House
Earlsfort Terrace
Dublin 2
Tel: 01 676 6144
Fax: 01 676 8727
Contact: Carolyn Walsh

Response Tech. Ltd.
Response House
Whitefriars
Aungier Street
Dublin 2
Tel: 01 478 4509
Fax: 01 478 4531
E-mail: marketing@response_grp.com
Contact : Dave Fitzgerald

Beacon Dodsworth
Garth Mews
Sim Balk Lane
Bishopthorpe
York YO2 1UE
England
Contact: Simon Perry

REFERENCES TO CHAPTER 9

Baker, Ken, John Birmingham and Colin McDonald (1979), "ACORN — A Classification of Residential Neighbourhoods", *Proceedings of the Market Research Society Conference*, London: The Market Research Society.

Baker, Ken, Paul Harris and John O'Brien (1989), "Data Fusion: An Appraisal and Experimental Evaluation", *Journal of the Market Research Society*, Vol. 31, No. 2, pp. 153–212.

Dibb, Sally, Lyndon Simkin, William M. Pride and O.C. Ferrell (1997), *Marketing: Concepts and Strategies*, Third European Edition, Boston: Houghton Mifflin.

Hallberg, Garth (1995), *All Consumers are not Created Equal*, New York: John Wiley.

Leventhal, Barry (1995), "Evaluation of Geodemographic Classifications", *Journal of Targeting, Measurement and Analysis for Marketing*, Vol. 4, No. 2, pp. 173–183.

Leventhal, Barry (1997), "An Approach to Fusing Market Research with Database Marketing", *Journal of the Market Research Society*, Vol. 39, No. 4, pp. 545–558.

Ozimek, John (1993), *Targeting for Success*, Berkshire: McGraw-Hill Book Company.

Raphel, Murray (1995), *Up the Loyalty Ladder*, Dublin: O'Brien Press.

Sleight, Peter (1997), *Targeting Consumers*, Second Edition, Henley-on-Thames, Oxfordshire: NTC Publications.

Chapter 10

DIRECT MARKETING AND PRIVACY

Kieran Devenish

Overview

Nowadays, direct marketers seem overly concerned with the mechanics of direct marketing (DM) and fail to address many of the wider issues. Already, there are growing demands from consumers that their right of personal privacy be fully respected by direct marketers. Failure to address these concerns will alienate potential customers and ultimately damage the direct marketing industry.

In this chapter, we examine the concept of privacy and look at its constituent elements. The importance of privacy is outlined, and the distinction between "data protection" and "privacy" is explained. Later, we consider the issue of privacy in Ireland. Finally, we briefly consider what might be done by the direct marketing industry to meet the privacy expectations of consumers.

PRIVACY: A CAUSE FOR CONCERN

W.H. Auden knew well that people like to receive mail. This comes across vividly in his wonderfully spirited poem "Night Mail";[1] he neatly captures the sense of anticipation and delight that people associate with the arrival of the post:

> Letters of thanks, letters from banks,
> Letters of joy from girl and boy,
> Receipted bills and invitations

---

[1] "Night Mail" (1936) in *Collected Shorter Poems* (1966).

> To inspect new stock[2] or to visit relations,
> And applications for situations,
> And timid lovers' declarations,
> And gossip, gossip from all the nations.

One might have imagined that, as people like to receive letters, the success of direct mail was almost assured. Certainly, it has many advantages over competing media.[3] Direct mail carries a targeted message; the potential for creativity and testing is enormous; the "clutter" of the marketplace is avoided; and, perhaps most importantly, there's a personal touch about it. What's more — as several studies have shown (Rogers, 1996: 219; O'Neill, 1996: Table 2) — the vast majority of people open their direct mail and at least glance at it.

But a key strength of the medium — the fact that it singles out people by name — has become a weakness. In most of the developed direct marketing countries in Europe, the growth in direct mail has been accompanied by an increase in consumer resistance to it (see, for example, Long et al, 1998).

In the past, consumer resentment could probably have been summed up in two equations: *unsolicited = unwanted* and *more = worse*. Unfortunately, little has been done then or since to reduce mail volumes. Now, the industry's once almost sacrosanct "right" to disseminate commercial information is under serious threat from a feisty, fickle, and formidable foe: the right to personal privacy.

Many practitioners are either unaware of, or undisturbed by, the extent of the problem. This lack of awareness is not helped by the fact that privacy issues are largely ignored in most of the standard textbooks. Indeed, in what is perhaps the most widely used direct marketing manual in Ireland[4] — a two-volume, 800-page textbook — just a single page is devoted to privacy (and it deals only with "data protection").[5]

---

[2] Note that even back in 1936, smart retailers were using direct mail to entice customers to "inspect new stock".

[3] Well summarised in, for example, Jenkins (1984: 34–36).

[4] *The Practitioner's Guide to Direct Marketing* (1995).

[5] This is nothing new. For example, Murrow and Hyman (1994) — mirroring concerns repeatedly raised by Schultz in editorials in the *Journal of Direct*

Moreover, even some of the most responsible marketers incorrectly assume that, provided they operate within the established data protection system and avail of the industry's mail and telephone preferences services, their obligations to respect consumers' privacy are satisfied.

Before we continue, it should be emphasised that while we will use the example of direct mail to illustrate some key points, the issue of privacy extends well beyond the direct mail sector. Indeed, the more intrusive the DM technique, the more serious the potential problem.

Telemarketing, for instance, is more likely to be adversely affected by privacy issues than traditional mail marketing. Also, there is a positive correlation between the amount of personal information gathered and the sensitivity of consumers. Those using advanced profiling technologies, for example, will face closer scrutiny than those using simpler tools (Korff, 1998: 78).

DATA PROTECTION AND PRIVACY

An important distinction must be drawn between "data protection" and "privacy". Though there is some overlap, the former is not a proxy for the latter.

"Privacy" has a wide spectrum; "data protection" has narrow range. "Privacy" tends to be vague and subjective; by contrast, "data protection" is reasonably well defined and relatively objective. While most practitioners are familiar with data protection requirements, relatively few seem alive to wider privacy issues.

WHAT IS PRIVACY?

There is no single, commonly accepted definition of "privacy". It means different things to different people. But though views on privacy may be vague and varied, there seems to be a large measure of agreement on its core elements.

Marketing — note that direct marketers now seem overly concerned with the mechanics of direct marketing and are failing to address many of the wider issues (e.g. privacy). They "now emphasise methodology at the expense of substance". See Murrow and Hyman (1994), p. 54.

In 1972, the UK's Committee on Privacy, chaired by Kenneth Younger, thoroughly examined the issue. They reviewed much of its vast body of literature and concurrently commissioned a major survey to gauge public opinion on privacy issues. Their Report (Younger, 1972) is a classic work. Written in plain language, it simplifies many of the key concepts involved.

Younger's survey revealed that people's ideas of privacy generally fell into two groups: *freedom from intrusion* and *privacy of information* (par. 100, p. 32). The Committee adopted and adapted these and, for the purposes of their Report, considered the right of privacy as possessing two main aspects:

> The first . . . is *freedom from intrusion* upon oneself, one's home, family and relationships. The second is *privacy of information*, that is the right to determine for oneself how and to what extent information about oneself is communicated to others. (par. 38, p. 10; emphasis added)

Aspects of Privacy

What most DM practitioners refer to as "data protection" is essentially the same as the "privacy of information" element shown above. The other aspect, freedom from intrusion, is less well known; and is thus worth examining further. However, before we do this, a couple of points deserve mention.

First, based on the combined weight of the medical and psychological evidence and the results of the public attitudes survey, Younger concluded:

> . . . that everyone needs some privacy, that some need it more than others, that the more you have the more you cherish it, that deprivation of privacy can be harmful, but so too can an excess of it, and that the effects of both vary from one person to another. (par. 105, p. 32)

Second, there are many different definitions of privacy. The Younger Committee shortlisted nine (Appendix K, p. 327); from these, two were selected[6] and then fashioned into the privacy elements shown above. That Younger preferred a particular brand of privacy does not invalidate the other, typically broader, definitions available. Indeed, their choice may simply reflect social attitudes in 1972; if their investigation was repeated now, their conclusions might differ.

That privacy is interpreted so subjectively — and the individual's need for it varies so widely — has profound implications for direct marketing. For example, a consumer who interprets privacy as "the right to be let alone"[7] might object to receiving a message from Santa Claus; another person, who thinks too much privacy is harmful, might welcome "cold calls".

Freedom from Intrusion

The growing demand for privacy can be partly explained by the fact that society is changing. It is becoming more urbanised; the pace of life is quickening; social bonds are weakening; and people are now less dependent on their neighbours than in the past. We are becoming more and more anonymous to those around us. This anonymity not only permits privacy but also fosters it. As Younger suggested, the more privacy you have, the more you prize it (par. 105, p. 32).

Pierce the individual's shield of anonymity and, almost by definition, you also invade their privacy. That may help us to understand why personally addressed, unrequested communications (such as unsolicited direct mail) are sometimes seen as intrusive and unwelcome.

If this point alone offered a complete rationale for consumer objections, one might reasonably conclude that *unaddressed* (i.e. non-personalised) mailings were largely inoffensive.

---

[6] Both taken from Westin (1970):

> 1. Viewed in terms of the relation of the individual to social participation, privacy is the voluntary and temporary withdrawal of a person from the general society through physical and psychological means, either in a state of solitude or small group intimacy or, when among larger groups, in a condition of anonymity or reserve.

> 2. Privacy is the claim of individuals, groups, or institutions to determine for themselves when, how and to what extent information about them is communicated to others.

[7] See, for example, Huttensteine (1985).

Now consider this question:

> Amongst your post one morning is a fat envelope addressed
> to "the Occupier" at your address. It contains a lot of glossy
> brochures advertising holidays in Spain. Would you regard
> the brochures as an invasion of your privacy?

Probably few, if any, DM practitioners would answer "yes" to that
question. Indeed, given the non-personalised nature of the mailing,
many might wonder how a privacy issue could arise at all.

Yet, when a similar question was put to consumers by Younger's
researchers, 14 per cent of respondents answered in the positive;
more disturbingly, a similar percentage thought that such mailings
should be prohibited by law (par. 412, p. 123).[8]

Though this example may now seem dated and irrelevant — it
relates to a once-off survey done in the UK in 1972 — it serves to reinforce a point made earlier: that privacy is often interpreted by consumers in fairly loose, but very personal, terms.

It is also useful to remember that privacy has a high emotive content. It follows that some of the "rational" arguments commonly advanced by the DM industry to offset criticism of direct mail (e.g. "if
you don't like the mailing, you can bin it") may be inappropriate.

PRIVACY AND DIRECT MARKETING IN IRELAND

"The issue of privacy", according to a major research study commissioned by the Irish Direct Marketing Association (IDMA), "is perhaps
the most important and sensitive issue shaping the future of direct
marketing in Ireland" (O'Neill, 1996: 92).

Some may genuinely doubt this. It might be argued, for example,
that many of the elements that conspired to create privacy problems
elsewhere do not yet exist in Ireland. Here, consumer complaints are
few; mail volumes are relatively low; lists are data protection com-
pliant; and concerns about DM and privacy are rarely the subject of
public debate.

In truth, some of these arguments do not survive close scrutiny.

---

[8] The question that followed tested public opinion about an addressed mailing
containing a brochure advertising an illustrated manual of sexual techniques.
This time, 67 per cent said it would invade their privacy; 72 per cent thought that
it should be prohibited by law.

Consider, for example, the statement that mail volumes in Ireland are low. It is true that the average Irish consumer received just 22 items of addressed direct mail in 1996[9] — about one-third of the European average. While this seems low, it is just an average figure. Some segments — higher income groups and urban dwellers, for example — receive more than others. The "average" also masks the fact that certain lists are more frequently used than others.

Further, these statistics relate to "addressed" mail only. Also coming through the letterbox are various leaflets, brochures, samples etc. Not everyone can readily distinguish "mail" and other advertising material. This tends to distort consumer perceptions of postal volumes and, in the process, tarnishes the image of "direct mail".

Next, the absence of official complaints does not, of itself, signify consumer interest in direct marketing materials or offers. (Alternatively, it might perhaps reflect apathetic resignation.) In any event, silence does not imply assent.

Now consider the following results of the IDMA Consumer Survey (O'Neill, 1996) carried out in late 1995. Consumers were asked:

"Would you be happy or not for companies selling the following types of services to contact you (a) by phone? or (b) by post?"

TABLE 10.1: CONSUMER ATTITUDES TO MAIL AND TELEPHONE CONTACTS

Service	By Phone		By Post	
	Happy	*Unhappy*	*Happy*	*Unhappy*
Entertainment	21%	75%	53%	39%
Restaurants, etc	20%	75%	49%	43%
Travel Services	20%	76%	56%	38%
Financial Services	12%	83%	48%	45%
Household Durables	11%	83%	46%	47%
Household Furniture	10%	84%	46%	46%
Clothes	11%	83%	46%	45%
Cars	11%	83%	42%	49%
Jobs and Appointments	36%	59%	57%	34%

Note: for sake of simplicity, the "Don't Knows" have been omitted.

---

[9] *Source*: PDMS (Private Direct Marketing Survey). Note, too, that there has been a nine-fold increase in mail volumes in 12 years.

Predictably enough, the results show that people are happier for companies to contact them by post than by phone. But given the vibrant DM environment in Ireland, the "approval rating" for postal contact is probably much lower than expected.

One possible explanation is that Irish consumers want to retain control over something (i.e. marketing materials) that might impinge on their privacy. That interpretation also helps to explain some of the other findings of the IDMA survey.

THE GROWING IMPORTANCE OF PRIVACY

That enormous store is placed by most people on the value of privacy was confirmed by the January 1997 Eurobarometer Survey Report (International Research Associates, 1997). It disclosed that 95 per cent of Europeans feel that it is important that the EU is trying to protect private lives and personal information (p. 32).

Another finding of the Eurobarometer poll was that two-thirds of Europeans did not know that laws existed to protect their private lives (p. 29). This is almost certain to lead to a determined effort by the authorities to educate consumers about their rights. After all, as the Irish Data Protection Commissioner succinctly stated in his 1995 Report: "Rights are of little use if people are not aware of them" (Glavey, 1995: 17).

In relation to data protection, the industry's trade associations have, at European level, fostered a regime which seeks to strike "a reasonable and fair balance" between the interests of direct marketers and individuals (Federation of European Direct Marketing, 1995: 3). And the recent EU Directive on Data Protection[10] — which aims to reconcile the competing rights of "commercial free speech" and "privacy" — was largely welcomed by the industry.

But by taking an industry-friendly, minimalist approach — a light legislative garment fitted loosely around self-regulation — this Directive is more likely to abate than abolish the very real concerns of consumers. The rather relaxed approach of the Directive is unlikely, for example, to convince DM-estranged consumers that unwanted direct mail is good for them.

---

[10] EU Directive 95/46/EC on the Protection of Individuals with Regard to the Processing of Personal Data.

ADDRESSING THE ISSUES

In this chapter, we have attempted to raise and discuss issues of privacy; the more difficult task of resolving the problems highlighted is beyond the scope of this text.

The following ideas are not meant to be prescriptive; rather, they are offered as prompts for discussion and debate.

Data Protection

Korff (1998: 50) suggests that

> . . . honest adherence to the letter *and spirit* of data protection should be seen . . . not as a bureaucratic hindrance . . . but rather as a contribution towards obtaining the trust of the consumer — without which the new opportunities for direct marketing in Europe [in particular, in connection with loyalty cards] will indeed be wasted.

But should direct marketers confine themselves to honest application of existing data protection rules? These are *minimum* requirements, and are unlikely to meet the increasing demands of consumers.

Data protection could be to direct marketing what Total Quality Management is to manufacturing industry — a means of winning customer confidence by continuous improvement.

Two simple examples might explain how they could achieve higher standards. First, data users could develop a Data Protection Charter for customers — a short, simply worded document designed to explain how personal information is held and used.

Next, all personally addressed, unsolicited direct mail might indicate the source of the recipient's name.

Freedom from Intrusion

A large proportion of the direct mail sent to Irish consumers is of little or no interest to them (O'Neill, 1996). For reasons given earlier, some consumers may also perceive that they already receive too much material through the letterbox.

The "Focus on the Future" Research (O'Neill, 1996: 102) suggests that for direct mail to succeed further in Ireland, it will have to move "quickly and collectively" from untargeted promotion towards a real two way dialogue with customers:

> This will also shift the practice and perception of direct mail away from a generally unacceptable exercise in postal cold calling, to an ideal situation in which most of the recipients of direct mail are both interested in it and willing to respond to it.

Too idealistic? Perhaps: it suggests a transition that none of our European counterparts has yet managed successfully. Of course, the fact that no easy remedy is available should not block the search for a solution.

Mail volumes might, perhaps, be voluntarily curbed. We could, for example, adopt the Dutch "sticker" system to assist those householders who object to receiving unaddressed, unsolicited material. And far more could be done to publicise the Mail Preference Service.

CONCLUSION

Throughout Europe, consumers are increasingly worried about their privacy. Those concerns need to be fully addressed. For that to happen, the DM industry must first acknowledge the existence and seriousness of the privacy problem. Responding to the consumer challenge will necessitate a radically fresh approach. If we are to succeed in the future, we need to be less concerned with the mechanics of DM and take heed of the wider issues.

REFERENCES TO CHAPTER 10

Federation of European Direct Marketing (1995), "Guide to the Common Position Draft of the EU Framework Directive on Data Protection and its Implications for Direct Marketing", Brussels: FEDM.

Glavey, F. (1995), "Sixth Annual Report of the Data Protection Commissioner, 1994", Dublin.

Huttensteine, M.L. (1985), "The Right to be Let Alone: A Descriptive Analysis of the Right to Privacy in Cases from 1880 through 1983", PhD Thesis published in North Carolina at Chapel Hill.

Institute of Direct Marketing (1995), *The Practitioner's Guide to Direct Marketing*, Middlesex: The Institute of Direct Marketing.

International Research Associates (1997), "Eurobarometer 46.1 — Information Technology and Data Privacy" Produced for the European Commission, Brussels.

Jenkins, V. (1984), *The Concept of Direct Marketing*, Melbourne: Australia Post, pp. 34–36.

Korff, D. (1998), "A Briefing on the EC Directive on Data Protection, with Particular Attention to the Implications of the Directive for the Direct Marketing Industry" (Unpublished), Brussels: Federation of European Direct Marketing.

Long, G., S.J. Angold and M.K. Hogg (1998), "Data, Privacy and Relationship Marketing: A Conundrum", *The Journal of Database Marketing*, Vol. 5, No. 3, p.231 (Abstract).

Murrow, J.L. and M.R. Hyman (1994), "Direct Marketing: Passages, Definitions, and Déjà Vu", *Journal of Direct Marketing*, Vol. 8, No. 3, Summer, p. 54.

O'Neill, G. (1996), *Focus on the Future: The Coming Boom in Direct Marketing* (Vols. 1 and 2), Dublin: Irish Direct Marketing Association.

Rogers, J.L. (1996), "Mail Advertising and Consumer Behavior", *Psychology and Marketing*, Vol. 13, No. 2, p. 219.

Westin, A. (1970), *Privacy and Freedom*, London: Bodley Head, p. 7.

Younger, K. (1972), *Report of the Committee on Privacy*, London: HMSO, Cmnd. 5012.

Chapter 11

MAILING LISTS AND DATA PROTECTION

Michael O'Donovan, Bill Moss *and* Pat Cody

Overview

"Where did you get my name from?" is a question that many people ask today. Direct marketers are increasingly using mailing lists to target potential customers in national and international markets. Lists are at the very core of direct marketing. In this chapter, we set out to define mailing lists and explain the importance of the mailing list for the direct market. We outline the internal and external sources of information used to compile lists. We profile the Irish list industry and the availability of lists. Finally we consider the data protection issues in using consumers' personal information.

WHAT IS A MAILING LIST?

The strict definition of a mailing list is: a list of persons, businesses, organisations or others, which is used to post something to them (a letter, a sample, a video, coupons). Baier (1983) views the list as a market segment and suggests that the list is the "place" of the four Ps of direct marketing. Lists are dynamic and perishable as people move away, marry or their circumstances change, and as such list management involves ongoing maintenance in order to deliver value.

In this chapter, however, we use the term to convey the sense of a list that enables you deliver your message to the properly targeted audience. As well as addresses, the list could contain other contact media such as:

- Telephone Numbers
- Fax Numbers

- E-mail addresses or other Internet vehicles
- Demographic zones (for unaddressed door-to-door leaflet drops).

THE IMPORTANCE OF THE LIST

Targeting customers is a critical factor in the success of a list. Of all the elements in a direct marketing campaign, the list is usually the second least expensive (after the envelope). Yet it is easily the most important one. The basic elements of a campaign usually consist of:

- Target Group (List)
- Product/Price
- Creative/Offer
- Envelope
- Response Media.

David Ogilvy, one of the world's foremost authorities on advertising, has estimated that the list is approximately twice as important to the campaign's success as either the product itself or the offer. You will not sell round-the-world cruises to a list of the unemployed, nor probably to a list of first-year university students — although you may get a large number of responses and an even larger number of complaints. If, however, the list is composed of well-to-do, newly retired couples, you may well overcome even a poor offer, or a boring creative approach, or a package in a brown manila envelope with no response card or Freephone number. At least you have a chance of success with the right audience.

For most of this chapter, we will examine how to put together the best list and how to do so legally and within the spirit of the Data Protection Act.

WHERE TO GET YOUR LIST

Lists come from internal and external sources. In general, your sources for a successful target group will be:

- Your own customer database (internal)
- Previous enquiries or past customers (internal)

- People who "look like" the above two groups (externally sourced); essentially you should profile your customers and prospects
  using any combination of the following:

  ◊   Geographical location

  ◊   Size of company

  ◊   Industry sector

  ◊   Age of business

- Groups that market research tell you should have an interest in
  your offer (externally sourced).

List Sources — Internal

There is no better source for a direct marketing campaign than your
own customer database. They know you, they may love even you,
and you carry familiarity and (one hopes) credibility. Mail them
early and mail them often. It will help if you keep this group as a
separately held database apart from — or linked to — your accounts
department. There are a number of application packages which will
help (ACT, Goldmine, Telemagic, etc.) but the important objective is
to keep it up-to-date — so as to be able to respond to price changes,
seasonal offers, and new products, to a segment who have shown
previous interest. (You also need to be sure that you have not kept
customers' details on the list longer than the Data Protection Act allows you to.)

   If possible, keep your prospect file in the same database, coded for
product interest. This is your strongest marketing list and the following section describes your best sources for keeping it that way.
One other important point — when you are building up your list,
make sure you will be entitled to use it. There is no point in going to
a lot of trouble and expense to construct a list if you then find that
you cannot use it because you have forgotten to comply with the
Data Protection Act (see "Collecting Information for Mailing Lists" in
the "Data Protection" section below).

How to Build up Your Own Internal List

Reception

The specific details of every company that visits you or contacts you should be recorded for your database.

Field Sales Force

Every legitimate show of interest should be logged with company name, details, person's name and title, date and product/service codes.

Telemarketing

This can be either your own list or one acquired from an outside agency. Keep track of all results. All too often, telemarketing campaigns are used for a quick fix and valuable medium- to long-range prospecting data are lost. Take the time to set it up for now and for the future.

Sales Promotion

Names gathered from exhibitions, coupons, bar-coded redemptions, competitions and the like are time-sensitive. Use them quickly, preferably within one year. These are not usually well-researched data, but are more like a snapshot in time, particularly with regard to consumers, and should be used to develop relationships from the start — not to gather dust.

List Sources — External

Desk Research

Good sources for prospects in the business sector are the tried and trusted directories such as Kompass, the IPA Yearbook, Golden Pages, and the myriad members' directories published by various trade associations (Ireland has over 300).

Internet

On the World Wide Web, you will find resources similar to published directories. Valuable prospects can be identified by searching the on-line directories available on literally thousands of sites. This is particularly useful for international prospects and for "top-slicing" major companies.

When you have to source external lists, there are three primary divisions:

Commercial Sources

These are the well-known companies that deal in lists. Usually they advertise what they have, declare the cost, and are not shy about urging you to use them.

Private Sources

These lists are commercially available but rarely advertised. They form only a secondary source of income to the organisations providing them. Examples include membership lists of professional and other similar bodies.

Exchange Lists

Some lists of responders (charity donors and some mail order buyers are two notable types) have been cleared vis-à-vis data protection but are not commercially available. They can, however, be exchanged for your customer database.

A well-known example is washing machine distributors "swapping" their list with detergent manufacturers. No direct competition; a perfect audience. After allowing for de-duplication, each party has a fresh group of prospects — and the consumer will receive a very good offer.

One must be careful here to ensure that all elements of the Data Protection Act have been considered. While this is covered in detail at the end of this chapter, the main point is that if a notification, such as an "opt-out" box, is used when gathering the name, the notification must contain the fact that, unless ticked, the data may be passed to third parties for direct marketing purposes or offers.

THE LIST INDUSTRY: HOW IT WORKS

The industry can be divided into five business categories:

1. List owners

2. List managers

3. Direct marketing or advertising agencies

4. Clients

5. List brokers.

List owners are the commercial and, in some cases, fraternal (Clubs, Trade Associations) organisations that actually possess the data and to whom all or the majority of the rental income accrues. In most cases, they are also responsible for gathering the information, data entry, updating, and protection of lists.

List managers are companies that act on behalf of list owners and carry out the technical side of list processing (data entry, list production, and marketing of the list). For this, they will charge the list owner a fee, typically 30–50 per cent of the list income. This is quite a common practice in the US and in the UK, where companies such as Mardev and Dudley Jenkins manage literally thousands of lists.

Advertising and direct marketing agencies work on behalf of the client and will therefore usually be responsible for selecting the list. Their fee is usually added to the cost of the list. Their primary function is twofold:

1. Working with the client to determine what target groups have been successful in the past

2. "Brainstorming" with the list owners/managers/brokers to select the final list(s).

Clients, of course, are self-explanatory. The only thing we will stress, in terms of their importance to the equation, is that you, or your agency, must be sure that the view of what target groups have historically responded is totally objective and not based on "gut feeling".

Finally, *List brokers*, operating independently on behalf of the client, recommend the best list for the campaign. Their commission, usually 20–25 per cent, is normally paid by the list owner. Their brief is to be objective so that the client gets the best possible result. There are currently (1998) five companies in Ireland who operate, at least to some degree, as list brokers.

LIST SOURCES — BUSINESS-TO-BUSINESS

The list industry, and particularly the list owners' market, is highly fragmented. We have identified at least 80 commercially available individual list sources. We name some of the major ones as examples of the general categories available in the sector.

Major Companies

Companies such as Kompass, Dun & Bradstreet, and *Business & Finance* are the main commercial list owners who track the top 10,000–20,000 Irish companies and provide in-depth information on each.

These companies generally track businesses in the categories of manufacturing, wholesale, business and financial services, but are usually weak in retailing, trades, professions and leisure. However, the amount of detail on each company they do track is quite exhaustive, including:

- Company age

- Parent data

- Export volume

- Export destination

- Credit rating

- Bankers

- Middle management.

Small Companies (Employing 1–10)

There are approximately 30,000–40,000 locations included in this "one-to-ten" employee sector, which are available from a number of list owners, such as Bill Moss and Associates, IDS and Thom's.

Farming (Agripost)

This is treated as a separate category. There are 85,000 known farmers who can be targeted by number of acres farmed or by type of agricultural activity such as dairy, beef and sugar beet. Agripost is owned by *The Farmer's Journal*.

Professionals

This sector includes solicitors, accountants, doctors and other professions and accounts for over 20,000 individuals and is used for targeting business products, services and also consumer goods such as cars, holidays and books.

Retail

This sector is similar to the small companies sector in size and includes shops, clothing, grocery, gift and hardware. The depth of data usually consists of the type of store, telephone number and proprietors' name and address.

Leisure

Table 11.1 highlights the number and type of leisure establishments in Ireland.

TABLE 11.1: LEISURE ESTABLISHMENTS IN IRELAND

Business Type	Number
Hotels	1,100
Bed & Breakfasts	4,500
Public Houses	8,000
Restaurants	3,000
Sports Clubs or Associations	3,000
Tourist Attractions	500

CRITERIA FOR SELECTION OF BUSINESS LISTS

Business lists are usually selected by the following criteria:

- Sector (specific activity in which the business is involved)

- Employee numbers

- Location (town, county, postcode or Postaim)

- Credit standing (does the company pay its bills?)

- Manufacturing/service/wholesale (general area of activity)

- Import/export (including volume, percentage turnover, and countries to which it exports).

LIST AVAILABILITY — CONSUMERS

Consumer lists in Ireland are a recent phenomenon. The first quality consumer lifestyle list, Targetpoint, was launched in early 1992. There are still only approximately 10–15 such lists.

However, the overall quality is quite high. For example, consumer lists in the US and the UK, which are considered the most developed, have a higher percentage of undeliverables ("gone aways"). The biggest contributing factor to this would be the tendency of consumers to change address much more frequently.

There are four distinct types of consumer lists:

- Lifestyle
- Mail Order Responsive
- Demographic
- Miscellaneous.

Lifestyle Lists

These are compiled through answers to questionnaires concerning people's homes, interests and hobbies, leisure time, automobiles, family size, etc. Some lists contain up to 250 categories. In Ireland, the current sources are PMI, NDL, Dublin Life and Consumer Sketch.

The questionnaires are distributed through a number of channels starting from standard direct mail such as Targetpoint (now PMI), through door drops (Dublin Life) and through to guarantee card questionnaires associated with the purchase of electrical and leisure goods (NDL).

These lists are used largely by two distinct groups.

- FMCG companies (soap, sweets, food and drink, etc.) for sales promotion activities.
- Distributors of more expensive consumer goods, usually relating to a person's particular interests (golf, foreign holidays, weekend breaks, home computers, etc.).

Mail Order Responsive Lists

These consist of consumers who have bought particular items through mail order. We may know what, how much and when people buy, but usually little other information (marital status, income, children, interests) is known. What is important is that they are known to be receptive to "distance selling". Examples would be Oxendales (clothing), Book Club of Ireland, Halbert's (heritage items), Studio Cards (giftware), *Fortune/Time* (magazines).

Demographic Lists

These are usually taken from the electoral register, with statistical census data applied at address level. Thus, we can assume if 40 per cent of the residents of a street or area have two or more cars, the entire area (that is, all people on the same street) would be a likely target group for an automotive product. This essentially is making an assumption about a household based on their address; with no useful postcodes, and many addresses only at townland level, these lists usually work best only in built-up areas.

In the UK, for example, each postcode represents an average of only 15 unique addresses. Compare this to Dublin, with 312,000 households covered by only 22 postcodes. Proper geo-coding would enable direct marketers to make a quantum leap in consumer targeting.

Chapters 1 and 9 contain more detailed analyses of geocoding and demographic lists.

Miscellaneous

Finally, we have at least three lists or list types that do not fall into the above categories but are well worth mentioning.

- *Loyalty Club Schemes* (Superquinn's Superclub, Dunnes Stores' Value Card and Tesco's Clubcard). These are based on what brand names and quantities of household goods, usually food, are purchased by members

- The *Shareholders List* consists of 100,000 Irish investors and can be rented based on the amount of the investment

- *Ticketline* consists of 175,000 consumers who have booked theatre, concert, or other events over the telephone by credit card.

LIST SOURCES — INTERNATIONAL

This is an area that requires experience such as clients with an export background, or third parties such as list brokers or agencies. The primary sources are highlighted in Table 11.2.

TABLE 11.2: INTERNATIONAL LIST SOURCES

	Lists and Data Sources	Directory
UK and Europe*	List Link	On-line
	Gold	CD-ROM
	Kompass/Reed	CD-ROM
USA**	SRDS	Directory and CD-ROM

* A compilation of the largest 2,000 European lists.

** This is a directory of 35,000 USA lists.

The secondary sources are probably a safer route:

- List brokers

- Your own agency

- The European, UK, and US Direct Marketing Associations.

Finally, here are some general points to be borne in mind when considering international lists:

- Usually more precise targeting is available than in Ireland

- They will have a lower unit cost than Irish lists

- They will generally be of lower quality.

QUALITY ISSUES — WHAT TO LOOK FOR IN A LIST

When acquiring a list, always ask the following questions:

1. Who owns it and how was it compiled (telephone, mailed questionnaire, etc.)?

2. When was it last updated and can it be selected based on oldest interview date?

3. Exactly what data does it contain (name, address, telephone/fax, SIC (industry code), size, sort codes (Postaim))?

4. What "gone away" percentage is to be expected and is there a guarantee? (In Ireland, between one and two per cent for a business list, two to four per cent for a "small business" list, and two per cent for consumer lists are generally accepted as reasonable "gone away" figures. By contrast, a UK business list may yield seven per cent or more by way of undeliverable addresses. Most Irish list owners will offer a guarantee of refunding the cost of the name, or the postage, or both, for every "gone away" returned to them. This, of course, enables them to keep their lists up to date.)

5. Are you entitled to have this list under data protection law? You can use a list containing individuals' data only if the person selling it to you has obtained their consent to make their information available to other parties.

6. Have companies similar to yours used the service successfully?

7. Are the prices quoted for rental or purchase?

TECHNICAL ISSUES

Most Irish lists are available in the following formats

-   *PC-compatible disk* (you will usually pay extra for a Mac version): This will allow you to personalise your mailing — *"Dear Mr Smith"* — as well as sort it geographically or by other selectors, and to track results more easily or print out reports/analysis

-   *Labels*: Less expensive and also useful when you do not wish to personalise a mailing

-   *Printout*: Used primarily for logging responses and for producing reports for telephone follow-up.

When selecting a hard copy (labels or printout), be sure of the sequence you wish to use, such as Postaim, alphabetic, county, sector.

PRICE

The answers to the questions in the section "Quality Issues — What to Look for in a List" should always be your determining factor when you consider two seemingly similar lists. The price should be the least of your concerns — as we have seen, the list is a very small part of the overall cost of a campaign, yet it can make or break the entire effort.

Nevertheless, here are some figures: as we go to print, the average cost of an Irish business list is £175/£200 per 1,000 names. Irish consumer lists vary from £70/£80 per 1,000 (demographic) to £135 per 1,000 for more targeted lists.

DATA PROTECTION

When information about a person is kept on computer, it becomes subject to the Data Protection Act, 1988. Even the simplest information, like names and addresses, are personal data under the Act if an individual can be identified from it. The Act is enforced by the Data Protection Commissioner, a Government appointee with extensive legal powers.

Fair Obtaining

The Act says that personal data must be *fairly obtained*. For information about someone to be fairly obtained, they must know — at the time it is obtained — who is obtaining it, what it is being obtained for and what will be done with it. Many complaints to the Data Protection Commissioner about mailing lists are essentially about whether this requirement has been met.

Collecting Information for Mailing Lists

The names on most mailing lists are obtained when someone gives personal information during some transaction. This is when fair obtaining must take place. Normally, the customer will clearly understand the primary purpose of the transaction — it may be a purchase by mail order or telephone, for example, or the opening of a bank account. But the vendor — the "data controller" — may also hope to add the information to a mailing list. This is a subsidiary purpose and the customer must be allowed to choose whether or not to have their data used for such purposes.

There is one situation in which a data controller does not need consent to add a customer's information to a mailing list. This is when a transaction is going to result in an on-going relationship and the data controller wants to add the customer to its own list. For example, when someone becomes a customer of a bank, the bank does not need consent to send them information subsequently about its own products and services.

But this is the only exception. If the data controller wants to mail a customer on behalf of other vendors or service providers, or if it wants to give or sell customer information to someone else for their use, then that is a subsidiary purpose and consent must be secured for it at the time the information is obtained.

Getting Consent During the First Transaction

This is why so many of the forms used to collect customer information for a transaction contain the so-called opt-out section. It usually contains wording like this (from the Bank of Ireland Visa Card application form):

> Please note that the details you are being asked to supply may be used to provide you with information about other products and services, either from the Bank of Ireland Group or which the Bank of Ireland Group have arranged exclusively for you with a third party. If you do not wish the information to be utilised for this purpose, please tick the box opposite.

In this case, Bank of Ireland Credit Card Services states clearly what it wants to do with the customer's information. It is not asking for the customer's consent to mail them about its own products, because once they have become a customer it does not need to. It is asking for the other consent that it *does* need — for mailings about products and services from other companies in the Bank of Ireland Group (because the customer is only applying for a Visa Card; they are not entering into a relationship with the rest of the Group) and of course for mailings from or on behalf of other parties outside the Group.

(There is nothing wrong with offering inducements to customers, such as gifts, to encourage them to consent to the use of their data for mailing purposes. As long as the matter is explained clearly to them, and they have a free choice, the data protection requirements are satisfied.)

Getting Consent at a Later Stage

However, different rules apply if a data controller has obtained customer information previously for a purpose that does not include direct mailing, and subsequently wants to use it for direct mailing. It must get the customer's consent for this additional use of personal data. But the Data Protection Commissioner believes that, in this case, the opt-out is not enough. There is a legal principle that states that consent cannot be obtained by silence. In other words, it is not enough to say, "I intend to do such-and-such, and unless you tell me not to, you will be deemed to have agreed to it". The opt-out box is sufficient at the time when a customer's personal data are first being obtained, as in the Bank of Ireland Visa Card example, because it appears on a form signed and sent back by the customer and the assumption can be made that they have looked at the box and decided not to tick it. But the same assumption cannot be made when consent is being looked for at a later stage in a relationship. At that stage, the consent must be positive — the customer must say, in effect, "Yes, I agree that you may do this with my information".

How Long May Information be Kept?

Under the Data Protection Act, information about people must be kept for a specified purpose or purposes, and must not be kept for longer than is necessary for those purposes. For mailing lists in general, the period for which information may be kept is more or less open-ended. But there are exceptions. In one case that the Data Protection Commissioner has dealt with, personal data were obtained from customers for one specific offer and the same people were mailed again over a year later for a different one. The main issue in this case was whether their consent had been obtained for the second mailing. But the data controller was also asked to consider whether it was justified in still having the data at all at that stage.

The Right of Access

The Data Protection Act gives a person a right to get a copy of any information kept on computer about them, by asking for it in writing and paying a fee of £5. A request of this kind must be responded to within 40 days of its arrival. (The Data Protection Commissioner frequently gets complaints about data controllers who have not understood this obligation or have not taken it seriously. In such cases, the Commissioner always enforces compliance.) In practice, this right of access is almost absolute. There are certain strictly limited exemptions, but it is difficult to imagine any of these applying to information kept for direct marketing purposes.

The Right to be Removed from a Mailing List

Anyone whose personal data are being used for direct marketing has an unqualified right under the Data Protection Act to stop that use at any time. That right exists even if they initially gave consent. (In this respect, the Irish Act is different from most others, including the UK one.) To exercise this right, a person must make a written request. That request must be put into effect within 40 days, and the individual must be told that this has been done. Here, too, the Data Protection Commissioner has received more than a few complaints of people's rights being disregarded, and has acted to enforce the provision. Recently (April 1998), the Freedom of Information Act has reinforced this right, although in reference to direct marketing, the 1998 Data Protection Act has always provided a very clear path for consumers to be removed from marketing lists.

THE FUTURE

Some say the future of direct marketing lies in the Internet. Others look at the average 15 per cent annual growth rate of direct marketing in Ireland since 1992 and say "If it ain't broke, don't fix it".

The truth is probably somewhere in between. Neither the telephone nor the fax has yet replaced mail as the number one media for direct marketing offers. Responses, however, are now as much by Freephone or fax as by reply card.

Our growth is limited only by legal and, to a lesser extent, environmental regulations. The Irish Direct Marketing Association has always promoted self-regulation. Its members must obey three separate codes of practice, each of which is more stringent than the law of the land requires:

- General code
- Telemarketing code
- Data protection.

In addition, of course, all members are bound by the general code for advertising, as published by the Advertising Standards Authority of Ireland.

Direct marketing is a combination of proper targeting, media selection and mix, ease of response, and, most important, proper identification of the respondent. Mail, the Internet, telephone, fax, door-to-door and off-the-page, are all part of what we loosely call relationship marketing. What we must not lose sight of is that it is a personal relationship, with both parties knowing each other's identity. As long as our targeting and use of media respects that fundamental relationship, our industry will continue to thrive.

REFERENCES TO CHAPTER 11

Baier, M. (1983), *Elements of Direct Marketing*, New York: McGraw-Hill, p. 183.

SUGGESTED READING

Code of Practice on Data Protection (Irish Direct Marketing Association).

Guide to the Data Protection Act, 1988 (Office of the Data Protection Commissioner).

PART THREE

Communications Strategy: Offers, Media and Creativity

Chapter 12

SALES PROMOTION

Laura Cuddihy *and* Helen Seymour[1]

Overview

This chapter charts the relationship between direct marketing and sales promotion. While these communications tools may be used both individually and complementarily, their over-arching advantage over other communication vehicles is their measurability.

Putting sales promotion into context requires an examination of its historical development, both internationally and in the Irish marketplace. There then follows an examination of the types of sales promotion tools available to a client, and an outline guide or framework to constructing and managing a sales promotion campaign is presented.

The chapter concludes with an examination of the integration achievable through the use of both sales promotion and direct marketing, using case examples to illustrate the role that each of these valuable communication tools can play in the delivery of a targeted, effective and measurable communications programme.

UNDERSTANDING SALES PROMOTION IN RELATION TO DIRECT MARKETING

Definitions of direct marketing and sales promotion are becoming increasingly blurred, as the two may sometimes do quite similar tasks. Often, sales promotion is used to increase uptake on a product or service through either value-increasing or value-adding methods.

[1] Acknowledgements: Aer Lingus, BMG Records, Coca-Cola, Dialogue Marketing Communications, Dimension, Elida Fabergé, Irish Institute of Sales Promotion Consultants, Nestlé, Premier Banking, Roisin Joyce, Watermarque Marketing Communications.

However, as illustrated throughout this text, direct marketing is also employed to achieve such objectives, albeit by addressing the target audience individually and taking the incentive personally to the customer. Depending on what area of marketing you currently study, practice, or consult in, you may have one of several views on sales promotion: as a standalone marketing tool or alternatively as an integral part of any communications activity, be it advertising, direct marketing or public relations. However, to form any type of opinion, one needs to be reasonably well equipped with the basic facts, which is what this chapter sets out to provide — both an understanding of sales promotion and sales promotion in relation to direct marketing.

THE HISTORY OF SALES PROMOTION

According to O'Connor (1997: 1) sales promotion, by virtue of an apocryphal tale, is the oldest profession in the world. Indeed, the first sales promotion took place in the Garden of Eden, and according to this story offered "free knowledge with every apple!". A joke this may be, but certainly the oldest form of promotion does go back nearly that far. Several lotteries are mentioned in the New Testament, and there is even one in the Old Testament (Numbers 26: 55–56) where Moses is instructed to run a census, after which land is to be divided amongst the Israelites. Lotteries were popular in the reigns of Augustus and Nero, who gave away slaves, property and other "trinkets" during festivities such as Saturnalia. However, the real explosion of sales promotion occurred about the middle of the 1800s, from which a number of examples survive (see Table 12.1).

The year 1844 saw the introduction of the first co-op "dividend" scheme and the Red Stamp Company of Yorkshire is recorded as trading in 1850, offering stamps from each item purchased which could then be redeemed against future purchases from the same outlet. However, it was not until the S&H Green Stamps Company was founded in the US in 1950 (followed by its British counterpart in 1958) that the trading stamp really acquired respectability. The next major development came in the 1870s, when Canadian Tobacconists started printing pictures on the protective cards in cigarette boxes.

TABLE 12.1: THE HISTORY OF SALES PROMOTION

Period	Sales Promotion Milestone
Middle Ages	Price promotion as an integral part of developing market economies
Early 19th century	Free gifts offered by retailers
1844	Introduction of first successful co-operative dividend scheme
1850s	Growth of trading stamps
1879	First cigarette card
Late 19th century	Puzzles, self-liquidation offers, coupons, special events
c1905	Probably the first sales promotion department: "Akeroyd's Circus" at Boots
1920s	Heyday of the prize contest, mystery shoppers, trade incentive schemes
1930	Launch of Robertson's free golly badge scheme
1932	Launch of Miss Pears annual competition
1939–52	Virtual absence of sales promotion
1962	Abolition of resale price maintenance ends wartime restraints — birth of money-off coupon
1974	Sales Promotion Code introduced in the UK
1976	Lotteries and Amusements Act allowed lotteries to be conducted for charitable purposes under licence
1980	Groups of independent Irish sales promotions companies form
1980/81	First Irish Code of Sales Promotion practice developed
1986	Attempts to form first Irish Institute of Sales Promotion fail — sales promotion market growing at a rapid rate.
1992	Irish companies compete in European Federation of Sales Promotion Consultants annual awards and win
1994	First IISPC conference on sales promotion is held
1997	IISPC delegate represents the Institute on the ASAI (Advertising Standards Authority of Ireland) — the first time Sales Promotion Consultants have ASAI representation
	The IISPC Newsletter is officially launched to IISPC's members
	The first IISPC education seminars are held

Towards the end of the nineteenth century, competitions began to appear. In 1894, Sunlight Soap gave away 232,000 prizes of books, bicycles and watches to consumers. The competition mechanic, although questionable by today's standards, was simple — consumers were awarded prizes based on the largest quantities of wrappers they sent in. Sears Roebuck devised one of the first "buy X get Y free" schemes, which offered consumers the chance to win a free bicycle if they persuaded their friends to buy a bicycle. However, not only had they to register for the scheme by sending $2 to Sears, they also had to have purchased a bicycle recently from the mailing list, so as promotions go, it was unlikely to have been very successful. In 1904, Quaker Oat consumers were invited to send 35 pack fronts to obtain four cereal bowls free of charge and could also obtain goods such as pipes, handkerchiefs, stockings, socks and silverware. In 1930, the famous Robertson's free golly made his first appearance, and apart from the Miss Pears annual competition which still (for the moment) runs, this must qualify as one of the longest-running promotions ever.

Between the outbreak of war in 1939 and the early 1950s, there was virtually no promotion at all; however, it was probably the austerity of this period that largely prompted the birth of the money-off coupon in the early 1950s. The coupon's actual advent was influenced greatly by the "new marketing" television commercials which accompanied the arrival of the supermarket. Interestingly enough, 85 per cent of commercials at this time were for detergents. The first version of Shell Make Money was created in the late 1950s. The Gaming and Lotteries Act of 1956 restricted the practice of lotteries to organisations specifically devised by the state. The first UK sales promotion code of practice was introduced in the UK in 1974 and the first Irish Sales Promotion Code of Practice was created in 1980.

SALES PROMOTION IN IRELAND

Sales promotion in Ireland has actively grown as an industry over the past 20 years, with a surge over the past decade. In the 1960s and 1970s, sales promotion in Ireland was viewed by advertising agencies and marketers as a secondary activity, falling more into the area of sales than marketing. Direct marketing had yet to be born and public relations was viewed as a separate activity altogether.

In the very late 1970s and early 1980s, demand for sales promotion was driven by the large FMCG companies, who had been using London agencies but required a local sales promotion resource. As this demand grew, a series of small companies specialising in sales promotions of varying kinds, ranging from supermarket sampling to coupon management to pub events, were founded, some of them aligned with UK or foreign companies, thus strengthening their resources and building their knowledge base. Global brands also assisted in the successful growth and development of sales promotion, as promotion experience from abroad was shared and new techniques were introduced.

In the 1980s, the subject of "integrated marketing", a concept well practised in the United States, became the focus of attention here and marketers began to adjust their thinking. Integrated marketing was based on creating an effective synergy between advertising, public relations, direct marketing, sales promotion and other brand activities to deliver one clear, consistent brand message to the consumer. The media environment was becoming increasingly cluttered, and there was a period of recession during the 1980s, which drove a demand for marketing budgets to work harder and perform more efficiently. These two factors contributed to the shifts in marketers' thinking as a requirement emerged for clear, consistent brand message co-ordination for maximum impact and cost efficiency. It was a dynamic period, particularly from a below-the-line viewpoint.

Direct marketing had at this point begun to make an impact in Irish marketing and the usage of public relations was increasing. The larger advertising agencies, particularly the multinationals, set up their own "below-the-line" divisions and independent sales promotions companies in the main continued to thrive. Marketers' promotion spends drove much of this development. These spends, which in the early 1980s had generally been 80 per cent above-the-line, 20 per cent below-the-line, by the early 1990s were 50:50 in many areas, with certain marketers spending more below-the-line than above.

In 1992, a group of Irish sales promotion companies successfully competed and won gold, silver and bronze awards in the EFSP (European Federation of Sales Promotion Consultants) awards. Subsequently, a number of leading Irish sales promotion consultants founded the Irish Institute of Sales Promotion Consultants (IISPC) "to promote the professional development of the sales promotion industry and to serve the needs of both practitioners and users".

This Institute's objectives set out:

- To be a benchmark for the ultimate in professionalism and self-regulation in sales promotion consultancy

- To act as a voice for the sales promotion industry in Ireland and in Europe, promoting sales promotion as a marketing tool

- To promote the professionalism of the industry amongst practitioners and users

- To develop an on-going education programme for both clients and agencies to encourage on-going professional development

- To monitor the legal and regulatory environment and to regulate all members and users through an appropriate code of ethics.

To achieve these objectives, the Institute board, comprising eight experienced practitioners, operates five committees — Events, Communications, Membership/Finance, Legal and Ethics and Education. In addition to this, they appoint a delegate to the EFSP to which the IISPC is aligned. In 1997, the Institute recorded 14 corporate and 19 associate members. All member details are printed in the IISPC Annual Yearbook, which also incorporates the official Irish Code Of Sales Promotion Practice. Although no definitive value has been placed on the sales promotion industry, "below-the-line" is estimated to be worth some £200 million. Industry analysts estimate that it will increase further over the next few years (O'Connor, 1997: 1).

DEFINING SALES PROMOTION

While there are many definitions of sales promotion, Chapman et al. (1994: 12) offer a particularly accurate contribution:

> Sales promotion comprises a range of tactical marketing techniques designed within a strategic framework to add value to a product or service in order to achieve specific sales and marketing objectives.

There are many who believe that sales promotion is merely a tactical, short-term, reactive tool. Those who do are short-sighted and, unlike

Chapman, miss the point. Chapman wisely acknowledges that, whilst sales promotion can be tactical, it can also contribute strategically and actively within the greater scheme of things.

TYPES OF SALES PROMOTIONS

Trade Sales Promotions

Broadly speaking, these sales promotions are directed at resellers who distribute products to ultimate consumers. Typically, they are part of a *push* marketing strategy that implies a forward thrust of effort and allocation of promotional resources to supporting the channel members. Trade sales promotions hope to accomplish four overall goals (Burnett, 1993: 392):

1. To develop in-store merchandising or other trade support (such as shelf space, feature pricing or use of point-of-sale materials)

2. To increase or decrease stock levels and eliminate peaks and valleys between seasonal items

3. To expand or improve distribution

4. To motivate channel members.

Types of trade sales promotions include trade allowances, point-of-purchase materials, trade contests and incentives, trade shows, co-operative advertising, vendor support programmes, and training programmes. As Ireland has a strong retailer concentration, the use of such types of sales promotions to defend existing business is commonplace.

Sales Force Sales Promotions

Such promotions aim to motivate a company's sales team to expend extra effort (generally on a short-term basis) in achieving stated company sales goals. They are best used to achieve specific goals such as getting new accounts, selling specific products or relieving certain overstocked inventory positions. Broad purposes, such as increasing overall sales and/or profits, are better achieved through sales management techniques. Burnett (1993: 387) identifies two categories of sales-force-directed sales promotions:

1. Supportive programmes designed partly by the sales promotion function in conjunction with sales management. Activities here would include sales meetings, sales manuals, sales portfolios, product models and company newsletters.

2. Motivational programmes, such as sales contests, designed to stimulate the achievement of sales objectives. Companies need to be judicious in the design and use of such promotions, as once initiated they can be difficult to discontinue. Equally problematical is the inevitable decline in sales which occurs once the promotion is concluded.

Like the other two major promotion types, sales promotions aimed at the sales force should be planned and integrated with the other marketing and sales activities in the company.

Consumer Sales Promotions

These promotions are extensively used to support a *pull* marketing strategy and are often in the eye of the storm when debates about the brand-building, as opposed to brand-damaging, role of sales promotions are taking place. In general, consumer sales promotions are incentives designed to stimulate trial or continued use of specific products or services.

Olsen and Shaw (1986) identified three broad categories of consumer sales promotions:

Immediate Gratification

Examples of sales promotion techniques that would fall into this category include money-off, reduced price packs, banded packs, bonus packs, instant point-of-purchase coupons, free samples/trials, instant wins, point-of-purchase displays, and free in-/on-pack gifts or premiums.

While some of these manipulate the price/quantity equation to *increase the value* of the product offering to consumers, others *add value* by bundling in an extra dimension to the core product, such as a free gift or a "piggy-back" complementary product. Peattie and Peattie (1993) argue that the "value-increasing" promotions cannot physically work for services, as there is no tangible product and therefore value-adding promotions are far more prevalent and suitable in services marketing.

Delayed Gratification

By definition, the consumer "reward" in this category of promotion is neither instant nor necessarily tangible. Typical examples of such techniques include coupons, competitions and continuity/collection schemes. As there are limited "winners", Olsen and Shaw (1986: 249) state that it makes more sense to talk about anticipated rather than actual rewards. Designers of such promotions must take purchasing and consumption patterns into account when setting out the tasks required by the consumer — otherwise the promotion may be viewed as less honest than immediate gratification tools. This perception would obviously have a negative effect on brand or store image. However, if correctly designed, these promotions create opportunities for consumer involvement and long-term relationship building. Consumers may be willingly stretched into buying more or sustaining purchasing patterns if they consider the mechanics reasonable and the outcome worthwhile.

Vicarious Gratification

These promotions can be very useful as part of an image-building exercise and include techniques such as charity donations, environmental donations and recycling mechanisms. Companies may use these types of promotions either for philanthropic reasons or for the achievement of purely commercial objectives. Whatever the corporate rationale for their use, consumers, on the other hand, may well derive a feeling of well-being through their indirect support of the nominated cause.

Sales promotion is evident around us on a day-to-day basis, in many shapes and forms. These can range from simple counter cards drawing attention to a new product or a special price offer to holiday or car competitions to magazine competitions, bill insert offers . . . the list is endless. Gaining an in-depth knowledge of the range of sales promotion types generally comes from years of practice, as does the understanding for how and when best to apply them. Table 12.2 sets out a summary of the main promotion types, the channels through which they can be implemented, the varying mechanics and some of the main user categories.

TABLE 12.2: SALES PROMOTION TYPOLOGY

Promotion Types	Channels	Mechanic Options	Categories
Direct	Multiples	Free draw	FMCG food and non-food
Joint	Wholesale	Instant win	
On-pack	Symbols	Collection	Consumer durables
In-store	Independent	Self-liquidation	Pharmaceuticals
Coupon	TSNs and	Competitions	Sports
Cross-product	CTNs*	Price	Clothing
Cross-group	Retail stores	promotions	Cosmetic
Cross-portfolio	Fast food	Combination tiers	Household goods
Events	restaurants	of all the above	Communications and
Staff	All direct		services
Trade	media		Business-to-business
			Trade and sales force

* TSNs: Tobacconists, stationery and newsagents
  CTNs: Confectionery, tobacconists and newsagents.

SALES PROMOTION — MAKING IT HAPPEN

Creating and implementing a sales promotion can, broadly speaking, be broken into the following groups of activities:

1. Concept generation

2. Mechanic development

3. Budget preparation

4. General management

5. Fulfilment

6. Post analysis.

Concept Generation

As in advertising, PR and direct marketing, the nucleus of any sales promotion concept development is the brief. In the case of sales promotion, key information required is illustrated in Figure 12.1.

FIGURE 12.1: DEVELOPING A SALES PROMOTION CONCEPT — THE PROCESS

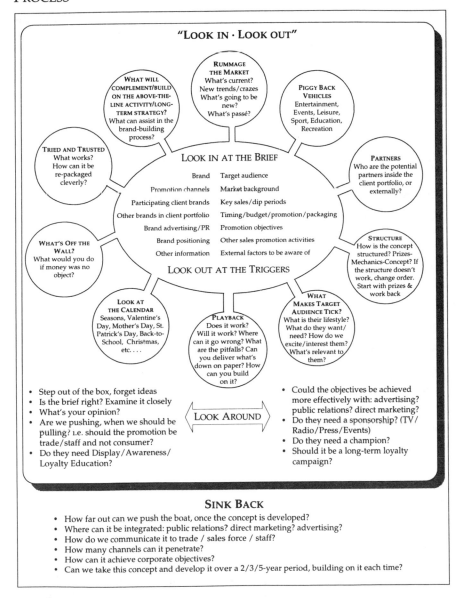

What brand(s) will participate in the promotion? What channels are they being sold through? What is the company's full portfolio of brands? What advertising/PR activities are being implemented? What is the brand positioning? Who are the target audience? What's the market background? (Gain a clear understanding of the environment you have to promote in) What are key sales/dip periods? What is the promotion timing/budget/objectives? If it's a physical product as opposed to a service, how is it packaged? What are the production/packaging lead times? Are there any external factors you need to be aware of?

All these factors will affect the type of sales promotion you construct — for example, in Figure 12.2, the client in question is a cola brand.

FIGURE 12.2: SAMPLE SALES PROMOTION BRIEF

Client	Soft drinks company
Promotion channels	• Multiples, independents, CTNs, Cash & Carry
Objectives	• Maximise summer sales opportunities • Generate measurable increased sales • Drive volume
Participating client brands	• Cola brand
Other brands in portfolio	• Orange and lemon soft drinks • Diet portfolio
Brand advertising/PR	• TV advertising, radio sponsorship
Brand positioning	• Fun/fashionable/cool/credible
Target audience	• 15–24s, highly brand conscious
Market background	• One major competitor — highly active • Own label growth
Key sales/dip periods	• Summertime — key sales period • Traditional dips — February and October
Timing	• June–August • Date of brief — January
Budget	• £60,000
Production/packaging	• 2-litre label — 8-week lead time • 6-pack shrink wrap — 8-week lead time • Cans — 12-week lead time
Other SP activities	• Previous sales promotions included mobile phones, watches and T-shirts all implemented on self-liquidating basis — all highly successful
Other information	• Company policy not to cross-promote • Cans contribute to 50% of summer business • Cash & carry drive 60% of can business • Shifts in grocery trade

There's no opportunity to cross-promote within the company portfolio because it's against company policy. Display is limited, so we'll need to brand the packs with the promotion message and ideally support with advertising to gain awareness for the promotion. The lead times for pack artwork are 20 weeks, so we'll need to action that as a priority. The budget is £60,000: once we take away artwork and production, what have we left for premiums/prizes? Can we associate with another party, such as a national chain of retail outlets, and get them to co-ordinate redemption? If so, what's in it for them — how do we sell it to them? Can we integrate with the existing radio sponsorship to assist in driving awareness for the promotion? Cans are key, so we need to look at special displays for cooler units. Cash & carry drive 60 per cent of can business, so we need a special cash & carry promotion to encourage them to drive the consumer promotion (push/pull effect).

The brief needs to be examined and re-examined during the process of developing a sales promotion concept. Figure 12.1 demonstrates that as you *look in* at the brief, so must you *look out* at the triggers, as in Figure 12.3.

Debating the brief is another important part of the concept development process. Why do we want a sales promotion? Could the brief be better answered with advertising, direct marketing, or PR? What's essential to the success of the promotion? Is it display? If so, structure a promotion that lends itself well to striking POS. The brief is for a consumer promotion, but could it be better achieved with a trade promotion which will guarantee key displays? Whilst it's reasonable to assume that a brief is accurate, it can be beneficial to challenge the thinking, and consider alternative approaches.

Once the promotion concept has been developed, you need to sit back and look at how it can be manipulated. You've developed it for one channel (supermarkets) but could it work well in another (forecourts)? How can it integrate with other marketing activities? Can it be developed as part of a long-term brand strategy? All *look around* issues on Figure 12.1 should be re-examined for each new sales promotion campaign.

FIGURE 12.3: LOOK OUT AT THE TRIGGERS

Look at the calendar	It's summer — what does the target audience want/need (sunglasses?)
What would you do if money was no object?	Oakley sunglasses?
Tried and trusted	What's a safe bet (cars, holidays, cash?)
What complements/ builds on the above-the-line imagery?	Does your prize/item enhance the brand building process?
Rummage the market	Read magazines, follow trends, especially where fun/fashionable brands are concerned. Stay in touch with what's happening.
Piggy-back vehicles	Look at entertainment/events (concepts) leisure/ sport (football) etc., and see if you can associate the brand with them for a sales promotion activity.
Partners	Beneficial from a budget point of view (cuts costs) and a brand positioning point of view (co-brand endorsement)
Structure	Sometimes, like writers, you hit a mental block when developing a concept. If you're not happy with your ideas, play around with your approach. Develop the mechanics first, instead of the prizes or vice versa.
What makes the target audience tick?	Key to a successful sales promotion. Consumers must want what you're offering in order to get them to participate.

Finally, playback: once you've developed an idea, go over it with a fine tooth-comb. Does it work? How and where can it go wrong? Can you deliver what's on paper? You must be 100 per cent confident that you can deliver before committing to your sales promotion activity.

Mechanic Development

"Even the best of ideas must eventually lead to work" (old practitioners' proverb).

Generally speaking, the mechanics of a sales promotion will be developed as part of the concept development process; however, once the promotion proceeds, these will inevitably need to be fine-tuned.

The best way to develop a promotion mechanic is to put yourself in the shoes of the different parties the promotion will affect — for example:

> I'm a consumer. I go into the store. How will I know there's a promotion on? *(Backboard)* I pick up a pack. How do I enter? *(Promotion copy needs to be simple and clear)* What's involved? *(Don't make mechanics too complex — the easier the method of participation, the higher the response)* What do I have to do to get my prize? *(Again, the least work from the consumer's point of view, the better)*

OR

> I'm a cash & carry owner. What's in this for me? *(Trade presenter outlining profit benefits/exclusive cash & carry promotion)* I'm a cash & carry customer. How do I know there's a promotion on? *(Special cash & carry displays — promotion flashes on the side of cash n' carry boxes/packs)*

Walk yourself through the promotion step-by-step in the eyes of the different parties that the promotion targets. Identify the obstacles/barriers they may overcome and find a solution to them.

In addition, consider all the third parties involved in the promotion — designers, printers, legal consultants, premium suppliers, promotion printers, etc. What has to be achieved with each one? Develop proper briefs for designers and production houses; consider potential pitfalls. Supply your legal people with a detailed promotion mechanic and consult them right through to finished artwork stage.

Where promotion partners are concerned, meet regularly in the mechanic development process; develop a clear understanding of what each party is committing to and document it in a formal contract. Where premium/prize fund suppliers are concerned, if you haven't dealt with them before, get references. Gain a clear understanding of their production process. What country are the goods coming from? What is the branding/production process? Can you have a printed sample? Can you view the first batch as they come off press? How will the items be delivered? What quantity will they be packed in? Will they be made up? Is assembly a separate cost? Failure to ask these types of questions can seriously affect the time you deliver your promotion, and the cost. If you did not allow for product assembly, for example, it may take two weeks and add £10,000 to your budget. It cannot be stressed enough how important it is to consider every aspect of the promotion process in advance.

Once you have considered the key issues, a critical path analysis is an excellent mechanic implementation tool, because not only does it itemise everything related to the promotion, it also puts a timing on it and key action dates. A sample sales promotion critical path analysis is set out in Figure 12.4.

FIGURE 12.4: SAMPLE CRITICAL PATH ANALYSIS

Item	Current status/next action	Action by
Artwork	Rough artwork to be developed for:	
	• 6 pack	
	• 2 litre	
	• can	
	• backboard	
	• leaflet	
	Comments/approval by	23/1/98
	F/A by	30/1/98
Copy	First draft copy by	10/1/98
	Comments/Alts by	15/1/98
	Final copy for F/A by	18/1/98
Production	Film for packs by	15/2/98
	Film for POS by	15/2/98
Legal	Legal approval on copy and artwork by	25/1/98
Prize fund	Prize fund ordered by	05/1/98
	Artwork for branding by	10/1/98
	Shipped in by	30/3/98
	Delivered to/on	03/4/98
PR/advertising	PR/advertising support in place by	05/5/98
Launch	Promotion in-trade on	05/5/98

Figure 12.4 is a sample only and will obviously differ from project to project. However, it does cover key areas of activity. Often several

areas will interrelate; for example, rough artwork and copy development go hand-in-hand and each will be fine-tuned alongside the other. A critical path works well from several points of view:

1. It allows you to examine all activities in context and pinpoint potential pitfalls

2. It acts as a driver — you know that if X does not happen by Y date, the process will be delayed

3. It encourages a sharper management process, which reduces the potential for error.

Budget Preparation

Inevitably, the preparation of a sales promotion budget will be intertwined with the overall mechanic development, as all the third parties are identified and quotes secured. The following are some key tips for constructing a budget:

1. Put a date and draft number on each budget. If additional costs are incurred or costs are saved, alter the budget as this happens, putting a new draft number and date on it each time. This helps track budget alterations.

2. Currency: if you're purchasing items from abroad, always adjust the currency accordingly, and highlight it on the budget as being subject to exchange rates. This can potentially increase/decrease the overall cost of the promotion.

3. Broadly group budget items into design/artwork, print production, prize fund, etc., and subtotal each group, so that at a glance you can analyse how much you're spending on each area, and consider whether or not it's appropriate. Can costs be saved or do you need to invest more?

4. Get all your quotes in writing and read them. Look at suppliers' terms and conditions — e.g. two weeks delivery from receipt of artwork; six weeks for shipping; 50 per cent payment upfront; 50 per cent on delivery — and make allowances for them in your critical path and your promotion mechanics.

General Management

Once a sales promotion is up and running, it will inevitably require some form of day-to-day/week-to-week management for its duration. The scale of management will vary from project to project. For example, an in-pub promotion utilising personnel will require daily outlet and personnel booking, collation and preparation of pub event report forms, pub merchandising co-ordination, etc. Conversely, an FMCG competition will require collection and sorting of entries and retail checks on key displays. Regardless of what level of general management is involved, it is important to consider it in advance of the promotion going in-trade and to agree the management process. If you haven't considered the fact that a six-month promotion is going to generate 20,000 entries a month, all of which have to be data-captured as the promotion runs, you will lose control.

Monitoring a sales promotion is also important, particularly if you want to measure responses to it. If you notice early in the promotion that awareness is low, or there is a poor response, you can pinpoint the problem and address the issue immediately. Similarly, if there is a strong response to the promotion when it first launches, you may decide to extend its duration and have time to order extra print/prizes.

Fulfilment

Fulfilment is an extremely important part of the sales promotion process. Additional sales guaranteed through the sales promotion will be short-lived if a consumer has to wait unnecessarily for their prize or offer delivery. Not only will all the goodwill generated be eroded, but the customer–brand relationship will also be damaged, if a sales promotion leaves them with a bad experience. Subsequently it cannot be stressed enough how important it is to follow through the promotion offer thoroughly and on time. This relates back to the general measurement process — a system for fulfilment should be put in place before the promotion starts, in order to ensure a positive close to the promotion in question.

Post-analysis

Regardless of how successful you think a sales promotion was, post-analysis is still important. Post-analysis:

- Can act as research for reasons behind a highly successful sales promotion, which can be considered when preparing future programmes

- Can identify and summarise key problem areas for an unsuccessful sales promotion, which again can be considered and actioned accordingly when preparing future programmes

- Can identify shifts in consumer attitudes to promotions, which may help you tailor future promotions

- Sometimes a sales promotion will not achieve one set of objectives, but in post-analysis, other benefits may become evident. For example, a sales promotion which did not generate the targeted sales increase, upon cross-reference with year-on-year figures may show the promotion to have held sales figures during a period which traditionally dips, or perhaps to have held market share during a period of aggressive price competition (such as own label). Research may pinpoint the sales promotion as having built the brand image or generated enormous goodwill with staff/retailers, the benefits of which are immeasurable.

A post-analysis document should be concise, and cover the following points:

- Promotion theme/offer

- Promotion timing

- Budget

- Target audience

- Channels

- Market environment prior to and during the promotion period

- Sales increase (during and after)

- Share increase

- Positives

- Negatives

- Key benefits

- Key problem areas

- Key learnings.

THE ROLE OF INTEGRATION

Shimp (1997: 16) defines integrated marketing communications (IMC) as a company's unified, co-ordinated effort to promote a brand concept through the use of multiple communication tools that "speak with a single voice".

He isolates five important features of IMC:

1. It must encourage some form of behavioural response and move people to action

2. It uses all forms of communication and all sources of brand or company contacts capable of reaching the target consumer

3. The IMC process starts with the customer or prospect and then works back to the brand communicator to determine the most appropriate and effective methods for developing persuasive communications programmes

4. Synergy can only be achieved through close co-ordination of all the communication elements being used

5. Implicitly, IMC requires building a relationship between the brand and the customer that leads to repeat purchases and perhaps even loyalty.

Powerful synergies are possible when sales promotions are integrated with other marketing communications tools. This is particularly so where price-based promotions are being used. Totten and Block (1994: 69) quote the example of a price promotion alone which produced a 15 per cent increase in sales volume. When combined with feature advertising, sales volume increased 19 per cent; when combined with feature advertising and point-of-purchase display, sales volume increased 24 per cent.

There are varying forms of sales promotion integration, the core ones being:

1. Integrating one or more sales promotion activities to assist in achieving strategic objectives

2. Integrating other marketing activities into a sales promotion to assist in creating maximum impact and generating the highest possible return

3. The reverse — integrating sales promotion into other marketing activities for their maximum effect and return.

Each of the above forms of integration has a different role to play, as demonstrated in Table 12.3.

In 1991, one of Coca-Cola's strategic marketing objectives was to successfully establish Diet Coke as a brand with a status of its own. This was achieved through a promotion-driven event "the Diet Coke Drive-in Movie", the first of its kind in Ireland. As demonstrated in Table 12.3, the campaign was totally integrated, embracing advertising, public relations, direct marketing and sales promotions. Sales promotion played a key role, targeting both trade and consumers in several channel types — supermarkets, pubs, fast food restaurants and offices. The sales promotion techniques employed ranged from simple sampling promotions, to an on-pack offer to win a convertible car, to ticket give-aways and movie memorabilia. In this case, sales promotion was effectively integrated into a campaign of marketing communications activities designed to achieve a strategic marketing goal, which it did. Post-event qualitative research clearly displayed a shift in consumer perceptions, which was further reinforced by sales figures.

In 1994, BMG Records wanted to inject some life into a traditionally "quiet" mid-price sales promotion which was implemented on an annual basis. Music marketing is highly competitive, with BMG's key competitors also implementing "mid-price" promotions throughout the marketing year. In addition, the retail environment is extremely busy with regular new album launches and label promotions. Consequently, attracting attention can be difficult. One of BMG's core objectives in the 1994 mid-price promotion was to attract consumer interest. To achieve this, the sales promotion concept, "thingy" (a luminous pink and yellow blob) was devised and integrated into a humorous teaser-style poster and radio advertising campaign which advised consumers of the £1.00/£1.50 price off wherever they saw a "thingy". A series of public relations news

TABLE 12.3: INTEGRATING SALES PROMOTION

Type	Objective	Example	Details	Results
1	Integrating one or more sales promotion activities to assist in achieving strategic objectives	**Diet Coke — 1991**	*Strategic brand objective: Establish Diet Coke as a brand with a status of its own*	Diet Coke firmly established as a brand with a status of its own
		• **TV advertising**	Old movie stars (Bogart, etc.) at a party with Elton John	
		• **Promotion event**	Diet Coke drive-in movies (the first in Ireland)	
		• **Sponsorship**	2FM co-event association	
		• **Public Relations**	*Late Late Show* TV launch	
			Extensive national and local press PR over a four-month period	
		• **Trade sales promotions**	Trade sales promotion giving away tickets to the event	
		• **Consumer sales promotions**	Sampling promotions prior to and at the event	
			National multiple sales promotion giving away a convertible car plus tickets to the movies	
			Pub promotions giving away tickets to the event	
			Fast food restaurant promotions giving away tickets to the event	
		• **Direct Marketing**	Direct sampling promotion to offices	

TABLE 12.3 CONTINUED

Type	Objective	Example	Details	Results
2	Integrating other marketing activities into a sales promotion to assist in creating maximum impact and generating the highest possible return	BMG Records (1994) • Sales promotion • 3D in-store POS/ merchandising • Advertising • Public Relations	*Mid-price range sales promotion* Basic price promotion across BMG's "mid-price" range Offered consumers £1.00/£5.00 off selected cassettes/CDs. "Thingy" concept developed to identify participating product 3D "Thingy" mobiles, shelf wobblers and staff T-shirts Series of "Thingy" teaser outdoor posters — series of humorous "Thingy" radio ads "Thingy" media releases to key media Local and national radio and press promotions	Integrating advertising and public relations into the campaign breathed life into the sales promotion, heightening awareness and creating maximum impact
3	Integrate sales promotion into other marketing activities for their maximum effect and return	Lynx (1997) • TV commercial • Sales promotion • Brand public relations	*Consumer Sales Promotion* TV commercial with *Friends* Jennifer Anniston. Primary feature of TV commercial was a lime green Volkswagen. Consumers offered the chance to win a lime green VW Beetle as per the one featured in the TV commercial Campaign of public relations activities including: • Launch photocall which recreated the characters from the TV commercial with the lime green VW • College, supermarket, high street sampling with Beetle • National and local press and radio promotions • Winner announcements — extensive trade, marketing, national and local press publicity	Sales promotion effectively added impact and longevity to TV advertising campaign and created a public relations vehicle through which substantial brand publicity was achieved, the imagery of which was consistent with, and again supported the above-the-line campaign

releases and press and radio PR promotions giving away product for the mid-price range further increased awareness for the campaign, resulting in increased consumer interest and subsequently a strong response. Here the sales promotion was integrated with advertising and public relations activities to allow it achieve maximum impact.

In 1997, Lynx Deodorants produced a TV commercial for the brand featuring *Friends* star Jennifer Anniston. Jennifer, however played a secondary and sadly submissive role to the commercial star, who despite his obvious "nerdy" appearance and demeanour attracted devoted female attention and male respect after applying Lynx deodorant. The main feature of the TV commercial was a lime green Volkswagen Beetle in which our hero parties around town with a beautiful model, leaving Jennifer Anniston at home ironing his shirts. The Lynx strapline in the TV commercial was "The Lynx Effect". A sales promotion was created specifically to integrate with and support the TV commercial. Entitled "The Lynx Effect", the promotion offered consumers the chance to win a lime green Volkswagen Beetle exactly like the one featured in the TV commercial (the best integration is simple stuff). The car, branded Lynx, with "Lynx Effect" registration plate was displayed in supermarkets nationwide and during the promotion period sales increased by 30 per cent year-on-year. All point of sale material depicted the title "The Lynx Effect" and a visual of the car. The promotion further created PR opportunities. A photocall replicating the TV commercial was held, which generated substantial press coverage. The car toured college campus sites sampling Lynx, and extensive radio and press promotions were implemented. The sales promotion and public relations activities integrated with each other and the TV commercial to deliver maximum brand impact. Consumers received a consistent set of images and messages on TV, radio, press and in-store over a sustained period of time.

INTEGRATING DIRECT MARKETING AND SALES PROMOTION

Examples of successfully integrated sales promotion and direct marketing campaigns are evident around us in numerous different forms. One of the most current is the hugely successful Superquinn Superclub. This direct loyalty promotion, which started in May 1993 and today has over 300,000 members, encourages customer loyalty through offering consumers a wide range of gifts, discount offers and cash-back schemes. Combining sales promotion and direct marketing in this case has been the key to the loyalty programme's success. Without the sales promotion offer, the direct campaign would not have the same effect; without the direct campaign, the promotion would never have reached the scale it has. In the case of Superclub, both are interdependent. However, sometimes sales promotion will be supported by direct marketing whilst, at other times a campaign will be direct-response driven, with sales promotion playing a secondary role, and, in certain instances, both will be an integral part of an advertising campaign. The case histories detailed below demonstrate the three variations:

CASE HISTORY 1 — DIRECT MARKETING SUPPORTING A SALES PROMOTION CAMPAIGN

Company	Nestlé Ireland
Brand	Fruit Pastilles
Sales Promotion	Dustin's Juicy Beaker

In Nestlé's case, the key driver was a sales promotion campaign involving Dustin the Turkey, the children's puppet TV celebrity. A cartoon illustration of Dustin was printed on a brightly-coloured children's drinking beaker ("Dustin's Juicy Beaker") which consumers could instantly collect with five specified Nestlé brands. The promotion was well received by key trade channels. However, Nestlé, recognising its sales potential, wanted to ensure that all channels had maximum penetration. Confectionery Tobacco and Newsagents (CTN) business is a key area for confectionery, and the majority of CTN owners purchase from cash & carry outlets. Promotions would generally be communicated to CTNs via a standard newsletter; however, for the Dustin promotion, a personalised letter from Dustin was posted all to all CTN owners, along with a Dustin-themed window sticker card and shelf talker. The direct campaign resulted in a strong response from CTN owners, driving them into cash & carry outlets early in the promotion period. Cash & carry owners responded by increasing orders for the promotion, which pushed the promotion out, giving it stronger exposure across the brand. In this case, direct marketing successfully supported and rounded out a sales promotion campaign, allowing it to realise maximum potential.

CASE HISTORY 2 — SALES PROMOTION SUPPORTING A DIRECT MARKETING CAMPAIGN

Company	Aer Lingus
Brand	Gold Circle Club
Direct Campaign	Gold Circle Frequent Flyer Initiative

Aer Lingus have a Gold Circle Club, predominantly for business travellers, through which members are offered a number of different benefits. The relationship between Aer Lingus and its Gold Circle Club members is largely managed through ongoing personalised direct marketing correspondence. As part of its direct marketing correspondence for 1997, and to encourage Gold Circle Club members to increase purchase during a pre-set period, Aer Lingus wrote to all members advising them of an incentive exclusive to them. It offered all Gold Circle Club members the chance to win one of ten luxury trips to the US Golf Open. At the end of the pre-set time period, 30 names were chosen at random. The number of times members were entered in the draw depended on the number of frequent flyer points earned during the pre-set time period. The 30 names chosen were each sent a gold golf ball inscribed with their name and invited to an exclusive Irish golf club to play a round of golf with Paul McGinley and other Irish golf professionals. After golf and lunch, Paul McGinley hit each of the 30 personalised golf balls to one of the greens. The 10 names measured nearest the pin were declared winners of the trips. The 20 runners-up all received secondary prizes. In this case, sales promotion was utilised to effectively support an on-going relationship marketing programme with Aer Lingus Gold Circle Club members, and to increase flight sales during a fixed period of time.

CASE HISTORY 3 — SALES PROMOTION AND
DIRECT MARKETING INTEGRATED INTO
AN OVERALL COMMUNICATIONS PROGRAMME

Company   Premier Banking
Brand   Banking and Insurance Services
Campaign   Generic

Premier Banking is without a doubt one of the best examples of a totally integrated communications programme. Established in November 1990, initially to provide bank loans by telephone, Premier has gone from strength to strength, adding insurance to its portfolio in 1994 and today servicing thousands of groups of different customers throughout the country.

When the service was first launched, direct response television, radio and press advertising were utilised in order to generate mass awareness and understanding of the service. All advertising respondents' information was data-captured as soon as each customer contacted the centre and all new contacts were tracked in line with the different advertising and promotional offers to measure success levels. Through a well-managed database programme, Premier were able successfully to build profiles on different customer groups.

Today, Premier is even more sophisticated in its communication. Whilst the launch phase mass-marketed the product, today Premier customise their communication to appeal to different customer groups. Different direct response advertising and promotional programmes are implemented to communicate to the different groups. For example, nurses will be targeted in publications relevant to them and receive personalised correspondence with relevant promotional offers; whilst business executives will be targeted through different media and a different set of personalised correspondence and promotional offers.

Premier Banking's activities are integrated "through-the-line" to their customers, employing advertising and promotional activities, all of which are direct-response driven. The foundation of all activity is their customer database, on which they measure responses, track market shifts, identify new customer groups, address customer needs, and ensure that all communication sent out in any shape or form is most relevant to its targeted recipient.

THE FUTURE FOR DIRECT MARKETING AND SALES PROMOTION

The lines between all types of communication are becoming increasingly blurred. The consumer doesn't go through the day considering "there's a nice advertisement", or "what an interesting direct campaign", or "what an effective sales promotion". Consumers simply react to the communications activity we present them with, regardless of the mix of activity. What is important from both the marketer's and practitioner's points of view is that we get the mix right for the brand in question, that the balance within that mix is appropriate, and that the best results are delivered all round.

On a practical level, the "specialists versus generalists" issue is still under debate. Specialists in PR, direct marketing, sales promotion and advertising will each bring a depth of experience and resource to the table. Generalists have in the past sometimes fallen down on areas in which they did not hold any depth of expertise; however, there have been substantial changes over the past five years, both in Ireland and abroad. Sales promotion and public relations agencies have merged. Direct marketing agencies have merged with sales promotion companies, or simply bought in the requisite skills. Large advertising agencies have merged with or taken over smaller sales promotion and public relations agencies. Although there are still large numbers of independent sales promotion, public relations and direct marketing agencies, current market trends indicate that there will be further such mergers, with practitioners moving towards providing "through-the-line" services for marketers.

Within this context, it is likely that sales promotion and direct marketing will continue to grow closer together. The two have always had a relationship; some of the earliest direct marketing activities offered sales promotion incentives to consumers as part of the overall campaign, and today campaigns such as the Superquinn Superclub clearly demonstrate how one can be integral to the other. That said, it is doubtful that the market will ever get to a stage where all sales promotion activity will have a direct marketing campaign attached to it or vice versa. However, they certainly won't grow apart, and what is important is that both marketers and practitioners have a strong understanding of and appreciation for both disciplines and that this is coupled with a practical working knowledge of each area. That way, when considering brand issues, a solid, balanced professional opinion can be developed, identifying the appropriate communications mix, to deliver the optimal results.

REFERENCES TO CHAPTER 12

Burnett, J.J. (1993), *Promotion Management*, Boston: Houghton Mifflin.

Chapman, A., K. Lawton and K. Lee (1994), "Sales Promotion . . . Getting Started!", *Promotions*, Dublin: Ryan Media, pp. 12–14.

O'Connor, J. (1997), "The History of Sales Promotion", Paper Presented at the IISPC "Do You Know Everything About Sales Promotion?" Education Seminar, Dublin, 15 October.

Olsen, C. and K. Shaw (1986), "Promotions — Just What are we Giving Away?", *Market Research Society, 1986 Conference Proceedings*, pp. 245–264.

Peattie, K. and S. Peattie (1993), "Sales Promotions — The Missing Link in Services Marketing", Paper Presented at Service Industries Management Research Unit Conference, "Managing Innovation in Services", Cardiff Business School, University of Wales, Cardiff, 5–7 April.

Shimp, T.A. (1997), *Advertising, Promotion, and Supplemental Aspects of Integrated Marketing Communications*, Fourth Edition, Fort Worth, TX: The Dryden Press.

Totten, J.C., and M.P. Block (1994), *Analyzing Sales Promotion*, Second Edition, Chicago: Dartnell, pp. 69–70.

Chapter 13

TELEMARKETING

Mary Lawlor, Tom Trainor *and* Susan Wheeler

Overview

In 1980, The Times *commented that "the most powerful marketing tool ever invented lies unused on desks up and down the country". They were, of course, talking about the telephone. Telemarketing today is by far the fastest growing communication medium, as businesses tap into the power of tele-communications and information technology to create stronger and more profitable relationships with their customers. Customer relationships are now considered to be highly valuable assets and as such require nurturing to achieve their full potential if businesses are to survive in an increasingly competitive marketplace. Over the last decade, as customer expectations have increased, instant service is expected in many industries, whether in business-to-business or consumer markets, ranging from financial services to home shopping. Customer service has become the key to competitive dif-ferentiation in every type of business, and telemarketing is now recognised as a very powerful strategy in the development of customer relationships.*

The new realities for today's marketers have radically altered the rules of the game. In some product markets facing slow growth or saturation, com-panies are plagued by intense competition and strive to maintain or consoli-date their position. In many of the new high-technology product markets, companies are experiencing fast growth; much of the literature suggests that this success comes from those companies establishing a dominant position in the early stages of market development. Continuous price wars between manufacturer and retailer brands, discounting and stock piling, and poorly designed promotions all ultimately combine to reduce total industry mar-gins. New corporate challenges arise from dwindling brand loyalty among consumers, fragmentation of mass media and mass markets. Essentially, companies are striving to find ways to get to know and treat their customers as individuals.

Maintaining a close relationship with each customer is not easy, par-
ticularly when large numbers of customers are involved and transactions
are becoming more impersonal. However, technological developments enable
the collection and management of large amounts of customer-specific infor-
mation, and this is central to personalised customer care. The growth of da-
tabases and targeted media and the resulting ability to segment mass
markets has enabled firms to integrate a variety of traditional and non-
traditional media to tailor their marketing to the customer. Marketers are
now seeking an active response to their advertising or sales message. They
recognise that dialogue with the consumer, whether it is a request for infor-
mation, a competition entry, or a sale, increases their results.

Telemarketing today is a sophisticated medium employed by major mul-
tinationals, as well as a growing body of Irish companies, as a vital and of-
ten central element of their marketing mix.

A British Telecom and Henley Centre report (1997) pointed out that
leading-edge companies such as Unilever, Federal Express and First Direct
have reorganised their business processes by adopting telemarketing tech-
nologies as part of their business strategy. Federal Express generates 54 per
cent of its customer leads through Freephone numbers. In Ireland, Esat
Digifone's 24-hour customer-care facility uses telemarketing for its billing,
technical support and complaints. Gateway 2000 has integrated its multi-
lingual call centre into its manufacturing plant to deal with sales, support
and customer services.

This chapter defines telemarketing and provides a summary of its typical
applications. International trends in telemarketing are outlined, as are the
factors influencing its growth. The chapter concludes with the strategic con-
siderations involved in the introduction of inbound and outbound telemar-
keting within a company.

TELEMARKETING: A DEFINITION

Telemarketing is increasingly viewed as having a broad strategic
function, rather than being just a narrow tactical element of a marketing communications plan, and this is reflected in the various definitions of telemarketing:

- "The systematic use of telephones as a communications channel
between an organisation and its customers" (Lawton, 1995)

- "Any measurable activity using the telephone to find, get, keep and develop customers" (Leiderman, 1990)

- "Managing the customer primarily through the medium of the telephone, using all the sales, marketing, systems and management disciplines of account management" (Stone et al., 1990)

- "Telephone marketing is the generic term for the planned and controlled use of the telephone in developing profitable relationships with customers, prospects, dealers, suppliers and shareholders" (Calvert, 1994).

There are two forms of telemarketing: inbound and outbound. Firms stimulate calls to their business through inbound telemarketing and generate calls from their business through outbound telemarketing.

INTERNATIONAL TRENDS IN TELEMARKETING

Telemarketing is experiencing explosive growth in Europe and the United States. The US telemarketing industry sells over $280 billion, amounting to a 400 per cent increase between 1982 and 1997. This increase was driven in part by a 65 per cent reduction in long-distance communications costs. The industry sustains four million jobs and it is predicted that telemarketing will be the number one industry in the world by the year 2000. A survey recently conducted by British Telecom with the Henley Centre (1997) found that the average American consumer uses the phone for six minutes per week to access goods or information, in contrast to a mere 30 seconds for a typical UK consumer. Three-quarters of an American sample surveyed said they had used Freephone numbers, compared to 25 per cent of the UK sample.

British Telecom and The Henley Centre (1997) have estimated that 670,000 Europeans will be working in call centres by the year 2001. In 1997, it was estimated that one in every 250 Europeans was employed in a call centre. In the UK, four per cent of the working population works in telemarketing. The volume of telephones has more than doubled in each decade since 1960 (Calvert, 1994). A growth rate of 40 percent in telemarketing is predicted in the next five years.

Around 15 million telemarketing calls are made in the UK each week. The Freefone (0800) and Lo-call (0345) numbers give an accurate measure of consumer-to-business calls. These numbers have experienced a 35 per cent growth in 1993 with 540 million calls to Freefone or Lo-call numbers. The findings of the British Telecom and The Henley Centre report (1997) suggest that the more experience consumers have of using the Freefone (0800) service, the more likely they are to prefer it to travelling to an outlet, or writing away for information.

TABLE 13.1: MARKET SECTORS USING TOLL-FREE SERVICES, THE US AND UK COMPARED

Industry Type	UK	US
Manufacturing	10%	36%
Financial services	35%	24%
Travel and transport	15%	17%
Retail and distribution	26%	9%
Other	14%	14%
Total	100%	100%

Source: Touche Ross, 1992, in The British Telecom and The Henley Centre Report (1997), p. 1.3.

TELEMARKETING IN IRELAND

In just four years, Ireland has emerged as the leader in the highly competitive call centre market in Europe, due to the joint efforts of Telecom Éireann and the IDA in marketing the concept of "Ireland Inc.". Since the early 1990s, over 55 major international companies have located their telephone sales, marketing and customer support in Ireland to service European markets by phone. In 1997, there were 4,500 people employed in call centres and this figure is forecast to double by the year 2000. Telemarketing has been applied to a wide variety of products and services, from hotel, car rental and airline reservations to computer hardware and software. Intelligent call centres, in which simple customer queries are handled automatically by computer, with staff concentrating on more complex queries, is the next stage in this development.

TABLE 13.2: FACTORS INFLUENCING THE GROWTH OF
TELEMARKETING IN IRELAND

Factor	Current Drivers	Result
Political	Drive towards fuller EU integration	Competition from new sources
	Emphasis on inward investment	Strategic shifts required
	Deregulation of markets	Squeeze on costs
	Trend toward privatisation	Greater drive for efficiency
Economic	Falling costs of communication	Increased commercial activity
	Increasing costs of labour	Lower employment levels
	Fragmentation of mass markets	More targeted marketing required
	Corporate restructuring	
	Business process re-engineering	
	Globalisation of companies	
Socio-Cultural	Shortage of language skills	Lower employment levels
	More educated consumer	More flexible work patterns
	Lifestyle shifts	More targeted marketing required
		Higher service expectations
		Mass customisation
Technological	Rapid development of equipment	More information
	More segmentation tools available	Greater efficiency
	Development of Internet	Fewer people
	Global communication networks	Increased competition
	Falling costs	

FACTORS INFLUENCING THE GROWTH OF TELEMARKETING IN IRELAND

Key drivers that have underpinned the growth in telemarketing in Ireland include the need for companies to target their marketing activity accurately to the level of the individual. There is also a change in consumer attitudes to the telephone as a way of ordering products and services. At a macro level, the increased use of technology, both telecommunications and computing, together with Irish government support for the telemarketing industry have contributed significantly to growth. Many Irish companies have redefined their business processes. Measurement, accountability and constant reviewing of activity are part of this new reality.

Table 13.2 outlines the factors influencing the development of direct marketing in general, and telemarketing in particular.

Political

Inward Investment

Recent governments have stimulated inward investment through industrial policies, attracting major American and European companies to set up call centres in Ireland. The call centre market is forecast to grow by 20 per cent per year to $5 billion by 1999. While the major users are currently in the financial services and travel sectors, expansion is predicted in the business-to-business sector. Table 13.3 highlights companies whose European call centres are located in Ireland.

TABLE 13.3: THE LARGEST TELESERVICING COMPANIES IN IRELAND

Company	No. Employed
UPS	900
IBM	750
Gateway 2000	700
Compaq	550
AOL Bertelsman	500
Oracle	400
Digital	400
American Airlines	220
Hertz	200
DER	175

Source: Business and Finance (October 1997)

All of these companies have call centres here: UPS, the world's largest package delivery company, whose Irish call centre handles over 5,000 calls per day; IBM has set up its customer support centre for PC users in Europe and the US; Best Western, the world's largest independently owned hotel chain with 300,000 rooms; Gateway 2000, the major PC manufacturer, employing 1,600 people in total at its centralised production unit and multilingual call centre in Dublin; Dell, the $10 billion PC manufacturer employs 300 in its telesales and support centre for Ireland and Britain in Bray; AOL Bertelsmann provides subscriber support for its 500,000 on-line customers across Europe from its call centre in Dublin; Oracle, the global software giant opened in Dublin in May 1997, starting with 200 employees selling to 20 different European countries by phone; and Ryanair, Korean Air and United Airlines have their call centres here.

An International Teleservices Forum has been formed, which involves companies working in the international teleservices sector in Ireland, using the telephone as their key business tool. This forum provides an opportunity for the industry to share information, evaluate technology and deal with other key industry issues.

Economic

There are many economic reasons for a firm to use telemarketing:

- To become more accessible to its customers, and potential customers

- To appear to have local presence in all served markets

- To provide higher levels of customer service

- To capture and use more detailed customer information

- To achieve lower costs of sale

- To gain economies of scale, consolidating an existing fragmented operation

- To benefit from lower overheads in lower labour-cost locations

- To reduce sales cycle times

- To expand the range of telephone applications being used

- To achieve consistency across borders.

Telemarketing can be organised as an operational business unit or call centre dedicated to the creation and maintenance of customer relationships over the telephone. It is a primary route to market for direct marketing companies. Call centres can enable a business to re-engineer its business processes, becoming a factory that makes calls.

Table 13.4 highlights the call centre applications that might be typically used by different industry sectors.

TABLE 13.4: CALL CENTRE APPLICATIONS

Industry Sector	Customer Service	Order Entry	Help Desk	Credit and Reservations	Outbound Telemarketing	Service Bureau
Computer/Software		×	×		×	×
Comms. Services	×	×	×			
Insurance/Banking	×		×	×	×	
Financial/Credit Bureau	×	×	×	×	×	×
Consumer Marketing	×	×				
Mail Order Houses	×	×			×	×
Publishing Houses	×	×				×
Transport/Travel	×	×		×		

Socio-cultural

Some of the key socio-cultural factors that have influenced the growth of telemarketing in Ireland are a skilled work force, changing demographics, image and attitude to telemarketing and an increase in the ownership of telephones.

Skills

Ireland has an abundance of well-educated young people; this, along with the strength of Telecom Éireann's infrastructures, both digital and fibre optic, forms the basis of Ireland's telemarketing success. There are currently 4,000 multi-lingual agents in place in Ireland, and it is estimated that this figure could rise to 10,000 by the end of the decade. Irish wages and social charges are substantially lower than most European countries. The IDA offers grants towards start-up costs, including capital investment, training, and employment grants.

Demographic

Changing work patterns in Ireland have also contributed to the growth of telemarketing. O'Neill (1996) points out that 30 per cent of the employee population engage in night work, 50 per cent work on Saturday, 33 per cent work on Sunday. Flexible working patterns are expected to become more common due in part to the growth in services and the liberalisation of trading hours. The growth in female employment has also contributed to this phenomenon. In 1970, five per cent of married women were in paid employment; it is forecast that, by the year 2000, 33 per cent of married women will be in paid employment.

The marketing implications are that: (1) companies need to and are able to target prospects and existing customers in their own homes, and (2) customers, with less time available, want to have the opportunity to contact companies at times that are convenient to them, resulting in the need for new communication and distribution channels.

Image and Attitudes

A study of direct marketing attitudes by Akaah et al. (1995) found that consumers with positive past direct marketing experience tend to exhibit positive direct marketing attitudes. The more positive consumers' attitudes are to direct marketing, the greater is the likelihood that they will purchase direct marketing products. There has been a shift in consumer behaviour in Ireland with changing lifestyles and the evolution of a "teleculture" contributing to the growth of telephone-based services such as direct insurance, telephone banking, home delivery of food and pre-booking of cinema tickets.

According to a survey undertaken by the *Sunday Business Post* (1998), one in five Irish adults possess a credit card, compared to four out of five in the US. The number of credit cards in circulation has doubled since the beginning of the last decade — from 760,000 in 1991 to 1.5 million in 1998. This method of payment for goods and services has contributed to the growth of telemarketing. In Ireland, 85 per cent of ABs use the telephone for consumer transactions, compared with 64 per cent of DEs. Eighty per cent of 15- to 49-year-olds use the phone similarly compared with 65 per cent of 50- to 64-year-olds and only 41 per cent of over-65-year-olds (O'Neill 1996).

The key issue for outbound telemarketers is knowing whom to call, when to call, and what to call about. If this is not done properly, the process can alienate customers, rather than attract and please them. In this lie the roots of the poor image that has dogged the industry; the response of smart efficient telemarketers is to maximise their use of information systems.

Telephone Ownership

Telephone ownership in Ireland has experienced rapid growth, with household telephone ownership more than doubling from 38 to 77 per cent since 1982. As a result, customers today expect easy communication, and the use of the telephone in business-to-business and business-to-consumer communications is customer-driven. According to O'Neill (1996), there is a new demand for retailing and other services outside opening hours and customers are seeking new ordering, buying and delivery channels.

Technology

The modern telecommunications infrastructure, generous government incentives, ten per cent corporation tax (currently due to last until 2010), and a highly educated young multilingual workforce have all contributed to Ireland's attractiveness as a call centre location. In many cases, Ireland offers the call centre investor more skilled staff, shorter pay-back period and higher return on investment.

Telecom Éireann has invested heavily in recent years to become equipped with one of the most advanced "feature-rich" networks in Europe. With diverse fibre-optic connections on all major routes, it delivers crystal clear connections world-wide. An intercontinental routing service provides a toll-free capability between Europe and the US. Telecom Éireann is the lowest cost service provider in the EU for international traffic in toll-free numbers.

STRATEGIC CONSIDERATIONS

In order to be most effective, the telemarketing process must be integrated into an overall strategy that defines the customers' needs and uses a scientific approach to matching the right offer to the right customer at the right time, within the context of an ongoing interactive relationship. It must therefore take into account the whole marketing philosophy. This requires careful business planning, clear objectives, efficient processes and robust monitoring and control systems. Systems that strategically integrate telemarketing with advertising and database programmes can assist in this task (Schlaphoff, 1996). Telemarketing is at the forefront of successful database marketing programme implementation, in that it can gather information, score the file and identify and deliver quality prospects for marketing communications activities.

In building a pathway from the strategic plan to the operational reality, a marketer might follow the high-level steps illustrated in Figure 13.1.

FIGURE 13.1: STRATEGIC PLAN FOR TELEMARKETING

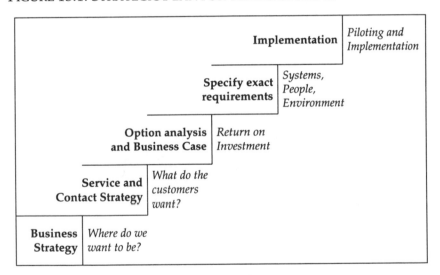

Business Strategy

A key objective of most companies is to differentiate themselves from others in the marketplace, and using telephone-based customer strategies can help. To achieve a genuinely competitive edge, a company must consistently deliver a superior level of service. This requires the most effective deployment of people, processes and systems in a highly structured way, so as to deliver "best practice". The "call centre" concept meets this need, providing a focused point of contact for the customer. Greater numbers of trained staff, better systems and processes, and specially designed environments facilitate longer hours of service, greater volumes of customer contacts, faster ordering and processing, greater language cover, and lower costs of sale. Managers must devise and follow a planning model in order to ensure that established best practices are aligned with their company's specific business situation and requirements. This involves both benchmarking and the development of bespoke processes, to ensure a strategy that both uses established call centre learning and responds to the particular needs of the business. The telephone is used to carry out more and varied business tasks. Transactions are becoming more complex, and the corresponding skill level required of agents is increasing. In some cases, all customer contact is exclusively over the telephone; the customer's perception of the company is therefore shaped directly by the interaction. We are experiencing a shift to the total "professionalisation" of the telemarketing operation. Table 13.5 highlights the shift in emphasis from a traditional approach to telemarketing to a more professional approach.

TABLE 13.5: PROFESSIONALISATION OF TELEMARKETING

Traditional Approach	Professional Approach
Cost-centred perspective	Revenue-centred perspective
Focus on volume sales	Focus on customer relationships
Junior staff	Experienced, professional staff
Standard handling of calls	Personalised handling of calls
Voice only	Multimedia
Local, regional, national	International, continental, global

Service and Contact Strategy

A firm considering using telemarketing must determine the level of service and contact required by its customers from the business. Telemarketing applications for servicing and contacting customers are constantly growing and may include any or all of those illustrated in Table 13.6.

TABLE 13.6: TELEMARKETING APPLICATIONS

• Information/brochure requests	• Inbound order taking
• Help-desk facilities	• Database/Lists building
• Lead generation	• Appointment setting
• Subscription renewals	• Telesales/sales support
• Account management	• Complaint handling
• Market research/surveys	• Customer care
• Testing new markets	• Debt collection

Option Analysis and Business Case

The benefits of telemarketing for a firm may include the following:

- *Cost efficiency*: The cost per contact or per sale is often lower than that of traditional field sales. According to the British Telecom and The Henley Centre report (1997), a personal sales call for a high technology product like a computer workstation can cost up to £350. A telesales call for a similar product can cost between £7 and £12.

- *Volumes*: Many more contacts can be made in shorter timeframes. The personal sales representative can typically make 12 to 15 effective primary contacts per day. In contrast, an effective telemarketer can place as many as 50 to 100 effective contacts in the same period.

- *Shortened sales cycle*: A protracted sales cycle for a complex product can be reduced. Telemarketing can also be employed to qualify leads for a personal sales representative.

- *Improved cash flow*: Sales made sooner pay sooner, and credit card payments may be taken.

- *Market expansion*: New territories and sectors may be entered without moving from your call centre.

- *Customer relations*: More contacts can gather more information, and enable more appropriate offers. Many companies have found that prospects and customers prefer telephone relationships because of convenience and time efficiency.

- *Market research*: Real-time market research can be conducted with customers.

There is an ongoing challenge for firms to balance the needs of the customers with the economic requirements of the business and also the continuous motivation and training of the telephone agents. The customer seeks fast, efficient response from a company and expects continuity of contact with staff to fulfil the "promise" made by the company. The fundamental mission of any business ought to be "satisfied customers". The company setting up a telemarketing operation has to balance the dual requirements to do so efficiently and profitably while recognising the need for continuous staff training.

Inbound and outbound telemarketing are different functions and combining them presents certain major challenges. Inbound calls are initiated by the customer, often prompted by a toll-free number appearing in direct mail or direct response media advertising. It is essentially consultative selling, as fact-finding is required to determine, firstly, why the customer called and, secondly, what their needs really are. There is a particular implication for skill levels of agents, who must be able to turn service calls into sales calls.

The outbound telemarketing efforts will be more targeted and should receive less resistance, because they are reaching only those respondents most likely to buy (Schlaphoff, 1996). Outbound is very specific, and is based on well-established sales and service contact processes, e.g. making appointments for sales representatives, sales calls to customers who do not warrant a personal visit, and magazine subscription sales are examples. A key task is to ensure that, if the agent establishes no customer need that can be satisfied through a sale, that the call is switched to a service focus. Many telemarketers believe that customer service and telemarketing are so closely related, they cannot be separated.

Specify Exact Requirements for People and Systems

As part of the strategic planning process for telemarketing, a company should specify the requirements for managing telemarketing staff and also the systems required to operate an outbound or inbound telemarketing operation.

Telemarketing People

Telemarketing is much more an intensely people-oriented business than a process or production centre. Recruiting, training and retaining effective "agents" or "telesales representatives" (TSRs) is a critical success factor, as they are the primary interface between customer and supplier. As such, they have a direct and critical impact on the company's customer service levels, corporate image, and sales performance.

Companies are constantly seeking better ways to recruit and select effective TSRs. Staff turnover is generally higher than average, and many move on to other telemarketing jobs. There is a growing body of psychological knowledge on telemarketing people, and more companies are incorporating this into selection processes.

The provision of a comprehensive and focused training programme is essential to the success of an effective telemarketing operation. On average, a call centre executive will receive six to eight weeks' training prior to dealing with customers. Such programmes usually include company and product knowledge, customer orientation, telephone techniques, systems appreciation and teamworking skills. Roleplays are always an integral part of training, and a supervisor will listen in to calls and provide feedback and coaching to improve performance. Each agent's progress is carefully charted, and improvement actions agreed. Well-designed and developed scripts will ensure the use of best dialogues, and these are often developed and improved by the agents themselves.

The role of management is to improve continuously the performance of the telemarketing operation. A key element of this is to keep the job interesting and challenging by designing activities and rewards to match the aspirations of both the business and the agents, in line with the demands and preferences of the customer. Competitions and reward systems are used to give recognition to the efforts of the staff. Incentives may include a prize for the friendliest operator or the best handled complaint. The business must measure the activities that make the greatest difference to performance. At the same time, being a "people person" is vital for call centre management, and this is not a numbers game.

Systems and Technology

By carefully monitoring response times, abandonment rates, customer segment performance and contacts per hour, customer acquisition costs can be reduced and response rates can be improved. A range of technological applications combining predictive dialling with call management programmes has made the task of managing and measuring telemarketing campaigns easier. Both agents and customer segments can be monitored hourly to determine success rates, and so marketing activities can be refined almost instantly.

Companies need state-of-the-art information systems to support the telemarketing organisation, along with the field sales force. These two groups should ideally operate as a tightly integrated sales team. To support this team-selling concept, a sales automation system based on remote client/server technology is required, allowing bi-directional transfer of information between the two groups.

Ireland has invested US$3.5 billion in recent years and as a result has one of the most advanced, feature-rich telecommunications networks in Europe, with diverse fibre optic connections on all major European routes. It delivers crystal clear connections world-wide. Features include an intercontinental routing service designed for companies with international call centres, which provides a toll-free capability between Europe and the US. Technology now allows immediate access to data (e.g. instant information on the caller's last order) plus update facilities, sophisticated call routing (e.g. re-routing a query to the relevant department), interactive voice systems including voice messaging and predictive dialling which increases the efficiency of outbound calling. Dedicated call centres now make sense in terms of cost efficiency, productivity, customer relations and corporate image (Calvert, 1994).

The integration of telecommunications and computers are facilitating the implementation of many new services. It now takes only a dozen keystrokes for a teleresponse operator to capture a name and address, resulting in the halving of costs for a direct response promotion. This has been made possible by the emergence of proprietary software which carries the 24.5 million UK addresses in Royal Mail's postal address file (PAF) and swiftly matches them to the given post code. Name, initials and postcode are requested and the address can then be confirmed, resulting in an average saving of 66 keystrokes, increasing efficiency and cost savings.

Teleresponse is seen as the major growth area for such systems. The UK and Ireland are expected to follow the example of the US, where 80 per cent of TV ads give telephone numbers; hence the forecast of explosive growth for the telemarketing industry over the next number of years.

A well-designed call traffic recording system is essential to measure the effectiveness of the telemarketing campaign. Systems can be designed to record call date and time, whether it was an inbound or outbound call, call destination, duration and cost. The agent's performance can also be evaluated and measured by the type of calls received and the success rates by sales and profit contribution. Other measures might include:

- Speed of answer

- Number of dialled and completed calls

- Number of calls taken

- Average duration

- Number of times the agent has got through to the customer

- Ratio of completed calls to dialled calls

- Comparison among agents

- Activity per hour

- Day/time comparisons

- Staff productivity on certain days/times

- Calls lost

- Abandoned calls.

Call centre efficiency can be improved by up to 25 per cent by analysing and "tweaking" variables. Because of the variables involved, it is difficult to generalise about activity rates. But a business-to-business outbound project can achieve up to eight completed calls per hour, depending on whether you are speaking to existing or new customers and the information you have. In a consumer campaign, up to 10 calls per hour can be achieved, and research would suggest that the total cost, including staff, telephone and fixed charges, of this activity is about £12 per hour.

It is better to reduce all fixed/variable costs to a cost per "active hour" of calling or receiving, rather than to a weekly or monthly cost. Variable costs are composed of staff and telephone expenditure. Budgeting for telephone costs on outbound requires a record of the number of dials and completed calls. What is the average call duration? What is the period actively spent on the phone? The greater part of the cost is in making the contact, possibly up to 90 per cent. If the primary objective is not achieved, it is expedient to find out more information, such as current supplier and next planned purchase.

A company must invest time, effort and money in the development and maintenance of good information systems. Telemarketing can be used as a database resource to drive prospect identification and programme tracking. Database staff will usually develop a customer profile for each of the company's products. The telemarketing team will usually develop a series of respondent profiles to determine how closely the respondent base matches the customer base. This ensures that the telemarketing operators are more likely to identify highly qualified prospects (Schlaphoff, 1996).

Implementation

Steps in Designing an Outbound Telemarketing Campaign

Outbound telemarketing is where the company contacts the customer and is mainly a business-to-business activity. Making appointments for sales reps, sales calls to customers who do not warrant a personal visit and magazine subscription sales are examples. Technology can make it more difficult to get through to some customers. The increasing popularity of voice mail means that telemarketing integrated with direct mail, rather than cold calling, is becoming essential. If an outbound call is relevant to the customer and that customer has a relationship with the company, they are likely to react positively to telemarketing. Table 13.7 highlights the steps involved in designing an outbound telemarketing campaign and the key issues to be considered at each stage.

TABLE 13.7: STEPS IN DESIGNING AN OUTBOUND TELEMARKETING CAMPAIGN

Stage	Activity	
Campaign objectives	Who?	MD/Financial controller/Mr/Mrs/Ms
	Which?	Geography/Company size/ geodemographic profile
	Why?	Reason for calling
	How many?	Number of contacts required
	How long?	Timescales
	How much?	Budgets
Campaign design	Stand-alone telemarketing campaign or part of an integrated marketing strategy? "Supporting" mail piece before or after the telephone call is made? Receptivity of the target audience to your approach? Secondary goals e.g. lead generation / database cleaning?	
The list	The right list is a critical step in developing a successful telemarketing campaign.	
Writing the script	Explain the reason for the call, a description of the product or service and the close. A well-designed script will be friendly, use conversational language, be to the point and involve the prospect throughout the dialogue.	
Script testing	Make five to ten calls to identify any changes which should be made.	
Recording information	What will the information be used for? How will the data be stored? Can the key records be accessed easily? What analysis is required?	
Campaign testing	Complete 50–100 calls to test and modify the campaign.	
Training	Ensure that telemarketing staff have a good knowledge of the company, its products/services and the market.	
Monitor	Monitor completed calls and the way the script is delivered.	
Analyse	Analyse results against initial campaign objectives.	

Steps in Designing an Inbound Telemarketing Campaign

The telephone is a dynamic medium that can add value to a company's communications and customer service needs in order to build customer relationships. The company can centralise all inbound communications from customers through one number such as a 1800 Freephone number, thereby enhancing the perceived customer service value. A company can use many opportunities to publicise its inbound telemarketing number in any or all of the following media:

- Press advertising
- Radio and TV advertising
- Posters and merchandising material
- Mailshots
- Statements, invoices, receipts
- Organisational letterheads, envelopes and other stationery
- Product packaging
- Membership cards.

TABLE 13.8: STEPS IN DESIGNING AN INBOUND TELEMARKETING CAMPAIGN

Stage	Activity
Freephone Number	Ensure optimum position in the medium and emphasise free, low cost or local rates
Access Hours	Decide on the hours that customers can call and inform them
Response	Ensure an in-house capacity for handling high call volumes
Objectives	Agree a structure before, during and after communication
Script	Provide guidelines for operators to capture extra information
Advertising source	Capture details of the medium which generated the call
Quantity vs. quality	Balance the need for high response rates with accuracy in data capture
Technology	Use technology to capture caller details and for information back-up, i.e. help screens, on-line credit card validation
Measurement	Design an assessment system to review results against goals

Agency Versus In-house

Many companies pilot a test marketing operation with an outside agency prior to setting up a dedicated in-house unit. This allows an opportunity to test before committing to significant investment. The agency also offers the benefits of experience and expertise achieved from other projects. If the results are positive and they can justify the call volumes, companies then look to developing "in-house" operations. Table 13.9 compares agency and in-house operation and the advantages and disadvantages of each.

TABLE 13.9: AGENCY AND IN-HOUSE COMPARED

Advantages of an agency	Disadvantages of an agency
Smaller initial investment	Loss of full control
Lower initial costs	Lack of familiarity
Greater ability to handle peaks/valleys	Frequent "busies" at call centre
Leverage experience	Financial instability
Advantages of in-house	**Disadvantages of in-house**
Control	Unfamiliar management problems
Ability to handle complex calls	Large capital outlay — inbound
Employee commitment	

The company deciding to set up its own "in-house" telemarketing operation should consider taking the following steps:

- Give management the flexibility to design incentive packages

- Make the work environment motivational and supportive

- Investigate all technology options to find the most appropriate

- Use telemarketing to enhance customer service

- Change the direction of your lead generation processes

- Consider the impact on your workforce — especially sales.

The final part of this chapter outlines the variety of special service numbers to be considered when setting up a telemarketing operation.

Access Number Types

An indication of the growth in the telemarketing industry in Ireland is the rapid increase in the usage of special service numbers, such as 1800/1850/1890, sometimes referred to as care-lines. Telecom Éireann has allocated over 2,000 numbers on its Freephone 1800 service since it was launched in 1990, and over nine million calls have so far been generated on the service.

As companies see the power of customer retention strategies over the continuous search for new customers, they are engaging in up-selling, cross-selling and range-selling alongside the establishment of customer care-lines. In the UK, Freephone and Lo-Call numbers alone are growing by 30 per cent a year. Customers using care-lines typically want advice on product choice before purchase, or details of product usage, while about 15 per cent of consumers use care-lines to complain. The most common questions include:

- "Where is my nearest stockist"?

- "Which of your products should I buy?"

- "How do I get the product to work?"

- "How can I get more out of my purchase?"

Manufacturers are using care-lines to deal with customer requests, and also to build powerful lifestyle databases on their customers. In the US, more than half the callers are asked for their name and ad-dress details. Research in the UK has shown that under-45 age groups were the most likely to use care-lines. Older age groups are more likely to return to the shop for advice or to complain. On US care-lines, 75 per cent of calls are at least initially handled by ma-chines; in the UK, the figure is 61 per cent.

Toll-free numbers were first introduced by AT&T in the USA in 1967. Today, 40 per cent of AT&T's daily US domestic traffic of 150 million calls goes to toll-free numbers, and American consumers view these as more of a right than a privilege. However, the market is still in its relative infancy in Europe. In the UK, toll-free usage is set to double by the year 2000 to stg£560 million, and it is predicted that, by 2000, the average consumer will spend an hour per year calling toll-free numbers. Already, one-in-four TV ads carry a toll-free number. June 1997 saw the introduction of number portability in the UK, as part of the deregulation of the market for Freephone, shared tariff numbers, and national rate services. Research by O'Neill (1996) indicates that companies using no charge and low charge numbers are perceived as being larger, more trustworthy, professional, and making a proactive statement about wanting their prospective customers' business. The following are the main special service numbers available from Telecom Éireann:

Toll-Free Access — Freephone 1800

A Freephone number can be called from anywhere in the country at no charge to the caller. The service provider pays for the call later.

Shared Tariff Access — CallSave 1850 / LoCall 1890

Using these numbers, callers are charged a distance-independent rate. There is a small threshold for the caller, and all callers are charged equally. The service provider pays the balance. This service effectively makes every customer in Ireland a local customer.

Premium Services — 1530 to 1580

Companies may use any of a range of six numbers to provide a range of services, information, advice or entertainment, over the phone. Calls may be answered by a recording or an operator.

International Freephone

With an international Freephone number, a caller in Berlin or Tokyo can dial free of charge direct to an office anywhere in Ireland. This direct marketing tool provides easy access to international markets, as it enables an Irish company to compete directly with local suppliers without heavy investment in overseas offices.

Alpha Numeric Numbers

With alpha-numeric key pads becoming standard on all new telephone sets, callers may dial by name as well as by number. In the US, common examples would be 1800-FLOWERS or (407)-W-DISNEY.

The following enhanced features are also available:

Origin Dependent Routing

This feature allows calls to be routed to different answering locations, depending on the service area in which they originate, enabling an international or national campaign to be localised.

Time Dependent Routing

This enables the re-routing of calls to different answering locations, depending on the time of day, or day of week. This is a cost-efficient method of providing continuous customer service.

Percentage Routing

This option allows calls to be routed to a number of different locations on a proportional basis, rather than exerting excess call pressure on one centre, e.g. 75 per cent calls to head office, and 25 per cent calls to a branch office.

Service Tone

This service informs the user, by means of a distinct tone, if an incoming call was dialled using a FreePhone 1800, CallSave 1850, or LoCall 1890 number, enabling the selection of a relevant script for handling the call.

The Telephone Preference Service

The Telephone Preference Service (TPS) was set up in the UK in 1995 by telecommunications and telemarketing companies. This allows consumers who do not wish to receive calls from unknown companies to have their names logged on a list that is checked by participating companies before campaigns begin.

THE FUTURE OF TELEMARKETING

Competition is expected to intensify in all markets and customers' expectations are continuously changing, resulting in more pressure on companies to find cost-effective marketing. Universal international Freephone numbers will provide a single toll-free number which a customer can use to call from different countries. This is expected to increase greatly the popularity of the international Freephone service globally. As the information society evolves, it is likely that the Internet will become more integrated into marketing strategies, enhancing telemarketing activity. The European call centre market is predicted to achieve further significant growth, as multinationals recognise the value of consolidating services to one location. Also, smaller companies will set up telemarketing facilities, either in-house or through outsourcing.

Outsourcing, currently growing at 30 per cent per annum, will provide a cost-effective means for medium and small companies to avail of telemarketing facilities without the requisite huge outlay on a call centre. The skills base derived from overseas call centres operating in Ireland will influence the diffusion of call centres in the indigenous sector. Consumer marketers will increase their use of telemarketing, as they develop customer management strategies to create competitive differential. Marketing will become further integrated, combining channel strategies into comprehensive approaches to managing lifetime customer relationships. Marketers are learning to respect the power of the telephone. Successful businesses understand both the limitations and potential of telemarketing. When managed carefully and in a structured way, the opportunities for creating competitive differential are significant.

TELEMARKETING CASE HISTORY: R&A BAILEY

Overview

R&A Bailey & Co. produces a wide range of cream liqueurs. Baileys Irish Cream was launched in Ireland in 1974, and internationally in 1975. As a market leader brand, it has reaped the benefits of product differentiation and has continuously sustained a strong market share by long being the world's number one liqueur brand.

R&A Bailey Philosophy

The company has a strong commitment to the Baileys brand. The management philosophy and the entire company's working regime is dedicated to the production of quality products. Great effort is directed at understanding the international consumer. The guiding philosophy behind the Baileys marketing strategy is "think global, act local". To make this effective, the international brand management team in Dublin works very closely with national marketing teams, suppliers and distributors to ensure that the most appropriate marketing tools are being used for every Baileys market.

The company strives to achieve customer satisfaction for the Baileys brand. Extensive qualitative and quantitative market research is undertaken regularly in global markets.

As part of its commitment to a quality brand, R&A Bailey decided in 1993 to develop its customer care ethos further. It recognised that by using the telephone more strategically, it would be able to build a stronger, closer relationship with customers, encouraging more loyalty and feedback. Talking "live" to a customer would provide a valuable insight into their concerns and priorities. The information gained through the customer service operations would keep R&A Bailey focused on customer needs.

Campaign Objectives

R&A Bailey wanted to satisfy its customers by supporting a quality product with a quality customer service. It also wanted to provide customers and prospects from all markets with an enhanced perception of the company's commitment to service, customer care and responsiveness, which would thus support brand values.

R&A Bailey provided a seamless channel through which customers and prospects from the various countries could access the company's services up to 24 hours a day. R&A Bailey required the service to provide product information by responding to customer queries, complaints and literature requests quickly, efficiently and in a professional and customer-friendly manner. In addition, they sought to develop and maintain a database where all responses received over the telephone would provide them with meaningful management information.

Target Audience

International Markets

An international customer care-line was established for Ireland, UK, USA, Germany, France and Australia initially.

Type of Caller

Consumers are segmented by usage rates and described as loyal drinkers of Baileys, occasional drinkers of Baileys and potential drinkers of Baileys. Distributors are mainly pubs selling Baileys. Other callers include non-drinkers of Baileys who would purchase the product as a gift for someone else and callers who are interested in finding out further information on the product (for example, doing a school project, studying the drinks industry). Competitors are also included in this category.

Strategy

The customer care-line focused on the delivery of high quality responses to customer calls and correspondence, initially dealing with calls from Ireland only. To cover the international spectrum, the customer service division was developed to handle calls from abroad and continues to do so under its Dublin-based centralised unit.

The platform for handling calls on the Baileys customer care-line is a combination of various elements:

A special Freephone number dedicated to each country is set up to divert to the customer service desk based in Dublin. When a customer calls an 0800 number in the UK, the call is routed to a trained English-speaking customer service advisor in Dublin and respectively for inbound calls from the US, Germany, France and Australia.

The majority of calls are generated from the Freeph

one number displayed on the back of the bottle, although it also appears on special promotional packs in certain markets at certain times. This encourages people to call if they have a query or complaint regarding the product. All calls are diverted to a centralised division capable of handling international as well as national calls and all information taken over the phone is logged onto a computerised database system so that every customer contact is tracked. The customer service centre deals with enquiries and complaints and also has a multitude of capabilities, including 24-hour accessibility, centralised response handling and instant data capturing.

An information/help screen facility acts as a full support mechanism for operators when taking a call and answering a particular question. It is a master database system covering all countries — this is the central hub of contact in terms of customer/prospect data, market research information and tracking each call that is taken. Lead generation opportunities are provided for the sales team, as well as future marketing opportunities for the marketing team. Requests for Baileys recipe booklets in addition to other merchandise can also be registered. The company provides a full customer service support for pub outlets and other distributors. In addition, periodical data can be analysed to build a profile of Baileys customers, which is reported by the telecentre to the marketing department regularly. There is an escalation process for more specific queries or complaints which have to be followed up; the customer service desk can simply transfer calls to the relevant department for action or flag the record on the database screen as a follow-up. This solution integrates all call centre functions appropriate to R&A Bailey's product range into one unique database and call-handling system that accommodates a variety of queries.

Customer Care Solution

The key factors that have contributed to the success of the operation are: (i) the database solution tailored to Baileys' customer care needs (ii) a reporting solution tailored to Baileys requirements (iii) trained and experienced telemarketing personnel and (iv) live telephone coverage.

A Database Solution Tailored to Baileys' Customer Care Needs

A special computerised database solution has been designed specially for the Baileys customer care-line. It is able to co-ordinate all inbound activity using user-friendly front-end screens.

It also includes an on-line information database (helpscreen) relevant to the country from where the call is being made, which provides the necessary facts and figures to the operator at the click of a mouse. For example, the operator can pull up, in seconds, key facts and figures about any Baileys product line — best before dates, product contents, nutritional information, shelf life and storage, case configuration, packaging requirements or batch numbers for the different product rotation cycles, if required. Alternatively, if the caller has a more particular query, the telemarketing operator can access additional information — brand information, other Bailey products, marketing and promotional activity, contact numbers for the various countries and departments within the company, or even internal guidelines like procedural information regarding the handling of complaints, giving out certain information, do's and don'ts, etc.

The database solution is designed to differentiate Baileys Ireland market information from that of the other markets it serves, and provides information relevant to each country — market profile, recipe ideas, question-and-answer breakdown. To achieve the aim of building a database, the solution enables operators to capture relevant caller details and market information quickly and accurately:

- Name, address, daytime/evening phone numbers, sex, state, zip code, country of origin;

- Media source: where did you see the phone number?

- Awareness: do you know where Baileys is made?

- Distribution: have you ever had difficulty in purchasing Baileys?

- Age profile: what age bracket do you fall into?

- Bottle size, bottle batch number;

- Impression of caller: negative, neutral or positive?

- Nature of call: enquiry dealt with over the phone, complaint;

- Request for myths booklet, request for recipe booklet, request for optic from pub outlet or follow-up call required.

In order to minimise errors, the database has been designed to include a series of dropdown menus and pick lists so that the operator need simply "point and click" on the relevant field rather than having to key in all the data from the start. Each call handled is dated, timed and registered with the name of the operator who logged the call, so everything about the call is recorded. There is also a facility for receiving or downloading up-to-date information from headquarters as well as the capability of analysing data, printing reports and extracting completed records in a variety of formats.

A Reporting Solution Tailored to Baileys Requirements

A unique reporting system has been set up in which all records captured over the phone by the customer service team and attached information can be reported in the correct format for further action or analysis when required. Data can be transferred by fax, disk or on-line via modem link or the Internet. In addition to the more formal reporting procedures, each country is updated regularly on progress and developments that arise so they can use the information for their own local efforts and marketing plans.

Trained and Experienced Telemarketing Personnel

The telephone operators are the first point of contact for any communication of this nature; therefore, as part of Baileys' mission to disseminate its commitment to service quality, the issue of briefing and training staff is an equally important element in the customer service mix.

All customer service operators who handle Baileys calls have the necessary language skills and have been trained in the core aspects of telephone techniques and customer care issues. Staff are trained in the operation of the database solution for every type of call scenario.

Live Telephone Coverage

Baileys offer a "live" 24-hour service for all markets, and all calls received are directed to operators who are trained and experienced to handle these calls. All calls are answered quickly and, when busy, there is a queuing facility for calls on hold which covers peak periods and thus minimises lost calls. The project management team is given a schedule of new marketing activity in each of the markets. This ensures that they are aware of potential call volumes at any given time and can anticipate busy periods.

Results

Call Volumes

Overall, this type of teleservicing function does not generate extremely high levels of call traffic. The care-line receives an average of 5,000 calls per year. The "qualitative" value and the "intangible" benefits of the Baileys customer care-line have contributed to the improvement in customer care for the company.

Intangible Benefits

The Baileys customer care centre is a more strategic and focused customer care service under one single division. It provides the capacity to handle inbound calls 24 hours a day. It is a central point of contact for customers, pub outlets and head office, thereby improving communication between all parties, where possible. The centre supplies front-line support and efficient customer service for all queries relating to Baileys products and promotional activity. It enables the company to capture data and any relevant comments, complaints or suggestions from callers, as well as market research/lifestyle/demographic information while callers are on the phone which can therefore be used for future direct marketing activities. It includes a call training facility, which can transfer a call to anywhere worldwide. This enables the customer service team to forward queries through to local Baileys offices or to the main sales division to achieve immediate "call completion". It includes a fulfilment service where recipe booklets/newsletters/merchandise material is sent out within 24 hours of receipt of the call.

Conclusion

Setting up an international customer care-line for Baileys has demonstrated that the company cares about its customers and what they think of their products. But one vital thing to remember is that such a service will amount to little or nothing unless a managed environment exists and unless there is the desire to improve continually ways of communicating with your customers.

REFERENCES TO CHAPTER 13

Akaah, I.P, K.K. Pradeep and L. Daulatram (1995), "Direct Marketing Attitudes", *Journal of Business Research*, Vol. 34, pp. 211–219.

Anderson, S. (1995), "Call Centre Profitability", *Go Direct*, November, p. 31.

British Telecom (1997), *Everything You Need to Know About BT Telemarketing*, London: Henley Centre.

Business and Finance (1997), "The Call Centre Conundrum", October 2, pp. 12–15.

Calvert, N. (1994), "Effective Methods of Measuring Bottom Line Input of Telephone Marketing", *Journal of Targeting, Measurement and Analysis for Marketing*, September, Vol. 2, pp. 155–167.

Cobb, R. (1994), "Conflict at the Tele-Bureaus" *Marketing*, 10 February, p. 19.

European Telephone Financial Services Report (1997), *Datamonitor*.

Finance (1995), "Telefinancial Services Set to Grow Fivefold", June, pp. 24–25.

Lawton, D. (1995), "Dial 'M' for Marketing", *Go Direct*, November.

Leiderman, Robert (1990), *The Telephone Book: How to Find, Get, Keep and Develop Customers*, McGraw-Hill Publishing.

Matthews, C. and B. Hanratty (1995), "Telemarketing From A–Z", Dublin: IDMA Conference.

O'Neill, G. (1996), *Focus on The Future: The Coming Boom in Direct Marketing*, Dublin: Henley Centre/IDMA Report.

Schlaphoff, E. (1996), "Turning a Telemarketing Programme into a Competitive Database Marketing Weapon", *The Journal of Database Marketing*, Vol. 4, No. 2, pp. 187–191.

Stone, M., A. Thomson and C. Wheeler (1990), *Telemanage Your Customers*, London: Gower Publishing.

Sunday Business Post, "Credit Card Survey — How They Compare", "Agenda", *Sunday Business Post*, 12 April.

Telebanking (1996), "New Number in the Cost/Income Battle", June, p. 4.

Chapter 14

THE ROLE OF DIRECT MAIL IN DIRECT MARKETING

Edel Foley *and* Matt Moran

Overview

This chapter looks at the growth of direct mail world-wide, the objectives of direct mail and its key benefits. We outline the growth of direct mail in Ireland and include a summary of the key postal services provided by An Post.

INTRODUCTION

The unhampered flow of mail is an accepted part of the Irish way of life. For over 200 years, the mail has served to tie the country and the world together. The postman or postwoman — the visible end of the now complex postal processing and delivery chain — has always been an institution whose importance is immortalised by the familiar inscription on the General Post Office in New York city: "Neither snow, nor rain, nor heat, nor gloom of night stays these couriers from the swift completion of their appointed rounds". The postman or postwoman is a familiar figure connecting people, no matter how great or small the geographical distance between them.

Direct Mail Comes of Age

In Ireland, the mail service is experiencing a renaissance as more and more businesses are realising the reach and flexibility of the medium for contacting customers and prospects at home or in the workplace. Direct mail accounts for almost nine per cent of total mail volume, and this figure is expected to increase substantially over the next five years. Corresponding figures for direct mail volume in the UK are currently 20 per cent of total mail, and in the USA 30 per cent. It is ironic that, even with the emergence of the information society, direct mail is maintaining its dominance as the key medium for direct marketing efforts worldwide, as the following figures show:

- UK business managers are sent an average of 15 items per week

- An average of 77 per cent of direct mail is opened and 63 per cent is read

- 88 per cent of consumers who have purchased in response to direct mail have been satisfied with purchases

- 81 per cent of consumers would reply again to the same company

- 80 per cent of the top 1,500 UK companies are using direct response advertising (UK Direct Mail Information Service, 1996).

Direct mail is the principal medium of direct marketing. It can be defined as any form of marketing communication that is delivered through the letterbox. This covers a wide range of printed media options: catalogues, letters, postcards, brochures, leaflets and newsletters being the most widely used. Developments in recent years include the emergence of the "magalogue", the use of bill and statement stuffers, and the use of the envelope itself as a promotional medium. Companies have adopted direct mail as part of an integrated marketing strategy, using such devices as the welcome letter, the application form, the issue of quotations or price announcements, and the despatch of samples or gifts, as opportunities to communicate with existing or potential customers.

Direct mail can be delivered in an addressed or unaddressed format. Addressed direct mail presupposes the availability of a mailing list, which may be developed from internal company records and/or external lists. Unaddressed direct mail can be targeted effectively using geodemographic or other segmentation criteria, and often offers better results than an out-of-date or unreliable list. For either option, response devices and incentives are used to boost the potential response rate.

Advances in computer technology have facilitated the growth of the volume of direct mail. The development of computerised databases and desktop publishing systems has encouraged even the smallest business to try direct mail. In Ireland, An Post's investment in automation software such as optical character reading (OCR) technology, and more centralised mail sorting operations, have enabled it to deliver increasing volumes of mail with a quality service. Technology also enables firms to sort mail by address in varying degrees before it is handed over to the post office. This in turn allows firms to avail of various discount schemes for bulk direct mail.

An unusual feature of the postal system in Ireland is the absence of a formal postcoding system. While simple district postcodes are in use in the Dublin area, there is no country-wide system in use. Rather than introduce postcodes, An Post has used OCR technology linked to the sorting system to develop a sophisticated National Address Directory. This means for example, that a letter addressed to Newport, County Mayo, is not confused with a letter addressed to Newport, County Tipperary. This system is felt to be a more appropriate "Irish solution to an Irish problem" than the enforcement of a postcoding system in a country which has large regions with a very fragmented population. A further addition to this system has been provided through Precision Marketing Information Ltd. (PMI), a joint venture between An Post and Equifax Europe, the world's largest data processing organisation. In 1996, PMI launched a national consumer database in Ireland which contained information on 1.2 million households. Using a combination of Electoral Register data, specialist software designed specifically for Irish addresses, and demographic and lifestyle data sourced from national surveys, PMI are now able to provide more targeted consumer prospect lists in a Geographical Information Systems (GIS) format. During 1998, it is planned to overlay PMI's 85,000 thoroughfares (streets/roads/townlands) with the District Electoral Divisions (DEDs) to provide a smaller unit of analysis. This will make demographic and lifestyle data available at individual thoroughfare level, facilitating targeting at the micro level.

Fraser-Robinson (1992) points out that mailing lists are getting shorter, due to more sophisticated targeting, a desire to improve response levels, and a drive for greater cost-effectiveness. The objective is to make direct mail more relevant to the receiving audience — a far cry from the traditional concept of "junk mail". The growth of relationship marketing has fostered an increased need to develop customer dialogue and response. Direct mail is the ideal medium for the establishment and maintenance of such relationships, either with businesses or individuals.

Changing Lifestyles Generate Growth

Growth in direct mail is also supported by changing Irish lifestyles — for example, the increasing number of women who have exchanged full-time housekeeping for a full-time or part-time job outside the home. Direct mail offers convenience and ease of purchasing to people in their homes or in their places of work. The depth of detailed product information that can be presented through direct mail is unmatched by other traditional advertising media such as press, TV or radio.

For example, direct mail offers an opportunity to describe complicated financial services in ways not possible in these other media. The financial services firm can explain in detail, on paper, the benefits, provisions, costs, and terms of what is being offered. The customer can examine the offer at their leisure in the comfort of their office or home and without pressure to decide in haste.

The Objectives of Direct Mail

More and more Irish firms from diverse sectors are becoming involved in the effective use of direct mail. The skilled implementation of direct mail:

- Improves the quality of sales and increases profitability
- Builds customer loyalty
- Identifies new product and service opportunities for the business
- Identifies and acquires new customers.

There is little doubt but that the skilled application of direct mail as an advertising and communications medium will help to improve business performance, whether a firm or organisation:

- Sells to other businesses at home or abroad
- Sells to consumers through retail or service outlets
- Sells to specific age or interest groups
- Has a sales force

- Wants to create awareness or to build business relationships

- Wants to conduct research

- Wants to raise funds.

Today, a key strategic lever in an increasing number of successful firms is the ability to identify customers and prospects by name. This enables them to make relevant offers that keep their customers coming back and purchasing more goods and services, and attracts new customers to their business. The objectives of any successful firm are to:

- Get existing customers to buy more of their products or services

- Bring past customers back to their business

- Win customers from their competitors

- Identify new opportunities to sell their products or services.

Direct mail, when planned and executed in an effective and professional manner, can assist in achieving these core objectives.

THE KEY BENEFITS OF DIRECT MAIL

Direct Mail is Selective

Direct mail is the only promotional medium offering the ability to target every single household and business address in Ireland. This enables a firm to be as selective as it likes in choosing a target audience. It can isolate individuals or groups of people most likely to be interested in a particular product or service. This selectivity enables it to make the direct mail piece totally relevant in content and design terms to this target group. Naturally, this means that direct mail has little wastage when used correctly, and this in turn contributes to its cost-effectiveness. For example, Lever Brothers (Irl.) Ltd. created a consumer database through a nationally organised sales promotion offer (see case study in Chapter 5). With this database, the firm could then make relevant offers through direct mail to selected groups of Irish consumers.

Targets can be selected on the basis of characteristics which are already known, or characteristics which are presumed to be indicators of a potential interest in purchasing. Known characteristics include the current order value of the customer, their name, address, job title, the area they live in and their current ownership status, e.g. if they already drive a particular make of car. Presumed characteristics include credit rating, geodemographic classification data such as that provided by the PMI database, time in current job, home ownership, proximity to the nearest sales outlet, and social class.

Direct Mail is Personal

Direct mail is the most personal form of advertising next to talking to individual customers or prospects face-to-face. As Fraser-Robinson (1992) puts it:

> Letters are intimate. For example, you read them to yourself. And if you decide to let someone else see your letter, then you do. Unusual for advertising that. Some of this intimacy has to do with the way they — as letters — are perceived. Some of it has to do with the fact that they are undoubtedly the only advertising message that starts "Dear" and ends "Yours".

All direct mail is personal. It speaks directly to the individual, without the pressure of the salesperson hovering in the background or the blitz of telemarketing calls. Following from this is the feature of personalisation: the ability to customise a mailing piece by name, title, address and whatever other details are deemed to be relevant. The strategist can decide whether to personalise and what form the personalisation will take, e.g. "Dear Ms O'Donnell", "Dear Account holder". The message can be individualised to each person according to their history of involvement with the sender. Modern computer technology provides for this important individualisation. Regular customers like to be recognised and hate to be treated as strangers. For example, First National Building Society can personalise and individualise a message to their customers depending on each customer's status with the company.

On occasion, an unusual approach to personalisation may win good results. One example of pesonalisation which went wrong but still worked for the client was the case of a UK financial services company marketing a special product to all of its well-off clients. It was nicknamed "Project Rich Bastards". For some strange reason, when all of the letters were posted, they went out with a letter addressed to "Dear Rich Bastard"! Luckily for the bank, most of the clients saw the funny side of it, because the promotion turned out to be a huge success (Sappal, 1996).

Direct Mail is Hard to Ignore

The personal character of direct mail ensures that, unlike the majority of advertising messages which bombard the individual, it gets noticed. For example, the Brown Thomas Group issues pre-sale shopping invitations to their regular customers and the turn-out shows how these get noticed and acted upon.

James and Li (1993) surveyed US consumers and direct marketing practitioners in an effort to find out what factors would most influence the opening of a piece of direct mail. Their consumer research suggested that the strongest influences on a mail piece being opened were an official-looking envelope, an envelope with a window, an envelope that looks like a bill, an indication of a free sample inside, a personalised envelope, and an address which looks handwritten. The actual number of pieces received on a particular day was not a strong influence. This was in some contrast to the practitioner research in the same study, which suggested that the most important factors to consider were the number of items received on a particular day, an envelope that looks official, an oversized envelope, an envelope that looks like a bill, an envelope with a window, the offer of a sweepstake or a free sample inside, personalisation, and an address that looks handwritten.

Well-targeted direct mail reaches the addressee in the privacy of their office or home. A professionally planned and executed mailshot then gets the desired attention. The relevance of the contents and the offer, over which the sender has total control, determines what action the addressee takes. In this context, cold mailings — those to prospects who have not heard of the company or done business with it before — are generally agreed to have a lower conversion rate than warm mailings — those directed at current customers and past enquirers.

Direct Mail is Versatile

The traditional media can impose severe physical restrictions on the creative format employed: restrictions of size and shape, colour, time and technique. Direct mail, in contrast, is virtually unrestricted in these aspects. One can send anything from a simple letter to an intricate three-dimensional object through the mail, direct to selected recipients. There is, in fact, only one restriction: the piece must be capable of delivery by the postal service. In the words of Fraser-Robinson (1992):

> Direct mail . . . gives you more opportunity to hold their attention than any other advertising medium. You can include colour, smell, sound, texture, shape. You can fashion your communications more artfully, more convincingly, than any other apart from actually sitting down with them and talking it through.

You can even enclose a free gift, or where practicable, an actual sample of your product. For example, when E.M. Halpin & Co. Ltd. in Limerick sent out a letter and brochure promoting Rombout's coffee, they also enclosed a sample, a filter and a plastic cup so that recipients could taste and smell the product. Likewise, Chivers Ireland Ltd. enclosed a sample sachet and money-off coupon with their promotion of Carbonell olive oil, whilst Barry's Tea distributed a set of four tea bags and a money-off coupon as a piece of unaddressed direct mail.

Direct Mail Can Be Timed

With press, TV, and radio, space has to be booked well in advance, and even then, restrictions on print space and airtime can make it extremely difficult to achieve topicality. Direct mail, however, can be timed by forward planning to coincide with any seasonal event, be linked to a special occasion, or be made to capitalise on something which could not be anticipated in advance. For example, Dairygold uses direct mail to the USA during autumn to sell its traditional Irish breakfast product during the Christmas season. Direct mail can also be a useful tool in the off-season, when teaser campaigns and special offers can be used to stimulate demand. Telephone companies use postcards to remind customers about forthcoming holiday weekends when international call rates are reduced. This is a cost-effective way of stimulating demand at a time when business call volumes are below normal.

With direct mail, the exact timing of the mailshot can be pre-planned. This also means that the response-handling process can be made more manageable by posting the piece in batches over a period of time — this would not be possible with most other media.

Direct Mail Can Be Tested

A very important advantage of direct mail is that it can be tested. Indeed, test runs, particularly for large mailings, are essential in planning a campaign. Testing allows the prediction of the final result with some degree of confidence.

Almost anything can be tested — for example, variations on the product or service, price, offer, creative approaches, mailing list, or payment method.

Direct Mail is Discreet

With almost every other medium, competitors know what is being advertised at the time the medium is used. With direct mail, no-one except the recipient knows what is being sent. Stone (1994) comments:

> In most advertising media, the advertising is an adjunct, not the main reason the person is watching the TV channel or reading the magazine. In direct mail, advertising arrives all by itself to be opened and read at the recipient's leisure. When it is read, there is nothing to compete with it for your prospect's attention.

Hence, competitors cannot respond to a direct mail campaign in the aggressive way that they can in other media. Club Tricot — part of the Blarney Woollen Mills Group — uses direct mail to make special offers on specific products to selected individuals, but their competitors are unaware of this at the time.

Direct Mail is the Easiest Form of Advertising to Respond To

The use of any of An Post's response services — Business Reply, Freepost or Vanity Freepost — gives customers an easy means to respond immediately to an offer or message without any cost to them, because the organiser of the campaign pays for the responses received. When AIB Credit Card Services undertake mailings to existing or potential cardholders, a Business Reply envelope or a Freepost address is always provided, to facilitate response. Depending on the nature of the business, recipients of direct mail can also be invited to respond by telephone, even Freephone.

Direct Mail Can Be Measured Accurately

How many people listened to your last radio ad or watched your last TV commercial? How many purchased your product or service as a result? What return did you get per pound on your last general advertising campaign? These are questions to which not just marketing managers but also finance directors and accountants need answers.

It is the measurable nature of direct mail that makes it such a powerful marketing tool. This feature makes it easy to calculate the cost of each enquiry and each conversion to sale. For example, in 1996 Henry Ford & Son Ltd. used direct mail exclusively in a promotion of their Mondeo model — this generated £2.45 million in sales over a three-month period. In summary, direct marketing success can be measured as the difference between the total turnover generated and the total costs incurred (Vogle, 1992).

Direct Mail is Easy to Evaluate

Evaluation of a campaign should not be confined entirely to consideration of profit. Regular users of the medium find that experience gained on one campaign usually leads to a better cost-effectiveness ratio in subsequent campaigns. In other words, it is an ongoing learning process resulting in greater efficiency and cost-effectiveness as indicated in the case study of Cockburn's Port at the end of this chapter.

The task of evaluation can be more effectively undertaken if one has, in advance, taken the time to understand what the recipients dislike about direct mail. In the UK, research conducted in 1989 and again in 1995 has highlighted some interesting changes in consumer attitudes. In both surveys, consumers had a positive attitude towards mailings — even cold mailings — about products or services that are of interest to the consumer. The 1995 survey, however, highlighted increasing concerns about where the company was sourcing names, and the fact that poorly targeted offers are viewed with increased suspicion (Table 14.1). The consumer has become more literate in the ways of direct marketing, and needs to be confident both of the company and of the offer itself (Croft, 1996).

TABLE 14.1: DISLIKES ABOUT RECEIVING DIRECT MAIL

	1989	1995
Not interested	10%	14%
Just throw it away	11%	9%
Intrusion	26%	9%
Too much of it	10%	8%
Waste of paper	8%	8%
Don't know how they get name and address	n/a	7%
Selling something you don't want	n/a	7%
Don't ask for it	7%	7%
Nothing	18%	23%

Source: Croft (1996).

GROWTH OF DIRECT MAIL IN IRELAND

The value of the advertising market in Ireland grew from £295 million in 1993 to £351 million in 1995. Table 14.2 shows the expected future growth in each medium up to the year 2000.

TABLE 14.2: EXPENDITURE TRENDS IN DIRECT MARKETING IN IRELAND

	Value of Expenditure — £ million					
	1995	*1996*	*1997*	*1998*	*1999*	*2000*
Total display advertising	271	294	316	338	362	386
Direct response advertising	29	32	34	37	40	43
Direct mail	69	77	84	92	101	110
Telemarketing	10	11	12	13	14	16
Total direct marketing	108	119	131	143	156	169
Total advertising	351	381	412	444	478	511

Source: Henley Centre Ireland (1996).

Hence, the growth predicted for the advertising market is 46 per cent over this period. Direct mail as an advertising medium is predicted to grow by 59 per cent over the same period, i.e. 13 per cent above the advertising market growth.

The Henley Centre report included some other conclusions in reference to direct mail:

- The value of direct marketing expenditure (including direct response advertising) in Ireland in 1993 was £88 million, split roughly as follows: direct mail, £56 million; direct response ads, £24 million; telemarketing, £8 million. In the same year, total display advertising spend was £240 million.

- Economic affluence is an important factor. A cross-sectional econometric analysis gave the elasticity of demand with respect to GDP, i.e. the increase in expenditure that could be expected with a 1 per cent n increase in nominal GDP. This was as follows for direct marketing media: direct mail, 1.35 per cent; direct response advertising, 1.16 per cent; telemarketing, 1.35 per cent; total direct marketing, 1.23 per cent.

The Henley Centre has predicted that the future rate of growth and share of spending on direct mail from 1995–2000 will be as follows:

TABLE 14.3: IRISH DIRECT MAIL — TRENDS FOR 1995–2000

	1995	1996	1997	1998	1999	2000
Rate of growth						
Direct mail	12%	11%	10%	9%	9%	9%
Total direct marketing	11%	11%	10%	9%	9%	8%
Share of spending						
Direct mail as percentage of total direct marketing	64%	64%	65%	65%	65%	65%
Direct marketing as percentage of total advertising	31%	31%	32%	32%	33%	33%

Source: Henley Centre Ireland (1996).

During this period, direct mail is predicted to grow by 43 per cent, but as a percentage of total direct marketing it will remain fairly static at 65 per cent. However, this indicates that direct mail will continue as the dominant medium of direct marketing.

The annual per capita receipt of addressed direct mail items in Europe between 1989 and 1996 are as shown in Table 14.4.

TABLE 14.4: TRENDS IN ADDRESSED DIRECT MAIL IN EUROPE (ITEMS PER CAPITA)

Country	1989	1996	Change
Switzerland	102	108	+5.9%
Belgium	76	87*	+14.5%
Sweden	73	67	–8.2%
Germany	60	81	+35.0%
France	50	64*	+28.0%
Finland	48	52	+8.3%
Norway	46	75	+63.0%
Denmark	47	46	–2.1%
United Kingdom	38	54	+42.1%
Netherlands	58	82	+41.4%
Spain	17	30	+76.5%
Ireland	11	22	+100.0%
Portugal	11	14	+27.3%
Poland	—	2	—
Average	47	56	+33.2%

Source: Postal Direct Marketing Services.

* 1995 figures, as 1996 figures are not available.

This table shows that, whilst the per capita receipt of direct mail in Ireland grew from 11 to 22 items, representing an increase of 100 per cent in this period, we rank third lowest in Europe, or 39 per cent of the European average of 56 items. The average letterbox is still far from saturation point — particularly if one notes that these statistics refer to addressed items only.

Postal volumes for addressed direct mail posted via the Postaim bulk discount service increased by 108 per cent during the period 1990–1996. The figure is only part of the picture, because direct mail not qualifying for bulk discount, and hence mailed through the standard postal system, is not included.

Attitudes to Direct Mail in Ireland

As the understanding of the practice and benefits of direct mail become more obvious to consumers, allied to better targeting, and a professional approach by mailers, Irish consumers have shown a more favourable attitude towards the medium. The Henley Centre report (1996) showed the following findings:

TABLE 14.5: CONSUMER ATTITUDES TO DIRECT MAIL IN IRELAND

Statement Put	Agree
The post is a good way of getting more information about products I am interested in	71%
If a company thinks I'm interested in something they are entitled to send me information about it	62%
I like receiving offers through the post for goods I might otherwise not know about	46%
I like to receive regular mailings from companies I know and trust	58%
I am more likely to buy again from a company that keeps in touch	48%
I am happy to provide personal details to a company if it means that they can provide me with a better service	43%

The attitude of marketing managers to direct marketing (where direct mail is the principal medium) has also improved in recent years. A survey of marketing managers in Ireland in 1995, conducted by the Henley Centre as part of the background to its 1996 report, stated that 65 per cent of those surveyed indicated that direct marketing would be much more important (34 per cent) or more important (31 per cent) to their future marketing strategy.

COMPETITION TO DIRECT MAIL

It is still too early to try to determine the likely effects new or emerging communications media such as the Internet or interactive TV might have on direct mail in the future. Many direct marketing practitioners believe that the Internet will in fact be complementary to direct mail in many situations. Already, Irish companies such as the Blarney Woollen Mills Group are using the Internet to create awareness, to promote and to sell directly, but also to support other direct marketing activities such as mail order. It also seems that Internet usage influences purchasing off-line, more so than on-line, to date.

It is fairly certain that electronic and home shopping is set to increase in Ireland, as it has in the UK and elsewhere in Europe and the US. This growth will be facilitated by consumers' desire for convenience and speed in a changing lifestyle environment. A study in the UK during 1996 by Cap Gemini business consultants indicated that 35 per cent of consumers want to be able to shop from home.

This shift in purchasing behaviour will complement mail order and direct mail buying as traditional barriers are broken down. Indeed, electronic shopping can also complement direct mail on the distribution side. For example, a leading UK travel agent expanding its Internet activities is proposing that customers be able to book and pay for holidays by credit card and order foreign currency from home. The tickets and foreign currency will then be delivered by post using a premium service. Another example is where purchases made on the Mainotelivisio's Internet sites in Finland are delivered by the Finnish Post, i.e. new mail order business is generated by the Internet.

An Post has indicated its committment to this important area of technology through the acquisition in 1996 of Ireland On-Line, the largest ISP (Internet service provider) in the Republic. This acquisition will facilitate the development of more integrated marketing strategies, incorporating both new and conventional technologies.

THE ROLE OF AN POST

As the provider of national and international postal services, An Post has a pivotal role to play in the direct marketing industry, particularly in direct mail. The company has developed a range of services over the past decade to meet the specific needs of this growing sector.

Equally important at the strategic level, An Post has invested in direct marketing infrastructure, principally through joint ventures, to assist the growth and development of the sector. This capital investment has brought international expertise to the Irish market.

Specialised Direct Mail Services

Apart from standard business mail, An Post provides specialised national and international services for direct marketers. The national services include the following:

Postaim

The brand name for nationally addressed direct mail posted in volumes of 2,000 plus. It gives substantial discounts off standard mail, depending on total number of pieces mailed in a single mailing or cumulative mailings over a 12-month period. Conditions such as presorting and deferred delivery apply. Variations in this service are introduced periodically, so it is advisable to check with An Post.

Publicity Post

The service allows an advertiser to deliver their message into every household or business in their target area without the need to address them. A target area can be as small as a postman's route, a town/city, or the entire country. The message can be a leaflet, letter, brochure, a product sample or any combination of these. Price is dependent on volume, and again deferred delivery applies.

Response Services — Business Reply and Freepost

Postal response services allow the advertiser's clients to respond to their message free of charge, i.e. the advertiser pays for the responses. The inclusion of either a Business Reply envelope or card or a Freepost address in a direct mail campaign has the following benefits:

- It makes it easier for the prospect to respond
- It generates more responses
- It controls the format of responses
- It measures response levels
- It provides data for the creation or updating of a marketing database
- It provides additional discount in the Postaim service.

Business Reply

Allows an advertiser to supply their clients with specially designed and approved pre-printed envelopes, cards or labels, which they can use to post back responses, e.g. a request for a brochure or for a sales representative to call.

Freepost

Like Business Reply, Freepost allows an advertiser to offer customers/prospects a free return postage facility. The sole difference between these two services is that with Freepost, it is not necessary to provide a pre-printed envelope or card — one simply registers a Freepost address to receive customer responses. Hence, Freepost can not only be used in direct mail, but also in other media such as press, radio or TV.

Vanity Freepost

Allows an advertiser to design their own personalised response address which is unique to their company. A word or phrase that describes the company or brand is chosen, and the word "Freepost" added.

To use these response services, an advertiser obtains a Business Response licence from An Post. The charges are an annual licence fee plus appropriate postage for responses received.

International Direct Mail

Ireland has an extremely high dependency on exports. Hence, direct mail forms an important part of the marketing activity of many exporters.

Bulk Direct Mail

An Post offers an international bulk direct mail service world-wide. This service offers substantial discount off standard international mail. Deferred delivery is a feature of the service.

Direct Injection

The complexities of exporting today are such that sometimes a company wants to indicate that it has a physical presence in another country where it wishes to do business through direct marketing techniques. To facilitate this market need, An Post has developed what is termed "direct injection" of mail into other countries, particularly in Europe.

Using this service, an exporter would generate their direct mail in the language and with the national postmark of the country of destination. An Post then conveys this mail to that country where it is "posted" as domestic mail. Such mail must comply with the national conditions of the country of delivery.

P.O. Box Facility

Where an exporter using direct injection of mail into a country wants to elicit postal responses from recipients there, An Post can provide a local P.O Box number in that country for responses, and arrange for these responses to be delivered to the exporter's Irish address.

International Business Reply

Direct mailers out of Ireland can also avail of International Business Reply from over 30 countries. As with national Business Reply, the mailer must obtain an annual licence and pre-print the reply envelopes in a specific format.

Customisation

An Post will discuss special arrangements or customisation with large international direct mailers where volume and/or frequency warrants special service.

Distribution and Logistics

Through its SDS division, An Post provides a range of distribution and logistics services nationally and internationally. Within Ireland, these include a timed next-day courier service (EMS) and a 24-hour business special, plus a regular parcel service. Internationally, services include EMS, Priority Air, and Economy, as well as direct injection into other countries.

SDS also operates added-value services such as Cash-on-Delivery (COD), where the purchase price of goods is collected from the addressee on delivery and remitted to the sender. The Parcel Forward service operates on the same basis as Business Reply in letter-post, e.g. a distributor can provide pre-printed special labels to his retail customers to return goods they no longer require.

Swiftpost

This is a priority letter service which ensures that a letter or small packet receives priority treatment in transit. Nationally, it gives next working day delivery, but it is not a guaranteed courier service. Internationally, delivery time is dependent on country of destination. For the modest extra charge, this service is ideal for fulfilment of small packets where fast delivery is desired, but courier charges are too expensive.

Advice and Consultancy Service

In order to assist Irish businesses to understand, plan, and implement direct mail strategies efficiently and cost-effectively, An Post provides a free advice and consultancy service through its team of trained and experienced sales consultants.

Support Infrastructure Created by An Post

An Post has helped the rapid development of the direct mail industry in Ireland by the creation of new infrastructure. This has involved substantial investment in joint venture operations such as Precision Marketing Information Ltd. and PrintPost Ltd.

Precision Marketing Information Ltd. (PMI)

A joint venture with Equifax Europe, the service offers a wide range of products and services to support the information needs of Irish companies wishing to use direct mail. PMI has developed the Irish Consumer Marketing Database (ICMD), which contains 2.6 million prospects in over one million households. It is the first database to provide comprehensive consumer information on the Irish Republic. It uses the most advanced software, specially developed to handle Irish names and addresses.

PMI also provides census and electoral register data as well as lifestyle and demographic information. Other services offered include file creation and management, profiling, thoroughfare prospecting, database management, address validation, response analysis, and bureau services and consultancy.

PrintPost Ltd.

PrintPost provides high volume personalised document processing, handling and mailing services to Irish companies. Using unique software and security controls, PrintPost enables a company to out-source the printing, enveloping and mailing of various documents, including transaction details (e.g. loyalty schemes) and direct mail.

Ireland On-Line

Through its electronic communications subsidiary — PostGEM — and conscious of the growing importance of this sector, An Post purchased Ireland On-Line (IOL) in 1996. IOL is the largest provider of Internet services in Ireland. An Post views this acquisition as an opportunity to integrate the electronic and printed media.

PRIVATE SECTOR INFRASTRUCTURE

Over the past decade, not only has the number and size of service providers in the private sector of the direct mail industry increased very substantially, but many of these have also invested heavily. The result now is that both the core competencies and the level of sophistication of the industry has improved dramatically.

As the direct mail market has grown, a number of the traditional advertising agencies have set up their own direct marketing operations, either in-house or at arms' length, to meet the new needs of their clients. At the same time a number of well-known international direct marketing agencies have set up operations in Ireland.

A decade ago, the focus would have been on the "tactical approach" in direct mail, but now a strong "strategic approach" by service providers is added to this. The annual IDMA Awards for Excellence demonstrate the growing capability of this industry, where the infrastructure and the personal and technical skills of the service providers are of international standards.

Mailing Preference Service

An important aspect of the direct mail industry is the Mailing Preference Service (MPS) introduced by the Irish Direct Marketing Association (IDMA) in 1997. This service ensures that anyone who doesn't want to receive personalised direct mail at their home address can make their preference known to direct mailers by completing an MPS application form, which is available from post offices nation-wide. The MPS register is made available by the IDMA to companies engaged in direct mail and to computer bureaux.

The IDMA operates a code of conduct for its members. This code, the MPS and the Data Protection Act are mechanisms which give comfort and protection to individuals who do not wish to receive direct mail at their home addresses.

CASE HISTORY: DIRECT MAIL IN ACTION — COCKBURN'S PORT

Cockburn's Port is a part of the product range of Grants of Ireland, wine and spirit merchants. In 1995, Grants decided to promote this brand and to increase its market share. To achieve this objective, direct mail was chosen as the most appropriate medium.

Market Background

At that time, Cockburn's was Ireland's number two port brand, with 13 per cent market share, after competitor Sandeman with 70 per cent market share. In 1990, sales of Cockburn's was 2,400 cases; by 1995, this had grown to 7,600 cases and had plateaued. Superquinn accounted for 11 per cent of sales. Grants set a sales target of 10,000 cases, equating to 20 per cent market share.

Campaign Objectives

Primary Objectives

- To encourage existing Cockburn's purchasers to trade up to Anno — a premium product

- To encourage non-Cockburn's Port purchasers to buy Cockburn's Special Reserve and thus foster permanent brand switching.

Secondary Objectives

- To communicate the heritage of Cockburn's and its various styles to over 5,000 port drinkers

- To encourage port consumers to perceive Cockburn's as a brand to be shared among friends in a social setting.

Execution of the Campaign

As Superquinn accounted for 11 per cent of sales, and Grants could gain sales information through the SuperClub database, the task of targeting the precise audience was made much easier. Using this database, 2,270 Cockburn's purchasers and 2,800 other port purchasers were identified. Access to the SuperClub database is always on the understanding that the company will provide the mailing piece, and SuperClub will supervise the actual mailing. This protects the integrity of the database, and assures SuperClub customers that they will only receive offers which have been vetted and deemed relevant to them.

It was necessary to create two separate direct mail pieces for these audiences. For existing Cockburn's purchasers, a personalised letter was created, introducing Anno LBV 1988 and including a money-off voucher worth £1.50, redeemable in Superquinn. On the reverse of the voucher, Superquinn Managing Director, Feargal Quinn allayed any possible fear by customers that their name and address details had been disclosed to Grants. He gave this guarantee:

> This offer has been sent to you directly through SuperClub.
> Your name and address has not been released to this or any
> other company.

In order to convey the maturity of the product, Grants printed the message "We have waited seven years to send you this letter" on the outside of the envelope.

For purchasers of other port brands, the letter focused on Cockburn's heritage and the Special Reserve brand. Again, the mailing included a £1.50 off voucher. The message on the outside of this envelope was "Spend more quality time with your friends. Start by reading this letter". The significance of this message was to portray the attribute of sociability of the product — an attribute which stems from the important friendships which exist between the various people involved in producing the product, including the grape growers.

Each of the two mailings included a full-colour product information leaflet to complement the letter by providing additional information and photographic images. Reflecting the maturity of the Cockburn's product, the message on the cover of the leaflet was "Time defines a superior port. Now is the perfect time to try one".

Cost of Campaign

The total cost of the campaign was £17,000. This included list usage, colour printing, postage, administration, production and agency fees.

Analysis of Results

As in any good direct mail campaign, the results were accurately measurable. Cockburn's sales in Superquinn increased as follows: Special Reserve, 53 per cent; Anno LBV, 273 per cent; Total, 110 per cent.

Amongst Cockburn's drinkers, 27 per cent traded up to Anno using the money-off voucher between October and December. During this period, this group purchased an average 2.02 times, giving a 100 per cent level of repurchasing *after* utilisation of the voucher.

Amongst non-drinkers of Cockburn's, 13 per. cent switched brands using the money-off voucher. During this period, this group purchased an average 1.51 times, i.e. 50 per cent of those using the voucher repurchased the product, thus giving seven per cent permanent brand switching.

The target set was achieved, with 10,100 cases being sold during the year. Apart from the successful sales results, the experience of this campaign prepared the way for the 1996 campaign and allowed Grants to build on the 1995 results, to further segment the database, and to test alternative mailing packs. In other words, evaluation of the campaign was not confined to consideration of sales and profit alone.

This campaign won the Gold Award in the direct mail business-to-consumer category in the IDMA Awards for Excellence in 1996.

(Thanks to Jim Farrelly, then Product Group Manager with Grants of Ireland and to Saatchi & Saatchi Direct for their assistance in writing this case study.)

REFERENCES TO CHAPTER 14

Cap Gemini (1996), *Customer Views on Remote Shopping*, London: Cap Gemini, p. 2.

Croft, M. (1996), "Clean-Up Operation", *Marketing Week*, 8 March, pp. 63–64.

Direct Mail Information Service, UK (1996), *1996 Statistics*, London: Direct Mail Information Service.

Fraser-Robinson, J. (1992), *The Essential Secrets of Effective Direct Mail*, Revised Edition, Maidenhead: McGraw-Hill.

Henley Centre Ireland (1996), *Focus on the Future: The Coming Boom in Direct Marketing*, Dublin: Henley Centre/Irish Direct Marketing Association.

James, E.L. and H. Li (1993), "Why Do Consumers Open Direct Mail?", *Journal of Direct Marketing*, Vol. 7, No. 3, pp. 37–39.

Postal Direct Marketing Services (1996), Chapter 3, *PDMS Guide for Cross-Border Direct Marketers*, Copenhagen: Postal Direct Marketing Services.

Sappal, P. (1996), "What a Cock-up!", *Direct Response*, Vol. 16, No. 12, December, p. 43.

Stone, R. (1994), *Successful Direct Marketing Methods*, New York: NYC Books, p. 3.

Vogle, S. (1992), *Handbook of Direct Mail*, Hemel Hempstead: Prentice Hall, p. 22.

Chapter 15

DIRECT MARKETING AND PRINT MEDIA IN IRELAND

Mairead Brady *and* Rosita Wolfe

Overview

Direct marketing uses an array of media to target customers. Among the most effective and creative are the print media. This is true even of this turbulent era when many of the classical marketing practices have been subsumed by new methods and new technologies. The traditional forms of print media advertising are newspapers and magazines, and these two advertising media have remained popular. The print media are particularly suitable for direct marketing and are widely used. As McCorkell (1997) states:

> *A very large proportion of all direct response expenditure goes on conventional space advertising in the press — national newspapers, consumer magazines and business magazines.*

This chapter considers the nature of the print media for direct marketing purposes and also the changes taking place within the media. It highlights the popularity and the use of the print media for direct marketing campaigns. The structure of print media in Ireland is outlined. Inserts are considered and how and why they work. The chapter concludes with the readership profiles and the research services available.

THE NATURE OF PRINT MEDIA FOR DIRECT MARKETING

The print media has witnessed dynamic changes over the last number of years. There has been a virtual revolution in the publishing industry and many of these changes have greatly benefited direct marketing's use of these media. The print media have always been popular with direct marketers. They were particularly important before the development of databases. Despite the increases in databases, the print media has still remained popular for direct marketing campaigns. Direct marketing's use of the print media has grown and developed over the years, and when used correctly, these media have proved to be very beneficial. In a lot of ways, the use of the print media for direct marketing campaigns has been key to the survival of these advertising media (Nash, 1994).

In 1997, press advertising in Ireland had a 46.6 per cent share of the advertising market, with a total spend of £158.52 million (Figure 15.1). It is difficult to state accurately what percentage of this is from direct response advertisements, but the level of direct response advertising is increasing all the time.

FIGURE 15.1: TOTAL ADVERTISING MARKET IN IRELAND (1997)

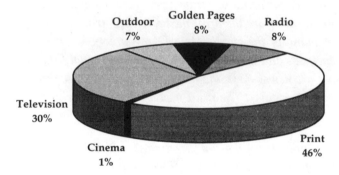

Source: Des O'Meara Advertising (January 1998)

O'Neill (1996a) estimated the share in Ireland at 39 per cent, which compares to 78 per cent in Britain. He predicted that over 75 per cent of Irish newspaper advertisements could contain direct response mechanisms by the year 2000. O'Neill (1996b) adds that over 300,000 Irish consumers have made inquiries or bought goods as a result of direct advertisements in newspapers. Goodwin (1995a) points out that, in Britain, 85 per cent of all large newspaper advertisements, and virtually 100 per cent of all classified advertisements, carry a coupon or telephone number to evoke a response. He adds that the response rate can be as high as tens of thousands for a single advertisement. This shows the power of this medium to generate results.

Conventional Advertising Compared to Direct Response Advertising

Nowadays conventional advertising in the print media and direct response advertising can be difficult to distinguish. When does a conventional advertisement become a direct response advertisement? Some practitioners would say that to use press and magazines effectively in direct marketing campaigns, it is not enough just to include a telephone number. The whole advertisement should be designed so that response-generation is the prime objective rather than an afterthought. When an advertisement is a direct response advertisement it will probably have a total focus on the response mechanism — a call to action from the advertisement. So you often see direct response advertisements which prominently feature sentences such as: "We have a seven-day help desk so if you want to get started call now . . ."; "Cut out this form and fax it to . . ." or "Call us 24 hours a day on . . .".

Planning for direct response requires a different focus to conventional advertising. Direct response advertisements:

- Can be tracked and the exact contribution to the objectives can be measured

- Are placed where the company feels they will get the best return and where historically they, or other companies, have received the best responses

- Contain the factor of diminishing returns. For conventional advertising the awareness of a company/product/service increases with the number and frequency of advertisements in a publication. The opposite is true for direct response advertising, where the replies fall dramatically with repetition. The best prospects are caught at the start of the campaign — these are the people who are favourable to direct response advertising and have a need for the product or service on offer.

Table 15.1 clearly illustrates the differences between conventional and direct response advertising.

TABLE 15.1: How Conventional and Direct Advertising Planning Differ

Conventional	Direct
• Schedules based on readership and frequency	• Schedules based on circulation and lifestyle
• High frequency repetition of simple message aimed at broad target audience	• Aim is for the widest possible (cost-effective) circulation
• Cumulative schedule builds coverage and reach	• Broad coverage of target prospects preferred to frequency (over frequency leads to diminishing returns)
• Employs a narrow band of titles with a high number of insertions	• A wide range of titles, each often carrying only one insertion per campaign
• Schedules planned with overall campaign objectives in mind	• Schedules built insertion by insertion, each of which is expected to pay its way
• Awareness/impact builds with repetition	• First insertion frequently most productive, followed by rapid falling off with repetition
• Planning based primarily on research data	• Planning based primarily on test results and performance
• Efficacy measured by research data including reading and noting	• Efficacy measured by results (e.g. cost per enquiry/sale)

Source: Goodwin (1995b)

CHANGES IN THE PRINT MEDIA

The print media industry is dynamic and ever-changing, and has been greatly affected by developments in technology. The major changes in this industry centre on increased economies of scale, the ability to reach niche markets profitably, smaller but still economical print runs, and desktop publishing. All of these are driving this industry forward. From a direct marketing point of view, many of the changes that have taken place have been greatly beneficial. Some of these are highlighted below:

- *Printing*: is faster and more economical.

- *Publishing*: There are more publications than ever before. This can be seen clearly from the range of choice on magazine racks.

- *Niche markets*: More publications are targeted at niche markets. *Irish Computer*, a magazine which focuses on a specific and well-defined target group, is a good example of this.

- *Increased sections within publications*: Many publications now include separate targeted sections. This is particularly true of newspapers. For instance, *The Irish Times* has a sports section on Mondays, an education section on Tuesdays, specials on Wednesdays, property on Thursdays and two business sections on Fridays.

- *Small but economical print runs*: The increased level of targeting in the print media is due to the fact that printing has become more economical; this is particularly true for smaller print runs, which were traditionally very expensive

- *Desktop publishing*: This allows companies to design and prepare their own advertisements

- *Internet*: Many publications are now appearing on the Internet, expanding the print media into new areas and in many cases new markets. *The Irish Times* on the Internet has found that a majority of hits are from America, where Irish Americans log on to the site

- *Increased speed and print quality*: Campaigns can now have an element of immediacy, as well as more creativity and colour than previously

- *Increased flexibility of the media*: As a result of developments in technology, placing and booking advertisements has become quicker and easier

- *Inserts*: The use of direct response insertions in newspapers and magazines are a relatively new development that is growing in popularity in Ireland.

THE POPULARITY OF THE PRINT MEDIA

With the growth in information technology and databases, the demise of print for direct marketing was predicted. This has not happened. As Jones (1993) points out, "on the contrary, many consumer and business-to-business direct marketers still consider magazine and newspaper advertising essential as a primary source of leads, sales, members or subscribers".

There is a variety of ways that the print media are used for direct marketing. One major advantage is that they can achieve a range of objectives. The main functions of newspaper and magazine advertising in relation to direct marketing are listed below:

1. *To generate direct sales*: In this case, the print advertisement is designed to encourage the customer to purchase. These are also called "off-the-page" sales and are achieved through a response coupon or telephone number. The customer contacts the company to buy the product or service after seeing the direct response advertisement. The growth in credit card and telephone ownership has increased this application. More and more people are buying products "sight unseen" than ever before.

2. *To generate enquiries and leads*: In this situation, the company wants the customer to make the initial contact and then they will follow through and endeavour to sell to them. The design of the advertisement is to create interest and to make the prospect respond. This is used when the prospect will need extra information before purchasing or when the company wants to select the prospects that they are interested in selling to, after they have made the initial enquiry.

3. *Database development and maintenance*: One of the important aspects of newspapers and magazines in direct marketing is to persuade prospects to identify themselves and thus allow a database to be compiled, which the company can then use to target suitable prospects.

   Once the respondents on a database have been exhausted, this is also a useful method for compiling new names for a database. Nash (1994) states that a good advertisement in this media has "the power to reach and identify prospects who can't be identified on existing mailing lists". A good example of this is the Swiftcall direct response advertisement (Figure 15.2). Swiftcall want companies to contact them if they are high users of international calls, as they may be able to offer them savings. The advertisement will also create a database for the company and/or add prospects to their existing database.

FIGURE 15.2: SWIFTCALL ADVERTISEMENT

4. *To find niche prospects*: Database development, alongside the targeting function, is particularly useful for niche markets, where potential customers may be difficult to locate. For example, companies can use specialist magazines to target specific prospects or they can target their direct response advertisement at the niche they are interested in.

5. *To create new markets*: The print media are very suitable for launching new products and services, particularly where no mailing list is available. By using these media, a company can target customers and compile a new mailing list for a new market from the responses generated. Subscription-based magazines can be very useful in this area, as a profile of the target reader is available which can be matched to the potential target market.

6. *To achieve more than one objective*: Direct marketing's use of print media often achieves more than one objective for the company. This is referred to as the double duty effect. Some examples are:

- Awareness and enquires

- Mail order sales and retail support

- Direct sales and enquiries

- Database updating and enquiries.

It is clear that multiple objectives can be achieved through the one advertisement and this is one of the benefits of direct response advertisements.

7. *To support other direct marketing activities*: Newspapers and magazines can support other direct marketing tactics like household delivery, direct mail or television. This type of support can often lend credibility and synergy to other aspects of the campaign and increase the enquiry rates. There is generally a predefined link in the campaign. Therefore, direct mail and telemarketing are often used for customer acquisition and for offering further information after the print media have generated the enquiry.

Why Companies Choose Print Advertising for Direct Marketing

When deciding on the use of print media for a direct marketing campaign, many factors have to be taken into account. In general, one of the best methods of looking at this is to study the difference between direct mail and the print media. The "shotgun" versus "sharpshooter" analogy can help here; the shotgun is the print media and the sharpshooter is targeted direct mail. Nash (1994) states that:

> if your targets are few, worthwhile and identified, nothing beats direct mail; but if they are hard to find, small in number or hard to identify, then there's nothing like a shotgun. It will be sure to hit something.

It is worth noting that direct mail and direct response advertisements in the print media are alternatives, and can achieve different objectives for the company. This is the same for the various choices of promotion campaigns that companies can opt for. The objectives of the campaign are all-important. The traditional trade-offs of reach, dominance, coverage and frequency are the same in this area. As with all marketing, the demands of the target customers will dictate what methods are used to attract their attention.

A study of the advantages and weaknesses of the print media for direct marketing campaigns will aid in the decision. The main advantages are outlined below:

- *Results measurement*: Each advertisement in each publication can be analysed separately and can therefore justify its individual contribution to the overall campaign.

- *Interactivity*: The customer is asked to do something — they are involved.

- *Immediacy of the campaign*: Direct response campaigns can produce immediate results — buy now, contact us today, and so on. In this way companies, can see the effect, or lack of effect, of their campaign immediately.

- *Economics*: The print media can be used as an alternative to direct mail and in some cases can reach a wider audience at a lower cost than direct mail. This has to be measured against the target audience needed, the standard of reply and so on.

- *Low production costs*: The costs are also relatively low as only one advertisement has to be produced.

- *Fast preparation*: This is a quick reaction medium and can therefore respond to situations as they develop. A good example of this was the "Get the boot in" newspaper campaign from the National Irish Bank. NIB placed direct response advertisements in a selection of national newspapers the day after AIB Bank increased their Visa card rates. The direct response advertisement highlighted their own low interest rates and showed how, with one phone call, the customer could switch over to their card. This was a very successful campaign with many customers converting to the National Irish Bank Visa card. Timing proved to be an important factor for this campaign.

- *Simple organisation*: In general, there is limited organisation involved. An advertisement is designed and placed in a suitable publication(s) and the back-up services are arranged.

- *Published rates and readership information*: All publications publish rate cards, making analysis of the various options relatively easy. It is worth pointing out that in Ireland most publications give discounts on the published rate card prices. Irish marketers are fortunate, as there is a wealth of marketing information available for each publication. This aids decision-making in the areas of targeting, inter-publication decisions, cost comparisons, etc.

- *Credibility*: Readers presume that the print media will stand behind the products/services they advertise. There is implied support for the product or service advertised in the publication. This is particularly true for magazines and many publications are very strict about the advertisements that they carry.

- *Reach*: The direct marketer can decide on publications, depending on the circulation and the target audience they reach.

- *Test opportunities*: The print media are suitable for testing offers and areas. By choosing different publications in different areas, the direct marketer can test a range of offers to alternative markets.

- *Skimming campaigns*: If the direct marketing offer is using a skimming strategy, then print can be a better medium than direct mail in some circumstances. This is because it can be more profitable to reach prospects in a less involved, less expensive print-media message, if the likely response rate is going to be low, but the return from each prospect will be high.

Some of the weaknesses of the print media with regard to direct marketing are as follows:

- *Lack of personalisation*: This is the shotgun analogy referred to earlier. This form of advertising is not a direct hit, as the advertiser has not personally contacted the prospect. There are many factors that will effect whether prospects will see the advertisement and/or respond to it.

- *Limited space*: The problem of clutter in the print media is a very definite weakness. The level of advertising in publications has increased and advertisements must compete for the customer's attention in a competitive environment.

- *Poor creative flexibility*: There are restrictions on how creative an advertisement can be in the print media. However, with a good designer and the added impact of colour advertisements, most companies nowadays can design eye-catching advertisements in the limited space available.

- *Need for support mechanisms*: The support mechanisms, like a telephone answering service for the direct marketing campaign, must also be prepared prior to the advertisement appearing in the publication. Such a service must be available for a longer period of time (as opposed to DRTV, where the service can coincide with the timing of the ad).

- *High visibility*: Once the advertisement appears, it is now a visible campaign and the competition are fully alerted to the offer and the company strategy. In using direct mail, a campaign can be run much more covertly.

- *Lower identified affinity*: This media is not as precisely targeted as direct mail, so you are in essence reaching a larger number of less motivated people.

For newspapers in the Irish market, the important attributes are their ability to achieve a very high level of penetration in each market, their high credibility and their immediacy. These are often offset by the media's lack of responsiveness and also the relatively small circulation figures. For magazines, the attributes are similar, with the added feature that magazines are perceived as the more responsive media, but there is increased clutter and intense competition. Magazines have the added advantage of shopping pages. This is where magazines accept small-space, mail-order advertisements in special sections. These sections can be very useful for direct marketing.

THE STRUCTURE OF THE PRINT MEDIA IN IRELAND

This section looks at the newspapers and magazines available for direct response campaigns in Ireland.

The Irish Newspaper Sector

There are a variety of newspapers available on the Irish market, divided into national, regional and foreign publications. On a very positive note, there is a high level of newspaper readership in Ireland, with the Joint National Readership Research (JNRR) for 1995/6 highlighting the fact that 59 per cent of all adults read a daily paper.

On the negative side, Irish newspapers are expensive, due to a combination of factors, including a lack of economies of scale, VAT at 12 per cent (the highest in Europe), and high staffing levels (Payne, 1996). The purchase prices of Irish newspapers are high at £1 for a Sunday paper and 85p for the main dailies. This compares to *The Times*, an English newspaper, which retails in Ireland at 30p.

As discussed previously, advertising in the national newspapers dominates total advertising expenditure. In 1997, £151.02 million was spent on national press advertising.

National Newspapers

The circulation figures for the main Irish national newspapers are listed in Table 15.2 with the costs for both a single column inch and a full page.

TABLE 15.2: IRISH NEWSPAPER CIRCULATION AND PRICES

Irish Newspapers	ABC Circulation Jan — Jun 96	SCI	Full page
Daily			
The Irish Times	102,460	£37.50	£14,850
The Irish Independent	157,393	£90.00	£14,350
The Examiner	52,011	£11.43	£5,750
The Star	86,602	£49.50	£4,950
The Evening Herald	118,942	£62.00	£5,400
Sunday			
The Sunday Independent	366,849	£100.00	£16,000
The Sunday Tribune	79,180	£52.00	£8,650
The Sunday Business Post	37,074	£32.50	£5,828
The Sunday World	299,680	£90.00	£8,400

Source: Media Advertising Promotions Sponsorship (MAPS), Association of Advertisers in Ireland, Directory 1997–1998.

Within the newspaper sector in Ireland, The Irish Independent Group has a dominant position and has some level of investment in almost 60 per cent of Irish newspaper titles. These include *The Irish Independent, The Sunday Independent, The Sunday World, The Star* and *The Sunday Tribune*. This is a very competitive market, but the fact that another Sunday newspaper — *Ireland on Sunday* — was launched in September 1997, is a sign of the potential in this market. The major developments in the Irish newspaper industry in recent years are the demise of The Irish Press Group, increasing circulation rates and growing foreign competition.

Newspapers in Ireland aim at fairly distinct target markets and therefore it is relatively easy for direct marketers to choose publications that might suit their target market. For example, *The Irish Times* targets the ABC classes, while *The Star* targets the DEF classes.

Regional Newspapers

The are over 40 regional weekly newspapers, which facilitates good targeting of the regional market. Many regional publications have gained market share over recent years due to:

- The preference for some people to incur the cost of one local paper a week rather than a daily national paper

- The improved quality of local newspapers, mainly due to competition from local radio

- The local nature of the news and advertisements, which create loyalty.

Many regional newspapers are very successful, such as *The Kilkenny People* or *The Limerick Leader*. An interesting development for regional newspapers is the expansion of *The Cork Examiner* to a national broadsheet, with a resulting change of name and emphasis. With such a proliferation of regional publications, it can be difficult to book advertising in all of them. As a result, a company, The Regional Newspaper Advertising Bureau carries out this task for companies.

Free Newspapers

Ireland has a good range of free titles. These titles are interesting from the point of view that they are delivered to the household, so the consumer does not have to make a purchase decision. The total revenue source for these publications is from advertisers, many of whom favour direct response advertisements. A sample of free sheet newspapers available in Dublin, including their single column inch cost and their cost per thousand (CPT) is given in Table 15.3.

TABLE 15.3: FREESHEET NEWSPAPERS

Freesheet	Circulation	Single Column Inch (SCI)	Cost per Thousand (CPT)
The Community Times	70,000	---------------	---------
Lifetimes	81,000	£30.00	37p
The North Wicklow Times	20,000	£13.50	68p
The Northside People	50,000	£21.00	42p
The Public Sector Times	17,000	£15.00	88p
The South and West Wicklow Times	10,500	£8.75	83p
The Dublin Mail	28,000	£16.00	57p
The Fitzwilliam Post	10,000	£14.00	£1.40
The South Dublin Life and Leisure Newspaper	51,000	£18.80	37p
The Southside People	54,000	£21.00	39p

Source: Golden Pages Marketing Department, Jan 1998.

British Newspapers

British newspapers have entered the Irish market and can be seen as a serious threat to the Irish newspaper industry. For example, in 1996, they accounted for 35 per cent of the Sunday paper sector. Rupert Murdoch's News International has a major operation in Ireland for *The Sunday Times*, *The News of The World* and *The Sun*. Murdoch sees Ireland "as a useful add-on for their products at a marginal cost" (Factfinder, 1994). The Mirror Group publishes *The Daily Mirror* in Ireland. The demise of *The Irish Press* titles can be viewed in the light of pressure from the strong sales of British tabloids on the Irish market. From a direct marketing point of view, the increase in titles gives the advertiser greater choice and more targeting ability.

The Irish Magazines Sector

Magazines have proven to be very important to the direct marketer. When used successfully they can have the same effect as a good retail shop for a manufacturer. "A magazine that performs constantly well for a variety of direct response advertisers is like a store in a low-rent, high traffic location" (Stone, 1996). Advertising revenue is the core revenue for most magazines and much of this comes from direct response advertising.

Off-the-Shelf Magazines

Irish off-the-shelf magazines can be divided into two main areas: business and consumer. In general, for Irish publications there are difficulties in maintaining and increasing market share in the magazine sector. McPartlin (1995) states that "consumer magazines with few exceptions have generally found it difficult to grow their sales base beyond 25,000 in the Irish market". Irish magazines account for five per cent of the Irish advertising market. The main Irish magazines are listed in Table 15.4.

TABLE 15.4: CIRCULATION OF CONSUMER & BUSINESS PUBLICATIONS

Consumer Publications	ABC Circulation, July–Dec 96
RTE Guide	170,049
Irish Farmers Journal	75,135
Woman's Way	67,300
Image	21,214
IT	20,900
U	21,050
Phoenix	17,494
Hot Press	21,033
Cara	70,000
Business Publications	**Circulation, July–Dec 96**
Business and Finance	11,307
Management	7,078
Accountancy Ireland	17,592
Stubbs Gazette	12,000/13,000
Marketing	3,000

Source: Media Advertising Promotions Sponsorship (MAPS), Association of Advertisers in Ireland, Directory 1997–1998.

In the consumer category there is competition between the titles, but the *RTE Guide* is by far the most popular. There is also extensive competition from British magazines. For example, *IT* magazine competes with British titles such as *Cosmopolitan, Marie Claire, Tatler,*

Harpers and Queen and *Hello*. Despite this, the four Irish women's titles (*Image, It, U* and *Woman's Way*) have maintained their circulation figures. This is because they are an Irish media for the Irish advertiser, in which Irish women can read about and purchase Irish products/services. These magazines have proven to be particularly useful for the direct marketing area.

For business publications, again there is intense competition in this market from British and American publications.

Subscription and Specialist Magazines

Many magazines are sold on subscription and this creates a well-targeted audience for the direct marketer. Many of the professional associations have magazines. A good example is the Marketing Institute of Ireland with *Marketing News*, which is delivered monthly to all members. Direct marketers know the exact target market of this publication and can target marketing professionals in Ireland through this publication. This is the main benefit of specialist subscription magazines.

More and more Irish specialist magazines are being published. Some examples are *Gaelic World, Irish Basketball, Irish Runner* and *The Irish Bridge Player*. Again, these are well-targeted publications, many of which are sold on subscription.

These subscription and specialist magazines also compete with the supplements to off-the-shelf magazines. Off-the-shelf magazines are inclined to extend their editorial contents and publish specialist sections within their publications. Therefore, they regularly produce standalone magazines, which are very useful for direct marketing.

INSERTS

The range of options for advertisers in the direct marketing area has remained very consistent. There are classified advertisements, standalone advertisements and inserts. Once inserts arrived, it became possible to enjoy the same quality of printing in newspapers and magazines as in direct mail. Their popularity in recent years has grown immensely and has added a new and different dimension to targeting within the print media. Inserts can be used in a variety of different ways and allow for campaign testing, measuring of response rates and accurate planning.

Why Inserts Work

Schultz et al. (1993) describe how consumers mentally accumulate information from marketing communications over time. Consumers can be expected to add information appearing in inserts to existing knowledge. Inserts are more cost-effective than conventional forms of advertising. They are adaptable to business, service and product areas. Goodwin (1995b) states that inserts work because they draw immediate attention before the reader has a chance to study the news, features or other advertisements. This makes them more responsive than space advertising. Bird (1993) goes so far as to describe the insert as the "chameleon of the business".

However, to be successful and get results, inserts need to "grab the eye and shake the complacency" (Lewis, 1996). This is the most important success factor, whereby the insert must dominate other inserts in the particular publication. The ability of inserts to target an audience gives them a distinct advantage over other marketing tools. It is possible that not only can regions be targeted, but magazines will often distribute inserts by industry type, profession, etc.

Jones (1995) discusses some of the advantages of inserts. These are format flexibility, good colour reproduction and control of reproduction. They also have an inherent advantage over direct mail in that exact timing is possible, since the insert arrives in a specific day's newspaper rather than whenever the mail is delivered. They also have a huge potential reach, which Reed (1996) feels is significant. He states that the size of the average campaign is important when making comparisons with other media. The use of inserts also allows cost-effective testing in small markets before the launch of the campaign. However, Jones (1995) does highlight some of the creative disadvantages of inserts. He states that in some markets there is a great deal of clutter among inserts. In addition, studies show that certain market segments almost never read them. He calls them a "mass medium with little opportunity to target prospects". In addition to this, he states that they may be effective only for relatively low-end, mass appeal products and services. Despite these views, inserts are "having phenomenal growth and show little sign of slowing up" (Fox, 1995).

Forms of Inserts

There are a number of different types of inserts. An insert is usually no larger than 5½" × 8½", an acceptable size to most companies. The insert placed in print media can also be easily used in other ways: placed as a take-one at a point of sale; as a package insert; included as a ride-along in regular communications; and as a billing or statement stuffer.

Full-page bind-ins are pre-printed by the advertiser and supplied to the publication for insertion in the magazine. The unit can include a perforated reply card, gummed areas for tokens or stamps, numbers for sweepstakes, pop-ups, or a variety of other techniques not possible with conventional soft-space. The unit is atypical, in that both sides of the bound-in card must be utilised, and the advertisement should be designed to conform to this. Stone (1996) states that the "bind-in insert card has created a world in which three, four, five or more direct response advertisers can all have the position impact once reserved for the cover advertisers alone".

Inserts that include coupons may be more salient than those inserts without coupons. It is possible that insert advertising positively affect sales of the advertised brand even to individuals who do not use the coupon. Secondly, coupons can negatively affect the sales of competitors' products, if consumers switch away from those brands to take advantage of the coupon.

Inserts in Newspapers and Magazines

Inserts offer a high-volume return, particularly when used with daily newspapers. There is more creativity and flexibility allowed compared to conventional space advertising. Creative inserts are highly visible, which means that readers are compelled to deal with them. Their flexibility is a distinct advantage for marketers, with greater formats allowed in terms of size and design, and this flexibility makes inserts more informative with more text and illustrative content. Segmentation is also possible, up to a point, by placing inserts in specific sections, e.g. men's products in the sports section, propositions of interest to youngsters in the Sunday comics, etc.

By choosing a magazine that is sold mainly by subscription, the waste factor is reduced and the insert can be more highly targeted to a specialist market.

The Cost of Inserts

The two main factors governing the cost of inserts are printing and insertion costs. When purchasing space for a page and an insert card, there is a higher cost — a space charge must be paid for the page and card and sometimes there is a separate binding charge. There is also a cost in printing the insert.

Because inserts tend to pull more impulse response, the average quality of response may be lower than for a conventional space advertisement. However, comparing the cost to other marketing tools, the increase in conventional advertising rates has meant the cost of inserts has become more competitive.

READERSHIP PROFILES AND RESEARCH SERVICES

When direct marketing uses newspapers and/or magazines, it is important to remember that the medium is the market — in other words, the publication that the direct response advertisement appears in is very very important. Therefore, there must be a logical affinity between the product/service and the reader of the publication. As Nash (1994) explained, "The quality of audience is more important than the quantity". To this end, the direct marketer needs plenty of readership and circulation information in order to choose the correct publication(s) for their campaign. In Ireland, this is mainly provided by an independent body who produce the Joint National Readership Research (JNRR) which is the "bible" for all direct marketers planning an Irish print media campaign.

Joint National Readership Research (JNRR)

The JNRR is produced annually and provides independent data for a selection of indigenous titles (Table 15.5). It produces a wealth of helpful information for direct marketers. The JNRR monitors various aspects of the print media including the following areas:

- *Coverage/Reach*: The number of people who read or looked at a copy of the publication during the timeframe of the publication.

TABLE 15.5: JNRR 1995/96 READERSHIP (AVERAGE ISSUE, SUNDAY NEWSPAPERS & MAGAZINES, ALL ADULTS)

	Total	Region					Community Type				Terminal Education Age				Lifestyle Clusters					
		Dublin	Rest Leinster	Munster	Cork City/Co	Conn/ Ulster	Urban	County Boros.	Other Urban	Rural	Primary	Secondary	Third Level	Student	Extrovert	Non-Conformist	Cultured	Homely	Ambitious	Conventional
Sample	5135	1550	1228	1387	550	970	2997	2017	980	2138	1258	2664	549	664	624	434	627	778	779	626
Universe Est.	2730 100%	832 100%	632 100%	770 100%	320 100%	496 100%	1630 100%	1104 100%	526 100%	1100 100%	606 100%	1462 100%	308 100%	354 100%	352 100%	239 100%	340 100%	391 100%	440 100%	290 100%
Any Sunday	1943 71%	561 67%	466 74%	562 73%	210 66%	354 71%	1109 68%	738 67%	371 70%	835 76%	368 61%	1066 73%	251 82%	257 73%	264 75%	144 60%	249 73%	308 79%	308 70%	175 60%
Sunday Independent	1185 43%	298 36%	301 48%	362 47%	121 38%	224 45%	629 39%	406 37%	224 43%	556 51%	206 34%	647 44%	184 60%	148 42%	168 48%	82 34%	169 50%	206 53%	145 33%	108 37%
Sunday World	1016 37%	251 30%	266 42%	299 39%	118 37%	200 40%	549 34%	342 31%	207 39%	467 42%	224 37%	579 40%	67 22%	146 41%	144 41%	65 27%	94 28%	168 43%	218 50%	100 35%
Sunday Tribune	251 9%	93 11%	40 6%	86 11%	46 14%	32 6%	164 10%	123 11%	41 8%	86 8%	20 3%	117 8%	75 24%	38 11%	36 10%	17 7%	57 17%	22 6%	22 5%	13 5%
Sunday Business Post	102 4%	48 6%	21 3%	24 3%	7 2%	9 2%	79 5%	59 5%	20 4%	23 2%	6 1%	50 3%	36 12%	10 3%	13 4%	11 4%	29 8%	6 1%	6 1%	2 1%
Magazines																				
RTE Guide (Weekly)	692 25%	136 16%	190 30%	248 32%	93 29%	118 24%	362 22%	203 18%	159 30%	330 30%	123 20%	386 26%	78 25%	105 30%	117 33%	37 15%	79 23%	114 29%	127 29%	55 19%
Woman's Way (Weekly)	304 11%	71 9%	83 13%	94 12%	44 14%	55 11%	175 11%	102 9%	74 14%	128 12%	58 10%	178 12%	27 9%	41 12%	66 19%	10 4%	24 7%	67 17%	53 12%	19 7%
Hot Press (Fortnightly)	63 2%	20 2%	14 2%	22 3%	11 3%	7 1%	48 3%	33 3%	14 3%	15 1%	3 –	28 2%	10 3%	23 6%	11 3%	4 2%	8 2%	1 –	21 5%	–
Image (Monthly)	146 5%	55 7%	25 4%	48 6%	23 7%	19 4%	99 6%	76 7%	23 4%	48 4%	13 2%	85 6%	30 10%	19 5%	44 12%	2 1%	17 5%	20 5%	23 5%	3 1%
IT (Monthly)	130 5%	37 4%	31 5%	51 7%	27 8%	12 2%	89 5%	60 5%	29 6%	42 4%	10 2%	77 5%	22 7%	22 6%	35 10%	1 –	19 6%	13 3%	24 6%	2 1%
U (Monthly)	139 5%	56 7%	23 4%	46 6%	22 7%	14 3%	98 6%	76 7%	23 4%	40 4%	11 2%	85 6%	21 7%	22 6%	41 12%	3 1%	21 6%	12 3%	26 6%	3 1%

- *Circulation/Readership*: Circulation is the number of copies sold, which compares to readership, the number of people who read the publication. Direct marketers feel that circulation is important, as only one person will enquire or purchase through the direct response mechanism. However, it must be noted that there are pass-on readers who do reply to direct response advertising.

- *Profiles*: Demographic profiles of readers of different publications.

- *Cumulative coverage*: Information on regular and occasional readers, as well as the profile of the average reader of the publication.

- *Duplication/sole readership*: The number of people who read only "one" or "more than one" publication within a publication category.

- *Product purchases and lifestyle issues*: They also provide extensive information in these areas. This is particularly useful for direct marketing. For example, it can provide a demographic breakdown of the percentage of people playing different types of sports in Ireland, cross-referenced by the publications they buy.

All this information allows direct marketers to carefully target their audience and to calculate average audiences, reach and readership frequency. O'Donoghue and Harper (1995) point out that the JNRR information "highlights the appropriateness of specific media to reach particular target groups".

Research Studies

There are also various annuals which provide information on all titles, their costs and some marketing information. An example of this would be Media Advertising Promotions Sponsorship (MAPS). These journals are extensively used by direct marketers.

From time to time, various independent studies are carried out. For example, The Henley Centre produced research in 1996 in relation to newspapers and direct marketing. This research pointed out that one in ten Irish adults responded to a direct response advertisement. The profile of the people who bought products from national newspaper "off-the-page" advertisements was also compiled. The profile was divided equally between male and female, aged 25–50, particularly ABs, and biased towards Dublin and Munster. This type of information is very useful for direct marketers. Their study of the favoured response mechanism showed that post was the clear favourite, with 42 per cent using this as the response mechanism of choice, followed by telephone at 37 per cent (O'Neill, 1996a). Again, this type of information is very appropriate when deciding on content, format and response mechanism for a direct response advertisement.

Testing Advertisement Copy

An important aspect of the print media for direct marketing is the ability to test advertisements in these media. This testing is available because many publications have split run options, where they will allow two or more versions of the advertisement to appear in different print runs. Therefore, there is often the option of running different advertisements in different areas and/or sections. This allows the advertiser to immediately test the effectiveness of various designs or offers and so on.

For testing to work effectively, it is necessary for the marketer to have control over all the variables such as colour, timing, positioning, etc. The tests should be kept as simple as possible, such as using an A-B split test, where one variable is changed to assess the difference and test the media. For example, a particular magazine or newspaper has one form of direct response advertisement in half of the issues, and the other in the remaining half.

For inserts, there are unlimited test opportunities, with the possibility of testing ten different inserts in one publication if necessary. Because you control the quality and content, you can use any creative technique and then test them out.

RESPONSE RATES

Direct mail uses a doubling rate and responses will arrive in a pattern suggestive of the way the mail is delivered and read. The same is true for magazines and newspapers. Daily papers are read immediately or never, and so the half-life point is less than a week away. For a Sunday paper, you can usually double the results that are in, as of the following Thursday.

Most monthly magazines have a doubling point about four weeks after the magazine's on-sale date. Weekly magazines have a similar pattern — once the returns start arriving, the halfway point is reached about 12 days later. An expiry date and coupons are seen to help responses. Stone (1996) states that the hard space such as business reply insert cards will come in faster than soft space, which requires the respondent to get an envelope and stamp.

Magazines with mostly subscription readers are usually received throughout the country at about the same time. The responses will come in as much as a week faster than responses from an off-the-shelf magazine which is picked up by readers over the month. Magazine response curves also vary by the editorial content. A magazine with a particularly interesting long article may be saved for weeks, keeping the responses coming in for a longer time.

MEDIA EVALUATION

Evaluation of the print media for direct marketing campaigns is similar to any media evaluation. The following evaluation criteria need to be considered: circulation/readership, geographic coverage, demographic coverage, frequency of publication, image of the publication, distribution, editorial content and affinity, volume and frequency discounts and responsiveness of the reader to direct marketing campaigns. These factors must be linked to the coverage and frequency that the campaign requires.

The most important feature of direct response advertisements is that the company can track the effectiveness of each advertisement when the consumer responds. As discussed earlier, it is very important to have an accurate profile of the target audience of the different publications, so that the direct marketer can compare the publication profiles to match the product and message with the right publication. Two major techniques used in the evaluation area are cost per thousand (CPT) and cost per response (CPR).

Cost per Thousand and Cost per Response

Media costs are usually measured in cost per thousand, which is the cost of reaching 1,000 members of the target population. The CPT is the cost of the advertisement multiplied by a thousand divided by the circulation of the publication. Several aspects of this technique need to be considered, including the audience quality, the audience attention probability and the editorial quality of the publication. A variation on this is the cost per response (order, lead, subscription and so on) technique. This is simply the cost of the advertisement divided by the number of responses. This is a very simple but effective device for direct marketing for tracking the results.

Evaluating the different media available to marketers is difficult, due to the fact that the decision will ultimately depend on the objectives of the campaign and the experiences of the marketer in using the different applications. In general, direct marketers will use a range of media. "Most active recruiters of new customers/prospects use all the available media options" (Goodwin, 1995).

CONCLUSION

The print media will continue to be used by direct marketers as a creative and active method to target customers in an increasingly dynamic and competitive environment. The structure of the print media in the Irish market lends itself very effectively to direct marketing campaigns. The level of professionalism and creativity in direct response advertising means that the Irish consumer is becoming more predisposed to direct marketing. The future predictions in this area are that direct marketing's use of the print media — newspapers, magazines and inserts — will continue to grow.

CASE HISTORY: THE OPEN UNIVERSITY BUSINESS SCHOOL:
MANAGEMENT DEVELOPMENT COURSES
Michelle Morris

Background

The Open University is a "virtual" university that specialises in offering a very wide range of courses and qualifications up to degree
level, specifically through distance learning. As such, it is unique —
students can use course materials and watch special TV programmes
instead of attending classes with continuous assessment by post as
the student progresses. Originally set up in the UK in 1966, The Open
University is regarded as the "university of second chance" for people who did not progress to third-level education first time around.

The Open University Business School was set up in 1985. Its objective was to focus specifically on offering management development courses, solely through distance learning. It has been very
successful, both in the UK and throughout Europe. More people are
currently studying with the Open University but this varies, depending on the country. For example, in Eastern European countries,
it would be perceived as the university of *only* chance.

The Open University Business School was launched in Ireland in
1995, offering three courses in management: Certificate, Diploma and
MBA. They sought to recruit via direct response press, using existing
advertising that had been developed in the UK. This was spectacularly unsuccessful. While the advertisements generated a poor response, the conversion rate was even weaker.

The Irish Market and Management Training

The Open University Business School faced challenges in the Irish
market that were quite different to those that they experienced in
other countries.

There is a growing acceptance of the value of training and development in Ireland, both among individuals and companies. One-
quarter of the population is under 25 years and well-educated, resulting in a great opportunity for further education, particularly in
career-related courses. However, Ireland has many reputable universities and business schools offering similar management courses to

those of The Open University Business School. Many of these are part-time and they have the advantage over The Open University Business School of being well established in the market. Unlike Eastern Europe, where a captive market was ready and waiting, in Ireland the market existed but would take some convincing about The Open University Business School concept.

Research

The Open University Business School hired Ogilvy and Mather Direct, a specialist direct marketing company, to conduct research into the perceptions of The Open University Business School in the Irish market. While some awareness of The Open University Business School was found to exist, many of the findings were negative — The Open University Business School was either not known or poorly regarded. In the latter category, some of the negative perceptions were deeply felt:

- *English*: At the emotional level, Irish people tend to reject anything English, while being favourably disposed to anything European or American

- *Practicality*: At the practical level, courses were perceived to be irrelevant to the Irish market and the qualification would be expected to have little status in Ireland

- *Outdated*: Old-fashioned associations, based on Open University early morning TV programmes, with presenters who were perceived to be the opposite of the cutting edge of business.

Target Audience

The main target audience for the initial activity were individual customers, split equally between male and female, aged 25–45 years. However, since their companies may be paying for their courses and since the University wanted to target companies at a later stage for group schemes, business-to-business segments were also recognised as an audience.

Strategy

The main obstacle to lead generation was the status of The Open University Business School's brand in Ireland. In order to generate the required level of leads, the brand's perception had to be altered.

Therefore the strategy had to establish a desirable brand for The Open University Business School to combat negative perceptions and then generate leads aggressively.

The campaign was divided into two phases: brand building and lead generation. However, both phases were deigned to assist each other, so the brand building phase encouraged a response and the lead generation phase sought to continue building the brand.

Media

The campaign period was between February/March and August/ September 1996. The budget allowed for the use of a single medium only. While a combination of outdoor and press would have been considered the ideal choice, it was decided to use press alone. For brand building, 10" X 4" colour advertisements in a mixture of national press and trade press were developed. For lead generation, solus, black and white advertisements were chosen (see Figure 15.3).

Creative Strategy

Initially, the recommendation was to reposition The Open University Business School in Ireland as The Open University *European* Business School, both to take advantage of the size of the school in Europe and to create a desirable, modern and enterprising image for the school. A more conservative positioning was eventually adopted.

Much use was made of The Open University Business School's colours which, by a happy coincidence, are blue and yellow — the same as the European Union colours. In addition, a visual device consisting of stars was developed, again to link in with the EU flag. In this way, the position was much more European and, therefore, acceptable. Even in black and white, the visual device of the stars allowed for a very strong visual link to the colour work.

Tired
of being
a yes man?

☐YES I want to fast-forward my career
       without putting my job on hold

Name ....

Job title ....

Company ....

Address ....

....

....

Daytime Telephone Number ....

II 23/01 '98

With The Open University Business School, there's no need to put your job on hold while you're gaining a management qualification. All our programmes, from Certificate level to MBA, are modular, giving you a choice over what and when you study and allowing you to develop your skills while remaining at work.

And because of this modular structure, you can start at Certificate level, then move on to Diploma and finally to MBA.

Take the first step to a better career now. For your prospectu return the coupon to The Open University Business School Holbrook House, Holles St, Dublin 2. Or send us a fax or 01 678 5442. Or E-mail: RC12-OBS@open.ac.uk. Or simply call **01 678 5399.**

The Open University

BUSINESS SCHOOL

EUROPE'S LEADING BUSINESS SCHOOL

FIGURE 15.3: DIRECT RESPONSE ADVERTISEMENTS
FOR OPEN UNIVERSITY

CUT THE COUPON TODAY. OR YOU MAY NEVER CUT IT.

I want to fast-forward my career with a management qualification from Europe's leading business school

Name ....

Job title ....

Company ....

Address ....

....

Daytime telephone ....
                                                        IT 26/01/98

With The Open University Business School, there's no need to put your job on hold while you're gaining a management qualification. All our programmes, from Certificate level to MBA, are modular, giving you a choice over what and when you study and allowing you to develop your skills while remaining at work.

And because of this modular structure, you can start at Certificate level, then move on to Diploma and finally to MBA. Take the first step to a better career now. For your prospectus return the coupon to The Open University Business School, Holbrook House, Holles St, Dublin 2. Or send us a fax on 01 678 5442. Or E-mail: RC12-OBS@open.ac.uk. Or simply call **01 678 5399.**

The Open University
BUSINESS SCHOOL

NEXT START DATE FOR ALL COURSES IS MAY 1998
APPLICATIONS CLOSE 13 MARCH 1998

---

fast forward YOUR career without putting YOUR job on hold

I'd like to know more about the (please tick)

❑ Certificate ❑ Diploma ❑ MBA course
        from Europe's leading business school

Name ....

Job title ....

Company ....

Address ....

Daytime telephone ....
                                                        IT 25/01/98

With The Open University Business School, there's no need to put your job on hold while you're gaining a management qualification. All our programmes, from Certificate level to MBA, are modular, giving you a choice over what and when you study and allowing you to develop your skills while remaining at work.

And because of this modular structure, you can start at Certificate level, then move on to Diploma and finally to MBA. Take the first step to a better career now. For your prospectus return the coupon to The Open University Business School, Holbrook House, Holles St, Dublin 2. Or send us a fax on 01 678 5442. Or E-mail: RC12-OBS@open.ac.uk. Or simply call **01 678 5399.**

The Open University
BUSINESS SCHOOL

NEXT START DATE FOR ALL COURSES IS MAY 1998
APPLICATIONS CLOSE 13 MARCH 1998

Improve your career prospects. sign on:

I want to fast-forward my career with a management qualification from Europe's leading business school

Name ....

Job title ....

Company ....

Address ....

Daytime telephone ....
                                                        IT 30/01/98

With The Open University Business School, there's no need to put your job on hold while you're gaining a management qualification. All our programmes, from Certificate level to MBA, are modular, giving you a choice over what and when you study and allowing you to develop your skills while remaining at work.

And because of this modular structure, you can start at Certificate level, then move on to Diploma and finally to MBA. Take the first step to a better career now. For your prospectus return the coupon to The Open University Business School, Holbrook House, Holles St, Dublin 2. Or send us a fax on 01 678 5442. Or E-mail: RC12-OBS@open.ac.uk. Or simply call **01 678 5399.**

The Open University
BUSINESS SCHOOL

NEXT START DATE FOR ALL COURSES IS MAY 1998
APPLICATIONS CLOSE 13 MARCH 1998

FIGURE 15.3 CONTINUED

A very important aspect of the creative strategy was the tone of voice used in the advertisements. To avoid any of the negative associations of being old-fashioned and stuffy, which would run counter to the required image, the tone of voice had to be up-to-the-minute, clever, even cheeky.

Finally, an unusual response mechanism was designed. The desired response methods were telephone, fax and e-mail, with post as the least favoured. But because coupons are known to lift readership and response, the mechanism was designed to look like a coupon.

Response

The conversion rate, measured by the number of candidates/ responses actually registering for one of the courses, was 27 per cent. This compared to an increase of 31 per cent on a previous control group. It illustrated that the dual objectives of building an acceptable brand in the Irish education market and encouraging interest was successful.

REFERENCES TO CHAPTER 15

Bird, D. (1993), *Commonsense Direct Marketing*, Third Edition, London: Kogan Page Ltd.

FACTfinder (1994), "Murdoch Sets Foot in Dublin", *Management*, June.

Fox, H.L. (1995), "Insert Sector Seeks Guarantees on Data", *Marketing*, 28 September, p. 12.

Golden Pages Ltd. — Marketing Department (1998), "Print Media Fact Sheet", Dublin: Golden Pages Ltd., p. 3.

Goodwin, J. (1995a), "Inserts — Press Advertising with Direct Mail Appeal", *The Practitioner's Guide to Direct Marketing*, Part 2, London: Institute of Direct Marketing.

Goodwin, J. (1995b), "Media Planning and the Role of Press Advertising", *The Practitioner's Guide to Direct Marketing*, Part 2, London: Institute of Direct Marketing.

Joint National Readership Research (JNRR), Volume 1 (1995/96), Dublin: Lansdowne Market Research.

Jones, J.K. (1995), *Creative Strategy in Direct Marketing*, Illinois: NTC Books.

Lewis, H.G. (1996), "Do Free Standing Inserts Pull?", *Direct Marketing*, Vol. 59, No. 8, pp. 42–44.

McCorkell, G. (1997), *Direct and Database Marketing*, London: Kogan Page Ltd.

McPartlin, P. (1995), "Media Strategy — Selecting and Scheduling Media in Ireland", in T. Meenaghan and P. O'Sullivan (eds.). *Marketing Communications in Ireland*, Dublin: Oak Tree Press.

Media Advertising Promotions Sponsorship (MAPS) (1998), Association of Advertisers in Ireland, Directory 1997–1998.

Nash, E. (1994), *Direct Marketing Strategy/Planning/Execution*, Third Edition, New York: McGraw-Hill, pp. 116–144.

Nash, E. (1992), *The Direct Marketing Handbook*, Second Edition, New York: McGraw-Hill.

O'Donoghue, A. and T. Harper (1995), "Media Research in Ireland", in T. Meenaghan and P. O'Sullivan (eds.), *Marketing Communications in Ireland*, Dublin: Oak Tree Press.

O'Meara, Des, and Partners (1998), *Overview of the Media*, Dublin: Des O'Meara and Partners, p. 1.

O'Neill, G. (1996a), "Direct Marketing — On the Threshold of a Revolution (FACTfinder)", *Irish Marketing Journal*, 1 May.

O'Neill, G. (1996b), *Focus on the Future — The Coming Boom in Direct Marketing*, Dublin: IDMA.

Payne, D. (1996), "Irish Press Report Looks Good on Paper", *The European*, 4 July, p. 28.

Reed, D. (1996), "Direct Marketing — Write to Reply — Exclusive", *Marketing Week*, 13 December.

Schultz, D.E., S.I. Tannenbaum and R.F. Lauterborn (1993), *Integrated Marketing Communications*, Chicago: NTC Business Books.

Stone, B. (1996), *Successful Direct Marketing Methods*, Fifth Edition, Chicago: NTC Business Books, pp. 237–281.

FURTHER READING

Bacon, M.S. (1992), *Do It Yourself Direct Marketing — Secrets for Small Business*, New York: John Wiley.

Hennessy, D. (1996), "Dataline: Ever Wonder About Women?", *RyanMedia*, Dublin: Fact Finder.

Lambkin, M. (1996), *The Irish Consumer Market*, Dublin: The Marketing Society.

Meenaghan, T. and P. O'Sullivan (1995), *Marketing Communications in Ireland*, Dublin: Oak Tree Press.

Reitman, J.I. (1995), *Beyond 2000: The Future of Direct Marketing*, Chicago: NTC Business Books.

Srinivasan, S.S., R.P. Leone and J.F. Mulhern (1995), "The Advertising Exposure Effect of Free Standing Inserts", *Journal of Advertising*, Vol. 24, Spring, p. 29.

Chapter 16

HOW TO MAKE YOUR COPY AND DESIGN WORK TOGETHER

Robert Hayes-McCoy *and* Ger Doherty

LET'S GET STARTED

You're now ready to enter the wonderful world of direct marketing creativity. The first thing you need to know is that creativity — especially direct marketing creativity — is ten per cent sublime imagination, 90 per cent hard boring graft.

So let's start with a bit of background and get some of the boring bits out of the way immediately. We are both direct marketing practitioners and while we work in entirely separate companies we join forces quite often to work on special assignments and projects for national and international clients.

Over the years we've developed a working formula that has not only produced some highly successful campaigns but along the way we've individually collected a very attractive string of national and international awards for our creative and copywriting work.

Essentially, our formula is encapsulated in one word: "Equality".

To be really successful, your copy and design must develop in careful tandem with each other, each complementing the other and both coming together to form a single powerful unified message.

WHAT'S IN IT FOR ME?

What you see should be reinforced in your mind by what you read and visa versa. And at every step of the way you have to keep in mind that there is a radio station which everybody — yes everybody — listens into 24-hours a day, morning, noon and night. If you can successfully tune into this station you are well on your way to creating a superb direct marketing message.

The station is called WII-FM. This stands for "What's in it for me?". Put simply, what this means is that you must always tell your readers what benefits they will get if they accept your offer.

The more benefits you can offer them, the more interesting your proposition is. And, of course, the more enticing your proposition is, the more you increase your chances of getting a higher than average response level.

The best way to open the creative process is to write down a short two or three paragraph section capturing the entire story of what your offer is all about. Wear your reader's shoes all the time, every time, so that it becomes second nature for you to automatically ask the question "What's in it for me?" on behalf of your reader.

Carefully list your answers to this question and you find something magical happening . . . your reader's proposition begins to unfold.

Write down your *proposition*. Polish it until it flows nice and smoothly off your tongue when you say it out loud. Then comes the hard bit. You must chip away at it until you have reduced the number of words it contains to an absolute minimum — and this may give you your headline!

But a Word of Caution!

Make absolutely sure that your headline is rooted in your product.

Don't make it too clever or people will get distracted. Don't make it too vague or people will simply miss the point. Clearly and unambiguously, what your headline must do is answer your reader's "WII-FM?".

Remember, the best headlines come from careful preparation, a crystal clear analysis of whom you are talking to, combined with a simple proposition. Put yourself in a position to *anticipate your customers' visual needs* — watch their TV, read their magazines.

Good direct marketing copy normally needs a great deal of information to make it work, which usually means that it's long. Don't be afraid of long copy, but remember — your reader will probably "skip read" it first. If they like what they see and read, they will normally go back and read every single word of it.

That's why DM copywriters often use bold face type and underlining in their copy. By doing this, they can highlight the important benefits (what's in it for me?) and actively help the reader to "skip read", while being careful to ensure that the skip reader first reads what the copywriter wants them to read.

SOME TIPS TO HELP YOU MAKE YOUR COPY AND DESIGN WORK TOGETHER

- There are a number of "magic" words that appear again and again in the headlines of many of the world's most successful direct marketing campaigns: *Free, Now, New, At last!, Breakthrough, Guarantee, You . . . you . . .* and *you!* Use these words in your headlines, if possible.

- Don't be shy. Never undersell yourself, your product or your service. Make your customer proud to be associated with you.

- Use endorsements to help support your product or service.

- Stay in love with KISS! (Keep It Simple Stupid!)

- Make yours an *"action"* headline instead of a "passive" headline. Avoid, if possible, writing in the past tense.

- *The more specific* you can make your headline, the better.

- Suit the headline you use to the medium in which you are appearing. For example, the headline on a full glossy brochure may need a different message than that on an ad in the newspaper.

- Use summaries, break up your copy with boxes, headlines, captions, sub-headings. It helps the "skip reader" to capture your message and it makes everything more lively to look at.

- Close carefully . . . telling your reader exactly what you want them to do. Take great care to be particularly explicit in this section. Remember, your prospects are virtually ready to reply. Don't undo all your good work by leaving them with any doubt or uncertainty in their minds.

- Use short words in your copy. They are more like the spoken word, people understand them and they feel more comfortable with them.

- Use short sentences and short paragraphs . . . people tend to skip read paragraphs that are longer than six lines.

- The more you use the word *"you"* the more personable and be-lievable your copy tends to be.

- Use type to get across your message. Cunning typography is one of the most important aspects of getting the visual look right.

How big should your type be?

The size of type that is comfortable to read varies as we grow older. This is due to a combination of reading skill, mental agility and eye-sight. New readers manage better with fairly large type, say 15 or more points in children's books, but teenagers can feel quite com-fortable with type as small as 9 points, as a look at their magazines will show.

Adult readers get on better with type between 10 and 13 points and older readers appreciate text in point sizes between 13 to 14. But be careful: larger point size for ordinary text can be perceived as be-ing patronising, unless you deliberately make it large for people with visual problems.

Serif versus Sans Serif Fonts

Old-style *serif* fonts have the advantage of being considerably quicker for most people to read than sans serif fonts. With serifs, word shapes are more distinctive and the eye skims easily along the line.

These old style fonts developed from handwriting using quills or wedge-tipped pens. They therefore have serifs, which are little tails at the extremities of the letters, such as these on the font which I am now using. This is a **Palatino** font.

This little "tail" is called a serif

Other serif fonts include **Times Roman**, which is perhaps the most familiar of all.

In the early twentieth century, fonts with a clean uncluttered appearance were designed. These are known by the French term *sans serif* (without serif). Examples are: **Helvetica** and **Arial**.

Helvetica

No "tail" — which is why this is a sans serif font.

Script fonts mimic handwriting. For example: *Brush Script* and *Mistral*. These are very hard to read, and can look somewhat dated, so don't use them overmuch.

Decorative fonts, of which there are an enormous number, are mainly designed for use in poster headlines, and they are sometimes called *display fonts.* They work best in large sizes so look somewhat odd in these examples: Playbill and **Kino**.

Boring!

Sans serif fonts can be clearer than serif fonts in small point sizes. A point to remember is that, because of the lack of variation in line thickness, pages of sans serif font can look very tedious.

Big Talk can be Ugly

Some fonts take on a different appearance when their size changes. When this occurs, some are quite pleasant on the eye in small sizes and others are better when large: Look at what happens to Courier . . . Look at what happens to Courier . . . Look at what happens to Courier . . .

Look at what happens to Courier . . .

DON'T OVERUSE CAPITAL LETTERS

Too much copy written in capital letters can have the opposite effect to what you might think. It can actually be very hard to read because it looks very monotonous and there isn't enough variation to help the eye relax.

Link Your Copy Visually!

Create the right atmosphere with art. Don't limit yourself to seeing the visual piece purely in terms of quality. A quality look is sometimes right, but it can be wrong too!

- Wherever possible, use photography for the sake of "realism".

- Don't use pictures or colour for the sake of it. Too many images and badly used colours *confuse the eye* of the reader.

- Be a Pied Piper! Pay careful attention to "tracking" — the way the mailing is designed can actually force the reader to open it in a certain way and read it in a certain sequence. This adds to the drama and the sense of involvement.

- Follow the Leader — but only if you understand where they are going. Look at successful campaigns. Know what makes them work . . . but make sure you put your own edge on it.

- Remember — *individuality is remembered by individuals.* What this means is: do not approach the job as if you are talking to a mass market. Put yourself in the shoes of your potential customer and address your copy and your design to them individually . . . after all, this is the essence of direct marketing.

Now Let's Just See How all this Works in Practice

Let's imagine that you have asked us to create a direct mail package that will sell something that we are all very familiar with: *A Cafetiere.*

The first thing that we must do is to decide who our target audience is. Since the mailing pack is going into the home, the audience is probably female/home-maker.

Then we've got to put ourselves in our reader's place and ask the question "what's in it for me if I buy this cafetiere?" When the two of us asked ourselves this question the first thing that immediately came into our minds was "Real coffee is great coffee, great taste, great smell, but . . . !

> . . . *Instant coffee is quick and clean!*

So what's in it for me is a slow, messy cup of great coffee? *No thanks!*

Don't be put off by negative thoughts like this. In fact, this is what makes the whole creativity challenge such fun. Because what we are about to do is make something slow and messy irresistibly attractive . . . so attractive that we are "proud to be associated with it" . . . and so proud to be associated with it that we are going to proudly add our names (Ger and Robert) to it and call it:

The Gerob Coffee Makers

Very quickly we wrote down three possible headlines:

1. *Have a cup of coffee.*

2. *Do you have time for a real cup of coffee?*

3. *Time to take the plunge!*

Now remember the rule: *The best headlines come from careful preparation, a crystal clear analysis of who you are talking to, combined with a simple proposition.*

And the other rule is: *The more specific you can make the headline the better.*

With this in mind we quickly rejected, as being far too offhand, the headline: *Have a cup of coffee.*

Next on the reject list was *Time to take the plunge*. While we liked the "sound" of this headline and we could see all kinds of interesting graphic design possibilities, such as a hand pushing down the plunger of the cafetiere, we rejected this one on the basis that *it wasn't clear enough* and the reader might not readily make the connection between the words "plunge" and "cafetiere".

So we are left with the clearest and simplest proposition of all:

Do you have time for a real cup of coffee?

The fact that this headline contains the magic word "you" left us in no doubt that we were making the correct decision.

FIGURE 16.1

Visuals

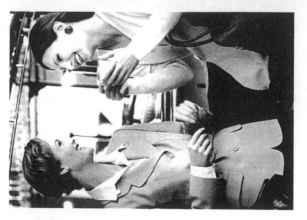

AND NOW FOR THE VISUALS TO LINK TO THE HEADLINES

After some time in the studio we had four possible visuals lined up to go with our chosen headline. And here they are in Figure 16.1 (Note: while all visuals were created in full colour, they are reproduced in black and white here):

- **Visual A:** features two smiling women enjoying a coffee break;

- **Visual B:** features two housewives enjoying coffee in the home;

- **Visual C:** Features a somewhat unusual shot of a Cafetiere containing real coffee;

- **Visual D:** Features a much more straightforward shot of the cafetiere.

Back to the "elimination" process that we used with the headline . . .

First to be rejected was Visual A. We felt that this had too much of a working atmosphere about it and might not go down well with the homemaker. We then rejected "C" on the basis that it was too obscure and didn't link in with our headline.

Whereas we liked "B", we felt that visual "D", featuring the attractive picture of the cafetiere, created a much stronger link with our headline: *Do you have time for a real cup of coffee?*

Have a look at Figure 16.2 and you'll quickly see how the "link" is established between the headline and the picture.

As you can see, we now have foundations of our Direct Mail campaign laid. We have a *concept, a headline* and the *main visual*.

THE NEXT STEP IS . . .

. . . to apply these three components to the different pieces of our direct mail pack. Since a "classical" direct mail pack has five different pieces as follows:

1. The Outer Envelope

2. The Letter

3. The Brochure

4. The Application Form

5. The reply envelope/Freephone number

We set out to tackle each of these pieces in the above order.

FIGURE 16.2

Do <u>you</u> have time for a real cup of coffee?

Outer Envelope

First off is the outer envelope. And the question is, "will we put a message or a picture on it"?

Figure 16.3 is the personalised envelope without a message on it — which we figured was somewhat plain and boring. So we added our headline to it and created Figure 16.4, using a bold red typeface.

But the moment we did this, we knew it was all wrong.

The red typeface looked angry and downright cheap. And it certainly didn't look very enticing. So we scrapped this immediately.

FIGURE 16.3

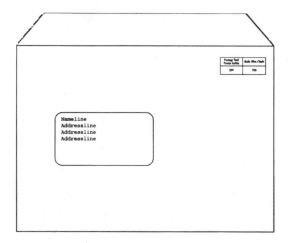

FIGURE 16.4

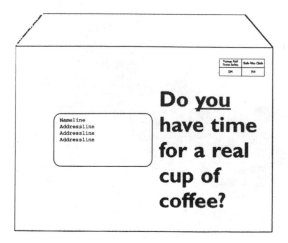

Next off the drawing board was Figure 16.5, which we both got quite excited about. And if you look carefully at the address window you'll see that we've actually managed to "personalise" the message on the outer envelope — i.e., *Ger . . . do you have time for a real cup of coffee?* Nice message . . . nice cafetiere . . . nice bright envelope. It was all beginning to come together for us, so we moved immediately to the letter.

FIGURE 16.5

The Letter

Our headline in the letter immediately established the link with the question on the outer envelope (Figure 16.6).

"Ger . . . of course you do!" Note how we used the same typeface to reinforce the link.

As you read through this letter, you'll quickly see that it's an extraordinarily friendly, chatty letter. It uses many of the magic words. Short paragraphs. Short sentences, underlining and boldface type for added impact. Some of the paragraphs are indented to make everything look nice and easy on the eye.

Look at the nice open, honest, signature, which was printed in blue ink. See how the price is clearly mentioned and how the response telephone number is presented in big bold print. Note how the magic word **FREE** is in bold capital letters. And do you notice something else too?

Notice how the letter is a "stand-alone" sales item. It tells you everything you need to know . . . to buy this special offer. And, of course, it has the direct marketing copywriter's all-important **PS** at the bottom of it. In the PS you'll find a call to action . . . buy before a certain date and you get something extra **FREE!** In this case the extra free gift is a "wonderful LCD alarm clock — a real beauty".

And note too, how we've used a warm friendly picture of a cup of coffee to make everything "look" as well as "read" attractively.

As is normal in direct mail packages, once the reader has read the letter, they turn immediately to the brochure (Figure 16.7).

The Brochure

For our brochure (carefully cut to the shape of a cafetiere), we presented our readers with a colourful cover showing them an approximate "real-size" Gerob Cafetiere featuring a slight variation of our headline: *"Now you can treat yourself to a real cup of coffee every morning!"*

What's in it for me? — What's in it for me is *a real treat!* (Figure 16.8).

FIGURE 16.6

INTERNATIONAL PURVEYORS *of the*
FINEST COFFEES & ACCOUTREMENTS

HAYES HOUSE, DOHERTY STREET, DUBLIN 2

Ger Doherty
Addressline
Addressline
Addressline

GER   ... OF COURSE YOU DO!

Dear Ger,

For years I used to drink instant coffee in the morning. Somehow it seemed quicker. It was just a matter of boiling the kettle and pouring the water over the coffee. And that was it!

But that was before I bought myself the Gerob Cafetiere. Now I enjoy the rich aroma and full flavour of fresh coffee every morning and it makes so much difference.

There's something unique about the way the Gerob Cafetiere holds on to the flavour of the finest coffee at its very best and, at the same time, releases that wonderful opulent smell of lightly roasted coffee beans. It's something for you to really look forward to ... especially when you're treating yourself to a few precious moments of time out from your busy day.

Making fresh coffee is so easy with a plunger-type Cafetiere. You just add boiling water to the medium ground coffee of your choice, wait 3-5 minutes, then push down the plunger, and you've got really fresh coffee without fuss.

And when, I tell you that the tried and tested Gerob Cafetiere now costs only **£19.99 + p&p,** I think you'll understand why it's so extraordinarily popular. One look at the enclosed brochure will quickly show you how attractive the Gerob Cafetiere is - a functional simplicity of design that's so elegant it's guaranteed to bring that extra touch of luxury to just about every occasion.

What's more, it comes to you with two **FREE** complimentary sachets of two of our most popular ground coffee beans. (More than enough for you and your friends to straightaway enjoy a cup of some of the world's finest coffee on us.)

If you'd like to take advantage of our special £19.99 + p&p offer price, complete the special order form attached to the enclosed brochure and return it to us immediately with your cheque. Better still, if you've a telephone nearby, why not call us now, for the price of a local call, on **1850 403 403** and order your Gerob Cafetiere by credit card.

We'll be delighted to hear from you ... after all, you do deserve this treat!

Yours sincerely,

Susan Mc Carthy

Susan Mc Carthy

Chief Coffee Blende

P.S. I have something very special for you if we receive your order before Friday 16th May 1997. It's a wonderful LCD Alarm clock - a real beauty! Keeping you on time - absolutely FREE!

FIGURE 16.7

FIGURE 16.8

Open up the brochure and your treat begins to unfold. But why don't you try a little experiment here and become a "skip reader" yourself. First just read the headlines and see how the combination of the headlines and the visuals work very well together to give you an immediate overall picture of a very attractive offer.

And note how the offer comes to you with two free sachets of coffee . . . *"more than enough for you and your friends to straightaway enjoy a cup of some of the world's finest coffee on us"*.

And yes! Immediately underneath this free offer is the call to action and your wonderful free gift of an alarm clock . . . all for £19.99 + p&p! It's a nice offer, so how do you take it up?

The answer is simple. You either fill in the response form or you pick up the telephone and place your order by Freephone, giving your credit card details (Figure 16.9).

But it was at this stage that we said STOP!

We knew that there was something wrong!

Somehow or other the alarm clock and the tidy little response form just didn't seem to fit comfortably with the warm friendly message of the letter and the relaxing feel of the brochure. Also, the more we thought about it, the more we realised that the "alarm clock" was all wrong.

It just didn't convey . . . relaxation. And furthermore, it didn't have any strong link with the cafetiere. So we decided to think again. And we're delighted that we did.

Because what we discovered was that we could buy a small one-cup cafetiere for the same price of the alarm clock. This got us quite excited, so we went back immediately and changed the PS of our letter. The new PS is in Figures 16.10 and 16.11.

Now we were really in business!

Look at the brochure now and you'll see what we did! We created a little flap showing the "baby" cafetiere. Have a look at Figure 16.12 and you'll see that we have created a real family feel . . . *Mammy, Daddy and baby cafetiere!*

FIGURE 16.9

Please send me my Gerob Cafetiere and my FREE Alarm Clock !

Name —————————————————

Address —————————————————

————————————————————————

Cheque ☐   Postal Order ☐

Credit Card   Visa ☐ MasterCard ☐

Credit Card Number

**FREEPHONE
1800 44 55 66**

FIGURE 16.10

INTERNATIONAL PURVEYORS *of the*
FINEST COFFEES & ACCOUTREMENTS

GEROB
COFFEE
MAKERS

HAYES HOUSE. DOHERTY STREET. DUBLIN 2

Ger Doherty

Addressline

Addressline

Addressline

GER   ... OF COURSE YOU DO!

Dear Ger,

For years I used to drink instant coffee in the morning. Somehow it seemed quicker. It was just a matter of boiling the kettle and pouring the water over the coffee. And that was it!

But that was before I bought myself the Gerob Cafetiere. Now I enjoy the rich aroma and full flavour of fresh coffee every morning and it makes so much difference.

There's something unique about the way the Gerob Cafetiere holds on to the flavour of the finest coffee at its very best and, at the same time, releases that wonderful opulent smell of lightly roasted coffee beans. It's something for you to really look forward to ... especially when you're treating yourself to a few precious moments of time out from your busy day.

Making fresh coffee is so easy with a plunger-type Cafetiere. You just add boiling water to the medium ground coffee of your choice, wait 3-5 minutes, then push down the plunger, and you've got really fresh coffee without fuss.

And when, I tell you that the tried and tested Gerob Cafetiere now costs only **£19.99 + p&p**, I think you'll understand why it's so extraordinarily popular. One look at the enclosed brochure will quickly show you how attractive the Gerob Cafetiere is - a functional simplicity of design that's so elegant it's guaranteed to bring that extra touch of luxury to just about every occasion.

What's more, it comes to you with two **FREE** complimentary sachets of two of our most popular ground coffee beans. (More than enough for you and your friends to straightaway enjoy a cup of some of the world's finest coffee on us.)

If you'd like to take advantage of our special £19.99 + p&p offer price, complete the special order form attached to the enclosed brochure and return it to us immediately with your cheque. Better still, if you've a telephone nearby, why not call us now, for the price of a local call, on **1850 403 403** and order your Gerob Cafetiere by credit card.

We'll be delighted to hear from you ... after all, you do deserve this treat!

Yours sincerely,

Susan Mc Carthy

Susan Mc Carthy

Chief Coffee Blende

PS: I have something very special for you if we receive your order before **Friday 16th May 1997,** It's a sparkling one-cup Gerob Cafetiere - a real beauty! And it will be yours **FREE!**

FIGURE 16.11

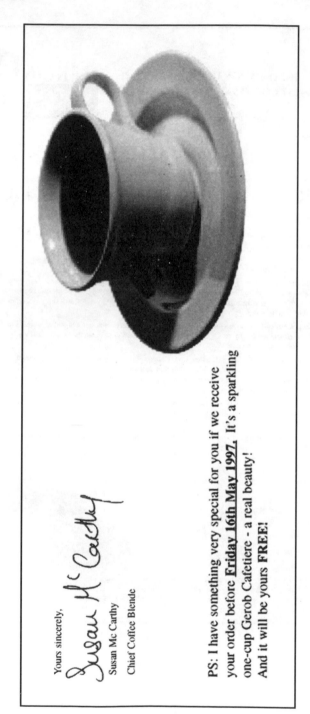

FIGURE 16.12

Back to the inside of the brochure and you'll see that we've changed the free gift on the bottom right hand corner and we've added on the response form in the shape of the baby cafetiere (Figures 16.13 and 16.14).

The little scissors symbol on the dotted line comes complete with instructions to cut off this response form and send it back to us in the Freepost envelope supplied.

Take another look at the response form and you'll quickly see how simple it is. There is plenty of space for the respondent to write their name comfortably (Figure 16.15). And once they have done this they put it in the supplied Freepost envelope.

The Reply Envelope

Most conventional reply envelopes are simple plain black and white jobs, which is a pity really, because with a little bit of imagination you can sometimes create an extra sales message at the vital point of response — but, unfortunately, most of the time, there are budget restrictions (Figure 16.16).

So what we decided to do was to reinforce the "quality" aspect of our offer by featuring the proud statement at the head of the envelope: *International Purveyors of the Finest Coffees & Accoutrements.*

And up in the top right hand corner where the stamp is normally put, we printed a clear, helpful message: "No Postage Necessary".

AND WE ARE READY TO MAIL OUT!

By now we have brought you step-by-step through the creative process of designing and writing an attractive direct mail offer.

We've shared our innermost creative thoughts, our proud moments and our mistakes (the dreaded alarm clock) with you. And if there is one over-riding message that is common to everything that we have done, it is . . .

Put yourself in your readers' place . . . every time!

Do this with both your copy and your visuals and you'll end up with a great response!

FIGURE 16.13

FIGURE 16.14

FIGURE 16.15

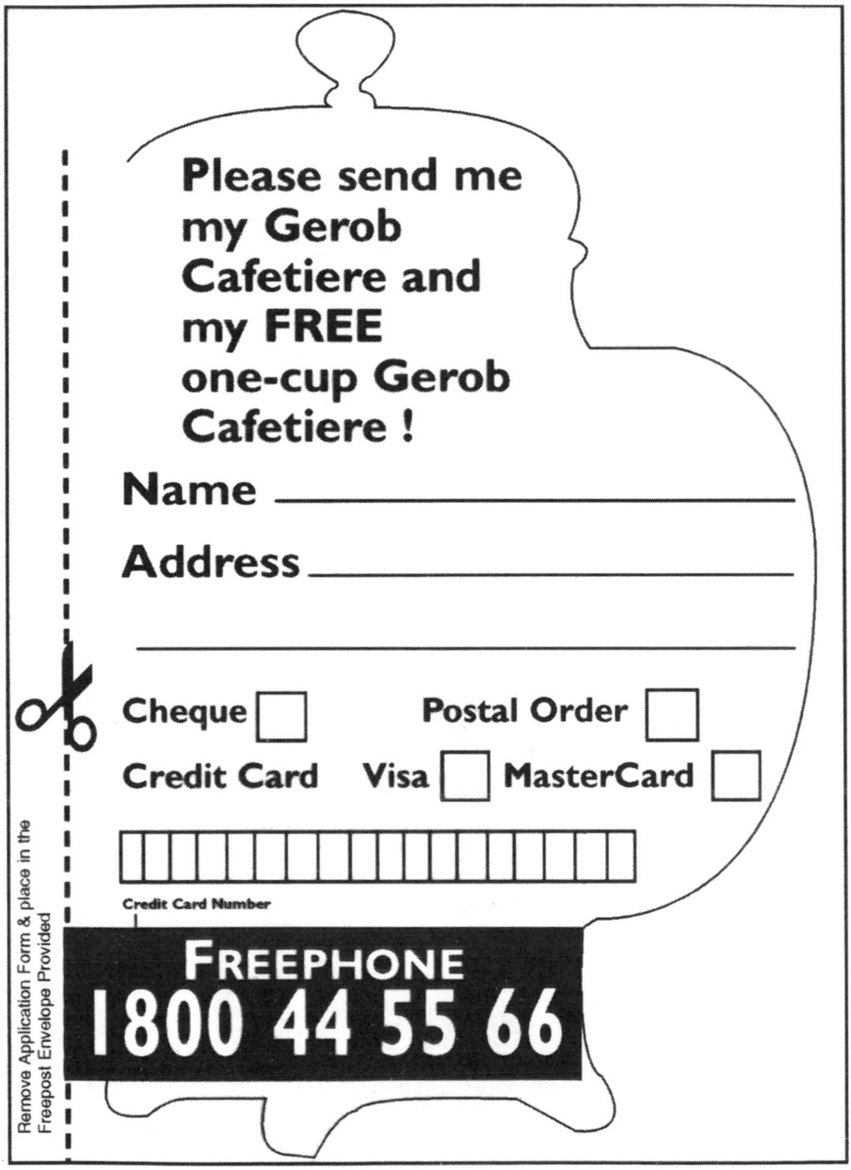

Please send me
my Gerob
Cafetiere and
my **FREE**
one-cup Gerob
Cafetiere !

Name _____

Address _____

_____

Cheque ☐   Postal Order ☐

Credit Card   Visa ☐ MasterCard ☐

Credit Card Number

Remove Application Form & place in the
Freepost Envelope Provided

FREEPHONE
1800 44 55 66

FIGURE 16.16

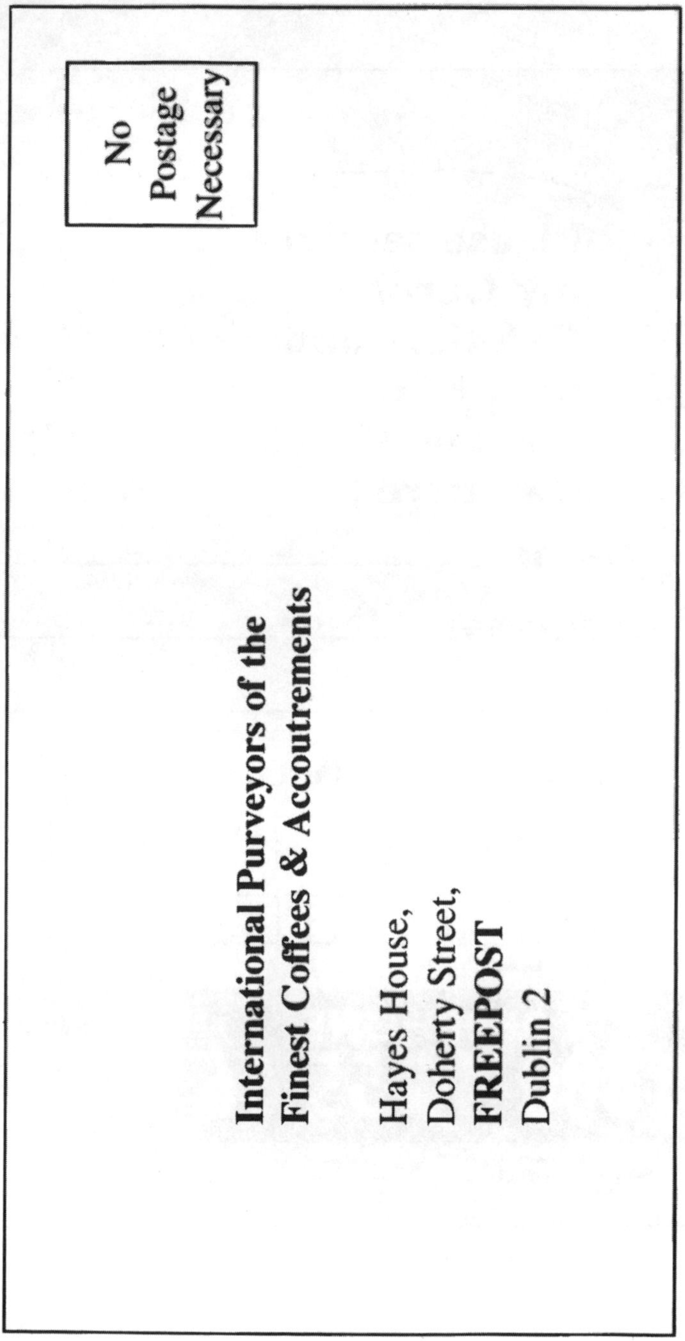

No
Postage
Necessary

**International Purveyors of the
Finest Coffees & Accoutrements**

Hayes House,
Doherty Street,
FREEPOST
Dublin 2

GEROB COFFEE MAKERS

PART FOUR

Emerging Technologies

Chapter 17

TELEVISION:
A TRANSFORMING MEDIUM

Bernice O'Connor

Overview

Television is one of the most exciting and interesting media in Ireland, due in no small part to major changes which are taking place at present in the industry. In the past decade, upwards of 80 satellite channels, the vast majority transmitting in the English language, can be received in Irish homes. The growth in cable, in MMDS systems and the expansion of satellite dishes, bear testament to an increasing appeal. Digital television is just around the corner, offering homes not just a greater choice of stations, but two-way data channels also. This means interactive TV and Internet access. Terrestrially, if all goes to plan, TV3 will go on air in September 1998, offering RTÉ television its first domestic competition.

This chapter will therefore look at this evolving medium, first of all in terms of terrestrial television — the changes taking place and those about to happen, which will influence the future of the industry. Secondly, the development and history of digital television will be explored, including the key players, the potential impact on viewing habits, and the emergence of interactive TV. Finally, the implications of all of these changes for direct marketing strategies will be considered.

TERRESTRIAL TELEVISION

Market Performance

As mentioned, there are upwards of 80 satellite channels presently beamed into this country. They have had an impact on the performance achieved by the main terrestrial stations; however, the main effect has been extreme fragmentation at the other end of the spectrum.

Figure 17.1 shows that the terrestrial stations still hold the lion's
share of the market — over half the country's adults remain loyal
RTÉ viewers in the afternoon/evening viewing segment.

FIGURE 17.1: REPUBLIC OF IRELAND NATIONAL AUDIENCE SHARE
(ADULTS, 14:00 TO 23:59, JANUARY–DECEMBER 1997)

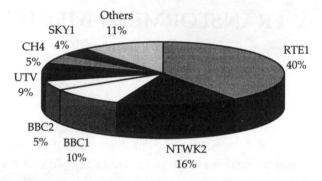

Source: AC Nielsen

Figure 17.2 illustrates the multichannel audience share — multichannel viewers are able to receive at least one other channel in addition to RTÉ1, Network 2 and TnaG and account for 71 per cent of
all households in the country. Significantly, even in this competitive
marketplace, RTÉ still has a market share of 41 per cent; the other
terrestrial stations show increased market share, and the "Others"
segment has increased to 14 per cent. This is a substantial figure, but
epitomises the fragmentation mentioned above, as the figure comprises the 40 or more other stations that AC Nielsen individually
measure, and the large number of stations with shares so small that
they are not individually measured.

FIGURE 17.2: REPUBLIC OF IRELAND MULTICHANNEL AUDIENCE
SHARE (ADULTS, 14:00 TO 23:59, JANUARY–DECEMBER 1997)

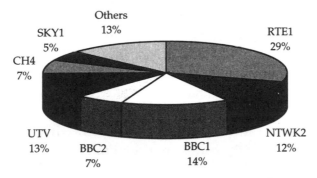

Source: AC Nielsen

Reach is defined as the number of people who saw an advertisement
or programme in a given schedule or broadcast period. A total television figure is not available, but an indication of the strength of television can be seen from Figure 18.3, which shows the high reach
figures achieved by RTÉ in 1997.

FIGURE 17.3: RTÉ TELEVISION: AVERAGE DAILY REACH, NATIONAL,
ADULTS, 1997

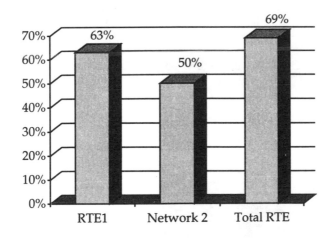

Source: AC Nielsen

Market Developments

The explosion in the number of channels has been matched by significant changes in television reception by individual households and a rapid growth in ownership of television-related products. The following charts document these changes from 1991 to 1997; Figure 17.4 illustrates the rise of multichannel and multisatellite reception and a corresponding decline in the number of terrestrial and dual-channel homes. In Figure 17.5, ownership of VCRs, remote control units and second television sets have almost doubled, while teletext homes have quadrupled in the period from 1991 to 1997.

FIGURE 17.4: TELEVISION RECEPTION

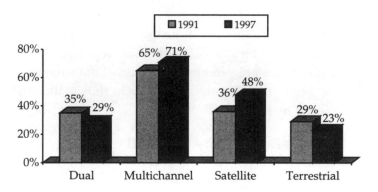

Source: AGBTAM/AC Nielsen

FIGURE 17.5: OWNERSHIP OF TV-RELATED GOODS (% OF HOUSEHOLDS WITH AT LEAST ONE TV)

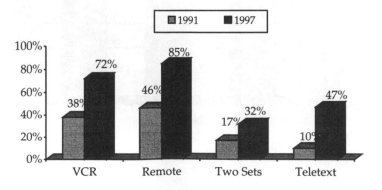

Source: AGBTAM/AC Nielsen

Individual channel penetration figures reflect the division of the market between 71 per cent multichannel and 29 per cent dual-channel reception homes — Figure 17.6.

FIGURE 17.6: CHANNEL PENETRATION

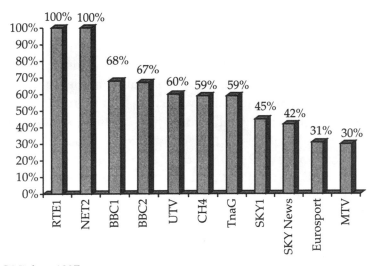

Source: AC Nielsen 1997

TnaG

The Irish-language television channel, launched on 31 October 1996, began 1998 with an official daily audience of 310,000 viewers, while over 1.1 million people tune in every week. After a shaky start dogged by technical problems — especially the fact that so many people could not receive the station — TnaG now boasts a greater audience share than established channels such as Sky News, EuroSport, MTV, Discovery and NBC. Coverage is expected to increase as additional work is done to its transmission network.

TV3

TV3 is expected to go on air in September 1998, offering RTÉ television its first domestic competition. The Canadian company CanWest is supplying the start-up finance and holds a 45 per cent stake in the station. Establishment costs will be quite small, between £15 million and £20 million. Transmission will be paid out of an annual rental to RTÉ, which will retain ownership of the transmission system. Can-

West is the world's largest non-US purchaser of Hollywood's television product and, through a recently acquired stake of 29.9 per cent in UTV, is expected to maximise co-operation between UTV and TV3.

TV3 will be allowed nine minutes of advertising per hour, compared to six minutes on RTÉ. The amount of new advertising will be significant and the industry is convinced that this explosion of advertising time will have the effect of reducing RTÉ's charges and growing television's share of the total advertising spend. TV3 claim that they will be competing with RTÉ for advertising spend, but not necessarily for viewers, and expects that its audience will come to a large extent from those watching British television.

TV3 believes that good production on these stations attracts an audience and will ensure that TV3 is seen as a national service. TV3 plans to broadcast 12 hours a day, with longer transmission periods at weekends. An outline of the programme schedule, as issued in 1995, included:

- A national dedicated news and current affairs service, both domestic and international. It is intended that news be produced in-house.

- A level of home-produced programmes exclusive to TV3. This will account for 15 per cent of total output and grow to 25 per cent by year five.

- A varied schedule of acquired material, selected to appeal to Irish viewers (MacConghail, 1997).

Industry experts differ as to the speed and extent of TV3's expected success. The majority feel that, like Today FM in radio, it will be a slow build-up. This is due in no small part to the level of home-production which will be broadcast — the expected two hours per day, including news, is not considered adequate to attract and sustain an audience in the Irish multichannel context.

Television Audience Measurement

In September 1996, AC Nielsen was awarded the contract for the measurement of audience viewing in the Republic of Ireland. The contract had been held by AGBTAM since the inception of the contract 35 years ago. The contract is awarded by RTÉ and IAPI — the

Institute of Advertising Practitioners in Ireland. Ratings information is still collected in the same way — overnight ratings obtained through "people-meters" attached to a sample of television sets. However, differences in the new contract include a larger number of sampling points, a non-clustered panel for greater geographic representation and 20 per cent forced turnover of the panel each year to avoid possible staleness. The software incorporated into the contract, called Imp*act, allows for more detailed analysis of ratings and includes modules that categorise programmes and quarter hours by rank and by profile, commercial break data, commercial activity data, reach and frequency and daypart optimisation for 150 standard audience categories and infinite user-defined audiences. A new module called Viewergraphics allows for audience analysis by viewing habits rather than demographics.

On 3 February 1998, RTÉ's Director of Sales and Marketing, Colm Molloy, made a momentous announcement to the industry at a seminar in UCD's Graduate School of Business on "Marketing and the Changing Face of Irish Broadcast Media". From September 1998, TV3 will become full partners with RTÉ and IAPI in the television audience measurement contract, and from 1 April 1998, this television rating service will be made available to any broadcaster who wishes to subscribe to it. In addition, data on all broadcasters who subscribe will be made available to the industry as a whole. This move has been widely welcomed by the advertising industry and, at the time of writing, both UTV and Channel 4 had expressed their interest in taking up the offer.

DIGITAL TELEVISION

Terrestrial, over-the-air television was the first delivery system for television. All services were clear to air — i.e. unencrypted. However, the maximum number of national television channels that could be squeezed into the allocated spectrum was five. Cable TV was developed in order to provide over ten channels. Cable TV is economically viable only in fairly densely populated urban areas. In order to provide more than ten channels in rural areas, MMDS was introduced in Ireland in the late 1980s. Despite more channel capacity, distribution costs are higher and combined coverage will never exceed 90 per cent, compared to greater than 99.5 per cent of terrestrial homes. Satellite cannot economically provide any local or regional variations in programmes, and in any case can only reach approximately 92 per cent of homes in Ireland. There is also the aspect of national interest, since it would likely be controlled by foreign interests distributing foreign programming, and any electronic commerce would take place outside Irish jurisdiction and involve transfers out of the Irish economy.

Digital terrestrial "over-the-air" television will be able to provide over 30 television programme services of standard definition pictures at start-up in 1999, increasing to over 100 programme services of standard definition when the existing analogue television transmitters are turned off in about ten years' time. An alternative would be to reduce the number of standard definition programmes from 100 and provide a smaller number of Extended Definition Television (EDTV) or High Definition Television (HDTV) services — perhaps 40–60 EDTV programme services. Cable, satellite and MMDS will be able to provide hundreds of standard definition television programme services — or a smaller number of EDTV or HDTV services. Moreover, all the distribution systems will have encryption — enabling different operators to bid for programme pay-per-view rights.

Internationally, the US and the UK have plans for digital launches in 1998. In the US, 26 television stations in the top markets will begin airing digital signals in the autumn of 1998, according to US Federal Communications Commission rules. In the UK, both the BBC and Sky are promising launches in 1998, and within a few months should be available in Ireland. One of the main reasons is to give them a head start on the development of the technology, and initially the offerings will be broadly similar to existing services. There will be more channels, better reception and some information services. On-line shopping and banking, Internet access, interactive television and a broad range of data services will eventually be on the cards (Casey, 1998).

Digital — Terrestrial, Cable, Satellite or MMDS System?

The different distribution systems (or mix of systems) adopted to broadcast digital television services in other countries has largely been a function of each market's unique characteristics, including elements such as topography, population density, existing broadcast infrastructure, as well as social and cultural factors.

RTÉ is of the opinion that a consideration of these factors indicates that Ireland is ideally suited to terrestrial distribution of digital television, rather than any other mode. The population is small and spread widely across remote rural areas. Mountain ranges add to the transmission difficulties. At present, 99 per cent of Ireland can receive RTÉ services. Viewers rightly expect that the national broadcasting service will continue to discharge its universal obligation in the digital era, providing the transmission infrastructure for terrestrial broadcasting. These factors preclude the cost-effective deployment of either cable or MMDS systems, and the cable companies argue that this is an important consideration, along with the greater number of channels, and easier and cheaper interactivity. They are committed to delivering digital television and the Internet during 1998 and to developing telephony opportunities after 2000 (Foley, 1998). Table 17.1 gives a comparison of the different digital delivery systems from an Irish perspective:

TABLE 17.1: COMPARISON OF DIFFERENT DIGITAL DELIVERY SYSTEMS

	Cable	MMDS	Satellite	Terrestrial
No. of Channels	>200	>100	>200	>100
Portable Reception	No	No	No	Yes
Local Programmes/Advertising	Yes	Yes	No	Yes
Cover (Ireland)	45–49%	25–35%	90–95%	97–99%
Video on Demand	Yes	No	No	No
Universal Service (Ireland)	No	No	No	Yes
National Control	Yes	Yes	No	Yes
Cost (in Irish context)	High	High	Medium	Low

Source: Branagan (1998)

Who will win is by no means simply a technical argument. If one system dominates, whoever controls the decoders for that system will have a major influence on what channels are carried and on what terms.

Viewing Habits

The large increase in the number of channels may not lead to massive fragmentation of the audience. Experience in the US has shown that, where 50+ channels have been available on large cable systems for many years, only 11 of those have 1 per cent or more share of viewing — this is portrayed by Figure 17.8 showing US viewing habits:

FIGURE 17.8: TV CHANNEL REPERTOIRE — US

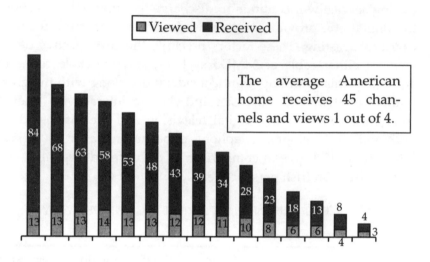

The average American home receives 45 channels and views 1 out of 4.

Source: AC Nielsen

By far the most important factor in determining which delivery system will win will be content. There is no point in having hundreds of channels if there is insufficient relevant content for the targeted audience. Local television news will be as cheap to produce as local radio news by 2005. Local information means local television news opt-outs from national services, local advertising and local data services. This will be possible because video and multimedia production equipment will become inexpensive within the next few years. It will be viable to serve population sizes as low as 250,000 with high quality multimedia information services.

Viewer Benefits

The extra capacity that digital television exploits can be used in a number of different ways to benefit viewers:

1. It offers greatly increased programming choice by allowing a larger number of channels to be broadcast easily and cost-effectively, opening the way for regional and local interests.

2. Digital television offers greatly enhanced sound and picture quality, alleviating problems associated with remote location and poor terrain.

3. The extra capacity afforded by digital compression allows data to be transmitted alongside visual and audio signals, resulting in a greatly enhanced entertainment and information experience.

4. The digital set-top boxes will be connected to a phone line, allowing interactivity with television programmes and facilitating services such as home shopping and electronic banking.

5. Digital terrestrial television ensures that every business, school, home and community in the country can be included in the Information Society.

Interactive Television

The term "interactive" is a central concept in direct marketing and points to the ability to address an individual, to gather and remember the response of that individual and to address the individual once more in a way that takes into account their unique response (Deighton, 1996).

Digital television will give advertisers potential to greatly increase the effectiveness of this communication. There will be numerous new advertising tactics including:

- *"Point and Click"*: an icon in an advertisement is clicked and information is automatically generated from a freephone number

- *"Point, Click and Save"*: a coupon is automatically credited to the viewer's frequent shopper card

- *Fact Sheets*: advertisements can be embedded in fact sheets from associated programmes that will automatically generate information and/or coupons.

For example, in a few years time, Ford will be marketing their third generation Ka. A highly sophisticated commercial is produced for the international market with some variations for different national markets. As the advertisement is broadcast, a pop-up icon appears on the side of the screen inviting the viewer to "point and click" the remote control for further information on the new Ka. This further information may be the detailed technical specifications, the range of colours available and a list of the local Ford dealers and any special offers they may have. This information will be a multimedia production with high presentation values — high quality text and graphics, some animation and, maybe, video and sound clips. It can be accessed within a few seconds on a "side" channel on the digital television or downloaded to a PC for later viewing and/or printing out on hard copy.

DIRECT MARKETING STRATEGY

Rowney (1995) defined direct marketing as a generic term for the use to which all media can be put in order to generate a direct communication with a potential or existing customer. DRTV, or direct response television, already exists as an important direct marketing tool (see the separate chapter on DRTV in this book) and its usefulness will be enhanced by the advent of the third national service, TV3. However, it is digital television which will completely change the face of DRTV. Digital television is where the powerful medium of television meets with a very powerful discipline and results in a marketing tool with all the essential characteristics of a successful direct marketing strategy, as identified by MacGowan (1995):

1. *Target*: Communications are targeted to the target market, using group or individual-specific information, and wastage is avoided.

2. *Interaction and Feedback*: This is the most distinctive feature of direct marketing, as it requires a response and the objective is to receive one. Digital television will have the effect of turning a non-response medium such as television into a pure direct medium.

3. *Control and Measurement*: Tracking and measurement of results and productivity is essential in any direct marketing campaign and a formulaic or scientific approach is guaranteed through digital television.

4. *Continuity*: Lifetime relationships can be created with the customer through enhanced customer retention and loyalty programmes.

CONCLUSION

There are major changes taking place in the television industry in Ireland — at present with terrestrial television and in the future with digital television. TnaG came on air in 1996 and TV3 is due to begin broadcasting in 1998. From 1 April 1998, other broadcasters into this country will be able to subscribe to the television audience measurement contract in order to view their ratings in the Republic of Ireland. Television reception by individual households is changing, and there is a rapid growth in the ownership of television-related products. All these factors will enhance DRTV tactics in direct marketing campaigns.

The full potential of television as a true direct marketing tool will, however, be seen with the advent of digital television, and the implications for advertisers' direct marketing strategies are enormous. Digital terrestrial distribution is arguably the best option for Ireland, but whatever distribution system is used, the bottom line is that for the first time data will be transmitted alongside visual and audio signals through telephone lines. This will result in powerful interactivity and lead to more targeted campaigns, which can be controlled and measured and can form the basis of lifetime relationships with customers.

REFERENCES TO CHAPTER 17

AC Nielsen (1998), Television Audience Measurement Contract from Sept. 1996.

AGBTAM, Television Audience Measurement Contract up to Sept. 1996.

Anon (1997), "Intel Tries to Turn Computers into TVs", *The Irish Times*, 19 December.

Branagan, P. (1988), *Digital Terrestrial Television — Towards an All Digital Future*, Dublin: RTÉ, January.

Casey, C. (1998), "Digital TV — Don't Wait for the Revolution", *Sunday Business Post*, 15 February.

Deighton, J. (1996), "The Future of Interactive Marketing", *Harvard Business Review*, November–December.

Foley, M. (1997), "310,000 Viewers Watch TnaG Daily", *The Irish Times*, 31 October.

Foley, M. (1998), "Cable Viewers to Have Access to Digital Television", *The Irish Times*, 4 February.

Foley, M. (1998), "RTÉ to Get First Domestic Competition in the Autumn", *The Irish Times*, 6 February.

MacConghail, M. (1997), "TV3 Says Programming Will Target the Young", *The Irish Times*, 3 November.

MacGowan, M. (1995), "Direct Marketing — Irish Perspectives", in T. Meenaghan and P. O'Sullivan (eds.), *Marketing Communications in Ireland*, Dublin: Oak Tree Press, pp. 532–545.

Molloy, C. (1998), "Marketing and the Changing Face of Irish Broadcast Media", UCD, 3 February.

Rowney, P. (1995), "What is Direct Marketing?", *Direct Response*, 19–26 March.

RTÉ (1998), "RTÉ and Digital Terrestrial Television", RTÉ Newsletter, Dublin.

Chapter 18

TELEVISION AND DIRECT RESPONSE ADVERTISING

Ben Kealy *and* Peter Crotty

Overview

Direct response advertising is one of the fastest-growing forms of advertising in Ireland today. The growth of direct response is particularly noticeable in the financial services industry, where a significant percentage of financial institutions offer either a Freephone or CallSave service to new and existing customers.

Research by Irish Marketing Surveys (1998) claims that, in the 1980s, there were 67 television stations broadcasting in Europe. By the early 1990s, this had more than doubled to 157 stations. It is predicted that, by 2000, the European market will be served by no less than 500 television stations. The IMS found that:

> *seven in ten Irish adults believe that it is a good thing to have more and more choice of TV channels. The under 25-year-olds are even more in favour. Nearly nine in every ten see proliferation as a good thing. Ireland is not alone in espousing the multi-channel ethos; most of our Western European neighbours tend to share this view.*

Direct response is not just about selling. It is ultimately about a relationship between a business and each of its individual customers, one that clearly delivers benefit to both parties. In this context, the telephone becomes a key relationship-building tool.

This chapter considers direct response advertising on television and how direct response buying differs from buying by conventional advertising. The factors involved in using the medium effectively are considered, as are the key measures of effectiveness. The chapter concludes with a case study of the EBS Building Society.

TELEVISION AS A DIRECT RESPONSE MEDIUM

Television is a very powerful medium in its effect on people's perceptions of a service or product. Consequently, it was only natural that direct marketers sought to harness this key attribute, combining it with traditional direct response "mechanisms" to generate enquiries or sales. The ability of television to reach large audiences was a key factor in its early success as a direct response medium. However, two key factors have recently come to mitigate against DRTV:

- Rising media costs — for example, the "all adults" airtime package increased by 11 per cent overall between 1996 and 1997 (added to already high production costs)

- Increased competition from overseas leading to fragmentation of audiences.

This has led to a change in strategy by many direct response advertisers, whereby some allocate their television budgets across other media, others are developing brand DRTV commercials and others yet again are becoming more selective than ever before in programme planning.

Increasingly, advertisers are turning to direct response TV. RTE estimates that one in ten commercials now carries a direct response number. Figures compiled by Channel 4 and British Telecom show that 25 per cent of that station's revenue comes from various forms of DRTV, as against the US, where almost 50 per cent of all commercials have a Freephone number.

Limited airtime availability and the high cost of advertising on RTE are slowing down the development of DRTV, to the extent that even the traditional DRTV advertisers are being cautious about their DRTV investment, as well as preventing new entrants to the market. It is expected that the provision of UTV on an all-Ireland basis and the launch of TV3 in September 1998 will increase the number of quality alternatives for advertisers.

In the case of TV3, it is anticipated that it will initially target Dublin, and this raises the question of whether the numbers will work in the short term for DRTV advertisers when the audience figures are likely to be relatively low. In addition, an increase in the number of digital TV channels will result in greater segmentation, with the possible downside of further media fragmentation.

How DRTV Buying Works

Buying direct response TV is different to buying traditional advertising. The marketer is not considering ratings and coverage impact, but rather what make people pick up the phone and call. Instead of buying awareness potential, the marketer is buying enquiries.

Brand advertising is evaluated by the effect it has on brand awareness figures, while direct response advertising is charged with the task of delivering the lowest possible media cost per capita.

Table 18.1 illustrates some of the main differences between traditional and DRTV media planning.

TABLE 18.1: DIFFERENCES BETWEEN TRADITIONAL AND DRTV MEDIA PLANNING

	Brand Media	DRTV Media
Objectives	To gain high coverage and frequency within a target audience	To generate consistent levels of in-bound calls to a live operated call centre
	To achieve high brand awareness figures in research	To generate the maximum numbers of enquiries possible, at the lowest possible cost per head
Strategy	High rating peak time spots, generally heavily weighted. Short bursts of activity, with a high volume of spots in order to reach as many people within the target market	A combination of peak and off-peak but more towards the off-peak
	Dominate the TV media in order to concentrate the consumer's mind on the product or service being advertised	Ongoing regular TV presence in order to generate a regular stream of enquiries
		Emphasis placed on cost-effective delivery of leads, not awareness, coverage and frequency, or audience delivery

Source: Browne (1997).

For the best possible results, a combination of both strategies is recommended. This strategy is sometimes called "brand response advertising". BRA seeks to generate in-bound calls from less cost-efficient segments of the programming schedule, thereby widening coverage of the target audience, generating a higher number of calls per spot, but sacrificing, to a degree, cost-efficiency. This strategy allows the marketing to become more creative in terms of media planning. It is possible to chase the target audience around the programming schedule in line with their viewing habits, thereby improving effective coverage whilst still remaining cost-efficient.

Unlike traditional advertisers, most direct players maintain a regular, if not constant presence across their chosen media. This continuous presence makes it possible for the direct marketer to commit to a guaranteed minimum spend.

According to a report by the ITV Network Centre (1993), there are a number of key factors that influence the planning and buying for DRTV, as distinct from conventional television buying. These factors are described in Table 18.2.

HOW TO USE THE MEDIUM EFFECTIVELY

Direct marketers use a number of proven methods to maximise response levels. These include using a voiceover to repeat the number more than once, explaining what the viewer has to do now, what they need to have ready (e.g. credit card) and to emphasise the benefits of calling. Equally important is the display of the telephone number. This should be on the screen for a minimum of 20 seconds, with a minimum size of two inches and centred on the screen.

According to Mathews (1997) "For companies who use direct response the advantages are great as long as they consider the following:

- Give the customer a reason to call

- Be prepared to deal with the calls when they happen

- Make sure the people handling the calls are properly trained

- Ensure your marketing department has advised your call centre."

TABLE 18.2: FACTORS INFLUENCING PLANNING AND BUYING

Conventional TV	DRTV
Coverage	
Coverage of at least 70 per cent would be considered normal.	A successful campaign may reach as little as 10 per cent of a station's audience.
Frequency	
Frequency levels vary greatly from one product category to another, but an average of "five opportunities to see" would be a common threshold level.	For well-known brands, response would be greater at first viewing and then decline with frequent repetition. For unknown brands, response tends to build, as repetition builds consumer confidence.
Programming	
Conventional advertisers seek high interest programming, assuming that viewers are more likely to give the commercial their full attention.	DRTV advertisers avoid "preference to view" programmes in favour of low-interest programmes, when it is easier to motivate people to call.
Peak Time	
The quality of a conventional TV schedule is often measured by the proportion of ratings in peak.	Peak time is rarely cost-effective for direct response advertising, and is often not even tested.
Commercial Length	
Commercials come in many lengths, but 30 seconds is still the most common.	The most popular length for direct response commercials (UK) is 90 seconds, although shorter lengths have been successfully used for certain products.
Campaign Period	
A burst would normally last between four and six weeks, sometimes extended to a low or "drip" weight.	A two-week test phase is normal, followed by a further campaign whose length is entirely dependent on profitability.
Test Areas (UK)	
The ideal test area would normally be an average area for the product or specific target audience.	The ideal test area will always be the best area for that product or service.
Evaluation	
Usually based on awareness or image. Evaluated as a campaign, not spot by spot.	Always based on directly attributable research — profit from the responses generated, each spot being measured separately.

Research was undertaken by Johnson (1996) concerning how to maximise the effectiveness of DRTV. In the UK, there was a growth of traditional DRTV advertisers in absolute terms, while, in addition, other non-traditional DRTV advertisers, such as mail order catalogues and telecommunications companies, had created a significant impact in increasing the popularity of the medium.

The research highlighted the improvement in response rates as a result of two main factors:

- Advertisers are becoming more experienced with DRTV advertising

- Viewers are getting more used to DRTV.

Through monitoring, the consistent characteristics of the commercials under research were noted, becoming what is considered industry-accepted guidelines for using the medium more effectively.

Weekend versus Weekday

Overall, the research identified that advertising during the week was more cost-efficient, with an average index of 105 for weekdays and 81 for weekends.

The only notable exception to this rule was the automotive industry. It was felt that this was due the fact that motor DRTV advertising is often more brand-based, with less concentration on response effort.

Time of Day

Daytime was the most response-efficient time, although generating less absolute response than the higher-rating times of day. This was consistent across all categories.

Length of Commercial

The longer the commercial, the better the response. However, this has to be balanced against the additional cost of a longer commercial, where the economic efficiencies have to be calculated. In addition, many shorter commercials, or combinations of 10-, 20- and 60-second commercials, showed how innovative creative treatment made for highly successful campaigns, bucking the "longer commercial rule".

Duration of Phone Number on Screen

The difference between having the telephone number displayed in the commercial for longer than ten seconds as against less than ten seconds was dramatic. A response index of 71 was noted for commercials where the number was displayed for less than ten seconds; the index for 11 seconds or more was 120.

Voiceover of the Telephone Number

It is widely accepted that including a voiceover of the phone number in the commercial will increase response — the real surprise was by how much. The index for a commercial with a voiceover was, on average, 144, as opposed to 39 without a voiceover. This difference was even more evident in the motor sector, with an index of 300 with a voiceover and 48 without.

Size of Telephone Number

This element of the research was incomplete. However, of the commercials where this was measured, the optimum size from a response efficiency criterion was between 6 and 10 per cent of screen size.

End or Centre Break

In conventional advertising, there is a preference for commercial breaks within programmes, as there is less audience movement and perhaps greater concentration. However, this does not necessarily hold true for DRTV commercials. For satellite TV and ITV, it was noted that there was little difference in the efficiency between centre and end breaks. With Channel 4, it was a different story — end breaks were found to be 25 per cent more efficient.

The reason for this is that people are less likely to use the phone when the next part of their programme is due to start soon; they are more likely to do so between programmes.

Type of Phone Number

Freephone was found to generate higher volumes of calls, but it is more expensive and there was a much higher rate of wasted calls. This is also the case in Ireland, and many advertisers have switched from 1800 to 1890 or 1850 numbers, with a reduction in quantity and cost but an increase in the quality of the caller.

Frequency/Weight of Campaign

In this case, the research attempted to identify what effect frequency actually had on response. The findings were somewhat contradictory to current thinking, in that they established that a more effective response is made from an advertisement that had been seen earlier that day, than either a new advertisement or an advertisement shown the previous day.

Lost Calls

Johnson (1996) measured the level of calls lost during the period of the exercise and it was calculated to be 37 per cent. The top eight advertisers did skew the results somewhat, but even when they were removed from the equation, the level of lost calls was 22 per cent. This served to underline the importance of adequate backup and support by the telemarketing bureau and the client working closely with the telemarketing bureau to minimise the risks.

MEASURES OF DRTV ADVERTISING EFFECTIVENESS

It is vitally important to have clear objectives and sufficient resources to handle the responses generated by direct response TV. Peak response from a spot will occur within five minutes of the advertisement appearing, and if the sale requires complex order-taking processes, it is necessary to have a large number of operators available to prevent the responses being lost. It is recommended that advertisers should conduct initial tests with artificially high manning levels, despite the higher costs that might be incurred. External response agencies might be unwilling to offer this facility, since they are usually paid on a per-call basis, and will lose money if operators' time is not fully maximised.

Another key phenomenon that has been identified in this area is that certain advertisements offering Freephone services are prone to generate high levels of what are known as "junk" calls or "nuisance" calls — i.e., time wasters, and young people who cannot buy the products or services. Advertisers need to be prepared for this and to monitor the levels of resources wasted in handling these calls.

Just as a press direct response campaign will have an initial schedule for a test programme, with subsequent bookings dependent on results, a television campaign can be booked on the same basis. Once feedback has been obtained on the results achieved by specific spots, buying can be matched to response-handling capabilities. Accurate and rapid media analysis is central to effective monitoring of results, to feed back into good media buying and planning.

As a direct response medium, DRTV is highly measurable and the traditional measurements are as relevant for television as they are for any media. The criteria for measurement include:

- Response per spot

- Conversion per spot

- Order value per spot

- Lifetime value per spot

- Wastage/hoax call levels

- Answered calls

- Unanswered calls

- Average call length

- Call type/nature of call

- Analysis by ad execution/length/offer

- Effect on other media (if double duty/support advertising).

In order to measure effectively, the marketer is required to work closely with the telemarketing department/bureau from the early planning stages of the campaign.

The overall media strategy requires planning in advance, setting down the buying criteria. Airtime is usually bought spot-by-spot in such a way that the individual and cumulative effectiveness of the spots can be measured. The schedule must also take into account the company response-handling capacity. The most effective way is to buy individual spots in high audience commercial breaks to begin with until response levels can be predicted. It is also wise to have excess staffing levels initially and reduce this as required in light of results.

Also, you must avoid unmanageable clashes between stations until the correct manning levels have been identified. Once initial results are available, the media buying is refined accordingly to increase further the campaign's effectiveness.

CONCLUSION

In summary, direct response television is growing, albeit at a slower rate than our European and American counterparts. Its success and future rate of growth is largely dependent on:

- Cost

- Media Fragmentation.

In the short to medium term, costs on their own are unlikely to come down, as demand for airtime is still very high and there is currently no indication that the pre-empt booking system currently practised in Ireland will be changed.

However, in the long term, the factors of cost and media fragmentation will inversely affect each other — as more media become a available, audiences will drop, as will demand for any one station/ medium, and consequently costs will reduce (or in the worst case scenario, the rate of increase will reduce).

The lesson to be learnt here is, as with any direct response medium, that you test, measure, evaluate and refine. The knowledge and skills exist to take advantage of DRTV; therefore, when the correct balance of the influencing factors is achieved, it will rapidly mushroom to UK levels.

CASE HISTORY: EBS BUILDING SOCIETY

Introduction

If you are looking to buy a property, there is a good chance that you will have called one of several financial institutions using direct response, on either a 1800 or 1850 telephone number. This would have been unheard of ten years ago. Direct response is now a typical marketing approach towards the changing consumer.

The growth in direct response has also been aided by the changing demands of clients in their search to create and invest in fully accountable advertising activity. In addition, the excellent telecommunications network in Ireland, together with the growing expertise of response handlers, has helped forge a path for what has become a major marketing consideration for all advertisers.

EBS's Experience . . . Why Direct?

EBS is a major Irish financial institution. It has assets of £2.6 billion, employs more than 600 people and operates from 150 offices throughout the country. It serves 53,000 borrowing customers and 400,000 savings' customers.

What makes EBS increasingly distinctive is its commitment to customer ownership. As a mutual building society, EBS is owned by its customers. Margins and costs are kept as low as possible to maximise value for these customers. Each year, a large proportion of the society's profits is returned to customers, through higher savings rates and lower borrowing rates. Not surprisingly in a customer-owned organisation, EBS attaches great importance to identifying and meeting the needs of customers. Since 1993, EBS's advertising has been in the form of direct response. The society has used direct response as part of integrated campaigns involving TV, radio, press and outdoor. But why go the direct route at EBS? There are a number of answers to this question:

- It is different

- It is measurable

- It allowed EBS to set up a specific team to handle responses, namely EBS*DIRECT*

- It is in keeping with the proposition "Talk to Us".

The discipline of direct response was, for EBS, a learning one. EBS established a specific team called EBS*DIRECT*, and initially began by giving the society a public face in the person of Adrian Taheny (General Manager — Marketing). He first appeared on TV in 1993. He spoke directly to camera, sitting on the edge of a desk and never moving. The Freephone number (1800 654 321) appeared at the end of the commercial and the response received that night was significant. Staff recall sitting by the phones and the buzz that they got as the first calls came through. EBS had arrived on the direct response scene.

The TV campaign developed over the years, initially using Adrian Taheny on his own, then bringing him into a "made-up" office in Ardmore Studios, and finally to the EBS Head Office in Westmoreland Street. EBS introduced new staff members into the TV ads and extended this into radio, press and outdoor advertising. The 1800 number, instead of appearing at the end, was on-screen for the entire commercial; this had the effect of significantly increasing responses.

From initially using the 1800 654 321 number, EBS switched to 1850 654 321 in early 1995. The switch was not a cost issue, but an attempt to reduce "nuisance calls". In 1993/94, when EBS used the 1800 number, the nuisance calls were at times as high as 70 per cent. Nuisance calls block the lines and stop genuine calls coming through. Staff motivation was another issue: answering seven or eight nuisance calls in a row and then answering a genuine call can frustrate staff and result in a genuine call being answered in an aggressive manner. When EBS switched to 1850 654 321, the amount of nuisance calls reduced significantly.

Apart from switching from the 1800 to 1850 number, EBS also started using Adrian Taheny and other staff on radio. This was less expensive than TV and allowed EBS greater flexibility with regard to timing and frequency. The use of radio also significantly reduced the amount of nuisance calls and enabled EBS to segment the market. The use of weekend radio, at a time when first-time buyers and those trading up in the mortgage market are house-hunting, was another first for a financial institution, and the competitors followed in time.

The outdoor campaigns followed, using local staff for each area; for example, a 48-sheet/SuperLite in Cork featured the local staff in

Cork. This form of advertising proved very successful at the local level. A cinema advertisement was designed specifically to target first-time buyers. Direct mail to existing customers was also part of the integrated campaign. Mailing to existing mortgage customers offering home improvement and personal loans, featuring staff from the "top-up" loans section and a dedicated 1850 654 327 number, generated a greater response.

At this stage, EBS have bought all the 1800/1850 numbers between 654 321 and 654 329. This enables EBS to use specific numbers for different campaigns and measure the responses. For example, 1850 654 326 is used for all savings advertising. More recently, EBS has bought "Vanity Numbers" — 1800/1850 MORTGAGE, HOMELOAN, SAVINGS, MUTUAL. Although these numbers are not in use in Ireland at present, it is expected that they will be used in the near future.

As a result of all of this direct response advertising, EBS was in a position to determine how well/badly an advertisement worked. For example, an advertisement at the break in *Coronation Street* would get minimal response, whereas an advertisement placed at the end of the soap would increase responses considerably. EBS learnt that viewers do not want to be disturbed while watching *Coronation Street*. The EBS also captured the following:

- How many calls EBS*DIRECT* received

- How many mortgage packs were issued

- The value of the mortgage packs sent to customers

- The number of enquiries handled

- The number of nuisance calls

- The cost per pack

- The number of follow-up sales calls.

By 1996, almost 50 per cent of the EBS advertising budget was spent on direct response TV, compared to 15 per cent by the other building societies — see Figure 18.1.

FIGURE 18.1: 1996 BUILDING SOCIETIES VERSUS EBS

Building Societies

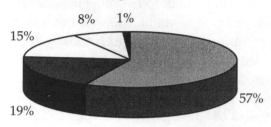

EBS

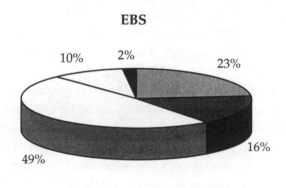

▨Press ■Radio ☐TV ☐Outdoor ■Cinema

Also in that year (1996), EBS opened its call centre, staffed by 50 tele-operators. New and existing customers could now call EBS and have all queries answered by one staff member, instead of going through the switchboard and being passed from operator to operator. The EBS*DIRECT* staff became part of the call centre and operate as one of its many teams.

By 1997, EBS was at the forefront of direct response advertising in Ireland. At this time, Adrian Taheny departed to FBD Insurance. This move resulted in EBS departing from TV to evaluate the brand strategy and in the meantime moving to press, where they could use very targeted campaigns in the Property Supplements of the *Irish Independent* and *Irish Times*.

FIGURE 18.2: 1997 BUILDING SOCIETIES VERSUS EBS

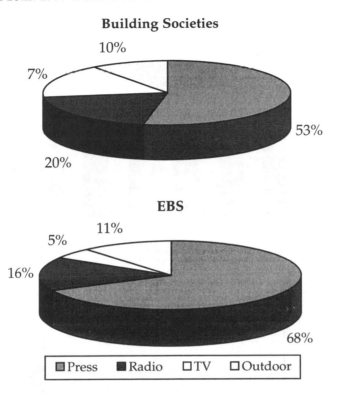

Building Societies

10%

7%

53%

20%

EBS

11%

5%

16%

68%

☐ Press ■ Radio ☐ TV ☐ Outdoor

Since EBS commenced using the direct response route for its advertising, it has seen its market share of the mortgage market increase significantly to a high of 17.5 per cent and its loan advances up to £626 million at the end of 1997.

In conclusion, EBS's direct response initiatives enabled the society to:

- Build Brand Awareness

- Measure performance of ads immediately

- Capture names and addresses of new and potential customers

- Open the way to follow-up sales calls.

FIGURE 18.3: EBS MARKET SHARE (ALL LENDERS; NET; RESIDENTIAL)

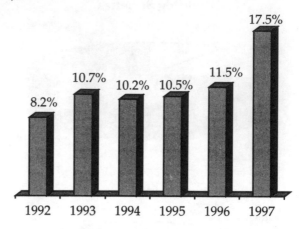

FIGURE 18.4: LOAN ADVANCES

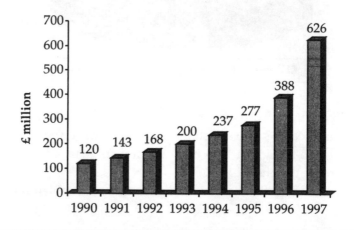

REFERENCES TO CHAPTER 18

Cole, A. (1997), "Teletalk Back", *Deadline*, Dec/Jan, pp. 14–15.

Browne, Julian (1997), "Direct Response Television, Masterclass", *Go Direct*, Nov/Dec.

ITV Network Centre (1993), *Guideline to Direct Response: How to Plan an Effective Direct Response TV Campaign*, London: ITV, p. 2.

Irish Marketing Surveys (1998), *Irish Marketing Surveys Newsletter*.

Johnson, H. (1996), "How to Maximise Effective Use of Direct Response TV", *Admap*, pp. 33–36.

Mathews, C. (1997), "Direct Response Television, Masterclass", *Go Direct*, Nov/Dec.

O'Neill, G. (1996), *Focus on The Future: The Coming Boom in Direct Marketing*, Dublin: Henley Centre/IDMA Report.

Chapter 19

THE INTERNET: IMPLICATIONS FOR MARKETING AND DIRECT MARKETING

Joseph Coughlan *and* Joy Redmond

Overview

The changes in telecommunications will be immense. Depending, possibly, on personal income, the average household will be linked by multiple cable or by radio with an immense variety of services, bringing people closer together all over the world (Childers, 1967).

Over 30 years on, Childers' prediction of a society interlinked by multiple cable or radio is on the verge of realisation. People all over the world are brought closer together by the Internet — the network of networks. However, the Internet is not limited to the household. "The Internet combines the power of modern telecommunications with the power of computers to create a giant world-wide network which will radically change business and society over the next five years" (McGovern, 1996). The Internet's impact on all aspects of business thinking and practice is immense.

This chapter outlines the effect of the Internet on marketing as a whole and on direct marketing specifically. The chapter opens with a brief discussion on the current status of global technological diffusion in the context of industrial economic history. A brief history and description of the Internet is then proffered, followed by a review of current Internet usage in Ireland. The application of the Internet to marketing in terms of "adding value" throughout the organisation is then outlined. The constant striving towards one-to-one marketing that lies at the heart of direct marketing is discussed and the question posed as to whether the Internet is the long-awaited vehicle to propel this. Practical advice on having an effective Web presence and promoting it online and offline is then given. The chapter closes with a discussion on some of the key issues pertaining to the future of the Internet.

WHERE ARE WE NOW?

In order to explain the impact of the Internet, and indeed all technology and information-based industries, on marketing practices, it is important to take a wider perspective and view the impact on society as a whole rather than solely on commercial aspects.

In an effort to understand industrial economic history, economists use various models or frameworks in an attempt to determine if any formal patterns emerge. Freeman and Perez (1988) identified five cycles based on the application and diffusion of key technologies and resources throughout advancing countries within the international economy. They have termed these diffusion cycles as "techno-economic paradigms" and named them as follows:

1. Early mechanisation (1770s to 1840s)

2. Steam power and railway (1830s to 1890s)

3. Electrical and heavy engineering (1880s to 1940s)

4. Fordist mass production (1930s to 1990s)

5. Information and communication (1980 to 2040s possibly).

Through an analysis of the previous four techno-economic paradigms, the authors noticed a distinct pattern in each cycle's adoption and diffusion of said key technologies. Apparently, each paradigm has a cycle of between 60 and 70 years, with 10 years in an emergent phase in a previous paradigm and 10 years in a declining phase in the ensuing paradigm. If the Internet and current information-related industries are viewed in terms of these techno-economic paradigms, then it appears that we are currently in the early years of the adoption phase, with approximately 40 more years before declining into the next era, which is as yet unknown.

This is not, however, a chapter on industrial economic history, but it serves as an interesting insight into advanced nations' current positions in terms of industrialisation. Freeman and Perez contend that each techno-economic paradigm is associated with a number of effects.

These effects are outlined below with some examples given in direct relation to Ireland and the Internet. Freeman and Perez did not relate the fifth techno-economic paradigm directly to the Internet, but to all technological advances of the late twentieth century.

- *The emergence of new industries based on the key technologies and resources*: In Ireland, software development, hardware and computer-related industries have been developing since the early 1980s.

- *Effective solutions to the limitations of previous techno-economic paradigms*: An important marketing implication of the move from Fordist mass production is the ability of organisations to adopt mass customisation and thus aspire to one-to-one marketing, which was impossible in the previous paradigms. Database technologies have allowed marketers to adopt new strategies of "one-to-many" communications, but the interactive or new media options available today now allow the marketer to communicate and operate on a one-to-one basis. This will be discussed in more detail later in the chapter.

- *New infrastructure at both national and international level*: In an Irish context, the technological infrastructure has been nurtured by EU funding and by the "industrialisation by invitation" policies of the late 1970s.

- *Countries gaining technological and economic leadership positions* from the application of key technologies and resources associated with the new paradigms:

  America is the unquestioned leader in the Internet race, while Europe consoles itself with being second and "catching up". In reality, there are few signs that Europe is indeed catching up. . . . There are signs, however, that while Europe ponders its dilemma, Asia will be racing ahead, embracing and exploiting the Internet and the long-term commercial opportunities that go with it (Nua, 1997a).

- *Significant changes in the spatial distribution* and distance between associated production factors (including land, labour and capital resources) and market locations (marketplaces and customers).

- *Shifts in population density and urbanisation.*

- *Radical changes in organisational forms associated with firms in new industries.*

- *New approaches to national and international regulation.*

- *New training and education systems*: The Internet and new media in general have radically transformed the concept of training and education. Education today is not confined to a classroom; technology now enables students to work from their own PCs. A good example of how new media technologies are extending the frontiers of education is the Irish company Knowledge Well, who produce CD-ROMs of various business courses. Students can work from their own PC, following tutorials on the CD-ROM, sit exams at their PCs and receive certificates and qualifications.

- *New innovative entrepreneurs*: This is the age of "computer-aided entrepreneurs" like Bill Gates, who earned his ranking as richest man in the world through technological innovation.

- *New political economists and philosophers*: Nicholas Negroponte, Marshall McLuhan and George Gilder are probably the most visible digital thinkers of our times.

THE INTERNET

The Internet is best described in its current state as a vast information utility, based around a global network system of dispersed information resources and a collection of information tools and applications (Coughlan, 1996). Without this interoperability, the Net would disintegrate into a patchwork of sealed-off cells and the increasing returns to scale so essential for continued growth and future profitability would collapse (National Academy of Sciences, 1996).

It has transformed rapidly from its initial military and academic usages into a global network that is revolutionising interpersonal communication. As a result of the increased number of people on the Internet, the amount of business is expected to grow dramatically (International Data Corporation, 1997). The most conservative estimates are a tenfold volume growth on current levels by the year 2000 (Miller, 1997):

> What is less certain than this rapid growth in users is the exact technological and institutional trajectory the Net's infrastruc-

ture will take in order to provide the capacity to meet the demand; the software upon which a seamless web depends; the
privacy, copyright, means of payment and policing safeguards
essential for reassuring both information suppliers and consumers; and the ease of use that can integrate the Net into
everyday life so that it becomes second nature, like switching
on a light, dialling a phone number (Miller, 1997).

The Internet is not a service as we commonly think of one. It is
emerging as the fulcrum of the information infrastructure.

Taking a cue from the history of how previous universal technologies diffused, it is not far-fetched to expect that the Net
will gradually reorganise how, what, where and when we
produce and consume (Miller, 1997).

The tools and applications of the Internet can be summarised in Table 19.1.

TABLE 19.1: TOOLS AND APPLICATIONS OF THE INTERNET

Information Search	Search mechanisms to locate requested information
File Transfer Protocol	Allows the transfer of files from one computer to another
Electronic Mail	Allows the exchange of electronic messages between users
Newsgroups	News and topic discussion groups where users participate on topics of interest to them
Mailing Lists	Groups of users with common interests receiving the same information
Chat	Allows large-group real-time text conversations over the Internet
World Wide Web	Multimedia hypertext interface for accessing resources and information

Source: Coughlan, 1996.

Users do not actually "use the Internet". Users use the various tools
of the Internet to perform different tasks (Cybersolve, 1997).

Ireland and the Internet

This section of the chapter attempts to provide the reader with an overview of Internet usage in Ireland. The first study was conducted in February 1997 by Nua Ltd. in conjunction with MIDAS-NET Ireland. The top 500 companies in Ireland were mailed questionnaires; the response rate was 42 per cent. The results are as follows:

- *Internet connection*: 74 per cent of respondent companies said they had a connection to the Net. Of the remaining 26 per cent, 47 per cent stated that they intended to get one over the next 12 months. If these expectations are accurate, then 86 per cent of respondents will have an Internet connection by 1998.

- *Importance of the Internet*: 18 per cent of respondents felt that the Internet was very important to their company with the remaining 82 per cent being evenly split as to the Internet being important and not very important. However, when asked about the possibility of change in levels of importance over the next 12 months, 89 per cent of respondents believe its importance will increase in 1998.

- *Need more information*: 63 per cent of companies responding stated that the Internet was something they needed to be more informed about.

- *World Wide Web (WWW)*: 56 per cent of respondents who have an Internet connection have a website. Of those, 47 per cent found it beneficial and 20 per cent stated it was very beneficial. According to ABT (1997), of their 2,800 exporting clients, 500 (18 per cent) currently have e-mail and only 200 (7 per cent) have home pages or websites.

- *Irish firms versus foreign-owned firms and Internet connections*: 64 per cent of Irish firms have an Internet connection, as opposed to 82 per cent of foreign-owned firms. Over the next 12 months, 22 per cent of Irish companies and 11 per cent of foreign-owned firms expect to get an Internet connection.

Profile of Irish Internet Users

The second source of information on Internet usage in Ireland involved an open-invitation online user survey that was hosted on the

Irish Internet Association (IIA) website in 1997 (IIA, 1997). A profile of Irish Internet users is given below in terms of age (Table 19.2), gender, level of education, who pays for access, place of access and finally respondent's views concerning payment for information.

TABLE 19.2: THE AGE OF IRISH INTERNET USERS

Age	Under 18	18–24	25–30	31–35	36–50	51–64	Over 65
Respondent	5.5%	17.7%	24.9%	15.3%	28.5%	7.0%	0.7%

- *Gender*: The ratio of males to females online in Ireland is 3:1.

- *Level of Education*: 70.1 per cent of respondents were third-level graduates.

- *Who pays?* Over 52 per cent of respondents pay for their own access. One-third of respondents' Internet accounts are paid for by employers, and parents account for 7 per cent. Schools account for 3.1 per cent, which indicates the low level of Internet access in schools throughout the country. However, Telecom Éireann announced, in September 1997, that £10 million would be invested over the next three years in providing Internet connections to every school in the State. The government also announced, in November 1997, plans to finance a £250 million investment in first-, second- and third-level institutions for Internet installations.

- *Primary Place of Access*: Almost 61 per cent of respondents' primary place of access is the home, with their place or work accounting for 35 per cent. The remaining four per cent are attributed to second- or third-level education and cyber cafes.

- *Pay for Information*: 50.6 per cent of users said they would not pay for information on the Internet. The remaining respondents said they would pay for information under certain conditions, such as a pay-by-view or pay-by-subscription option.

MARKETING OPPORTUNITIES ON THE INTERNET

Marketing is an ever-evolving discipline. It builds on past experience while taking advantage of new opportunities. Each new challenge demands a firm grasp of what has gone before,

> a clear picture of the present situation, and an understanding
> of the most attractive options at the moment (Rapp and
> Collins, 1995).

As a preface to outlining the marketing opportunities on the Internet, the marketing concept will be reintroduced. Marketing is a way of doing business, a critical philosophy in today's competitive marketplace. Marketing hones in on all the facets of the organisation and examines how each facet adds value to the customer. Block (1997) defines value as giving the customer more than they expect you will give them. Increasing perceived customer value leads to greater customer satisfaction, implying superior marketing.

Marketing has always existed. Marketing has always communicated a particular message to a particular audience using the available media of a particular era. It is the efficiency and effectiveness of communicating that message to that audience that distinguishes optimal marketing from mediocrity. Every now and again, new media and tools emerge. It is incumbent upon the marketer to try to understand these new challenges and adapt accordingly. New media will not obliterate the old, but will rather offer the marketer more options to be better equipped in a competitive marketplace. Certainly one can continue using the traditional media, but actively evading new marketing media will deny the possibility of optimal marketing. Less than optimal perceived customer value is the opportunity cost associated with such evasion.

The Internet — The Marketing Challenge

> The Internet is not only a marketing vehicle, it's become a
> marketing challenge, requiring companies to adapt age-old
> promotional techniques and develop new ones (Mullich,
> 1995).

The Internet challenges the traditional approaches to accomplishing marketing, not the philosophy of marketing itself. It empowers the consumer/user in a way that, decades ago, we would never have envisaged. "The customer has always been king but the new technologies make that more transparent" (Rushbrook, 1995).

It challenges our ideas of ourselves and our offerings. It creates a new spirit of enterprise — the computer-aided entrepreneur. It challenges industry by creating opportunities for new industries that, overnight, could render our services obsolete. Most importantly, the Internet challenges the traditional concept of value.

> The core values that apply with traditional media don't change when someone gets behind a computer screen; what changes is the consumer's expectation about the delivery system (Melin, 1997).

The Internet — Implications for Improved Marketing

> Because of its rapid growth and its global nature, the Internet should be understood and considered, in particular by marketers, as a potential new and evolving advertising, marketing, sales, distribution, communication and support medium (Coughlan, 1996).

As marketing is not just sales or advertising, but about consistently adding value, the Internet's application to marketing is not just about sales or advertising, but about adding value. In order to explain the impact of the Internet on marketing practice, we have adapted the Ellsworth and Ellsworth (1996: 228) model entitled "the reasons companies typically use the web". Each element will be discussed in detail below.

1. Communication
   - Internal, networking
   - External, vendors, customers, suppliers.

2. Data Transfer
   - Between sites
   - To/from other companies
   - On the road staff.

3. Information Retrieval/Research/Utilisation
   - Marketing research
   - New materials
   - Training

- Professional development.

4. Cost Containment

   - Alternative communications

   - Telephone

   - Mail

   - Personnel, efficiency of customer support, telecommunication, reduce the need for meetings.

5. Collaboration/Product Development

   - Workgroups.

6. Marketing research

   - Primary

   - Secondary

   - Surveys.

7. Sales

   - Distribution channels

   - Online sales.

Communication

The Internet is radically transforming both internal and external business communications. When discussing the Internet in terms of communication, it is essential to outline the different network options available — *intranets*, *extranets* and the Internet.

An intranet is a WWW network developed for internal communications within the organisation, which can only be accessed by people in the organisation and which is protected from those outside the organisation by "firewalls". An extranet is somewhat similar to an intranet except that it can also be accessed by other parties outside the organisation, namely suppliers and vendors, who receive permission from the organisation to use it. The Internet consists of all networks that choose to be networked. Recent media scares regarding security and privacy have led companies to opt for either intranets or extranets. However, powerful encryption software is now available to reduce the likelihood of privacy invasion on the Internet.

The key aspect of communicating both internally and with third parties, such as vendors or suppliers, is that it enables real-time interaction. The main difference between communicating with customers or prospects through the Internet and through traditional media is the direction of the communication flow, i.e. consumer demand pull versus the marketer's push model. Traditionally, the marketer pushed information and advertisements on to the mass market; the WWW enables the consumer to decide who they want to contact and what information they require. Therefore, the most impressive attribute of WWW communication is that it truly is one-to-one.

Data Transfer

File transfer protocol (FTP) is a program that facilitates the transfer of files between different locations at very high speeds. The most common use is the transfer of files from a remote site to the local, originating site.

Information Retrieval/Research/Utilisation

Companies can download real-time information off the Internet. The Internet is an abyss of business and industry-specific information. If an individual does not have the know-how or the time to "surf" for industry news, one option is to exploit push technology, whereby you enrol in a filtering service, paying a subscription each month to receive information relevant to your organisation via e-mail. Many international research organisations have a web presence and it is worth visiting their sites and doing keyword searches relevant to your industry. The full reports can cost anything up to £20,000, but usually the research findings or executive summaries are published free online. The Internet is an invaluable resource if looking to build relationships with other organisations. An advanced keyword search in specific countries yields many potential partners. If their web address is given, you can learn about their offerings, coverage, rates and so on. The Internet is abundant in training and professional development facilities pertaining to almost every industry.

Cost Containment

Most of the "hype" regarding the Web's application to business concerns its communication and sales potential. The Web's cost-saving capabilities seldom receive much attention when a company is promised a global market of greater than 90 million.

Sun Microsystems reported savings of over $4 million with "Sun-Solve Online" since they re-engineered information processes on the WWW (Chase, 1996). Sun Microsystems employs a call centre team to handle numerous inbound customer and technical support phone calls every year; through a vigorous analysis of the most common calls, the responses can be transferred to the "frequently asked questions" (FAQ) section of the company website, where the customer can search the questions applicable and self-solve their problems. The result is twofold: call centre staffing needs are reduced dramatically as requests are now "self-service" and there is a higher probability of the customer retaining the knowledge.

Another study by IBM in 1995 reported that online catalogues can save firms up to 25 per cent in processing costs and reduce cycle time by up to 62 per cent (Chase, 1996). Indeed, the use of the Internet could not only dramatically reduce business costs but also give a company a competitive edge in terms of reduced cycle times and faster product development. However, Stil and Zimmerman (1996) maintain that "much of the web's growth will be based on a transfer of commerce from other less efficient direct response and retail distribution channels".

Collaboration/Product Development

Groupware is software that enables several users to work on the same document at the same time. The potential of groupware is enormous: pan-national teams can work in real time on projects in industries where time to market is critical.

An example would be a cross-national information systems design where systems analysts can send and retrieve designs and/or *telnet* into another location (a capability that enables access to remote computers) to create or modify a design. Therefore, the design is created under the guidance of a selection of managers, and by designers from varied backgrounds. Time differences are eradicated, as one team can work long after the other teams have already finished their day's work, and subsequent teams can pick up where the last team left off the following morning (Granger and Schroeder, 1996).

Marketing Research

As mentioned earlier, there is tremendous potential for both primary and secondary research on the Internet. Primary research, exemplified by surveys, are very common and are frequently seen on websites. The benefit of carrying out primary research on a company website lies not only in its immediacy and interactivity, but also in the fact that the respondent has chosen to visit your site and is therefore quite affable towards your company or, one can at least assume, is a member of your target audience. The IIA online user survey is a prime example.

The Internet is also an effective launching pad for prototypes of new products, particularly beta-testing of software, in which a software company sends a pre-release version (either a simulation or the actual product time-locked) of their software product to current customers or prospects and invites feedback to see if the product has all the required features.

Sales

Organisations are finding more efficient and direct routes to their customers, removing the need for intermediaries. Dell Computers sell $3 million worth of computer hardware per day from their website. They also allow customers to "build" a computer to their own technical specifications —the order is then processed online and fulfilled within 24 hours. Levi's Jeans allow web browsers to design their own jeans particular to their individual shape. Such innovative uses of the interactive capabilities of the WWW ensure its successful application to business.

DIRECT MARKETING ON THE INTERNET

With media proliferation, splintering of audiences and the rise of a heterogeneous, IT-literate society, marketing as we know it is experiencing a revolution. Central to this revolution are the changes in the marketing media — changes that are central to the tenets of direct marketing. The Internet and other media have facilitated "integration, control, targeting and continuity, the four cornerstones upon which good direct marketing practice is based" (McCorkell, 1992).

Direct marketing has always embraced new technology, and the Internet is no exception. The challenge is not the technology, but the application of solid business principles to this dynamic marketing environment (Phillips, 1996).

In order for the Internet to be a viable segment for the direct marketer, it must be accessible, measurable, substantial, differentiable and actionable (Mehta and Sivadas, 1996).

- The target audience is accessible through electronic mail, websites, newsgroups and chat forums online as well as through the traditional methods of communication

- With approximately 90 million people on the Net, the Internet constitutes a substantial segment (Nua, 1997b)

- Measurability is possible through "hits statistics" from websites and from page impressions

- The members of a segment must respond differently to differing marketing mix elements

- Finally, in order to be a viable segment, effective programmes should be capable of being formulated for attracting and serving the segment: the segment should be actionable.

Mehta and Sivadas (1996) found that Internet users form a global segment. They found few differences between domestic (US) and international users. Because it is necessary that segments exhibit homogenous buying behaviour (Dibb et al., 1997), these findings suggest the similarity between respondents across countries poses some interesting questions for the direct marketer.

Electronic mail (e-mail) is the communications tool of today. It is now possible to send a message to tens of thousands of people instantaneously for less than a quarter of the cost of a direct mailing (Ellsworth and Ellsworth, 1995).

This process is called bulk e-mail. However, there is one important distinction between traditional paper-based and the new electronic direct mail: the cost to the recipient. With e-mail, the recipient is paying to receive your message. Most people online pay their

Internet service provider (ISP) a monthly or annual fee to join and also pay for their time online through their telephone bill.

Sending long messages to individuals who have little interest in your product or service offering ("spamming"), will only serve to alienate potential customers and may also damage the reputation of your organisation. The reaction to the receipt of "cyberjunk" is to send multiple negative e-mails to the sender (Shultz, 1994). This process is called "flaming" and can result in an ISP disconnecting the sender and charging them for the damage they have caused to their system. "For any company not exclusively Net-based, the certainty of alienating the vast majority of message recipients cannot be worth the effort" (Gellman, 1997). Currently in the US, injunctions are being sought by ISPs for revenue lost and for damage to reputation. Some ISPs have gone so far as to forbid the practice of sending bulk unsolicited e-mails (CNet, 1997).

Autoresponders — programs that automatically and immediately respond to an incoming message with pre-defined characteristics — can be used to combat the problem of long messages. A typical campaign would work as follows. A short e-mail is sent out to the targets, who are invited to send a reply in a specified format if they desire more information. The replies are dealt with by the autoresponder and the complete information is only sent out to the targets who have requested it. This so-called "teaser" campaign is proving quite successful. This is similar to print media campaigns, where direct response advertising is used to invite prospects to apply for further information, with the added advantage of ease of response.

Targeting and Response Rates

This all leads back to one of the tenets of direct marketing: that of targeting. Internet users are more receptive to targeted marketing communication efforts than untargeted (Mehta and Sivadas, 1995). In order to target, you need a list. As with traditional list acquisition, there are a number of firms that sell lists and there is also the possibility of compiling your own list from the e-mail addresses of individuals who visit your website or request information from you.

The providers of traditional lists are now including e-mail addresses in their offerings. All the problems that can be ascribed to traditional lists can be ascribed to e-mail lists, with one additional feature. This is that individuals change their ISP, and thus their e-mail address, quite frequently.

However, the Internet offers another means of building lists. There are newsgroups and discussion groups on almost every subject imaginable on the Internet. This is a group of people who have a particular interest in a topic. There are programs available that will search the groups and extract the e-mail addresses from them, thus supplying the direct marketer with a list that includes prospects in the particular segment that is to be targeted. This allows the marketer to find narrower segments through self-reported interests (Mehta and Sivadas, 1995).

Response rates are also higher with direct e-mail. It may happen that, when direct mail comes in the door, it is discarded without being examined. When direct e-mail is used, the examination rates are higher (Coughlan, 1996).

One-to-One Marketing

Direct marketing strives to achieve one-to-one marketing. The Internet is an ideal vehicle to propel direct marketing to this end. "Using the new media of the one-to-one future, you will be able to communicate directly with consumers, individually, rather than shouting at them, in groups" (Peppers and Rogers, 1995).

While some believe that the Internet is a mass market (NOP Research Group, 1997), many believe that it allows for a one-to-one experience between the individual and the marketer, because it is customer-driven and dialogue-oriented. "This profound promise, of mass customisation to 'markets of one', changes the way direct marketing programs are conceptualised and delivered" (Scofield, 1997). The marketer can market to the individual's needs, not to the broad needs of a target audience. With intensified competition in the marketplace, this can be of great benefit to the marketer. The Internet provides a mechanism for one-to-one marketing called *closed-loop digital marketing* (CDM).

CDM gains information about the individual from several sources: in-house data sources, web-driven forms that the customer completes, traditional data sources and the interaction of the customer with the organisation's web presence (Scofield, 1997). CDM consists of four steps that form a closed loop:

1. Identifying a market segment

2. Deploying a communication strategy

3. Measuring effectiveness

4. Automatically correcting the communication.

This process is supported by sophisticated analysis using neural-network and database technologies. The outcome is "real-time tracking" of Internet customers, with little extra effort and the benefit of gaining time series data on their interactive experiences (Scofield, 1997). The promise of CDM is building long-term customer loyalty.

Customisation implies personalisation. Personalisation requires learning the interests of customers (Scofield, 1997). There are two levels of customisation that can be achieved. By the nature of the medium, the individual can choose what to access, and therefore each individual's experience is unique. On another level, the individual can visit a site that is unique to them, customised to their individual needs. The site changes for each individual in response to the stored information about the individual (Cybersolve, 1997).

Information is stored in a text file, called a "cookie" file, on the user's computer. It is written to by the site and includes information about the user, i.e. what pages they visited. This information can be accessed by the site when the user returns, thus allowing the site to customise itself for the user. On-the-fly page-building programs let you develop a number of static pages, but as your visitors look for more information, new pages are custom-built and personalised in real time to offer a tailored response for each customer (Ahl and Temes, 1997).

Advantages of direct marketing through the Internet include:

- Saves money and helps to stretch the marketing budget

- Saves time and cuts steps from the traditional marketing process

- Offers customers another way to purchase

- Provides a wealth of relevant content

- Interactivity

- Offers instant international reach

- Lowers barriers to entry and offers equal opportunity access to markets

- Offers direct feedback

- Can use multimedia tools to get message across

- Can offer more convenience to both companies and customers

- Provides the option of one-to-one relationship building (Stil and Zimmerman, 1996).

Building an Internet Presence

Previous sections of this chapter have outlined the commercial application of the Internet and various examples of both marketing and direct marketing tactics were also given. This section gives practical advice on evaluating and exploiting the Internet for your business.

Duncan (1997) asserts that there are seven steps to building an effective online presence, as outlined below:

1. *Research all available options to determine how to integrate online media most effectively with your current marketing programme.* Read up on the Internet before spending time and money on something which may not be the optimal solution. Talk with some ISPs (such as Indigo and Ireland OnLine) to get an idea of costs and service offerings. Do not, however, limit yourself to ISPs, as there are a number of innovative companies in Ireland who do not offer Internet connection but may prove a more effective option for your organisation in terms of service, design backgrounds and Internet marketing know-how. Perhaps a better option is to research ISPs for best deals relating to Internet connection fees and then research the varied and growing number of Internet specialist companies in Ireland. An example of one such Internet specialist company is Newmedia Design — a relatively new and highly respected small company whose background is predominantly graphic design. They emphasise the importance of a site that is visually pleasing, thinking of the browser's online experience. But they also adopt a serious marketing approach in terms of service offerings to clients, volunteering ways of approaching the design in terms of adding value. After all Internet avenues are researched, the next step is to decide on the purpose of the

Internet presence — informational, transactional, lead generation? Each purpose will determine what type of web strategy will be most effective.

2. *Determine which type of presence will yield the best result at the lowest cost.* Choices include: WWW homepage, Store Front, Classified Ad, Online Shopping Mall. A comprehensive online marketing plan should be developed that is integrated into the current marketing strategy. An example of this is researching sites that your target audience currently visit.

3. *Identify and articulate the "information value" of your product or service.* What types of information are currently available to your prospects? Which of those can you develop to be of maximum interest to your market? Will you set them up to be downloaded on the spot or will you demand registration or prospect qualifications to send later by e-mail?

4. *Translate these values into interactive copy and design with particular attention to attractive, effectively digitised graphics.* This is where the Blue Peter Principle comes into effect — don't try this at home, as it is imperative when investing in a Web presence to set about it in the right way, so as to avoid later disappointment. Make sure, if outsourcing the website design, to employ designers who have learned HTML, not programmers who know HTML and have no idea of design.

5. *Structure information values with hypertext links to related, user-selectable values and marketing opportunities.* Offer point and click links to other sites of interest to your target market; they will reciprocate, helping to build your Web traffic.

6. *Determine viability of concurrent message support (having your message available in different ways on the medium).* This can be achieved through postings on appropriate Internet directories, newsgroups, mailing lists, forums and message boards.

7. *Support your online marketing investment with appropriate media advertising, direct mail and public relations efforts.*

Promoting the Web Presence

Once your company has a website and Internet connection, it is not enough to sit pretty on the WWW, hoping that a global market of over 90 million consumers will tap into your website (Nua, 1997b). You have to pave a path to your site so that your target audience can find you. An effective web presence requires the promotion of the site both on- and offline. Online promotion involves the use of extensive inbound and outbound Internet marketing strategies and techniques. Offline promotion requires a company to use the traditional communication and marketing media to draw attention to their web presence. Before any discussion on how to promote a web presence, it is essential to ascertain how current Internet users find websites. The graph below shows the results of a recent WWW user survey.

FIGURE 19.1: HOW DO USERS FIND THE WEBSITES THEY VISIT?

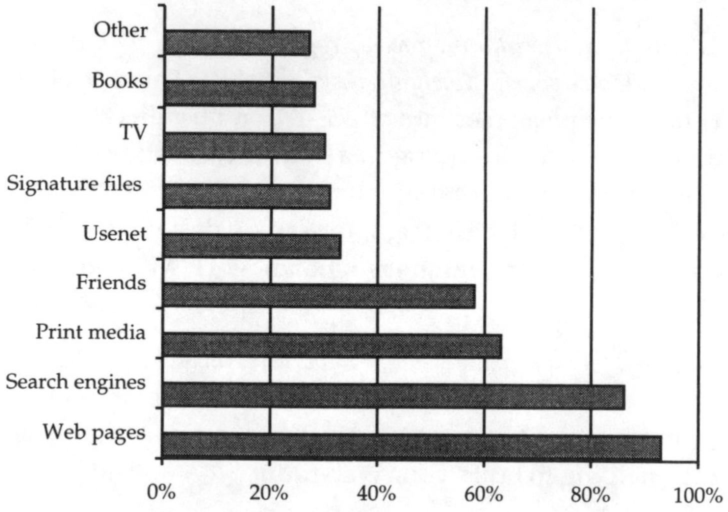

Source: WWW User Surveys Graphics, Visualisation, and Usability Center at Georgia Institute of Technology, 1997.

Online Web Presence Promotion

As mentioned above, effective promotion of a website involves inbound and outbound Internet marketing tactics.

Inbound Internet marketing refers to any tactics employed to boost the number of visitors to your site. Figure 19.1 illustrates that the two most effective guides to finding sites online are through other web pages and through search engines. The most common methods of inbound Internet marketing are outlined below. The simplest method of promoting a website online is by establishing links with other sites that attract your target audience and offering reciprocity. These can be hypertext links (which connect automatically to your site if clicked on) or static links (which show the web address). An example of this method of online promotion in an Irish context would be if *The Irish Times* displayed an icon of a property company in its Thursday online edition. Membership of industry associations, such as the Irish Internet Association (www.iia.ie), will provide hypertext links from their busy site to your site.

The use of "banners" is another method of online inbound Internet marketing. Banners are online advertisements, which can also be either hypertext or static, and work in much the same way as traditional media, i.e. paying for advertising space in places likely to attract your target audience. The use of signature files is a simple and automatic way of getting your web address around the WWW and it costs nothing. A signature file is an option on every e-mail software package that allows you to insert details of your choice to appear automatically at the end of every e-mail that you send. Such details include your name and contact details, including your web address.

The final area of inbound Internet marketing involves the use of search engines. Search engines are services that help a user find sites in their areas of interest. The most well-known and used search engines include Altavista, Excite, Lycos, Infoseek and Yahoo. When a user is looking for sites in a particular field of interest, they type in keywords relevant to their search. Typically, a list of hundreds of website addresses appears. The key challenge is to establish a presence at the top of that list. How? Most search engines sort and present this list according to how relevant the sites are to the user's search topic. Hitting the top of the list is not easy, but the use of tags and the clever placement of descriptive text and key words when writing the body of your web pages increases the probability. Most search engine sites give advice on the selection criteria of the engine and these should be consulted when drafting the text of the site. Search engines can be daunting to the novice, and one should not be discouraged in adopting a web presence based on bad experiences of being lost or unable to find the information required. Patience is a virtue where the Net is concerned.

Outbound Internet marketing strategy refers to any technique on the Internet that is proactive and takes you to the customer, rather than being inactive, waiting for the customer to come to you.

Traynor Kitching & Associates (1997) outline the following five techniques of outbound Internet marketing.

- *Reminder Notices* usually highlight activities about the company, new products and new sections on the site. This is useful, as only users genuinely interested will register and then enter your site when an area of interest attracts them, leading to more targeted traffic.

- *Profiled Information Streams* involve sending customised information to subscribers based on their own information needs. This is useful when a company has a large portfolio of products and services.

- *E-mailed Newsletters* act as an extension to the website which strengthen the corporate image and create a sense of an online community for readers. An Irish success story in this case is Nua Internet Developers with their "Nua Internet Surveys", which has a weekly readership of 90,000 people.

- *Discussion List Participation*

- *Online Conferences.*

For the last two techniques above to be successful, the list members must be part of the target audience. They offer an opportunity for a targeted forum to promote an organisation's knowledge of the industry in an informative and informal way.

Offline Web Presence Marketing

As the title suggests, offline web presence marketing involves promoting the web address through any available means other than the Internet, namely conventional media and corporate stationery. The insertion of web addresses in broadcast and print advertisements has increased dramatically over the past ten months; the recent inclusion of the RTE web address on the credits of the news is an example.

Including your web address on all corporate literature is a good first step, but a compelling reason to visit the site is essential. Offering a facility or service not available in other media is a possibility. For example, Tayto have a website where you can order boxes of crisps online and arrange for them to be delivered to people abroad in one sitting. Another possibility is simply offering advice or information free to visitors. Many drinks companies offer cocktail recipes and invite users to upload their own recipes. An additional way of promoting the web address is through magazines — including the web address in a small classified section in the back of a publication read by your target audience. This is an inexpensive option. Most Irish publications feature articles on the Internet and the WWW in every other issue. Try writing a press release to the editors informing them of your website; it will have to be something interesting or exciting to gain attention. Try anything — since you have invested in a web presence, you may as well invest a little more in promoting that presence.

Food for Thought — The Future

"Many equate technology with taxes — inevitable. They are right" (Maguire, 1996). This quote illustrates the inescapable truth: the Internet is here to stay. The precise targeting of consumer groups and direct communication with the customer through technology such as the Internet makes for more cost-effective direct marketing.

This does not mean that marketing costs will be reduced by interactive technology, but it will make marketing communication more efficient. Ubiquitous and mobile technology will broadly extend the number of places where a business can capture and process information and thus be effectively present (Haeckel, 1994).

The need for information searching and browsing will always exist. The Internet will "evolve into a mix of push and pull demand" (Cybersolve, 1997). The introduction of "push" technology will deliver data to the user. The pioneer of this technology was a company called Pointcast. Under this system, the user subscribes to specific information channels, and can view the information as it is produced, without having to search for it. Pointcast and its competitors are "similar to the television broadcast model in which users subscribe to specific channels of information and where information is constantly updated" (Formenski, 1997). The advantage to the direct marketer is customised information. The information is specific to the needs of the user and also saves time, as the user is not required to search for the information.

There are many myths prevailing about the legality of doing business on the Internet. "The Internet is not a lawless place . . . the same basic laws apply" (McGovern, 1996). One example is the law of copyright. "The cost of making digital copies is zero, copies are exact, copies are simple to create and the quality does not diminish according to the number of copies made" (Cybersolve, 1997). The judicial issues are new and undeveloped. This may be true in the specific context of the Internet, but the experience with respect to marketing by telephone and fax — all new media in their day — exists (Forster, 1997). Domain names also create concerns. When a domain name is registered, many companies seek to protect it by trademark. However, different countries have different policies with regard to trademarks (Cybersolve, 1997). Different nations also have different policies on content regulation. Commerce conducted via the Internet will be subject to differing tax laws in differing jurisdictions, since electronic commerce will cross borders. The way forward is an international treaty on the Internet.

In the current model of technology, companies are investing significant resources in software for their employees. The Internet can offer an alternative. Instead of hosting all the software on each personal computer, the software is hosted at another location and is accessed on demand by each employee from a network computer. The network computer usually has limited memory, evoking memories of the "dumb terminals" of old.

The network computer is perhaps not appropriate for all employees, but has become especially relevant for customer service. The maintenance of such a system is less complex from an administrator's viewpoint. It is also a cheaper method of software distribution. The individual organisation does not have to pay for multiple copies of expensive software, but can subscribe to a service where the required number of copies is available on demand.

Such products represent a move away from the concept of selling software by the copy towards charging the user each time the software is used. "Software objects differ from tangible objects in being fundamentally unable to monitor their copying but trivially able to monitor their use" (Cox, 1992). This new selling concept is a viable anti-piracy measure, as counting how many times software has been invoked is relatively easy (McGovern, 1996).

The future of the Internet is in the hands of the users. In a survey by FIND/SVP in 1997, users were asked what they saw as the future of the Internet (Figure 19.2).

FIGURE 19.2: THE FUTURE OF THE INTERNET

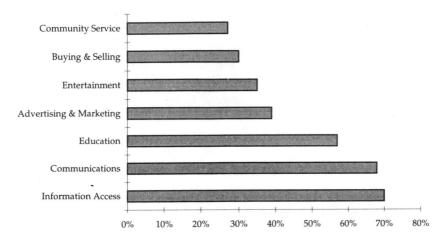

Source: FIND/SVP (1997).

Communication and information access emerged as being the main items that users felt were going to be important for them. This is something that direct marketing can build on; information-rich and innovative campaigns can meet these expectations.

Security is a major issue on the Internet. Secure electronic transaction (SET) is an emerging standard for secure electronic commerce, developed and approved by a group of companies including VISA, Mastercard, American Express and Microsoft (Sympatico, 1997). This uses encryption techniques. "To encrypt something means to scramble and jumble it about, so that if someone looks at it, it is just a bunch of characters and numbers" (McGovern, 1996). The recipient will have software to "de-crypt" the message. There are also security issues with regard to online crime, such as unauthorised access to remote computers. Businesses are developing firewalls to deny access to those who should not have access. The Internet allows for anonymity, which creates its own problems for conducting business.

However, this can be overcome through the use of encryption. An Irish company, Baltimore Technologies, is at the leading edge of encryption software development.

The Internet has many wonderful and revolutionary advantages, but it is not a medium that should as yet be depended upon for time- or business-critical functions. The fact that the infrastructure is under strain is understandable, as no-one believed it would have so many users from its quite specialised beginnings (McGovern, 1996).

Sound, animation, online video, virtual reality: these are some of the new technologies that are appearing on the Internet.

> The current bandwidths are too small to handle such large amounts of data in a timely manner. In the future, all these plumbing problems will be resolved and when that happens the Web will rule . . . mercilessly because of mass accessibility (Diorio and Diorio, 1997).

CONCLUSION

It has been stressed that the Internet, still in the embryonic stages of development, is here to stay and "it is critical for firms to hop on now and start riding the experience curve. You have to be online to understand online" (Hoffman, 1997). However, the need to adopt a strategic approach when considering a web presence is critical, i.e. using the same decision-making processes as you would with any other media or in terms of overall business strategy. Jumping on the bandwagon and going online without thoroughly researching the options for your organisation can only lead to disappointment, which is regretful when a media as multi-faceted as the Internet is not exploited. Neither is hoping that the Internet is the answer to all organisational weaknesses the attitude to adopt.

> In the world of business, too, digital technology has its limits. It cannot sell an otherwise weak product, make a bad business plan work, or salvage inept marketing programmes, inadequate channel distribution and inappropriate pricing strategies (Burnstein and Kline, 1995).

The Internet is not the answer, but it is a powerful interactive media that, when used effectively, can reap many rewards. Certainly, companies can continue to prosper without it, but mere survival is not the axiom of commerce. Optimisation is every organisation's goal and if the Internet propels an organisation closer to achieving that goal, it should not be ignored. In ten years' time, it will be just another option in the marketer's toolkit, a standard marketing practice with very little fuss. Invention has always been celebrated by few and feared by many in the early days. Those in the know believed that nobody would ever speak face-to-face again when the telephone was invented. Technology is changing so fast these days that this chapter is already dated. However laborious it is to keep up, that is no argument to reject change, as the implications of technology for marketing will outweigh the pains of pace. We end with a quotation which typifies the experience of being digitally connected to the world. Literally translated, it means, "Traveller, there is no path, you make the path as you walk".

> Caminante no hay camino se hace el camino, al andar.
> — Antonio Machado

REFERENCES

ABT (1997), "Irish Exporters Target Worldwide Internet Sales", www.irish-trade.ie.

Ahl, D. and P. Temes (1997), "E-commerce's Future: Page Building, Phone", www.dmnews.com/web_marketing.html.

Block, W. (1997), "Laughing all the Way", www.bookinfo.com.

Burnstein, D. and D. Kline (1995) *Road Warriors: Dreams and Nightmares along the Information Highway*, New York: Dutton Books.

Chase, L. (1996), "Reality Check: the Net is a Better Money Saver than Money Maker", www. chaseonline.com/marketing/hr.html.

Childers, E. (1967) in "Ireland: the Digital Age — the Internet", www.forbairt.ie/internet.html

CNet (1997), "31 Percent Increase in Internet Sales", www.cnet.com.

Coughlan, C. (1996), "Wild Future Stuff — New and Emerging Media Technologies", *Irish Marketing Journal*, Vol. 9, No. 1, April.

Cox, B. (1992), "What If There is a Silver Bullet and the Competition Gets it First?", *Journal of Object Oriented Programming*, Vol. 3.

Cybersolve (1997), "Marketing on the Internet", www.cybersolve.com

Dibb, S., L. Simkin, W. Pride and O. Ferrell (1997), *Marketing: Concepts and Strategies*, Boston: Houghton Mifflin.

Diorio, T. and D. Diorio (1997), "The Valley of Decision: Web Presence or Interactive CD Presentation?", www.d10r10.com/text.html.

Duncan, G. (1997), "Learning to Sell in CyberSpace", www.DMWorld.com.

Ellsworth, J. and M. Ellsworth (1995), *Marketing on the Internet: Multimedia Strategies for the World Wide Web*, New York: Wiley.

Ellsworth, J. and M. Ellsworth (1996), *The Internet Business Book*, New York: Wiley, p. 228.

FIND/SVP (1997), "How Users see the Future of the Internet" in "Nua Internet Surveys: Graphs and Charts: Internet Future", www.nua.ie/surveys.

Formenski, T. (1997), *A Better Way to Stay in Touch, Doing Financial Business Online*, London: Financial Times Surveys and *.net*.

Forster, C. (1997), "Financial Services and the Internet", *ACCA Financial Services Newsletter*, Issue 44, November/December, p. 5.

Freeman, C. and C. Perez (1988), "Structural Crisis of Adjustment, Business Cycles and Investment Behaviour" in G. Dosi, C. Freeman, R. Nelson, G. Silverberg, and L. Soete (eds.), *Technical Change and Economic Theory*, London: Pinter, pp. 1–19.

Gellman, R. (1997), *Why is Spam So Boringly, Predictably Time-Consuming?*, www.dmnews.com.

Granger, M. and D. Schroeder (1996), "Integrating the Internet into the Business Environment", *Internet Research: Electronic Networking Applications and Policy*, Vol. 6, pp. 2–3.

Haeckel, S. (1994), "Managing the Information Intensive Firm of 2001" in R. Battenberg, R. Glazer and J. Little (eds.), *The Marketing*

Information Revolution, Boston, MA: Harvard Business School Press.

Hoffman, D. (1997), "The Vision of an Accomplished Web Marketer", www.december.com/cmc/mag/1996/jun/hoffman.html.

IIA (1997), "Irish Internet Association Online User Survey", www.iia.ie/survey/.

International Data Corporation (1997), "Dramatic Growth of Web Commerce", www.idcresearch.com/f/HNR/ic2001f.htm.

Maguire, T. (1996), "Global Electronic Connections" in *IDMA Brave New Media Conference Proceedings*, Dublin: IDMA.

McCorkell, G. (1992), *Why Direct Marketing Remains Poised for Further Growth — The Practitioners Guide to Direct Marketing*, London: Institute of Direct Marketing.

McGovern, G. (1996), "State of the Net" in *IDMA Brave New Media Conference Proceedings*, Dublin: Irish Direct Marketing Association.

McGovern, G. (1997), "New Thinking: Ownership in the Digital Age" in *Electronic Newsletter*, Dublin: Nua Ltd.

Mehta, R. and E. Sivadas (1995), "Direct Marketing on the Internet: An Empirical Assessment of Consumer Attitudes", *Journal of Direct Marketing*, Vol. 9, No. 3, Summer, 21–31.

Mehta, R. and E. Sivadas (1996), "International Direct Marketing on the Internet: Do Internet Users form a Global Segment?", *Journal of Direct Marketing*, Vol. 10, No. 1, Winter, 15–22.

Melin (1997) in R. Heath (1997) "Working the Web", www.marketingtools.com.

Midas-Net Ireland (1997), "Second Irish Internet/Multimedia Survey", www.midas.ie/2ndSurvey.html.

Miller, R. (1997), "The Internet in Twenty Years: Cyberspace, the Next Frontier?", www.oecd.org/sge/au/highligh.htm.

Mullich, J. (1995), "Web Sale Opportunities: Dangers Abound", *Technology and Marketplace*, April.

National Academy of Sciences (1996), *The Unpredictable Uncertainty: Information Infrastructure Through 2000*, Washington: National Academy Press.

NOP Research Group (1997), "Surveys", www.nopres.co.uk/internet.htm.

Nua (1997a), "Consolidation of the Internet and America Leads, Asia follows, Europe Ponders", in "Nua Internet Surveys — Review and Analysis", Dublin: Nua, July/August, www.nua.ie.

Nua (1997b), "Nua's How Many Online", www.nua.ie/howmany.html.

Peppers, D. and Rogers, M. (1995), "A New Marketing Paradigm: Share of Customers, Not Market Share", *Planning Review*, March/April.

Phillips, P. (1996), "Gold Fever in Cyberspace" in A. Baines and S. Lloyd (eds.), *The Handbook of International Direct Marketing*, Third Edition, London: Kogan Page.

Rapp, S. and S. Collins (1995) *The New Maxi-marketing*, McGraw-Hill, New York.

Rushbrook, L. (1995), "Buying in the Cybermarket", *Marketing*, March.

Scofield, C. (1997), "CDM Lets Programs Get Personal", www.dmnews.com/web_marketing.html.

Shultz, D.E. (1994), "From the Editor: Will the Information Highway Be Filled with Cyberjunk and Roadkill", *Journal of Direct Marketing*, Vol. 8, No. 3, Summer, 3–5.

Stil, A. and R. Zimmerman (1996), "Direct Marketing Through the Internet," Unpublished Thesis, Rotterdam: College of Economics and Business.

Sympatico (1997), "What is a Secure Electronic Transaction (SET)?", www.nf.sympatico.ca/Sympatico_Help/Advisories/set.html.

Traynor Kitching & Associates (1997), "Outbound Internet Marketing", www.u-net.com.

Chapter 20

VIRTUAL SHOPPING

Alan Leibert

Overview

Traditionally, people purchased goods face to face in markets and shops. Once a person was known to a shopkeeper, they could telephone orders and receive goods by delivery. Later the concept of mail order developed with delivery by post, courier or personalised delivery service. Mail order flourished as the suppliers of the service allowed their customers to pay off on a weekly basis for the goods they purchased. This gave access to the consumer marketplace for the less well off.

In recent times, as the nation has become more mobile, local shopping parades have given way to city centre shops; still more recently, the out-of-town shopping mall has flourished. With each change, the previous methods of shopping have remained but have declined somewhat in their success. For example, local shopping parades housing local owner-occupier shops have declined in favour of out-of-town shopping malls; while traditional mail-order companies are in decline as the nation becomes more affluent.

Nevertheless, the full range of shopping possibilities has remained, with some routes to market comparing better than others. Virtual shopping is a new route to market that may be likened to electronic mail order. With virtual shopping, the customer purchases electronically using some form of computer interface, probably pays at the time of order with a credit card, and receives the goods via some form of delivery service similar to that employed in mail order.

This chapter raises some of the issues involved in virtual shopping. It looks at the technologies involved, which include the telephone, the personal computer, television and the Internet. The chapter concludes with a marketing case history of Virtual Precincts Limited and the SmartZone virtual shopping mall.

VIRTUAL SHOPPING — THE ISSUES

Before dealing with the details of virtual shopping, there are some key issues that must be noted:

- Virtual shopping will never eclipse other methods of shopping, particularly face-to-face trading, since some goods need to be examined or tried on before purchase. Indeed, virtual shopping may well enhance face-to-face shopping as the purchaser may use virtual shopping to check upon stock availability and carry out a shop-to-shop price comparison before embarking on a visit to the high street.

- Virtual shopping may well work to the benefit of the small shopkeeper rather than the large retailer, since in a virtual world all shops are equal. Position does not count and shops are all of infinite size. What is significant is the price and quality of goods held — the traditional retail benefit, and the expertise with which the virtual shop is built and presented — which implies the quality of bought-in programming expertise.

- Since virtual shops are of infinite size, all stock may be presented. This overcomes the real-shop limitations of shops with a large stock range, such as bookshops; those with bulky stock, such as furniture suppliers; and those with expensive stock, such as jewellers.

- Payment is invariably made or committed at the time of purchase, but an electronic terminal will not accept cash or cheques. Therefore, plastic cards are implied. At the present time, this pushes virtual shopping up-market; however, the development of the smart-card-based electronic purse (see the separate chapter in this book), which is analogous to cash, will permit those without bank accounts to trade electronically.

It is believed that virtual shopping will develop rapidly in the coming years, capturing up to 20 per cent of the available retail marketplace. It is uncertain whether it will displace other methods of shopping or simply expand the retail marketplace; probably the answer is a little of both.

VIRTUAL SHOPPING — THE TECHNOLOGY

Telephone

So how does a person interact with a computer system to shop electronically? At one level, a person could simply use their telephone, enter goods codes on the keypad and receive computer-generated spoken responses. But this would be rather tedious, and it is more likely that this type of virtual shopping will develop only as telephones develop to include large displays with a graphics capability.

Such telephones are being developed under names such as transaction phones. In general, they contain a small computer, a credit card reader, an extended keypad to include alphabetic characters and a multi-line graphics display panel. It should be noted that, at the same time as these land-based telephones are being developed, so are mobile phones such as the Nokia 9000 mobile phone, personal organisers and pocket computers. In essence, we have a convergent set of technologies leading to a low-cost, multi-function transaction terminal that may be used for virtual shopping, among many other things.

With this type of device, one simply has to dial up the appropriate shopping service or electronic vendor, scan stock, place orders and make payment. Although the technology was still in its infancy in the late 1980s, the Keyline shopping service was set up to provide this type of virtual shopping and the Keyline terminal was built along the lines described above. It was not a success, primarily because the man–machine interface was not sufficiently attractive or simple enough for all to use.

The Home PC

The moral of the Keyline story is that if you make shopping difficult, the customer will not buy. Indeed, as will be discussed later, exactly the same moral applies to the many retail failures that tried selling via the Internet. However, before talking about the Internet, let us continue to pursue the issue of man–machine interface.

We have seen above that the telephone and products derived from it may make attractive electronic commerce terminals for some applications, but not for shopping, even if the shopper had printed product sheets in front of them — goods and prices change too rapidly.

A clearly better customer interface for virtual shopping is the home PC. Using a PC, one has the full power of multimedia graphics and sound. Goods may be displayed in colour and rotated, and video clips may be shown. In the US, where the PC is more prevalent in the home, and where it is treated more as a commodity product like the telephone, the PC is fast-becoming accepted as a virtual shopping terminal. However, the same is not true of the UK and Ireland, and even less so for the non-English-speaking countries.

The Television Set

The ideal shopping terminal would be one that the shopper is well used to using, has a large colour screen interface, is common in most households and is found in convenient locations in the home. This is, of course, the television set; in combination with an appropriate interface unit or "set-top box", it makes the ideal home shopping terminal. In this mode, the television set plus set-top box is the equivalent of a PC.

So having identified a sensible man-machine interface, the next step is to consider the nature of service required for virtual shopping, which will identify the requirement for the necessary backing infrastructure for a useful virtual shopping service. In its simplest mode, virtual shopping implies connection to a remote computer, so that the shopper may interact to browse goods, find out more about an item, purchase goods, pay for them and arrange delivery.

Clearly an interactive service is required. The most obvious connection for virtual shopping would be a telephone line; however, other good candidates would be the fibre cable television connection or some form of radio system such as that offered in the UK by Ionica. At this point we should consider the Internet.

The Internet/World Wide Web

The Internet/World Wide Web offers two key components for virtual shopping:

- A standard interface

- Access to world-wide databases.

The standard interface means that interface equipment can be built which will be guaranteed to work with all Internet-compatible services, while access to world-wide databases opens up a whole world of shopping to the customer. Any vendor anywhere in the world can create a virtual shop database on the Internet and start selling products.

Nevertheless, the Internet as it stands does not offer a good virtual shopping environment, for the following reasons:

- It is an open environment, which means that anyone can set up a virtual shop. There are no controls and the shopper has no idea whether or not the goods will be delivered, or even which country the virtual shop is operating from.

- The shopper has no idea about where their payment is going, whether it is being hacked and whether this gives criminals access to their credit card account.

- Because each vendor sets up its own virtual shop, the look and feel of each is different, which can be very confusing to the shopper.

- Finding shops that sell specific items is very difficult. One has to "surf the Net", using search engines such as Yahoo and Infoseek. Can the little old lady at home really do this?

- Performance can be abysmal, regardless of the communication line speed between the terminal and the local Internet service provider. This means that working one's way through shop departments can be very tedious. To see any form of graphic, let alone a video clip, can be nigh on impossible.

There are various solutions that have evolved to overcome these problems and certainly in time, the Internet will become very much better and Internet shopping more practical. Nevertheless, at the moment, Internet shopping is really for business-to-business corporate activity and the "anorak brigade".

Virtual Shopping Malls

One way to improve Internet shopping is to group shops together into "virtual shopping malls". These have the advantage of being easily found, they can guarantee that goods will be delivered, they can provide a secure and certified payment mechanism and they can mandate a common look and feel interface to the shops on the mall; although only a few do this. However, what they cannot do is improve access performance.

Access performance may be improved by placing the shopping mall database onto the local Internet service provider's server. To make this service easy to find, and indeed to make it the preferred customer service, the Internet service provider will create a direct pointer to the virtual shopping service as the user logs on to the Internet. In fact, the service may be such that open access to the Internet is barred or made difficult, while a range of local services are offered via a simple interface. This is the type of service offered by WebTV and NetChannel.

The usability of virtual shopping, given a local shopping mall, will then be dependent on the nature of the connection between the Internet service provider and the customer. A normal telephone line connection up to 33 Kb/s is simply too slow, as graphics display still takes too long for interesting shop- and product-browsing. An ISDN line running at 64 Kb/s is adequate for graphics, but too slow for video clips and anything but the smallest Java Applets. On the other hand, a broadband link of 2 Mb/s, as offered by the fibre cable operators via a cable modem service or a fully digital service, is adequate for all purposes.

CASE HISTORY: VIRTUAL PRECINCTS LIMITED

Virtual Precincts Limited offers the SmartZone™ broadband shopping mall direct to shoppers at television terminals, PCs and kiosk terminals in public places. The service is run as an Intranet service — that is, it is Internet compatible but not available on the open Internet — at 2 Mb/s over the fibre cable television network. Using this configuration, the shopper sees an instant real-time multimedia shopping mall down which they can "walk" and enter shops. Inside the shop, they can see helper video clips, rotate products, change colours, etc., depending on the way the retailer wishes to present its goods. The virtual shopping experience is at least as good as the shopper's children's video games such as Doom.

The shopper carrying out virtual shopping will typically be sitting at home watching television and will switch to their Internet service. The managed Internet service provider service will offer the viewer a series of "managed" Internet services, including the SmartZone™ virtual shopping mall. The shopper can enter the mall and "go shopping".

Besides "shopping trips", the shopper may impulse buy. Consider a person watching a television programme when the ads come on. An ad is shown promoting a product that the person wishes to purchase. No waiting until the next day — just flick over to SmartZone™ and make the purchase. Consider the marketing benefits that brings.

It is expected that shops on the virtual mall will be smaller shops that cannot afford to take space in the out-of-town mall, those that have fulfilment mechanisms in place such as direct marketing outlets, and those that presently do not sell retail but wish to, for example manufacturers and importers. So the virtual mall will contain a wide variety of interesting shops selling many different goods and services.

The national implementation of SmartZone™ is based around Intranet servers located around the country. This allows virtual shops to be replicated or mirrored around the country to provide national coverage. It also allows some shops only to be represented locally in local malls. So the shop without a national distribution capability can service just its local community. Even the local pizza delivery service may be represented on a local mall.

Besides service delivery to the home, virtual shopping will be made available at many other locations via kiosks, PC terminals and television sets. Key locations will include large office blocks, business parks, hotels, hospitals, clubs, universities and airport lounges. That is, anywhere a person can be found in a warm, dry and comfortable location where there is no ready access to real shops. It is expected that virtual shopping from non-home locations will prove to be equally as significant as home shopping, although home virtual shopping will probably dominate through sheer weight of numbers.

Virtual Precincts Limited, in building the SmartZone™ shopping mall, is starting in the UK with UK-based virtual shops. It intends to expand this to include retailers who do not have a physical presence in the UK but wish to sell there. Subsequently, it will take SmartZone™ into other countries and sell UK goods into those countries. The end result will be an international global virtual shopping city.

Virtual Precincts Limited is but one example of the growing trend towards virtual shopping which, in the very near future, will be available to all of us.

Chapter 21

SMART CARDS

Joanne Reader

Overview

Since the first plastic payment card was issued in the UK in the 1960s, the concept of payment tokens, and the plastic card as a medium, have developed considerably. This chapter outlines the growth in payment cards and the issues that their success has created, together with details of the background to smart cards and the associated benefits for marketers. The main part of this chapter focuses on the applications that the smart card can support and the benefits of each for the supplier and consumer. The final part of this chapter contains a case study of one such application, the electronic purse.

SMART CARDS DEFINED

A smart card is a normal plastic card with a silicon microchip embedded into the front or reverse in order to provide security/fraud control and store additional data.

Plastic cards are now part of our everyday lives, with more than two-thirds of adults in Britain carrying a debit or credit card. In 1995, some 54 million payment cards in the UK were used to buy £68 billion worth of goods and services at a vast array of retail outlets and businesses. By the year 2000, it is predicted that the volume of purchases by plastic cards will reach some three billion per year in the UK. In Ireland, there are currently 1.5 million payment cards, which are used to buy £2.5 billion worth of goods and services.

However, a symptom of the success of plastic cards is card fraud. Measures such as the increase in online authorisations (card issuer approval), the lowering of the floor limits, over which authorisations are obtained, the use of "Hot Card" files (lost, stolen and cancelled cards) and the use of knowledge-based systems, have all helped to cut plastic card fraud losses (from stolen cards) from an all-time high of £165 million in 1991 to £97 million in 1994.

Despite such co-ordinated and effective action between banks and retailers, there is still concern over the level of losses from counterfeit. Although this only represents about ten per cent of UK fraud losses, counterfeit fraud is an area of potential growth.

In a bid to stop plastic card fraudsters in their tracks, banks and building societies are creating new chip-based plastic cards, or smart cards as they are commonly known. A silicon microchip (a wafer of semi-conductor forming an integrated circuit) is embedded into an ordinary plastic card to turn it into a chip card. There are two types of chip cards:

- The less sophisticated chip does not contain a microprocessor, although data can still be stored securely

- The more sophisticated type of chip contains a microprocessor, enabling it to perform complicated mathematical calculations used in security functions.

Chip cards can therefore be used to provide a highly secure card authentication method (CAM) which aims to ensure that the plastic card is genuine and not counterfeit.

The majority of plastic cards use magnetic stripe technology for data storage and security, although the information can easily be copied onto a counterfeit card, allowing fraud to take place. The counterfeit card can look exactly the same as the genuine article and there is no way of detecting it at the point of sale. The technology required to copy data from a chip card to a counterfeit card is beyond the ability of present-day fraudsters. The information sent online to the card issuer to authenticate the card changes for every transaction. This is because the chip, as a microprocessor, is able to validate the identity by the use of cryptography. Cryptography is a means of sending the receiving messages in code. Each chip contains data that are transmitted during its electronic conversations with the card reader or point-of-sale terminal in an online situation to the card issuer. The data are encoded during all transmissions using cryptography. This cryptographic information is confirmed by either the card reader or the card issuer using cryptographic techniques. A further coded message can be sent back to the card by the issuer. The card will confirm this encoded message using sophisticated cryptographic techniques. The coded messages are constructed using a secret key and a complicated mathematical formula. The key is held securely by the card issuer and cannot be extracted or copied. It is also programmed securely into the chip during manufacture. The combination of the key and cryptography, together with the physical constraints imposed by the chip, provide a secure environment.

Also, any attempt to physically remove the chip from the card in order to copy it would cause the chip to "blow a fuse" and it could not be copied.

The first chip card was devised in 1970 by Kunitaka Arimura of the Arimura Technology Institute in Japan. In 1974, a Frenchman, Roland Moreno, patented the chip card concept and this heralded the start of the chip card revolution in France. The French government recognised the potential of the chip card and the opportunity that the technology offered to two of its main industries in bringing them into the twenty-first century. The French government invested $27 billion in the modernisation of its telecommunications and in the conversion of the banking system. Chip card technology helped reduce the volume of cheques being processed (three million in 1980) by providing an electronic online service. There are now over 22 million debit cards with a chip in France.

SMART CARD BENEFITS

Each chip can currently store the equivalent of about four pages of information in its memory, whilst magnetic stripes hold just four lines. As a result, chip cards offer far more to the banks, retailers and consumers than just fraud prevention. With their capacity to store large amounts of account and transaction data, chip cards are opening up the possibility of providing customers with multiple applications on the same plastic card. The smart card scheme operators and card issuers are interested in multi-application cards for a number of reasons, besides the fraud prevention benefits previously outlined:

- The business case for smart cards requires more revenue to justify the current expense of converting cards and the supporting infrastructures to be chip-capable

- In order to create acceptance and demand amongst consumers and retailers, greater value is demanded, particularly in the case where some retailers' expenditure is required to create a chip-based point-of-sale infrastructure

- The hardware costs of creating multi-application capability are little different to those required to create a single application

- Any multi-application card product offering in a given market will force competition on the basis of similar or superior propositions

- The technology and associated systems are readily available for implementation and exploitation, and it is only the pace at which the consumer and retailer will accept change that dictates progress

- If consumers and retailers can obtain multi-application capability for the same price or start-up cost as a single application, then it is inevitable that demand will focus on multi-application products.

SMART CARD APPLICATIONS

A multi-application card is essentially a smart card containing two or more software-driven applications or uses. Through this software the smart card is destined to change fundamentally the way that consumers buy products, receive and use services, and the way that marketers sell products and deliver services. Today, multi-application card products are more prevalent in theory than in practice, but the opportunities include:

- *Electronic Purse or Stored Value*: The capability of the chip to store money, units or a token of value which can be used for low-value purchases which would traditionally be made in cash, and where transaction speed is normally important

- *Loyalty*: The use of a chip card as both the loyalty token and the data capture and transfer mechanism, linked to a given scheme operator

- *Cardholder Verification Methods*: To enable verification at the point of sale that the person presenting the card is actually the cardholder

- *Electronic Banking*: Secure banking from the home, office or place of education

- *Electronic Shopping*: Secure shopping over the Internet and other such networks from the comfort of the home, office or place of education

- *Information Storage*: The use of the data capacity of the chip to store personalised and non-personalised data such as passport details, driving licence information, membership details, etc.

- *Access Control*: To provide a token for authorised access in companies, educational establishments, military sites, clubs and societies, etc.

In order to assess the changes that will be required of marketers as a result of the smart card revolution, it is necessary to consider each of the potential applications or benefits in more detail.

Electronic Purse

Firstly, the electronic purse or stored value card application, which in its simplest form has been around for a number of years, as the origins of the concept lie in the phonecard. Since this time, increasing numbers of products have been developed in transport, car parking and vending, although the technology platform on which they were based, and the fact that they could only be used for one type of purchase, meant that their spread has been limited. Since the advent of the chip card, to which the traditional phonecard is being converted, a number of large co-ordinated, multi-usage electronic purse schemes have emerged as alternatives to cash for low-value purchases.

Early electronic purse applications have been created using stand-alone cards, although the more recent pilots and trials have begun introducing electronic purse applications that reside on the chip of an existing payment card, creating multi-application cards. We now have a situation where the card issuer or bank can provide the consumer with added value and encourage increased usage of their payment card, with the ultimate promise of ensuring that they do not need to carry cash. Electronic purse schemes are being launched all around the world, with notable examples of schemes including Visa Cash, Mondex and Proton. For more details of the electronic purse application, see the case study at the end of the chapter.

Loyalty

Within an increasingly competitive sales environment, retailers are challenged with safeguarding their existing customer base, growing and expanding their businesses, improving profitability and creating a customer database. However, the features of smart cards that create these advantages (intelligence, data storage capacity and security) bring challenges for the retailer — for example, providing security to protect the cardholder without inconvenience at the point of sale, getting the relevant data onto the card in the first instance, managing a potentially large, fragmented database and interfacing new hardware to ensure that delays are avoided at the checkout.

Most businesses considering developing a loyalty scheme aim for short-term financial gain, long-term customer relationships and improved targeting of customer communication, whilst the consumer demands achievable rewards in realistic timescales, supported by relevant and effective communication and an easy-to-use mechanism. The smart card in achieving this also assists marketers in providing visual promotion of the scheme to reinforce the brand and act as a constant reminder to the customer that they have a relationship with the retailer. Although smart loyalty cards are being applied in multi-retailer consortiums, we have yet to see a multi-application smart loyalty card, despite the fact that this is now technically feasible. However, in an age when alliances are becoming more commonplace, it is only a matter of time.

Cardholder Verification Methods

There has been considerable discussion about the benefits of smart cards in the fight against counterfeit, although the microchip brings with it the opportunity to introduce cardholder verification methods (CVM) to ensure that the presenter of the card is actually the cardholder. CVM is based on the principle of the chip storing the digitised data for checking against that presented by the cardholder to the point-of-sale terminal. Various methods are being researched by the banks. These include the use of PINs (personal identification numbers) at the point of sale, which would help to reduce cardholder disputes, although it is not a unique identifier of the cardholder and could be compromised. There are also a number of biometric methods in research, such as fingerprint scanning, signature dynamics (the way that the signature is formed), retina scanning, voice pattern recognition, hand geometry and facial pattern recognition. For a method to be adopted, it must have a minute false rejection rate, not disadvantage any customer types, have cost effective enrolment and be feasible at the point of sale. The ultimate CVM is probably DNA, although as with many of the methods described, it may not find favour with the consumer, or provide sufficient benefits for the retailer and consumer to accept.

Electronic Banking and Home Shopping

Electronic banking and home shopping are a 1990s development that, although feasible without the smart card, will actually grow in importance and usage with it. Much has been made of the security issues that surround trading across networks, and the increased risk for both cardholders and retailers. With the smart card, and the development of complementary technology enabling PCs to read the chip on a smart card just as a traditional point-of-sale would, many banks are developing electronic banking and shopping services. These developments support the move to chip technology by the banks and retail loyalty schemes and enables these organisations to respond to the demands of the increasingly discerning, busy consumer who has greater access to technology.

Information Storage

Microchips today only use a fraction of the inherent data storage capacity, presenting opportunities for this additional capacity to be rented by third parties. One such use of this unused capacity is the storage of information about the cardholder, be it social security data, national insurance numbers, driving licence or passport details or simply membership details. For the primary application owner, the existence of additional data only serves to strengthen the cardholder's attachment to the card and loyalty to the primary application provider, whilst the retailers have the potential to collect additional data about the cardholder for the fields that they are authorised to access. To date, exploitation of this type of application on a multi-application card is really only in evidence in universities and other educational establishments where the card issuer (the university) owns all applications. For this type of development to succeed in a more open environment will require resolution of issues such as card ownership, branding and data protection, before card issuers can even begin to tackle the complex task of consumer awareness and education.

Access Control

The final potential application that I would like to highlight is the ability of the smart card to be used for access control. Tokens of identification for access are not a new phenomenon, but the smart card brings with it the ability to configure variable access privileges, which can be amended by downloading changes to the card readers to update the card next time it is presented. This type of application is being heavily adopted in environments such as military sites and educational establishments where the justification for the scheme has been based upon the opportunities that the smart card technology presents for multiple applications. In these environments, multi-application cards provide a range of benefits for the scheme operator through cost savings and new income streams, and benefits for the consumer through added value services, convenience and the need to carry only one card in a world which is increasingly being dominated by plastic cards.

Whilst smart cards are issued free of charge from the banks and other scheme operators, single card applications are likely to continue in isolation for some time to come. However, as soon as consumers have to pay for their smart cards, their needs will only be satisfied by multi-application cards where each application creates consumer benefits and consumers have control over the applications that reside on their cards. Clearly this creates a whole new set of challenges for the marketers in co-ordinating complementary applications, protecting branding and effectively communicating the applications and delivery channels. However, through the advent of the smart card, marketers will be able to respond more effectively to the demands of consumers for choice, convenience, personalisation, security and access.

SMART CARDS IN IRELAND

Although not the pioneers of smart card technology, Ireland has produced a host of innovative companies who are becoming well-respected in international markets for their contribution to the development and exploitation of smart cards. In addition, a number of banks, local authorities and transport operators are providing their own contribution through leading-edge smart card trials.

One example of such a development is the CAROLAN project in Dublin. The CAROLAN project represents a card-based offline linked payment for transport networks. The purpose of the CAROLAN project is to provide a way of integrating the ticketing systems from a number of different transport mechanisms using different operators through a common payment method. Based in Dublin city centre and in the suburb of Bray, approximately 25 kilometres from the city, CAROLAN combines off-street parking, local bus services, the suburban rail system and late-night bus services. From the first quarter of 1998, approximately 3,000 consumers will be using a common smart card, which utilises three applications: integrated transport ticketing; shopping/parking loyalty point scheme and an electronic purse. The trial will run for six months, during which time the concepts will be validated.

A second project in Ireland, the Cardlink project, run by the Eastern Health Board, demonstrates the diversity of applications for smart cards by enabling key aspects of health records to be transferred to this secure, portable electronic form. As a result, data is more readily available where and when required, and the patient can be supplied with a portable medical record. Cardlink is part of a Europe-wide project which aims to enhance the mobility of European citizens, promote communication amongst health care professionals and drive the standardisation of smart cards in the health industry. Two associated benefits are that transcription errors can be reduced and the data can be extracted in the language appropriate to the country in which the patient is being treated, rather than the country in which the data was applied. By February 1999, it is estimated that 200,000 cards will have been issued to a cross-section of patient types.

The final example of smart card applications being trialed in Ireland is a trial of the Visa Cash electronic purse by AIB Bank and Bank of Ireland, in partnership with Telecom Éireann, the state telephone company. The trial, which is due to commence towards the end of 1998, will take place in Ennis, Ireland's "Information Age Town", which has been chosen by Telecom Éireann to become a multi-million pound test-bed for a whole range of new technologies. Up to 15,000 Visa Cash cards will be issued by the two Banks at the start of the 18-month programme. Like the UK Visa Cash trial in Leeds, the Ennis trial will use state-of-the-art public key technology, which is an important step towards the development of an inter-operable system. Up to 300 retailers in Ennis will accept Visa Cash, ranging from car parks and vending machines, to grocery and hardware stores.

Case Study — The UK Visa Cash Trial

Background to Visa Cash

In the UK some 80 per cent of all consumer transactions are still made in cash, and although a walk down any high street in any town or city would suggest that the use of plastic cards is a way of life, they still account for less volume than cheques. If we take a look at plastic card usage by value, then the picture moves slightly more into focus, with 28 pence in every pound spent on a plastic card.

The trends in payments may be of little surprise: a general increase in the use of plastic cards, with a steady decline in cheques, which has been apparent since the introduction of the debit card in the late 1980s. As for cash, in most environments there simply is no alternative, and for some things we may never want there to be, but more often than not cash causes delays and frustration. How many times have you stood at a pay-and-display machine in a car park only to discover that you don't have enough change, or that you don't have the right coins and the machine is only too happy to pocket the rest? How many times have you stood in a queue when you only want a newspaper or a drink and the person in front of you insists on getting rid of all their loose change as though they had just raided their child's piggy bank? These are common occurrences, which, in the absence of any alternative to cash, we all learn to live with.

The Growth in Stored Value Cards

Probably the earliest example of a stored value card is a telecomms card, purchased with value on it, decremented during use, and thrown away (or retained as a collector's item through clever marketing) when it is empty. Perhaps slow to take off, but soon gaining momentum as payphones are increasingly converted to card phones, and the cards themselves become easier to obtain. For the consumer, the benefits are clear: you don't have to wait in the cash queue, you don't need the correct change, and you only pay for what you use. For the telecomms provider, the benefits are significant: no cash to collect, greater loyalty (if only while the customer still has the card), increased purchase value and some free advertising thrown in for good measure (as consumers carry a card with your brand on it). It is hardly surprising that other heavy cash acceptors began to create their own stored value card schemes, with a particular dominance in the vending, passenger transport and car-parking sectors. It is now possible to have another four pieces of plastic, just as the supermarket loyalty card explosion is beginning.

It is little wonder that at this time the banks and card schemes, such as Visa and Mastercard, began to take an interest. Consumer demand for stored-value cards emerged as an alternative to cash in a number of open environments without creating separate pieces of plastic. Consequently, the likes of Visa Cash were born as a stored value card product, or electronic purse as it is commonly called, which can be used in a number of traditional low-value, cash-based environments.

The Visa Cash Stored Value Card Product

As a payment product, three broad card types can be produced: disposable (purchased with value stored and disposed of after use); re-loadable (value transferred from a connecting account), and feature re-loadable (as per re-loadable, except the plastic contains a second application, usually either debit or credit). Visa Cash is an auditable system containing a central archive of transactions. Once the consumer has value loaded onto their card, the actual transaction takes a matter of seconds. They simply insert their card into the card reader on the point-of-sale device and press the accept button if they are happy with the price keyed in by the retailer or generated by the machine, if in an unattended environment such as vending or car parking. The consumer has an opportunity to view their card balance before and after the transaction, and because the transaction requires no authorisation, PIN, signature or additional receipt, it is quick and convenient.

Visa Cash World-wide

To date, over six million Visa Cash cards have been issued in 18 locations world-wide. Notable examples include Barcelona, Buenos Aires, Hong Kong, Rio de Janeiro, Toronto and New York — but perhaps the most prestigious was Atlanta, to coincide with the Olympic Games in 1996. The Atlanta trial was predominantly based on disposable Visa Cash cards, due to the temporary nature of the target market. The trial was a great success, with over 1.5 million cards being issued, and it inspired many other countries, including the UK, to develop their own Visa Cash trials. Today, in Atlanta, Visa Cash is being expanded geographically to allow more residents and retailers to take advantage of the product.

Although most of the countries where Visa Cash is being trialled have very different cultures and environments, there are still lessons that other pioneers can learn. In Atlanta, it was appropriate for the vast majority of the cards to be disposable, although one of the key findings from the research was that consumers don't really want another plastic card, and what they would really like is Visa Cash added to their existing payment card. One of the most important checkpoints for any Visa Cash trial is the average transaction value, since Visa Cash is aimed at low-value, traditionally cash-based transactions where other payment methods are not appropriate. The average transaction value from the world-wide trials has been under £3.00, which says a great deal about the success of the retailer selection and the cardholder education. It is inevitable that every trial will have a "killer application" which makes more consumers want to use the card. In Atlanta, this was the mass transit system, in Australia the soft drinks machines and in New York the laundry machines. In the UK, research suggests that this may well be car parking.

The UK Visa Cash Trial

Commencing during the last quarter of 1997, the UK Visa Cash trial is taking place in Leeds and is supported by six UK Banks. The scope of the trial includes up to 2,000 points of sale, 65,000 cards and 60 load devices. In addition to the centre and south of the city of Leeds, the point-of-sale and load-device infrastructure will also cover the vicinity of the bus and train stations in five commuter satellite sites: Bradford, Dewsbury, Halifax, Pudsey and Wakefield. As transport is an important application for the trial, the satellite sites ensure that commuters have the ability to use Visa Cash at their destination.

In response to consumer research, Visa Cash will focus on three main sectors: the machine sector, the mobile sector and general small value retail. Within the machine sector, Visa Cash will be accepted in car parks, vending machines and payphones, whilst the mobile sector will focus on train and bus ticket sales. The final sector is more all-encompassing and includes fast food, pubs, newsagents, bakeries, chemists, etc. — the general criterion being those environments where transactions are traditionally cash-based and of low value.

There are a number of different card types in the UK trial, ranging from standalone re-loadable Visa Cash cards to feature re-loadable cards, which also contain a debit or credit card application. As a result, Visa Cash will be tested amongst a broad range of consumer types. The maximum amount of value that can be loaded onto a Visa Cash card is £50, although there is no minimum load or transaction value. Consumers are able to load their cards at any one of the 60 load devices situated in the trial area by transferring value from a linked account (credit card or bank account, depending upon the card type). The load devices are situated in car parks, bus and train stations, shopping centres and shopping precincts, so that consumers can reload their cards in the places where they run out of value.

The Key Players for the Success of Visa Cash

The success of the Visa Cash trial is dependent upon the benefits realised by consumers and retailers alike. The future of Visa Cash will in addition to this depend upon the benefits that the banks can realise, even if this is sometime in the future. For the consumer, Visa Cash provides a fast and convenient alternative to cash, which in unattended environments such as car parks and vending means that the exact change is no longer required. For the retailer, Visa Cash can improve cash handling costs and productivity, reduce change errors and increase the speed of the transaction process. Less cash means less risk from theft, fraud and counterfeit, with payments guaranteed. In addition, retailers can respond to consumer demand for acceptance and improve customer service.

The Future of Electronic Purse

To some extent, and certainly for the UK, it is too early to say what the future will bring. However, there are some established precedents, not least of all the success of other world-wide Visa Cash trials, from which preparation for the UK trial has no doubt benefited. Assuming a successful outcome, one of the key items on the agenda, which is already a priority for the card industry, is that of interoperability between product types and across borders. Although cash transaction volumes have remained relatively constant for some time at around 80 per cent, there may soon be real alternatives to cash for low value payments, which enable a decline on a similar scale to that of cheques following the introduction of the debit card. The year 1966 marked the launch of the first credit card in the UK by Barclaycard, and although not an overnight success, there are now some 60 million payment cards in the UK. There is little doubt that the electronic purse is here to stay, and like credit cards have a successful future ahead of them.

REFERENCES TO CHAPTER 21

Allen, C.A., W.J. Barr and R. Schultz (1996), *Smart Cards: Seizing Strategic Business Opportunities — The Smart Card Forum*, USA: Irwin Professional Publishing.

Dreifus, H.N. and J.T. Monk (1997), *Smart Cards: A Guide to Building and Managing Smart Card Applications*, UK: John Wiley and Sons.

QMS (1997), *Smart Card 1997 — Convention Proceedings*, Peterborough: Quality Marketing Services Ltd.

Rankl, W., W. Effing and R. Wolfgang (1997), *Smart Card Handbook*, London: John Wiley and Sons.

SMI (1997), *Optimising on the Potential of the Electronic Purse — Conference Proceedings*, London: SMI Ltd.

Zoreda, J.L. and J.M. Oton (1994), *Smart Cards*, US: Artech House.

Chapter 22

SALES AND MARKETING TECHNOLOGY

Áine Cassidy

Overview

This chapter looks at how direct marketing is integrating with other functions such as sales, telemarketing and customer service. The changes that have led to this development are highlighted, with specific attention paid to the growing importance of the changing customer. As technology is the key enabler of this development, the chapter then examines the evolution of sales, marketing, call centre and customer service technology. Finally, a case study on Ark Life, AIB's life and pensions company, shows how one company has been integrating its sales, marketing, customer service and call centre functions.

Integrated direct marketing is very often associated with integrating different media such as mail, telephone and direct response advertising or integrating direct marketing activity with other marketing activity, such as PR and brand advertising. However, there is another side to the coin that is too often ignored — that is, integrating direct marketing with other customer-interfacing functions such as sales and customer service. If direct marketing is about building individual, long-term, profitable relationships with customers, then all customer contact with an organisation must be considered. There is no point in having a telemarketing department that is fully briefed on all aspects of marketing and trained to cross-sell to customers, if the customer service department — i.e. the department the customer is most likely to contact — has not got adequate telephone training. Equally, the point-of-sale, where the customer actually purchases, provides the most powerful time to gather information and build customer relationships — the basic aim of the direct marketer.

Direct marketers often spend significant amounts on acquiring information to overlay on their databases, yet the information gleaned at the point-of-sale is not always captured or is only accessible by the salesperson. The following section considers how these functions can be integrated.

SYSTEMS AND SOFTWARE

One method is through internal marketing, training and communications. The key enabler, however, is technology, particularly the integration of systems and software. Many marketing departments have their own standalone marketing database system, but in order to increase the value of this tool, sales and customer service staff could be given access to update it.

The concept of contact management is crucial where a number of people within an organisation may be in contact with one single customer. This feature allows all contacts to be recorded, so that in advance of any planned contact, the user can check to see who was last in contact with this person and what the outcome was. Many companies are recognising this and are developing customer databases that integrate with field points-of-sale and customer servicing solutions.

Marketing has evolved to focus more on developing long-term relationships with customers. Other departments have a role to play in relationship-building activities. As a result, the role of marketing is expanding and extending beyond the marketing department.

THE CHANGING BUSINESS ENVIRONMENT

This section considers the importance of the customer, how they are changing and how markets are evolving.

Customers

Customers are becoming more sophisticated, knowledgeable, demanding and, also, less loyal to companies. This disloyalty has resulted in the emergence of loyalty schemes, such as those introduced by the major grocery retailers. Customer expectations have increased and they are dissatisfied if they are not met. Customers also have more disposable income and less time. They own more technology than ever and this is increasing (telephones, televisions, videos, mobile phones, personal computers, etc.). The amount of choice available to consumers has increased dramatically in recent years to the point of confusion, in some cases.

Products and services are available through more and different distribution channels than before, such as ATMs, direct/telephone selling and Internet marketing. Consumer markets are fragmenting and shrinking, due in part to a globalisation of markets and products.

Keeping customers satisfied and coming back is essential to long-term relationships and profit. However, customer retention does not imply customer satisfaction, or vice versa. Sixty-five to 85 per cent of customers who defect say they were satisfied or very satisfied with their previous supplier (Reichheld, 1993). This would suggest that customers are becoming less loyal and will move to another supplier more easily than in the past.

In some situations, customers are reluctant to switch suppliers due to inertia and the effort involved; for example, changing one's mortgage involves high switching costs. This false loyalty is misleading in monopolies or where there is a lack of choice for the consumer.

Brian Joiner (1994) maintains that customer satisfaction is not sufficient and what is required is to "delight" the customer. Professor Noriki Kano's model of customer perception identifies three characteristics:

- *"Must-be"*: what the customer expects to be present, taken for granted

- *"More is better"*: characteristics that satisfy the customer and at various scales can dissatisfy or at the other end delight the customer, e.g. speed of response to a query

- *"Delighter"*: unexpected characteristics that surprise or delight the customer.

To retain customers, we need to find ways to "delight" on an ongoing basis. This involves knowing the customer and developing a long-term relationship with them.

This author recently came across a website developed by an irate customer who had received poor service from an airline and his website was dedicated to telling the world about this. Also, like-minded people sent in details of any bad experience they had dealing with this company and these were added to the website. Poor customer service in this case led to very bad PR for this company. Complaints are an unusual area and there is much written on the subject. However, modern marketing theory suggests that companies should invite complaints and develop complaint-handling strategies. A problem solved can often increase customer loyalty.

Clearly, whilst customer focus has been around for a long time, the customer of the 1990s is a demanding, knowledgeable and disloyal one. The focus on trying to develop personalised, targeted and meaningful dialogue with individual customers in ways that delight them is the aim of modern marketing.

Competition

Competition in the marketplace is intense. This is further exacerbated by the increasing cost of sales and the overall reduction of margins on products and services. Companies are under pressure to reduce costs, while at the same time there is increased emphasis on customer service, which often suffers when a cost-cutting exercise is undertaken.

Customer service expectations have increased dramatically in recent years. Consumer choice means that you can go elsewhere if you receive poor customer service. The key enabler to all of this change is the revolutionary advances in telecommunications and computer technology that have taken place and continue to do so.

The Marketing Function

The marketing function is undergoing radical change. The costs of sales and account management have increased dramatically in recent years and customer care and service by telephone or "telecare" has become more prevalent. In an effort to control costs, companies are continuously exploring new ways to increase productivity; this has resulted in more communications over the phone. Sales people are required to specialise in the selling function. Customer care, prospecting, lead generation and qualification have become head-office-based functions, more specifically those of the telemarketing team. This has developed the telemarketing role and improved it as a career path, from its early days of "telesales".

The development of telemarketing centres in recent years has evolved from a small number of operators in the marketing department to the development of a front-end call centre for the entire company, employing multi-skilled operators so that customer and prospect enquiries are more efficiently handled by one person. Call centres have replaced the switchboard, customer service centre and telemarketing centre. As marketers have traditionally been the owners of call centres, this has moved marketing, and specifically direct marketing, into the realms of sales and customer service, whereas traditional marketing was typically a completely separate function.

Technology has been a key driver in redefining the marketing function. This will continue as more and more companies invest in sales, marketing and call centre systems with telecommunications linking remote users and the head-office function.

TECHNOLOGY

This section focuses on the technologies used within the sales, marketing, call centre and customer service functions. Emerging technologies are considered and it is demonstrated how technology from different functions must be integrated for a company to be truly customer-focused.

FIGURE 22.1: INTEGRATING TECHNOLOGIES

Sales Force Automation

The role of the sales force is expanding. A variety of new roles are emerging, including understanding the customer, analysing the market, planning, information gathering, sales forecasting, technology operation, customer service and after sales service. The salesperson now has a new armoury, including mobile phone, voicemail, laptop, palmtop and home modem, each providing them with links to head office. The information available reduces administration time, which should mean more time in front of customers.

Traditionally, the salesperson had little information, was rarely managed and was just expected to sell the product. "In the coming decade, not only will the sales executive preside over some radical changes in selling, he will also be under a microscope as never before" (O'Connell and Keenan, 1990). Technology has radically changed the role of sales, particularly through transfer of information. These advances in technology and communications have also made sales personnel more accountable and their activities more transparent.

Moriarty and Swartz (1989) estimated that sales would increase by at least 10 to 30 per cent as a result of automation. They cited specific examples of companies where additional benefits, including reduced sales force attrition of 40 per cent and reduced costs in recruitment and training, paid for the system in one year. Additional benefits are the information available for decision-making and improved customer relationships. Moriarty and Swartz also predict the demise of any company if they fail to automate within five years. The sales process is becoming more complex, products are being tailored to customer needs and product development cycles are shortening. We have already seen that the cost of sales is increasing and the role of the salesperson is changing. The use of technology is critical to the salesperson of the 1990s to allow them to know their customer and offer the level of customer service that is expected of them. Sending and receiving information on a daily basis is essential, as it saves time and gives the salesperson accurate and up-to-date information.

Typical sales applications of new technologies include:

- Contact management: recording details of all contacts and actions and providing a comprehensive picture of each customer

- Territory management and allocation

- Sales forecasting

- Sales activity management

- Diary management — may include alarm/reminder system

- MIS for sales management

- Customer account management

- Application form completion

- Database development and management

- Mailing facility, e.g. standard letters and mail-merge facility

- Analysis and reporting function

- Quotations

- Product or service presentation/demonstration.

To fully embrace technology, salespeople need to change their work practices and develop new skills. The benefits of the system, both to the company and in particular to the salesperson, need to be carefully explained before any system can be adopted. Sales force systems need to be easy to use and flexible. Ideally, salespeople should be involved in developing and testing the system. The salespeople used for pilot testing should be selected based on positive attitude, as they will become champions for the system. Crucial to the success of sales force automation is the development and testing of the remote communications mechanism, as file transfer and communications processes are complex. Finally, it is essential to have a comprehensive training programme and helpdesk support function in place to ensure that sales force automation is a success.

Marketing Technology

Rapp and Collins (1989) define database marketing as:

> the ability of a company to use the vast potential of today's computer and telecommunications technology to drive customer-oriented programmes in a personalised, articulated and cost-effective manner.

Database marketing gives strategic advantage through better use of customer and marketing information to build long-term customer relationships. Good quality data allow the marketer to understand the marketplace and the customer better and to manage communications with the customer by creating a dialogue through one-to-one marketing.

Typical marketing applications include the following:

Data Management

- Importing and exporting of lists and databases

- Manual data entry

- De-duplication and address verification.

Analysis

- Segmentation

- Customer profiling

- Scoring and modelling

- Testing.

Customer Communications

- Contact history record of all customer communications

- Generation of customer contacts at appropriate times, etc.

- Customer loyalty schemes and customer care programmes

- Customer account management.

Campaign Management

- Selection of customer grouping for campaign purposes

- Personalisation

- Ensuring each step of campaign is carried out (e.g. direct mail, telemarketing, etc.)

- Response analysis

- Budgeting

- Reporting.

Management Information

- Management information system

- Decision support systems

- Executive information systems.

Issues to be considered are the interfaces between systems, different data formats, data modelling, database design, data quality and maintenance. The ability to import data from various sources into the database is important and quality name and address management is essential. Also, a single picture of the relationship with the client gives an improved understanding of the customer and this can be used to influence sales and marketing activity.

A recent development with marketing databases is the development of data warehouses and the concepts of data mining and neural networks. A data warehouse is a very large database that holds transactional, historical and customer data and makes it available for decision-making. Analysis is based on a snapshot of company performance. Data warehouses are usually custom-built and are time-consuming and expensive to develop. They are limited to large companies, due to size and amount of information, resources required and their relative infancy.

Data mining seeks data correlations that may assist in gaining an insight into customer behaviour. Financial companies have been successfully using data mining techniques for fraud prevention, credit scoring, product development and cross-selling.

Neural networking is based on the concept of pattern recognition and the computer learning from experience and adapting its responses as a result. The marketing function will typically be responsible for data maintenance and management. Ongoing maintenance, de-duplication and data cleaning must be allocated dedicated resources, as data quickly become out-of-date and cease to provide meaningful information and may even result in incorrectly targeted or addressed information being sent to customers, which could result in the customer being more upset than if no communication had been received at all.

Call Centre Technology

Many companies now use the telephone as a major sales, marketing and customer service channel (see also Chapter 13 on telemarketing). The main aim of telemarketing systems is to facilitate two-way communications with customers by phone. Applications include:

- *Automatic Call Distribution (ACD)*: automatically sends the call to the next available agent and plays messages/music while the customer is on hold

- *Interactive Voice Response (IVR)*: combines an auto-attendant and voicemail. This allows the caller to make selections using a touch-tone phone; often one option will be to talk to an operator or leave a message.

- *Computer telephony integration (CTI)*: this links telephony and technology and gives the operator access to the customer record from the database during the call.

- *Call (and screen) transfer*: ability to send a call and details to another operator

- *Auto-dialling*: predictive and preview dialling. Predictive dialling or power dialling automatically dials numbers on a list and only delivers answered calls to an available operator with the appropriate details on screen. The dialler also monitors the number of calls answered to determine how many calls it should dial to keep operators busy without abandoning answered calls. As conditions change, it will alter its dialling rate. All unanswered, engaged or answering machine responses are rescheduled and recalled automatically. Preview dialling allows the operator to preview customer details before the system is activated to dial a number.

- *Call list management*: managing call queues, rescheduling of calls, allocating calls to operators, ensuring calls are made on time, removing calls from queues and so on.

- *Diary management* and appointment-setting

- *Direct sales,* i.e. allowing the customer to buy the product or service by phone

- *Information provision/fulfilment*: ensuring the customer receives the information requested

- *Contact management*: providing a complete picture of all contacts with a customer

- *Scripting/prompting*: operators are taken through a script which prompts them for information, where necessary

- *Reporting and statistics*: detailed information can be made available by operator, shift, team, campaign, etc.

- *Voicemail for after-hours*

- *Caller line identification*: when the caller phones in, their telephone number is recognised and their customer record presented to the operator.

A key issue for call centre solutions is performance — customer search, screen update and navigation need to be speedy, ensuring that dialogue with the customer is not obstructed. Systems must be easy to use and all information required should be made available or easy to navigate. Benefits include increased sales and productivity gains, improvement in customer service, staff morale and reporting and statistics.

In addition, call centre technology can go further than increasing productivity and efficiency — it can make customer service seamless. Customers want their calls to be answered quickly and for the operator to be empowered to deal with their query. ACD technology allows calls to be answered sequentially, ensuring maximum operator efficiency, and also gives the caller the option of leaving a message. ACD technology can present its own customer service problems if the customer is left waiting and it is not a toll-free number.

Interactive voice response is used particularly by banks and credit card companies for account balances and also in the publishing/ entertainment industry for information, horoscopes and competitions. Voice processing and the latest technology of voice recognition are not proving very popular, as they are perceived as being impersonal. However, whether people demand this personalised service is largely dependent on the industry.

Customer Service Technology

Customer service guru Ron Zemke (1990) believes that organisations that focus on customer service grow twice as fast as those that do not, increase their market share three to four times more and can also charge a premium price for their product/service. Clutterbuck (1991) states that employees are not empowered to deal with problems. Also, they rarely have objectives and are, by and large, superficial.

Systems are now available to support complex customer service operations to assist in problem diagnosis and respond to complaints. Complaint systems are becoming more prevalent and quite often are made available to all customer-interfacing functions, including sales and customer service. Complaints are recorded, tracked, managed and analysed to ensure that they are resolved quickly and prioritised by senior management. Many companies actively encourage complaints, as research indicates that a resolved complaint can increase customer loyalty.

Imaging systems also allow documents such as customer application forms and all customer correspondence to be replicated on screen. This provides customer service representatives with very accurate information to handle customer queries.

Emerging Technologies

Neural networks, data mining and voice recognition have already been referred to as emerging technologies. Cybermarketing or Internet marketing is having a significant impact on sales, marketing and customer service functions. The Internet is being used in a number of ways, including electronic mail, the World Wide Web and the setting up of Intranets for distributors and/or customers to access. Interactive TV, home shopping, CD-ROM, virtual reality and multimedia kiosks are other technologies that are also developing (see the separate chapters in this book on the most important technologies from the point of view of the direct marketer).

Integrating Technologies

The sales function must be integrated into the company's strategy and recognised as a core activity — salespeople must be viewed as customer relationship managers. Sales training should be provided in customer relationships and technology, not just customer acquisition. Sales management is now making greater use of information to manage the sales force and to implement control systems.

Technology will not replace people. It can offer improved effectiveness and enhance the capabilities of the marketer, salesperson and customer service agent. In the future, the current customer service centres will integrate more with marketing and more proactively seek customer contact. The reactive (inbound) and proactive (outbound) arms of call centres will integrate with customer service, allowing the customer to enquire and purchase in one place.

Many companies now collect information on web pages and via e-mail and send it to their central database; automatic responses are then generated (interactive web response). This may result in actions being created for sales/marketing/call centre personnel — for example, following up an information pack request.

The roles of sales, customer service, telemarketing and marketing are blurring as each is focusing more and more on customer relationship management. As their systems become more integrated, these functions become more and more dependent on each other. This demands more internal communications, planning and synchronisation and has expanded the role of marketing across the organisation.

SALES AND MARKETING TECHNOLOGY PROJECT PLANNING

There are a number of key guidelines in running a successful sales and marketing technology project. It is essential for the company to be both customer- and technology-focused. Below are a number of stages to consider in the process of developing a system for sales, marketing and/or customer service.

1. Overview of Company

Stating the current situation, work practices, systems and resources in the company. In this phase, the scale of the project should be clarified — identify the activities or processes to be automated. Whether the process can be improved through automation needs to be investigated. It is also important not to simply replicate a paper-based system. All sales and marketing processes should be reviewed to determine how they can be integrated. The preparation of a business case is essential.

2. Develop a Requirements Specification

This should include both business and technical requirements. In this document, it is important to concentrate on tasks that can add value for the customer, such as all customer information being available to salespeople, customer service and telephone operators.

3. Prepare a Budget

In this process, account for hidden costs and intangible benefits.

4. Identify Appropriate Suppliers and Packages

There are several directories available that will list possible software packages that may meet your requirements. Developing a bespoke system is always an option, but this can be costly, both in terms of time and financial resources. Proprietary solutions are also available, where an external supplier and/or your own IT function may customise the product to meet your specific requirements.

5. Evaluate and Select the Packages/Supplier

If the system has a lot of customisation and interface development, it is important to select a supplier with whom you can work closely. Alternatively, while most off-the-shelf packages may not allow much customisation and may only meet 80 per cent of your requirements, if cost and time are significant factors, you may be prepared to forfeit some of your functionality requirements to achieve a quick, low-cost solution.

6. Pinpoint Roles and Responsibilities

Clarify the role of staff responsible for selecting, designing and operating the system. In particular, because of the convergence of business and technology, it is important to appoint a business project manager and a technical project manager. The business project manager will be responsible for the requirements specification and the design and functionality of the system, whereas the technical project manager will assume a stronger role in development and implementation. However, both should work as a team throughout the project. A project sponsor is also required at executive level. The project managers should report to the sponsor on an ongoing basis and ensure that the project is delivered on time and within budget.

7. Develop a Project Plan

This should be realistic, achievable and assign responsibilities.

8. Customise

This involves prototype development, documentation of design, system customisation and acceptance testing.

9. Implementation

This includes data conversion, definition of business processes and change management, training, system rollout and finally a post-implementation review. The first stage of implementation is often a pilot, which is a live test of the system. If sufficient testing has been done, this should be the equivalent of the start of the rollout, rather than a test where new bugs are being found.

Background

Ark Life is AIB's life and pensions company. The company is independent and its administration, marketing, finance and personnel and IT functions are based in Ark Life's Head Office. Ark Life employs approximately 115 financial planning consultants (FPCs), based in AIB Bank branches, with each consultant covering an average of two branches each. The AIB Bank branch staff engage in prospecting and setting up appointments for the consultancy force. Since its inception in 1991, Ark Life has therefore been heavily reliant on AIB branch staff for referrals.

During 1995, Ark Life had reached a significant stage in its growth, and senior management recognised the need to invest in sales and marketing technology to achieve further desired growth.

This section reviews the Ark Life customer focus and the technology and systems in place at that time. It also describes how marketing campaigns (in particular the customer service review campaign) and advertising responses were handled prior to the introduction of a sales and marketing system.

Customer Service Focus

One of Ark Life's key differentiators is its "customer service promise". Each customer is assured when they make a purchase that they will be contacted on a yearly basis for a financial review (customer service review or CSR). The customer also receives an annual policy statement, customer magazines and direct mail. This contact strategy was designed to differentiate Ark from the typical life assurance sales "sell and run" image and to offer excellent customer service so that customers will remain loyal.

Sales Technology

The consultancy force used laptops at the point-of-sale to undertake "factfinds", where they captured vital information to analyse customers' needs and provide quotations and recommendations. The system they used for this is called WinPOS. Details of factfinds were stored on the FPC's laptop. The type of information gathered included demographic, lifestyle, financial and affordability. However, this information was held only locally by FPCs.

Accounts Database

When the customer purchased a policy, application form and policy history details were captured at Head Office on a system called Capsil, held on a mini-computer (AS400). However, FPCs had no access to this information, which resulted in a lot of telephone calls from FPCs to Head Office, enquiring about policy details.

Imaging

An imaging and workflow system had also been implemented at Ark Life, so that communications and forms relating to a customer could be scanned into the system, providing customer service staff with more detailed and comprehensive information about customers.

Marketing Campaign Administration

The marketing department was reliant on the IT department to run queries on the Capsil database system. All marketing campaigns were driven by this database. Extracting information for a campaign was also a lengthy process. These extracts would be passed to a mailing house. In addition, a number of campaigns were run internally by the IT department, such as the customer service review (CSR) campaign. All campaigns required the provision of information sheets about customers to FPCs where they were involved in follow-up.

Customer Service Review (CSR) Campaign

Details and dates of upcoming CSRs were mailed to FPCs on a weekly basis, with an individual sheet for each customer containing policy information. The FPCs could make the telephone call to book an appointment or could request that this contact be made by Ark Life's telemarketing function (in which case they would send the sheets to the call centre).

This annual review campaign was run by the IT Department, who ran a query each week to generate the list of customers for review. They then produced letters to be mailed to the customer, prospect sheets for the salesforce (for follow-up purposes) and listings for sales management. This process was very paper-intensive.

Advertising

Ark Life's advertising included press, radio, bank and Visa statement inserts. In recent years, a reply device was used in all advertising to generate post and telephone queries. Ark Life recognised the value of engaging in direct response advertising. This provided an opportunity to sell the consultancy service to respondents. These calls are handled by the call centre function.

Ark Life has also established a website and enquiries are handled by the marketing department. All responses to advertising were stored in prospect databases, as the Capsil system only allowed the addition of customers who had purchased a policy.

Oxygen Sales and Marketing System

In 1995, Ark Life recognised that it required a system for sales force automation, in particular to provide FPCs with the information that was held about customers at Head Office (for example, policy information and policy values). It also identified the need for a marketing system for analysis, campaign management and telemarketing, in order to plan more targeted campaigns and to run ongoing campaigns such as CSR in a more automated way. In reviewing packages and suppliers, the key challenge for Ark Life was to purchase a software package that integrated both sales and marketing functionality. A further requirement was to find a supplier that could integrate the Capsil system and the field point-of-sale system, WinPOS. Finally, a system called Oxygen (developed by Integrated Sales Systems in the UK) was selected in early 1996. It had excellent sales functionality, and the company had a strong communications and interface development experience. ISS was in the process of developing a campaign management module and involved Ark Life in the development phase. This module was also planned to integrate seamlessly with the sales functionality and would be completed within the timeframe of the project.

Oxygen Sales and Marketing System

Oxygen was required to process information from both the laptop point-of-sale system and the Capsil policy administration system. Complex interfaces were set up to handle this and administration utilities handled the merging and de-duplication of data in this process. Additional utilities were made available for manual merging, deduplication and territory management. Every laptop would be connected to a modem each evening and communications would take place during the night between each laptop and the main server at head office. This communication updates information — policy and customer information, policy values, diary entries and actions ("to do's") — on the laptop, retrieves new information added to the laptop that day and sends and receives electronic mail.

Customer Information

The major benefit of this is FPCs and Head Office users have access to all of the information available about the customer, be it information acquired at the point-of-sale, application form information, policy payment or performance history.

Contact Management

In addition, each contact made with a customer is recorded on the system as an "event". When an FPC meets a customer for a consultation, this is automatically recorded in an event history log. Every mailing sent to the customer from the campaign management module is recorded as a mail event. Other *ad hoc* events such as incoming mail or telephone calls can also be recorded, thus providing a complete picture of all contact with the customer.

Diary Management

Each Oxygen user has access to all diaries. This allows call centre staff to make appointments for FPCs in a diary that is updated on a daily basis. It also allows sales managers to book meetings and training sessions with their teams. Prior to the implementation of Oxygen, all of these meetings and appointments were confirmed individually to FPCs by phone.

Management Information and Reporting

Sales forecasting and sales activity management are made possible by detailed management information on sales activities. This allows FPCs and their managers to plan more effectively.

Non-customers

Prospects and suspects (such as respondents to campaigns or bought-in lists) can be added to the Oxygen database and allocated to an FPC if required.

Territory Management

Each customer is linked to an AIB branch and therefore to an FPC. If an FPC looks after two branches, they hold the customer records for all of the Ark Life customers for those branches. Prospects are allocated by geographic location to AIB branches. Also, if an FPC is looking after another FPC's branch for a day, they can be granted temporary access to individual customer records.

Analysis

Oxygen contains a function called Organise, which is an analysis and selection tool. This can be used to run queries and identify campaign lists. Any field or combination of fields on the database can be used. This tool is used to drive Ark Life marketing campaigns. An additional analysis tool is currently being sourced by Ark to allow more detailed analysis of the customer base.

To Do's

One of the key features of Oxygen is the ability to set "to do's" or actions for the sales force or the call centre staff. These to do's can be automatically sent from a campaign listing, thus removing the need for information sheets to be mailed to the FPCs and call centre. To do's are also linked to individual customer records, so both the FPC and the call centre would have full customer information.

To do's can also be forwarded from one user to another. For example, if an FPC wanted the call centre to handle some of their CSR campaign telephone follow-ups, they can forward them directly to the call centre.

Campaign Management

The campaign management function is linked to the Organise function to select customers or prospects for a campaign, or they can also be extracted using SQL (Structured Query Language, a standard method for database interrogation). Campaign lists can then be checked for duplicates and to validate address data.

This function is also linked to to do's and events. If a campaign involves sending out a direct mail letter and this is to be followed up by the relevant FPC for that customer, a to do (e.g. "Pension letter sent — Follow up with a phone call") can be set for the campaign and this will automatically send an individual to do for each customer to the relevant FPC. Alternatively, if one wanted the call centre to follow up the mailing, to do's for the call centre could be set, so that the entire campaign list goes to it. And finally, if required, an event can be automatically created for each campaign member to record in the event log that a letter was mailed to them. The campaign management function also includes campaign planning and responses can be analysed using the management information and reporting system for campaigns.

Saleslan Telemarketing System

The role of the Ark Life internal telemarketing function ("Customer Communications Centre") is primarily to:

- Make annual review appointments for the consultancy force

- Handle inbound telephone calls from direct response advertising using Freefone (radio, press, statement inserts, take-ones, etc.)

- Make outbound telephone contact with customers to develop and retain customers.

Previously, operators had access to the Capsil policy system, the imaging and workflow system, but most of their work was paper-driven.

Within the business requirements for Oxygen, telemarketing functionality was identified as a key need, particularly as Ark Life had just recently set up the call centre within the marketing function.

As Oxygen did not have any of this functionality, a separate system was sourced. The main telemarketing applications required were telephony (e.g. ACD and IVR), computer telephony integration, scripting and a detailed reporting function. It was very important that the chosen solution would integrate with the Oxygen system. The system selected was Saleslan, which satisfied all of the requirements and offered significant flexibility in amending scripts and designing new scripts, without the need to involve programming staff.

In the search for a solution, many of the systems available appeared to offer either telephony or scripting, but not many had both. With a relatively small call centre, the cost of two separate systems would have been prohibitive. Scripts had already been developed for all Ark campaigns, so these were easily set up on the Saleslan system. A tool has also been provided to Ark, so that scripts can easily be added to or amended by a business user.

Initially, a standalone Saleslan system was set up, taking an extract from Oxygen of the customers to be called each week as part of the CSR campaign. It was also populated with basic information on all Ark customers. This provided a very good test of the system prior to Oxygen integration. Due to time constraints, Oxygen was being rolled out to the sales force first and the Saleslan integration was the second phase of the Oxygen project, due to complete mid-1998. The aim was to start using Saleslan as soon as possible.

The call list was worked through by each of the operators, and where a customer could not be contacted, the call would be rescheduled. Each of Ark's Freefone numbers was diverted to Saleslan, so when a customer or prospect phoned in, the correct script would be presented to the operator and, if a customer phoned, the customer details were available to them (Ark Life will eventually automate this when available). Saleslan offers very detailed reporting, which has improved the information available for managing the operation, both in terms of operator performance and campaign planning.

Ark Life is in the process of integrating Oxygen and Saleslan, with a project completion date of mid-1998. This will allow automation of the movement of call lists (to do's) from Oxygen campaigns to Saleslan and improved computer telephony integration, so that the complete Oxygen database will be available to operators, rather than a reduced snapshot. Responses to advertising campaigns and Internet enquiries will automatically be added from the Saleslan script to the Oxygen database if they are not already on the system. When FPCs forward to do's to the call centre, this will automatically go straight into the call list. The creation of events will be facilitated, as there will be improved navigation between Saleslan and Oxygen.

Future Developments

As Oxygen and Saleslan are integrated, the roles of sales, marketing and call centre are merging. These operations are becoming paperless and less administration-bound. They are working more closely to achieve long-term customer relationships and the lines between these functions are blurring into "relationship marketing".

Ark views the Oxygen and Saleslan projects as ongoing. Implementation results in a lot of feedback from users. This has, and will, result in enhancements and continued development to the system. Neither ISS nor Saleslan are standing still with their products and are looking to improve and expand them, through user groups and R&D. One thing about IT projects in this area is they never end!

The Ark Life customer service and switchboard functions are still separate. In the future, these may be integrated into the emerging "relationship marketing" function.

REFERENCES TO CHAPTER 22

Clutterbuck, David (1991), "Why Customer Care Programmes Don't Work", *Managing Service Quality*, March, pp. 125–126.

Gorski, Debbie and Jonathan Ingram (1994), *The Price Waterhouse Sales and Marketing Software Handbook 1994*, Price Waterhouse/ Pitman Publishing.

Hartley, Bob and Michael W. Starkey (eds.) (1996), *The Management of Sales and Customer Relationships*, International Thomson Business Press.

Joiner, B.L. (1994), *Fourth Generation Management*, New York: McGraw-Hill.

Kotler, Philip (1991), *Marketing Management*, Seventh edition, Englewood Cliffs, NJ: Prentice Hall.

Moriarty, Rowland T. and Gordon Swartz (1989), "Automation to Boost Sales and Marketing", *Harvard Business Review*, Jan/Feb, pp. 100–108.

O'Connell, William A. and William Keenan, Jnr (1990), "The Shape of Things to Come", *Sales & Marketing Management*, Jan., pp. 36–41.

O'Connor, John and Eamonn Galvin (1997) *Marketing & Information Technology*, London: Pitman Publishing.

Peppers, Don and Martha Rogers (1994), *The One-to-One Future — Building Business Relationships One Customer at a Time*, Judy Piatkus (Publishers) Ltd.

Rapp, S. and T. Collins (1989), *The Great Marketing Turnaround*, Englewood Cliffs, NJ: Prentice Hall.

Reichheld, F.F. (1993) "Loyalty-Based Management", *Harvard Business Review*, March.

Zemke, Ron (1990), "Managing Service Quality", BBC Training Video.

PART FIVE

Implementation of the Direct Marketing Strategy

Chapter 23

CAMPAIGN MANAGEMENT AND BUDGETING

Valerie Gannon

Overview

Direct marketing involves a high degree of management, particularly of the campaign budget. This chapter takes the reader through the main stages of the campaign management process, including budgeting, and draws on some useful and practical tools from the sphere of project management.

DIRECT MARKETING AS PROJECT MANAGEMENT

Direct marketing involves the management of many campaigns a year, all differing in operational detail, and drawing on a wide variety of suppliers and resources. As each campaign is customised and must achieve targets, be on budget and meet deadlines, it can quite clearly be viewed a separate project.

A specialised branch of management has developed since the 1950s, focusing specifically on the skills essential to managing projects. Processes and procedures which developed in industry for the management of large-scale and complex projects have been increasingly in common use in the general management arena, across a spectrum of industries, and project management is now a profession in its own right.

According to Lock (1992), "the principal identifying characteristic of a project is its novelty". In addition, he points out that all projects have three sets of objectives in common: to achieve certain goals to certain quality levels, to a budget, and to predetermined timescales.

It is useful to visualise the project as a jigsaw puzzle:

> The project management process is the method needed to clearly and simply identify each piece, its place in the pattern and in relation to all other pieces, each of which must be included in work breakdown (Lock, 1992).

Project management tools and techniques are thus ideally suited to the management of direct marketing, and the jigsaw analogy is very apt. The many operational details of each individual direct marketing campaign must fit into a larger picture, which comprises all direct marketing activity for the year. For this larger picture to remain in focus, for all the pieces of the jigsaw puzzle to finally fit together, a single manager is required.

All projects have project managers, who have overall responsibility for achieving targets, on budget, to deadlines, and must designate responsibility for component parts of the project. The basic steps to planning a project are as follows:

- Setting the plan
- Compiling the task list
- Costing the task list
- Planning timescales.

In the subsequent implementation phase the steps are:

- Communicating the plan
- Monitoring and control
- Reviewing the project (adapted from Lock, 1992).

Each of these specific steps of project management will now be examined in the direct marketing context.

GETTING FROM STRATEGY TO THE IMPLEMENTATION PLAN

A campaign plan is determined by the tactics that derive from overall direct marketing objectives, and the strategy chosen to achieve these. The entire planning process begins with a strategic exercise, where a situational analysis is conducted, reviewing both the company and the competitive environment. Setting objectives is a crucial part of this planning process. Holder (1992) identifies three possible company objectives — improving profitability, growing market share, and improving cash flow — and seven sub-objectives for improving profitability.

Once the situation analysis has been conducted, and objectives chosen, it is now possible to determine which tactics will be used to achieve which objectives. The three together — objectives, strategy and tactics — form the marketing plan. As Mounsey and Stone (1990) point out, if the company uses only direct marketing to reach customers, then the marketing and direct marketing plans are one and the same. But of course the direct marketer (or direct marketing department) is very often working within a general marketing department.

Where the latter is the case, then setting the direct marketing plan will be a two-stage process. In this case, the next step is to decide which marketing objectives, as set out in the overall marketing plan, can be best achieved through *direct* marketing. For example, is direct marketing to be used for:

- Gaining more business from existing customers?

- Reducing promotional costs?

- Positioning and branding? (Mounsey and Stone, 1990: 27–28)

Therefore, the direct marketing planning process is either a one-stage process (where the marketing plan and the direct marketing plan are one and the same), or a two-stage process (where the overall marketing plan is first set, and the direct marketing plan then set, based on which objectives are best achieved via direct, as opposed to general, marketing techniques).

Once the direct marketing plan is in place, it is then possible to quantify objectives by setting targets and deciding how performance will be measured. Once all of this has been done, it is possible to draw up campaign plans.

In planning the campaign, the relationship between the direct marketing plan and campaign plans should be dynamic to allow for benefits from some key advantages of direct marketing, among which are rapid learning from experience and the ability to test and then generalise to the whole market (Mounsey and Stone, 1990).

The first stage in putting together a campaign plan, which determines exactly what tasks are involved, will now be reviewed.

COMPILING THE TASK LIST

Once the direct marketing plan is in place, the next stage is what Mounsey and Stone (1990: 33–49) describe as "developing the campaign", which involves media planning and testing, developing offers, deciding on the creative approach and so on. All of these concerns are covered in detail in other chapters of this volume. Here, the task list will be compiled: outlining in as much detail as possible each constituent activity and event of the campaign. This will allow for detailed project planning regarding scheduling and implementation to be undertaken.

However, prior to compiling the detailed task list, it is necessary to decide which suppliers will be used. In practice, deciding which supplier implements which stages of the campaign is in fact part of the task list. One fulfilment house may offer a fuller set of services than another, one telemarketing agency offer fulfilment services, another none and so on. So the decision regarding which suppliers to use is also a decision about which tasks to outsource.

Supplier Selection

Any direct marketing campaign will involve work from several different suppliers. No budget can be completed until accurate quotations have been received, and no quotations can be used until suppliers have been chosen.

Direct marketing suppliers include some or all of the following:

- Direct marketing agencies (often the lead supplier managing other relationships)

- Media buyers

- Fulfilment houses

- Mailing houses

- List suppliers and brokers

- Computer bureaux

- Data providers

- Telemarketing agencies

- Print production houses.

Spending time selecting the right supplier is obviously important for the success of a single campaign. More importantly, finding the right supplier fit early on can lay the basis for an ongoing relationship and eliminate the cost in management time of shopping around again for the next campaign.

Recommendations from industry peers or from other suppliers are often a starting point for finding the right company. If certain aspects of the campaign are likely to dominate, it is advisable to choose the relevant key suppliers first. The telemarketing agency chosen may have an existing relationship with a fulfilment company, for example, which means that these two suppliers have worked together before and that their relationship does not have to be managed too closely. The Irish Direct Marketing Association produces a very useful annual directory of members and services (IDMA, 1997).

As with the choosing of any supplier, criteria such as quality, reliability, experience and price are of course key determinants. However, for a long-term direct marketing supplier relationship, a number of specific criteria should be employed:

Account Management

- Will there be a dedicated account manager who will champion the project internally?

- At the very least will there be a single point of contact for the project within the company?

- Does this person display the empathy and understanding of the company, product and brief?

Creativity

- Does the company show sufficient creativity (particularly important in the choice of a direct marketing agency)?

- Can the executives add value, and identify potential problems and opportunities? Are they likely to offer lateral solutions to blockages in the campaign process?

Communication

- Are they clear and timely communicators?

- Will they fit with the other choice of suppliers and provide the necessary openness and flexibility?

- Can they be relied upon to communicate directly with other suppliers without constant client intervention?

The Task List

Once suppliers have been chosen, it is now possible to put together an itemised list of activities and events that will constitute individual campaigns. Responsibility for individual tasks can be assigned. This will form the basis for detailed time planning, which will be examined in the section on planning the timescales and scheduling the campaign. Suppliers can now be asked for quotations, which will be used to establish the budget.

COSTING THE TASK LIST: QUANTITATIVE PLANNING TECHNIQUES

As McCorkell (1997: 67) explains:

> Direct marketers begin their planning . . . by calculating how many sales can be made for nothing, then how many can be made for very little and continue until it ceases to be profitable to make any more sales [which is] the only sensible way to construct a marketing budget, yet . . . most companies do not actually budget this way.

This is what Nash (1995) refers to as the "task-based budget".

In other words, where traditional marketing budgets have been constructed on the basis of historical precedent, direct marketers (should) begin with projected sales, determine the campaign plan and tasks deriving from this, decide on a required profit, and then budget accordingly.

A number of quantitative planning techniques used by direct marketers in advance of setting a budget will now be examined, namely: basic cost and response measures, allowable marketing cost, and lifetime values. The section concludes with a summary of the steps and techniques that should be used in setting a budget.

Basic Direct Marketing Measures

The basic units of measure for direct marketers are on a cost-per-thousand or response/order/sale-per-thousand basis. This allows comparison of like with like, whether in terms of quotations from suppliers or performance of campaigns, offers, media and so on and is calculated simply as follows:

Cost per thousand:

$$\frac{\text{Total cost}}{\text{Total quantity}} \times 1,000$$

Response per thousand:

$$\frac{\text{Total response}}{\text{Total mailed}} \times 1,000$$

Cost per order:

$$\frac{\text{Total cost}}{\text{Total orders}} \times 1,000$$

Allowable Marketing Cost

The traditional direct marketing approach to allocating expenditure across activities has been to project likely sales from each activity, decide on the required profit and set the promotional expenditure accordingly. This is known as the allowable marketing cost or sometimes the "allowable cost per order" or "marketing allowable" and is calculated as follows:

Selling Price – Returns = Net Order Value

Net Order Value – (Costs + Required Profit Margin) = Allowable Marketing Costs

This approach has been widely used and is a useful rule of thumb. However, Weetch (1992) points out a number of limitations to using the allowable marketing cost calculation, and suggests some ways of overcoming these or turning them into benefits (see Table 23.1).

TABLE 23.1: LIMITATIONS OF THE ALLOWABLE MARKETING COST
CALCULATION AND SUGGESTED SOLUTIONS

Limitations	Overcoming Limitations
Assumption of fixed price	Run calculations based on different prices
Sales must be predicted	Projective, true, but valuable in terms of tracking actual versus predicted sales
Promotion is function of price and sales	In fact, sales are a function of promotion and price, so our calculations should also be run based on different prices
Decisions are based on profit maximisation at level of individual sale, not on basis of entire campaign	Run calculations at campaign level rather than at individual sale level
Does not take into account the long-term value of the customer	Another set of calculations to account for this is required

Source: Adapted from Weetch (1992: 6–8).

Lifetime Values

As just seen above, establishing the allowable marketing cost does not take any account of the lifetime value of a customer. Since direct marketing seeks to establish a long-term one-to-one relationship with the customer, it follows that any decisions about recruitment costs and ongoing promotional costs must take into account the value of the customer over the life of the relationship.

The length of this relationship forms the basis for calculating lifetime values, and will depend on a number of factors; for example:

- *Target Market*: If the product is aimed at 9- to 14-year-olds, the lifetime length is five years by definition

- *Product Category*: A baby-wear company cannot hope to have a relationship with customers spanning their entire lives, while a car manufacturer could, for example.

If the company has an established trading history and an accurate record of consumer purchases, then lifetime values can be calculated historically. However, if the company has just begun to trade, or just begun to track customer purchasing patterns, then lifetime values can only be calculated on a projective basis. Obviously, historical calculations have the advantage of being based on known customer behaviour. But projective calculations allow the direct marketer to include scenarios based on potential market conditions in the future (Courtheoux, 1992).

Net Present Value

Before examining either the historical or projective methods of calculating lifetime value, it is essential to take into account the time value of money. One pound earned from a customer today has a greater value than one pound earned from a customer in five years' time. Therefore, all lifetime value calculations must take into account the discounted cash flow from the customer, or what is also called the net present value of the customer's purchases:

Formula for discount rate: $\dfrac{1}{(1+r)^n}$

where r = rate of interest expressed as a decimal, e.g. 10% = 0.1; n = number of years to be discounted.

So for example if the interest rate over the number of years in question is 5 per cent, then the calculation would be as follows:

Year	Formula	Discount Factor
Year 0 (Now)	$\dfrac{1}{(1+0.05)^0} = \dfrac{1}{1}$	1
Year 1 (One year's time)	$\dfrac{1}{(1+0.05)^1} = \dfrac{1}{1.05}$	0.9524
Year 2 (Two years' time)	$\dfrac{1}{(1+0.05)^2} = \dfrac{1}{1.1025}$	0.9070
Year 3 (Three years' time)	$\dfrac{1}{(1+0.05)^3} = \dfrac{1}{1.1576}$	0.8639

Calculating Historical Lifetime Value

When calculated on a historical basis, the lifetime value of a notional customer is always based on the aggregate of group behaviour in the past. It is best to analyse behaviour for specific groups of customers with shared characteristics — for example, all customers recruited via a particular campaign (Courtheoux, 1992).

Once the group has been chosen, all costs and revenues for the group are calculated over the period in question, by time-segments as appropriate to the company and product (campaign, season, quarter, year, etc.). The discount factor is then applied across each time-segment to give the net present value, or discounted contribution, of the customer activity at point of recruitment. This is year zero in the example outlined below, where the interest rate has been five per cent over each year in question, just as in our earlier example for net present value.

Quarter 1	Total Revenues	Total Costs	Total Contribution*	Discounted Contribution
Year 0	1,000	600	400	(× 1) = 400.00
Year 1	2,200	1,500	700	(× 0.9524) = 666.68
Year 2	4,300	3,100	1,200	(× 0.9070) = 1,088.40
Year 3	3,500	1,800	1,700	(× 0.8639) = 1,468.63
Total	11,000	7,000	4,000	3,623.71

*Total revenues *less* total costs.

Calculating Projective Lifetime Values

Where no historical data are available on customer performance, then any recent data available must be used to divide customers by recency, frequency and value, into groups or cells. Average contribution is estimated, based on these data and likely forward movements and contributions projected. A discount factor is applied, just as for historical lifetime values in the example above (Courtheoux, 1992).

Budgeting

Successful budgeting for direct marketing is no different from budgeting for other business activities, in that it involves making accurate projections of the various component costs. All budgeting should start with lifetime value calculation, as this will determine the choice of profit levels on recruiting new customers and maintaining existing customers. The next step is to determine allowable marketing costs, as outlined above. Then a budget can be set at campaign level, and must take into account the nature of each individual campaign. Are sales expected off-the-page, for example, or will initial enquiries be followed up with an information pack, and then by a telephone follow-up? In other words, is it a one-step, two-step or multistage campaign? (See "Managing a Lead-Generation Program" in Stone, 1996)

Determining the cost components of the task list is the next step, and can only be done once suppliers have been chosen. Typically, these will involve the following:

- Media costs

- Agency costs

- Production and print costs

- Bureau costs

- Mailing costs

- Response costs

- Fulfilment costs

- Other costs such as bad debts, returns, etc.

As Nash points out, it may be possible to determine at the campaign planning stage along which path, among a number of possible alternatives, the campaign may progress. If this is the case, "where there are alternatives, their effect should be clearly expressed". In addition, "if it is not yet possible to forecast results from recommended mailing to media insertions, a range of possible [costs] should be shown, with the economic effect of each worked out and shown" (Nash, 1995: 55).

Always remember to allow for contingencies, where some or all of the variables may perform differently from projections. This is especially important on first direct marketing efforts by companies, where there is no historical picture for comparison. Cost overruns are always a possibility, as will be seen when discussing control of suppliers.

The final step is to combine all projected campaign budgets into a master budget for the year.

Summary – Budgeting Steps

- Establish lifetime values

- Determine allowable marketing cost

- Outline stages of campaign

- Establish component cost of each campaign from task list

- Allow for contingencies

- Combine all campaign budgets into master budget.

PLANNING THE TIMESCALES: SCHEDULING THE CAMPAIGN

Lock (1992) points out that time scheduling can be determined by two opposing sets of considerations. Either the time to complete the campaign is determined on the basis of aggregate time taken to complete individual project components, or an end-date requirement is already in place. Remember that time schedules determined by an end-date requirement may sometimes allow a time period *longer* than necessary to complete the campaign; the temptation may arise to do more than planned, and therefore run over budget.

In practice, time is usually at a premium, and schedules tend to be dictated by end-date requirements. For example, a product must be launched in quarter two to meet a summer demand, or the campaign must be complete by the end of quarter three to meet year-end sales targets, and so on. Ideally, a balance must be struck between the two determinants of the schedule, and ways found to optimise the schedule, whether by overlapping, condensing or running tasks in parallel.

Time Scheduling Techniques

All time schedules must be communicated in written form, and the clearer that form, the greater the ease and clarity of adhering to the schedule for all concerned. A number of forms can be used for time scheduling:

Timetables

Timetables are the most basic form of written schedule acceptable, and are in day-to-day use for all sorts of management applications. However, they do not give any visual dimension to the project, nor to they encompass any of the interdependencies of the various project elements.

Bar Charts

These are a visual representation of the plan, where the horizontal axis is proportional to the timescales, and can be coded for ease of interpretation. Standard wall-hung kits are available from office equipment suppliers. Specialised project planning bar charts are called Gantt charts. They can be used to represent milestones, critical milestones, activities which can float (can move in time and delay another activity but not the whole project) and free-float (can move in time but do not delay anything). According to Hamilton (1997: 307), bar charts are probably most useful for shorter, simpler projects, otherwise they should be seen "as an end presentation method of other scheduling methods". Like timetables, of course, they cannot show interdependencies between tasks.

FIGURE 23.1: A SAMPLE BAR CHART

WBS Number	Activity Description	Weeks
1.1.1	Establish Theme and Topics	
1.1.2	Obtain Speakers	
1.1.3	Prepare Hand-out Materials	This shows a "hammock" for 1.1.3.1 and 1.1.3.2
1.1.3.1	Obtain Ditto from Speakers	
1.1.3.2	Prepare/Print Handouts	
1.2.1	Set Conference Date	
1.2.2	Select/Commit Conference Location	
1.2.3	Confirm Arrangements	
1.3.1	Develop and	

Source: Reproduced from Hamilton (1997: 306)

Network-based Planning

Network analysis is the generic term for a variety of project planning methods, the best known of which are critical path method (CPM) and programme evaluation and review technique (PERT). Both networks use left-to-right arrow diagrams to represent the flow of activities and events.

- *CPM*: This scheduling method uses a notation known as activity on node (AON), where boxes (nodes) are used to represent the flow, sequence and relationship between activities.

- *PERT*: PERT uses the activity on arrow notation (AOA). Here, each node represents an event such as the starting point or end of an activity which takes no time, while it is the arrows which represent the activity. Each node is given a number as a means of identifying the various activities. Emphasis is placed on the time taken for completion of each activity, based on a probable duration calculated as follows:

t_o = the most optimistic duration

t_m = the most likely duration

t_p = the most pessimistic duration.

From these three a probable duration for each task is calculated which is noted as

t_e = the estimated duration

Hamilton illustrates how CPM and PERT employ the AON and AOA notations respectively in the diagram reproduced below. However, the distinction between the differing notations has, he says, "virtually disappeared in practice" (Hamilton, 1997: 322).

FIGURE 23.2: COMPARISON OF CPM AND PERT DIAGRAMS

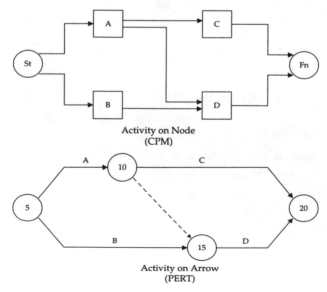

Source: Reproduced from Hamilton (1997: 321)

Using Software

A variety of software products are available for some or all of the above tools (*Microsoft Project*, for example). In addition, Mounsey and Stone (1990) point out that computerising campaign management forms, if only on a word-processing or spreadsheet package, can save a great deal of time. Campaign management forms are discussed below.

The above only gives the barest outline of what is involved in time-scheduling techniques and critical path network analysis in particular. These tools are most commonly applied in industrial, engineering and construction contexts, often at a very sophisticated level. However, this should not discourage the direct marketer. As Lock (1992: 188) points out, "the basic elements of network notation are simple" and it should be possible to acquire "a working knowledge of logic diagram preparation in one day".

All campaigns must, of course, by definition be scheduled in some way. The more sophisticated the time-scheduling technique, the more management time it can take, which can become a self-defeating exercise and a drain on the project manager. Time scheduling techniques are, after all, designed to optimise time management, not to become an end in themselves. The resources at the direct marketers' disposal and their own time management will dictate the level of sophistication and detail at which the tools are used.

COMMUNICATING THE PLAN: BRIEFING AND CAMPAIGN FORMS

Briefing

Whether the company manages supplier relationships, or has them managed in part or entirely by a direct marketing agency acting on its behalf, it is vital that all requirements, deadlines and reporting lines are clear and well established from the very start. Any supplier can only be as good as the briefing they receive. Often the test of a good supplier is their ability to interrogate and even improve upon the brief.

Bird (1993) provides useful insights into briefing a direct marketing agency when he says that

> The quality of the *thinking* that the agency delivers to you in a presentation will depend almost entirely upon the quality of the brief you give them. . . . Discussion as between equals will get you *much* further (p. 333).

and that

> vague briefs result in vague work. . . . *the* most vital contribution to successful work is . . . probably ensuring that agency and client have jointly agreed on the brief before the work begins (pp. 349–350).

Collective Briefing

Where there are a number of suppliers — in other words where the entire campaign has not been outsourced to a single one-stop direct marketing agency — then bring all suppliers (or at least the key ones) together once they have been chosen. The decision on which suppliers to include in this collective briefing may depend on the campaign length, or on an ongoing relationship. If in doubt, include all suppliers. This collective briefing will achieve in one step what would otherwise take valuable management time. Specifically, it will enable:

- Establishment of inter-supplier relationships

- Establishment of inter-supplier dependency: who needs what, from whom, by when

- Assignment of supplier responsibilities and key deliverables

- Determining of time lines

- Clarification that all parties accept and commit to what is agreed.

The supplier team, like the internal team, is composed of humans, subject to the same temptations to blame someone else when slippages or problems occur. A collective briefing can have the added advantage of lessening this temptation.

Campaign Forms

Remember to coincide or follow up any briefing, whether collective or individual, with a written confirmation of what was agreed. At the very least, a general revised briefing document should be circulated to all suppliers, while individual suppliers will obviously require relevant detail. Here, the advantages of working repeatedly with the same supplier who understands your system are clear. Andersen et al. (1987) suggest the use of a document distribution matrix to keep control of which forms have been circulated, to whom and when.

Because of the level of detail in planning and rolling-out a direct marketing campaign, the use of campaign forms is highly advisable. While standard forms can be customised to individual company requirements over time, they are nonetheless a very good starting point, particularly if this is a first direct marketing campaign for the company, or the first time a dedicated direct marketing function has been employed.

Documentation is essential at all stages of a campaign. Verbal instructions are a precarious basis on which to implement a complex and detailed campaign, as will testify any direct marketer who has heard the immortal words, "You never told me that". Forms are a systematic method of ensuring that all necessary actions are carried out at the required time. Andersen et al. (1987) recommend use of both a project responsibility chart — who is responsible for what *areas*, and an activity responsibility chart — who is responsible for what *tasks*, both with scheduled milestones.

Mounsey and Stone (1990) have developed a series of forms specifically for direct marketing projects. They offer 29 forms in total, not all of which will be relevant in all cases. However, they identify five master forms which they believe "should be mandatory as part of the process for translating the marketing plan into campaign plans", and these are reproduced here (Mounsey and Stone, 1990: 89–161).

FORM 1: CAMPAIGN DEFINITION AND ACCOUNTABILITIES

Campaign Name _____   Code _____

Originator _____   Date of issue _____

Description of requirement _____

_____

Planned launch date _____   Planned close date _____

Measurement Criteria _____

_____

Campaign Manager _____   Internal Clients _____

Implementer's Name   *Implementer Workload*

_____   _____ days between _____ & _____

_____   _____ days between _____ & _____ etc.

Suppliers:

Company   Contact Name   Objective of company on campaign

1. _____   _____   _____

2. _____   _____   _____ etc.

Others on circulation list for all campaign documentation

(keep to minimum) _____ etc.

FORM 2: CAMPAIGN COVERAGE

Campaign Name _____   Code _____

Originator _____   Date of issue _____

Test or roll-out _____

Object of test _____

If test, roll-out strategy _____

_____

Country/Region involvement:

Country/Region   Type of involvement

1. _____   _____

2. _____   _____ etc.

FORM 3: OBJECTIVES AND STRATEGY

Campaign Name _____   Code _____

Originator _____   Date of issue _____

Objectives of marketing strategy of which campaign forms part

1. _____

2. _____ etc.

Main elements of overall marketing strategy

1. _____

2. _____ etc.

Promotional objectives

1. _____

2. _____ etc.

Required consistency with other campaigns and activities

1. _____

2. _____ etc.

Desired customer response

1. _____

2. _____ etc.

Proposition — key issue/offer from prospect's point of view

_____

_____ etc.

Previous promotional activity targeted at the same audience

_____

_____ etc.

FORM 4: PRODUCT OR PROGRAMME DETAIL

Campaign Name _____   Code _____

Originator _____   Date of issue _____

Products/services/programmes to be promoted/offered   Code

1. _____   _____

2. _____   _____ etc.

Product or programme attributes

Product/service/programme 1

Price _____

Features _____

Benefits _____

Position relative to similar products/services/programmes in portfolio

_____

(and so on for each product/service/programme)

FORM 5: MARKET DETAIL

Campaign Name _____   Code _____

Originator _____   Date of issue _____

Target markets (customer types)

1. _____

2. _____ etc.

Relevant customer perceptions

_____

_____

Direct competition

Company   Product   Comment (e.g. SWOT vs. your offering)

_____   _____   _____

_____   _____   _____

Source of Forms: Mounsey and Stone (1990), pp. 89–161

MONITORING AND CONTROL

Key Performance Measures

The key performance measures chosen for any campaign will naturally depend on the campaign objectives set. If the campaign objective is to generate leads or inquiries, for example, then volume of leads or inquiries generated will be the measure of success. The more common performance indicators are listed in Table 23.2.

Management Reporting

Mounsey and Stone (1990: 73–79) recommend the adoption of a series of formal campaign statuses and authorities, which provides the project manager and senior management with at-a-glance information regarding individual campaigns. Campaign statuses they suggest using are as follows:

- *Operational Statuses*: Provisional, submitted, approved, budgeted, under development, live, completed, closed

- *Management Statuses*: Current, cancelled, deferred, absorbed.

TABLE 23.2: COMMON PERFORMANCE MEASURES

Key Performance Measure	Indicates
Cost per 1,000 contacts	Cost of reaching every 1,000 contacts
Cost per decision-maker contact	Cost of reaching each decision-maker (lead-generation programmes)
Response/enquiry/lead rate	Responses/enquiries/leads achieved overall
Order/sales rate	Orders/sales achieved overall
Cost per response/enquiry/lead	Cost per response/enquiry/lead achieved
Cost per order/sale	Cost per order/sale achieved
Cost per response/enquiry by media	Relative effectiveness of media in generating responses/enquiries
Cost per order/sale by media	Relative effectiveness of media in generating sales
Profit per order/sale	Incremental profit margin
Profit aggregate	Overall profit margin
Response/enquiry by type	Relative success of different products/offers in generating responses/enquiries
Order/sale by type	Relative success of different products/offers in generating sales
Response or order by type by media	Relative success of different product/offers in generating responses/sales in various media

Monitoring and Controlling Suppliers

Once the campaign is underway, it is essential to keep tight control of suppliers, not just to ensure that they meet deadlines, but to avoid the escalation of costs. Cost overruns are a perennial problem, sometimes originating with the client if the original plan has not been clearly thought through.

Mounsey and Stone (1990: 168–170) point to a number of reasons why cost overruns can occur:

- Last minute copy deadlines and missed approval deadlines

- Lack of criteria for judging supplier costs

- Lack of negotiation with suppliers

- Lack of feeling about cost-accountability

- Lack of supplier cost-control

- Lack of cost-control system.

Any of the above should act as a red light to the project manager, and as a signal to review the budget. However, the difficulties of borrowing from one part of the budget to pay for another are intractable. The ultimate solution is to avoid the problem in the first place by planning thoroughly.

Negotiating a contract with a supplier in advance can help to avoid some cost over-run problems. Obviously, the level of detail involved in any contract will depend on the client–supplier relationship. But at the very least, a contract should specify the deliverables, costs and timescales (Mounsey and Stone, 1990). As Andersen et al. (1987) point out, progress meetings and progress reports are a key element in monitoring and controlling projects at all levels.

Summary: Keys to Avoiding Cost Overruns

- Brief closely

- Obtain detailed quotations

- Negotiate contracts with suppliers

- Monitor closely for red-light warnings

- Review budget as campaign progresses.

FURTHER READING

Most direct marketing literature does not focus on campaign management at all, with at most a chapter or perhaps part of a chapter, given over to the management of processes and procedures. Probably the best single reference is P. Mounsey and M. Stone (1990), *Managing Direct Marketing*. B. Stone (1996), *Successful Direct Marketing Methods*, has a very good chapter on "Managing a Lead-Generation Program". For further reading on project management, the best starting point is D. Lock (1992), *Project Management* or Andersen et al. (1987), *Goal Directed Project Management*. A. Hamilton's (1997) *Management by Projects* is an excellent in-depth textbook which more serious students of the subject should consult.

REFERENCES TO CHAPTER 23

Andersen, E.S., K.V. Grude, T. Haug and R.J. Turner (1987), *Goal Directed Project Management*, London: Kogan Page and Coopers & Lybrand.

Bird, D. (1993), *Commonsense Direct Marketing*, Third Edition, London: Kogan Page.

Courtheoux, R. (1992), "Calculating the Lifetime Value of a Customer", in B. Halsey (ed.), *The Practitioner's Guide to Direct Marketing*, Middlesex: The Institute of Direct Marketing.

Hamilton, A. (1997), *Management by Projects*, Dublin: Oak Tree Press.

Holder, D. (1992), "Planning a Direct Marketing Strategy", in B. Halsey (ed.), *The Practitioner's Guide to Direct Marketing*, Middlesex: The Institute of Direct Marketing.

IDMA (1997), *The Irish Direct Marketing Association Members and Services Directory 1997/1998*, Dublin: Ryanho Publications and Irish Direct Marketing Association.

Lock, D. (1992), *Project Management*, Fifth Edition, Aldershot: Gower.

McCorkell, G. (1997), *Direct and Database Marketing*, London: Kogan Page and The Institute of Direct Marketing.

Mounsey, P. and M. Stone (1990), *Managing Direct Marketing*, Surrey: Croner Publications and The Institute of Direct Marketing.

Nash, E. (1995), *Direct Marketing: Strategy, Planning & Execution*, Third Edition, New York: McGraw Hill.

Stone, B. (1996), *Successful Direct Marketing Methods*, Fifth Edition, Chicago: NTC Business Books.

Weetch, R. (1992), "Budgeting, Costing, Evaluation for Non-financial Managers", in B. Halsey (ed.), *The Practitioner's Guide to Direct Marketing*, Middlesex: The Institute of Direct Marketing.

Chapter 24

FULFILMENT AND CUSTOMER CARE MANAGEMENT

John Keane *and* Maria Keane

Overview

The essence of direct marketing is the creation of one-to-one communications that will hopefully create sales, influence opinions and build long-term customer relationships, all leading to sustained growth and profitability for the companies driving the strategies.

In this chapter, the writers explore the issues arising from the need to plan and manage fulfilment and customer care. The first section concentrates on fulfilment, the second section highlights the importance of customer care and the final section examines customer complaint management.

FULFILMENT[1]

It is important to understand that, depending upon the media chosen to deliver individual campaigns and the actual offer made, the methods of responding to customer communication(s) may vary greatly. The outbound communication resulting from a customer response, whether intended as a once-off or as a complicated trigger mailing/phone response, is generally defined as fulfilment.

Delivering the Promise

Those working in fulfilment see their job as "delivering the final promise". This promise should form the basis for a continued relationship. Detailed planning will precede successful fulfilment, clear

---

[1] Special thanks to Sinead O'Connell for research on fulfilment

policies (especially regarding customer care) and objectives, which are tangible and specific to the offer being made.

The crucial aspect of the fulfilment process is that it interfaces with real customers (and/or prospects) on a one-to-one level and at a point when the customer has sought to do business. Any customer dissatisfied, during or as a result of the fulfilment process, will represent a real financial loss. Successful fulfilment should lead to satisfied customers and the probability of a long-term and profitable customer relationship.

Evidence indicates that today's customers are better educated and fiercely demanding. They will know what they want, be aware of their "rights" and be very unforgiving, in contrast to customers in the 1980s.

The need to accommodate such characteristics must form the basis of developing a fulfilment process. The positive import of such policies can be enormous and gives proof to the concept of the lifetime customer. The planning necessary and policies required in developing a basic fulfilment process, and the necessary management reporting are set out in Figure 24.1.

The process will only be effective if sound policies are set in place, especially in terms of customer need. Clear policies should cover each stage in the process, so that if any should break down, action can be taken or put in train to rectify the situation.

The Policies

- *Campaign Champion*: Most companies will put one executive in day-to-day control, i.e. a champion of the campaign. This executive will have the authority to take action to see through the governing policies. The executive should frequently oversee the processing functions being implemented.

- *Customer Care*: The policies set out under this heading will mostly be based on the premise of "The customer is King" and statements like "customers make pay-days possible". The benefit of the doubt should always be given to the customer, and in circumstances where the process breaks down (e.g. an out-of-stock situation), the customer should always be contacted, to

FIGURE 24.1: FULFILMENT PROCESS (MANY ELEMENTS WILL HAPPEN SIMULTANEOUSLY)

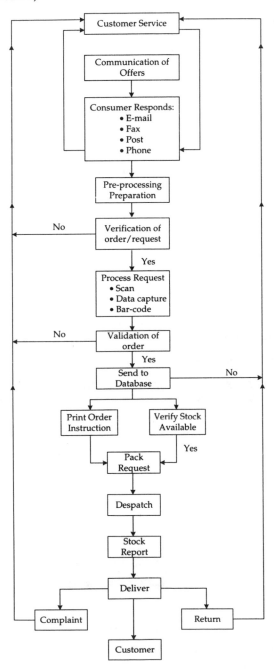

explain the situation and make further offers. The importance of this particular element is expanded upon in the second and third sections of this chapter. As will be seen from Figure 24.1, at any point in the process, if it is possible that a customer could be misunderstood, the process should revert to customer care.

- *Stock Management* and the policies overlaying this function will determine the level of stocks to be put in place at the opening of the offer, the re-ordering threshold, and the review system based on actual versus projected responses. The policy governing the agreement with the suppliers will be crucial; for example, a two-days or say a three-week delivery schedule would have a huge impact on how the process and customer policy will evolve.

- *Turnaround Time*: The overseeing executive must ensure and receive regular reports on the actual agreed time to despatch goods/information. Depending upon the method of communication to and from the customers, turnaround times could be set as low as same day or as high as several weeks.

- *Tolerance Levels*: This will cover areas where a customer fails to meet the requirements and yet may be treated as a bona-fide application; for example:

  - Received after closing date — some days' grace may be allowed

  - Insufficient Payment — a level of acceptance may be set so that if the applicant pays within, say, 50 pence or 90 per cent of the price set

  - Unanswered question(s), which form part of the offer requirement; a policy will be set as to whether such applicants should be treated as bona fide applications or sent to customer service. Most companies will agree a tolerance depending upon the relevance of the questions asked to the offer being made.

- *Payment*: Most credit card and electronic payments can be cleared on-line; postal orders and money orders are guaranteed. Cheques will pose a problem and a policy must be put in place to process applications in "good faith" or await formal clearance from the bank. The policy used will have an effect on batch processing.

A policy regarding payments that are rejected by a financial institution will need to be stated; for example, all can be sent to customer services who will be required to contact the customer with a view to overcoming the problem or simply reject the application file.

- *Insurance*: A policy will need to be agreed as to whether to insure stocks while in transit or not

- *Reporting*: The level and frequency of reporting on the campaign will have to be set and clearly monitored by management

- *Special Limitation*: A policy should be clearly stated covering any limitations on the offer examples, age eligibility, signature requirement, one per household, specific ways of paying, and/or specific credit cards acceptable.

- *Address Validation*: Once a customer's address information is data-captured, it will normally be run through some form of validation to determine if the address information is sufficient to enable deliverability, or if the address can be enhanced without compromising its integrity. Validated and/or standardised addresses form an important secondary usage, as, depending upon the policy set, they will allow analysis to household level; access to profiled data; and linkage to census data relevant to the area of address.

The Fulfilment Process

As can be seen on Figure 24.1, many of the processes will happen simultaneously, especially if they are driven by computer technology. The process designed here reflects how most campaigns are managed in Ireland. The emphasis will always be on customer care.

In planning the process, each element should be questioned in terms of its acceptability, deliverability and understandability of the targeted customer.

Communication of the Offer/Customer Responses

The fulfilment process will begin as soon as communication has been completed. Communication can be delivered in many forms, e.g. direct response television; direct response radio; mailing and follow-up mailings; e-mail; telephone; fax; press; or from various combinations of the foregoing.

In Ireland, most responses will be received via telephone and mail, although fax and especially e-mail are growing very quickly.

Category Responses

Normally responses will be categorised by the method of response i.e. fax, e-mail, telephone or mail. Each method will arrive through a different communication channel and in different formats, e.g.

- *E-mail*: Download from PC

- *Mail*: Written/typed format

- *Fax*: As mail, except electronic delivery

- *Phone*: Verbal communication.

Each method will most probably be processed separately until the process reaches the address validation stage or the database stage.

Normally, responses will be:

- Coded by method of receipt

- Maintained in batch(es) of specified numbers, e.g. 100, 200, etc.

- Each batch given a unique number (URN)

- Each batch day dated

- Each batch referenced by the person who processed it to begin with, and by the person who is subsequently accountable at each stage of the process.

Verification of Order/Requirement

Before processing an order/request, it is imperative to verify that each response meets the offer's requirements. If money is required, are the relevant details completed in a way that will be acceptable to the relevant financial institution? For example, cheques should be made payable to the company, crossed, and the account holder's address should be written on the reverse. The cheque must be signed and dated, and the written amount must equal the figures.

Verify that all entry conditions are completed; these may include the completion of a questionnaire and/or specific questions relating to the granting of credit and/or insurance approval.

Process Response Information

This will involve the physical transferring of the data supplied by a customer onto the company's computer system. There are various methods used, including:

- Scanning material

- Barcode reading material

- Capturing data manually onto computer system.

Scanning will only be effective if pre-prepared stationery is supplied to the customer, usually with the customer's address pre-printed; otherwise the address may have to be data-captured manually.

Where a barcode is pre-printed onto the stationery, a swipe through a barcode reader will call up the customer address and file information. Process time can therefore be reduced substantially.

Manual data capture is the most used method and by definition the slowest way to process data. Every effort should be made at the pre-planning stage to reduce the cost impact of manual data capture.

Validation Process/Database

At this point, the final decision on whether to accept and deliver the customer order/request will be made.

If payment is required, then clearance of payment will be sought. For credit cards, this is normally completed via "on-line" clearance, a process available from most credit card companies in Ireland. Otherwise, clearance can take two or three days. However, most credit card companies will guarantee payment up to a specified level.

Postal order or bank drafts are essentially guaranteed payments and do not need advance clearance. Cheques will require lodgement and some days to be cleared. The company policy will determine whether to process "in good faith" or await clearance.

Normally the address is validated and standardised to ensure that goods can be delivered; the database can also be examined to see if a customer already has a record. If they already have a record, their status can be ascertained. If not, the area in which they live may suggest whether they are a good prospect. Finally, the data supplied can be checked to see if it conflicts with or updates previous data.

Once the customer request has met with all the aforementioned requirements the processing system will request the order to be prepared for despatch.

Print Order/Invoice

The process will cause an order request to be printed. This will detail the goods or information piece(s) to be despatched. This document will be used to pick the items to be despatched and will normally accompany the goods when delivered in the form of an address carrier and delivery docket. In some cases, the order request will simply prompt the computer to print the information pack requested or even a contract. This is done using a lettershop process that prints personalised communications.

The order request may in addition cause an invoice/terms of credit to be printed and despatched.

Where the goods or information sought are not available, the print request will be flagged and identified to customer service to initiate its corporate policy.

Pack Request/Despatch

Goods may need to be picked and packed as per the order request document. The physical packing may be done by machines or people, who will pick the goods requested from stock. The items must be collated and packed for despatch. Despatch of orders/requests are normally despatched via mail, courier, e-mail, phone or fax.

Stock Report/Management Reporting

The control and management of stock levels is a key requirement of profitability. A balance between ongoing demand and investment in stock can be the key to success. There are various software models available to support the prediction of stock levels; however, a mix of experience and technology is the best basis for setting stock levels.

Decisions can always be made with regular and accurate information. Information on response levels, the mix of goods/information sought, and the actual stock levels should be provided on a daily basis at the beginning of the offer, later reducing to bi-weekly.

This information, combined with experience and various stock-predicting models, will alert the company to the need to provide stocks. The results lead in many cases to more economical physical stock levels, reduced back orders, and less warehousing charges.

Stock reporting, mixed with response and despatch rates, will form the basis for in-depth reports covering all aspects of the fulfilment process. This information will assist in the management of a campaign and become part of the corporate experience for future planning.

Returns/Complaints

Following delivery of a customer request, the final element of the fulfilment process will be to handle returns or customer complaints.

The policies set down by management as to how returns and complaints are managed will have a lasting effect on the relationships with their customers, and should be addressed positively through customer service. Returns must be analysed to identify why they were returned, such as:

* Wrong goods/size/information

* Moved address / gone away

* Goods received damaged.

The lessons to be learned for future campaigns can be extremely useful, and the analysis can identify in-built failures within the process, which can be rectified to give a better service in the future.

The Fulfilment Process — In-house or Outsourced?

Because of the specialised nature of the skills required in managing the process of fulfilment and the enormous investment required in the areas of telemarketing and computer software, many companies tend to outsource this function, or at least part of it.

However, many of the largest mail order companies provide in-house facilities, as do many banking and insurance companies. Part of the IDA's success has been in attracting both in-house telecentres and outsourcing telemarketing specialists to locate in Ireland.

The decision about whether to outsource or to keep the fulfilment process in-house will be very much determined by an examination of the costs/benefits to the company. If there is likely to be an on-going requirement for fulfilment and the economics are right, then companies may develop an in-house facility. However, some companies who have created the necessary volume may decide not to proceed with in-house fulfilment, as they feel it does not form part of their core business.

Companies who outsource will do so in the main because of the intolerable demand the provision of such a service would create on their management and existing resources.

CUSTOMER CARE MANAGEMENT

Defining Customer Care

Customer care has a significant role to play in the management of the social interchange between the customer and the service provider. The way this process is managed is pivotal to a successful direct marketing relationship. The ultimate driving force of a customer care programme is customer satisfaction and loyalty.

Customer care is partly a function of good management, good marketing and good people. Demonstrating care, concern and spontaneity, problem-solving and effecting successful service recoveries essentially underpin good customer care. Customers need to be valued and feel that their custom is important. Furthermore, it has to be the *same standard of care*, however small the request, or however difficult the customer (Johnson, 1994).

Customer care must have its roots in a company's culture and corporate beliefs. It starts with an attitude which covers every aspect of customer relations from the first moment a potential customer hears about, and comes in contact with, the business. Primarily, it must become a management attitude that transcends the organisation. The customer care philosophy must be seen to emanate from senior management, be respected and required as a professional standard and visibly seen to be important by all key management personnel. Customer care must be a fundamental value, driven by policy into every facet of the business. It must be incorporated into recruitment, induction, training, design, delivery and distribution functions. As Johnson (1994) points out, *care* means instilling two important words into the everyday lives of those in contact with customers — and those who are not. These words are *belonging* and *belief*. Staff and management need to be part of a company that cares about its staff, its products/services, and its customers. Everyone must feel that they are part of the customer care programme. It only exists when all employees want and believe it to be vital and understand how it is attainable.

The key to success in customer care lies in:

- Senior management supporting the initiative with ongoing commitment

- Full knowledge of the needs, expectations and attitudes of both internal and external customers

- Involving all employees in both setting and constantly improving service standards

- Establishing methods of measuring the standards of service quality provided at regular intervals

- Developing systems and structures to enable people at the customer interface to take customer care decisions on their own initiative

- Provision of customer-oriented training and reward systems.

Benefits of a Customer Care programme

The benefits of a customer care programme include:

- Ability to command higher relative price without affecting market share

- Lower marketing costs

- Increased customer loyalty

- Reduced vulnerability to price wars

- Low customer turnover

- Ability to attract and maintain high calibre staff, together with enhancing the morale of existing staff

- Increased opportunity for cross-selling

- It achieves a maximum number of advocates who sell on for the company through positive word-of-mouth

- Repeat business

- Reputation for being a caring, customer-oriented business

- It establishes a shared sense of organisational purpose

- It improves communication at all levels of the organisation.

Defining the Standards of Customer Care

An important factor in the consistency of service delivery is the establishment of standards of customer care. The quality of customer care delivered by customer-contact personnel is critically influenced by the standards against which they are evaluated and compensated. Standards signal to contact personnel what management and customer priorities are, and what type of performance really counts. When service standards are absent or when the standards in place do not reflect customers' expectations (e.g. if bank cashiers are judged solely on how well they balance their cash), quality of customer care is likely to suffer. Likewise, when organisations provide a uniform standard of service, irrespective of customers' needs, there is a danger that customers may form the impression that they are just another number, rather than a valued individual. In contrast, when there are standards reflecting what customers expect (e.g. courteous treatment, quick response and fulfilled responses), the quality of customer care is likely to be enhanced (Zeithamal et al., 1990).

There are some essential guidelines for setting standards (Cook, 1992; Johnson, 1994). Standards must be:

- *Realistic* and *achievable*: You cannot achieve the impossible

- *Descriptive*: explain what can and should be achieved

- *Understood*: Clear, concise, with proper guidelines

- *Properly communicated* in an easy to understand form, written down, and circulated to everyone in the organisation

- *Capable of measurement* by all those involved, including the customer.

Regularly reviewing standards against performance is important to reflect changes in care demands, staff ability or new product/service ranges. This can be achieved by monitoring internal and external customer satisfaction levels against performance standards. Monitoring and measurement techniques include customer surveys, observation and self-assessment techniques, focus groups, customer panels, analysis of complaints and compliments. The ultimate responsibility for monitoring and review must lie with management, but staff and customers have an important role to play in undertaking this task. The "cycle of control" in Figure 24.2 illustrates how this is achieved.

FIGURE 24.2: THE CYCLE OF CONTROL FOR CARE OF CUSTOMERS

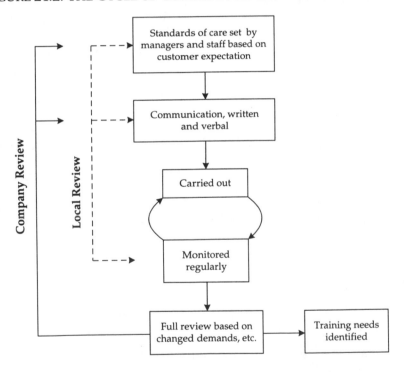

Source: Johnson (1994), p. 70.

Staff members must be convinced that performance cannot be measured without standards. Consequently, it is imperative that staff and management are involved, together, in the formulation of customer care standards, to engender long-term commitment.

The setting of standards should incorporate "hard" (task-oriented) as well as "soft" (people-oriented) standards. Hard standards, which are quantifiable, are more easily formulated, since they deal with the mechanics of how the product/service is delivered. For example, to process all complaints within 24 hours, to answer the phone within three rings. Soft standards are qualitative and often difficult to set and maintain, yet are crucial, since they give substance to hard standards. Soft standards can cover areas such as courtesy, appearance and communication skills. Standards should not be set too rigidly; rather the minimum requirements should be defined and staff empowered to use their own initiative. Standards, in this respect, form the basis of the service delivery customers can expect from an organisation.

Standards may be set for both the external and internal customer. For the external customer, each customer encounter point (telephone, counter, correspondence, etc.) should have a checklist outlining the agreed standards formulated for each team member. The following are examples of typical telephone standards:

- Answer the phone within three rings

- Greeting should be "Good morning/afternoon, company name, staff name"

- Follow by "May I help you?"

- Listen carefully to the message and repeat or question to ensure that the correct information is received

- Obtain and use the caller's name

- Do not leave a caller on hold for more than 20 seconds; after that time, ask the caller if they wish to continue holding, or if they would like you to call them back

- Always keep the caller informed of what you are doing, e.g., "I am transferring you to Mark in our customer services section"

- Explain fully all details solicited when handing over a call

- If the person required is unavailable, seek other assistance where possible; otherwise offer to phone the caller back

- Thank the caller for phoning

- Ensure that the message is received by the appropriate personnel and actioned.

Many of the aforementioned standards are common sense, but evidence shows that much of it is forgotten and unused. Standards must become part of the day-to-day running of a team and establish the "norms" of behaviour — thus ensuring service consistency. To be effective, service standards must not only reflect customers' expectations, but also be backed up by adequate and appropriate resources such as people, systems and technology (Zeithamal et al., 1990).

COMPLAINT MANAGEMENT

An important element of customer care programmes should involve the systematic collection and analysis of complaints. Customer complaints can provide important information about the failures and inadequacies in the service system. If rectified, compiled and analysed, complaints can become an inexpensive and continuous source of adjustment for the service process. Complaints also offer opportunities for managers and contact personnel to interact with customers, thereby learning detailed and rich information about products and services (Zeithamal et al., 1990).

The role of the complaint management function, as represented in Figure 24.3, is twofold: individual complaint handling and aggregate complaint analysis (Gower, 1996; Schibrowsky, 1994; Fornell, 1992; Fornell, 1981; Fornell and Wernerfelt, 1987).

FIGURE 24.3: THE ROLE OF COMPLAINT MANAGEMENT

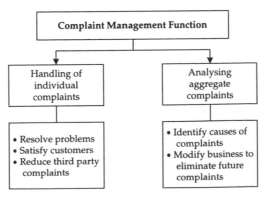

Source: Adapted from Schibrowsky (1994), pp.15–26.

Complaint Handling

The *complaint-handling* function is designed to address individual complaints in an attempt to redress consumer dissatisfaction immediately (Fornell and Westbrook, 1984). The objective of complaint handling is to turn dissatisfied customers into satisfied and loyal ones, thereby increasing their lifetime value to the organisation (De Ruyter and Brack, 1993; Stewart, 1994). Efficiency in complaint handling usually refers to the procedures involved and the steps taken to ensure rapid turnover of complaints, accurate and fair responses to consumers, and low complaint processing costs.

Research shows that for organisations that endeavour to resolve complaints, over half actually reinforce negative reactions, leading to increased customer frustration (Hart et al., 1990). While a poorly handled complaint results in negative effect toward either the product or service, well-handled complaints alter the consumer's final disposition toward the complaint encounter positively. Positive evaluations of customer complaint encounters can be perceived as "second-order" satisfaction and help to build customer loyalty and higher levels of repurchase intention (Gilly and Gelb, 1982; Gilly and Stevenson, 1988; Westbrook, 1987; TARP, 1986; Clark et al., 1992; Cooke, 1987; Goodwin and Ross, 1990; Resnik and Harmon, 1983; Etzel and Silverman, 1981; Bitner et al., 1990, Blodgett et al., 1995). The following is a ten-step approach to handling customer complaints effectively:

1. Provide adequate privacy for the complainant

2. Take ownership and present a positive and confident attitude to resolving the problem

3. Listen attentively to the customer

4. Remain calm and objective and keep your emotions in check

5. Establish the facts and complaint validity by asking questions

6. Record key information to avoid question duplication

7. Agree a course of action which is acceptable to the customer

8. Keep the complainant informed of progress in resolving the problem

9. Follow up the complaint until the customer is satisfied

10. Record and disseminate complaint information to appropriate personnel to prevent a reoccurrence.

It is important to recognise that in some instances a consumer may not have a legitimate complaint and may never be reasonably satisfied. However, successful companies work towards developing strategies which ensure that all complaints are investigated and responded to with the appropriate urgency expected by the customer.

Aggregate Complaint Analysis

Complaints must be analysed in a manner that allows the firm to make the changes necessary to eliminate the causes of complaints. Aggregate complaint information should be used to formulate managerial strategies designed to reduce the negative effects of complaining. The key benefit associated with aggregate complaint analysis is that it allows the company to manage its business proactively, helping to identify consumer problems that occur over time, and possibly across different service offerings (Fornell, 1981; Fornell and Wernerfelt, 1987; 1988; Gilly and Stevenson, 1988; Gilly et al., 1991; Schwartz and Saxe, 1991). The role of effective complaint management in maximising customer satisfaction and increasing customer loyalty is summarised in Figure 24.4.

FIGURE 24.4: FORMULA FOR MAXIMISING CUSTOMER SATISFACTION AND BRAND LOYALTY

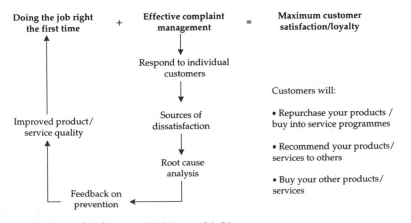

Source: Seelos and Adamson (1994), pp. 26–31

The essence of the formula in Figure 24.4 lies in problem prevention, through feedback and root-cause analysis. An effective customer care programme can prevent many complaints. However, customer care which springs into action after a service failure occurs can lead to customer retention and loyalty.

Benefits of Complaint Management

Empirical evidence (Fornell, 1992; Fornell and Wernerfelt, 1987, Goodwin and Ross, 1992: Mitchell and Critchlow, 1993; Barnard, 1996) suggests that:

- A dissatisfied customer, once persuaded to stay, is more loyal and thus more valuable than before
- Generous complaint management is likely to generate positive consumer word-of-mouth communications, and company image is, therefore, enhanced
- Solutions can be found to enhance customer satisfaction by using data on service issues which are causing problems for customers
- Consumer complaints can be a useful source of design and new product development ideas
- Complaint redress helps reduce the risks consumers associate with a purchase and engenders customer confidence
- Customer perceptions of quality increase as complaint analysis is used as a method of quality control
- Cross-selling opportunities increase.

From an internal company point of view, complaint analysis:

- Affords the company the opportunity of looking at its business from the customer's point of view
- Helps tie operational decisions, issues and problems back to customer satisfaction
- Provides the firm with an objective look at the big picture, based on numbers and not supposition
- Provides a summary overview of the level of satisfaction the firm is delivering
- Enables the firm to establish complaint benchmarks to monitor the effectiveness of the customer service program over time.

TABLE 24.1: A FRAMEWORK FOR FULFILMENT AND RESPONSE
HANDLING

1. *Planning*	It is essential that fulfilment is an integral part of the planning and review process from the beginning, since it represents the methodology used to deliver both the creative and the offer.
2. *Weight*	As most fulfilment exercises concern direct mail and subsequently postage weight is important, since most postage rates are governed by weight.
3. *Machine vs. Man*	Since manpower is a costly overhead, it is more cost-effective to: • Aim for a mechanical fulfilment solution; or • Consider using an outside contractor as opposed to staying in-house.
4. *Proofing*	Check and double-check all aspects of the planned communication, including proof-reading all copy, examination of the legal requirements in relation to any offer being made, terms and conditions and computer data (including live data samples).
5. *The Promise, the Offer*	It is essential to ensure, due to direct one-to-one communication with either an existing customer or a potential client, that promises or offers made can be met.
6. *Stock*	It is necessary to ensure sufficient stock is either available or on short-term call-off to meet a worst/best response scenario. The stocking level equation should take account of the highest possible redemption levels.
7. *Resource*	Ensure that there are adequate resources to meet both statutory requirements and respondents' expectations. Customers/prospects invited to a company by phone or post reasonably assume that they will get either an immediate response, or the goods/incentives within the time specified in the offer.
8. *Suppliers/ Bureau*	The offer/promise contained in the original communication is the *company's* offer or promise. If the company chooses to engage a fulfilment bureau, then there is no scope for derogation of the company's responsibilities. As far as the customer/prospect is concerned, it is the company and their representative that they are dealing with. Every precaution should be taken when choosing a supplier/bureau. This includes visiting the fulfilment house, making sure that they are a member of a relevant trade association and asking for and taking up user referrals.
9. *Legalities*	It is essential to be aware of, and adhere to, all legal and associations' codes of conduct. These include, amongst others, the Sale of Goods Act, the Data Protection Act, and the IDMA and IISP Codes of Conduct.

Source: Martin Biddle, head of Marketing and Sales, PMI Ltd.

REFERENCES

Barnard, Robert (1996), "Improving Customer Service through Measuring Retention", *Journal of Targeting, Measurement and Analysis for Marketing*, Vol. 5, No. 2, pp. 104–110.

Bitner, Mary Jo, Bernard M. Booms and Mary S. Tetreault (1990), "The Service Encounter: Diagnosing Favourable and Unfavourable Incidents", *Journal of Marketing*, Vol. 54, January, pp. 71–85.

Blodgett, Jeffrey G., K.C. Wakefield and J.H. Barnes (1995), "The Effects of Customer Service on Consumer Complaining Behaviour", *Journal of Services Marketing*, Vol. 9, No. 4, pp. 31–42.

Clark, G.L., P. Kaminski and D.R. Rink (1992), "Consumer Complaints: Advice on How Companies Should Respond, Based on an Empirical Study", *Journal of Consumer Marketing*, Vol. 6, No. 3, Summer, pp. 5–14.

Cook, Sarah (1992), *Customer Care: Implementing Total Quality in Today's Service-Driven Organisation*, London: Kogan Page Limited, pp. 119–131.

Cooke E. (1987), "Post-shipment Services: Turning Consumer Complaints into Assets", *Journal of Business and Industrial Marketing*, Vol. 15, No. 2, Winter, pp. 17–22.

De Ruyter, Ko and Antoni Brack (1993), "European Legal Developments in Product Safety and Liability: The Role of Customer Complaint Management as a Defensive Marketing Tool", *International Journal of Research in Marketing*, Vol. 10, pp. 153–164.

Etzel, Michael J., and Bernard I. Silverman (1981), "A Managerial Perspective on Directions for Retail Customer Dissatisfaction Research", *Journal of Retailing*, Vol. 57, Fall, pp. 124–136.

Fornell, Claes (1981), "Increasing the Organisational Influence of Corporate Consumer Affairs Departments", *Journal of Consumer Affairs*, Vol. 15, Winter, pp. 191–213.

Fornell, Claes (1992), "A National Consumer Satisfaction Barometer: The Swedish Experience," *Journal of Marketing*, Vol. 56, January, pp. 6–21.

Fornell, C and B. Wernerfelt (1987), "Defensive Marketing Strategy by Customer Complaint Management: A Theoretical Analysis ", *Journal of Marketing Research*, Vol. 24, pp. 337–346.

Fornell, C and B. Wernerfelt (1988), "A Model for Customer Complaint Management", *Journal of Marketing Science*, Vol. 7, No. 3, pp. 287–298.

Fornell, Claes and Robert A. Westbrook (1984), "The Vicious Circle of Consumer Complaints", *Journal of Marketing*, Vol. 48, Summer, pp. 68–78.

Gilly, M.C. and B.D. Gelb (1982), "Post-purchase Consumer Processes and the Complaining Consumer", Vol. 9, December, pp. 323–329.

Gilly, M.C. and W.B. Stevenson (1988), "Complaint Management in the Health Care Organisation", *Journal of Consumer Satisfaction, Dissatisfaction and Complaining Behaviour*, Vol. 1, pp. 93–98.

Gilly, M., W. Stevenson and L. Yale (1991), "Dynamics of Complaint Management in Service Organisations", *Journal of Consumer Affairs*, Vol. 9, pp. 295–322.

Goodwin, Cathy and Ivan Ross (1990), "Consumer Evaluations of Responses to Complaints: What's Fair and Why", *Journal of Consumer Marketing*, Vol. 7, No. 2, Spring, pp. 39–47.

Goodwin, Cathy and Ivan Ross (1992), "Consumer Responses to Service Failures: Influence of Procedural and International Fairness Perceptions", *Journal of Business Research*, Vol. 25, September, pp. 149–163.

Gower, Tom (1996), *Dealing with Customer Complaints*, Avebury: Gower Publishing Limited, pp. 107.

Hart, Christopher W.L., James L. Heskett, and W. Earl Sasser, Jr. (1990), "The Profitable Art of Service Recovery", *Harvard Business Review*, Vol. 68, July–August, pp. 148–156.

Johnson, Simon (1994), *Ready-made Activities for Customer Care Skills*, The Institute of Management Foundation, Pitman Publishing, London.

Mitchell, V.W. and C. Critchlow (1993), "Dealing with Complaints: a Survey of UK Grocery Suppliers", *International Journal of Retail and Distribution Management*, Vol. 21, No. 2, pp. 15–22.

Resnik, A.R. and R.R. Harmon (1983), "Consumer Complaints and Managerial Response: A Holistic Approach", *Journal of Marketing*, Vol. 47, No. 1, Winter, pp. 86–97.

Schibrowsky, John A. et al. (1994), "Gaining a Competitive Advantage by Analysing Aggregate Complaints", *Journal of Consumer Marketing*, Vol. 1, No. 1, pp. 15–26.

Schwartz, L. and P. Saxe (1991), "Risk Management for Survival", *Direct Marketing*, February, pp. 37–38.

Seelos, Lilo and Colm Adamson (1994), "Redefining NHS Complaint Handling — the Real Challenge", *International Journal of Health Care Quality Association*, Vol. 7, No. 6, pp. 26–31.

Stewart, Kate (1994), "Customer Exit: Loyalty Issues in Retail Banking", *Irish Marketing Review*, Vol. 7, pp. 45–53.

TARP (1986), *Consumer Complaint Handling in America: An Update Study*, Washington DC: White House Office of Consumer Affairs (Technical Assistance Research Programs).

Westbrook, R.A. (1987), "Product/Consumption-based Affective Responses and Post-Purchase Processes", *Journal of Marketing Research*, Vol. 24, No. 3, August, pp. 258–275.

Zeithamal, Valerie A., A. Parasuraman and Leonard L. Berry (1990), *Delivering Quality Service: Balancing Customer Perceptions and Expectations*, New York: The Free Press, p. 41.

Chapter 25

THE INTIMATE FUTURE: THE OUTLOOK FOR DIRECT MARKETING IN IRELAND

Gerard O'Neill

Overview

This concluding chapter sets out our thoughts on future prospects for direct marketing in Ireland, standing back from the focus on practice addressed in previous chapters. In particular, this chapter will focus on the findings of research carried out for the Irish Direct Marketing Association in 1996 relating to the industry's future, with particular regard the following issues:

1. *The acceptability of direct marketing communications to consumers*

2. *The emerging shape of the direct marketing industry*

3. *Scenarios for the future of the direct marketing market in Ireland*

4. *Forecasts for the future value of direct marketing.*

THE ACCEPTABILITY OF DIRECT MARKETING

One of the key drivers of growth — though perhaps not the most obvious — is the synergy between the main direct marketing media. More developed strategies now incorporate telemarketing and direct response advertising in addition to direct mail. Likewise, many telemarketing campaigns will often follow up a response to, say, a freefone number by mailing out additional details or an application form inviting the respondent to post back their reply.

As a result, Irish consumers are becoming educated on the benefits of both telemarketing and direct mail, as well as on replying via either means to direct response advertisements on television or the radio, or in newspapers and magazines. Thus the *interdependence* of direct marketing tools ensures that there is a positive, reinforcing circle of usage, growth and additional usage.

An example of this interdependence in action can be seen from the IDMA research. About a quarter of a million Irish adults responded to information received in the post in the 12 months prior to the survey. Among those responding to direct mail, a number of key groups were represented:

- Women tend to be more likely to respond to direct mail than men in both Ireland and the UK (especially married women in Ireland)

- Respondents tend to be aged under 35 in Ireland (older in the UK)

- Respondents tend to be in the C1C2 (middle class) and F (farmers) social classes in Ireland (13 per cent of C2s had responded) and more C2DE (lower class) in the UK.

The majority of those who reply to items received in the post tend to do so by post (in both Britain and Ireland). But a key figure to note is that nearly three in ten respondents actually do so by telephone — highlighting the degree of consumer comfort with using several different direct marketing media. Regarding different sub-segments and their preferences for responding to direct mail, it should be noted that:

- Irish women are much more likely than Irish men to reply by post (63 per cent compared with 47 per cent), while British men and women are equally as likely to do so

- Men, on the other hand, are much more likely to reply to direct mail by phone than women (39 per cent compared with 17 per cent) — in line with the UK's experience

- Preferences are fairly consistent across most age groups, in both countries

- Social class variations give postal respondents to direct mail an upmarket bias in Ireland (64 per cent of ABC1s (higher social class) — though it is more C1C2 in the UK); while telephone respondents are biased downmarket in Ireland (30 per cent of

C2DEs) — while in the UK it is more evenly spread across the social classes

- With regard to regional variations, those outside Dublin prefer to respond by post to their direct mail, and those in Dublin tend to prefer to respond by telephone.

A key finding from our research is that people are much happier for companies to contact them by post than by phone, but that they much prefer to follow up the contact by phone rather than by post in most instances. For example, in financial services, while 48 per cent of adults are happy to be contacted by post, only 12 per cent are happy to be contacted by phone. There is considerable resistance to the concept of being contacted by phone in general, with over three-quarters of consumers saying that they would not be happy to be contacted by phone regarding most of the services. That still leaves an average of 15–20 per cent who would be happy either way. These latter tend to be:

- Equally male and female

- Predominantly from younger age groups (under 49)

- Not especially skewed towards one social class grouping or another

- Where there is an area bias it is usually in favour of those in urban areas rather than in rural areas.

This contrasts substantially with the answers for postal contacts, with, in some instances, over half of the respondents saying that they would be happy to be contacted by post. In terms of the profile of these more positive respondents, they tend to be:

- Equally male and female

- From younger age groups (under 49), but with quite high proportions of over 50s also, indicating that they would be happy to receive materials in the post (45 per cent and more of this age group for certain products, such as financial services)

- For many products, there is little or no social class variation in terms of satisfaction with receiving materials from companies through the post, though in the case of clothing there is a more downmarket bias (52 per cent of C2DEs are happy to be contacted via the post compared with 38 per cent of ABC1s)

- Generally, Dubliners are less happy to be contacted than consumers in the rest of Ireland, giving rise to a generally higher level of satisfaction with contact by post in rural areas than in urban areas.

These findings point to a future in which we will see the interdependence of the core direct marketing media become more clearly recognised by direct marketing practitioners, and more effectively utilised to satisfy customer requirements for choice in how they contact and keep in touch with companies.

THE EMERGING SHAPE OF THE DIRECT MARKETING INDUSTRY

The economics of direct marketing are expected to change substantially up to the end of the decade. Falling prices associated with the core costs of direct marketing will accelerate the trend already evident towards greater use of direct marketing, as falling prices bring it increasingly within the budgets of almost all companies.

In the survey of IDMA members, respondents were asked to relate how they expected a number of key direct marketing costs to change over the next five years. The first related to the cost of telemarketing services, and it is clear that the balance of opinion expects that these will fall as we approach the year 2000. Though a much higher proportion expect direct mail costs to remain unchanged over the next five years, among those who do expect to see changes, the balance is clearly in favour of a fall in direct mail costs.

Finally, with regard to direct marketing costs, respondents were asked to indicate whether they expected to see the cost of printing services rising, falling or remaining the same over the same period. A majority of Irish direct marketing practitioners expect that printing services will become more expensive over the next few years. A key issue will be to what extent such a development is likely to offset the anticipated falls in other direct marketing costs.

If it is more than offset, then the net effect will be a reduction in aggregate direct marketing costs for most practitioners (assuming there is a direct mail and printing component to their campaigns).

This in turn will mean that the growth in direct marketing expenditure attributable to economic growth will receive a further stimulus from nominal and even real price reductions in the case of postal and telecommunications charges. On the other hand, if the expected increase in printing service costs is not offset by the other price reductions, then an aggregate rise in direct marketing costs could partially offset the growth arising from the underlying trend in the economy.

Among direct marketing practitioners in Ireland, there is currently a very positive and bullish attitude towards the export potential for direct marketing over the next five years. Over eight in ten respondents to the IDMA survey expected exports of direct marketing services by Irish-based companies to rise, with no respondent expecting a decline. Asked to indicate what they considered to be the main export opportunity for Irish direct marketing service companies, they noted the following:

- *Telemarketing Services*: Clearly, the success of Ireland as a centre for call-centre and other telemarketing service operations has signalled to many Irish practitioners the great potential there is in Europe, and even globally, for Irish service providers to deliver their services via telemarketing-type operations.

- *Educated Work Force*: This was seen not so much as an opportunity as an enabling factor in the growth of overseas export opportunities (subject to ensuring an adequate quantity and quality of potential employees).

- *The Internet*: The very ubiquity of discussions about the Internet in the context of new direct marketing and home shopping practice leads many practitioners to sense that Ireland is well placed to exploit the potential of the Internet and the World Wide Web to sell and to deliver direct marketing services.

- *Direct Mail*: The future of direct marketing exports is not seen entirely in terms of telecommunications. A number of respondents suggested that Ireland could become an important hub for North Atlantic mail services, which in turn would enable direct marketers in Ireland to use that positioning to develop international direct mail and fulfilment operations.

Respondents were also asked to indicated what they thought would be the main barriers to the realisation of export opportunities:

- *Cost Competitiveness*: This issue was seen as key, especially with regard to direct marketing costs (such as those referred to in the previous section) and to labour and tax costs.

- *Peripheral Location*: Partly related to the first point, the very nature of direct marketing practice in Europe, with its emphasis on next-day deliveries and quick responses makes Ireland a hard place to sell as a location for a direct marketing operation serving all of Europe.

- *Market Intelligence*: For some respondents, simply finding out about direct marketing opportunities is itself the biggest obstacle to export growth.

On balance, however, most of the comments in the IDMA member survey were favourable towards the idea of increased exports and of Irish practitioners playing a part in that increase. The benefits of such a role for Irish direct marketers should, of course, mean growth in employment in direct marketing in Ireland.

Given the importance of services in general to employment growth in Ireland, as in the rest of Europe, it is essential that we look at the potential for direct marketing to play a part in securing job growth in the future. In the survey of IDMA members, those providing direct marketing services were asked about the numbers of employees their companies presently have.

Over two-thirds of direct marketing service providers in Ireland employ fewer than 26 people. However, as with services generally, small businesses are increasingly recognised as the source of most sustainable job increases in modern economies. Research has shown that Ireland's direct marketing service providers will play a similar role. Almost all direct marketing service providers expect to increase their employee numbers over the next five years. This not only reflects the generally positive attitudes of such companies towards the future, but also reflects the simple fact that direct marketing services are people-intensive, and as such have the potential to be a key source of job creation in the future.

Just how significant a part that could be is illustrated with reference to experiences in the United States. Recently, the US Direct Marketing Association published a detailed report on the economic impact of direct marketing on the US economy. The following table is a presentation of their findings and forecasts with regard to employment in direct marketing.

The allocations of direct marketing employment within the business-to-consumer and business-to-business markets are shown (Table 25.1).

TABLE 25.1: DIRECT MARKETING EMPLOYMENT BY MARKET IN THE UNITED STATES

Market	1994 (actual)	1995 (estimated)	2000 (forecast)	Growth 1995–2000
DM Consumer Market	58.7%	58.3%	56.1%	+16.3%
DM Business-to-Business Market	41.3%	41.7%	43.9%	+27.3%
Total US Employment (millions)	116,300	119,500	129,200	+8.1%
DM Employment (% US Economy)	15.7%	16.0%	17.8%	+8.8%

Source: The Wefa Group (1996), *The Economic Impact: US Direct Marketing Today*, US Direct Marketing Association.

There are a number of key points to note about the table:

- The share of business-to-business direct marketing employment will grow as a percentage of total DM employment over the next five years

- Total DM employment as a percentage of the US workforce will grow to nearly 18 per cent (almost one in five jobs) by the year 2000, as a result of a higher rate of job growth than in the labour market generally.

In Ireland, we are still a very long way from this level of development of the direct marketing industry. But the potential is there to narrow the gap over the next five to ten years.

SCENARIOS FOR THE FUTURE OF DIRECT MARKETING IN IRELAND

Given the complex range of variables influencing the future for direct marketing, the most appropriate approach to assessing the future for direct marketing is to examine different scenarios that allow for alternative outcomes for the variables under discussion. Scenarios are a planning tool designed to provide the following benefits:

1. A thorough assessment of the future market environment

2. An appreciation of the range of possible futures that lie ahead

3. Insights that can be fed into the strategy formation process.

Scenarios do not replace planning and forecasting. Rather, they act as a means of linking the task of scanning market change in a turbulent environment to strategic planning. Scenarios are therefore about being ready, not about being right. They are used to tease out the potential sequence of events in the future, and to guide businesses and industries in the preparation of plans to deal with such sequences. Scenarios are essentially a creative technique, designed to enable managers and planners to prepare an honest and comprehensive assessment of the future.

The approach taken in the original IDMA study was to run a workshop in which invited participants addressed the full range of social, technological, economic, environmental and political (STEEP) changes affecting the future of direct marketing in Ireland.

From a number of suggestions, two axes were selected in order to prepare a future map. Using the customer/consumer axis as our vertical dimension and the industry axis as the horizontal dimension, a two-dimensional map for evaluation of future scenarios was created. The two axes give four quadrants, each one of which represents a possible scenario for the future of direct marketing. On the maps, the consensus view as to both the current and future locations of the direct marketing "market" are indicated.

In the case of *business users* of direct marketing (Figure 25.1), the dominant axis of uncertainty with regard to the users' axis was expected to be the extent to which they are focused primarily on the short-term returns to their direct marketing activities, or the extent to which they become focused on the long-term contribution of direct marketing strategy to future profits.

FIGURE 25.1: BUSINESS USERS OF DIRECT MARKETING — KEY AXES
OF UNCERTAINTY

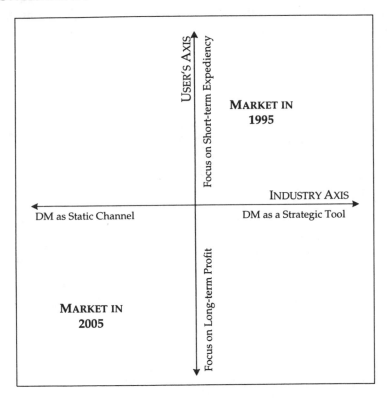

The map suggests that the usage of direct marketing by businesses is currently focused on short-term returns, using direct marketing as a sales promoting tool. Looking ahead to 2005, the potential exists for business usage of direct marketing to become much more strategic, playing a key role in generating long-term profits.

As for the *direct marketing industry* (Figure 25.2), the key axis of uncertainty for the industry looking ahead to the next ten years is the extent to which direct marketing is simply seen (and sold) as another marketing tool, or the extent to which its wider role as a delivery channel is realised.

But of course, all of this depends on the willingness of consumers to respond to direct marketing. Our future map for consumers has on the vertical axis a spectrum ranging from "acceptance" of direct marketing at one end, to "rejection" at the other end. For the direct marketing industry, the key axis of uncertainty is one with "transaction focus" at one end (where direct marketing is used as a tool for generating one-off sales), and "relationship focus" at the other end (whereby direct marketing becomes the key strategic resource for building one-to-one relationships with key customers).

FIGURE 25.2: CONSUMERS AND DIRECT MARKETING — KEY AXES OF UNCERTAINTY

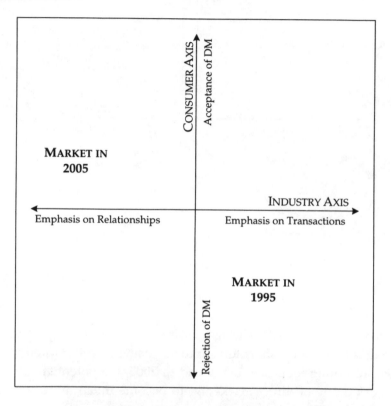

Our future map suggests that with regard to consumers and direct marketing, the present situation is biased more towards the "rejection" end of the consumer axis, and the "transaction" end of the industry axis. We anticipate that direct marketing to consumers will move upwards and leftwards across the future map over time, as a result of increasing experience of and confidence with direct marketing on the part of the consumer, and as a result of the growing recognition of the true power of direct marketing for relationship marketing purposes on the part of the industry and its clients.

Of course, it is possible that the future course of direct marketing in Ireland set out in the above maps could be very different from our consensus scenarios. Another scenario could simply see it staying where it is on both maps. On the other hand, business users might decide to use direct marketing as a delivery channel to achieve short-term rather than long-term ambitions. Likewise, consumers might become more accepting of direct marketing, even though its usage remains predominantly one of maximising transactions.

However, it is the IDMA's view that the current momentum behind direct marketing practice and usage in Ireland, and the expectations noted on the part of Irish consumers, are such that the future indicated in the maps is still the most likely. Just what that future might look like in terms of expenditure on direct marketing services is the subject of the next section.

FORECASTS FOR THE FUTURE VALUE OF DIRECT MARKETING

In the IDMA survey, marketing managers were asked to indicate their likely plans for marketing expenditure up to the year 2000 (beyond 1996). It was found that the main direct marketing media — telemarketing and direct mail — were in the top three media expected to benefit from increased expenditure in the medium term, with television in between them.

A further indication of the expected role of direct marketing in advertising and marketing strategies in the medium term is shown by the same marketing managers' responses to a question asking them, "How important do you expect direct marketing (including direct mail, telemarketing and direct response advertising) will be to your future marketing strategy?" Thirty-four per cent indicated that it would become much more important, with 31 per cent choosing "A little more important".

Clearly, most marketing managers expect to increase the role of direct marketing in their marketing strategies. To explore the impact of this on the different direct marketing media in more detail, the respondents to the survey of IDMA members were asked to indicate the extent to which they expected selected direct marketing media to become more important up to the year 2000. Direct mail expenditure was expected to grow fastest of all the DM media, followed by outbound telemarketing, and by inbound telemarketing, in that order.

Direct mail and telemarketing are expected to dominate the growth in direct marketing expenditure over the next few years, with direct response advertising lagging some way behind. This is supported by econometric models of direct marketing in Europe. Table 25.2 uses EU and Henley Centre forecasts for Irish GDP growth over the next five years (the main driver of expenditure growth in the models) to predict likely expenditure.

TABLE 25.2: THE FUTURE VALUE OF DIRECT MARKETING EXPENDITURE IN IRELAND

	1995	1996	1997	1998	1999	2000
Value of Expenditure — £ million						
Total display advertising	271	294	316	338	362	386
Direct response advertising	29	32	34	37	40	43
Total direct mail	69	77	84	92	101	110
Total telemarketing	10	11	12	13	14	16
Total direct marketing	108	119	131	143	156	169
Advertising and direct marketing	351	381	412	444	478	511
Rate of Growth						
Total display advertising	9%	8%	8%	7%	7%	7%
Display advertising excluding DR	9%	8%	7%	7%	7%	6%
Direct response advertising	10%	9%	9%	8%	8%	8%
Total direct mail	12%	11%	10%	9%	9%	9%
Total telemarketing	12%	11%	10%	9%	9%	9%
Total direct marketing	11%	11%	10%	9%	9%	8%
Advertising and direct marketing	9%	9%	8%	8%	8%	7%
Share of Spending						
DR advertising as % total display	11%	11%	11%	11%	11%	11%
DR advertising as % total DM	27%	26%	26%	26%	26%	25%
Direct mail as % total DM	64%	64%	65%	65%	65%	65%
Telemarketing as % total DM	9%	9%	9%	9%	9%	9%
Direct marketing as % total	31%	31%	32%	32%	33%	33%

The table (based on 1996 economic projections) reveals that, among other things, total expenditure on advertising and direct marketing in Ireland will exceed half a billion pounds by the year 2000, while total expenditure on direct marketing will reach nearly £170 million.

The share of direct marketing in total expenditure will rise towards a third of the total in the year 2000 (compared with 29 per cent in 1993) — driven by the higher growth rate of direct marketing expenditure compared with display or above-the-line expenditure. Within total direct marketing, the share of direct mail will remain dominant, with little anticipated change, on the basis of these models, in the share of the other direct marketing media.

This is in contrast to the US, where direct mail is expected to decline as a proportion of total direct marketing expenditure, while telemarketing and DRTV are expected to grow in share.

These forecasts for Ireland are essentially projections based on an assumption that the primary influence on the value of expenditure will be economic growth, and that Ireland's pattern of direct marketing expenditure will gradually evolve towards the average European pattern as our standard of living similarly converges towards the average.

These forecasts have not allowed for "structural changes" to the marketplace that might arise in the event of, say, new media emerging (such as the Internet) or large changes to key direct marketing costs (e.g. postal and telephone tariff restructuring). These and other variables might well lead to a different outcome for the year 2000.

Indeed, given the potential for quantum changes in business practices with regard both to direct marketing in general and to telemarketing in particular (as phone ownership in Ireland tends towards the European norm), our forecasts for the relative shares of the different direct marketing media may change more rapidly than implied in the above table.

Nevertheless, these forecasts are consistent with the scenarios set out in the previous section, in that it is anticipated that the double-digit rate of growth in direct marketing expenditure described in the earlier table for Ireland will only be realised through a greater focus on the use of direct marketing as a delivery channel and as a resource for building long-term, profitable relationships with key customers.

CONCLUSION: DIRECT MARKETING'S FUTURE

From the above analysis, it is clear that a boom in direct marketing in Ireland is near. The reasons for this are various, and relate to economic and social changes on the one hand, and to technological and corporate strategic changes on the other. The marketing managers in the IDMA survey who expected direct marketing to become more important in their future marketing strategies were asked to indicate why they thought that this would be the case. A number of reasons recurred throughout the responses:

- *Targeting*: Simply being able to identify with whom to communicate — by name and address — is an increasingly attractive feature of direct marketing to all marketing managers

- *Measurability*: It follows that with targeting there is also greater potential to measure the effectiveness of expenditure on direct marketing campaigns

- *Cost Effectiveness*: Both of the above also mean that marketing managers can quickly assess where their money is being well spent — and where it is not

- *Accountability*: All three of the above are manifestations of a greater onus on marketing managers, whether users of direct marketing or not, to justify their expenditure on advertising and promotions and to take responsibility for ensuring that the money is spent wisely and effectively.

For perhaps 10–15 years now, the application of information and telecommunications technologies has been gradually moving out of the finance department into the distribution and delivery department, and is now finally making strong headway in the marketing department. These applications include the systematic application of transaction data collation and analysis and its fusion with individual customer information, including non-financial data on demographic and lifestyle characteristics. These are not the exclusive practice of financial service and airline marketers. The heart of marketing strategy is being transformed in markets as diverse as:

- *Retailing*: The Tesco Club Card and Superquinn's Superclub initiative, for example.

- *Media*: In the UK, the development of a one million plus database of readers by *The Daily Telegraph* that is now being used to implement multi-layered marketing campaigns which fuse newspaper advertising with direct marketing.

- *Cars*: Ford's initiative in the area of car maintenance services aimed at existing Ford drivers using database marketing techniques.

- *FMCG*: The development of stealth marketing strategies using databases and direct marketing by Unilever, Heinz, and Procter & Gamble, among many others.

All of this activity is aimed at one simple objective: to know each customer's needs better than potential competitors. All of this is leading towards "The Intimate Future" — in other words, a future in which companies will strive to secure competitive advantage *one customer at a time* by knowing each individual customer's needs and preferences better than any competing company.

The growth of computing power and the fall in its price has — within the past five years — put within the grasp of mass marketers the kind of purchasing information and customer understanding that was previously the exclusive domain of banks, allowing more and more mass marketers to become "relationship marketers". Likewise, the growth of new sources of competition has meant that *nobody* can afford to ignore the imperative to improve the quantity and quality of knowledge they possess about *each* of their customers. Not even the banks can ignore this imperative — as they watch retailers and telecommunications companies enter the most lucrative parts of the financial services sector equipped with their new-found knowledge of relationship marketing.

More importantly, it works. IDMA research shows that nearly half of all Irish consumers and four in ten UK consumers "would be more likely to buy from a company that keeps in touch".

Those consumers who are most open to the potential of relationship marketing include:

- Women in Ireland, especially single women (50 per cent of whom agree with the statement)

- Younger age groups in both Britain and Ireland, essentially those aged under 40

- Those from higher social income groups in Ireland (ABC1) and from middle income groups in the UK (C1C2)

- People living in rural rather than urban areas.

At the heart of the intimate future is trust. The expectations and activities of the company with regard to its relationship marketing strategy must be properly meshed with the needs and experiences of the consumer if the relationship is to work properly. For the company, a relationship marketing strategy built upon an integrated direct marketing campaign will have the following key elements:

- *Definition of Segments*: The company will only want to have a relationship with its most profitable customers; hence the need for segmentation by profit and lifetime value

- *Clearly Set Objectives*: Once the segments have been identified, the next step will be to set short-, medium- and long-term objectives for each segment in terms of recruitment, retention and return on the marketing investment

- *Communications Programmes*: There then follows a series or parallel set of programmes designed to communicate with each customer within each target segment

- *Re-Purchase*: The name of the game — relationship marketing recognises that we are all in the same business, i.e. the "repeat business" business; the heart of the strategy is to get consumers to buy not just once but repeatedly through the lifetime of their need for the product or service that the company is selling

- *Capture Responses*: From the dialogue that ensues from the relationship, the responses of customers (and even key non-customers) should be captured, stored and analysed

- *Build Database*: From all of this the company will acquire its most important asset, its database of customers and the histories of the relationships with those customers that will enable the company to revisit its segmentation strategy and objectives, and to evolve continuously its marketing strategy to meet the changing circumstances of its relationships with its customers.

On the consumer side of the relationship, a different but equally important sequence exists:

- *Accessibility*: For the consumer, this is the most important test, at least at the outset, of the value of their relationship with a company — how easily and quickly can they get what they want from the company, how they want it?

- *Emotional Experience*: Thereafter, the emotional associations with the product or service brand have to live up to expectations; if they do this, then the consumer will post-rationalise their purchase

- *Re-purchase Rewarded*: There also must be clear benefits to maintaining and sustaining the relationship with one company rather than exploring the alternatives on offer from others; in other words, loyalty must pay and be seen to pay

- *Reinforced Rational Reasons*: Rewards will also help with the post-rationalisation of a positive emotional experience

- *Communication*: There must be opportunities for the customer to learn about what the company has new to offer, and for the company to get feedback about what the customer wants, ideally in a way in which the customer feels in control of the dialogue

- *Recommendations*: The creation of a "word of mouth" culture among satisfied customers can be a very powerful way of amplifying the communications process — turning each customer into an advocate for the company's products or services

- *Re-purchase*: The litmus test for the consumer as well — whether their ongoing experiences of doing business with a company justifies the investment they have made in dialogue with the company and in sharing personal information with it as well.

To conclude, there are three key elements to future direct marketing strategies aimed at developing long-term, profitable relationships:

1. *Target*: By definition, the Pareto Principle tells us that we must focus our attention on those target segments that have the greatest potential or that would pose the greatest loss if they were to defect — it is this requirement for precision that qualifies direct marketing more than any other marketing tool or tactic

2. *Test*: Be prepared to invest in "fast failures" and "short cul-de-sacs"; in other words, do your research in real time, using short burst and micro-targeted direct marketing campaigns to find out what works, what does not, and what to do next

3. *Trim*: The beauty of all of this is that one can actually focus and re-focus activities to become truly engaged in a one-to-one dialogue with the most important customers, turning them into strategic partners for the lifetime of the relationship.

By doing so, the success of both the marketing strategy and the long-term success of the company will be secured. When the day comes that direct marketing is placed at the heart of business strategy for all of Ireland's major advertisers, then Irish direct marketing will finally have realised the potential now evident — a potential rightly described as the coming boom in direct marketing.

REFERENCES

O'Neill, Gerard (1996), *Focus on the Future — The Coming Boom in Direct Marketing in Ireland*, Dublin: Irish Direct Marketing Association.

The Wefa Group (1996), *The Economic Impact: US Direct Marketing Today*, New York: US Direct Marketing Association.

INDEX